FITZGERALD

FITZGERALD

SELECTED WORKS

edited by
JOANNA RICHARDSON

Rupert Hart-Davis

SOHO SQUARE LONDON

1962

PRINTED IN GREAT BRITAIN BY
WESTERN PRINTING SERVICES LTD, BRISTOL

CONTENTS

INTRODUCTION

EDWARD FITZGERALD translated the *Rubáiyát* of Omar Khayyám. That, in one brief sentence, is all that most people know of
him; and it would, alone, be sufficient memorial for any man of
letters. But it is not a fair memorial to FitzGerald; for we owe
him a number of other translations from Latin, Greek, Spanish
and Persian, and one of them at least, his version of Attár's *Bird-
Parliament*, is a poetic achievement of high order. And we owe
him, too, a more original contribution to literature: something
that should, I think, have earned him immortality had he never
taken up Persian, never heard of Omar Khayyám. This is his
correspondence.

The letters of FitzGerald belong to the great tradition of
English letter-writing; they are among the best letters in our
language. At times (and there is no more magnificent comparison) they recall the humour, power and felicity of Keats. And
yet this is the first comprehensive selection of FitzGerald's
letters to appear since his editor and literary executor, William
Aldis Wright, published the works of FitzGerald in 1902–3.
There have, it is true, been a volume of his letters to his friend
Donne, a volume of his letters to his publisher, Bernard Quaritch,
and a volume of letters to Bernard Barton. But these are hard to
come by; the Aldis Wright editions are scarce and (when discovered) quite prohibitive. There has not been a single book
which took them all into account, and included unpublished
correspondence. I have examined all the published letters of
FitzGerald, and I am most grateful to Mr Norman Colbeck for
letting me reproduce an unpublished letter to W. B. Scott, and
to Mr Kenneth Basham for letting me use FitzGerald's letters
to his father, Horace Basham. I hope that this selection, if not

complete and definitive, will at least be an introduction to Fitz-Gerald the letter-writer. It is an introduction that can only lead to admiration and affection.

Edward Purcell was born near Ipswich on 31 March 1809. He was the son of John Purcell and Mary Purcell (*née* FitzGerald): a woman of strong character, celebrated beauty, and (on her father's death, when the family took his name) of exceptional wealth. He was educated at the Grammar School at Bury St Edmunds, where he was more addicted to friendships than to work, and at Trinity College, Cambridge, where he took a pass degree and formed other devoted friendships (one of them with Thackeray). After a brief interlude in France, FitzGerald settled down to become, as he expressed it, "a great bear." He made his home at Boulge Cottage, a somewhat ramshackle cottage at the gates of Boulge Hall, the family's Suffolk estate; and there, with a parrot, Beauty Bob, a cat, a retriever, and a housekeeper, Mrs Faiers, he began to lead an existence which seemed "like a pirated copy of the peace of God." Occasionally he made trips to London, stayed in bachelor lodgings, and enjoyed theatres, art exhibitions, and the company of his bachelor friends. Sometimes he made excursions to places of interest, or stayed with close acquaintances in various parts of the country. But for the most part he stayed in Suffolk, observing Nature with the love of Keats, or White of Selborne; taking a little part in country life, and reading voraciously. It was this self-imposed isolation, and his natural Irish sociability, that made him converse by letter with his friends. He wrote as he talked, "whatever about-ly"; and that, after all, is the best way to write letters.

His friendships were many: the three most famous were perhaps his friendships with Thackeray, Tennyson and Carlyle; and those, of course, are reflected in the letters here. He was well acquainted with Fanny Kemble (daughter of Mrs Kemble, the actress), and with the Rev. George Crabbe (son of the poet). It was his friendship with Edward Byles Cowell, the orientalist, that led him to Persian translation and so to Omar Khayyám; and it was, I think, his failure to have married Cowell's wife (the former Elizabeth Charlesworth) that confirmed FitzGerald in his lonely, rather melancholy existence. In 1856, moved by a wildly

8

mistaken sense of chivalry, he married the middle-aged daughter of his late friend, Bernard Barton, the Quaker poet. It was a foregone, unrelieved disaster, reflected in his work on Omar Khayyám: "Omar," so he wrote, "seems to breathe a sort of Consolation"; it is also reflected in FitzGerald's correspondence. And then his marriage dissolves, and he reverts to his bachelor existence, turns to his sailing, his herring-fishing, his friendship with Posh Fletcher, the Lowestoft fisherman, and to his reading, writing and translation. He moves from cottage to lodging, and from lodging to private house: to become, as he gaily signs himself, the Laird of Littlegrange. But the fact remains that the tenor of his life hardly changes from the time he leaves Cambridge in 1830 to the day he dies, 14 June 1883. The blithe, monocled figure in Thackeray's painting becomes the tired, unkempt and elderly bachelor in the Cade photographs, and then the frail, purblind old man, in his Inverness cape, pointed out as he potters along the Suffolk roads. But FitzGerald's way of life remains constant for half a century; and his character, too, hardly changes, except, perhaps, to become a trifle more melancholy. It is a remarkably constant picture that we see in the letters.

To say that FitzGerald had a Keatsian, Elian humour is almost to repeat a platitude. But he did have such a humour, and it shines out from his letters: subtle, uproarious, quiet, unexpected. We see his touching modesty, his love of nature, his visual sense, his gusto, his warmth in friendship, his erudition, his generosity, his wistfulness, his charm. FitzGerald is entirely disarming: there is a childlike innocence about him. And it is, perhaps, his innocence that most enthrals us, for it is the innocence, the lasting freshness and candour, of genius.

J.R.

Much of the correspondence given here, and all FitzGerald's other work, is taken from his *Letters and Literary Remains*, edited by W. Aldis Wright (1902–3); I have omitted some of Fitz-Gerald's footnotes.

J.R.

CHRONOLOGICAL TABLE

1809	Edward Purcell born at the White House, Bredfield, Suffolk, on 31 March: the son of Mary Purcell (*née* FitzGerald) and Edward Purcell.
1816	Purcell family moves to France.
1818	Mrs Purcell's father dies, leaving her a fortune; the family assume the name of FitzGerald and return to England.
1821	Edward FitzGerald sent to King Edward VI School, Bury St Edmunds.
1826	FitzGerald matriculates at Trinity College, Cambridge.
1830	FitzGerald graduates, and pays a brief visit to Paris with Thackeray.
1835	The FitzGerald family move to Boulge Hall, Woodbridge, Suffolk.
1837	FitzGerald settles in Boulge Cottage.
1842	First meeting with Carlyle, 15 September.
1844	FitzGerald collects information on Cromwell's Lincolnshire campaign for Carlyle.
1846	Working on *Euphranor, A Dialogue on Youth*.
1849	Death of Bernard Barton, 19 February. FitzGerald edits and introduces a selection from his work.
1851	*Euphranor* published.
1852	*Polonius: A Collection of Wise Saws and Modern Instances* published.
1853	Publication of *Six Dramas from Calderon, freely translated by Edward FitzGerald*. FitzGerald translating Sádi.
1855	Carlyle stays with FitzGerald at Farlingay, near Woodbridge, in August.
1856	*Salámán and Absál* published. FitzGerald reads the *Rubáiyát* of Omar Khayyám, which Edward Cowell has discovered in Oxford. Cowell takes up appointment as Professor of History at the Presidency College, Calcutta. FitzGerald marries Lucy Barton in Chichester, 4 November.
1857	FitzGerald separates from his wife, and translates much of the *Rubáiyát*.
1859	Bernard Quaritch publishes FitzGerald's translation of the *Rubáiyát*, 9 April.

1860	FitzGerald moves to lodgings in Market Hill, Woodbridge.
1861	Quaritch reduces the translations from 5s. to 1d. and leaves them in his bargain box. They are later discovered by the editor of the *Saturday Review*, and by the Pre-Raphaelites.
1864	FitzGerald buys a cottage on the outskirts of Woodbridge; he has it enlarged but continues to live in Market Hill. He meets Joseph (Posh) Fletcher.
1867	The lugger *Meum and Tuum* is built. FitzGerald and Posh become partners in herring-fishing.
1868	Enlarged edition of the *Rubáiyát*.
1870	Partnership with Posh Fletcher dissolved.
1872	Third edition of the *Rubáiyát*.
1873	FitzGerald evicted from his rooms in Market Hill.
1874	Moves to his 'château,' Grange Farm, later known as Little Grange.
1876	Formally acknowledged as the translator of the *Rubáiyát*. He publishes "an impudent version of the Agamemnon."
1879	Fourth edition of the *Rubáiyát*.
1880 and 1881	Translations of Sophocles privately distributed.
1882	*Readings in Crabbe* published by Quaritch.
1883	FitzGerald dies at George Crabbe's rectory, Merton, Norfolk, on 14 June. Buried in Boulge churchyard, 19 June.

MEMOIR OF
BERNARD
BARTON

[*Selections from the Poems and Letters of Bernard Barton*, edited by his daughter, was published by Hall, Virtue and Co. in 1849. From a letter to W. B. Donne (see pages 550–1) it is clear that FitzGerald was responsible for most of the editorial work of selection, as well as for the Memoir of Bernard Barton signed with his initials which was included in the book.]

MEMOIR OF
BERNARD BARTON

———————

(*From a letter of Bernard Barton's*)

"2 *mo*, 11, 1839.

"Thy cordial approval of my brother John's hearty wish to bring us back to the simple habits of the olden time, induces me to ask thee if I mentioned in either of my late letters the curious old papers he stumbled on in hunting through the repositories of our late excellent spinster sister? I quite forget whether I did or not; so I will not at a venture repeat all the items. But he found an inventory of the goods and chattels of our great-grandfather, John Barton of Ive-Gill, a little hamlet about five or seven miles from Carlisle; by which it seems our progenitor was one of those truly patriarchal personages, a Cumbrian statesman—living on his own little estate, and drawing from it all things needful for himself and his family. I will be bound for it my good brother was more gratified at finding his earliest traceable ancestor such an one than if he had found him in the college of heralds with *gules purpure* and argent emblazoned as his bearings. The total amount of his stock, independent of house, land, and any money he might have, seems by the valuation to have been £61 6s., and the copy of his admission to his little estate gives the fine as £5, so that I suppose its annual value was then estimated at £2 15s. This was about a century back. Yet this man was the chief means of building the little chapel in the dale, still standing. (He was a churchman.) I doubt not he was a fine simple-hearted noble-minded yeoman, in his day, and I am very proud of him. Why did his son, my grandfather, after whom I was named, ever leave that pleasant dale, and go and set up a manufactory in

15

Carlisle; inventing a piece of machinery* for which he had a medal from the Royal Society?—so says Pennant. Methinks he had better have abode in the old grey stone, slate-covered homestead on the banks of that pretty brooklet the Ive! But I bear his name, so I will not quarrel with his memory."

Thus far Bernard Barton traces the history of his family. And it appears that, as his grandfather's mechanical genius drew him away from the pastoral life at Ive-Gill, so his father, who was of a literary turn, reconciled himself with difficulty to the manufactory he inherited at Carlisle. "I always," he wrote, "perused a Locke, an Addison, or a Pope, with delight, and ever sat down to my ledger with a sort of disgust;" and he at one time determined to quit a business in which he had been "neither successfully nor agreeably engaged," and become "a minister of some sect of religion—it will *then* be time," he says, "to determine of what sect, when I am enabled to judge of their respective merits. But this I will freely confess to you, that if there be any one of them, the tenets of which are more favourable to rational religion than the one in which I have been brought up, I shall be so far from thinking it a crime, that I cannot but consider it my duty to embrace it." This, however, was written when he was very young. He never gave up business, but changed one business for another, and shifted the scene of its transaction. His religious inquiries led to a more decided result. He very soon left the Church of England, and became a member of the Society of Friends.

About the same time he married a Quaker lady, Mary Done, of a Cheshire family. She bore him several children: but only three lived to maturity; two daughters, of whom the elder, Maria, distinguished herself, afterward, as the author of many useful children's books under her married name, Hack; and one son, Bernard, the poet, who was born on January 31, 1784.

* The manufactory was one of calico-printing. The "piece of machinery" is thus described by Pennant:—"Saw at Mr Bernard Barton's a pleasing sight of twelve little girls spinning at once at a horizontal wheel, which set twelve bobbins in motion; yet so contrived, that should any accident happen to one, the motion of that might be stopped without any impediment to the others."

16

Shortly before Bernard's birth, however, John Barton had removed to London, where he engaged in something of the same business he had quitted at Carlisle, but where he probably found society and interests more suited to his taste. I do not know whether he ever acted as minister in his Society; but his name appears on one record of their most valuable endeavours. The Quakers had from the very time of George Fox distinguished themselves by their opposition to slavery: a like feeling had gradually been growing up in other quarters of England; and in 1787 a mixed committee of twelve persons was appointed to promote the Abolition of the Slave-trade; Wilberforce engaging to second them with all his influence in parliament. Among these twelve stands the name of John Barton, in honourable companionship with that of Thomas Clarkson.

"I lost my mother," again writes B.B., "when I was only a few days old; and my father married again in my infancy so wisely and so happily, that I knew not but his second wife was my own mother, till I learned it years after at a boarding school." The name of this amiable step-mother was Elizabeth Horne; a Quaker also; daughter of a merchant, who, with his house in London and villa at Tottenham, was an object of B.B.'s earliest regard and latest recollection. "Some of my first recollections," he wrote fifty years after, "are, looking out of his parlour windows at Bankside on the busy Thames, with its ever-changing scene, and the dome of St Paul's rising out of the smoke on the other side of the river. But my most delightful recollections of boyhood are connected with the fine old country-house in a green lane diverging from the high road which runs through Tottenham. I would give seven years of life as it now is, for a week of that which I then led. It was a large old house, with an iron palisade and a pair of iron gates in front, and a huge stone eagle on each pier. Leading up to the steps by which you went up to the hall door, was a wide gravel walk, bordered in summer time by huge tubs, in which were orange and lemon trees, and in the centre of the grass-plot stood a tub yet huger, holding an enormous aloe. The hall itself, to my fancy then lofty and wide as a cathedral would seem now, was a famous place for battledore and shuttlecock; and behind was a garden, equal to that of old Alcinous himself. My favourite walk was one of turf by a long strait pond, bordered with lime-trees. But the whole demesne was the fairy ground of my childhood; and its presiding genius was grandpapa. He must have been a handsome man in his youth, for I remember him at nearly eighty, a very fine looking one, even in the decay of mind and body. In the morning a velvet cap; by dinner, a flaxen wig; and features always expressive of benignity and placid cheerfulness. When he walked out into the garden, his cocked hat and amber-headed cane completed his costume. To the recollection of this delightful personage, I am, I think, indebted for many soothing and pleasing associations with old age."

John Barton did not live to see the only child—a son—that was born to him by this second marriage. He had some time before quitted London, and taken partnership in a malting business at Hertford, where he died, in the prime of life. After his death his widow returned to Tottenham, and there with her son and stepchildren continued for some time to reside.

In due time, Bernard was sent to a much-esteemed Quaker school at Ipswich: returning always to spend his holidays at Tottenham. When fourteen years old, he was apprenticed to Mr Samuel Jesup, a shopkeeper at Halstead in Essex. "There I stood," he writes, "for eight years behind the counter of the corner shop at the top of Halstead Hill, kept to this day" (Nov. 9, 1828) "by my old master, and still worthy uncle S. Jesup."

In 1806 he went to Woodbridge; and a year after married Lucy Jesup, the niece of his former master, and entered into partnership with her brother as coal and corn merchant. But she died a year after marriage, in giving birth to the only child, who now survives them both; and he, perhaps sickened with the scene of his blighted love,* and finding, like his father, that he

---

* The following verses were published in his first volume:—

O thou from earth for ever fled!
Whose reliques lie among the dead,
With daisied verdure overspread,
        My Lucy!

For many a weary day gone by,
How many a solitary sigh
I've heaved for thee, no longer nigh,
        My Lucy!

had less taste for the ledger than for literature, almost directly quitted Woodbridge, and engaged himself as private tutor in the family of Mr Waterhouse, a merchant in Liverpool. There Bernard Barton had some family connexions; and there also he was kindly received and entertained by the Roscoe family, who were old acquaintances of his father and mother.

And if to grieve I cease awhile,
I look for that enchanting smile
Which all my cares could once beguile
        My Lucy!

But ah! in vain—the blameless art
Which used to soothe my troubled heart
Is lost with thee, my better part,
        My Lucy!

Thy converse, innocently free,
That made the fiends of fancy flee,
Ah then I feel the want of thee,
        My Lucy!

Nor is it for myself alone
That I thy early death bemoan;
Our infant now is *all my own*,
        My Lucy!

Couldst thou a guardian angel prove
To the dear offspring of our love,
Until it reach the realms above,
        My Lucy!

Could thy angelic spirit stray,
Unseen companion of my way,
As onward drags the weary day,
        My Lucy!

And when the midnight hour shall close
Mine eyes in short unsound repose,
Couldst thou but whisper off my woes,
        My Lucy!

Then, though thy loss I must deplore,
Till next we meet to part no more
I'd wait the grasp that from me tore
        My Lucy!

For, be my life but spent like thine,
With joy shall I that life resign,
And fly to thee, for ever mine,
        My Lucy!

After a year's residence in Liverpool, he returned to Wood-bridge, and there became clerk in Messrs Alexander's bank—a kind of office which secures certain, if small, remuneration, without any of the anxiety of business; and there he continued for forty years, working till within two days of his death.

He had always been fond of books; was one of the most active members of a Woodbridge Book Club, which he only quitted a month or two before he died; and had written and sent to his friends occasional copies of verse. In 1812 he published his first volume of Poems, called "Metrical Effusions," and began a correspondence with Southey, who continued to give him most kind and wise advice for many years. A complimentary copy of verses which he had addressed to the author of the "Queen's Wake," (just then come into notice,) brought him long and vehement letters from the Ettrick Shepherd, full of thanks to Barton and praises of himself; and along with all this, a tragedy "that will astonish the world ten times more than the 'Queen's Wake' has done," a tragedy with so many characters in it of equal importance "that justice cannot be done it in Edinburgh," and therefore the author confidentially intrusts it to Bernard Barton to get it represented in London. Theatres, and managers of theatres, being rather out of the Quaker poet's way, he called into council Capel Lofft, with whom he also corresponded, and from whom he received flying visits in the course of Lofft's attendance at the county sessions. Lofft took the matter into consideration, and promised all assistance, but on the whole dis-suaded Hogg from trying London managers; he himself having sent them three tragedies of his own; and others by friends of "transcendent merit, equal to Miss Baillie's," all of which had fallen on barren ground.

In 1818 Bernard Barton published by subscription a thin 4to volume—"Poems by an Amateur,"—and shortly afterward appeared under the auspices of a London publisher in a volume of "Poems," which, being favourably reviewed in the Edinburgh, reached a fourth edition by 1825. In 1822 came out his "Napoleon," which he managed to get dedicated and presented to George the Fourth. And now being launched upon the public with a favouring gale, he pushed forward with an eagerness that was little to his ultimate advantage. Between 1822 and 1828 he published five volumes of verse. Each of these contained many pretty poems; but many that were very hasty, and written more as task-work, when the mind was already wearied with the desk-labours of the day; not waiting for the occasion to suggest, nor the impulse to improve. Of this he was warned by his friends, and of the danger of making himself too cheap with publishers and the public. But the advice of others had little weight in the hour of success with one so inexperienced and so hopeful as himself. And there was in Bernard Barton a certain boyish impetuosity in pursuit of anything he had at heart, that age itself scarcely could subdue. Thus it was with his correspondence; and thus it was with his poetry. He wrote always with great facility, almost unretarded by that worst labour of correction; for he was not fastidious himself about exactness of thought or of harmony of numbers, and he could scarce comprehend why the public should be less easily satisfied. Or if he did labour—and labour he did at that time—still it was at task-work of a kind he liked. He loved poetry for its own sake, whether to read or to compose, and felt assured that he was employing his own talent in the cause of virtue and religion, and the blameless affections of men. No doubt he also liked praise; though not in any degree proportional to his eagerness in publishing; but inversely, rather. Very vain men are seldom so careless in the production of that from which they expect their reward. And Barton soon seemed to forget one book in the preparation of another; and in time to forget the contents of all, except a few pieces that arose more directly from his heart, and so naturally attached themselves to his memory. And there was in him one great sign of the absence of any inordinate vanity—the total want of envy. He was quite as anxious others should publish as himself; would never believe there could be too much poetry abroad; would scarce admit a fault in the verses of others, whether private friends or public authors, though after a while (as in his own case) his mind silently and unconsciously adopted only what was good in them. A much more likely motive for this mistaken activity of publication is, the desire to add to the slender income of his clerkship. For Bernard Barton was a generous, and not a provident man; and, few and modest as were his wants, he did not usually manage to square them to the still narrower limit of his means.

But apart from all these motives, the preparation of a book was amusement and excitement to one who had little enough of it in the ordinary routine of daily life: treaties with publishers—arrangements of printing—correspondence with friends on the subject—and, when the little volume was at last afloat, watching it for a while somewhat as a boy watches a paper boat committed to the sea.

His health appears to have suffered from his exertions. He writes to friends complaining of low spirits, head-ache, etc., the usual effect of sedentary habits, late hours, and overtasked brain. Charles Lamb advises after his usual fashion: some grains of sterling available truth amid a heap of jests.* Southey replies more gravely, in a letter that should be read and marked by every student.

"Keswick, 27 Jan., 1822.

"I am much pleased with the 'Poet's Lot'—no, not with his lot, but with the verses in which he describes it. But let me ask you—are you not pursuing your studies intemperately, and to the danger of your health? To be 'writing long after midnight' and 'with a miserable head-ache' is what no man can do with impunity; and what no pressure of business, no ardour of com-

---

* "You are too much apprehensive about your complaint. I know many that are always ailing of it, and live on to a good old age. I know a merry fellow (you partly know him) who, when his medical adviser told him he had drunk away all *that part*, congratulated himself (now his liver was gone) that he should be the longest liver of the two. The best way in these cases is to keep yourself as ignorant as you can—as ignorant as the world was before Galen—of the entire inner constructions of the animal man; not to be conscious of a midriff; to hold kidneys (save of sheep and swine) to be an agreeable fiction; not to know whereabouts the gall grows; to account the circulation of the blood a mere idle whim of Harvey's; to acknowledge no mechanism not visible. For, once fix the seat of your disorder, and your fancies flux into it like so many bad humours. Those medical gentry choose each his favourite part, one takes the lungs—another the aforesaid liver, and refers to that whatever in the animal economy is amiss. Above all, use exercise, take a little more spirituous liquors, learn to smoke, continue to keep a good conscience, and avoid tamperings with hard terms of art—viscosity, schirrosity, and those bugbears by which simple patients are scared into their graves. Believe the general sense of the mercantile world, which holds that desks are not deadly. It is the mind, good B.B., and not the limbs, that taints by long sitting. Think of the patience of tailors—think how long the Lord Chancellor sits—think of the brooding hen."

position, has ever made me do. I beseech you, remember the
fate of Kirke White;—and remember that if you sacrifice your
health (not to say your life) in the same manner, you will be
held up to your own community as a warning—not as an example
for imitation. The spirit which disturbed poor Scott of Amwell
in his last illness will fasten upon your name; and your fate will
be instanced to prove the inconsistency of your pursuits with
that sobriety and evenness of mind which Quakerism requires,
and is intended to produce.—

"You will take this as it is meant, I am sure.

"My friend, go early to bed;—and if you eat suppers, read
afterwards, but never compose, that you may lie down with a
quiet intellect. There is an intellectual as well as a religious peace
of mind;—and without the former, be assured there can be no
health for a poet. God bless you,

Yours very truly,
R. SOUTHEY."

Mr Barton had even entertained an idea of quitting the bank
altogether, and trusting to his pen for subsistence.—An unwise
scheme in all men: most unwise in one who had so little tact
with the public as himself. From this, however, he was fortunately diverted by all the friends to whom he communicated his
design.* Charles Lamb thus wrote to him:—

* So long ago as the date of his first volume he had written to Lord Byron
on the subject; who thus answered him:—

"St James's Street, June 1, 1812.

"Sir,

The most satisfactory answer to the concluding part of your letter is, that
Mr Murray will re-publish your volume if you still retain your inclination
for the experiment, which I trust will be successful. Some weeks ago my
friend Mr Rogers showed me some of the Stanzas in MS., and I then expressed my opinion of their merit, which a further perusal of the printed
volume has given me no reason to revoke. I mention this as it may not be
disagreeable to you to learn that I entertained a very favourable opinion of
your power before I was aware that such sentiments were reciprocal.—
Waiving your obliging expressions as to my own productions, for which I
thank you very sincerely, and assure you that I think not lightly of the praise
of one whose approbation is valuable; will you allow me to talk to you
candidly, not critically, on the subject of yours?—You will not suspect me
of a wish to discourage, since I pointed out to the publisher the propriety of
complying with your wishes. I think more highly of your poetical talents than

"9th January, 1823.

"Throw yourself on the world without any rational plan of support beyond what the chance employ of booksellers would afford you!!!

"Throw yourself rather, my dear Sir, from the steep Tarpeian rock, slap-dash headlong upon iron spikes. If you have but five consolatory minutes between the desk and the bed, make much of them, and live a century in them, rather than turn slave to the booksellers. They are Turks and Tartars when they have poor authors at their beck. Hitherto you have been at arm's length from them. Come not within their grasp. I have known many authors want for bread—some repining—others enjoying the blest security of a counting-house—all agreeing they had rather have been tailors, weavers,—what not?—rather than the things they were. I have known some starved, some to go mad, one dear friend literally dying in a workhouse. You know not what a rapacious, dishonest set these booksellers are. Ask even Southey, who (a single case almost) has made a fortune by book-drudgery, what he has found them. O you know not, may you never know! the miseries of subsisting by authorship! 'Tis a pretty appendage it would perhaps gratify you to hear expressed, for I believe, from what I observe of your mind, that you are above flattery.—To come to the point, you deserve success; but we knew before Addison wrote his Cato, that desert does not always command it. But suppose it attained—

'You know what ills the author's life assail,
Toil, envy, want, the *patron*, and the jail.'—

Do not renounce writing, but never trust entirely to authorship. If you have a profession, retain it, it will be like Prior's fellowship, a last and sure resource.—Compare Mr Rogers with other authors of the day; assuredly he is among the first of living poets, but is it to that he owes his station in society and his intimacy in the best circles? no, it is to his prudence and respectability. The world (a bad one I own) courts him because he has no occasion to court it.—He is a poet, nor is he less so because he was something more.—I am not sorry to hear that you are not tempted by the vicinity of Capel Lofft, Esq., though if he had done for you what he has for the Bloomfields I should never have laughed at his rage for patronizing.—But a truly well constituted mind will ever be independent.—That you may be so is my sincere wish; and if others think as well of your poetry as I do, you will have no cause to complain of your readers.—Believe me,

Your obliged and obedient Servant,
BYRON."

24

to a situation like yours or mine; but a slavery worse than all slavery, to be a bookseller's dependant, to drudge your brains for pots of ale and breasts of mutton, to change your free thoughts and voluntary numbers for ungracious task-work. The booksellers hate us. The reason I take to be, that, contrary to other trades, in which the master gets all the credit, (a jeweller or silversmith for instance,) and the journeyman, who really does the fine work, is in the background: in *our* work the world gives all the credit to *us*, whom *they* consider as *their* journeymen, and therefore do they hate us, and cheat us, and oppress us, and would wring the blood of us out, to put another sixpence in their mechanic pouches.

.   .   .   .   .

"Keep to your bank, and the bank will keep you. Trust not to the public: you may hang, starve, drown yourself for any thing that worthy personage cares. I bless every star that Providence, not seeing good to make me independent, has seen it next good to settle me upon the stable foundation of Leadenhall. Sit down, good B.B., in the banking office: what! is there not from six to eleven, P.M., six days in the week, and is there not all Sunday? Fie, what a superfluity of man's time, if you could think so! Enough for relaxation, mirth, converse, poetry, good thoughts, quiet thoughts. O the corroding, torturing, tormenting thoughts that disturb the brain of the unlucky wight, who must draw upon it for daily sustenance! Henceforth I retract all my fond complaints of mercantile employment—look upon them as lovers' quarrels. I was but half in earnest. Welcome dead timber of a desk that gives me life. A little grumbling is a wholesome medicine for the spleen, but in my inner heart do I approve and embrace this our close but unharassing way of life. I am quite serious.

Yours truly,
C. LAMB."

In 1824, however, his income received a handsome addition from another quarter. A few members of his Society, including some of the wealthier of his own family, raised £1200 among them for his benefit. Mr Shewell of Ipswich, who was one of the main contributors to this fund, writes to me that the scheme originated with Joseph John Gurney:—"one of those innumerable acts of kindness and beneficence which marked his character, and the *measure* of which will never be known upon the earth." Nor was the measure of it known in this instance; for of the large sum that he handed in as the subscription of several, Mr Shewell thinks he was "a larger donor than he chose to acknowledge." The money thus raised was vested in the name of Mr Shewell, and its yearly interest paid to Bernard Barton; till, in 1839, the greater part of it was laid out in buying that old house and the land round it, which Mr Barton so much loved as the habitation of his wife's mother, Martha Jesup.

It seems that he felt some delicacy at first in accepting this munificent testimony which his own people offered to his talents. But here again Lamb assisted him with plain, sincere, and wise advice.

"March 24th, 1824.

"DEAR B.B.,

I hasten to say that if my opinion can strengthen you in your choice it is decisive for your acceptance of what has been so handsomely offered. I can see nothing injurious to your most honourable sense. Think that you are called to a poetical ministry —nothing worse—the minister is worthy of his hire.

"The only objection I feel is founded on a fear that the acceptance may be a temptation to you to let fall the bone (hard as it is) which is in your mouth, and must afford tolerable pickings, for the shadow of independence. You cannot propose to become independent on what the low state of interest could afford you from such a principal as you mention; and the most graceful excuse for the acceptance would be, that it left you free to your voluntary functions: that is the less *light* part of the scruple. It has no darker shade. I put in *darker*, because of the ambiguity of the word light, which Donne, in his admirable poem on the Metempsychosis, has so ingeniously illustrated in his invocation—

'Make my *dark heavy* poem *light* and *light*—'

where the two senses of *light* are opposed to different opposites. A trifling criticism.—I can see no reason for any scruple then but what arises from your own interest; which is in your own power, of course, to solve. If you still have doubts, read over Sanderson's 'Cases of Conscience,' and Jeremy Taylor's 'Ductor Dubitantium;' the first a moderate octavo, the latter a folio of nine hundred close pages: and when you have thoroughly digested the admirable reasons *pro* and *con* which they give for every possible case, you will be—just as wise as when you began. Every man is his own best casuist; and, after all, as Ephraim Smooth, in the pleasant comedy of Wild Oats, has it, 'There is no harm in a guinea.' *A fortiori*, there is less in two thousand.

"I therefore most sincerely congratulate with you, excepting so far as excepted above. If you have fair prospects of adding to the principal, cut the bank; but in either case, do not refuse an honest service. Your heart tells you it is not offered to bribe you *from* any duty, but *to* a duty which you feel to be your vocation.

Farewell heartily,

C.L."

While Mr Barton had been busy publishing, his correspondence with literary people had greatly increased. The drawers and boxes which at last received the overflowings of his capacious Quaker pockets, (and he scarcely ever destroyed a letter,) contain a multitude of letters from literary people, dead or living. Beside those from Southey and Lamb, there are many from Charles Lloyd—simple, noble, and kind, telling of his many Poems—of a Romance in six volumes he was then copying out with his own hand for the seventh time;—from old Lloyd, the father, into whose hands Barton's letters occasionally fell by mistake, telling of his son's many books, but "that it is easier to write them than to gain numerous readers;"—from old Mr Plumptre, who mourns the insensibility of publishers to his castigated editions of Gay and Dibdin—leaving one letter midway, to go to his "spring task of pruning the gooseberries and currants." There are also girlish letters from L.E.L.; and feminine ones from Mrs Hemans. Of living authors there are many letters from Mitford, Bowring, Conder, Mrs Opie, C. B. Tayler, the Howitts, etc.

Owing to Mr Barton's circumstances, his connexion with most of these persons was solely by letter. He went indeed occasionally to Hadleigh, where Dr Drake then flourished, and Mr

Tayler was curate;—to Mr Mitford's at Benhall;—* and he visited Charles Lamb once or twice in London and at Islington. He once also met Southey at Thomas Clarkson's at Playford, in the spring of 1824. But the rest of the persons whose letters I have just mentioned, I believe he never saw. And thus perhaps he acquired a habit of writing that supplied the place of personal intercourse. Confined to a town where there was but little stirring in the literary way, he naturally travelled out of it by letter, for communication on those matters; and this habit gradually extended itself to acquaintances not literary, whom he seemed as happy to converse with by letter as face to face. His correspondence with Mr Clemesha arose out of their meeting once, and only once, by chance in the commercial room of an inn. And with Mrs Sutton, who, beside other matters of interest, could tell him about the "North Countrie," from which his ancestors came, and which he always loved in fancy, (for he never saw it,) —he kept up a correspondence of nearly thirty years, though he and she never met to give form and substance to their visionary conceptions of one another.

From the year 1828, his books, as well as his correspondence with those "whose talk was of" books, declined; and soon after this he seemed to settle down contentedly into that quiet course of life in which he continued to the end. His literary talents, social amiability, and blameless character made him respected,

* Here is one of the notes that used to call B.B. to Benhall in those days.

"Benhall, 1820

"My dear Poet,

We got your note to-day. We are at home and shall be glad to see you, but hope you will not swim here; in other words, we think it better that you should wait, till we can seat you under a chestnut and listen to your oracular sayings. We hope that, like your sister of the woods, you are in full song; she does not print, I think; we hope you do; seeing that you beat her in sense, though she has a little the advantage in melody. Together you will make a pretty duet in our groves. You have both your defects; she devours glow-worms, you take snuff; she is in a great hurry to go away, and you are prodigious slow in arriving; she sings at night, when nobody can hear her, and you write for Ackermann, which nobody thinks of reading. In spite of all this, you will get a hundred a year from the king, and settle at Woodbridge; in another month, she will find no more flies, and set off for Egypt.

Truly yours,

J.M."

liked, and courted among his neighbours. Few, high or low, but were glad to see him at his customary place in the bank, from which he smiled a kindly greeting, or came down with friendly open hand, and some frank words of family inquiry—perhaps with the offer of a pinch from his never-failing snuff-box—or the withdrawal of the visitor, if more intimate, to see some letter or copy of verses, just received or just composed, or some picture just purchased. Few, high or low, but were glad to have him at their tables; where he was equally pleasant and equally pleased, whether with the fine folks at the Hall, or with the homely company at the Farm; carrying every where indifferently the same good feeling, good spirits, and good manners; and by a happy frankness of nature, that did not too precisely measure its utterance on such occasions, checkering the conventional gentility of the drawing-room with some humours of humbler life, which in turn he refined with a little sprinkling of literature.—Now too, after having long lived in a house that was just big enough to sit and sleep in, while he was obliged to board with the ladies of a Quaker school over the way,* he obtained a convenient house of his own, where he got his books and pictures about him. But, more than all this, his daughter was now grown up to be his housekeeper and companion. And amiable as Bernard Barton was in social life, his amiability in this little *tête-à-tête* household of his was yet a fairer thing to behold; so completely was all authority absorbed into confidence, and into love—

> "A constant flow of love, that knew no fall,
>   Ne'er roughen'd by those cataracts and breaks
>   That humour interposed too often makes,"

but gliding on uninterruptedly for twenty years, until death concealed its current from all human witness.

In earlier life Bernard Barton had been a fair pedestrian; and was fond of walking over to the house of his friend Arthur Biddell at Playford. There, beside the instructive and agreeable society of his host and hostess, he used to meet George Airy,

---

* Where he writes a letter one day, but he knows not if intelligibly; "for all hands are busy round me to clap, to starch, to iron, to plait—in plain English, 'tis washing-day; and I am now writing close to a table in which is a bason of starch, caps, kerchiefs, etc., and busy hands and tongues round it."

now Astronomer Royal, then a lad of wonderful promise; with whom he had many a discussion about poetry, and Sir Walter's last new novel, a volume of which perhaps the poet had brought in his pocket. Mr Biddell, at one time, lent him a horse to expedite his journeys to and fro, and to refresh him with some wholesome change of exercise. But of that Barton soon tired. He gradually got to dislike exercise very much; and no doubt greatly injured his health by its disuse. But it was not to be wondered at, that having spent the day in the uncongenial task of "figure-work," as he called it, he should covet his evenings for books, or verses, or social intercourse. It was very difficult to get him out even for a stroll in the garden after dinner, or along the banks of his favourite Deben on a summer evening. He would, after going a little way, with much humorous grumbling at the useless fatigue he was put to endure, stop short of a sudden, and, sitting down in the long grass by the river-side, watch the tide run past, and the well-known vessels gliding into harbour, or dropping down to pursue their voyage under the stars at sea, until his companions, returning from their prolonged walk, drew him to his feet again, to saunter homeward far more willingly than he set forth, with the prospect of the easy chair, the book, and the cheerful supper before him.

His excursions rarely extended beyond a few miles round Woodbridge—to the vale of Dedham, Constable's birth-place and painting-room; or to the neighbouring sea-coast, loved for its own sake—and few could love the sea and the heaths beside it better than he did—but doubly dear to him from its association with the memory and poetry of Crabbe. Once or twice he went as far as Hampshire on a visit to his brother; and once he visited Mr W. B. Donne, at Mattishall, in Norfolk, where he saw many portraits and mementoes of his favourite poet Cowper, Mr Donne's kinsman. That which most interested him there was Mrs Bodham, ninety years old, and almost blind, but with all the courtesy of the old school about her—once the "Rose" whom Cowper had played with at Catfield parsonage when both were children together, and whom until 1790, when she revived their acquaintance by sending him his mother's picture, he had thought "withered and fallen from the stalk." Such little excursions it might be absurd to record of other men; but they were some of the few that Bernard Barton could take, and from their rare occurrence, and the simplicity of his nature, they made a strong impression upon him.

He still continued to write verses, as well on private occasions as for annuals; and in 1836 published another volume, chiefly composed of such fragments. In 1845 came out his last volume; which he got permission to dedicate to the Queen. He sent also a copy of it to Sir Robert Peel, then prime minister, with whom he had already corresponded slightly on the subject of the income tax, which Mr Barton thought pressed rather unduly on clerks, and others, whose narrow income was only for life. Sir Robert asked him to dinner at Whitehall.—"Twenty years ago," writes Barton, "such a summons had elated and exhilarated me—now I feel humbled and depressed at it. Why?—but that I verge on the period when the lighting down of the grasshopper is a burden, and desire itself begins to fail."—He went, however, and was sincerely pleased with the courtesy, and astonished at the social ease, of a man who had so many and so heavy cares on his shoulders. When the Quaker poet was first ushered into the room, there were but three guests assembled, of whom he little expected to know one. But the mutual exclamations of "George Airy!" and "Bernard Barton!" soon satisfied Sir Robert as to his country guest's feeling at home at the great town dinner.

On leaving office a year after, Sir Robert recommended him to the queen for an annual pension of £100:—one of the last acts, as the retiring minister intimated, of his official career, and one he should always reflect on with pleasure.—B. Barton gratefully accepted the boon. And to the very close of life he continued, after his fashion, to send letters and occasional poems to Sir Robert, and to receive a few kind words in reply.

In 1844 died Bernard's eldest sister, Maria Hack. She was five or six years older than himself; very like him in the face; and had been his instructress ("a sort of oracle to me," he says) when both were children. "It is a heavy blow to me," he writes, "for Maria is almost the first human being I remember to have fondly loved, or been fondly loved by—the only living participant in my first and earliest recollections. When I lose her, I had almost as well never have been a child; for she only knew me as such—and the best and brightest of memories are apt to grow dim when they can be no more reflected." "She was just older enough than I," he elsewhere says, "to recollect distinctly what I have a confused glimmering of—about our house at Hertford —even of hers at Carlisle."

Mr Barton had for many years been an *ailing* man, though he never was, I believe, *dangerously* ill (as it is called) till the last year of his life. He took very little care of himself; laughed at all rules of diet, except temperance; and had for nearly forty years, as he said, "taken almost as little exercise as a mile-stone, and far less fresh air." Some years before his death he had been warned of a liability to disease in the heart, an intimation he did not regard, as he never felt pain in that region. Nor did he to that refer the increased distress he began to feel in exertion of any kind, walking fast or going up-stairs, a distress which he looked upon as the disease of old age, and which he used to give vent to in half-humorous groans, that seemed to many of his friends rather expressive of his dislike to exercise, than implying any serious inconvenience from it. But probably the disease that partly arose from inactivity now became the true apology for it. During the last year of his life, too, some loss of his little fortune, and some perplexity in his affairs, not so distressing because of any present inconvenience to himself, as in the prospect of future evil to one whom he loved as himself, may have increased the disease within him, and hastened its final blow.

Towards the end of 1848 the evil symptoms increased much upon him; and, shortly after Christmas, it was found that the disease was far advanced. He consented to have his diet regulated; protesting humorously against the small glass of small beer allowed him in place of the temperate allowance of generous port, or ale, to which he was accustomed. He fulfilled his daily duty in the bank,* only remitting (as he was peremptorily bid) his attendance there after his four o'clock dinner.† And though

* He had written of himself, some years before, "I shall go on making figures till Death makes me a cipher."

† For which he half accused himself as "*a skulker.*" And of late years, when the day account of the bank had not come quite right by the usual hour of closing, and it seemed necessary to carry on business late into the evening, he would sometimes come up wearied to his room, saying—"Well, we've got all right but a shilling, and I've left my boys" (as he called the younger clerks) "to puzzle that out." But even then he would get up from "Rob Roy"

32

not able to go out to his friends, he was glad to see them at his own house to the last.

Here is a letter, written a few days before his death, to one of his kindest and most hospitable friends.

"2 *mo*, 14, 1849.

"My dear old Friend—Thy home-brewed has been duly received, and I drank a glass yesterday with relish, but I must not indulge too often—for I make slow way, if any, toward recovery, and at times go on puffing, panting, groaning, and making a variety of noises, not unlike a loco-motive at first starting; more to give vent to my own discomfort, than for the delectation of those around me. So I am not fit to go into company, and cannot guess when I shall. However, I am free from much acute suffering, and not so much hypp'd as might be forgiven in a man who has such trouble about his breathing that it naturally puts him on thinking how long he may be able to breathe at all. But if the hairs of one's head are numbered, so, by a parity of reasoning, are the puffs of our bellows. I write not in levity, though I use homely words. I do not think J—— sees any present cause of serious alarm, but I do not think he sees, on the other hand, much prospect of speedy recovery, if of entire recovery at all. The thing has been coming on for years; and cannot be cured at once, if at all. A man can't poke over desk or table for forty years without putting some of the machinery of the chest out of sorts. As the evenings get warm and light we shall see what gentle exercise and a little fresh air can do. In the last few days too I have been in solicitude about a little pet niece of mine dying, if not dead, at York: this has somewhat worried me, and agitation or excitement is as bad for me as work or quickness of motion. Yet, after all, I have really more to be thankful for than to grumble about. I have no very acute pain, a skeely doctor, a good nurse, kind solicitous friends, a remission of the worst part of my desk hours—so why should I fret? Love to the younkers.

Thine,

B."

or the "Antiquary" every now and then, and go to peep through the curtain of a window that opens upon the back of the bank, and, if he saw the great gas-lamp flaming within, announce with a half comical sympathy, that "they were still at it"; or, when the lamp was at last existinguished, would return to his chair more happily, now that his partners were liberated.

On Monday, February 19, he was unable to get into the bank, having passed a very unquiet night—the first night of distress, he thankfully said, that his illness had caused him. He suffered during the day; but welcomed as usual the friends who came to see him as he lay on his sofa; and wrote a few *notes*—for his correspondence must now, as he had humorously lamented, become as short-breathed as himself. In the evening, at half-past eight, as he was yet conversing cheerfully with a friend, he rose up, went to his bed-room, and suddenly rang the bell. He was found by his daughter—dying. Assistance was sent for; but all assistance was vain. "In a few minutes more," says the note despatched from the house of death that night, "all distress was over on *his* part—and that warm kind heart is still for ever."

The Letters and Poems that follow are very faithful revelations of Bernard Barton's soul; of the genuine piety to God, good-will to men, and cheerful guileless spirit, which animated him, not only while writing in the undisturbed seclusion of the closet, but (what is a very different matter) through the walk and practice of daily life. They prove also his intimate acquaintance with the Bible, and his deep appreciation of many beautiful passages which might escape a common reader.

The Letters show, that while he had well considered, and well approved, the pure principles of Quakerism, he was equally liberal in his recognition of other forms of Christianity. He could attend the *church*, or the *chapel*, if the *meeting* were not at hand; and once assisted in raising money to build a new *Established Church* in Woodbridge. And while he was sometimes roused to defend Dissent from the vulgar attacks of High Church and Tory, he could also give the bishops a good word when they were unjustly assailed.

While duly conforming to the usages of his Society on all proper occasions, he could forget *thee* and *thou* while mixing in social intercourse with people of another vocabulary, and smile at the Reviewer who reproved him for using the heathen name *November* in his Poems. "I find," he said, "these names of the months the prescriptive dialect of *poetry*, used as such by many members of our Society before me—'sans peur et sans reproche;'

34

and I use them accordingly, asking no questions for conscience' sake, as to their origin. Yet while I do this, I can give my cordial tribute of approval to the scruples of our early friends, who advocate a simpler nomenclature. I can quite understand and respect their simplicity and godly sincerity; and I conceive that I have duly shown my reverence for their scruples in adhering *personally* to their dialect, and only using another *poetically*. Ask the British Friend the name of the planet with a belt round it, and he would say, Saturn; at the peril, and on the pain, of excommunication."

As to his politics, he always used to call himself, "a Whig of the old school." Perhaps, like most men in easy circumstances, he grew more averse to change as he grew older. He thus writes to a friend in 1845, during the heats occasioned by the proposed Repeal of the Corn Laws:—"Queer times these, and strange events. I feel most shamefully indifferent about the whole affair; but my political fever has long since spent itself. It was about its height when they sent Burdett to the Tower. It has cooled down wonderfully since then. He went there, to the best of my recollection, in the character of Burns's Sir William Wallace—

'Great patriot hero—ill-requited chief;'—

and dwindled down afterwards to 'Old Glory.' No more patriots for me." But Bernard Barton did not trouble himself much about politics. He occasionally grew interested when the interests of those he loved were at stake; and his affections generally guided his judgment. Hence he was always against a Repeal of the Corn Laws, because he loved Suffolk farmers, Suffolk labourers, and Suffolk fields. Occasionally he took part in the election of a friend to Parliament—writing in prose or verse in the county papers. And here also, though he more willingly sided with the Liberal interest, he would put out a hand to help the good old Tory at a pinch.

He was equally tolerant of men, and free of acquaintance. So long as men were honest, (and he was slow to suspect them to be otherwise,) and reasonably agreeable, (and he was easily pleased,) he could find company in them. "My temperament," he writes, "is, as far as a man can judge of himself, eminently social. I am wont to live out of myself, and to cling to anything or anybody

35

loveable within my reach." I have before said that he was equally welcome and equally at ease, whether at the Hall or at the Farm; himself indifferent to rank, though he gave every one his title, not wondering even at those of his own community, who, unmindful perhaps of the military implication, owned to the soft impeachment of *Esquire*. But no where was he more amiable than in some of those humbler meetings—about the fire in the *keeping-room* at Christmas, or under the walnut-tree in summer. He had his cheerful remembrances with the old; a playful word for the young—especially with children, whom he loved and was loved by.—Or, on some summer afternoon, perhaps, at the little inn on the heath, or by the river-side—or when, after a pleasant pic-nic on the sea-shore, we drifted homeward up the river, while the breeze died away at sunset, and the heron, at last startled by our gliding boat, slowly rose from the ooze over which the tide was momentarily encroaching.

By nature, as well as by discipline perhaps, he had a great dislike to most violent occasions of feeling and manifestations of it, whether in real life or story. Many years ago he entreated the author of "May you like it," who had written some tales of powerful interest, to write others "where the appeals to one's feelings were perhaps less frequent—I mean one's sympathetic feelings with suffering virtue—and the more pleasurable emotions called forth by the spectacle of quiet, unobtrusive, domestic happiness more dwelt on." And when Mr Tayler had long neglected to answer a letter, Barton humorously proposed to rob him on the highway, in hopes of recovering an interest by crime which he supposed every-day good conduct had lost. Even in Walter Scott, his great favourite, he seemed to relish the humorous parts more than the pathetic;—Bailie Nicol Jarvie's dilemmas at Glennaquoich, rather than Fergus Mac Ivor's trial; and Oldbuck and his sister Grizel rather than the scenes at the fisherman's cottage. Indeed, many, I dare say, of those who only know Barton by his poetry, will be surprised to hear how much humour he had in himself, and how much he relished it in others. Especially, perhaps, in later life, when men have commonly had quite enough of "domestic tragedy," and are glad to laugh when they can.

With little critical knowledge of pictures, he was very fond of them, especially such as represented scenery familiar to him—the shady lane, the heath, the corn-field, the village, the sea-shore. And he loved after coming away from the bank to sit in his room and watch the twilight steal over his landscapes as over the real face of nature, and then lit up again by fire or candle light. Nor could any itinerant picture-dealer pass Mr Barton's door without calling to tempt him to a new purchase. And then was B.B. to be seen, just come up from the bank, with broad-brim and spectacles on, examining some picture set before him on a chair in the most advantageous light; the dealer recommending, and Barton wavering, until partly by money, and partly by exchange of some older favourites, with perhaps a snuff-box thrown in to turn the scale; a bargain was concluded—generally to B.B.'s great disadvantage and great content. Then friends were called in to admire; and letters written to describe; and the picture taken up to his bed-room to be seen by candle light on going to bed, and by the morning sun on awaking; then hung up in the best place in the best room; till in time perhaps it was itself exchanged away for some newer favourite.

He was not learned—in language, science, or philosophy. Nor did he care for the loftiest kinds of poetry—"the heroics," as he called it. His favourite authors were those that dealt most in humour, good sense, domestic feeling, and pastoral description —Goldsmith, Cowper, Wordsworth in his lowlier moods, and Crabbe. One of his favourite prose books was Boswell's Johnson; of which he knew all the good things by heart, an inexhaustible store for a country dinner-table. And many will long remember him as he used to sit at table, his snuff-box in his hand, and a glass of genial wine before him, repeating some favourite passage, and glancing his fine brown eyes about him as he recited.

But perhaps his favourite prose book was Scott's Novels. These he seemed never tired of reading, and hearing read. During the last four or five winters I have gone through several of the best of these with him—generally on one night in each week—Saturday night, that left him free to the prospect of Sunday's relaxation. Then was the volume taken down impatiently from the shelf almost before tea was over; and at last, when the room was clear, candles snuffed, and fire stirred, he would read out, or listen to, those fine stories, anticipating with a glance, or an impatient ejaculation of pleasure, the good things he knew were coming—which he liked all the better for knowing they were coming—relishing them afresh in the fresh enjoyment of his companion, to whom they were less familiar; until the modest supper coming in closed the book, and recalled him to his cheerful hospitality.

Of the literary merits of this volume, others, less biassed than myself by personal and local regards, will better judge. But the Editor, to whom, as well as the Memoir, the task of making any observations of this kind usually falls, has desired me to say a few words on the subject.

The Letters, judging from internal evidence as well as from all personal knowledge of the author's habits, were for the most part written off with the same careless ingenuousness that characterized his conversation. "I have no alternative," he said, "between not writing at all, and writing what first comes into my head." In both cases the same cause seems to me to produce the same agreeable effect.

The Letters on graver subjects are doubtless the result of graver "foregone conclusion,"—but equally spontaneous in point of utterance, without any effort at style whatever.

If the Letters here published are better than the mass of those they are selected from, it is because better topics happened to present themselves to one who, though he wrote so much, had perhaps as little of new or animating to write about as most men.

The Poems, if not written off as easily as the Letters, were probably as little elaborated as any that ever were published. Without claiming for them the highest attributes of poetry, (which the author never pretended to,) we may surely say they abound in genuine feeling and elegant fancy expressed in easy, and often very felicitous, verse. These qualities employed in illustrating the religious and domestic affections, and the pastoral scenery with which such affections are perhaps most generally associated, have made Bernard Barton, as he desired to be, a household poet with a large class of readers—a class, who, as they may be supposed to welcome such poetry as being the articulate voice of those good feelings yearning in their own bosoms, one may hope will continue and increase in England.

While in many of these Poems it is the spirit within that redeems an imperfect form—just as it lights up the irregular features of a face into beauty—there are many which will surely abide the test of severer criticism. Such are several of the Sonnets; which, if they have not (and they do not aim at) the power and grandeur, are also free from the pedantic stiffness of so many English Sonnets. Surely that one "To my Daughter," is very beautiful in all respects.

Some of the lighter pieces—"To Joanna," "To a young Housewife," &c., partake much of Cowper's playful grace. And some on the decline of life, and the religious consolations attending it, are very touching.

Charles Lamb said the verses "To the Memory of Bloomfield" were "sweet with Doric delicacy." May not one say the same of those "On Leiston Abbey," "Cowper's Rural Walks," on "Some Pictures," and others of the shorter descriptive pieces? Indeed, utterly incongruous as at first may seem the Quaker clerk and the ancient Greek Idyllist, some of these little poems recall to me the inscriptions in the Greek Anthology—not in any particular passages, but in their general air of simplicity, leisurely elegance, and quiet unimpassioned pensiveness.

Finally, what Southey said of *one* of Barton's volumes—"there are many rich passages and frequent felicity of expression"—may modestly be said of these selections from ten. Not only is the fundamental thought of many of them very beautiful—as in the poems, "To a Friend in Distress," "The Deserted Nest," "Thought in a Garden," etc.,—but there are many verses whose melody will linger in the ear, and many images that will abide in the memory. Such surely are those of men's hearts brightening up at Christmas "like a fire new stirred,"—of the stream that leaps along over the pebbles "like happy hearts by holiday made light,"—of the solitary tomb showing from afar like a lamb in the meadow. And in the poem called "A Dream,"—a dream the poet really had,—how beautiful is that chorus of the friends of her youth who surround the central vision of his departed wife, and who, much as the dreamer wonders they do not see she is a spirit, and silent as she remains to their greetings, still with countenances of "blameless mirth," like some of Correggio's angel attendants, press around her without awe or hesitation, repeating "welcome, welcome!" as to one suddenly returned to them from some earthly absence only, and not from beyond the dead—from heaven.

E.F.G.

EUPHRANOR

[*Euphranor, A Dialogue on Youth*, was first published by William Pickering in 1851. Further editions, much revised by the author, appeared in 1855 and 1882. The 1882 edition was subtitled *A May-Day Conversation at Cambridge*, "*'Tis Forty Years Since*," and provides the text used by Aldis Wright. All the editions were anonymous.]

EUPHRANOR

DURING the time of my pretending to practise Medicine at Cambridge, I was aroused, one fine forenoon of May, by the sound of some one coming up my staircase, two or three steps at a time it seemed to me; then, directly after, a smart rapping at the door; and, before I could say, "Come in," Euphranor had opened it, and, striding up to me, seized my arm with his usual eagerness, and told me I must go out with him—"It was such a day—sun shining—breeze blowing—hedges and trees in full leaf.—He had been to Chesterton, (he said,) and pull'd back with a man who now left him in the lurch; and I must take his place." I told him what a poor hand at the oar I was, and, such walnut-shells as these Cambridge boats were, I was sure a strong fellow like him must rejoice in getting a whole Eight-oar to himself once in a while. He laughed, and said, "The pace, the pace was the thing—However, that was all nothing, but—in short, I must go with him, whether for a row, or a walk in the fields, or a game of Billiards at Chesterton—whatever I liked— only go I must." After a little more banter, about some possible Patients, I got up; closed some very weary medical Treatise I was reading; on with coat and hat; and in three minutes we had run downstairs, out into the open air; where both of us calling out together "What a day!" it was, we struck out briskly for the old Wooden Bridge, where Euphranor said his boat was lying.

"By-the-by," said I, as we went along, "it would be a charity to knock up poor Lexilogus, and carry him along with us."

Not much of a charity, Euphranor thought—Lexilogus would so much rather be left with his books. Which I declared was the very reason he should be taken from them; and Euphranor, who was quite good-humour'd, and wish'd Lexilogus all well, (for we were all three Yorkshiremen, whose families lived no great distance asunder,) easily consented. So, without more ado, we turn'd into Trinity Great gate, and round by the right up a staircase to the attic where Lexilogus kept.

The door was *sported*, as they say, but I knew he must be within; so, using the privilege of an old friend, I shouted to him through the letter-slit. Presently we heard the sound of books falling, and soon after Lexilogus' thin, pale, and spectacled face appear'd at the half-open'd door. He was always glad to see me, I believe, howsoever I disturb'd him; and he smiled as he laid his hand in mine, rather than return'd its pressure: working hard, as he was, poor fellow, for a Fellowship that should repay all the expense of sending him to College.

The tea-things were still on the table, and I asked him (though I knew well enough) if he were so fashionable as only just to have breakfasted?

"Oh—long ago—directly after morning Chapel."

I then told him he must put his books away, and come out on the river with Euphranor and myself.

"He could not possibly," he thought;—"not so early, at least —preparing for some Examination, or course of Lectures——"

"Come, come, my good fellow," said Euphranor, "that is the very reason, says the Doctor; and he will have his way. So make haste."

I then told him (what I then suddenly remember'd) that, beside other reasons, his old Aunt, a Cambridge tradesman's widow whom I attended, and whom Lexilogus help'd to support out of his own little savings, wanted to see him on some business. He should go with us to Chesterton, where she lodged; visit her while Euphranor and I play'd a game or two of Billiards at the Inn; and afterwards (for I knew how little of an oars-man he was) we would all three take a good stretch into the fields together.

He supposed "we should be back in good time"; about which I would make no condition; and he then resign'd himself to Destiny. While he was busy changing and brushing his clothes, Euphranor, who had walk'd somewhat impatiently about the room, looking now at the books, and now through the window at some white pigeons wheeling about in the clear sky, went up to the mantelpiece and call'd out, "What a fine new pair of screens Lexilogus had got! the present, doubtless, of some fair Lady."

Lexilogus said they were a present from his sister on his birthday; and coming up to me, brush in hand, asked if I recognised the views represented on them?

"Quite well, quite well," I said—"the old Church—the Yew tree—the Parsonage—one cannot mistake them."

"And were they not beautifully done?"

And I answer'd without hesitation, "they were;" for I knew the girl who had painted them, and that (whatever they might be in point of Art) a still finer spirit had guided her hand.

At last, after a little hesitation as to whether he should wear cap and gown, (which I decided he should, for this time only, *not*,) Lexilogus was ready; and calling out on the staircase to some invisible Bed-maker, that his books should not be meddled with, we ran downstairs, crossed the Great Court—through the Screens, as they are call'd, perpetually travers'd by Gyp, Cook, Bed-maker, and redolent of perpetual Dinner;—and so, through the cloisters of Neville's Court, out upon the open green before the Library. The sun shone broad on the new-shaven expanse of grass, while holiday-seeming people saunter'd along the Riverside, and under the trees, now flourishing in freshest green—the Chestnut especially in full fan, and leaning down his white cones over the sluggish current, which seem'd indeed fitter for the slow merchandise of coal, than to wash the walls and flow through the groves of Academe.

We now consider'd that we had miss'd our proper point of embarkation; but this was easily set right at a slight expense of College propriety. Euphranor calling out to some one who had his boat in charge along with others by the wooden bridge, we descended the grassy slope, stepp'd in, with due caution on the part of Lexilogus and myself, and settled the order of our voyage. Euphranor and I were to pull, and Lexilogus (as I at first proposed) to steer. But seeing he was somewhat shy of meddling in the matter, I agreed to take all the blame of my own awkwardness on myself.

"And just take care of this, will you, Lexilogus?" said Euphranor, handing him a book which fell out of the pocket of the coat he was taking off.

45

"Oh, books, books!" I exclaimed. "I thought we were to steer clear of them, at any rate. Now we shall have Lexilogus reading all the way, instead of looking about him, and inhaling the fresh air unalloy'd. What is it—Greek, Algebra, German, or what?"

"None of these, however," Euphranor said, "but only Digby's Godefridus;" and then asking me whether I was ready, and I calling out, "Ay, ay, Sir," our oars plash'd in the water. Safe through the main arch of Trinity bridge, we shot past the Library, I exerting myself so strenuously (as bad rowers are apt to do), that I almost drove the boat upon a very unobtrusive angle of the College buildings. This danger past, however, we got on better; Euphranor often looking behind him to anticipate our way, and counteracting with his experienced oar the many mis-directions of mine. Amid all this, he had leisure to ask me if I knew those same Digby books?

"Some of them," I told him—"the 'Broad Stone of Honour,' for one; indeed I had the first Protestant edition of it, now very rare."

"But not so good as the enlarged Catholic," said Euphranor, "of which this Godefridus is part."

"Perhaps not," I replied; "but then, on the other hand, *not* so Catholic; which you and Lexilogus will agree with me is much in its favour."

Which I said slyly, because of Euphranor's being rather taken with the Oxford doctrine just then coming into vogue.

"You cannot forgive him that," said he.

"Nay, nay," said I, "one can forgive a true man anything."

And then Euphranor ask'd me, "Did I not remember Digby himself at College?—perhaps know him?"

"Not *that*," I answer'd, "but remember'd him very well. A grand, swarthy Fellow, who might have stept out of the canvas of some knightly portrait of his Father's hall—perhaps the living image of one sleeping under some cross-legg'd Effigies in the Church."

"And, Hare says, really the Knight at heart that he represented in his Books."

"At least," I answered, "he pull'd a very good stroke on the river, where I am now labouring so awkwardly."

46

In which and other such talk, interrupted by the little accidents of our voyage, we had threaded our way through the closely-packt barges at Magdalen; through the Locks; and so for a pull of three or four miles down the river and back again to the Ferry; where we surrender'd our boat, and footed it over the fields to Chesterton, at whose Church we came just as its quiet chimes were preluding Twelve o'clock. Close by was the humble house whither Lexilogus was bound. I look'd in for a moment at the old lady, and left him with her, privately desiring him to join us as soon as he could at the Three Tuns Inn, which I preferr'd to any younger rival, because of the many pleasant hours I had spent there in my own College days, some twenty years ago.

When Euphranor and I got there, we found all the tables occupied; but one, as usual, would be at our service before long. Meanwhile, ordering some light ale after us, we went into the Bowling-green, with its Lilac bushes now in full bloom and full odour; and there we found, sitting alone upon a bench, Lycion, with a cigar in his mouth, and rolling the bowls about lazily with his foot.

"What! Lycion! and all alone!" I call'd out.

He nodded to us both—waiting, he said, till some men had finish'd a pool of billiards upstairs—a great bore—for it was only just begun! and one of the fellows "a man I particularly detest."

"Come and console yourself with some ale, then," said I. "Are you ever foolish enough to go pulling on the river, as we have been doing?"

"Not very often in hot weather; he did not see the use," he said, "of perspiring to no purpose."

"Just so," replied I, "though Euphranor has not turn'd a hair, you see, owing to the good condition he is in. But here comes our liquor; and 'Sweet is Pleasure after Pain,' at any rate."

We then sat down in one of those little arbours cut into the Lilac bushes round the Bowling-green; and while Euphranor and I were quaffing each a glass of Home-brew'd, Lycion took up the volume of Digby, which Euphranor had laid on the table.

"Ah, Lycion," said Euphranor, putting down his glass, "there is one would have put you up to a longer and stronger pull than we have had to-day."

"Chivalry——" said Lycion, glancing carelessly over the

47

leaves; "Don't you remember,"—addressing me—"what an absurd thing that Eglinton Tournament was? What a complete failure! There was the Queen of Beauty on her throne—Lady Seymour—who alone of all the whole affair was *not* a sham— and the Heralds, and the Knights in full Armour on their horses —they had been practising for months, I believe—but unluckily, at the very moment of Onset, the rain began, and the Knights threw down their lances, and put up their umbrellas."

I laugh'd, and said I remembered something like it had oc- curr'd, though not to that umbrella-point, which I thought was a theatrical, or Louis Philippe Burlesque on the affair. And I asked Euphranor "what he had to say in defence of the Tourna- ment"?

"Nothing at all," he replied. "It *was* a silly thing, and fit to be laughed at for the very reason that it *was* a sham, as Lycion says. As Digby himself tells us," he went on, taking the Book, and rapidly turning over the leaves—"Here it is"—and he read: " 'The error that leads men to doubt of this first proposition'—that is, you know, that Chivalry is not a thing past, but, like all things of Beauty, eternal—'the error that leads men to doubt of this first proposition consists in their supposing that Tournaments, and steel Panoply, and Coat arms, and Aristocratic institutions, are essential to Chivalry; whereas, these are, in fact, only accidental attendants upon it, subject to the influence of Time, which changes all such things.' "

"I suppose," said Lycion, "your man—whatever his name is —would carry us back to the days of King Arthur, and the Seven Champions, whenever they were—that one used to read about when a Child? I thought Don Quixote had put an end to all that long ago."

"Well, *he*, at any rate," said Euphranor, "did not depend on fine Accoutrement for his Chivalry."

"Nay," said I, "but did he *not* believe in his rusty armour— perhaps even the paste-board Visor he fitted to it—as impregnable as the Cause——"

"And some old Barber's bason as the Helmet of Mambrino," interposed Lycion——

"And his poor Roxinante not to be surpass'd by the Bavieca of the Cid; believed in all this, I say, as really as in the Windmills and Wine-skins being the Giants and Sorcerers he was to annihilate?"

"To be sure he did," said Lycion; "but Euphranor's Round-table men—many of them great rascals, I believe—knew a real Dragon, or Giant—when they met him—better than Don Quixote."

"Perhaps, however," said I, who saw Euphranor's colour rising, "he and Digby would tell us that all such Giants and Dragons may be taken for Symbols of certain Forms of Evil which his Knights went about to encounter and exterminate."

"Of course," said Euphranor, with an indignant snort, "every Child knows that: then as now to be met with and put down in whatsoever shapes they appear as long as Tyranny and Oppression exist."

"Till finally extinguisht, as they crop up, by Euphranor and his Successors," said Lycion.

"Does not Carlyle somewhere talk to us of a 'Chivalry of Labour'?" said I; "that henceforward not "*Arms* and the Man,' but '*Tools* and the Man,' are to furnish the Epic of the world."

"Oh, well," said Lycion, "if the 'Table-Round' turn into a Tailor's Board—'Charge, Chester, charge!' say I—only not exorbitantly for the Coat you provide for us—which indeed, like true Knights, I believe you should provide for us gratis."

"Yes, my dear fellow," said I, laughing, "but then *You* must not sit idle, smoking your cigar, in the midst of it; but, as your Ancestors led on mail'd troops at Agincourt, so must you put yourself, shears in hand, at the head of this Host, and become what Carlyle calls 'a Captain of Industry,' a Master-tailor, leading on a host of Journeymen to fresh fields and conquests new."

"Besides," said Euphranor, who did not like Carlyle, nor relish this sudden descent of his hobby, "surely Chivalry will never want a good Cause to maintain, whether private or public. As Tennyson says, King Arthur, who was carried away wounded to the island valley of Avilion, returns to us in the shape of a 'modern Gentleman' who may be challenged, even in these later days, to no mock Tournament, Lycion, in his Country's defence, and with something other than the Doctor's shears at his side."

To this Lycion, however, only turn'd his cigar in his mouth by

way of reply, and look'd somewhat superciliously at his Antagon-
ist. And I, who had been looking into the leaves of the Book that
Euphranor had left open, said:

"Here we are, as usual, discussing without having yet agreed
on the terms we are using. Euphranor has told us, on the word
of his Hero, what Chivalry is *not*: let him read what it *is* that
we are talking about."

I then handed him the Book to read to us, while Lycion, lying
down on the grass, with his hat over his eyes, composed himself
to inattention. And Euphranor read:

"Chivalry is only a name for that general Spirit or state of
mind, which disposes men to Heroic and Generous actions; and
keeps them conversant with all that is Beautiful and Sublime in
the Intellectual and Moral world. It will be found that, in the
absence of conservative principles, this Spirit more generally
prevails in Youth than in the later periods of men's lives: and,
as the Heroic is always the earliest age in the history of nations,
so Youth, the first period of human life, may be considered as
the Heroic or Chivalrous age of each separate Man; and there
are few so unhappy as to have grown up without having experienced its influence, and having derived the advantage of being
able to enrich their imaginations, and to soothe their hours of
sorrow, with its romantic recollections. The Anglo-Saxons distinguished the period between Childhood and Manhood by the
term 'Cnihthade,' Knighthood: a term which still continued to
indicate the connexion between Youth and Chivalry, when
Knights were styled 'Children,' as in the historic song beginning

'Child Rowland to the dark tower came:'

an excellent expression, no doubt; for every Boy and Youth is,
in his mind and sentiments, a Knight, and essentially a Son of
Chivalry. Nature is fine in him. Nothing but the circumstance of
a singular and most degrading system of Education can ever
totally destroy the action of this general law. Therefore, as long
as there has been, or shall be, a succession of sweet Springs in
Man's Intellectual World; as long as there have been, or shall be,
Young men to grow up to maturity; and until all Youthful life
shall be dead, and its source withered for ever; so long must there
have been, and must there continue to be, the spirit of noble

Chivalry. To understand therefore this first and, as it were, natural Chivalry, we have only to observe the features of the Youthful age, of which examples surround us. For, as Demipho says of young men:

'Ecce autem similia omnia: omnes congruunt:
Unum cognoris, omnes noris.'

Mark the courage of him who is green and fresh in this Old world. Amyntas beheld and dreaded the insolence of the Persians; but not so Alexander, the son of Amyntas, ἅτε νέος τε ἐών, καὶ κακῶν ἀπαθὴς (says Herodotus) οὐδαμῶς ἔτι κατέχειν οἷός τε ἦν. When Jason had related to his companions the conditions imposed by the King, the first impression was that of horror and despondency: till Peleus rose up boldly, and said,

Ὥρη μητιάασθαι ὅ κ᾽ ἔρξομεν οὐ μὲν ἔολπα
Βουλῆς εἶναι ὄνειαρ, ὅσον τ᾽ ἐπὶ κάρτεϊ χειρῶν.

'If Jason be unwilling to attempt it, I and the rest will undertake the enterprise; for what more can we suffer than death?' And then instantly rose up Telamon and Idas, and the sons of Tyndarus, and Œnides, although

οὐδέ περ ὅσσον ἐπανθιόωντας ἰούλους
Ἀντέλλων.

But Argus, the Nestor of the party, restrained their impetuous valour."

"Scarce the Down upon their lips, you see," said I, "Freshmen;—so that you, Euphranor, who are now Bachelor of Arts, and whose upper lip at least begins to show the stubble of repeated harvests, are, alas, fast declining from that golden prime of Knighthood, while Lycion here, whose shavings might almost be counted——"

Here Lycion, who had endured the reading with an occasional yawn, said he wish'd "those fellows upstairs would finish their pool."

"And see again," continued I, taking the book from Euphranor's hands—"after telling us that Chivalry is mainly but another name for Youth, Digby proceeds to define more particularly what *that* is—'It is a remark of Lord Bacon, that "for the Moral part, Youth will have the pre-eminence, as Age hath for the

Politic;" and this has always been the opinion which is allied to that other belief, that the Heroic (the Homeric age) was the most Virtuous age of Greece. When Demosthenes is desirous of expressing any great and generous sentiment, he uses the term νεανικὸν φρόνημα'—and by the way," added I, looking up parenthetically from the book, "the Persians, I am told, employ the same word for Youth and Courage—'and it is the saying of Plautus, when surprise is evinced at the Benevolence of an old man, "Benignitas hujus ut Adolescentuli est." There is no difference, says the Philosopher, between Youthful Age and Youthful Character; and what this is cannot be better evinced than in the very words of Aristotle: "The Young are ardent in Desire, and what they do is from Affection; they are tractable and delicate; they earnestly desire and are quickly appeased; their wishes are intense, without comprehending much, as the thirst and hunger of the weary; they are passionate and hasty, and liable to be surprised by anger; for being ambitious of Honour, they cannot endure to be despised, but are indignant when they suffer injustice: they love Honour, but still more Victory; for Youth desires superiority, and victory is superiority, and both of these they love more than Riches; for as to these, of all things, they care for them the least. They are not of corrupt manners, but are Innocent, from not having beheld much wickedness; and they are credulous, from having been seldom deceived; and Sanguine in hope, for, like persons who are drunk with wine, they are inflamed by nature, and from their having had but little experience of Fortune. And they live by Hope, for Hope is of the future, but Memory of the past, and to Youth the Future is everything, the Past but little; they hope all things, and remember nothing: and it is easy to deceive them, for the reasons which have been given; for they are willing to hope, and are full of Courage, being passionate and hasty, of which tempers it is the nature of one not to fear, and of the other to inspire confidence; and they are easily put to Shame, for they have no resources to set aside the precepts which they have learned: and they have lofty souls, for they have never been disgraced or brought low, and they are unacquainted with Necessity; they prefer Honour to Advantage, Virtue to Expediency; for they live by Affection rather than by Reason, and Reason is concerned with Expediency, but Affection with Honour: and they are warm friends and hearty companions, more than other men, because they delight in Fellowship, and judge of nothing by Utility, and therefore not their friends; and they chiefly err in doing all things over much, for they keep no medium. They love much, and they dislike much, and so in everything, and this arises from their idea that they know everything. And their faults consist more in Insolence than in actual wrong; and they are full of Mercy, because they regard all men as good, and more virtuous than they are; for they measure others by their own Innocence; so that they suppose every man suffers wrongfully." ' So that Lycion, you see," said I, looking up from the book, and tapping on the top of his hat, "is, in virtue of his eighteen Summers only, a Knight of Nature's own dubbing—yes, and here we have a list of the very qualities which constitute him one of the Order. And all the time he is pretending to be careless, indolent, and worldly, he is really bursting with suppressed Energy, Generosity, and Devotion."

"I did not try to understand your English any more than your Greek," said Lycion; "but if I can't help being the very fine Fellow whom I think you were reading about, why, I want to know what is the use of writing books about it for my edification."

"O yes, my dear fellow," said I, "it is like giving you an Inventory of your goods, which else you lose, or even fling away, in your march to Manhood—which you are so eager to reach. Only to repent when gotten there; for I see Digby goes on— 'What is termed *Entering the World*'—which Manhood of course must do—'assuming its Principles and Maxims'—which usually follows—'is nothing else but departing into those regions to which the souls of the Homeric Heroes went sorrowing—

" 'ὃν πότμον γοόωσα, λιποῦσ' ἁδροτῆτα καὶ ἥβην.' "

"Ah, you remember," said Euphranor, "how Lamb's friend, looking upon the Eton Boys in their Cricket-field, sighed 'to think of so many fine Lads so soon turning into frivolous Members of Parliament!' "

"But why 'frivolous'?" said Lycion.

"Ay, why 'frivolous'?" echoed I, "when entering on the Field where, Euphranor tells us, their Knightly service may be call'd into action."

"Perhaps," said Euphranor, "entering before sufficiently equipp'd for that part of their calling."

"Well," said Lycion, "the Laws of England determine otherwise, and that is enough for me, and, I suppose, for her, whatever your ancient or modern pedants say to the contrary."

"You mean," said I, "in settling Twenty-one as the Age of 'Discretion,' sufficient to manage, not your own affairs only, but those of the Nation also?"

The hat nodded.

"Not yet, perhaps, accepted for a Parliamentary Knight complete," said I, "so much as Squire to some more experienced, if not more valiant, Leader. Only providing that Neoptolemus do not fall into the hands of a too politic Ulysses, and under him lose that generous Moral, whose Inventory is otherwise apt to get lost among the benches of St Stephen's—in spite of preliminary Prayer."

"Aristotle's Master, I think," added Euphranor, with some mock gravity, "would not allow any to become Judges in his Republic till near to middle life, lest acquaintance with Wrong should harden them into a distrust of Humanity: and acquaintance with Diplomacy is said to be little less dangerous."

"Though, by-the-way," interposed I, "was not Plato's Master accused of perplexing those simple Affections and Impulses of Youth by his Dialectic, and making premature Sophists of the Etonians of Athens?"

"By Aristophanes, you mean," said Euphranor, with no mock gravity now; "whose gross caricature help'd Anytus and Co. to that Accusation which ended in the murder of the best and wisest Man of all Antiquity."

"Well, perhaps," said I, "he had been sufficiently punish'd by that termagant Wife of his—whom, by-the-way, he may have taught to argue with him instead of to obey. Just as that Son of poor old Strepsiades, in what you call the Aristophanic Caricature, is taught to rebel against parental authority, instead of doing as he was bidden; as he would himself have the Horses to do that he was spending so much of his Father's money upon: and as we would have our own Horses, Dogs, and Children,—and young Knights."

"You have got your Heroes into fine company, Euphranor,"

54

said Lycion, who, while seeming inattentive to all that went against him, was quick enough to catch at any turn in his favour.

"Why, let me see," said I, taking up the book again, and running my eye over the passage—"yes,—'*Ardent of desire,*'—'*Tractable,*'—some of them at least—'*Without comprehending much*'—'*Ambitious*'—'*Despisers of Riches*'—'*Warm friends and hearty Companions*'—really very characteristic of the better breed of Dogs and Horses. And why not? The Horse, you know, has given his very name to Chivalry, because of his association in the Heroic Enterprises of Men,—*El mas Hidalgo Bruto*, Calderon calls him. He was sometimes buried, I think, along with our heroic Ancestors—just as some favourite wife was buried along with her husband in the East. So the Muse sings of those who believe their faithful Dog will accompany them to the World of Spirits—as even some wise and good Christian men have thought it not impossible he may, not only because of his Moral, but——"

"Well," said Euphranor, "we need not trouble ourselves about carrying the question quite so far."

"Oh, do not drop your poor kinsman just when you are going into good Company," said Lycion.

"By-the-way, Lycion," said I, "has not your Parliament a 'Whipper-in' of its more dilatory members—or of those often of the younger ones, I think, who may be diverting themselves with some stray scent elsewhere?"

To this he only replied with a long whiff from his Cigar; but Euphranor said:

"Well, come, Lycion, let us take the Doctor at his word, and turn it against himself. For if you and I, in virtue of our Youth, are so inspired with all this Moral that he talks of—why, we—or, rather, you—*are* wanted in Parliament, not only to follow like Dog and Horse, as he pretends, but also to take the lead; so as the Generous counsel, the νεανικὸν φρόνημα, of Youth, may vivify and ennoble the cold Politic of Age."

"Well, I remember hearing of a young Senator," said I, "who, in my younger days, was celebrated for his faculty of Cock-crowing by way of waking up his more drowsy Seniors, I suppose, about the small hours of the morning—or, perhaps, in token of Victory over an unexpected Minority."

"No, no," said Euphranor, laughing, "I mean seriously; as in the passage we read from Digby, Amyntas, the Man of Policy, was wrong, and his son Alexander right."

But oddly enough, as I remember'd the story in Herodotus, by a device which smack'd more of Policy than Generosity. "But in the other case, Argus, I suppose, was not so wrong in restraining the impetuosity of his Youthful Crew, who,—is it not credibly thought?—would have fail'd, but for Medea's unexpected magical assistance."

Euphranor was not clear about this.

"Besides," said I, "does not this very νεανικὸν φρόνημα of yours result from that νεανικὸν condition—ἔθος, do you call it? —of Body, in which Youth as assuredly profits as in the Moral, and which assuredly flows, as from a Fountain of 'Jouvence that rises and runs in the open' Field rather than in the Hall of St Stephen's, where indeed it is rather likely to get clogg'd, if not altogether dried up? As, for instance, *Animal Spirit, Animal Courage, Sanguine Temper,* and so forth—all which, by the way, says Aristotle, inflame Youth not at all like Reasonable people, but *'like persons drunk with wine'*—all which, for better or worse, is fermented by Cricket from good Roast Beef into pure Blood, Muscle—and Moral."

"Chivalry refined into patent Essence of Beef!" said Euphranor, only half-amused.

"I hope you like the taste of it," said Lycion, under his hat.

"Well, at any rate," said I, laughing, "those young Argonauts needed a good stock of it to work a much heavier craft than we have been pulling to-day, when the wind fail'd them. And yet, with all their animal Inebriation—whencesoever derived—so tractable in their Moral as to submit at once to their Politic Leader—Argus, was it not?"

" 'The Nestor of the Party,' Digby calls him," said Euphranor, "good, old, garrulous, Nestor, whom, somehow, I think one seems to feel more at home with than any of the Homeric Heroes."

"Aye, *he* was entitled to crow in the Grecian Parliament, fine 'Old Cock' as he was, about the gallant exploits of his Youth, being at threescore so active in Body as in Spirit, that Agamemnon declares, I think, that Troy would soon come down had he but a few more such Generals. Ah yes, Euphranor! could one by so full Apprenticeship of Youth become so thoroughly season'd with its Spirit, that all the Reason of Manhood, and Politic of Age, and Experience of the World, should serve not to freeze, but to direct, the genial Current of the Soul, so that—

'Ev'n while the vital Heat retreats below,
Ev'n while the hoary head is lost in Snow,
The *Life* is in the leaf, and still between
The fits of falling Snow appears the streaky Green'—

that Boy's Heart within the Man's never ceasing to throb and tremble, even to remotest Age—then indeed your Senate would need no other Youth than its Elders to vivify their counsel, or could admit the Young without danger of corrupting them by ignoble Policy."

"Well, come," said Euphranor gaily, after my rather sententious peroration, "Lycion need not be condemn'd to enter Parliament—or even 'The World'—unless he pleases, for some twenty years to come, if he will follow Pythagoras, who, you know, Doctor, devotes the first forty years of his Man's allotted Eighty to Childhood and Youth; a dispensation which you and I at least shall not quarrel with."

"No, nor anyone else, I should suppose," said I. "Think, my dear Lycion, what a privilege for you to have yet more than twenty good years' expatiation in the Elysian Cricket-field of Youth before pent up in that Close Borough of your Father's! And Euphranor, whom we thought fast slipping out of his Prime as his Youth attained a beard, is in fact only just entering upon it. And, most wonderful of all, I, who not only have myself enter'd the World, but made my bread by bringing others into it these fifteen years, have myself only just ceased to be a Boy!"

What reply Lycion might have deign'd to all this, I know not; for just now one of his friends looked out again from the Billiard-room window, and called out to him, "the coast was clear." On which Lycion getting up, and muttering something about its being a pity we did not go back to Trap-ball, and I retorting that we could carry it forward into Life with us, he carelessly nodded to us both, and with an "*Au Revoir*" lounged with his Cigar into the house.

Then Euphranor and I took each a draught of the good liquor which Lycion had declined to share with us; and, on setting down his tumbler, he said:

"Ah! you should have heard our friend Skythrops commenting on that Inventory of Youth, as you call it, which he happen'd to open upon in my rooms the other day."

"Perhaps the book is rather apt to open there of its own accord," said I. "Well—and what did Skythrops say?"

"Oh, you may anticipate—'the same old Heathen talk,' he said—'very well for a Pagan to write, and a Papist to quote'— and, according to you, Doctor, for Horse and Dog to participate in, and for Bullock to supply."

"But I had been mainly bantering Lycion," I said; "as Euphranor also, I supposed, with his Pythagorean disposition of Life. Lycion would not much have cared had I derived them from the angels. As for that Animal condition to which I had partly referr'd them, we Doctors were of old notorious on that score, not choosing your Moralist and Philosopher to carry off all the fee. But, 'The Cobbler to his Last'—or, the Tailor to his Goose, if I might be call'd in, as only I profess'd, to accommodate the outer Man with what Sterne calls his Jerkin, leaving its Lining to your Philosopher and Divine."

"Sterne!" ejaculated Euphranor; "just like him—Soul and Body all of a piece."

"Nay, nay," said I, laughing; "your Lining is often of a finer material, you know."

"And often of a coarser, as in Sterne's own case, I believe."

"Well, then, I would turn Mason, or Bricklayer," I said; "and confine myself to the House of Clay, in which, as the Poets tell us, the Soul is Tenant—'The Body's Guest'—as Sir Walter Raleigh calls him; would that do?"

"Better, at any rate, than Jerkin and Lining."

But here the same difficulty presented itself. For, however essentially distinct the Tenant from his Lodging, his Health, as we of the material Faculty believed, in some measure depended on the salubrity of the House, in which he is not merely a Guest, but a Prisoner, and from which I knew Euphranor thought he was forbidden to escape by any violent self-extrication. Dryden indeed tells us of—

"A fiery Soul that, working out his way,
Fretted the pigmy Body to decay,
And o'er-informed this Tenement of Clay."—

"But *that* was the Soul of an Achitophel," Euphranor argued, "whose collapse, whether beginning from within or without, was of less than little moment to the world. But the truly grand Soul possesses himself in peace, or, if he suffer from self-neglect, or over-exertion in striving after the good of others—why, that same Dryden—or Waller, it may be—says that such an one becomes, not weaker, but stronger, by that Bodily decay, whether of Infirmity, or of Old Age, which lets in new light through the chinks of dilapidation—if not, as my loftier Wordsworth has it, some rays of that Original Glory which he brought with him to be darken'd in the Body at Birth."

"But then," I said, "if your crazy Cottage won't fall to pieces at once, but, after the manner of creaking gates, go creaking—or, as the Sailors say of their boats 'complaining' on—making the Tenant, and most likely all his Neighbours, complain also, and perpetually calling on the Tenant for repairs, and this when he wants to be about other more important Business of his own? To think how much time—and patience—a Divine Soul has to waste over some little bit of Cheese, perhaps, that, owing to bad drainage, will stick in the stomach of an otherwise Seraphic Doctor."

Euphranor laughed a little; and I went on: "Better surely, for all sakes, to build up for her—as far as we may—for we cannot yet ensure the foundation—a spacious, airy, and wholesome Tenement becoming so Divine a Tenant, of so strong a foundation and masonry as to resist the wear and tear of Elements without, and herself within. Yes; and a *handsome* house withal—unless indeed you think the handsome Soul will fashion that about herself from within—like a shell—which, so far as her Top-storey, where she is supposed chiefly to reside, I think may be the case."

"Ah," said Euphranor, "one of the most beautiful of all human Souls, as I think, could scarce accomplish that."

"Socrates?" said I. "No; but did not he profess that his Soul was naturally an ugly soul to begin with? So, by the time he had beautified her within, it was too late to re-front her Outside,

59

which had case-hardened, I suppose. But did not he accompany Alcibiades, not only because of his Spiritual, but also of his Physical Beauty, in which, as in the Phidian statues, the Divine Original of Man was supposed to reflect Himself, and which has been accepted as such by Christian Art, and indeed by all Peoples who are furthest removed from that of the Beast?"

"Even of Dog and Horse?" said Euphranor, smiling.

"Even my sturdy old Philosopher Montaigne—who, by the way, declares that he rates 'La Beauté à deux doigts de la Bonté . . . non seulement aux hommes qui me servent, mais aux bêtes aussi;' quotes your Aristotle, saying that we owe a sort of Homage to those who resemble the Statues of the Gods as to the Statues themselves. And thus Socrates may have felt about Alcibiades, who, in those earlier and better days when Socrates knew him, might almost be taken as a counterpart of the Picture of Youth, with all its Virtues and defects, which Aristotle has drawn for us."

"Or, what do you say, Doctor, to Aristotle's own Pupil, Alexander, who turned out a yet more astonishing Phenomenon? —I wonder, Doctor, what you, with all your theories, would have done had such an 'Enfant terrible' as either of them been put into your hands."

"Well, at any rate, I should have the advantage of first laying hold of him on coming into the World, which was not the case with Aristotle, or with the Doctors of his time, was it?"

Euphranor thought not.

"However, I know not yet whether I have ever had an Infant Hero of any kind to deal with; none, certainly, who gave any indication of any such 'clouds of glory' as your Wordsworth tells of, even when just arrived from their several homes—in Alexander's case, of a somewhat sulphureous nature, according to Skythrops, I doubt. No, nor of any young Wordsworth neither under our diviner auspices."

"Nay, but," said Euphranor, "he tells us that our Birth is but a 'Sleep and a Forgetting' of something which must take some waking-time to develope."

"But which, if I remember aright, is to begin to darken 'with shades of the Prison-house,' as Wordsworth calls it, that begin to close about 'the growing Boy.' But I am too much of a

Philistine, as you Germans have it, to comprehend the Transcendental. All I know is, that I have not yet detected any signs of the 'Heaven that lies about our Infancy,' nor for some while after—no, not even peeping through those windows through which the Soul is said more immediately to look, but as yet with no more speculation in them than those of the poor whelp of the Dog we talked of—in spite of a nine days' start of him."

"Nevertheless," said Euphranor, "I have heard tell of another Poet's saying that he knew of no human out-look so solemn as that from an Infant's Eyes; and how it was from those of his own he learn'd that those of the Divine Child in Raffaelle's Sistine Madonna were not over-charged with expression, as he had previously thought they might be."

"I think," said I, "you must have heard of that from me, who certainly did hear something like it from the Poet himself, who used to let fall—not lay down—the word that settled the question, æsthetic or other, which others hammer'd after in vain. Yes; that was on occasion, I think, of his having watch'd his Child one morning '*worshipping the Sunbeam on the Bed-post*'— I suppose the worship of Wonder, such as I have heard grown-up Children tell of at first sight of the Alps, or Niagara; or such stay-at-home Islanders as ourselves at first sight of the Sea, from such a height as Flamborough Head."

"Some farther-seeing Wonder than dog or kitten are conscious of, at any rate," said Euphranor.

"Ah, who knows? I have seen both of them watching that very Sunbeam too—the Kitten perhaps playing with it, to be sure. If but the Philosopher or Poet could live in the Child's or kitten's Brain for a while! The Bed-post Sun-worship, however, was of a Child of several months—and Raffaelle's—a full year old, would you say?"

"Nay, you know about such matters better than I," said Euphranor, laughing.

"Well, however it may be with young Wordsworth, Raffaelle's child certainly *was* 'drawing Clouds of Glory' from *His* Home, and we may suppose him conscious of it—yes, and of his Mission to dispense that glory to the World. And I remember how the same Poet also noticed the Attitude of the Child, which might otherwise seem somewhat too magisterial for his age."

61

Euphranor knew the Picture by Engraving only; but he observed how the Divine Mother's eyes also were dilated, not as with Human Mother's Love, but as with awe and Wonder at the Infant she was presenting to the World, as if silently saying, "Behold your King!"

"Why," said I, "do not some of you believe the 'Clouds of Glory' to have been drawn directly from herself?"

"Nonsense, nonsense, Doctor—you know better, as did Raffaelle also, I believe, in spite of the Pope."

"Well, well," said I, "your Wordsworth Boy has also his Divine Mission to fulfil in confessing that of Raffaelle's. But, however it may be with that Mother and Child, does not one— of your Germans, I think—say that, with us mortals, it is from the Mother's eyes that Religion dawns into the Child's Soul?— the Religion of Love, at first, I suppose, in gratitude for the flowing breast and feeding hand below."

"Perhaps—in some degree," said Euphranor. "As you were saying of that Sun-worshipper, one cannot fathom how far the Child may see into the Mother's eyes any more than all that is to be read in them."

"To be developed between them thereafter, I suppose," said I, "when the Mother's lips interpret the Revelation of her Eyes, and lead up from her Love to the perception of some Invisible Parent of all."

"Ah," said Euphranor, "how well I remember learning to repeat after her, every morning and night, 'Our Father which art in Heaven.'"

"In your little white Surplice, like Sir Joshua's little Samuel— on whom the Light is dawning direct from Heaven, I think— from Him to whom you were half-articulately praying to 'make me a good Boy' to them. And, by-and-by, Watts and Jane Taylor's, of the Star Daisy in the grass, and the Stars in Heaven,

"For ever singing as they shine,
The Hand that made us is Divine."

"Ah," said Euphranor, "and beautiful some of those early things of Watts and Jane Taylor are. They run in my head still."

"As why should they not?" said I, "you being yet in your Childhood, you know. Why, I, who have left it some way behind

62

me, to be sure, am constantly reminded of them in the nurseries I am so often call'd into from which they are not yet banisht by more æsthetic verse. As also, I must say, of some yet more early, and profane, such as 'Rock-a-bye Baby on the Tree-top,' with that catastrophe which never fail'd to 'bring the House down' along with the Bough which is,—Mother's Arms. Then there was 'Little Bopeep' whose stray flock came back to her of themselves, carrying their tails behind them—and 'Little Boy Blue' who was less fortunate. Ah, what a pretty little picture he makes 'under the haycock'—like one of your Greek Idylls, I think, and quite 'suitable to this present Month of May,' as old Izaak says. Let me hear if you remember it, Sir."

And Euphranor, like a good boy, repeated the verses.

"And then," said I, "the echoes of those old London Bells whose Ancestors once recall'd Whittington back to be their Lord Mayor; and now communicating from their several Steeples as to how the account with St Clement's was to be paid—which, by-the-by, I remember being thus summarily settled by an old College Friend of mine—

" 'Confound you all!'
Said the Great bell of Paul; "

only, I am afraid, with something more Athanasian than 'Confound'—though he was not then a Dignitary of the Church. Then that Tragedy of 'Cock Robin'—the Fly that saw it with that little Eye of his—and the Owl with his spade and '*Showl*'— proper old word that too—and the Bull who the Bell could pull —and—but I doubt whether you will approve of the Rook reading the Burial Service, nor do I like bringing the Lark, only for a rhyme's sake, down from Heaven, to make the responses. And all this illustrated by appropriate—'Gays,' as they call them in Suffolk—and recited, if not intoned, according to the different Characters."

"Plato's 'Music of Education,' I suppose," said Euphranor.

"Yes," said I, warming with my subject; "and then, beside the True Histories of Dog and Horse whose example is to be followed, Fables that treat of others, Lions, Eagles, Asses, Foxes, Cocks, and other feather'd or four-footed Creatures, who, as in Cock Robin's case, talk as well as act, but with a Moral—

more or less commendable—provided *the* Moral be dropt. Then as your punning friend Plato, you told me, says that *Thaumas*—Wonder—is Father of Iris, who directly communicates between Heaven and Earth—as in the case of that Bed-post-kissing Apollo—you, being a pious man, doubtless had your Giants, Genii, Enchanters, Fairies, Ogres, Witches, Ghosts——"

But Euphranor was decidedly against admitting any Ghost into the Nursery, and even Witches, remembering little Lamb's childish terror at Her of Endor.

"Oh, but," said I, "*She* was a real Witch, you know, though represented by Stackhouse; who need not figure among the Musicians, to be sure. You, however, as Lycion says, have your Giants and Dragons to play with—by way of Symbol, if you please—and you must not grudge your younger Brethren in Arms that redoubtable JACK who slew the Giants whom you are to slay over again, and who for that very purpose climb'd up a Bean-stalk some way at least to Heaven—an Allegory that, as Sir Thomas Browne says, 'admits of a wide solution.' "

"Ah," said my companion, "I remember how you used to climb up the Poplar in our garden by way of Bean-stalk, looking out upon us now and then, till lost among the branches. You could not do that now, Doctor."

"No more than I could up Jack's own Bean-stalk. I was a thin slip of a Knight then, not long turned of Twenty, I suppose—almost more like a Giant than a Jack to the rest of you—but Children do not mind such disproportions. No—I could better play one of the three Bears growling for his mess of porridge now. But, in default of my transcendental illustration of Jack, he and his like are well represented in such Effigies as your friend Plato never dream'd of in his philosophy, though Phidias and Praxiteles may have sketcht for their Children what now is multiplied by Engraving into every Nursery."

"Not to mention Printing, to read about what is represented," said Euphranor.

"I do not know what to say about *that*," said I. "Does not your Philosopher repudiate any but Oral instruction?"

"Notwithstanding all which, I am afraid we must learn to read," said Euphranor, "in these degenerate days."

"Well, if needs must," said I, "you may learn in the most

musical way of all. Do you not remember the practice of our Forefathers?

> "To Master John, the Chamber-maid
> A Horn-book gives of Ginger-bread;
> And, that the Child may learn the better,
> As he can name, he eats the Letter."

"Oh, how I used to wish," said Euphranor, "there had been any such royal road to Grammar which one had to stumble over some years after!"

"Well," said I, "but there is now, I believe, a Comic Grammar—as well as a Comic History of Rome—and of England."

"Say no more of all that, pray, Doctor. The old 'Propria quæ maribus' was better Music, uncouth as it was, and almost as puzzling as an Oracle. I am sure it is only now—when I try—that I understand the meaning of the rule I then repeated mechanically—like a Parrot, you would say."

"Sufficiently intelligible, however," said I, "to be mechanically applied in distinguishing the different parts of Speech, and how related to one another; how a verb governs an accusative, and an adjective agrees with a noun; to all which you are guided by certain terminations of *us*, *a*, *um*, and *do*, *das*, *dat*, and so on; till you are able to put the scattered words together, and so ford through a sentence. And the old uncouth Music, as you call it, nevertheless served to fix those rules in the memory."

"But all that is changed now!" said Euphranor; "Nominative and Accusative are turned into Subjective and Objective, and what not."

"Darkening the unintelligible to Boys," said I, "whatever it may afterwards to men. 'Floreat Etona!' say I, with her old Lily, and 'Propria quæ maribus,' always providing there be not too much of it—even could it be construed, like the Alphabet, into Gingerbread."

"Well," said Euphranor, "I think you took pretty good care that we should not suffer an indigestion of the latter, when you were among us at home, Doctor. What with mounting that Bean-stalk yourself, and clearing us out of the Schoolroom into

C

the Garden, wet or dry, regardless of Aunt's screaming from the window for us to come in, when a Cloud was coming up in the Sky——"

"Or a little dew lying on the Grass."

"Why, I believe you would have a Child's shoes made with holes in them on purpose to let in water, as Locke recommends," said Euphranor, laughing.

"I wouldn't keep him within for having none, whole shoes, or whole clothes—no, nor *any*—only the Police would interfere."

"But the Child catches cold."

"Put him to bed and dose him."

"But he dies."

"Then, as a sensible woman said, 'is provided for.' Your own Plato, I think, says it is better the weakly ones should die at once; and the Spartans, I think, kill'd them off."

"Come, come, Doctor," said Euphranor. "I really think you gave us colds on purpose to be called in to cure them."

"No, no; that was before I was a Doctor, you know. But I doubt that I was the Lord of Mis-rule sometimes, though, by the way, I am certain that I sometimes recommended a remedy, not when you were sick, but when you were sorry—without a cause—I mean, obstinate, or self-willed against the little Discipline you had to submit to."

Euphranor looked comically at me.

"Yes," said I, "you know—a slap on that part where the Rod is to be applied in after years—and which I had, not long before, suffered myself."

"*That* is almost out of date now, along with other Spartan severities even in Criminal cases," said Euphranor.

"Yes, and the more the pity in both cases. How much better in the Child's than being shut up, or additionally tasked—revenging a temporary wrong with a lasting injury. And, as for your public Criminal—my wonder is that even modern squeamishness does not see that a public application of the Rod or Lash on the bare back in the Market-place would be more likely to daunt the Culprit, and all Beholders, from future Misdemeanour than months of imprisonment, well-boarded, lodged, and cared for, at the Country's cost."

"Nevertheless," said Euphranor, "I do not remember your

66

Advice being taken in our case, much as I, for one, may have
deserved it."

"No," said I; "your Father was gone, you know, and your
Mother too tender-hearted—indulgent, I might say."

"Which, with all your Spartan discipline, I know you think
the better extreme," said Euphranor.

"Oh, far the better!" said I—"letting the *Truth* come to the
surface—the ugliest Truth better than the fairest Falsehood
which Fear naturally brings with it, and all the better for deter-
mining outwardly, as we Doctors say, than repressed to rankle
within. Why, even without fear of spank or Rod, you remember
how your Wordsworth's little Harry was taught the practice of
Lying, who, simply being teased with well-meaning questions as
to *why* he liked one place better than another, caught at a
Weather-cock for a reason *why*. Your mother was wiser than that.
I dare say she did not bother you about the meaning of the
Catechism she taught you, provided you generally understood
that you were to keep your hands from picking and stealing, and
your tongue from evil-speaking, lying, and slandering. She did
not insist, as Skythrops would have had you, on your owning
yourselves Children of the Devil."

"No, no!"

"I should not even wonder if, staunch Churchwoman as she
was, she did not condemn you to go more than once of a Sunday
to Church—perhaps not to be shut up for two hours' morning
Service in a Pew, without being allowed to go to sleep there; nor
tease you about Text and Sermon afterward. For, if she had,
you would not, I believe, have been the determined Churchman
you are."

"Ah, I remember so well," said Euphranor, "her telling a
stricter neighbour of ours that, for all she saw, the Child generally grew up with clean opposite inclinations and ways of thinking, from the Parent."

"Yes," said I, "that is the way from Parent to Child, and from
Generation to Generation; and so the World goes round."

"And we—Brothers and Sister, I mean"—said Euphranor,
"now catch ourselves constantly saying how right she was in
the few things we ever thought her mistaken about. God bless
her!"

67

He took a long pull at his glass, and was silent some little while—she had died a few years ago—and then he said:

"However, even she began in time to find 'the Boys too much for her,' as she said—for which you, Doctor, as you say, are partly accountable; besides, we should have our livelihood to earn, unlike your born Heroes; and must begin to work sooner rather than later. Our Friend Skythrops' *ipse* had already warned her of our innate, and steadily growing, Depravity, and, when I was seven or eight years old, came to propose taking me under his wing, at what he called his 'Seminary for young Gentlemen.'"

"I see him," said I, "coming up the shrubbery walk in a white tie, and with a face of determined asperity—the edge of the Axe now turned *toward* the Criminal. Aye, I was gone away to Edinburgh by that time; indeed I think he waited till I was well out of the way. Well, what did he say?"

"Oh, he explained his scheme, whatever it was——"

"And—oh, I can tell you—some eight or ten hours a day of Grammar and Arithmetic, Globes, History, and as Dickens says, 'General Christianity'; and, by way of Recreation, two hours' daily walk with himself and his sallow Pupils, two and two along the High-road, improved with a running commentary by Skythrops—with perhaps a little gymnastic gallows in his gravel Play-ground, without room or time for any generous exercise. Your Mother, I hope, gave him a biscuit and a glass of Sherry, and, with all due thanks, let him go back the way he came."

"His Plan does not please you, Doctor?"

"And if it did—and it only wanted reversing—*he* would not. No Boy with any Blood in his veins can profit from a Teacher trying to graft from dead wood upon the living sapling. Even the poor Women's *Preparatory Establishments* for 'Young Gentlemen' are better; however narrow their notions and routine, they do not at heart dislike a little of the Devil in the other sex, however intolerant of him in their own."

"Well, we were committed to neither," said Euphranor, "but to a nice young Fellow who came to be Curate in the Parish, and who taught us at home, little but well—among other things—a little Cricket."

"Bravo!" said I.

68

"Then Uncle James, you know, hearing that I was rather of a studious turn—'serious,' he called it—took it into his head that one of his Brother's family should be a Parson, and so undertook to pay my way at Westminster, which he thought an aristocratic School, and handy for him in the City. In which, perhaps, you do not disagree with him, Doctor?"

"No," said I; "though not bred up at any of them myself, I must confess I love the great ancient, Royal, aye, and aristocratic Foundations—Eton with her 'Henry's holy Shade'—why, Gray's verses were enough to endear it to me—and under the walls of his Royal Castle, all reflected in the water of old Father Thames, as he glides down the valley; and Winchester with her William of Wykeham entomb'd in the Cathedral he built beside his School—"

"And *West*minster, if you please, Doctor, under the Shadow of its glorious old Abbey, where Kings are crown'd and buried, and with Eton's own River flowing beside it in ampler proportions."

"Though not so sweet," said I. "However, excepting that fouler water—and fouler air—and some other less wholesome associations inseparable from such a City, I am quite ready to pray for your Westminster among those other 'Royal and Religious Foundations' whom the Preacher invites us to pray for at St Mary's. But with Eton we began, you know, looking with Charles Lamb and his Friend at the fine Lads there playing; and there I will leave them to enjoy it while they may, 'strangers yet to Pain'—and Parliament—to sublime their Beefsteak into Chivalry in that famous Cricket-field of theirs by the side of old Father Thames murmuring of so many Generations of chivalric Ancestors."

"We must call down Lycion to return thanks for *that* compliment," said Euphranor; "he is an Eton man, as were his Fathers before him, you know, and, I think, proud, as your Etonians are, of his School, in spite of his affected Indifference."

"Do you know what sort of a Lad he was while there?" said I.

"Oh, always the Gentleman."

"Perhaps somewhat too much so for a Boy."

"No, no, I do not mean that—I mean essentially honourable, truthful, and not deficient in courage, I believe, whenever it was

69

called for; but indolent, and perhaps fonder too of the last new Novel, and the Cigar and Easy-chair, to exert himself in the way you like."

"Preparing for the Club, Opera, Opera-glass, '*Déjeuner dansant*,' etcetera, if not for active service in Parliament. Eton should provide for those indolent Children of hers."

"Well, she has provided her field, and old Father Thames, as you say, and Boys are supposed to take pretty good care of themselves in making use of them."

"Not always, however, as we see in Lycion's case, nor of others, who, if they do not 'sacrifice the Living Man to the Dead Languages,' dissipate him among the Fine Arts, Music, Poetry, Painting, and the like, in the interval. Why, did not those very Greeks of whom you make so much—and, as I believe, your modern Germans—make Gymnastic a necessary part of their education?"

"But you would not have Eton Boys compelled to climb and tumble like monkeys over gymnastic poles and gallows as we saw with Skythrops' 'Young Gentlemen'?"

"Perhaps not; but what do you say now to some good Military Drill, with March, Counter-march, Encounter, Bivouac 'Wacht am Rhein'—Encampment—that is, by Father Thames—and such-like Exercises for which Eton has ample room, and which no less a Man—although a Poet—than John Milton, enjoin'd as the proper preparation for War, and, *I* say, carrying along with them a sense of Order, Self-restraint, and Mutual Dependence, no less necessary in all the relations of Peace?"

"We might all of us have been the better for that, I suppose," said Euphranor.

"And only think," said I, "if—as in some German School— Fellenberg's, I think—there were, beside the Play-ground, a piece of Arable to *work in*—perhaps at a daily wage of provender according to the work done—what illumination might some young Lycion receive, as to the condition of the Poor, 'unquenchable by logic and statistics,' says Carlyle, 'when he comes, as Duke of Logwood, to legislate in Parliament.'"

"Better Log than Brute, however," answer'd Euphranor. "You must beware, Doctor, lest with all your Ploughing and other Beef-compelling Accomplishments you do not sink the Man in

the Animal, as was much the case with our 'Hereditary Rulers'
of some hundred years ago."

" '*Μηδὲν ἄγαν*,' " said I; "let us but lay in—when only laid
in it can be—such a store of that same well-concocted stuff as
shall last us all Life's journey through, with all its ups and downs.
Nothing, say the Hunters, that Blood and Bone won't get over."

"Be there a good Rider to guide him!" said Euphranor; "and
that, in Man's case, I take it is—if not yet the Reason we talked
of—a Moral such as no Beast that breathes is conscious of. You
talk of this Animal virtue, and that—why, for instance, is there
not a *moral*, as distinguisht from an *animal* Courage, to face, not
only the sudden danger of the field, but something far-off coming, far foreseen, and far more terrible—Cranmer's, for instance——"

"Which," said I, "had all but failed—all the more honour for
triumphing at last! But Hugh Latimer, I think, had wrought
along with his Father's hinds in Leicestershire. Anyhow, there
is no harm in having two strings to your Bow, whichever of them
be the strongest. The immortal Soul, obliged, as she is, to take
the Field of Mortality, would not be the worse for being mounted
on a good Animal, though I must not say with the Hunters, till
the Rider seems 'part of his horse.' As to your Reason—he is apt
to *crane* a little too much over the hedge, as they say, till, by too
long considering the '*How*,' he comes to question the '*Why*,' and,
the longer looking, the less liking, shirks it altogether, or by his
Indecision brings Horse and Rider into the Ditch. Hamlet lets
us into the secret—luckily for us enacting the very moral he
descants on—when he reflects on his own imbecility of action:

> "Whether it be
> Bestial oblivion, or some craven scruple
> Of thinking too precisely on the Event,
> A thought which, quarter'd, hath but one part Wisdom,
> And ever three parts Coward—I do not know
> Why yet I live to say, '*This thing's to do*,'
> Sith I have Cause, and Will, and Strength, and Means,
> To do't."

Not in his case surely '*oblivion*,' with such reminders, super-
natural and other, as he had: nor as in our case, with the Ditch

before our Eyes: nor want of Courage, which was his Royal inheritance; but the *Will*, which he reckon'd on as surely as on Strength and Means—was he so sure of *that*? He had previously told us how 'The native hue of Resolution'—how like that glow upon the cheek of healthy Youth!—

"The native hue of Resolution
Is sicklied o'er with the pale cast of Thought,
And Enterprizes of great pith and moment
With this regard their currents turn awry,
And lose the name of Action."

He had, he tells his College Friends, foregone his '*Custom of Exercises*'—among others, perhaps, his Cricket, at Wittenberg too soon, and taken to reasoning about 'To be, or not to be'—otherwise he would surely have bowl'd his wicked uncle down at once."

"Though not without calling 'Play!' I hope," said Euphranor, laughing.

"At any rate, not while his Adversary's back was turned, and so far prepared, inasmuch as he was engaged in repentant Prayer. And that is the reason Hamlet gives for not then despatching him, lest, being so employ'd, he should escape the future punishment of his crime. An odd motive for the youthful Moral to have *reasoned* itself into."

"His Father had been cut off unprepared, and perhaps, according to the Moral of those days, could only be avenged by such a plenary Expiation."

"Perhaps; or, perhaps—and Shakespeare himself may not have known exactly why—Hamlet only made it an excuse for delaying what he had to do, as delay he does, till vengeance seems beyond his reach when he suffers himself to be sent out of the country. For you know the *Habit* of Resolving without Doing, as in the Closet, gradually snaps the connexion between them, and the case becomes chronically hopeless."

Euphranor said that I had stolen that fine Moral of mine from a Volume of "Newman's Sermons" which he had lent me, as I agreed with him was probably the case; and then he said:

"Well, Bowling down a King is, I suppose, a ticklish Business, and the Bowler may miss his aim by being too long about taking it: but, in Cricket proper, I have most wonder'd at the Batter who has to decide whether to block, strike, or tip, in that twinkling of an eye between the ball's delivery, and its arrival at his wicket."

"Yes," said I, "and the Boxer who puts in a blow with one hand at the same moment of warding one off with the other."

" 'Gladiatorem in arenâ,' " said Euphranor.

"Yes; what is called '*Presence of mind,*' where there is no time to '*make it up.*' And all the more necessary and remarkable in proportion to the Danger involved. As when the Hunter's horse falling with him in full cry, he braces himself, between saddle and ground, to pitch clear of his horse—as Fielding tells us that brave old Parson Adams did, when probably thinking less of his horse than of those Sermons he carried in his saddle-bags."

"Ah!" said Euphranor, "Parson Adams was so far a lucky man to have a Horse at all, which we poor fellows now can hardly afford. I remember how I used to envy those who—for the fun, if for nothing else—followed brave old Sedgwick across country, through brier, through mire. Ah! *that* was a Lecture after your own heart, Doctor; something more than peripatetic, and from one with plenty of the Boy in him when over Seventy, I believe."

"Well, there again," said I, "your great Schools might condescend to take another hint from abroad where some one—Fellenberg again, I think—had a Riding-house in his much poorer School, where you might learn not only to sit your horse if ever able to provide one for yourself, but also to saddle, bridle, rub him down, with the *ss'ss-s'ss'* which I fancy was heard on the morning of Agincourt—if, by the way, one horse was left in all the host."

"Well, come," said Euphranor, "the Gladiator, at any rate, is gone—and the Boxer after him—and the Hunter, I think, going after both; perhaps the very Horse he rides gradually to be put away by Steam into some Museum among the extinct Species that Man has no longer room or business for."

"Nevertheless," said I, "War is *not* gone with the Gladiator, and cannon and rifle yet leave room for hand-to-hand conflict, as may one day—which God forbid!—come to proof in our own sea-girt Island. If safe from abroad, some Ruffian may still

C*

assault you in some shady lane—nay, in your own parlour—at home, when you have nothing but your own strong arm, and ready soul to direct it. Accidents will happen in the best-regulated families. The House will take fire, the Coach will break down, the Boat will upset;—is there no gentleman who can swim, to save himself and others? no one do more to save the Maid snoring in the garret, than helplessly looking on—or turning away? Some one is taken ill at midnight; John is drunk in bed; is there no Gentleman can saddle Dobbin—much less get a Collar over his Head, or the Crupper over his tail, without such awkwardness as brings on his abdomen the kick he fears, and spoils him for the journey? And I do maintain," I continued, "having now gotten 'the bit between my teeth'—maintain against all Comers that, independent of any bodily action on their part, these, and the like Accomplishments, as you call them, do carry with them, and, I will say, with the Soul incorporate, that habitual Instinct of Courage, Resolution, and Decision, which, together with the Good Humour which good animal Condition goes so far to ensure, do, I say, prepare and arm the Man not only against the greater, but against those minor Trials of Life which are so far harder to encounter because of perpetually cropping up; and thus do cause him to radiate, if through a narrow circle, yet, through that, imperceptibly to the whole world, a happier atmosphere about him than could be inspired by Closet-loads of Poetry, Metaphysic, and Divinity. No doubt there is danger, as you say, of the Animal overpowering the Rational, as, I maintain, equally so of the reverse; no doubt the high-mettled Colt will be likeliest to run riot, as may my Lad, inflamed with Aristotle's 'Wine of Youth,' into excesses which even the virtuous Berkeley says are the more curable as lying in the Passions; whereas, says he, 'the dry Rogue who sets up for Judgment is incorrigible.' But, whatever be the result, VIGOUR, of Body, as of Spirit, one must have, subject like all good things to the worst corruption—Strength itself, even of Evil, being a kind of *Virtus* which Time, if not good Counsel, is pretty sure to moderate; whereas Weakness is the one radical and Incurable Evil, increasing with every year of Life.—Which fine Moral, or to that effect, you will also find somewhere in those Sermons, whose Authority I know you cannot doubt."

"And thus," said Euphranor, "after this long tirade, you turn out the young Knight from Cricket on the World."

"Nay," said I, "did I not tell you from the first I would not meddle with your Digby any more than your Wordsworth? I have only been talking of ordinary mankind so as to provide for Locke's '*totus, teres*,' and—except in the matter of waistband—'*rotundus*' man, sufficiently accoutred for the campaign of ordinary Life. And yet, on second thought, I do not see why he should not do very fairly well for one of the 'Table round,' if King Arthur himself is to be looked for, and found, as the Poet says, in the 'Modern Gentleman,' whose 'stateliest port' will not be due to the Reading-desk or Easy-chair. At any rate, he will be sufficiently qualified, not only to shoot the Pheasant and hunt the Fox, but even to sit on the Bench of Magistrates—or even of Parliament—not unprovided with a quotation or two from Horace or Virgil."

Euphranor could not deny that, laughing.

"Or if obliged, poor fellow—Younger son, perhaps—to *do* something to earn him Bread—or Claret—for his Old Age, if not prematurely knocked on the head—whether not well-qualified for Soldier or Sailor?"

"Nor that."

"As for the Church, (which is your other Gentlemanly Profession,) you know your Bishop can consecrate Tom or Blifil equally by that Imposition——"

"Doctor, Doctor," broke in Euphranor, "you have been talking very well; don't spoil it by one of your grimaces."

"Well, well," said I,—"Oh, but there is still THE LAW, in which I would rather trust myself with Tom than Blifil," added I. "Well, what else? Surgery? which is said to need 'the Lion's Heart.'"

"But also the Lady's Hand," replied he, smiling.

"Not in drawing one of the Molares, I assure you. However, thus far I do not seem to have indisposed him for the Professions which his Rank usually opens to him; or perhaps even, if he had what you call a Genius in any direction, might, amid all his Beef-compelling Exercises, light upon something, as Pan a-hunting, and, as it were 'unaware,' says Bacon, discover'd that Ceres whom the more seriously-searching Gods had looked for in vain."

75

"Not for the sake of *Rent*, I hope," said Euphranor, laughing.

"Or even a turn for looking into Digby and Aristotle, as into a Mirror—could he but distinguish his own face in it."

Euphranor, upon whose face no sign of any such self-consciousness appeared, sat for a little while silent, and then said:

"Do you remember that fine passage in Aristophanes' Clouds —lying libel as it is—between the Δίκαιος and Ἄδικος Λόγος ?"

"I had forgotten," I said, "my little Latin and less Greek:" and he declared I must however read this scene over again with him. "It is, you see, Old Athens pleading against Young; whom after denouncing, for relinquishing the hardy Discipline and simple severe Exercises that reared the Μαραθωνομάχους Ἄνδρας, for the Warm Bath, the Dance, and the Law Court; he suddenly turns to the Young Man who stands hesitating between them, and in those Verses, musical—

’Αλλ’ οὖν λιπαρός γε καὶ εὐανθής—"

"Come, my good fellow," said I, "you must interpret." And Euphranor, looking down, in undertone repeated:

"O listen to me, and so shall you be stout-hearted and fresh as a Daisy:

Not ready to chatter on every matter, nor bent over books till you're hazy:

No splitter of straws, no dab at the Laws, making black seem white so cunning:

But scamp'ring down out o' the town, and over the green Meadow running.

Race, wrestle, and play with your fellows so gay, like so many Birds of a feather,

All breathing of Youth, Good-humour, and Truth, in the time of the jolly Spring weather,

In the jolly Spring-time, when the Poplar and Lime dishevel their tresses together."

"Well, but go on," said I, when he stopp'd, "I am sure there is something more of it, now you recall the passage to me— about broad shoulders and——"

But this was all he had cared to remember.

I then asked him who was the translator; to which he replied

76

with a shy smile, 'twas more a paraphrase than a translation, and I might criticize it as I liked. To which I had not much to object, I said—perhaps the trees "dishevelling their tresses" a little Cockney; which he agreed it was. And then, turning off, observed how the degradation which Aristophanes satirized in the Athenian youth went on and on, so that, when Rome came to help Greece against Philip of Macedon, the Athenians, says Livy, could contribute little to the common cause but declamation and despatches—"quibus solum valent."

"Aye," said I, "and to think that when Livy was so writing of Athens, his own Rome was just beginning to go downhill in the same way and for the same causes: when, says Horace, the Boy of gentle blood, adept enough at feats of trivial dexterity, had no seat on the Horse, nor courage to follow the Hounds: unlike those early times, when Heroic Father begot and bred Heroic Son; Generation following Generation, crown'd with Laurel and with Oak; under a system of Education, the same Livy says, handed down, as it were an Art, from the very foundation of Rome, and filling her Parliament with Generals, each equal, he rhetorically declares, to Alexander.—But come, my dear fellow," said I, jumping up, "here have I been holding forth like a little Socrates, while the day is passing over our heads. We have forgotten poor Lexilogus, who (I should not wonder) may have stolen away, like your fox, to Cambridge."

Euphranor, who seemed to linger yet awhile, nevertheless follow'd my example. On looking at my watch I saw we could not take anything like the walk we had proposed and yet be at home by their College dinner;* so as it was I who had wasted the day, I would stand the expense, I said, of dinner at the Inn: after which we could all return at our ease to Cambridge in the Evening. As we were leaving the Bowling-Green, I called up to Lycion, who thereupon appeared at the Billiard-room window with his coat off, and asked him if he had nearly finish'd his Game. By way of answer, he asked us if we had done with our Ogres and Giants; whom, on the contrary, I said, we were now running away from that we might live to fight another day— would he come with us into the fields for a walk? or, if he meant to go on with his Billiards, would he dine with us on our return?

* Then at 3.30 p.m.

"Not walk with us," he said; and when I spoke of dinner again, seemed rather to hesitate; but at last said, "Very well;" and, nodding to us, retired with his cue into the room.

Then Euphranor and I, leaving the necessary orders within, return'd a little way to look for Lexilogus, whom we soon saw, like a man of honour as he was, coming on his way to meet us. In less than a minute we had met; and he apologized for having been delay'd by one of Aunt Martha's asthma-fits, during which he had not liked to leave her.

After a brief condolence, we all three turn'd back; and I told him how, after all, Euphranor and I had play'd no Billiards, but had been arguing all the time about Digby and his books.

Lexilogus smiled, but made no remark, being naturally little given to Speech. But the day was delightful, and we walk'd briskly along the road, conversing on many topics, till a little further on we got into the fields. These—for it had been a warm May—were now almost in their Prime, (and that of the Year, Crabbe used to say, fell with the mowing,) crop-thick with Daisy, Clover, and Buttercup; and, as we went along, Euphranor, whose thoughts still ran on what we had been talking about, quoted from Chaucer whom we had lately been looking at together:

> "Embrouded was he as it were a Mede,
>   Alle ful of fresshe Floures, white and rede,"

and added, "What a picture was that, by the way, of a young Knight!"

I had half-forgotten the passage, and Lexilogus had never read Chaucer: so I begg'd Euphranor to repeat it; which he did, with an occasional pause in his Memory, and jog from mine.

> "With him ther was his Sone, a yonge Squier,
>   A Lover, and a lusty Bacheler,
>   With Lockes crull, as they were laide in presse;
>   Of Twenty yere of age he was, I gesse;
>   Of his Stature he was of even lengthe,
>   And wonderly deliver, and grete of Strengthe;
>   And he hadde be somtime in Chevachie,
>   In Flaundres, in Artois, and in Picardie,

And borne him wel, as of so litel space,
In hope to stonden in his Ladies grace.
Embrouded was he as it were a Mede,
Alle ful of fresshe Floures, white and rede;
Singing he was, or floyting alle the day;
He was as fresshe as is the moneth of May:
Short was his Goune, with sleves long and wide,
Wel coude he sitte on Hors, and fayre ride;
He coude Songes make, and well endite,
Juste, and eke dance, and wel pourtraie and write.
So hote he loved, that by nightertale
He slep no more than doth the Nightingale.
Curteis he was, lowly, and servisable,
And carf before his Fader at the table."

"Chaucer, however," said Euphranor, when he had finished the passage, "credited his young Squire with other Accomplishments than you would trust him with, Doctor. See, he dances, draws, and even indites songs—somewhat of a Dilettante, after all."

"But also," I added, "is of 'grete Strengthe,' 'coude fayre ride,' having already 'borne him wel in Chevachie.' Besides," continued I, (who had not yet subsided, I suppose, from the long swell of my former sententiousness,) "in those days, you know, there was scarce any Reading, which now, for better or worse, occupies so much of our time; Men left that to Clerk and Schoolman; contented, as we before agreed, to follow their bidding to Pilgrimage and Holy war. Some of those gentler Accomplishments may then have been needed to soften manners, just as rougher ones to strengthen ours. And, long after that, Sir Philip Sidney might well indulge in a little Sonneteering, amid all those public services which ended at Zutfen; as later on, in the Stuart days, Lord Dorset troll off—'*To all you Ladies now on Land,*' from the Fleet that was just going into Action off the coast of Holland."

"Even Master Samuel Pepys," said Euphranor, laughing, "might sit with a good grace down to practise his '*Beauty retire,*' after riding to Huntingdon and back, as might Parson Adams have done many years after."

"They were both prefigured among those Canterbury Pilgrims so many years before," said I. "Only think of it! Some nine-and-twenty, I think, 'by aventure yfalle in feleweship,' High and Low, Rich and Poor, Saint and Sinner, Cleric and Lay, Knight, Ploughman, Prioress, Wife of Bath, Shipman, hunting Abbot-like Monk, Poor Parson—(Adams' Progenitor)—Webster (Pepys')—on rough-riding 'Stot' or ambling Palfrey, marshall'd by mine Host of the Tabard to the music of the Miller's Bagpipes, on their sacred errand to St Thomas'; and one among them taking note of all in Verse still fresh as the air of those Kentish hills they travelled over on that April morning four hundred years ago."

"Lydgate too, I remember," said Euphranor, "tells of Chaucer's good-humour'd encouragement of his Brother-poets —I cannot now recollect the lines," he added, after pausing a little.

"A famous Man of Business too," said I, "employ'd by Princes at home and abroad. And ready to fight as to write; having, he says, when some City people had accused him of Untruth, 'prepared his body for Mars his doing, if any contraried his saws.' "

"A Poet after your own heart, Doctor, sound in wind and limb, Mind and Body. In general, however, they are said to be a sickly, irritable, inactive, and solitary race."

"Not our 'Canterbury Pilgrim' for one," said I; "no, nor his successor, William Shakespeare, who, after a somewhat roving Knighthood in the country, became a Player, Play-wright, and Play-manager in London, where, after managing (as not all managers do) to make a sufficient fortune, he returned home again to settle in his native Stratford—whither by the way he had made occasional Pilgrimages before—on horseback, of course—putting up—for the night—at the Angel of Oxford— about which some stories are told——"

"As fabulous as probably those of his poaching in earlier days," said Euphranor.

"Well, however that may be—and I constantly believe in the poaching part of the Story—to Stratford he finally retired, where he built a house, and planted Mulberries, and kept company with John-a-Combe, and the neighbouring Knights and Squires— except perhaps the Lucys—as merrily as with the Wits of London; all the while supplying his own little 'Globe'—and, from it, 'the Great globe itself,' with certain manuscripts, in which (say his Fellow-players and first Editors) Head and hand went so easily together as scarce to leave a blot on the pages they travell'd over."

"Somewhat resembling Sir Walter Scott's, I think," said Euphranor, "in that love for Country home, and Country neighbour—aye, and somewhat also in that easy intercourse between Head and hand in composition which those who knew them tell of—however unequal in the result. Do you remember Lockhart's saying how glibly Sir Walter's pen was heard to canter over the paper, before 'Atra Cura' saddled herself behind him?"

"Ah, yes," said I; " 'Magician of the North' they call'd him in my own boyish days; and such he is to me now; though maybe not an Archi-magus like him of Stratford, to set me down in Rome, Athens, Egypt, with their Heroes, Heroines, and Commoners, moving and talking as living men and women about me, howsoever 'larger than human' through the breath of Imagination in which he has clothed them."

"Somebody—your Carlyle, I believe," said Euphranor, "lays it down that Sir Walter's Characters are in general fashioned from without to within—the reverse of Shakespeare's way—and Nature's."

"What," said I, "according to old Sartor's theory, beginning from the over-coat of temporary Circumstance, through the temporary Tailor's 'Just-au-corps,' till arriving at such centre of Humanity as may lie within the bodily jerkin we talk'd of?"

"Something of that sort, I suppose," said Euphranor; "but an you love me, Doctor, no more of that odious old jerkin, whether Sterne's or Carlyle's."

"Well," said I, "if the Sartor's charge hold good, it must lie against the Heroes and Heroines of the later, half-historical, Romances; in which, nevertheless, are scenes where our Elizabeth, and James, and Lewis of France figure, that seem to me as good in Character and Circumstance as any in that Henry the Eighth, which has always till quite lately been accepted for Shakespeare's. But Sartor's self will hardly maintain his charge against the Deanses, Dumbiedykes, Ochiltrees, Baillies, and others of the bonâ-fide *Scotch* Novels, with the likes of whom

Scott fell 'in feleweship' from a Boy, riding about the country—
'born to be a trooper,' he said of himself; no, nor with the Brad-
wardines, Balfours, Maccombicks, Macbriars, and others, High-
lander, Lowlander, Royalist, Roundhead, Churchman, or Coven-
anter, whom he animated with the true Scottish blood which ran
in himself as well as in those he lived among, and so peopled
those Stories which are become Household History to us. I declare that I scarce know whether Macbeth's blasted heath would
move me more than did the first sight of the Lammermoor Hills
when I rounded the Scottish coast on first going to Edinburgh;
or of that ancient 'Heart of Mid-Lothian' when I got there. But
the domestic Tragedy naturally comes more nearly home to the
bosom of your Philistine."

"Sir Walter's stately neighbour across the Tweed," said
Euphranor, "took no great account of his Novels, and none at all
of his Verse—though, by the way, he did call him 'Great Minstrel
of the Border' after revisiting Yarrow in his company; perhaps
he meant it only of the Minstrelsy which Scott collected, you
know."

"Wordsworth?" said I—"a man of the Milton rather than of
the Chaucer and Shakespeare type—without humour, like the
rest of his Brethren of the Lake."

"Not but he loves Chaucer as much as you can, Doctor, for
those fresh touches of Nature, and tenderness of Heart—insomuch that he has re-cast the Jew of Lincoln's Story into a form
more available for modern readers."

"And successfully?"

"Ask Lexilogus—Ah! I forget that he never read Chaucer; but
I know that he loves Wordsworth next to his own Cowper."

Lexilogus believed that he liked the Poem in question, but he
was not so familiar with it as with many other of Wordsworth's
pieces.

"Ah, you and I, Euphranor," said I, "must one day teach
Lexilogus the original before he is become too great a Don to
heed such matters."

Lexilogus smiled, and Euphranor said that before that time
came Lexilogus and he would teach me in return to love Wordsworth more than I did—or pretended to do. Not only the Poet,
but the Man, he said, who loved his Home as well as Shakespeare

and Scott loved theirs—aye, and his Country Neighbours too, though perhaps in a sedater way; and, as so many of his Poems show, as sensible as Sir Walter of the sterling virtues of the Mountaineers and Dalesmen he lived among, though, maybe, not of their humour.

"Was he not also pretty exact in his office of stamp-distributor among them?" asked I.

"Come, you must not quarrel, Doctor, with the Business which, as with Chaucer and Shakespeare, may have kept the Poetic Element in due proportion with the rest—including, by the way, such a store of your Animal, laid in from constant climbing the mountain, and skating on the lake, that he may still be seen, I am told, at near upon Eighty, travelling with the shadow of the cloud up Helvellyn."

"Bravo, Old Man of the Mountains!" said I. "But, nevertheless, it would not have been amiss with him had he been sent earlier, and further, from his mountain-mother's lap, and had some of his—conceit, I must not call it—Pride, then—taken out of him by a freer intercourse with men."

"I suppose," said Euphranor, again laughing, "you would knock a young Apollo about like the rest of us common pottery?"

"I think I *should* send young Wordsworth to that Military Drill of ours, and see if some rough-riding would not draw some of that dangerous Sensibility which 'young Edwin' is apt to mistake for poetical Genius."

"Gray had more than that in him, I know," said Euphranor; "but I doubt what might have become of his poetry had such been the discipline of his Eton day."

"Perhaps something better—perhaps nothing at all—and *he* the happier man."

"But not *you*, Doctor—for the loss of his Elegy—with all your talk."

"No; I am always remembering, and always forgetting it; remembering, I mean, the several stanzas, and forgetting how they link together; partly, perhaps, because of each being so severally elaborated. Neither Yeomanry Drill—nor daily Plough —drove the Muse out of Burns."

"Nor the Melancholy neither, for that matter," said Euphranor. "Those 'Banks and braes' of his could not bestow on him even the 'momentary joy' which those Eton fields 'beloved in vain' breathed into the heart of Gray."

"Are you not forgetting," said I, "that Burns was not then singing of himself, but of some forsaken damsel, as appears by the second stanza? which few, by the way, care to remember. As unremember'd it may have been," I continued, after a pause, "by the only living—and like to live—Poet I had known, when, so many years after, he found himself beside that 'bonnie Doon' and—whether it were from recollection of poor Burns, or of 'the days that are no more' which haunt us all, I know not—I think he did not know—but, he somehow 'broke' as he told me, 'broke into a passion of tears.'—Of tears, which during a pretty long and intimate intercourse, I had never seen glisten in his eye but once, when reading Virgil—'dear old Virgil,' as he call'd him—together: and then of the burning of Troy in the Second Æneid —whether moved by the catastrophe's self, or the majesty of the Verse it is told in—or, as before, scarce knowing why. For, as King Arthur shall bear witness, no young Edwin he, though, as a great Poet, comprehending all the softer stops of human Emotion in that Register where the Intellectual, no less than what is call'd the Poetical, faculty predominated. As all who knew him know, a Man at all points, Euphranor—like your Digby, of grand proportion and feature, significant of that inward Chivalry, becoming his ancient and honourable race; when himself a 'Yongé Squire,' like him in Chaucer 'of grete strength,' that could hurl the crow-bar further than any of the neighbouring clowns, whose humours, as well as of their betters,—Knight, Squire, Landlord and Land-tenant,—he took quiet note of, like Chaucer himself. Like your Wordsworth on the Mountain, he too, when a Lad, abroad on the Wold; sometimes of a night with the Shepherd; watching not only the Flock on the greensward, but also

> "The fleecy Star that bears
> Andromeda far off Atlantic seas"

along with those other Zodiacal constellations which Aries, I think, leads over the field of Heaven. He then observed also some of those uncertain phenomena of Night: unsurmised apparitions of the Northern Aurora, by some shy glimpses of which no

winter—no, nor even summer—night, he said, was utterly unvisited; and those strange voices, whether of creeping brook, or
copses muttering to themselves far off—perhaps the yet more
impossible Sea—together with 'other sounds we know not whence
they come,' says Crabbe, but all inaudible to the ear of Day. He
was not then, I suppose, unless the Word spontaneously came
upon him, thinking how to turn what he saw and heard into
Verse; a premeditation that is very likely to defeat itself, previously breathing, as it were, upon the mirror which is to receive
the Image that most assuredly flashes Reality into words."

Something to this effect I said, though, were it but for lack of
walking breath, at no so long-winded a stretch of eloquence. And
then Euphranor, whose lungs were in so much better order than
mine, though I had left him so little opportunity for using them,
took up where I left off, and partly read, and partly told us of a
delightful passage from his Godefridus, to this effect, that, if the
Poet could not invent, neither could his Reader understand him,
when he told of Ulysses and Diomed listening to the crane clang-
ing in the marsh by night, without having *experienced* something
of the sort. And so we went on, partly in jest, partly in earnest,
drawing Philosophers of all kinds into the same net in which we
had entangled the Poet and his Critic—How the Moralist who
worked alone in his closet was apt to mismeasure Humanity, and
be very angry when the cloth he cut out for him would not fit—
how the best Histories were written by those who themselves
had been actors in them—Gibbon, one of the next best, I believe,
recording how the discipline of the Hampshire Militia he served
as Captain in—how odd he must have looked in the uniform!—
enlighten'd him as to the evolutions of a Roman Legion—And
so on a great deal more; till, suddenly observing how the sun had
declined from his meridian, I look'd at my watch, and ask'd my
companions did not they begin to feel hungry, like myself? They
agreed with me; and we turn'd homeward: and as Lexilogus had
hitherto borne so little part in the conversation, I began to question him about Herodotus and Strabo, (whose books I had seen
lying open upon his table,) and drew from him some information
about the courses of the Nile and the Danube, and the Geography
of the Old World: till, all of a sudden, our conversation skipt
from Olympus, I think, to the hills of Yorkshire—our own old

hills—and the old friends and neighbours who dwelt among them. And as we were thus talking, we heard what seemed to us the galloping of Horses behind us, (for we were now again upon the road,) and, looking back as they were just coming up, I recognised Phidippus for one of the riders, with two others whom I did not know. I held up my hand, and call'd out to him as he was passing; and Phidippus, drawing up his Horse all snorting and agitated with her arrested course, wheel'd back and came alongside of us.

I ask'd him what he was about, galloping along the road; I thought scientific men were more tender of their horses' legs and feet. But the roads, he said, were quite soft with the late rains; and they were only trying each other's speed for a mile or so.

By this time his two companions had pulled up some way forward, and were calling him to come on; but he said, laughing, "they had quite enough of it," and address'd himself with many a "Steady!" and "So! So!" to pacify Miss Middleton, as he called her, who still caper'd, plung'd, and snatch'd at her bridle; his friends shouting louder and louder—"Why the Devil he didn't come on?"

He waved his hand to them in return; and with a "Confound" and "Deuce take the Fellow," they set off away toward the town. On which Miss Middleton began afresh, plunging, and blowing out a peony nostril after her flying fellows; until, what with their dwindling in distance, and some expostulation address'd to her by her Master as to a fractious Child, she seem'd to make up her mind to the indignity, and composed herself to go pretty quietly beside us.

I then asked him did he not remember Lexilogus,—(Euphranor he had already recognised,)—and Phidippus who really had not hitherto seen who it was, (Lexilogus looking shyly down all the while,) call'd out heartily to him, and wheeling his mare suddenly behind us, took hold of his hand, and began to inquire about his family in Yorkshire.

"One would suppose," said I, "you two fellows had not met for years."

"It was true," Phidippus said, "they did not meet as often as he wish'd; but Lexilogus would not come to his rooms, and he

86

did not like to disturb Lexilogus at his books; and so the time went on."

I then inquired about his own reading, which, though not much, was not utterly neglected, it seemed; and he said he had meant to ask one of us to beat something into his stupid head this summer in Yorkshire.

Lexilogus, I knew, meant to stop at Cambridge all the long Vacation; but Euphranor said he should be at home, for anything he then knew, and they could talk the matter over when the time came. We then again fell to talking of our County; and among other things I asked Phidippus if his horse were Yorkshire,—of old famous for its breed, as well as of Riders,—and how long he had had her, and so forth.

Yorkshire she was, a present from his Father, "and a great pet," he said, bending down his head, which Miss Middleton answered by a dip of hers, shaking the bit in her mouth, and breaking into a little canter, which however was easily suppress'd.

"Miss Middleton?" said I—"what, by Bay Middleton out of Coquette, by Tomboy out of High-Life Below-Stairs, right up to Mahomet and his Mares?"

"Right," he answered, laughing, "as far as Bay Middleton was concerned."

"But, Phidippus," said I, "she's as black as a coal!"

"And so was her Dam, a Yorkshire Mare," he answered; which, I said, saved the credit of all parties. Might she perhaps be descended from our famous "Yorkshire Jenny," renowned in Newmarket Verse? But Phidippus had never heard of "Yorkshire Jenny," nor of the Ballad, which I promised to acquaint him with, if he would stop on his way back, and dine with us at Chesterton, where his Mare might have her Dinner too—all of us Yorkshiremen except Lycion, whom he knew a little of. There was to be a Boat-race, however, in the evening, which Phidippus said he must leave us to attend, if dine with us he did; for though not one of the Crew on this occasion, (not being one of the best,) he must yet see his own Trinity keep the head of the River. As to that, I said, we were all bound the same way, which indeed Euphranor had proposed before; and so the whole affair was settled.

As we went along, I began questioning him concerning some of those Equestrian difficulties which Euphranor and I had been talking of: all which Phidippus thought was only my usual banter—"he was no Judge—I must ask older hands," and so forth—until we reach'd the Inn, when I begg'd Euphranor to order dinner at once, while I and Lexilogus accompanied Phidippus to the Stable. There, after giving his mare in charge to the hostler with due directions as to her toilet and table, he took off her saddle and bridle himself, and adjusted the head-stall. Then, follow'd out of the stable by her flaming eye and pointed ears, he too pausing a moment on the threshold to ask me, "was she not a Beauty?" (for he persisted in the delusion of my knowing more of the matter than I chose to confess,) we cross'd over into the house.

There, having wash'd our hands and faces, we went up into the Billiard-room, where we found Euphranor and Lycion playing,—Lycion very lazily, like a man who had already too much of it, but yet nothing better to do. After a short while, the girl came to tell us all was ready; and, after that slight hesitation as to precedence which Englishmen rarely forget on the least ceremonious occasions,—Lexilogus, in particular, pausing timidly at the door, and Euphranor pushing him gently forward,—we got down to the little Parlour, very airy and pleasant, with its windows opening on the bowling-green, the table laid with a clean white cloth, and upon that a dish of smoking beef-steak, at which I, as master of the Feast, and, as Euphranor slyly intimated, otherwise entitled, sat down to officiate. For some time the clatter of knife and fork, and the pouring of ale, went on, mix'd with some conversation among the young men about College matters: till Lycion began to tell us of a gay Ball he had lately been at, and of the Families there; among whom he named three young Ladies from a neighbouring County, by far the handsomest women present, he said.

"And very accomplish'd too, I am told," said Euphranor.

"Oh, as for that," replied Lycion, "they *Valse* very well." He hated "your accomplished women," he said.

"Well, there," said Euphranor, "I suppose the Doctor will agree with you."

I said, that certainly *Valsing* would be no great use to me personally—unless, as some Lady of equal size and greater rank had said, I could meet with a concave partner.

"One knows so exactly," said Lycion, "what the Doctor would choose,—a woman

> "Well versed in the Arts
> Of Pies, Puddings, and Tarts,"

as one used to read of somewhere, I remember."

"Not forgetting," said I, "the being able to help in compounding a pill or a plaister; which I dare say your Great-grandmother knew something about, Lycion, for in those days, you know, Great ladies studied Simples. Well, so I am fitted,—as Lycion is to be with one who can *Valse* through life with him."

> "And follow so the ever-rolling Year
> With profitable labour to their graves,"

added Euphranor, laughing.

"I don't want to marry her," said Lycion testily.

"Then Euphranor," said I, "will advertise for a 'Strong-minded' Female, able to read Plato with him, and Wordsworth, and Digby, and become a Mother of Heroes. As to Phidippus there is no doubt—Diana Vernon—"

But Phidippus disclaimed any taste for Sporting ladies.

"Well, come," said I, passing round a bottle of sherry I had just call'd for, "every man to his liking, only all of you taking care to secure the accomplishments of Health and Good-humour."

"Ah! there it is, out at last!" cried Euphranor, clapping his hands; "I knew the Doctor would choose for us as Frederick for his Grenadiers."

"So you may accommodate me," said I, "with a motto from another old Song whenever my time comes;

> " 'Give Isaac the Nymph who no beauty can boast,
> But Health and Good-humour to make her his toast.'

Well, every man to his fancy—Here's to mine!—And when we have finish'd the bottle, which seems about equal to one more errand round the table, we will adjourn, if you like, to the Bowling-green, which Euphranor will tell us was the goodly custom of our Forefathers, and I can recommend as a very wholesome after-dinner exercise."

"Not, however, till we have the Doctor's famous Ballad about Miss Middleton's possible Great-Great-Grandmother," cried Euphranor, "by way of Pindaric close to this Heroic entertainment, sung from the Chair, who probably composed it——"

"As little as could sing it," I assured him.

"Oh, I remember, it was the Jockey who rode her!"

"Perhaps only his Helper," answered I; such bad grammar, and rhyme, and altogether want of what your man—how do you call him—G. O. E. T. H. E.—'Gewty,' will that do?—calls, I believe, *Art*."

"Who nevertheless once declares," said Euphranor, "that the Ballad was scarcely possible but to those who simply saw with their Eyes, heard with their Ears—and, I really think he said, fought with their fists,—I suppose also felt with their hearts—without any notion of '*Art*'—although Goethe himself, Schiller, and Rückert, and other of your æsthetic Germans, Doctor, have latterly done best in that line, I believe."

"Better than Cowper's 'Royal George,' " said I, "where every word of the narrative *tells*, as from a Seaman's lips?"

"*That* is something before our time, Doctor."

"Better then than some of Campbell's which follow'd it? or some of Sir Walter's? or 'The Lord of Burleigh,' which is later than all? But enough that my poor Jock may chance to sing of his Mare as well as Shenstone of his Strephon and Delia."

"Or more modern Bards of Cocles in the Tiber, or Regulus in the Tub," said Euphranor.—"But come! Song from the Chair!" he call'd out, tapping his glass on the table, which Phidippus echoed with his.

So with a prelusive "Well then," I began—

" 'I'll sing you a Song, and a merry, merry Song'—

By the way, Phidippus, what an odd notion of merriment is a Jockey's, if this Song be a sample. I think I have observed they have grave, taciturn faces, especially when old, which they soon get to look. Is this from much wasting, to carry little Flesh—and large—Responsibility?"

"Doctor, Doctor, leave your—faces, and begin!" interrupted Euphranor. "I must call the Chair to Order."

Thus admonish'd, with some slight interpolations, (to be jump'd by the Æsthetic,) I repeated the poor Ballad which, dropt I know not how nor when into my ear, had managed, as others we had talk'd of, to chink itself in some corner of a memory that should have been occupied with other professional jargon than a "Jockey's."

I

"I'll sing you a Song, and a merry, merry Song,
  Concerning our Yorkshire Jen;
Who never yet ran with Horse or Mare,
  That ever she cared for a pin.

II

When first she came to Newmarket town,
  The Sportsmen all view'd her around;
All the cry was, 'Alas, poor wench,
  Thou never can run this ground!'

III

When they came to the starting-post,
  The Mare look'd very smart;
And let them all say what they will,
  She never lost her start—

—which I don't quite understand, by the way: do you, Lycion?"
—No answer.

IV

"When they got to the Two-mile post,
  Poor Jenny was cast behind:
She was cast behind, she was cast behind,
  All for to take her wind.

V

When they got to the Three-mile post,
  The mare look'd very pale—
(Phidippus!"—His knee moved under the table—)
  "SHE LAID DOWN HER EARS ON HER BONNY NECK,
  AND BY THEM ALL DID SHE SAIL;

VI   (*Accelerando.*)

'Come follow me, come follow me,
    All you who run so neat;
And ere that you catch me again,
    I'll make you well to sweat.'

VII   (*Grandioso.*)

When she got to the Winning-post,
    The people all gave a shout:.
And Jenny click'd up her Lily-white foot,
    And jump'd like any Buck.

VIII

The Jockey said to her, 'This race you have run,
    This race for me you have got;
You could gallop it all over again,
    When the rest could hardly trot!'

"They were Four-mile Heats in those days, you see, would
pose your modern Middletons, though Miss Jenny, laying back
her ears—away from catching the Wind, some think—and otherwise '*pale*,' with the distended vein and starting sinew of that
Three-mile crisis, nevertheless on coming triumphantly in,
click'd up that lily-white foot of hers, (of which *one*, I have heard
say, is as good a sign, as all four white are a bad,) and could, as
the Jockey thought, have gallop'd it all over again—Can't you
see him, Phidippus, for once forgetful of his professional
stoicism, (but I don't think Jockeys were quite so politic then,)
bending forward to pat the bonny Neck that measured the
Victory, as he rides her slowly back to the—*Weighing-house*, is
it—? follow'd by the scarlet-coated Horsemen and shouting
People of those days?—all silent, and pass'd away for ever now,
unless from the memory of one pursy Doctor, who, were she
but alive, would hardly know Jenny's head from her tail— And
now will you have any more wine?" said I, holding up the empty
decanter.

Phidippus, hastily finishing his glass, jump'd up; and, the
others following him with more or less alacrity, we all sallied

forth on the Bowling-green. As soon as there, Lycion of course pull'd out his Cigar-case, (which he had eyed, I saw, with really good-humoured resignation during the Ballad,) and offer'd it all round, telling Phidippus he could recommend the contents as some of Pontet's best. But Phidippus did not smoke, he said; which, together with his declining to bet on the Boat-race, caused Lycion, I thought, to look on him with some indulgence.

And now Jack was rolled upon the green; and I bowl'd after him first, pretty well; then Euphranor still better; then Lycion, with great indifference, and indifferent success; then Phidippus, who about rivall'd me; and last of all, Lexilogus, whom Phidippus had been instructing in the mystery of the bias with some little side-rolls along the turf, and who, he said, only wanted a little practice to play as well as the best of us.

Meanwhile, the shadows lengthen'd along the grass, and after several bouts of play, Phidippus, who had to ride round by Cambridge, said he must be off in time to see his friends start. We should soon follow, I said; and Euphranor asked him to his rooms after the race. But Phidippus was engaged to sup with his crew.

"Where you will all be drunk," said I.

"No; there," said he, "you are quite mistaken, Doctor."

"Well, well," I said, "away, then, to your race and your supper."

"Μετὰ σώφρονος ἡλικιώτου," added Euphranor, smiling.

"Μετὰ, 'with,' or 'after,'" said Phidippus, putting on his gloves.

"Well, go on, Sir," said I,—"Σώφρονος?"

"A temperate—something or other—"

" ᾽Ηλικιώτου?"

"Supper?"—he hesitated, smiling—" 'After a temperate supper'?"

"Go down, Sir; go down this instant!" I roar'd out to him as he ran from the bowling-green. And in a few minutes we heard his mare's feet shuffling over the stable threshold, and directly afterwards breaking into a retreating canter beyond.

Shortly after this, the rest of us agreed it was time to be gone. We walk'd along the fields by the Church, (purposely to ask about the sick Lady by the way,) cross'd the Ferry, and mingled

with the crowd upon the opposite shore; Townsmen and Gownsmen, with the tassell'd Fellow-commoner sprinkled here and
there—Reading men and Sporting men—Fellows, and even
Masters of Colleges, not indifferent to the prowess of their
respective Crews—all these, conversing on all sorts of topics,
from the slang in *Bell's Life* to the last new German Revelation,
and moving in ever-changing groups down the shore of the
river, at whose farther bend was a little knot of Ladies gathered
up on a green knoll faced and illuminated by the beams of the
setting sun. Beyond which point was at length heard some indistinct shouting, which gradually increased, until "They are
off—they are coming!" suspended other conversation among ourselves; and suddenly the head of the first boat turn'd the corner;
and then another close upon it; and then a third; the crews
pulling with all their might compacted into perfect rhythm; and
the crowd on shore turning round to follow along with them,
waving hats and caps, and cheering, "Bravo, St John's!" "Go it,
Trinity!"—the high crest and blowing forelock of Phidippus's
mare, and he himself shouting encouragement to his crew, conspicuous over all—until, the boats reaching us, we also were
caught up in the returning tide of spectators, and hurried back
toward the goal; where we arrived just in time to see the Ensign
of Trinity lowered from its pride of place, and the Eagle of St
John's soaring there instead. Then, waiting a little while to hear
how the winner had won, and the loser lost, and watching
Phidippus engaged in eager conversation with his defeated
brethren, I took Euphranor and Lexilogus under either arm,
(Lycion having got into better company elsewhere,) and walk'd
home with them across the meadow leading to the town, whither
the dusky troops of Gownsmen with all their confused voices
seem'd as it were evaporating in the twilight, while a Nightingale
began to be heard among the flowering Chestnuts of Jesus.

PREFACE TO
POLONIUS

[*Polonius : A Collection of Wise Saws and Modern Instances*, was published by Pickering in 1852.]

PREFACE TO
POLONIUS

FEW books are duller than books of Aphorisms and Apophthegms. A Jest-book is, proverbially, no joke; a Wit-book, perhaps, worse; but dullest of all, probably, is the Moral-book, which this little volume pretends to be. So with men: the Jester, the Wit, and the Moralist, each wearisome in proportion as each deals exclusively in his one commodity. "Too much of one thing," says Fuller, "is good for nothing."

Bacon's "Apophthegms" seem to me the best collection of many men's sayings; the greatest variety of wisdom, good sense, wit, humour, and even simple "naiveté," (as one must call it for want of a native word,) all told in a style whose dignity and antiquity (together with perhaps our secret consciousness of the gravity and even tragic greatness of the narrator) add a particular humour to the lighter stories.

Johnson said Selden's Table-talk was worth all the French "Ana" together. Here also we find wit, humour, fancy, and good sense alternating, something as one has heard in some scholarly English gentleman's after-dinner talk—the best English common-sense in the best common English. It outlives, I believe, all Selden's books; and is probably much better, collected even imperfectly by another, than if he had put it together himself.

What would become of Johnson if Boswell had not done as much for his talk? If the Doctor himself, or some of his more serious admirers, had recorded it!

And (leaving alone Epictetus, à Kempis, and other Moral aphorists) most of the collections of this nature I have seen, are made up mainly from Johnson and the Essayists of the last century, his predecessors and imitators; when English thought and language had lost so much of their vigour, freshness, freedom, and picturesqueness—so much, in short, of their native character, under the French polish that came in with the second Charles. When one lights upon, "He who"—"The man who"—"Of all the virtues that adorn the breast"—&c.,—one is tempted to swear, with Sir Peter Teazle, against all "*sentiment*," and shut the book. How glad should we be to have Addison's Table-talk as we have Johnson's! and how much better are Spence's Anecdotes of Pope's Conversation than Pope's own letters!

If a scanty reader could, for the use of yet scantier readers than himself, put together a few sentences of the wise, and also of the less wise,—(and Tom Tyers said a good thing or two in his day,)—from Plato, Bacon, Rochefoucauld, Goethe, Carlyle, and others,—a little Truth, new or old, each after his kind—nay, of Truism too, (into which all truth must ultimately be dogs-eared,) and which, perhaps, "the wit of one, and the wisdom of many," has preserved in the shape of some nameless and dateless Proverbs which yet "retain life and vigour," and widen into new relations with the widening world—

Not a book of *Beauties*—other than as all who have the best to tell, have also naturally the best way of telling it; nor of the "limbs and outward flourishes" of Truth, however eloquent; but in general, and as far as I understand, of clear, decided, wholesome, and available insight into our nature and duties. "Brevity is the soul of *Wit*," in a far wider sense than as we now use the word. "As the centre of the greatest circle," says Sir Edward Coke, "is but a little prick, so the matter of even the biggest business lies in a little room." So the "Sentences of the Seven" are said to be epitomes of whole systems of philosophy: which also Carlyle says is the case with many a homely proverb. Anyhow that famous Μηδὲν ἄγαν, the boundary law of Goodness itself, as of all other things, (if one could only know how to apply it,) brings one up with a wholesome halt every now and then, and no where more fitly than in a book of this kind, though, as usual, I am just now violating in the very act of vindicating it.

The grand Truisms of life only life itself is said to bring to life. We hear them from grandam and nurse, write them in copy-books, but only understand them as years turn up occasions for practising or experiencing them. Nay, the longest and most eventful life scarce suffices to teach us the most important of all. It is Death, says Sir Walter Raleigh, "that puts into a man all the wisdom of the world without speaking a word." Only when we have to part with a thing do we feel its value—unless indeed *after* we have parted with it—a very serious consideration.

When Sir Walter Scott lay dying, he called for his son-in-law, and while the Tweed murmured through the woods, and a September sun lit up the towers, whose growth he had watched so eagerly, said to him, "Be a good man; only that can comfort you when you come to lie here!" "*Be a good man!*" To that threadbare Truism shrunk all that gorgeous tapestry of written and real Romance!

"You knew all this," wrote Johnson to Mrs Thrale, rallying for a little while from his final attack—"You knew all this, and I thought that I knew it too: but I know it now with a new conviction."

Perhaps, next to realizing all this in our own lives, (when just too late,) we become most sensible of it in reading the lives and deaths of others, such as Scott's and Johnson's; when we see all the years of life, with all their ambitions, loves, animosities, schemes of action—all the "curas supervacuas, spes inanes, et inexspectatos exitus hujus fugacissimæ vitæ"—summed up in a volume or two; and what seemed so long a history to them, but a Winter's Tale to us.

Death itself was no Truism to Adam and Eve, nor to many of their successors, I suppose; nay, some of their very latest descendants, it is said, have doubted if it be an inevitable necessity of life: others, with more probability, whether a man can fully comprehend its inevitableness till life itself be half over; beginning to believe he must Die about the same time he begins to believe he is a Fool.

"As are the leaves on the trees, even so are man's generations;
    This is the truest verse ever a poet has sung:
Nevertheless few hearing it hear; Hope, flattering alway,
    Lives in the bosom of all—reigns in the blood of the Young."

"And why," says the note-book of one 'nel mezzo del cammin

di nostra vita,' "does one day still linger in my memory? I had
started one fine October morning on a ramble through the villages that lie beside the Ouse. In high health and cloudless spirits,
one regret perhaps hanging upon the horizon of the heart, I
walked through Sharnbrook up the hill, and paused by the
church on the summit to look about me. The sun shone, the
clouds flew, the yellow trees shook in the wind, the river rippled
in breadths of light and dark; rooks and daws wheeled and cawed
aloft in the changing spaces of blue above the spire; the churchyard all still in the sunshine below."

Old Shallow was not very sensible of Death even when moralizing about old Double's—"Certain, 'tis very certain, Death, as
the Psalmist saith, is certain to all—all shall die—How a good
yoke of bullocks at Stamford fair?"

Could we but on our journey hear the Truisms of life called
out to us, not by Chapone, Cogan, &c., but by such a voice as
called out to Sir Lancelot and Sir Galahad, when they were
about to part in the forest—"Thynke for to doo wel; for the one
shall never see the other before the dredeful day of dome!"

Our ancestors were fond of such monitory Truisms inscribed
upon dials, clocks, and fronts of buildings; as that of "Time and
Tide tarry for no man," still to be seen on the Temple sundial;
and that still sterner one I have read of, "Go about your business"—not even moralizing upon me. I dare say those who
came suddenly and unaware upon the Γνῶθι Σεαυτόν over the
Delphian temple were brought to a stand for a while, some
thrown back into themselves by it, others (and those probably
much the greater number) seeing nothing at all in it.

The parapet balustrade round the roof of Castle Ashby, in
Northamptonshire, is carved into the letters, "NISI DOMINUS
CUSTODIAT DOMUM, FRUSTRA VIGILAT QUI CUSTODIT
EAM." This is not amis to decipher as you come up the long
avenue some summer or autumn day, and to moralize upon after-
wards at the little "Rose and Crown" at Yardley, if such good
Home-brewed be there as used to be before I knew I was to
die.

We move away the grass from a tombstone, itself half buried,
to get at any trite memento of mortality, where it preaches more
to us than many new volumes of hot-pressed morals. Not but

we can feel the warning whisper too, when Jeremy Taylor tells us that one day the bell shall toll, and it shall be asked, "For whom?" and answered, "For *us*."

Some of these Truisms come home to us also in the shape of old Proverbs, quickened by wit, fancy, rhyme, alliteration, &c. These have been well defined to be "the Wit of one and the Wisdom of many;" and are in some measure therefore historical indexes of the nation that originates or retains them. Our English Proverbs abound with good sense, energy, and courage, as compactly expressed as may be; making them properly enough the ready money of a people more apt to act than talk. "They drive the nail home in discourse," says Ray, "and clench it with the strongest conviction."

A thoughtful Frenchman says that nearly all which expresses any decided opinion has "quelque chose de métrique, ou de mesure." So as even so bare-faced a truism as "Of two evils choose the least," (superfluous reason, and no rhyme at all!) is not without its secret poetic charm. How much vain hesitation has it not cut short!

So that if Cogan and Chapone had not been made poetical by the gods, but only brief—

Sometimes indeed our old friend the Proverb gets too much clipt in his course of circulation: as in the case of that very important business to all Englishmen, a Cold—"STUFF A COLD AND STARVE A FEVER," has been grievously misconstrued, so as to bring on the fever it was meant to prevent.

Certainly Dr Johnson (who could hit hard too) not only did not always drive the nail home, but made it a nail of wax, which Fuller truly says you can't drive at all. "These sorrowful meditations," the Doctor says of Prince Rasselas, "fastened on his mind; he passed four months in resolving to lose no more time in idle resolves; and was awakened to more vigorous exertion by hearing a maid, who had broken a porcelain cup, remark that 'what cannot be repaired is not to be regretted.' "

But perhaps this was a Maid of Honour. If so, however, it proves that Maids of Honour of Rasselas' court did not talk like those of George the Second's. Witness jolly Mary Bellenden's letters to Lady Suffolk.

Swift has a fashionable dialogue almost made up of vulgar

adages, which I should have thought the Beaux and Belles left to the Mary Bellendens and Country Squires of his day—

"Grounding their fat faiths on old country proverbs."

Nor do I see any trace of it in the comedies of Congreve, Vanbrugh, &c.

Erasmus says that the Proverb is "a nonnullis Græcorum," thus defined, λόγος ὠφέλιμος ἐν τῷ βίῳ, ἐν μετρίᾳ παρακρύψει πολὺ τὸ χρήσιμον ἔχων ἐν ἑαυτῷ. The definition, it might seem at first, rather of a Fable, or Parable, than a Proverb. But, beside that the titles of many fables *do* become proverbs—"Fox and Grapes," "Dog in Manger," &c., the title including the whole signification, (like those "Sentences of the Seven,")—so many of our best proverbs *are* little whole fables in themselves; as when we say, "The Fat sow knows not what the Lean one thinks," &c.

We are fantastic, histrionic creatures; having so much of the fool, loving a mixture of the lie, loving to get our fellow-creatures into our scrapes and make them play our parts—the Ass of our dulness, the Fox of our cunning, and so on—in whose several natures those of our Neighbours, as we think, come to a climax. Certainly, swollen Wealth is well enacted by the fat Sow reclining in her sty, as a Dowager in an opera-box, serenely unconscious of all her kindred's leanness without. The phrase "rolling in wealth" too suggests the same fable.

Indeed, is not every Metaphor (without which we cannot speak five words) in some sort a Fable—one thing spoken of under the likeness of another? And how easy (if need were) it is to dramatize, for instance, Bacon's figure of discovering the depth, not by looking on the surface ever so long, but beginning to *sound* it!

And are these Fables so fabulous after all? If beasts do not really rise to the level on which we amuse ourselves by putting them, we have an easy way of really sinking to theirs. It is no fable surely that Circe *bodily* transformed the captives of Sensuality into apes, hogs, and goats; as Cunning, Hypocrisy, and Rapacity, graft us with the sharp noses, sidelong eyes, and stealthy gait, of wolves, hyænas, foxes, and serpents; sometimes, as in old fable too, the misfeatures and foul expressions of two baser animal passions—as lust and cunning for instance, with perhaps cruelty beside—conforming man into a double or triple monster, more hideous than any single beast. On the other hand, our more generous dispositions determine outwardly into the large aspect of the lion, or the horse's speaking eye and inspired nostril. "There are innumerable animals to which man may degrade his image, inward and outward; only a few to which he can properly (and that in the Affections only) level it: but it is an ideal and invisible type to which he must erect it."

"Such kind of parabolical wisdom," says Bacon, "was much more in use in the ancient times, as by the Fables of Æsop, and the brief Sentences of the Seven, and the use of hieroglyphics may appear. And the cause was, for that it was then of necessity to express any point of reason which was more sharp or subtled than the vulgar in that manner, because men in those times wanted both variety of examples and subtlety of conceit; and as Hieroglyphics were before letters, so Parables were before arguments."

We cannot doubt that Christianity itself made way by means of such Parables as never were uttered before or after. Imagine (be it with reverence) that Jeremy Bentham had had the promulgation of it!

And as this figurative teaching was best for simple people, "even now," adds Bacon, "such Parables do retain much life and vigour, because Reason cannot be so sensible, nor examples so fit." Next to the Bible parables, I believe John Bunyan remains the most effective preacher, among the poor, to this day.

Nor is it only simple matters for simple people that admit such illustration. Again, Bacon says, "It is a rule that whatsoever science is not consonant to presuppositions must pray in aid of Similitudes." "Neither Philosopher nor Historiographer," says Sir Philip Sidney, "could at the first have entered into the gates of popular judgments, if they had not taken a great Passport of Poetry," which deals so in Similitudes. "For he" (the poet) "doth not only show the way, but giveth so sweet a prospect into the way as will entice any man to enter into it. Nay, he doth, as if your journey should lie through a fair vineyard, at the very first give you a cluster of grapes, that, full of that taste, you may long to pass further."

Who can doubt that Plato wins us to his Wisdom by that skin

and body of Poetry in which Sir Philip declares his philosophy is clothed? Not the sententious oracle of one wise man, but evolved dramatically by many like ourselves. The scene opens in Old Athens, which his genius continues for us for ever new; the morning dawns; a breeze from the Ægæan flutters upon our foreheads; the rising sun tips the friezes of the Parthenon, and gradually slants upon the house in whose yet twilight courts gather a company of white-vested, whispering guests, "expecting till that fountain of wisdom," Protagoras, should arise.

Carlyle notices, as one of Goethe's chief gifts, "his emblematic intellect, his never-failing tendency to transform into *shape*, into *life*, the feeling that may dwell in him. Every thing has *form*, has visual existence; the poet's imagination *bodies forth* the forms of things unseen, and his pen turns them into shape." The same is, I believe, remarkable, probably *too* remarkable, in Richter: and is especially characteristic of Carlyle himself, who to a figurative genius, like Goethe's, adds a passion which Goethe either had not or chose to suppress, which brands the truth double-deep. And who can doubt that Bacon, could it possibly have been his own, would have clothed Bentham's bare argument with cloth of gold?

He says again, "Reasons plainly delivered, and always after one manner, especially with fine and fastidious minds, enter heavily and dully; whereas, if they be varied, and have more life and vigour put into them by these forms and imaginations, they carry a stronger apprehension, and many times win the mind to a resolution." Which, if it be true in any matter, most of all surely in morals, for the most part so old, so trite, and, in this naughty world, so dull. Are not *all* minds grown "fine and fastidious" in these matters, apt to close against any but the most musical voice?

Which also (to join the snake's head and tail of this rambling overgrown Preface) may account, rightly or wrongly, for my rejection of those essayists aforesaid, (who crippled their native genius by a style which has left them "more of the ballast than the sail,") and my adoption of earlier and later writers. Not, as I said before, in copious draughts of their eloquence—and what pages of Bacon and Browne it is far easier to bear than forbear! —but where the writer has gone to the heart of a matter, the

centre of the circle, hit the nail on the head and driven it home—
Proverb-wise, in fact. For in proportion as any writer tells the
truth, and tells it figuratively or poetically, and yet so as to lie in
a nutshell, he cuts up sooner or later into proverbs shorter or
longer, and gradually gets down into general circulation.

Some extracts are from note books, where the author's name
was forgot; some from the conversation of friends that must alike
remain anonymous; and some that glance but lightly at the truth
are not without purpose inserted to relieve a book of dogmatic
morals. "Durum et durum non faciunt murum."

And now Mountain opens and discovers—

POLONIUS.

THE PAINTER
OF HIS OWN
DISHONOUR

[*Six Dramas of Calderon*, freely translated by Edward Fitz-Gerald, was published by Pickering in 1853. Besides *The Painter of His Own Dishonour*, printed here, the dramas were: *Keep Your Own Secret*; *Gil Perez, the Gallician*; *Three Judgments at a Blow*; *The Mayor of Zalamea*; and *Beware of Smooth Water*.]

ADVERTISEMENT

In apologizing for the publication of so free translations of so famous a poet as Calderon, I must plead, first, that I have not meddled with any of his more famous plays; not one of those on my list being mentioned with any praise, or included in any selection that I know of, except the homely Mayor of Zalamea. Four of these six indeed, as many others in Calderon, may be lookt on as a better kind of what we call melodramas. Such plays as the *Magico Prodigioso* and the *Vida es Sueño* (I cannot rank the *Principe Constante* among them) require another translator, and, I think, form of translation.

Secondly, I do not believe an exact translation of this poet can be very successful; retaining so much that, whether real or dramatic Spanish passion, is still bombast to English ears, and confounds otherwise distinct outlines of character; Conceits that were a fashion of the day; or idioms that, true and intelligible to one nation, check the current of sympathy in others to which they are unfamiliar; violations of the probable, nay *possible*, that shock even healthy romantic licence; repetitions of thoughts and images that Calderon used (and smiled at) as so much stage properties—so much, in short, that is not Calderon's own better self, but concession to private haste or public taste by one who so often relied upon some striking dramatic crisis for success with a not very accurate audience, and who, for whatever reason, was ever averse from any of his dramas being printed.

Choosing therefore such less famous plays as still seemed to me suited to English taste, and to that form of verse in which our dramatic passion prefers to run, I have, while faithfully trying to retain what was fine and efficient, sunk, reduced, altered, and replaced, much that seemed not; simplified some perplexities, and curtailed or omitted scenes that seemed to mar the breadth of general effect, supplying such omissions by some lines of after-narrative; and in some measure have tried to compensate for the fulness of sonorous Spanish, which Saxon English at least must forego, by a compression which has its own charm to Saxon ears.

That this, if proper to be done at all, might be better done by others, I do not doubt. Nay, on looking back over these pages, I see where in some cases the Spanish individuality might better have been retained, and northern idiom spared; and doubtless there are many inaccuracies I am not yet aware of. But if these plays prove interesting to the English reader, I and he may be very sure that, whatever of Spain and Calderon be lost, there must be a good deal retained; and I think he should excuse the licence of my version till some other interests him as well at less expense of fidelity.

I hope my *Graciosos* will not be blamed for occasional anachronisms not uncharacteristic of their vocation.

THE PAINTER OF HIS OWN
DISHONOUR

DRAMATIS PERSONÆ

FEDERIGO,	*Prince of Orsino.*
CELIO,	*his Friend.*
DON LUIS,	*Governor of Naples.*
PORCIA,	*his Daughter.*
ALVARO,	*his Son.*
FABIO,	
BELARDO,	*their Servants.*
JULIA,	
DON JUAN ROCA.	
SERAFINA,	*his Wife.*
DON PEDRO,	*his Father-in-law.*
LEONELO,	*their Servants.*
FLORA,	

MASKERS, MUSICIANS, SAILORS, &c.

ACT I

SCENE I.—*A Room in* DON LUIS' *palace at Naples.—Enter* DON
LUIS *and* DON JUAN *meeting.*

LUIS: Once more, a thousand times once more, Don Juan,
    Come to my heart.
JUAN: And every fresh embrace
    Rivet our ancient friendship faster yet!
LUIS: Amen to that! Come, let me look at you—
    Why, you seem well—
JUAN: So well, so young, so nimble,
    I will not try to say how well, so much
    My words and your conception must fall short
    Of my full satisfaction.
LUIS: How glad am I
    To have you back in Naples!
JUAN: Ah, Don Luis,
    Happier so much than when I last was here,
    Nay, than I ever thought that I could be.
LUIS: How so?
JUAN: Why, when I came this way before,
    I told you (do you not remember it?)
    How teased I was by relatives and friends
    To marry—little then disposed to love—
    Marriage perhaps the last thing in my thoughts—
    Liking to spend the spring time of my youth
    In lonely study.
LUIS: Ay, ay, I remember:
    Nothing but books, books, books—still day and night
    Nothing but books; or, fairly drowsed by them,
    By way of respite to that melancholy,
    The palette and the pencil—
    In which you got to such a mastery
    As smote the senseless canvas into life.
    O, I remember all—not only, Juan,

When you were here, but I with you in Spain,
What fights we had about it!

JUAN: So it was—
However, partly wearied, partly moved
By pity at my friends' anxieties,
Who press'd upon me what a shame it were
If such a title and estate as mine
Should lack a lineal inheritor,
At length I yielded—
Fanned from the embers of my later years
A passion which had slept in those of youth,
And took to wife my cousin Serafina,
The daughter of Don Pedro Castellano.

LUIS: I know; you showed me when you last were here
The portrait of your wife that was to be,
And I congratulated you.

JUAN: Well now
Still more congratulate me—as much more
As she is fairer than the miniature
We both enamoured of. At the first glance
I knew myself no more myself, but hers,
Another (and how much a happier!) man.

LUIS: Had I the thousand tongues, and those of brass,
That Homer wished for, they should utter all
Congratulation. Witty too, I hear,
As beautiful?

JUAN: Yourself shall judge of all,
For even now my lady comes; awhile
To walk the Flora of your shores, and then
Over your seas float Venus-like away.

LUIS: Not *that*, till she have graced our gardens long,
If once we get her here. But is she here?

JUAN: Close by—she and her father, who would needs
See her abroad; and I push'd on before
To apprize you of our numbers—so much more
Than when I first proposed to be your guest,
That I entreat you—

LUIS: What?

JUAN: —to let us go,

And find our inn at once—not over-load
Your house.

LUIS: Don Juan, you do me an affront—
What if all Naples came along with you?—
My heart—yes, and my house—should welcome them.

JUAN: I know. But yet—

LUIS: But yet, no more "but yets"—
Come to my house, or else my heart shall close
Its doors upon you.

JUAN: Nay, I dare not peril
A friendship—

LUIS: Why, were't not a great affront
To such a friendship—when you learn besides,
I have but held this government till now
Only to do you such a courtesy.

JUAN: But how is this?

LUIS: Sickness and age on-coming,
I had determined to retire on what
Estate I had—no need of other wealth—
Beside, Alvaro's death—my only son—

JUAN: Nay, you have so felicitated me,
I needs must *you*, Don Luis, whose last letter
Told of a gleam of hope in that dark quarter.

LUIS: A sickly gleam—you know the ship he sail'd in
Was by another vessel, just escaped
The selfsame storm, seen to go down—it seem'd
With all her souls on board.

JUAN: But how assured
'Twas your son's ship?—

LUIS: Alas, so many friends
Were on the watch for him at Barcelona,
Whither his ship was bound, but never came—
Beside the very messenger that brought
The gleam of hope, premised the tragedy—
A little piece of wreck,
That floated to the coast of Spain, and thence
Sent to my hands, with these words scratcht upon't—
"*Escaped alive, Alvaro.*"

JUAN: When was this?

LUIS: Oh, months ago, and since no tidings heard,
   In spite of all inquiry. But we will hope.
   Meanwhile, Serafina—when will she be here?
JUAN: She must be close to Naples now.
LUIS: Go then,
   Tell her from me—
   I go not forth to bid her welcome, only
   That I may make that welcome sure at home.
JUAN: I'll tell her so. But—
LUIS: What! another *"But"*?
   No more of that. Away with you.—Porcia! [*Exit* JUAN.

Enter PORCIA.

   Daughter, you know (I have repeated it
   A thousand times, I think) the obligation
   I owe Don Juan Roca.
PORCIA: Sir, indeed
   I've often heard you talk of him.
LUIS: Then listen.
   He and his wife are coming here to-day—
   Directly.
PORCIA: Serafina!
LUIS: Yes.
   To be our guests, till they set sail for Spain;
   I trust long first—
PORCIA: And I. How glad I am!
LUIS: You! what should make you glad?
PORCIA: That Serafina,
   So long my playmate, shall be now my guest.
LUIS: Ay! I forgot—that's well, too—
   Let us be rivals in their entertainment.
   See that the servants, Porcia, dress their rooms
   As speedily and handsomely as may be.
PORCIA: What haste can do (which brings its own excuse)
   I'll do—'tis long a proverb hereabout
   That you are Entertainer-general,
   Rather than Governor, of Naples.
LUIS: Ay,
   I like to honour all who come this way.

Enter LEONELO.

LEONELO: Peace to this house!—and not only that, but a story beside.—A company of soldiers coming to a certain village, a fellow of the place calls out for *two* to be billeted on him. "What!" says a neighbour, "you want a double share of what every one else tries to shirk altogether?" "Yes," says he, "for the more nuisance they are while they stay, the more glad one is of their going." In illustration of which, and also of my master's orders, I crave your Lordship's hand, and your Ladyship's foot, to kiss.

LUIS: Welcome, good Leonelo. I was afraid I had overlooked you in receiving your master.

PORCIA: And how does marriage agree with you, Leonelo?

LEONELO: One gentleman asked another to dine: but such an ill-ordered dinner that the capon was cold, and the wine hot. Finding which, the guest dips a leg of the capon into the wine. And when his host asks him what he's about—"Only making the wine heat the capon, and the capon cool the wine," says he. Now just this happened in my marriage. My wife was rather too young, and I rather too old; so, as it is hoped—

PORCIA: Foolery, foolery, always!—tell me how Serafina is—

LEONELO: In a coach.

PORCIA: What answer is that?

LEONELO: A very sufficient one—since a coach includes happiness, pride, and (a modern author says) respectability.

PORCIA: How so?

LEONELO: Why, a certain lady died lately, and for some reason or other, they got leave to carry her to the grave in a coach. Directly they got her in,—the body, I mean,—it began to fidget—and when they called out to the coachman—"Drive to St Sepulchre's!"—"No!" screams she,—"I won't go there yet. Drive to the Prado first; and when I have had a turn there, they may bury me where they please."

LUIS: How can you let your tongue run on so!

LEONELO: I'll tell you. A certain man in Barcelona had five or six children: and he gave them each to eat—

VOICES (*within*): Way there! way!

PORCIA: They are coming.

LEONELO: And in so doing, take that story out of my mouth.

117

Enter JULIA.

JULIA: Signor, your guests are just alighting.

LUIS: Come, Porcia—

LEONELO: (No, no, stop you and listen to me about those dear
children.)

PORCIA: They are coming upstairs—at the door—

Enter DON JUAN *leading* SERAFINA, DON PEDRO,
and FLORA—*all in travelling dress.*

LUIS: Your hand, fair Serafina, whose bright eyes
Seem to have drawn his lustre from the sun,
To fill my house withal;—a poor receptacle
Of such a visitor.

PORCIA: Nay, 'tis for me
To blush for that, in quality of hostess;
Yet, though you come to shame my house-keeping,
Thrice welcome, Serafina.

SERAFINA: How answer both,
Being too poor in compliment for either!
I'll not attempt it.

PEDRO: I am vext, Don Luis,
My son-in-law should put this burden on you.

LUIS: Nay, vex not me by saying so.—What burden?
The having such an honour as to be
Your servant?—

LEONELO: Here's a dish of compliments!

FLORA: Better than you can feed your mistress with.

                              (*Guns heard without.*)

JUAN: What guns are those?

Enter FABIO.

FABIO: The citadel, my lord,
Makes signal of two galleys in full sail
Coming to port.

LUIS: More guests! the more the merrier!

PEDRO: The merrier for them, but scarce for you,
Don Luis.

LUIS: Nay, good fortune comes like bad,
All of a heap. What think you, should it be,

As I suspect it is, the Prince Orsino
Returning; whom, in love and duty bound,
I shall receive and welcome—

JUAN: Once again,
Don Luis, give me leave—

LUIS: And once again.
And once for all, I shall *not* give you leave.
Prithee, no more—
All will be easily arranged. Porcia,
You know your guest's apartments—show her thither:
I'll soon be back with you.

PEDRO: Permit us, sir,
To attend you to the port, and wait upon
His Highness.

LUIS: I dare not refuse that trouble,
Seeing what honour in the prince's eyes
Your company will lend me.

LEONELO: And methinks
I will go with you too.

JUAN: What, for that purpose?

LEONELO: Yes—and because perhaps among the crowd
I shall find some to whom I may relate
That story of the children and their meat.

[*Exeunt* DON LUIS, PEDRO, JUAN, LEONELO, FABIO, &c.

SERAFINA: Porcia, are they gone?

PORCIA: They are.

SERAFINA: Then I may weep.

PORCIA: Tears, Serafina!

SERAFINA: Nay, they would not stay
Longer unshed. I would not if I could
Hide them from you, Porcia. Why should I,
Who know too well the fount from which they flow?

PORCIA: I only know you weep—no more than that.

SERAFINA: Yet 'tis the seeing you again, again
Unlocks them—is it that you do resent
The discontinuance of our early love,
And that you *will* not understand me?

PORCIA: Nay,—
What can I say!

SERAFINA: Let us be *quite* alone.

PORCIA: Julia, leave us.

SERAFINA: Flora, go with her.

JULIA: Come, shall we go up to the gallery,
And see the ships come in?

FLORA: Madame, so please you.
[*Exeunt* FLORA *and* JULIA.

SERAFINA: Well, are we *quite* alone?

PORCIA: Yes, quite.

SERAFINA: All gone,
And none to overhear us?

PORCIA: None.

SERAFINA: Porcia,
You knew me once when I was happy!

PORCIA: Yes,
Or thought you so—

SERAFINA: But now most miserable!

PORCIA: How so, my Serafina?

SERAFINA: You shall hear.
Yes, my Porcia, you remember it,—
That happy, happy time when you and I
Were so united that, our hearts attun'd
To perfect unison, one might believe
That but one soul within two bodies lodg'd.
This you remember?

PORCIA: Oh, how could I forget!

SERAFINA: Think it not strange that so far back I trace
The first beginnings of *another* love,
Whose last sigh having now to breathe, whose last
Farewell to sigh, and whose deceased hopes
In one last obsequy to commemorate,
I tell it over to you point by point
From first to last—by such full utterance
My pent up soul perchance may find relief.

PORCIA: Speak, Serafina.

SERAFINA: You have not forgot
Neither, how that close intimacy of ours
Brought with it of necessity some courtesies
Between me and your brother, Don Alvaro—

Whose very name, oh wretched that I am!
Makes memory, like a trodden viper, turn,
And fix a fang in me not sharp enough
To slay at once, but with a lingering death
Infect my life—

PORCIA: Nay, calm yourself.

SERAFINA: We met,
Porcia—and from those idle meetings love
Sprang up between us both—for though 'tis true
That at the first I laugh'd at his advances,
And turn'd his boyish suit into disdain,
Yet true it also is that in my heart
There lurk'd a lingering feeling yet behind,
Which if not wholly love, at least was liking,
In the sweet twilight of whose unris'n sun
My soul as yet walk'd hesitatingly.
For, my Porcia, there is not a woman,
Say what she will, and virtuous as you please,
Who, being lov'd, resents it: and could he
Who most his mistress's disfavour mourns
Look deeply down enough into her heart,
He'd see, however high she carries it,
Some grateful recognition lurking there
Under the muffle of affected scorn.
You know how I repell'd your brother's suit:
How ever when he wrote to me I tore
His letters—would not listen when he spoke—
And when, relying on my love for you,
Through you he tried to whisper his for me,
I quarrell'd with yourself—quarrell'd the more
The more you spoke for him. He wept—I laugh'd;
Knelt in my path—I turn'd another way;
Though who had seen deep down into my heart,
Had also seen love struggling hard with pride.
Enough—at last one evening as I sat
Beside a window looking on the sea,
Wrapt in the gathering night he stole unseen
Beside me. After whispering all those vows
Of love which lovers use, and I pass by,

He press'd me to be his. Touch'd by the hour,
The mask of scorn fell from my heart, and Love
Reveal'd himself, and from that very time
Grew unconceal'd between us—yet, Porcia,
Upon mine honour, (for I tell thee *all*,)
Always in honour bounded. At that time
In an ill hour my father plann'd a marriage
Between me and Don Juan—yours, you know,
Came here to Naples, whence he sent your brother,
I know not on what business, into Spain;
And we agreed, I mean Alvaro and I,
Rather than vex two fathers at one time
By any declaration of our vows,
'Twere best to keep them secret—at the least,
Till his return from Spain. Ah, Porcia,
When yet did love not thrive by secrecy?
We parted—he relying on my promise,
I on his quick return. Oh, mad are those
Who, knowing that a storm is up, will yet
Put out to sea. Alvaro went—my father
Urged on this marriage with my cousin. Oh!—

PORCIA: You are ill, Serafina!

SERAFINA: Nothing—nothing—
I reason'd—wept—implor'd—excus'd—delay'd—
In vain—O mercy, Heaven!

PORCIA: Tell me no more:
It is too much for you.

SERAFINA: Then suddenly
We heard that he was dead—your brother—drown'd—
They married me—and now perhaps he lives.
They say—Porcia, can it be?—I know not
Whether to hope or dread if that be true:—
And every wind that blows your father hope
Makes my blood cold; I know that I shall meet him,
Here or upon the seas—dead or live—
Methinks I see him now!—Help! help!   [*Swoons.*

PORCIA: Serafina!—
She has fainted!—Julia! Flora!—

Enter ALVARO.

ALVARO: My Porcia!

PORCIA: Alvaro! (*They embrace.*)

ALVARO: I have outrun the shower of compliment
On my escapes—which you shall hear anon—
To catch you to my heart.

PORCIA: Oh joy and terror!
Look there!—

ALVARO: Serafina!
And sleeping too!

PORCIA: Oh, swooning! see to her
Till I get help.   [*Exit.*

SERAFINA (*in her swoon*): Mercy, mercy!
Alvaro, slay me not!—I am not guilty!—
Indeed I am not!—

ALVARO: She dreams—and dreams of me—but very strangely—
Serafina!—

SERAFINA (*waking*): Dead!—or return'd alive to curse and slay
me!—
But I am innocent!—I could not help—
They told me you were dead—and are you not?—
And I must marry him—

ALVARO: Must marry?—whom?—
Why, you are dreaming still—
Awake!—'tis your Alvaro—   (*Offers to embrace her.*)

SERAFINA: No, no, no—
I dare not—

ALVARO: Dare not!

Enter PORCIA, FLORA, JULIA.

PORCIA: Quick, quick!

FLORA: My lady!

JULIA: My lord alive again!

ALVARO: Porcia, come hither—I am not alive,
Till I have heard the truth—nay, if't be true
That she has hinted and my heart forebodes,
I shall be worse than dead—
                              [*Retires with* PORCIA *to back of Stage.*

Enter JUAN *and* PEDRO.

JUAN: What is the matter?—
    My Serafina!
PEDRO: We have hurried back,
    Told of your sudden seizure—What is it?
SERAFINA: The very heart within me turn'd to ice.
JUAN: But you are better now?—
SERAFINA: Yes—better—pray,
    Be not uneasy for me.
ALVARO (*to* PORCIA *in the rear*): This is true then!
PORCIA: Nay, nay, be not so desperate, Alvaro,
    Hearing but half the story—no fault of hers—
    I'll tell you all anon. Come, Serafina,
    I'll see you to your chamber.
PEDRO: She will be better soon—
JUAN: Lean upon me, my love—so—so.
ALVARO: Oh, fury!
SERAFINA: Oh, would to heaven these steps should be my last,
    Leading not to my chamber, but my grave!
PORCIA (*to* ALVARO): Wait here—compose yourself—I shall be
    back
    Directly.   [*Exeunt* PORCIA, SERAFINA, *and* JUAN.
ALVARO: She is married—broke her troth—
    And I escaped from death and slavery
    To find her—but the prince!—Oh weariness!

Enter the PRINCE ORSINO, CELIO, DON LUIS, *and Train.*

PRINCE: Each day, Don Luis, I become your debtor
    For some new courtesy.
LUIS: My lord, 'tis I
    Who by such small instalments of my duty
    Strive to pay back in part the many favours
    You shower upon your servant. And this last,
    Of bringing back Alvaro to my arms,
    Not all my life, nor life itself, could pay.
PRINCE: Small thanks to me, Don Luis; but indeed
    The strangest chance—two chances—two escapes—
    First from the sinking ship upon a spar,
    Then from the Algerine who pick'd him up,

Carried him captive off—
He first adroitly through their fingers slipping
That little harbinger of hope to you,
And then, at last, himself escaping back
To Barcelona, where you know I was—
If glad to welcome, house, and entertain
Any distrest Italian, how much more,
Both for his own sake and for yours, your son,
So making him, I trust, a friend for life.

ALVARO: Rather a humble follower, my lord.

LUIS: I have no words to thank you—we shall hear
The whole tale from Alvaro by and by—
To make us merry—once so sad to him.
Meanwhile, Alvaro, thou hast seen thy sister?

ALVARO: Yes, sir—

LUIS: Oh what a joy 'tis to see thee!

PRINCE: A day of general joy.

ALVARO (*aside*):   Indeed!—

PRINCE: Especially
To her, Alvaro—

ALVARO: Sir?

PRINCE: I mean your sister.

ALVARO: Yes, my lord—no—I am not sure, my lord—
A friend of hers is suddenly so ill,
My sister is uneasy—

LUIS: Serafina!
Indeed!—I know your Highness will forgive
My seeing to her straight.   [*Exit.*

ALVARO: And I, my lord,
Would fain see some old faces once again
As soon as may be.

PRINCE: Nay, no more excuse—
Follow your pleasure.

ALVARO (*aside*):   'Tis no friend I seek,
But my one deadliest enemy—myself.   [*Exit.*

PRINCE: Celio, I think we have well nigh exhausted
The world of compliment, and wasted it:
For I begin to doubt that word and deed
Are wasted all in vain.

CELIO: How so, my lord?

PRINCE: Why, if I never am to see Porcia
     Whom I have come so far and fast to see—

CELIO: *Never*, my lord! her father's guest is ill,
     And she for a few minutes—

PRINCE: *Minutes*, Celio!
     Knowest thou not minutes are years to lovers?

CELIO: I know that lovers are strange animals.

PRINCE: Ah, you have never loved.

CELIO: No, good my lord,
     I'm but a looker-on; or in the market
     Just give and take the current coin of love—
     Love her that loves me; and, if she forget,
     Forget her too.

PRINCE: Ah, then I cannot wonder
     You wonder so at my impatience;
     For he that cannot love, can be no judge
     Of him that does.

CELIO: How so?

PRINCE: I'll tell thee, Celio.
     He who far off beholds another dancing,
     Even one who dances best, and all the time
     Hears not the music that he dances to,
     Thinks him a madman, apprehending not
     The law that rules his else eccentric action.
     So he that's in himself insensible
     Of love's sweet influence, misjudges him
     Who moves according to love's melody:
     And knowing not that all these sighs and tears,
     Ejaculations, and impatiences,
     Are necessary changes of a measure,
     Which the divine musician plays, may call
     The lover crazy; which he would not do
     Did he within his own heart hear the tune
     Play'd by the great musician of the world.

CELIO: Well, I might answer, that, far off or near
     Hearing or not the melody you tell of,
     The man is mad who dances to it. But
     Here is your music.

Enter PORCIA.

PORCIA: I left my brother here but now.

PRINCE: But now,
    Sweet Porcia, you see he is not here—
    By that so seeming earnest search for him
    Scarce recognising me, if you would hint
    At any seeming slight of mine toward you
    I plead not guilty—

PORCIA: You mistake, my lord—
    Did I believe my recognition
    Of any moment to your Excellency,
    I might perhaps evince it in complaint,
    But not in slight.

PRINCE: Complaint!—

PORCIA: Yes, sir—complaint.

PRINCE: Complaint of what? I knowing, Porcia,
    And you too knowing well, the constant love
    That I have borne you since the happy day
    When first we met in Naples—

PORCIA: No, my lord—
    You mean my love to you, not yours to me—
    Unwearied through your long forgetful absence.

PRINCE: How easily, Porcia, would my love
    Prove to you its unchanged integrity,
    Were it not that our friends—

PORCIA: Your friends indeed,
    Who stop a lame apology at the outset.

Enter SERAFINA.

SERAFINA: I cannot rest, Porcia, and am come
    To seek it in your arms—but who is this?

PORCIA: The Prince Orsino.

SERAFINA: Pardon me, my lord—
    I knew you not—coming so hurriedly,
    And in much perturbation.

PRINCE: Nay, lady,
    I owe you thanks for an embarrassment
    Which hides my own.

SERAFINA: Let it excuse beside

What other courtesies I owe your Highness,
But scarce have words to pay. Heaven guard your Highness—
  Suffer me to retire.   [*Exit.*

PORCIA: I needs must after her, my lord. But tell me,
  When shall I hear your vindication?—
  To-night?
PRINCE: Ay, my Porcia, if you will.
PORCIA: Till night farewell, then.   [*Exit.*
PRINCE: Farewell.—Celio,
  Didst ever see so fair an apparition,
  As her who came and went so suddenly?
CELIO: Indeed, so sweetly mannered when surprised,
  She must be exquisite in her composure.
PRINCE: Who is she?
CELIO: Nay, my lord, just come with you,
  I know as little—
  What! a new tune to dance to?—
PRINCE: In good time,
  Here comes Alvaro.

     Enter ALVARO.

ALVARO: How restless is the sickness of the soul!
  I scarce had got me from this fatal place,
  And back again—
PRINCE: Alvaro!
ALVARO: My lord—
PRINCE: Who is the lady that was here anon?
ALVARO: Lady, my lord—what lady?—
PRINCE: She that went
  A moment hence—I mean your sister's guest.
ALVARO: (This drop was wanting!)
  My lord, the daughter of a nobleman
  Of very ancient blood—
  Don Pedro Castellano.
PRINCE: And her name?
ALVARO: Serafina.
PRINCE: And a most seraphic lady!
ALVARO: You never saw her, sir, before?

PRINCE: No, surely.

ALVARO (*aside*): Would I had never done so!

PRINCE: And in the hasty glimpse I had,
    I guess her mistress of as fair a mind
    As face.

ALVARO: Yes, sir—

PRINCE: She lives in Naples, eh?

ALVARO: No—on her way
    To Spain, I think—

PRINCE: Indeed!—To Spain. Why that?

ALVARO: (How much more will he ask?)
    My lord, her husband—

PRINCE: She is married then?—

ALVARO: Torture!

PRINCE: And who so blest to call her his,
    Alvaro?

ALVARO: Sir, Don Juan Roca, her cousin.

PRINCE: Roca? Don Juan Roca? Do I know him?

ALVARO: I think you must; he came, sir, with my father
    To wait upon your Grace.

PRINCE: Don Juan Roca!
    No; I do not remember him—should not
    Know him again.

Enter DON LUIS.

LUIS: My lord, if my old love
    And service for your Highness may deserve
    A favour at your hands—

PRINCE: They only wait
    Until your tongue has named it.

LUIS: This it is then—
    The captain of the galleys, good my lord,
    In which your Highness came,
    Tells me that, having landed you, he lies
    Under strict orders to return again
    Within an hour.

PRINCE: 'Tis true.

LUIS: Now, good my lord,
    The ships, when they go back, must carry with them

Some friends who, long time look'd for, just are come,
And whom I fain—

PRINCE: Nay, utter not a wish
I know I must unwillingly deny.

ALVARO: Confusion on confusion!

PRINCE: I have pledg'd
My word to Don Garcia of Toledo,
The galleys should not pass an hour at Naples.
I feel for you,—and for my self, alas!
So sweet a freight they carry with them. But
I dare not—and what folly to adore
A Beauty lost to me before I found it!

                    [*Exeunt* PRINCE *and* CELIO.

LUIS: And those I so had long'd for, to avenge
Their long estrangement by as long a welcome,
Snatcht from me almost ere we'd shaken hands!—
Is not this ill, Alvaro?

ALVARO: Ill indeed.

LUIS: And, as they needs must go, my hospitality,
Foil'd in its spring, must turn to wound myself
By speeding their departure.   (*Going.*)

ALVARO: Sir, a moment.
Although his Highness would not, or could not,
Grant you the boon your services deserv'd,
Let not that, I beseech you, indispose you
From granting one to me.

LUIS: What is't, Alvaro?
'Twere strange could I refuse you anything.

ALVARO: You sent me, sir, on state affairs to Spain,
But being wreckt and captur'd, as you know,
All went undone.
Another opportunity now offers;
The ships are ready, let me go and do
That which perforce I left undone before.

LUIS: What else could'st thou have askt,
In all the category of my means,
Which I, methinks, had grudg'd thee! No, Alvaro,

The treacherous sea must not again be trusted
With the dear promise of my only son.
ALVARO: Nay, for that very reason, I entreat you
To let me go, sir. Let it not be thought
The blood that I inherited of you
Quail'd at a common danger.
LUIS: I admire
Your resolution, but you must not go,
At least not now.
Beside, the business you were sent upon
Is done by other hands, or let go by
For ever.
ALVARO: Nay, sir—
LUIS: Nay, Alvaro.   [*Exit.*
ALVARO: He is resolved. And Serafina,
To whose divinity I offered up
My heart of hearts, a purer sacrifice
Than ever yet on pagan altar blaz'd,
Has play'd me false, is married to another,
And now will fly away on winds and seas,
As fleeting as herself.
Then what remains but that I die? My death
The necessary shadow of that marriage!
Comfort!—what boots it looking after that
Which never can be found? The worst is come,
Which 'twere a blind and childish waste of hope
To front with any visage but despair.
Ev'n that one single solace, were there one,
Of ringing my despair into her ears,
Fails me. Time presses; the accursed breeze
Blows foully fair. The vessel flaps her sails
That is to bear her from me. Look, she comes—
And from before her dawning beauty all
I had to say fades from my swimming brain,
And chokes upon my tongue.

Enter SERAFINA, *drest as at first, and* PORCIA.

PORCIA: And must we part so quickly?—

SERAFINA: When does happiness
    Last longer?
ALVARO: Never!—who best can answer that?
    I standing by, why ask it of another?
    At least when speaking of such happiness
    As, perjur'd woman, thy false presence brings!
SERAFINA: Alvaro, for Heaven's sake spare me the pang
    Of these unjust reproaches.
ALVARO: What! unjust!
SERAFINA: Why, is it not unjust, condemning one
    Without defence?
ALVARO: Without defence indeed!
SERAFINA: Not that I have not a most just defence,
    But that you will not listen.
ALVARO: Serafina,
    I listen'd; but what wholly satisfies
    The criminal may ill suffice the judge;
    And in love's court especially, a word
    Has quite a different meaning to the soul
    Of speaker and of hearer. Yet once more,
    Speak.
SERAFINA: To what purpose? I can but repeat
    What I have told your sister, and she you,—
    What on the sudden waking from my swoon,
    I, who had thought you dead so long, Alvaro,
    Spoke in my terror, suddenly seeing you
    Alive, before me.
ALVARO: I were better, then,
    Dead than alive?
SERAFINA: I know not—were you dead
    I might in honour weep for you, Alvaro;
    Living, I must not.
ALVARO: Nay then, whether you
    Forswear me living or lament me dead,
    Now you must hear me; if you strike the wound,
    Is it not just that you should hear the cry?
SERAFINA: I must not.
ALVARO: But I say you must.
SERAFINA: Porcia,

Will you not help me when my life and honour
Are thus at stake?
ALVARO: Porcia's duty lies
In keeping watch that no one interrupt us.
PORCIA: Between the two confus'd, I yield at last
To him, both as my brother, Serafina,
And for his love to you. Compose yourself;
I shall be close at hand, no harm can happen.
And let him weep at least who has lost all.   [*Exit.*
SERAFINA: If I am forc'd to hear you then, Alvaro,
You shall hear me too, once more, once for all,
Freely confessing that I loved you once;
Ay, long and truly loved you. When all hope
Of being yours with your reported death
Had died, then, yielding to my father's wish,
I wed another, and am—what I am.
So help me Heaven, Alvaro, this is all!
ALVARO: How can I answer if you weep?
SERAFINA: No, no,
I do not weep, or, if I do, 'tis but
My eyes,—no more, no deeper.
ALVARO: Is 't possible you can so readily
Turn warm compassion into cold disdain!
And are your better pulses so controll'd
By a cold heart, that, to enhance the triumph
Over the wretched victim of your eyes,
You make the fount of tears to stop or flow
Just as you please? If so, teach me the trick,
As the last courtesy you will vouchsafe me.
SERAFINA: Alvaro, when I think of what I was,
My tears will forth; but when of what I am,
My honour bids them cease.
ALVARO: You *do* feel then—
SERAFINA: Nay, I'll deny it not.
ALVARO: That, being another's—
SERAFINA: Nay, no argument—
ALVARO: These tears—
SERAFINA: What tears?
ALVARO: Are the relenting rain

133

On which the Iris of my hope may ride;
Or a sweet dew—

SERAFINA: Alvaro—

ALVARO: That foretells
That better day when in these arms again—

SERAFINA: Those arms! Alvaro, when that day shall come
May heaven's thunder strike me dead at once!

                                 (*Cannon within.*)

Mercy, what's that?

Enter PORCIA.

PORCIA: A signal from the ship,
'Tis time: your father and Don Juan now
Are coming for you.

ALVARO: O heavens!

PORCIA: Compose yourself,
And you, Alvaro— (*Motions him back.*)

Enter DON JUAN, LUIS, PEDRO, LEONELO, &c.

LUIS: Lady, believe how sadly I am come
To do you this last office.

JUAN: Trembling still?—
But come, perhaps the sea-breeze, in requital
Of bearing us away from those we love,
May yet revive you.

LUIS: Well, if it must be so,
Lady, your hand. Porcia, come with us.

                     [*Exeunt all but* ALVARO.

ACT II

JUAN: Are you not wearied sitting?
SERAFINA: Surely not
    Till you be wearied painting.
JUAN: Oh, so much
    As I have wish'd to have that divine face
    Painted, and by myself, I now begin
    To wish I had not wish'd it.
SERAFINA: But why so?
JUAN: Because I must be worsted in the trial
    I have brought on myself.
SERAFINA: You to despair,
    Who never are outdone but by yourself!
JUAN: Even so.
SERAFINA: But *why* so?
JUAN: Shall I tell you why?
    Painters, you know, (just turn your head a little,)
    Are nature's apes, whose uglier semblances,
    Made up of disproportion and excess,
    Like apes, they easily can imitate:
    But whose more gracious aspect, the result
    Of subtlest symmetries, they only outrage,
    Turning true beauty into caricature.
    The perfecter her beauty, the more complex
    And hard to follow; but her perfection
    Impossible.
SERAFINA: That I dare say is true,
    But surely not in point with me, whose face
    Is surely far from perfect.
JUAN: Far indeed
    From what is perfect call'd, but far beyond,

    Not short of it; so that indeed my reason
    Was none at all.

SERAFINA: Well now then the true reason
    Of your disgust.

JUAN: Yet scarcely my disgust,
    When you continue still the cause of it.
    Well then, to take the matter up again—
    The object of this act, (pray, look at me,
    And do not laugh, Serafina,) is to seize
    Those subtlest symmetries that, as I said,
    Are subtlest in the loveliest; and though
    It has been half the study of my life
    To recognise and represent true beauty,
    I had not dreamt of such excess of it
    As yours; nor can I, when before my eyes,
    Take the clear image in my trembling soul;
    And therefore if that face of yours exceed
    Imagination, and imagination
    (As it must do) the pencil; then my picture
    Can be but the poor shadow of a shade.
    Besides,—

SERAFINA: Can there be any thing besides?

JUAN: 'Tis said that fire and light, and air and snow,
    Cannot be painted; how much less a face
    Where they are so distinct, yet so compounded,
    As needs must drive the artist to depair!
    I'll give it up.—(*Throws away his brushes*, &c.) The light
     begins to fail too.
    And Serafina, pray remember this,
    If, tempted ever by your loveliness,
    And fresh presumption that forgets defeat,
    I'd have you sit again, allow me not,—
    It does but vex me.

SERAFINA: Nay, if it do that
    I will not, Juan, or let me die for it,—
    Come, there's an oath upon't.

JUAN: A proper curse
    On that rebellious face.

Enter LEONELO.

LEONELO: And here comes in a story:—
A man got suddenly deaf, and seeing the people about him moving their lips, quoth he, "What the devil makes you all dumb?" never thinking for a moment the fault might be in himself. So it is with you, who lay the blame on a face that all the world is praising, and not on your own want of skill to paint it.

JUAN: Not a very apt illustration, Leonelo, as you would admit if you heard what I was saying before you came in. But, whose soever the fault, I am the sufferer. I will no more of it, however. Come, I will abroad.

SERAFINA: Whither, my lord?

JUAN: Down to the pier, with the sea and the fresh air, to dispel my vexation.

SERAFINA: By quitting me?

JUAN: I might indeed say so, since the sight of you is the perpetual trophy of my defeat. But what if I leave you in order to return with a double zest?

SERAFINA: Nay, nay, with no such pretty speeches hope to delude me; I know what it is. The carnival with its fair masks.

JUAN: A mask abroad when I have that face at home!

SERAFINA: Nay, nay, I know you.

JUAN: Better than I do myself?

SERAFINA: What wife does not?

LEONELO: Just so. A German and the priest of his village coming to high words one day, because the man blew his swine's horn under the priest's window, the priest calls out in a rage, "I'll denounce your horns to the parish, I will!" which the man's wife overhearing in the scullery, she cries out, "Halloa, neighbour, here is the priest revealing my confession!"

SERAFINA: What impertinence, Leonelo!

LEONELO: Very well then, listen to this; a certain man in Barcelona had five or six children, and one day—

JUAN: Peace, foolish fellow.

LEONELO: Those poor children will never get the meat well into their mouths.

E* 137

JUAN: Farewell, my love, awhile.

[*Exeunt* JUAN *and* LEONELO.

SERAFINA: Farewell, my lord.
Thou little wicked Cupid,
I am amused to find how by degrees
The wound your arrows in my bosom made,
And made to run so fast with tears, is healing.
Yea, how those very arrows and the bow
That did such mischief, being snapt asunder—
Thyself art tamed to a good household child.

Enter FLORA, *out of breath.*

FLORA: O madam!

SERAFINA: Well, Flora, what now?

FLORA: O madam, there is a man down-stairs!

SERAFINA: Well?

FLORA: Drest sailor-like.

SERAFINA: Well?

FLORA: He will not go away unless I give this letter into your hands.

SERAFINA: Into my hands? from whom?

FLORA: From the lady Porcia he says, madam.

SERAFINA: From Porcia, well, and what frightens you?

FLORA: Nothing, madam, and yet—

SERAFINA: And yet there is something.

FLORA: O, my lady, if this should be Don Alvaro!

SERAFINA: Don Alvaro! what makes you think that?

FLORA: I am sure it is he.

SERAFINA: But did you tell him you knew him?

FLORA: I could not help, madam, in my surprise.

SERAFINA: And what said he then?

FLORA: That I must tell you he was here.

SERAFINA: Alvaro!—
Flora, go back, tell him you dared not tell me,
Fearful of my rebuke, and say beside,
As of your own advice, that it is fit,
Both for himself and me,
That he depart immediately.

FLORA: Yes, madam.

As she is going, enter ALVARO, *as a Sailor.*

ALVARO: No need. Seeing Don Juan leave his house,
    I have made bold to enter, and have heard
    What Flora need not to repeat.

SERAFINA: Nay, sir,
    Rather it seems as if you had not heard;
    Seeing the most emphatic errand was
    To bid you hence.

ALVARO: So might it seem perhaps,
    Inexorable beauty: but you know
    How one delinquency another breeds;
    And having come so far, and thus disguised,
    Only to worship at your shrine, Serafina,
    (I dare not talk of love,) I do beseech you
    Do not so frown at my temerity,
    As to reject the homage that it brings.

SERAFINA: Don Alvaro,
    If thus far I have listen'd, think it not
    Warrant of further importunity.
    I could not help it—'tis with dread and terror
    That I have heard thus much; I now beseech you,
    Since you profess you came to honour me,
    Show that you did so truly by an act
    That shall become your honour well as mine.

ALVARO: Speak, Serafina.

SERAFINA: Leave me so at once,
    And without further parley,
    That I may be assured *you* are assured
    That lapse of time, my duty as a wife,
    My husband's love for me, and mine for him,
    My station and my name, all have so changed me,
    That winds and waves might sooner overturn
    Not the oak only,
    But the eternal rock on which it grows,
    Than you my heart, though sea and sky themselves
    Join'd in the tempest of your sighs and tears.

ALVARO: But what if I remember other times

When Serafina was no stubborn oak,
Resisting wind and wave, but a fair flower
That open'd to the sun of early love,
And follow'd him along the golden day:
No barren heartless rock,
But a fair temple in whose sanctuary
Love was the idol, daily and nightly fed
With sacrifice of one whole human heart.

SERAFINA: I do not say 'twas not so;
But, sir, to carry back the metaphor
Your ingenuity has turn'd against me,
That tender flower, transplanted it may be
To other skies and soil, might in good time
Strike down such roots and strengthen such a stem
As were not to be shook: the temple, too,
Though seeming slight to look on, being yet
Of nature's fundamental marble built,
When once that foolish idol was dethroned,
And the true God set up into his place,
Might stand unscathed in sanctity and worship,
For ages and for ages.

ALVARO: Serafina,
Why talk to me of ages, when the account
Of my misfortune and your cruelty
Measures itself by hours, and not by years!
It was but yesterday you loved me, yes,
Loved me, and (let the metaphor run on)
I never will believe it ever was,
Or is, or ever can be possible
That the fair flower so soon forgot the sun
To which so long she owed and turn'd her beauty,
To love the baser mould in which she grew:
Or that the temple could so soon renounce
Her old god, true god too while he was there,
For any cold and sober deity
Which you may venerate, but cannot love,
Newly set up.

SERAFINA: I must leave metaphor,
And take to sober sense; nor is it right.

Alvaro, that you strive
To choke the virtuous present with the past,
Which, when it was the past, was virtuous too,
But would be guilty if reiterate.
Nor is it right, nor courteous, certainly,
Doubting what I declare of my own heart;
Nay, you who do yourself affirm, Alvaro,
How well I loved you when such love was lawful,
Are bound to credit me when I declare
That love is now another's.

ALVARO: Serafina—

JUAN (*speaking within*): Light, light, there!

Enter FLORA *hurriedly.*

FLORA: Madam, my lord, my lord.

ALVARO: Confusion!

SERAFINA: O ye heavens!

FLORA: The old lover's story.
Brother or husband sure to interrupt.

JUAN (*within*): A light there, Flora! Serafina! night
Set in, and not a lamp lit in the house?

ALVARO: He comes.

SERAFINA: And I am lost!

FLORA: Quick, Don Alvaro,
Into this closet, till my lord be gone
Into his chamber; in, in, in!

ALVARO: My fears
Are all for you, not for myself.   [*Hides in the closet.*

FLORA: In, in!   [*Exit.*

JUAN (*entering*): How is it there's no light?

SERAFINA: She had forgot—
But here it comes.

Enter FLORA *with lights.*

'Twas kind of you my lord,—
So quickly back again—
Sooner than I expected.

JUAN: Yes, a friend
Caught hold of me just as I reach'd the pier,
And told me to get home again.

SERAFINA (*aside*):   My heart!
JUAN: And wherefore do you think?
SERAFINA: Nay, I know not.
JUAN: To tell you of a festival, Serafina,
      Preparing in your honour.
SERAFINA (*aside*):   I breathe again.
JUAN: The story's this. It is the carnival,
      You know, and, by a very ancient usage,
      To-morrow all the folk of Barcelona,
      Highest as well as lowest, men and women,
      Go abroad mask'd to dance and see the shows.
      And you being newly come, they have devised
      A dance and banquet for you, to be held
      In Don Diego's palace, looking forth
      So pleasantly (do you remember it?)
      Upon the sea. And therefore for their sakes,
      And mine, my Serafina, you must for once
      Eclipse that fair face with the ugly mask;
      I'll find you fitting dress,—what say you?
SERAFINA: Nay,
      What should I say but that your will is mine,
      In this as evermore?
      And now you speak of dress, there are ev'n now
      Some patterns brought me in the nick of time
      To choose from, in my chamber; prithee come,
      And help me judge.
JUAN: I would that not your robe
      Only, but all the ground on which you walk
      Were laced with diamond.
SERAFINA: What not done yet
      With compliment? Come—come.   (*She takes a light.*)
JUAN: But wherefore this?
SERAFINA: My duty is to wait upon you.
JUAN: No.
      Take the lamp, Flora.
SERAFINA: Flora waits on me,
      And I on you.
JUAN: What humour's this?
      But be it as you will.   [*Exeunt* JUAN *and* SERAFINA.

FLORA (*letting out* ALVARO): Now is the time, Signor Alvaro!
    hist!
    The coast is clear, but silently and swiftly—
    Follow—but, hush! stop! wait!
ALVARO: What now?
FLORA: A moment!
    Back, back, 'tis Leonelo.
ALVARO: Put out the light, I can slip past him.
FLORA (*falls putting out light*): No sooner said than done.
    O Lord, Lord, Lord!

Enter LEONELO.

LEONELO: What is the matter?
FLORA: The matter is, I have fallen.
LEONELO: Into temptation?
FLORA: It is well, sir, if I have not broken my leg; here, sir,
    cease your gibing, and get this lamp lighted directly.
LEONELO (*stumbling over* ALVARO): Halloa!
FLORA: What now?
LEONELO: I've fallen now, and on your temptation I think, for
    it has got a beard.
ALVARO (*groping his way*): The fool! but I can find the door.
                                          [*Exit.*

LEONELO: There goes some one!
FLORA: The man's mad!
LEONELO: Am I? Halloa! halloa, there!

Enter JUAN *with light.*

JUAN: What is the matter?
FLORA: Nothing, nothing, my lord.
LEONELO: Nothing? I say it is something, a great—
FLORA: My lord, going to shut the door, I stumbled, fell, and
    put out the light, that's all.
LEONELO: And I stumbled too.
JUAN: Well?
LEONELO: Over a man.
JUAN: In this chamber?
LEONELO: Yes, and—

FLORA: Nonsense! my lord, he stumbled against *me*, as we both
floundered in the dark.

LEONELO: You! What have you done with your beard then?

JUAN: Are you mad? or is this some foolery?

LEONELO: My lord, I swear I stumbled over a fellow here.

JUAN (*aside*): And she so anxious to light me to her chamber!
what is all this? Take the lamp, Leonelo. Though partly I
think you have been dreaming, I will yet search the house;
come with me. I will draw the sting of suspicion at once, come
what come may.   [*Draws sword and exit.*

FLORA (*to* LEONELO): All of your work. A murrain on your
         head,
     Making this pother.

LEONELO: Minx! what is said, is said.
                              [*Exeunt severally.*

SCENE II.—*The garden of* DON LUIS' *palace at Naples; a window with a balcony on one side, or in front:—night. Enter the*
PRINCE *and* CELIO *muffled up.*

CELIO: Still sighing? pardon me, your Highness, but
     This melancholy is a riddle to me.

PRINCE: Ah, Celio, so strange a thing is love,
     The sighs you think are melancholy sighs,
     Yet are not so; I have indeed drunk poison,
     But love the taste of it.

CELIO: I used to think
     'Twas all of being away from your Porcia;
     But now when better starr'd, her brother absent,
     Her father unsuspicious, at her bidding
     Night after night you come beneath her lattice,
     And yet—

PRINCE: If Porcia be not the cause
     Of my complaint she cannot be the cure:
     Yet (such is love's pathology) she serves
     To soothe the wound another made.

CELIO: Who then was she, my lord, for whose fair sake
     You cannot either love this loving lady,
     Nor leave her?

PRINCE: I would tell you, Celio,
    But you would laugh at me.
CELIO: Tell me, however.
PRINCE: Rememberest not the lady whom we saw
    For a few minutes, like some lovely vision,
    In this same house a little while ago,
    Not Porcia, but her diviner guest?
CELIO: Oh, I remember; is it then to be
    The speciality of your Highness' love,
    That, whereas other men's dies off by absence,
    Yours quickens—if it can be love at all
    Caught from one transitory glance?
PRINCE: Nay, Celio;
    Because a cloud may cover up the sun
    At his first step into the firmament,
    Are we to say he never rose at all?
    Are we to say the lightning did not flash
    Because it did but flash, or that the fountain
    Never ran fresh because it ran so fast
    Into its briny cradle and its grave?
    My love, if 'twere but of one moment born,
    And but a moment living, yet was love;
    And love it *is*, now living with my life.   (*A harp heard.*)
CELIO: O fine comparisons! but hark, I hear
    The widow'd turtle in the leaves away
    Calling her faithless mate.
PRINCE: Yes, Celio, 'tis
    Porcia—if she sings to me of *love*,
    I am to approach the window; but if *jealousy*,
    I am to keep aloof. Listen!
PORCIA (*singing within*):

        Of all the shafts to Cupid's bow,
           The first is tipt with fire;
        All bare their bosoms to the blow,
           And call the wound Desire.

              (*She appears at the window.*)

PRINCE: Ah! I was waiting, lovely Porcia,

    Till your voice drew me by the notes of love,
    Or distanc'd me by those of jealousy.
PORCIA: Which needs not music, prince, to signify,
    Being love's plain, prose history.
PRINCE: Not always;
    For instance, I know one,
    Who, to refute your theory, Porcia,
    Attracts men by her jealousy as much
    As she repels them by her love.
PORCIA: Nay, then
    Men must be stranger beings than I thought.
PRINCE: I know not how that is, I only know
    That in love's empire, as in other empires,
    Rebellion sometimes prospers.
PORCIA: That the night
    Would give us leave to argue out their point!
    Which yet I fear it will not.
PRINCE: Why?
PORCIA: My father,
    Who frets about my brother's sudden absence,
    Sits up enditing letters after him;
    And therefore I have brought my harp, that while
    We talk together I may touch the strings,
    So as he, hearing me so occupied,
    May not suspect or ask for me. Besides,
    We can talk under cover of the music.
PRINCE: Not the first time that love has found himself
    Fretted, Porcia.
PORCIA: Oh, the wretched jest!
    But listen—
    The music is for him, the words for you,
    For I have much to tell you underneath
    This mask of music.   (*Plays on the harp.*)
    You know my father has been long resolv'd
    To quit this government, and to return
    To his own country place—which resolution,
    First taken on my brother's suppos'd death,
    My brother's sudden absence has revived;
    And brought to a head—so much so, that to-morrow,

  To-morrow, he has settled to depart
  To Bellaflor—I scarce can say the words—
  But let my tears—
PRINCE: 'Tis well that you should mask
  Ill news under sweet music: though, indeed,
  A treason to make sweet the poison'd cup.
PORCIA: Who more than I—

    Enter JULIA *within, hurried.*

JULIA: Madam, madam, your father
  Is gone into the garden—I hear his steps.
PORCIA: Nay then—(*Sings*):

    Love's second is a poison'd dart,
     And Jealousy is nam'd:
    Which carries poison to the heart
     Desire had first inflam'd.

PRINCE: She sings of jealousy—we must retire;
  Hist, Celio!   [CELIO *and* PRINCE *retreat.*

    Enter LUIS.

JULIA: Who's there?
PORCIA: Speak!
LUIS: Oh, I, Porcia,
  Who writing in my study, and much troubled
  About your brother, was seduc'd away
  By your harp's pleasant sound and the cool night,
  To take a turn in the garden.
PORCIA.   Yes, sir, here
  I sit, enjoying the cool air that blows
  Up from the shore among the whispering leaves.
LUIS: What better? but, Porcia, it grows late,
  And chilly, I think: and though I'd have you here
  Singing like a nightingale the whole night through,
  It must not be. Will you come in? [*Exit.*
PORCIA: Directly—
  I've but a moment.
PRINCE (*entering*): And you shall not need
  Repeat the love call, for I heard—

PORCIA (*playing as she speaks*):   Nay, listen,
And that attentively. To-morrow, then,
We go to Bellaflor, (you know the place,)—
There in the hill-top, hid among the trees,
Is an old castle; ours, but scarcely us'd,
And kept by an old man who loves me well,
And can be secret. And if you should come
That way by chance, as hunting it may be,
I think we yet may meet.
LUIS (*within*):   Porcia!
PORCIA: Sir!
LUIS (*within*): It's time, indeed, to shut your window.
PORCIA: Hark,
I dare no longer.
PRINCE: Then farewell!
PORCIA: Farewell!
Remember Bellaflor: while you retreat
Among the trees, I still shall sing to you
Of love; not that dark shape of jealousy,
But in the weeds of absence.
PRINCE: A descant
That suits us both,—(*aside*) but on a different theme.
PORCIA (*singing*):

> The last of Cupid's arrows all
>   With heavy lead is set;
> That vainly weeping lovers call
>   Repentance or Regret.

[*As she retires still singing from the window within, the*
PRINCE *and* CELIO *retire back into the garden.*

SCENE III. *A street before* DON DIEGO'S *house in Barcelona.*—
Enter ALVARO *and* FABIO, *masked : other Masks pass across, and
into* DIEGO'S *house.*

ALVARO: This is the place; here will I wait till she comes by.
I know her dress, but I dared not follow her till myself disguised.
FABIO: And no doubt, sir, you will find good opportunity of
talking to her. 'Tis the old and acknowledged usage of this

season, that any one may accost any one so long as both are masked, and so neither supposed to know the other.

ALVARO: Oh, a brave usage, and a brave invention that of the Carnival! One may accost whom one pleases, and whisper what one wiil, under the very ears of husband, father, or duenna!

FABIO: So received a custom, that even among this hot-headed jealous people of Spain, no mortal quarrel has yet arisen on these occasions, though plenty to provoke it.

ALVARO: Look! the Masks are coming; I hear the music within. She must soon be here. Let us withdraw round this corner till she come. [*Exeunt.*

SCENE IV.—*A garden leading down to the sea; on one side a Portico.—Masks singing and dancing: in the course of which enter and mix with them,* JUAN, SERAFINA, LEONELO, *and* FLORA, *and afterwards* ALVARO; *all masked.*

CHORUS

Tantara, tantara, come follow me all,
Carnival, Carnival, Carnival.
Follow me, follow me, nobody ask;
Crazy is Carnival under the mask.
Follow me, follow me, nobody knows;
Under the mask is under the rose.
Tantara, tantara, &c.

JUAN: How like you all this uproar?

SERAFINA: O quite well.

JUAN (*aside*): And so should I,
      Did not a shadow from that darken'd room
      Trail after me. But why torment myself!

LEONELO: My lord, the dancers wait.

JUAN (*to the musicians*): Pardon me. Strike up!

VOICES: Strike up! strike up!

A VOICE: The castanets!

VOICES: The castanets! the castanets!

MUSICIAN: What will you have?

VOICES: The Tarazana! the Tarazana!

      [*A dance, during which* ALVARO *observes* SERAFINA.

149

FABIO: You recognise her?

ALVARO: Yes, Fabio, my heart
Would recognise her under any dress,
And under any mask.

FABIO: Now is your time.

ALVARO (*to* SERAFINA): Mask, will you dance with me?

SERAFINA: No, Cavalier;
You come too late.

ALVARO: Too late?

SERAFINA: I am engag'd.

ALVARO: Nevertheless—

SERAFINA: Nay, sir, I am not apt
To change my mind.

ALVARO: I hop'd that in my favour
You might perhaps.

SERAFINA: 'Twas a delusion.

ALVARO: But,
Fair Mask, didst never change thy mind before?

SERAFINA: Perhaps once—to such purpose that that *once*
Forbids all other.

JUAN: Serafina, the Mask
Has askt your hand to dance. On these occasions
You must permit him, whether known or not.
Unknown, the usage of the time allows;
If known, 'twere more discourteous to refuse.

SERAFINA: My lord, 'twas chiefly upon your account
That I refus'd to dance with him; if you
Desire it, I am ready.

JUAN: How, my love,
On my account?

SERAFINA: Liking your company
Much better.

JUAN: Nay, take the humour of the time,
And dance with him. (*Aside*) I marvel who it is
That follows Serafina, and to whom,
The very indisposition that she shows,
Argues a kind of secret inclination.

ALVARO: Well, do you still reject me?—

SERAFINA: I am bidden
    To dance with you; what measure will you call?
ALVARO: Play "Love lies bleeding!"
SERAFINA: But why that?—
ALVARO: Because
    The spirit of the tune and of the words
    Moves with my heart, and gives me leave beside
    Amid its soft and slow divisions
    To gaze on you and whisper in your ear.

(*A minuet by the Masks: during which* ALVARO *constantly whispers* SERAFINA, *who seems distrest; after some time, they return in the figure to the front of the Stage.*)

SERAFINA: I've heard enough, sir; save for courtesy
    Too much. No more.
ALVARO: Brief as the happiness
    That once was mine! But—
SERAFINA: Stay, sir, I will hear
    No more. I had not danc'd with you at all,
    But that I wish'd to tell you once for all
    How hopeless is your passion—the great danger
    Your coming hither put and puts me to,
    And that not my honour only, but my life,
    Depends upon your quitting me at once,
    Now and for ever.
ALVARO: Serafina!
SERAFINA (*aloud*):   I am tired;
    Pardon me, friends, I cannot dance.
JUAN: My love,
    What is't? Unwell?
SERAFINA: I know not.
A WOMAN: Stop the ball!
ANOTHER: All in her honour too!
ANOTHER: What is the matter?
JUAN: You are but tir'd with dancing.
SERAFINA: No, no, no,
    Let us go home.
JUAN: Pardon us, friends,
    Continue you your revels; we will go

Into the house awhile, and rest; I think
The heat and dancing have distrest her much,
But she'll be better. To your dance again.
Come, Serafina. (*Aside*) Leonelo! hither!
Find out the Mask that with your lady danc'd.

LEONELO: I'll watch him to the world's end—or beyond,
If need be.

JUAN: Good—Come, Serafina.

[*Exeunt* JUAN *and* SERAFINA.

ALVARO: So end my hopes for ever. Fool! who seeking
For what once lost could never more be found,
Like to a child after a rainbow running—
Leaving my father, who had only just
Recover'd me to his old heart again,
Without adieu—equipp'd this Brigantine
(Down to the bottom may she go with me!)
In chase of this—not Serafina—no—
But this false Siren,
Who draws me with the music of her beauty,
To leave me in destruction.

LEONELO (*watching him*): This must be some monk, who knows
of some better entertainment elsewhere.

ALVARO: And after all,
Not one kind word of welcome or of thanks,
But that her life depended on my leaving her,
Who would for her have sacrificed my own
In any way but that. But it is done!
Henceforward I renounce all hope; henceforth—
And why not all despair?—the world is wide,
Eh, Fabio? and the good old saw says well
That fortune at the worst must surely mend.
Let us to sea, the ship is ready; come,
Away with all this foolery. (*Throws off mask, &c.*)

LEONELO: Here is a harlequin sailor!

FABIO: Well resolv'd.

ALVARO: Wear them what other fool may list,
I'll straight aboard, and if the wind and sea
Can rise as they were wont, I'll stretch all sail

Toward the perdition she consigns me to.
Halloa there! (*Whistles.*)

Enter SAILORS.

SAILOR: Captain?
ALVARO: How is't for a cruise?
SAILOR: Oh, never better; just a breeze to keep
    The ship from looking in her glass too long.
ALVARO: Aboard, aboard then! Farewell all my hopes;
    My love, farewell for ever!
VOICES (*within*):   Fire! fire! fire!
ALL: What's this?
VOICES: Fire! fire! in Don Diego's palace!
    Help! help!
ALVARO: She there! my life shall save the life
    She said it jeopardied.

As he is going out, enter JUAN *with* SERAFINA *fainted in
his arms.*

JUAN: Friends! Gentlemen! if you would help in this calamity,
take charge for a moment of this most precious thing of all,
till I return.
ALVARO (*taking* SERAFINA *in his arms*): Trust me, sir.
                              [JUAN *rushes off.*
LEONELO: Stop, my lord, stop a moment—he is gone, and this
man—
ALVARO: Serafina in my arms! my ship at hand!
    O love, O destiny!—aboard, aboard—
    O 'tis the merriest proverb of them all,
    How one man rises by his neighbour's fall.
                    [*Exit, carrying off* SERAFINA.
LEONELO: Halloa! stop him! stop him! it is my mistress; Don
Juan! my lord! my lord! the rascal has carried her off! my
lord! my lord!   [*Runs after* ALVARO.
FIRST VOICE IN THE CROWD: The fire is getting under.
SECOND VOICE: No lives lost?
THIRD VOICE: Only, they say, one poor girl of the lady Sera-
fina's.

Enter DON JUAN *hurriedly.*

JUAN: I thought I heard Leonelo calling me—But where is
Serafina? This is the place—yes—Serafina! I left them here—
taken her perhaps fainting as she was for help. Gentlemen,
have you seen any here with a lady, fainted, in their charge—a
sailor, I think?

FIRST MAN: Not I, sir.

SECOND MAN: Nor I.

THIRD MAN: Stay, I think there were some sailors with a lady
in their arms.

JUAN: And where—

Enter LEONELO *breathless.*

LEONELO: Oh, my lord, my lord!

JUAN: Speak!

LEONELO: The Mask who danced with my lady—

JUAN: Where is she?

LEONELO: Was the sailor you gave her in charge to—He has
carried her off.

JUAN: The Mask! the sailor!

LEONELO: I saw him throw off his disguise, and now he has
carried her off—to the shore—to sea—to the ship there now
spreading her sails in the harbour.

JUAN: Man! beware lest I blast thee!

LEONELO: As if I were the sailor! I tell you I ran after them,
shouted, struggled, but was pushed aside, knocked down—

JUAN: To the shore, to the shore! follow me!

VOICES: What is the matter?

JUAN: What I dare not name till it be avenged; Pirate!—Ruffian!
Oh fool, I might have guessed—but I will find them through
water and fire too. To the shore!

[*Exit* JUAN, LEONELO *after him; confusion, &c.*

ACT III

SCENE I.—*A room in* DON LUIS' *country-house near Naples.*
Enter DON LUIS *reading a letter.*

LUIS: "You bid me tell you why it is Don Juan Roca has not
written to you so long: and though it be pain to do so, I dare
no longer defer answering you. At a carnival dance here, the
palace of Don Diego de Cordona, in which the festival was
held, took fire so suddenly, as people had much ado to escape
with their lives. Don Juan's wife fainting from terror, he
carried her out, and gave her in charge to a sailor standing
near, while he himself returned to help at the fire. No doubt
this sailor was a pirate: for he carried her off to his ship and
set sail immediately. Don Juan returning and finding her gone
rushes madly after; casts himself into the sea in his rage and
desperation; is rescued half drowned, and taken to his house,
from which he was missed—he and his servant Leonelo—
some days ago, taking scarce any thing with him, and leaving
no hint of whither he is gone. And since that hour we have
heard nothing of him, or of Serafina."

> My heart prevents my eyes from reading more.
> O heavens! to what chance and danger is
> The fortune of the happiest, and still more
> The honour of the noblest, liable!
> Ill fortune we may bear, and, if we choose,
> Sit folded in despair with dignity;
> But honour needs must wince before a straw,
> And never rest until it be avenged.
> To know where Juan is, and by his side
> To put myself, and run all risk with him
> Till he were righted, and the offender too,
> I'd give my life and all I'm worth; no corner
> In the wide earth but we would ferret it,
> Until—Porcia!

Enter PORCIA.

PORCIA: Pray, sir, pardon me,
          But I would know what vexes you, you stand
          Angrily talking to yourself alone:
          This letter in your hand—What is it, sir?
LUIS: Nothing, nothing, Porcia; (for Juan's sake
          I must dissemble)—Nay, I have received
          A letter upon business that annoys me.
PORCIA: I'm sorry, sir, for that, for I had come
          To ask a favour of you.
LUIS: Well, why not?
PORCIA: They say that those who ask unseasonably
          Must be content with a refusal.
LUIS: Nay,
          Between us two no season's out of season.
PORCIA: So? then I'll ask. Alvaro—
LUIS: All but that!
          Ask me not that way.
PORCIA: Then 'tis *not* the season.
LUIS: The season for all else but that which never
          Can be in season. How often have I told you
          Never to speak to me again of him!
PORCIA: What has my brother done, sir, after all,
          To make you so inveterate?
LUIS: What done!
          To leave my house, to which I only just
          Had welcom'd him as only a father can,
          Without adieu, or word of when or where,
          And then as suddenly come back, forsooth,
          Knock at my door, as if he had but made
          A morning call, and think to find it open—
          It and my heart—open to him as ever.
PORCIA: But may not, sir, the thoughtlessness of youth
          Be some excuse? Pray you remember, sir,
          How on a sudden you yourself determin'd
          To leave the cheerful city and come here,
          Among dull woods and fields, and savage people;
          And surely 'twas no wonder that my brother

Should, ill advis'd, no doubt, but naturally,
Slip for a month back to the busy world
To which his very dangers had endear'd him.
And now to prove
How much he feels your anger and his fault,
Since his return he has lived quietly,
I might say almost *eremitically*,
Up in the mountain, yet more solitary
And still than this is, doing penance there.
Let me plead for him, sir; let him come down,
To kiss your hand and see you once again.

LUIS: He should be grateful to you, Porcia—
    Well, let him come.

PORCIA: Bless you for saying so!
    I'll go myself to him this evening,
    And tell him this good news.

LUIS: Do so. Ah me!
    That all were settled thus! Did I but know
    Where Juan is, and where his enemy!   [*Exit.*

JULIA (*entering*): Well, madam, you have gain'd your point.

PORCIA: Yes, Julia,
    Two points; for, first, my brother will come back;
    And, secondly, so doing, leave the old castle
    At my disposal, where the Prince and I
    May meet together in security.
    I'll write to Alvaro now, and do you tell
    The messenger who brought his letter hither,
    I'll go this evening up the mountain. So
    Belardo, the old porter,
    Who knows and loves me well, will look for me,
    And understand the purpose of my going.

JULIA: Ah, now I see, beside his bow and arrows,
    Love arms himself with trick and stratagem.

PORCIA: And something else; give me my Arquebuss;
    So, Love and I perchance, as says the song,
    May hit a hart, as we shall go along.

SCENE II.—*A room in* DON LUIS' *castle in the hills.*—*Enter* ALVARO *and* FABIO.

ALVARO: How is't with Serafina?
FABIO: Nay, you know.
          Ever the same.
ALVARO: You mean still weeping?
FABIO: Ay.
ALVARO: Yes, from the hour when, fainting in my arms,
          She pass'd from raging flame to the wild seas,
          And opening those heavenly eyes again,
          Still with the hue of death upon her cheek,
          She saw herself in my ship—in my power,—
          She has not ceas'd to weep; all my caresses
          Unable to console her.
          I fondly hoped that she—

                    Enter SERAFINA.

SERAFINA: Good Fabio,   [*Exit* FABIO.
          Leave us awhile. "You fondly hoped," Alvaro—
          So much I heard, connected with my name;
          And I perhaps have something on that text
          Would clear the matter up to both of us.
          "You fondly hoped"—was't not that I might be
          So frail, so lost to shame, and so inconstant,
          That for the loss of husband, home, and honour,
          Lost in one day, I might console myself
          With being in his arms, who robb'd me of all!
          Was't this you hoped?
ALVARO: No, Serafina, but—
SERAFINA: But what?
ALVARO: And yet perhaps 'twas that I hop'd—
          The very desperation of my act
          Bringing its pardon with it, soon or late,
          Seeing, the very element of love
          Is rashness, that he finds his best excuse
          In having none at all. Ah, Serafina,
          How greatly must he love, who all for love
          Perils the hope of being loved at all!

SERAFINA: Poor argument! I rather draw that he
Who ventures on such desperate acts can have
No true respect for her he outrages,
And therefore no true love. No, daring traitor—
But I'll not strive to break the heart of flint,
But wear it with my tears. Hear me, Alvaro,
In pity—in mercy—hear me.
This thing is done, there is no remedy,
Let us not waste the time in arguing
What better had been done; the stars so rul'd it—
Yea, providence that rules the stars. Well then,
What next? Alvaro, I would speak of this;
And if't be right I owe you any thing,
Be it for this one boon, a patient hearing.
Listen to me—
I never draw a breath but 'tis on fire
With Juan's vengeance; never move a step
But think I see his fierce eyes glaring at me
From some dark corner of this desolate house
In which my youth is buried. And what gain *you*
By all this crime and misery? My body,
But not my soul; without possessing which,
Beauty itself is but a breathing corpse,
But a cold marble statue, unsuffus'd
With the responsive hue of sympathy,
Possess'd, but not enjoy'd.
Oh, ill betide that villain love, not love,
That all its object and affection finds
In the mere contact of encircling arms!
But if this move you not—consider, Alvaro—
Don Juan is a nobleman—as such
Bound to avenge his honour; he must know
'Twas you who did this monstrous act, for Flora
Would tell him all. There is one remedy:
'Tis this, that you, despairing of my love,
Which you can never gain—forego me quite,
And give me up to some cold convent's cloister,
Where buried I may wear away—

ALVARO: No more,

159

Rather than give you up again, Serafina,
Pray heaven's thunder—   (*Shot within.*)

SERAFINA: Again, this dreadful omen!
'Tis for my death!

ALVARO: Fear not—Belardo! ho!
What shot was that?

Enter BELARDO.

BELARDO: Your sister Porcia
Is coming up the mountain; nay, is now
At the very gate.

SERAFINA: O, whither must I go!

ALVARO: Belardo, lead her hence.

BELARDO: Not that way, sir,
By which your sister enters.

ALVARO: In here then.
I'll go and meet Porcia.

SERAFINA: Mercy, heaven!
[*She goes in at one door, as* PORCIA *enters by another.*

ALVARO: How now, Porcia, you look pleased to-day!

PORCIA: And well I may—for two reasons, Alvaro.

ALVARO: Well, what are they?

PORCIA: First, I have got my father to relax in his humour
against you.

ALVARO: My good sister!

PORCIA: So as he will see you at Bellaflor this very evening.

ALVARO: Good! and your second reason?

PORCIA: That coming up the pass, I made the crowning shot of
my life with this arquebuss—a hare at full speed—flying, I
might say.

ALVARO: Give you joy of both your hits, Porcia.

PORCIA: I am so proud of the last (though glad of the first,
Alvaro) that I shall try my luck and skill a little longer about
the castle this evening.

ALVARO: So—

PORCIA: You will not wait for me, but go down at once to
Bellaflor, and show my father you value his forgiveness by
your haste to acknowledge it.

ALVARO: You say well; but you will go with me?

PORCIA: Fear not, I shall soon be after you.

ALVARO: Well, if so, then—(*apart to* BELARDO,) Belardo, re-member you get the lady to her room directly my sister is gone out.

PORCIA: Our roads lie together as far as the gate at least. (*Aside to* BELARDO.) If the Prince happen to come hither, tell him to wait for me, Belardo; I shall be back directly. Come, brother.

[*Exeunt* ALVARO *and* PORCIA.

BELARDO: They say a Pander is a good business; and yet here am I ministering both to brother and sister with very little profit at the year's end.

SERAFINA (*entering cautiously*): Porcia's gone?

BELARDO: Yes, she is gone.

SERAFINA: Had she resolved on going into the room where I was she could have done it; there was neither key nor bolt within. But she is gone and I can get to my own.

BELARDO: No.

SERAFINA: Belardo! why?

BELARDO: Some one coming.

SERAFINA: Again! [*She hides as before.*

Enter PRINCE.

PRINCE: How now, Belardo, where is your mistress? she ad-vised me her brother would be away, and she here this evening.

BELARDO: Your Highness comes in good time. She went with him, but will be back directly. She is here.

Enter PORCIA.

PORCIA: Not far behind, you see. Scarce had he taken the turn to Bellaflor, when I turn'd back.

PRINCE: How shall I thank you for this favour?

PORCIA: My brother's living here has been the reason of our not meeting before: but that is remedied for the future.

PRINCE: And how?

PORCIA: He is at last reconciled to my father, and is even now gone home, to Bellaflor.

PRINCE (*aside*): My heart thanks you but little, being away with

F   161

another; but if I cannot avenge memory, I will thus try and deceive or amuse it. My lovely Porcia!

BELARDO (*aside*): She hears every word they say!

PORCIA: Ah, you flatter still.

PRINCE: Flatter!

PORCIA: Do I not know there is a Siren at Naples—

PRINCE: Porcia, to prove to you how unfounded that suspicion is, I have these many days wholly quitted Naples, and, out of a melancholy that has taken hold of me, now live retired in a little Villa hard by this: you may imagine at least one reason for my doing so. And so enchanted am I with my solitude, that till this evening (when you broke it as I could wish) I have not once stirred abroad; my only occupation being to watch some pictures that I am having done, by the best masters of Italy and of Spain too; one of which country I have happened on, who might compete with Apelles. As I told you, I have spent whole days in watching them at work.

PORCIA: My jealousy whispered—

Enter BELARDO.

BELARDO: Unlucky to be sure.

PORCIA: What now?

BELARDO: What can make your brother return so suddenly?

PORCIA: My brother!

BELARDO: He is now at the gate.

PORCIA: He must suspect the Prince! O, my lord, hide yourself.

PRINCE: Where?

PORCIA: Any where!—quick! here.

[*She puts him where* SERAFINA *is.*

PRINCE: For your sake, Porcia.

Enter ALVARO.

ALVARO: I cannot be easy till I am assured that Serafina—— Porcia here?

PORCIA: Alvaro!

ALVARO: You left me on a sudden?

PORCIA: I was tired, and came back for rest.

ALVARO: So—

PORCIA: But you?

ALVARO: I bethought me that, considering my father's late
indisposition toward me, it were better you were at my side
when I went to him.

PORCIA: So—

ALVARO: So that if he should relapse into ill-humour, you know
how to direct him.

PORCIA: Well, shall we start again together?

ALVARO: Is not that best?

PORCIA: As you please.

ALVARO (*aside*): She will not then stumble on Serafina.

PORCIA (*aside*): I shall so get him out of the Prince's way.

[*Exeunt* PORCIA *and* ALVARO.

BELARDO: Now then the two imprison'd ones get out.

Enter the PRINCE, *and* SERAFINA, *her hand before her face.*

SERAFINA: In vain—you shall not know me.

PRINCE: Nay, in vain
You try to be unknown.

SERAFINA: Consider—

PRINCE: Nay,
Down with that little hand, too small a cloud
To hide the heaven of your beauty from me.
Lady, I know you—but one such. And know
That love himself has wrought a miracle,
To this unlikeliest place, by means unlikeliest,
Bringing us here together.

BELARDO: Only this was wanting to the plot! The sister's gallant
in love with the brother's mistress!

SERAFINA: Generous Orsino! if I try in vain
To hide me from you—wretched that I am
To have to hide at all—but the less wretched
Being unmaskt by your nobility—
I ask this mercy at your feet; betray not
The secret chance has now betray'd to you.
I am a wretched woman, you a Prince.
Grant me this boon; and yet one more, to leave me
To weep my miseries in solitude.

PRINCE: Madam, your prayer is not in vain. Your name,
Upon the word and honour of a Prince,

Shall never pass my lips.
And for that second wish, hardest of all,
I yet will pay for one delicious glance
The greatest price I can, by leaving you.
Farewell—you owe me more anxiety
Than you believe.

SERAFINA: I shall not be asham'd
To own the debt, though hopeless to repay it.
But heav'n shall do that for me. Farewell, my lord.

PRINCE: Farewell.   [*Exeunt* PRINCE *and* SERAFINA.

BELARDO: I wonder if they know the ancient line,
    "I'll keep your secret, only you keep mine."   [*Exit.*

SCENE III.—*The* PRINCE'S *Villa.—Enter* DON JUAN *in poor apparel; and* CELIO.

CELIO: Your business with the Prince, sir?

JUAN: Only to speak
About a picture I have finish'd for him.

CELIO: He is not here at present; not, I think,
Return'd from hunting.

JUAN: Will he soon be home?

CELIO: I cannot speak to that, sir.   [*Exit* CELIO.

JUAN: Why, what a fate is mine!
All of a sudden—but I dare not say it;
Scarce could I of myself believe it, if
I told it to myself; so with some things
'Tis easier to bear, than hear of them;
And how much happens daily in this strange world,
Far easier to be done than be believed.
Who could have thought that I, being what I was
A few days back, am what I am; to this
Reduc'd by that name *Honour*; whose nice laws,
Accurst be he who framed!
Little he knew the essence of the thing
He legislated for, who put my honour
Into another's hand; made my free right
Another's slave, for others to abuse,
And then myself before the world arraign'd,

To answer for a crime against myself!
And one being vain enough to make the law,
How came the silly world to follow it,
Like sheep to their own slaughter! And in all
This silly world is there a greater victim
To its accursed custom than myself!

Enter LEONELO, *poorly drest.*

LEONELO: Yes, one,
    Who follows your misfortunes, and picks up
    The crumbs of misery that fall from you;
    My chief subsistence now.

JUAN: And I have left
    Country and home to chase this enemy,
    Of whom as yet no vestige—

LEONELO: And no wonder,
    Seeing he travels with you.

JUAN: In these rags—

LEONELO: And very hungry; and so we come at last
    To Naples; for what purpose?

JUAN: Why, if't be
    Some former lover; would he not return
    To his own country, and hers?

LEONELO: In which meanwhile
    We starve, without a stiver in our pockets,
    While friends swarm round us, if you would, my lord,
    Reveal yourself.

JUAN: Shorn of my honour? No!

LEONELO: And I, not being shorn of appetite,
    Would publish my disgraceful want of food
    To all the world. There is Don Luis now,
    Your ancient friend.

JUAN: What friend but, if he be
    True to himself and me, must be my enemy,
    And either wholly turn his face away,
    Or look at me with pity and contempt?
    I will reveal myself to no one, nay,
    Reveal *myself* I cannot,—not myself
    Until I be aveng'd.

LEONELO: And so you make
The painter's trade your stalking-horse,
To track your enemy, and in these rags
Come to the Prince.
JUAN: Oh let me die in rags,
Rather than he should recognise me! Once
He saw me—
LEONELO: O my lord, fear not for that;
Hunger, and rags, and sleeplessness, and anguish,
Have chang'd you so your oldest friend would pass you.
JUAN: They have that merit then. But see—the Prince.

Enter PRINCE.

I kiss your Highness' hand.
PRINCE: Well, Spaniard,
What would you with me?
JUAN: I waited on your Highness,
To tell you of a picture I had finisht.
Thinking your Grace might like—
PRINCE: I thank you, sir.
What is the subject?
JUAN: Hercules, my lord;
Wherein (unless I do deceive myself)
I think the fair and terrible are join'd
With some success.
PRINCE: As how?
JUAN: As thus, my lord.
The point I have chosen in that history
Is where the faithless Centaur carries off
Deijanira, while beyond the river
Stands Hercules with such a face and gesture
As not a man, I think, who looks on it,
But would exclaim, "Jealousy and Revenge!"
PRINCE: I long to see it.
JUAN: That is the main group;
But far away, among the tangled thicks
Of a dark mountain gap, this Hercules
Fires his own funeral pile to the smoky clouds.

And I would have this motto for the whole,
"So Jealousy in its own flames expires."
PRINCE: Not only do I like the subject well,
  But now especially, being deeply scorcht,
  Not with the flame that burn'd up Hercules,
  But that for which the unlucky Centaur died.
JUAN: Indeed, my lord.
PRINCE: Indeed—and, having done
  This picture for me, you shall set about
  One other.
JUAN: At your pleasure.
PRINCE: You shall know then,
  That of a certain lady whom but once
  I saw, and for a moment, I became
  Infatuated so, her memory
  Every where and for ever, day and night,
  Pursues me. Hopeless of obtaining her,
  And ev'n of ever seeing her again,
  Chance has discover'd to me where she lives
  Conceal'd—I know not why, but so it is—
  And 'twould at least console my hopeless love,
  To have her picture. You are a foreigner
  Who know not nor are known by any here,
  So I can better trust you with a secret
  I dare not even to herself reveal.
JUAN: I'll do my best to serve you; but I fear,
  If she be such a creature as you say,
  That I shall fail to satisfy myself
  Or you.
PRINCE: Why so?
JUAN: I tried at such a face
  Once.
PRINCE: Nay, I know that beauty's subtlest essence
  Is most impossible to seize. But yet
  I shall commit this business to your hands
  Most confidently.
JUAN: I'll do my best.
PRINCE: Come then,
  Remembering this business must be done
      167

       With all despatch and secrecy. Yourself
       Must not be seen by her, nor I, who know not
       (I told you) how or why she should be there;
       But my authority, and a little gold,
       (At least, I hope,) shall set the door ajar,
       That you may catch a sight of her. Myself
       Will be at hand, and ready to protect you
       Against all danger.

JUAN: I will trust your Highness,
       And also (let me say so) trust myself,
       Although but a poor painter.

PRINCE: I believe it;
       And each of us shall play his part, I think,
       That neither shall depart unsatisfied.   [*Exit* PRINCE.

JUAN: Perhaps, but not as you suppose. Leonelo,
       Put up my brushes and my colours, and—
       My pistols with them.

LEONELO: Pistols! Is't to paint
       In body colour?

JUAN: Put them up.

LEONELO: And whither
       Are we to carry them?

JUAN: I do not know.
       Whither the Prince shall carry me, I go.   [*Exeunt.*

SCENE IV.—*A room in* DON LUIS' *Villa.*—*Enter* LUIS *and*
ALVARO.

ALVARO: Now, sir, that (thanks to Porcia) you have open'd
       Your arms to me once more, I cannot rest
       (So favour ever calls for favour) till
       You tell me what the inward trouble is
       That mars your outward feature. I was cause
       Of so much trouble to you, that I dread
       Lest of this also, which with troubled looks
       You still keep speaking to yourself apart,
       Like people in a play.

LUIS: Alvaro, no.
       Thank God, this trouble lies not at your door.
       Let that suffice.

ALVARO: You will not trust me, sir?

LUIS: Why will you press me? since you must be told,
    It is about my friend—Don Juan Roca.

ALVARO: Don Juan!

LUIS: Yes, Don Juan.

ALVARO: What of him?
    (I'll drink the cup at once!) (*aside*).

LUIS: What evil star
    Made him my friend!

ALVARO: Too true! (*aside*). But what has happen'd?

LUIS: Why will you know? and should I dare to tell
    My friend's dishonour? Well, no more than this—
    Some wretch—some villain—some accursed—but
    Be there bad name enough to brand him by,
    I have not breath for it—nor is it well
    For you or for myself—has ravisht from him
    His wife, his Serafina.
    And I, O God! not able to avenge him!

ALVARO (*aside*): Does he know all? and knowing whose the
        crime,
    Cannot, he says, avenge it on his son?
    Shall I then tell, and gain at least the grace
    Of a confession? Hear me, sir.

LUIS: Nay, nay,
    I know what you would say, how vain it is
    To vex myself who cannot help my friend—
    We neither knowing who the villain is,
    Nor whither both are fled: heaven! if we did,
    I should not now be idly moaning here.

ALVARO: All's safe! (*aside*). Nor I, sir; give me but a clue,
    (Not only for Don Juan's sake, but yours,)
    I'll track the villain through the world.

LUIS: Alvaro,
    Your words are music to me.

ALVARO: Still, my father,
    I will say what to say you said was vain.
    Until some clue be found, let not this grief
    Consume you so.

LUIS: Such wounds are hard to heal.

Yet, quicken'd by your courage, and to show
How well I like your counsel—come, Alvaro,
I will with you to your hill castle there;
That which has been your banishment so long,
Shall witness now our reconciliation.
We'll go this evening—now—together.

ALVARO: Good, sir.
But pardon me, let me go on before
To apprize Belardo of your going thither—
And also Serafina! (*apart*).   [*Exit.*

LUIS: Be it so!

JULIA (*entering*): My lord, Don Pedro is without, and fain
Would speak to you.

LUIS: Admit him, Julia.
The wound re-opens—Serafina's father!
No doubt upon what errand.

Enter DON PEDRO.

PEDRO: Ah, Don Luis,
Your arms! (*They embrace.*)

LUIS: Don Pedro, I must surely thank
The cause to which my poor retirement owes
This honour.

PEDRO: Yet a thankless cause, Don Luis.
These many days I have heard nothing of
Don Juan and my daughter; they neither write
Themselves, nor any one to whom I write
To ask about them answers to the purpose.
What may this mean? I have come hither thinking
That you, who are the model of all friends,
May deal more clearly with me. You may think
What I endure from this suspense. In mercy
Relieve me from it quickly.

LUIS (*aside*):   Poor old man;
What shall I say? tell his grey hairs at once
The ruin of his honour and his love?

PEDRO: You pause, my lord!

LUIS: And yet I need not wonder,
I nothing hear of them if you do not.

PEDRO: And you know nothing of them?

Enter PORCIA *hurriedly.*

PORCIA: Sir, I hear
  You are going (are you not?) this evening
  To the castle, with my brother.
  But who is this?
PEDRO: Ever your slave, sweet lady.
PORCIA: Oh, pardon me, my lord.
LUIS: Nay, pardon *me*
  That I cut short your compliments, Porcia.
  (This interruption, come so opportune,
  Shall carry what ill news I have to tell
  Into the open air at least.) Don Pedro,
  I am going to the mountain, as she says;
  You to the city; for some way at least
  Our roads are one, and I would talk with you
  About this business without interruption.
  Will't please you come?
PEDRO: Your pleasure's mine. Adieu,
  Fair lady.
PORCIA: Farewell, sir.
LUIS: Porcia, you
  Will follow in the carriage.   [*Exeunt* LUIS *and* PEDRO.
PORCIA: And should go
  More gladly, were my lover there to meet me.   [*Exit.*

SCENE V.—*The garden under* ALVARO'S *castle.—A large grated
door in the centre.—Enter* PRINCE, JUAN, LEONELO, *and*
BELARDO.

PRINCE (*to* BELARDO): You know your office; take this diamond by way of thanks.
BELARDO: I know little of diamonds but that they sell for less
  than you give for them. But this [*to* JUAN] is to be your post.
JUAN: I am ready.
PRINCE: Remember, Spaniard, it is for *me* you run this hazard,
  if there be any; I shall be close at hand to protect you. Be not
  frightened.

JUAN: Your Highness does not know me: were it otherwise,
danger cannot well appal him whom sorrows like mine have
left alive.

BELARDO: And, another time—doubloons, not diamonds.

[Exeunt PRINCE *and* LEONELO.

Here she mostly comes of an evening, poor lady, to soothe
herself, walking and sitting here by the hour together. This is
where you are to be. Go in; and mind you make no noise.

[Puts JUAN *into the grated door, and locks it.*

JUAN (*through the grated window*): But what are you about?

BELARDO: Locking the door to make all sure.

JUAN: But had it not better be unlockt in case—

BELARDO: Hush! she comes.

JUAN: My palette then.

Enter SERAFINA.

SERAFINA: How often and how often do I draw
My resolution out upon one side,
And all my armed sorrows on the other,
To fight the self-same battle o'er again!

JUAN: He stands in the way; I cannot see her face.

BELARDO: Still weeping, madam?

SERAFINA: Wonder not, Belardo:
The only balm I have. You pity me:
Leave me alone then for a while, Belardo;
The breeze that creeps along the whispering trees
Makes me feel drowsy.

JUAN (*to* BELARDO, *whispering*): She turns her head away,
I cannot see her still.

SERAFINA: What noise was that?

BELARDO: Madam?

SERAFINA: I thought I heard a whisper.

BELARDO: Only
The breeze, I think. If you would turn this way,
I think 'twould blow upon you cooler.

SERAFINA: Perhaps it will.
Thank you. I am very miserable and very weary.

BELARDO: She sleeps: that is the lady.
Make most of time.   *[Exit.*

172

JUAN: Yes. Now then for my pencil.
    Serafina! found at last! Whose place is this?
    The Prince? no! But the stray'd lamb being here,
    The wolf is not far off. She sleeps! I thought
    The guilty never slept: and look some tears
    Still lingering on the white rose of her cheek.
    Be those the drops, I wonder,
    Of guilty anguish, or of chaste despair?
    This death-like image is the sculptor's task,
    Not mine.
    Or is it I who sleep, and dream all this,
    And dream beside, that once before I tried
    To paint that face—the daylight drawing in
    As now—and when somehow the lamp was out,
    A man—I fail'd: and what love fail'd to do,
    Shall hate accomplish? She said then, if ever
    She suffer'd me to draw her face again,
    Might she die for it. Into its inmost depth
    Heav'n drew that idle word, and it returns
    In thunder.
SERAFINA (*dreaming*): Juan! Husband! on my knees.
    Oh Juan—slay me not!

    Enter ALVARO; *she wakes and rushes to him.*

                       Alvaro,
    Save me, oh save me from him!
ALVARO: So the wretch
    Thrives by another's wretchedness. My love!
JUAN: Alvaro, by the heavens!
ALVARO: Calm yourself;
    You must withdraw awhile. Come in with me.
JUAN: Villain!
SERAFINA (*clinging to* ALVARO): What's that?
JUAN (*shaking at the door*):   The door is fast;
    Open it, I say!—
    Then die, thou and thy paramour!
  [*Shoots a pistol at each through the grating.—Both fall:*
    SERAFINA *into the arms of* BELARDO, *who has come in during*
    the noise.—Then directly enter DON LUIS, PEDRO, PORCIA.

LUIS: What noise is this?

SERAFINA: My father!—in your arms
To die;—not by your hand—Forgive me—Oh!   [*Dies.*

PEDRO (*taking her in his arms*): My Serafina!

LUIS: And Alvaro!

ALVARO: Ay,
But do not curse me now!   [*Dies.*

Enter the PRINCE *and* LEONELO.

LEONELO: They must have found him out.

PRINCE: Whoever dares
Molest him, answers it to me. Open the door.
But what is this?   [BELARDO *unlocks the door.*

JUAN (*coming out*): A picture—
Done by the Painter of his own Dishonour
In blood.
I am Don Juan Roca. Such revenge
As each would have of me, now let him take,
As far as one life holds. Don Pedro, who
Gave me that lovely creature for a bride,
And I return to him a bloody corpse;
Don Luis, who beholds his bosom's son
Slain by his bosom friend; and you, my lord,
Who, for your favours, might expect a piece
In some far other style of art than this:
Deal with me as you list; 'twill be a mercy
To swell this complement of death with mine;
For all I had to do is done, and life
Is worse than nothing now.

PRINCE: Get you to horse,
And leave the wind behind you.

LUIS: Nay, my lord,
Whom should he fly from? not from me at least,
Who lov'd his honour as my own, and would
Myself have help'd him in a just revenge,
Ev'n on an only son.

PEDRO: I cannot speak,
But I bow down these miserable gray hairs

To other arbitration than the sword;
Ev'n to your Highness' justice.

PRINCE: Be it so.
Meanwhile—

JUAN: Meanwhile, my lord, let me depart;
Free, if you will, or not. But let me go,
Nor wound these fathers with the sight of one,
Who has cut off the blossom of their age:
Yea, and his own, more miserable than all.
They know me; that I am a gentleman,
Not cruel, nor without what seem'd due cause
Put on this bloody business of my honour;
Which having done, I will be answerable
Here and elsewhere, to all for all.

PRINCE: Depart
In peace.

JUAN: In peace! Come, Leonelo.

[He goes out slowly, followed by LEONELO: *and the curtain falls.*

Some alterations of this play were made with a view to the English stage,
where, in spite of the slightness of many parts, I still think it might be tried.
    Its companion play, the *Medico de su Honra*, is far more famous; has some
more terrible, perhaps some finer, situations; but inferior, I think, in variety
of scene, character, and incident.

SALÁMÁN AND ABSÁL

AN ALLEGORY

TRANSLATED FROM THE
PERSIAN OF JÁMÍ

[*Salámán and Absál, An Allegory, Translated from the Persian of Jámí,* was published by J. W. Parker in 1856. Subsequent editions, much revised, and without the letter to Cowell, appeared in 1856 and 1871, and with *The Rubáiyát of Omar Khayyám,* in 1879.]

LETTER TO PROFESSOR COWELL

My dear Cowell,

Two years ago, when we began (I for the first time) to read this Poem together, I wanted you to translate it, as something that should interest a few who are worth interesting. You, however, did not see the way clear then, and had Aristotle pulling you by one Shoulder and Prakrit Vararuchi by the other, so as indeed to have hindered you up to this time completing a Version of Hafiz' best Odes which you had then happily begun. So, continuing to like old Jámí more and more, I must try my hand upon him; and here is my reduced Version of a small Original. What Scholarship it has is yours, my Master in Persian, and so much beside; who are no further answerable for *all* than by well liking and wishing publisht what you may scarce have Leisure to find due fault with.

Had all the Poem been like Parts, it would have been all translated, and in such Prose lines as you measure Hafiz in, and such as any one should adopt who does not feel himself so much of a Poet as him he translates and some he translates for—before whom it is best to lay the raw material as genuine as may be, to work up to their own better Fancies. But, unlike Hafiz' best—(whose Sonnets are sometimes as close packt as Shakespeare's, which they resemble in more ways than one)—Jámí, you know, like his Countrymen generally, is very diffuse in what he tells and his way of telling it. The very structure of the Persian Couplet—(here, like people on the Stage, I am repeating to you what you know, with an Eye to the small Audience beyond)—so often ending with the same Word, or Two Words, if but the foregoing Syllable secure a lawful Rhyme, so often makes the Second Line but a slightly varied Repetition, or Modification of the First, and gets slowly over Ground often hardly worth gaining. This iteration is common indeed to the Hebrew Psalms and Proverbs—where, however, the Value of the Repetition is different. In your Hafiz also, not Two only, but Eight or Ten

Lines perhaps are tied to the same Close of Two—or *Three*—words; a verbal Ingenuity as much valued in the East as better Thought. And how many of all the Odes called his, more and fewer in various Copies, do you yourself care to deal with?—And in the better ones how often some lines, as I think for this reason, unworthy of the Rest—interpolated perhaps from the Mouths of his many Devotees, Mystical and Sensual—or crept into Manuscripts of which he never arranged or corrected one from the First?

This, together with the confined Action of Persian Grammar, whose organic simplicity seems to me its difficulty when applied, makes the Line by Line Translation of a Poem not line by line precious tedious in proportion to its length. Especially—(what the Sonnet does not feel)—in the Narrative; which I found when once eased in its Collar, and yet missing somewhat of rhythmical Amble, somehow, and not without resistance on my part, swerved into that "easy road" of Verse—easiest as unbeset with any exigencies of Rhyme. Those little Stories, too, which you thought untractable, but which have their Use as well as Humour by way of quaint Interlude Music between the little Acts, felt ill at ease in solemn Lowth-Isaiah Prose, and had learn'd their tune, you know, before even Hiawatha came to teach people to quarrel about it. Till, one part drawing on another, the Whole grew to the present form.

As for the much bodily omitted—it may be readily guessed that an Asiatic of the 15th Century might say much on such a subject that an Englishman of the 19th would not care to read. Not that our Jámí is ever *licentious* like his Contemporary Chaucer, nor like Chaucer's Posterity in Times that called themselves more Civil. But better Men will not now endure a simplicity of Speech that Worse men abuse. Then the many more, and foolisher, Stories—preliminary Te Deums to Allah and Allah's-shadow Sháh—very much about Alef Noses, Eyebrows like inverted Núns, drunken Narcissus Eyes—and that eternal Moon Face which never wanes from Persia—of all which there is surely enough in this Glimpse of the Original. No doubt some Oriental character escapes—the Story sometimes becomes too Skin and Bone without due interval of even Stupid and Bad. Of the two Evils?—At least what I have chosen is least in point of bulk;

scarcely in proportion with the length of its Apology which, as usual, probably discharges one's own Conscience at too great a Price; people at once turning against you the Arms they might have wanted had you not laid them down. However it may be with this, I am sure a complete Translation—even in Prose— would not have been a readable one—which, after all, is a useful property of most Books, even of Poetry.

In studying the Original, you know, one gets contentedly carried over barren Ground in a new Land of Language— excited by chasing any new Game that will but show Sport; the most worthless to win asking perhaps all the sharper Energy to pursue, and so far yielding all the more Satisfaction when run down. Especially, cheered on as I was by such a Huntsman as poor Dog of a Persian Scholar never hunted with before; and moreover—but that was rather in the Spanish Sierras—by the Presence of a Lady in the Field, silently brightening about us like Aurora's Self, or chiming in with musical Encouragement that all we started and ran down must be Royal Game!

Ah, happy Days! When shall we Three meet again—when dip in that unreturning Tide of Time and Circumstance!—In those Meadows far from the World, it seemed, as Salámán's Island— before an Iron Railway broke the Heart of that Happy Valley whose Gossip was the Mill-wheel, and Visitors the Summer Airs that momentarily ruffled the sleepy Stream that turned it as they chased one another over to lose themselves in Whispers in the Copse beyond. Or returning—I suppose you remember whose Lines they are—

> When Winter Skies were tinged with Crimson still
> Where Thornbush nestles on the quiet hill,
> And the live Amber round the setting Sun,
> Lighting the Labourer home whose Work is done,
> Burn'd like a Golden Angel-ground above
> The solitary Home of Peace and Love—

at such an hour drawing home together for a fireside Night of it with Æschylus or Calderon in the Cottage, whose walls, modest almost as those of the Poor who clustered—and with good reason—round, make to my Eyes the Towered Crown of Oxford hanging in the Horizon, and with all Honour won, but

181

a dingy Vapour in Comparison. And now, should they beckon from the terrible Ganges, and this little Book begun as a happy Record of past, and pledge perhaps of future, Fellowship in Study, darken already with the shadow of everlasting Farewell!

But to turn from you Two to a Public—nearly as numerous— (with whom, by the way, this Letter may die without a name that *you* know very well how to supply),—here is the best I could make of Jámí's Poem—"Ouvrage de peu d'étendue," says the Biographie Universelle, and, whatever that means, here collapsed into a nutshell Epic indeed; whose Story however, if nothing else, may interest some Scholars as one of Persian Mysticism—perhaps the grand Mystery of all Religions—an Allegory fairly devised and carried out—dramatically culminating as it goes on; and told as to this day the East loves to tell her Story, illustrated by Fables and Tales, so often (as we read in the latest Travels) at the expense of the poor Arab of the Desert.

The Proper Names—and some other Words peculiar to the East—are printed as near as may be to their native shape and sound—"Sulaymán" for Solomon—"Yúsuf" for Joseph, &c., as being not only more musical, but retaining their Oriental flavour unalloyed with European Association. The *accented* Vowels are to be pronounced long, as in Italian—Salámán—Absál—Shírín, &c.

The Original is in rhymed Couplets of this measure—

$$- \cup - - \mid - \cup - - \mid - \cup - \mid \mid$$

which those who like Monkish Latin may remember in

Dum Salámán verba Regis cogitat,
Pectus intrá de profundis æstuat.

or in English—by way of asking, "your Clemency for us and for our Tragedy"—

Of Salámán and of Absál hear the Song;
Little wants Man here below, nor little long.

[1856]

NOTICE OF JÁMÍ'S LIFE

Drawn from Rosenzweig's "Biographische Notizen" of the Poet

NÚRUDDÍN ABDURRAHMAN, Son of Mauláná Nizámuddín Ahmed, and descended on the Mother's side from One of the Four great "FATHERS" of Islam, was born A.H. 817, A.D. 1414, in Jám, a little Town of Khorásán, whither his Grandfather had removed from Desht of Ispahán and from which the poet ultimately took his Takhallus, or Poetic name, JÁMÍ. This word also signifies "A Cup;" wherefore, he says, "Born in Jám, and dipt in the '*Jám*' of Holy Lore, for a double reason I must be called JÁMÍ in the Book of Song." He was celebrated afterwards in other Oriental Titles—"Lord of Poets"—"Elephant of Wisdom," &c., but latterly liked to call himself "The Ancient of Herát," where he mainly resided, and eventually died.

When Five Years old he received the name of Núruddín, the "Light of Faith," and even so early began to show the Metal, and take the Stamp that distinguished him through Life. In 1419, a famous Sheikh, Khwájah Mohammed Pársá, then in the last Year of his Life, was being carried through Jám. "I was not then Five Years old," says Jámí, "and my Father, who with his Friends went forth to salute him, had me carried on the Shoulders of one of the Family and set down before the Litter of the Sheikh, who gave a Nosegay into my hand. Sixty Years have passed, and methinks I now see before me the bright Image of the Holy Man, and feel the Blessing of his Aspect, from which I date my after Devotion to that Brotherhood in which I hope to be enrolled."

So again, when Mauláná Fakhruddín Loristání had alighted at his Mother's house—"I was then so little that he set me upon his Knee, and with his Fingers drawing the Letters of 'ALÍ' and 'OMAR' in the Air, laughed with delight to hear me spell them. He also by his Goodness sowed in my Heart the Seed of his Devotion, which has grown to Increase within me—in which I hope to live, and in which to die. Oh God! Dervish let me live,

183

and Dervish die; and in the Company of the Dervish do Thou quicken me to life again!"

Jámí first went to a School at Herát; and afterward to one founded by the Great Timúr at Samarcand. There he not only outstript his Fellow-students in the very Encyclopædic Studies of Persian Education, but even puzzled his Doctors in Logic, Astronomy, and Theology; who, however, with unresenting Gravity welcomed him—"Lo! a new Light added to our Galaxy!" —And among them in the wider Field of Samarcand he might have liked to remain, had not a Dream recalled him to Herát. A Vision of the Great Súfí Master there, Mohammed Saaduddín Káshgharí, appeared to him in his Sleep, and bade him return to One who would satisfy all Desire. Jámí returned to Herát; he saw the Sheikh discoursing with his Disciples by the Door of the Great Mosque; day after day passed him by without daring to present himself; but the Master's Eye was upon him; day by day drew him nearer and nearer—till at last the Sheikh announces to those about him—"Lo! this Day have I taken a Falcon in my Snare!"

Under him Jámí began his Súfí Noviciate, with such Devotion, both to Study and Master, that going, he tells us, but for one Summer Holiday into the Country, a single Line sufficed to "lure the Tassel-gentle back again;"

"Lo! here am I, and Thou look'st on the Rose!"

By-and-by he withdrew, by due course of Súfí Instruction, into Solitude so long and profound, that on his return to Men he had almost lost the Power of Converse with them. At last, when duly taught, and duly authorized to teach as Súfí Doctor, he yet would not take upon himself so to do, though solicited by those who had seen such a Vision of him as had drawn himself to Herát; and not till the Evening of his Life was he to be seen taking that place by the Mosque which his departed Master had been used to occupy before.

Meanwhile he had become Poet, which no doubt winged his Reputation and Doctrine far and wide through a People so susceptible of poetic impulse.

"A Thousand times," he says, "I have repented of such Employment; but I could no more shirk it than one can shirk

184

what the Pen of Fate has written on his Forehead"—"As Poet
I have resounded through the World; Heaven filled itself with
my Song, and the Bride of Time adorned her Ears and Neck
with the Pearls of my Verse, whose coming Caravan the Persian
Háfiz and Saadí came forth gladly to salute, and the Indian
Khosrau and Hasan hailed as a Wonder of the World." "The
Kings of India and Rúm greet me by Letter: the Lords of Irák
and Tabríz load me with Gifts; and what shall I say of those of
Khorásán, who drown me in an Ocean of Munificence?"

This, though Oriental, is scarcely bombast. Jámí was honoured
by Princes at home and abroad, at the very time they were cutting one another's Throats; by his own Sultan Abú Saïd; by
Hasan Beg of Mesopotamia—"Lord of Tabríz"—by whom Abú
Saïd was defeated, dethroned, and slain; by Mohammed II of
Turkey—"King of Rúm"—who in his turn defeated Hasan; and
lastly by Husein Mírzá Baikará, who somehow made away with
the Prince whom Hasan had set up in Abú Saïd's Place at Herát.
Such is the House that Jack builds in Persia.

As Hasan Beg, however—the USUNCASSAN of old European
Annals—is singularly connected with the present Poem, and
with probably the most important event in Jámí's Life, I will
briefly follow the Steps that led to that as well as other Princely
Intercourse.

In A.H. 877, A.D. 1472, Jámí set off on his Pilgrimage to Mecca,
as every True Believer who could afford it was expected once in
his Life to do. He, and, on his Account, the Caravan he went
with, were honourably and safely escorted through the inter-
jacent Countries by order of their several Potentates as far as
Baghdád. There Jámí fell into trouble by the Treachery of a
Follower whom he had reproved, and who misquoted his Verse
into disparagement of ALí, the Darling Imám of Persia. This,
getting wind at Baghdád, was there brought to solemn Tribunal.
Jámí came victoriously off; his Accuser was pilloried with a
dockt Beard in Baghdád Market-place: but the Poet was so ill
pleased with the stupidity of those who had believed the Report,
that, in an after Poem, he called for a Cup of Wine to seal up
Lips of whose Utterance the Men of Baghdád were unworthy.

After four months' stay there, during which he visited at
Helleh the Tomb of Alí's Son Husein, who had fallen at Kerbela,

he set forth again—to Najaf, (where he says his Camel sprang forward at sight of Alí's own Tomb)—crossed the Desert in twenty-two days, continually meditating on the Prophet's Glory, to Medina; and so at last to MECCA, where, as he sang in a Ghazal, he went through all Mohammedan Ceremony with a Mystical Understanding of his Own.

He then turned Homeward: was entertained for forty-five days at Damascus, which he left the very Day before the Turkish Mohammed's Envoys come with 5000 Ducats to carry him to Constantinople. On arriving at Amida, the Capital of Mesopotamia, he found War broken out and in full Flame between that Sultan and Hasan Beg, King of the Country, who caused Jámí to be honourably escorted through the dangerous Roads to Tabríz; there received him in full Díván, and would fain have him abide at his Court awhile. Jámí, however, was intent on Home, and once more seeing his aged Mother—for *he* was turned of Sixty—and at last reached Herát in the Month of Shaabán, 1473, after the Average Year's absence.

This is the HASAN, "in the Name and Nature *Handsome*" (and so described by some Venetian Ambassadors of the Time), who was Father of YAKÚB BEG, to whom Jámí dedicated the following Poem; and who, after the due murder of an Elder Brother, succeeded to the Throne; till all the Dynasties of "Black and White Sheep" together were swept away a few years after by Ismaíl, Founder of the Sofí Dynasty in Persia.

Arrived at home, Jámí found Husein Mírzá Baikará, last of the Timuridæ, seated on the Throne there, and ready to receive him with open Arms. Nizámuddín Alí Shír, Husein's Vizír, a Poet too, had hailed in Verse the Poet's Advent from Damascus as "The Moon rising in the West;" and they both continued affectionately to honour him as long as he lived.

Jámí sickened of his mortal Illness on the 13th of Moharrem, 1492—a Sunday. His Pulse began to fail on the following Friday, about the Hour of Morning Prayer, and stopped at the very moment when the Muezzin began to call to Evening. He had lived Eighty-one Years. Sultan Husein undertook the pompous Burial of one whose Glory it was to have lived and died in Dervish Poverty; the Dignitaries of the Kingdom followed him to the Grave; where twenty days afterward was recited in pre-

sence of the Sultan and his Court an Eulogy composed by the
Vizír, who also laid the first Stone of a Monument to his Friend's
Memory—the first Stone of "Tarbet'i Jámí," in the Street of
Meshhed, a principal Thoro'fare of the City of Herát. For, says
Rosenzweig, it must be kept in mind that Jámí was reverenced
not only as a Poet and Philosopher, but as a Saint also; who not
only might work a Miracle himself, but leave such a Power
lingering about his Tomb. It was known that an Arab, who had
falsely accused him of selling a Camel he knew to be unsound,
died very shortly after, as Jámí had predicted, and on the very
selfsame spot where the Camel fell. And that libellous Rogue at
Baghdád—he, putting his hand into his Horse's Nose-bag to see
if the beast had finisht his Corn, had his Forefinger bitten off by
the same—from which "Verstümmlung" he soon died—I suppose, as he ought, of Lock-jaw.

The Persians, who are adepts at much elegant Ingenuity, are
fond of commemorating Events by some analogous Word or
Sentence whose Letters, cabalistically corresponding to certain
Numbers, compose the Date required. In Jámí's case they have
hit upon the word "KÁs," A Cup, whose signification brings
his own name to Memory, and whose relative letters make up his
81 years. They have *Táríkhs* also for remembering the Year of
his Death: Rosenzweig gives some; but Ouseley the prettiest of
all;—

> Dúd az Khorásán bar ámed—
> "The smoke" of Sighs "went up from Khorásán."

No Biographer, says Rosenzweig cautiously, records of Jámí's
having more than one Wife (Granddaughter of his Master
Sheikh) and Four Sons; which, however, are Five too many for
the Doctrine of this Poem. Of the Sons, Three died Infant; and
the Fourth (born to him in very old Age), and for whom he wrote
some Elementary Tracts, and the more famous "Beháristán,"
lived but a few years, and was remembered by his Father in the
Preface to his Khiradnáma-i Iskander—Alexander's Wisdom-
book—which perhaps had also been begun for the Boy's Instruction. He had likewise a nephew, one Mauláná Abdullah, who was
ambitious of following his Uncle's Footsteps in Poetry. Jámí
first dissuaded him; then, by way of trial whether he had a

Talent as well as a Taste, bade him imitate Firdausí's Satire on Sháh Mahmúd. The Nephew did so well, that Jámí then encouraged him to proceed; himself wrote the first Couplet of his First (and most celebrated) Poem—Laila and Majnún—

> This Book of which the Pen has now laid the Foundation,
> May the diploma of Acceptance one day befall it,—

and Abdullah went on to write that and four other Poems which Persia continues to delight in to the present day, remembering their Author under his Takhallus of HÁTIFÍ—"The Voice from Heaven"—and Last of the classic Poets of Persia.

Of Jámí's literary Offspring, Rosenzweig numbers forty-four. But Shír Khán Lúdí in his "Memoirs of the Poets," says Ouseley, accounts him Author of Ninety-nine Volumes of Grammar, Poetry, and Theology, which, he says, "continue to be universally admired in all parts of the Eastern World, Irán, Túrán, and Hindústán"—copied some of them into precious Manuscripts, illuminated with Gold and Painting, by the greatest Penmen and Artists of the time; one such—the "Beháristán"—said to have cost some thousands of pounds—autographed as their own by two Sovereign Descendants of TIMÚR; and now reposited away from "the Drums and Tramplings" of Oriental Conquest in the tranquil seclusion of an English library.

With us, his Name is almost wholly associated with his "Yúsuf and Zulaikhá;" the "Beháristán" aforesaid: and this present "Salámán and Absál," which he tells us is like to be the last product of his Old Age. And these three Poems count for three of the brother Stars of that Constellation into which his seven best Mystical Poems are clustered under the name of "HEFT AURANG"—those "SEVEN THRONES" to which we of the West and North give our characteristic name of "Great Bear" and "Charles's Wain."

This particular Salámán Star, which thus conspicuously figures in Eastern eyes, but is reduced to one of very inferior magnitude as seen through this English Version,—is one of many Allegories under which the Persian Mystic symbolized an esoteric doctrine which he dared not—and probably could not

—more intelligibly reveal. As usual with such Poems in the story-loving East, the main Fable is intersected at every turn with some other subsidiary story, more or less illustrative of the matter in hand: many of these of a comic and grotesque Character mimicking the more serious, as may the Gracioso of the Spanish Drama. As for the metre of the Poem, it is the same as that adopted by Attár, Jeláluddín and other such Poets—and styled, as I have heard, the "Metre Royal"—although not having been used by Firdausí for his Sháh-námeh. Thus it runs:

$$- \cup -- \mid - \cup -- \mid - \cup - \mid$$

a pace which, to those not used to it, seems to bring one up with too sudden a halt at the end of every line to promise easy travelling through an Epic. It may be represented in Monkish Latin Quantity:

> Dum Salámán verba Regis cogitat,
> Pectus illi de profundis æstuat;

or by English accent in two lines that may also plead for us and our Allegory:

> Of Salámán and of Absál hear the Song;
> Little wants man here below, nor little long.

SALÁMÁN AND ABSÁL

PRELIMINARY INVOCATION

OH Thou, whose Spirit through this universe,
In which Thou dost involve thyself diffused,
Shall so perchance irradiate human clay
That men, suddenly dazzled, lose themselves
In ecstasy before a mortal shrine
Whose Light is but a Shade of the Divine;
Not till thy Secret Beauty through the cheek
Of LAILA smite doth she inflame MAJNÚN;
And not till Thou have kindled SHÍRÍN'S Eyes
The hearts of those two Rivals swell with blood.
For Loved and Lover are not but by Thee,
Nor Beauty;—mortal Beauty but the veil
Thy Heavenly hides behind, and from itself
Feeds, and our hearts yearn after as a Bride
That glances past us veil'd—but ever so
That none the veil from what it hides may know.
How long wilt thou continue thus the World
To cozen with the fantom of a veil
From which thou only peepest? I would be
Thy Lover, and thine only—I, mine eyes
Seal'd in the light of Thee to all but Thee,
Yea, in the revelation of Thyself
Lost to Myself, and all that Self is not
Within the Double world that is but One.
Thou lurkest under all the forms of Thought,
Under the form of all Created things;
Look where I may, still nothing I discern

But Thee throughout this Universe, wherein
Thyself Thou dost reflect, and through those eyes
Of him whom MAN thou madest, scrutinize.
To thy Harím DIVIDUALITY
No entrance finds—no word of THIS and THAT;
Do Thou my separate and derivéd Self
Make one with thy Essential! Leave me room
On that Diván which leaves no room for Twain;
Lest, like the simple Arab in the tale,
I grow perplext, oh God! 'twixt "ME" and "THEE;"
If *I*—this Spirit that inspires me whence?
If *THOU*—then what this sensual Impotence?

From the solitary Desert
Up to Baghdád came a simple
    Arab; there amid the rout
Grew bewilder'd of the countless
People, hither, thither, running,
Coming, going, meeting, parting,
Clamour, clatter, and confusion,
    All about him and about.
Travel-wearied, hubbub-dizzy,
Would the simple Arab fain
Get to sleep—"But then, on waking,
"How," quoth he, "amid so many
    Waking know Myself again?"
So, to make the matter certain,
Strung a gourd about his ankle,
And, into a corner creeping,
Baghdád and Himself and People
    Soon were blotted from his brain.
But one that heard him and divined
His purpose, slily crept behind;
From the Sleeper's ankle clipping,
    Round his own the pumpkin tied,
    And laid him down to sleep beside.
By and by the Arab waking
Looks directly for his Signal—

Sees it on another's Ankle—
Cries aloud, "Oh Good-for-nothing
Rascal to perplex me so!
That by you I am bewilder'd,
Whether I be I or no!
If I—the Pumpkin why on You?
If You*—then Where am I, and* Who?"

AND yet, how long, O Jámí, stringing Verse,
Pearl after pearl, on that old Harp of thine?
Year after year attuning some new Song,
The breath of some old Story? Life is gone,
And that last song is not the last; my Soul
Is spent—and still a Story to be told!
And I, whose back is crooked as the Harp
I still keep tuning through the Night till Day!
That harp untuned by Time—the harper's hand
Shaking with Age—how shall the harper's hand
Repair its cunning, and the sweet old harp
Be modulated as of old? Methinks
'Twere time to break and cast it in the fire;
The vain old harp, that, breathing from its strings
No music more to charm the ears of men,
May, from its scented ashes, as it burns,
Breathe resignation to the Harper's soul,
Now that his body looks to dissolution.
My teeth fall out—my two eyes see no more
Till by Feringhí glasses turn'd to four;*
Pain sits with me sitting behind my knees,
From which I hardly rise unhelpt of hand;
I bow down to my root, and like a Child
Yearn, as is likely, to my Mother Earth,
Upon whose bosom I shall cease to weep,
And on my Mother's bosom fall asleep.†

* First notice of Spectacles in Oriental Poetry, perhaps.
† The same Figure is found in Chaucer's "Pardoner's Tale," and, I think,
in other western poems of that era.

The House in ruin, and its music heard
No more within, nor at the door of speech,
Better in silence and oblivion
To fold me head and foot, remembering
What THE VOICE whisper'd in the Master's ear—
"No longer think of Rhyme, but think of ME!"—
Of WHOM?—Of HIM whose Palace the SOUL is,
And Treasure-house—who notices and knows
Its income and out-going, and *then* comes
To fill it when the Stranger is departed.
Yea; but whose Shadow being Earthly Kings,
Their Attributes, their Wrath and Favour, His,—
Lo! in the meditation of His glory,
The SHÁH whose subject upon Earth I am,
As he of Heaven's, comes on me unaware,
And suddenly arrests me for his due.
Therefore for one last travel, and as brief
As may become the feeble breath of Age,
My weary pen once more drinks of the well,
Whence, of the Mortal writing, I may read
Anticipation of the Invisible.

One who travell'd in the Desert
Saw MAJNÚN *where he was sitting*
All alone like a Magician
    Tracing Letters in the Sand.
"Oh distracted Lover! writing
What the Sword wind of the Desert
Undeciphers so that no one
    After you shall understand."
MAJNÚN *answer'd—"I am writing*
Only for myself, and only
  'LAILA,'—*if for ever* 'LAILA'
Writing, in that Word a Volume,
Over which for ever poring,
From her very Name I sip
In Fancy, till I drink, her Lip."

THE STORY

Part I

A SHÁH there was who ruled the realm of Yún,*
And wore the Ring of Empire of Sikander;
And in his reign A SAGE, of such report
For Insight reaching quite beyond the Veil,
The Wise men from all quarters of the World,
To catch the jewel falling from his lips
Out of the secret treasure as he went,
Went in a girdle round him.—Which THE SHÁH
Observing, took him to his secresy;
Stirr'd not a step, nor set design afoot,
Without the Prophet's sanction; till, so counsell'd,
From Káf to Káf† reach'd his Dominion:
No People, and no Prince that over them
The ring of Empire wore, but under his
Bow'd down in Battle; rising then in Peace
Under his Justice grew, secure from wrong,
And in their strength was his Dominion strong.
The SHÁH that has not Wisdom in himself,
Nor has a Wise one for his Counsellor,
The wand of his Authority falls short,
And his Dominion crumbles at the base.
For he, discerning not the characters
Of Tyranny and Justice, confounds both,
Making the World a desert, and Redress
A fantom-water of the Wilderness.

---

* Or "YAVAN," Son of Japhet, from whom the country was called "YÚNAN"—IONIA, meant by the Persians to express Greece generally. Sikander is, of course, Alexander the Great.

† The Fabulous Mountain supposed by Asiatics to surround the World, binding the Horizon on all sides.

God said to the Prophet David—
"David, whom I have exalted
From the sheep to be my People's
  Shepherd, by your Justice my
    Revelation justify.
Lest the misbelieving—yea,
The Fire-adoring Princes rather
Be my Prophets, who fulfil,
Knowing not my WORD, *my* WILL."

———————

ONE night THE SHÁH of Yúnan as he sate
Contemplating his measureless extent
Of Empire, and the glory wherewithal,
As with a garment robed, he ruled alone;
Then found he nothing wanted to his heart
Unless a Son, who, while he lived, might share,
And, after him, his robe of Empire wear.
And then he turned him to THE SAGE, and said:
"O Darling of the soul of IFLATÚN;*
To whom with all his school ARISTO bows;
Yea, thou that an ELEVENTH to the TEN
INTELLIGENCES addest: Thou hast read
The yet unutter'd secret of my Heart;
Answer—Of all that man desires of God
Is any blessing greater than a Son?
Man's prime Desire; by whom his name and he
Shall live beyond himself; by whom his eyes
Shine living, and his dust with roses blows.
A Foot for thee to stand on, and an Arm
To lean by; sharp in battle as a sword;
Salt of the banquet-table; and a tower
Of salutary counsel in Diván;
One in whose youth a Father shall prolong
His years, and in his strength continue strong."

* Iflatún, Plato: Aristo, Aristotle: both renowned in the East to this Day.

When the shrewd SAGE had heard THE SHÁH's discourse
In commendation of a Son, he said:
"Thus much of a *Good* Son, whose wholesome growth
Approves the root he grew from. But for one
Kneaded of *Evil*—well, could one revoke
His generation, and as early pull
Him and his vices from the string of Time.
Like Noah's, puff'd with insolence and pride,
Who, reckless of his Father's warning call,
Was by the voice of ALLAH from the door
Of refuge in his Father's Ark debarr'd,
And perish'd in the Deluge. And as none
    Who long for children may their children choose,
Beware of teazing Allah for a Son,
    Whom having, you may have to pray to lose."

Sick at heart for want of Children,
Ran before the Saint a Fellow,
Catching at his garment, crying,
        "Master, hear and help me! Pray
        That ALLAH *from the barren clay*
Raise me up a fresh young Cypress,
Who my longing eyes may lighten,
And not let me like a vapour
        Unremember'd pass away."
But the Dervish said—"Consider;
        Wisely let the matter rest
In the hands of ALLAH *wholly,*
Who, whatever we are after,
        Understands our business best."
Still the man persisted—"Master,
I shall perish in my longing:
Help, and set my prayer a-going!"
        Then the Dervish raised his hand—
        From the mystic Hunting-land
Of Darkness to the Father's arms
        A musky Fawn of China drew—
A Boy—who, when the shoot of Passion

In his Nature planted grew,
Took to drinking, dicing, drabbing.
From a corner of the house-top
Ill-insulting honest women,
Dagger-drawing on the husband;
*   And for many a city-brawl*
Still before the Cadi summon'd,
*   Still the Father pays for all.*
Day and night the youngster's doings
Such—the city's talk and scandal;
Neither counsel, threat, entreaty,
Moved him—till the desperate Father
Once more to the Dervish running,
Catches at his garment—crying—
"Oh my only Hope and Helper!
One more Prayer! That God, who laid,
Would take this trouble from my head!"
But the Saint replied "Remember
"How that very Day I warn'd you
Not with blind petition ALLAH
Trouble to your own confusion;
*   Unto whom remains no more*
To pray for, save that He may pardon
*   What so rashly pray'd before."*

"So much for the result; and for the means—
Oh SHÁH, who would not be himself a slave,
Which SHÁH least should, and of an appetite
Among the basest of his slaves enslaved—
Better let Azrael find him on his throne
Of Empire sitting childless and alone,
Than his untainted Majesty resign
To that seditious drink, of which one draught
Still for another and another craves,
Till it become a noose to draw the Crown
From off thy brows—about thy lips a ring,
Of which the rope is in a Woman's hand,
To lead thyself the road of Nothing down.

197

For what is *She*? A foolish, faithless thing—
A very Káfir in rapacity;
Robe her in all the rainbow-tinted woof
Of Susa, shot with rays of sunny Gold;
Deck her with jewel thick as Night with star;
Pamper her appetite with Houri fruit
Of Paradise, and fill her jewell'd cup
From the green-mantled Prophet's Well of Life—
One little twist of temper—all your cost
Goes all for nothing: and, as for yourself—
Look! On your bosom she may lie for years;
　But, get you gone a moment out of sight,
And she forgets you—worse, if, as you turn,
　Her eyes on any younger Lover light."

———

Once upon the Throne together
Telling one another Secrets,
Sate SULAYMÁN *and* BALKÍS;*
The Hearts of both were turn'd to Truth,
Unsullied by Deception.
First the King of Faith SULAYMÁN
　　Spoke—"However just and wise
Reported, none of all the many
Suitors to my palace thronging
　　But afar I scrutinize;
And He who comes not empty-handed
　　Grows to Honour in mine Eyes."
After this, BALKÍS *a Secret*
From her hidden bosom utter'd,
Saying—"Never night or morning
Comely Youth before me passes
Whom I look not after, longing"—

"If this, as wise Firdausí says, the curse
Of better women, what then of the worse?"

———

———

* Solomon and the Queen of Sheba, who, it appears, is no worse in one
way than Solomon in another, unless in Oriental Eyes.

THE SAGE his satire ended; and THE SHÁH,
Determined on his purpose, but the means
Resigning to Supreme Intelligence,
With Magic-mighty Wisdom his own WILL
Colleagued, and wrought his own accomplishment.
For Lo! from Darkness came to Light A CHILD,
Of carnal composition unattaint;
A Perfume from the realm of Wisdom wafted;
A Rosebud blowing on the Royal stem;
The crowning Jewel of the Crown; a Star
Under whose augury triumph'd the Throne.
For whom dividing, and again in one
Whole perfect Jewel re-uniting, those
Twin Jewel-words, SALÁMAT and ASMÁN,*
They hail'd him by the title of SALÁMÁN.
And whereas from no Mother milk he drew,
They chose for him a Nurse—her name ABSÁL—
So young, the opening roses of her breast
But just had budded to an infant's lip;
So beautiful, as from the silver line
Dividing the musk-harvest of her hair
Down to her foot that trampled crowns of Kings,
A Moon of beauty full; who thus elect
Should in the garment of her bounty fold
SALÁMÁN of auspicious augury,
Should feed him with the flowing of her breast.
And, once her eyes had open'd upon Him,
They closed to all the world beside, and fed
For ever doating on her Royal jewel
Close in his golden cradle casketed:
Opening and closing which her day's delight,
To gaze upon his heart–inflaming cheek,—
Upon the Babe whom, if she could, she would
Have cradled as the Baby of her eye.
In rose and musk she wash'd him—to his lip
Press'd the pure sugar from the honeycomb;
And when, day over, she withdrew her milk,

* SALÁMAT, Security from Evil; ASMÁN, Heaven.

She made, and having laid him in, his bed,
Burn'd all night like a taper o'er his head.

And still as Morning came, and as he grew,
Finer than any bridal-puppet, which
To prove another's love a woman sends,
She trick'd him up—with fresh Collyrium dew
Touch'd his narcissus eyes—the musky locks
Divided from his forehead—and embraced
With gold and ruby girdle his fine waist.

So for seven years she rear'd and tended him:
Nay, when his still-increasing moon of Youth
Into the further Sign of Manhood pass'd,
Pursued him yet, till full fourteen his years,
Fourteen-day full the beauty of his face,
That rode high in a hundred thousand hearts.
For, when SALÁMÁN was but half-lance high,
Lance-like he struck a wound in every one,
And shook down splendour round him like a Sun.

———

SOON as the Lord of Heav'n had sprung his horse
Over horizon into the blue field,
SALÁMÁN kindled with the wine of sleep,
Mounted a barb of fire for the Maidán;
He and a troop of Princes—Kings in blood,
Kings in the kingdom-troubling tribe of beauty,
All young in years and courage, bat in hand
Gallop'd a-field, toss'd down the golden ball
And chased, so many crescent Moons a-full;
And, all alike intent upon the Game,
SALÁMÁN still would carry from them all
The prize, and shouting "Hál!" drive home the ball.

This done, SALÁMÁN bent him as a bow
To Archery—from Masters of the craft
Call'd for an unstrung bow—himself the cord

Fitted unhelpt,* and nimbly with his hand
Twanging made cry, and drew it to his ear:
Then, fixing the three-feather'd fowl, discharged:
And whether aiming at the fawn a-foot,
Or bird on wing, direct his arrow flew,
Like the true Soul that cannot but go true.

———————

WHEN night came, that releases man from toil,
He play'd the chess of social intercourse;
Prepared his banquet-hall like Paradise,
Summon'd his Houri-faced musicians,
And, when his brain grew warm with wine, the veil
Flung off him of reserve: taking a harp,
Between its dry string and his finger quick
Struck fire: or catching up a lute, as if
A child for chastisement, would pinch its ear
To wailing that should agéd eyes make weep.
Now like the Nightingale he sang alone;
Now with another lip to lip; and now
Together blending voice and instrument;
And thus with his associates night he spent.

His Soul rejoiced in knowledge of all kind;
The fine edge of his Wit would split a hair,
And in the noose of apprehension catch
A meaning ere articulate in word;
Close as the knitted jewel of Parwín
His jewel Verse he strung; his Rhetoric
Enlarging like the Mourners of the Bier.†
And when he took the nimble reed in hand
To run the errand of his Thought along
Its paper field—the character he traced,

* Bows being so gradually stiffened, according to the age and strength of
the Archer, as at last to need five Hundred-weight of pressure to bend, says
an old Translation of Chardin.

† The Pleiades and the Great Bear. This is otherwise prettily applied in the
Anvári Soheili—"When one grows poor, his Friends, heretofore compact as
THE PLEIADES, disperse wide asunder as THE MOURNERS."

Fine on the lip of Youth as the first hair,
Drove Penmen, as that Lovers, to despair.

His Bounty like a Sea was fathomless
That bubbled up with jewel, and flung pearl
Where'er it touch'd, but drew not back again;
It was a Heav'n that rain'd on all below
Dirhems for drops—

                 But here that inward Voice
Arrested and rebuked me—"Foolish Jámí!
Wearing that indefatigable pen
In celebration of an alien SHÁH
Whose Throne, not grounded in the Eternal World,
If YESTERDAY it were, TO-DAY is not,
TO-MORROW cannot be."* But I replied;
"Oh Fount of Light!—under an alien name
I shadow One upon whose head the Crown
WAS and yet Is, and SHALL BE; whose Firmán
The Kingdoms Sev'n of this World, and the Seas,
And the Sev'n Heavens, alike are subject to.
Good luck to him who under other Name
Instructed us that Glory to disguise
To which the Initiate scarce dare lift his eyes."

Sate a Lover in a garden
All alone, apostrophizing
Many a flower and shrub about him,
    And the lights of Heav'n above.
Nightingaling thus, a Noodle
Heard him, and, completely puzzled,
"What," quoth he, "and you a Lover,
Raving, not about your Mistress,
But about the stars and roses—

* The Hero of the Story being of YÚNAN—IONIA, or Greece generally
(the Persian Geography not being very precise)—and so not of THE FAITH.

> What have these to do with Love?"
> Answer'd he; "Oh thou that aimest
> Wide of Love, and Lovers' language
>   Wholly misinterpreting;
> Sun and Moon are but my Lady's
>   Self, as any Lover knows;
> Hyacinth I said, and meant her
>   Hair—her cheek was in the rose—
> And I myself the wretched weed
>   That in her cypress shadow grows."

AND now the cypress stature of Salámán
Had reached his top, and now to blossom full
The garden of his Beauty: and Absál,
Fairest of hers, as of his fellows he
The fairest, long'd to gather from the tree.
But, for that flower upon the lofty stem
Of Glory grew to which her hand fell short,
She now with woman's sorcery began
To conjure as she might within her reach.
The darkness of her eyes she darken'd round
With surma, to benight him in mid day,
And over them adorn'd and arch'd the bows
To wound him there when lost: her musky locks
Into so many snaky ringlets curl'd,
In which Temptation nestled o'er the cheek
Whose rose she kindled with vermilion dew,
And then one subtle grain of musk laid there,
The bird of that belovéd heart to snare.
Sometimes in passing with a laugh would break
The pearl-enclosing ruby of her lips;
Or, busied in the room, as by mischance
Would let the lifted sleeve disclose awhile
The vein of silver running up within:
Or, rising as in haste, her golden anklets
Clash, at whose sudden summons to bring down
Under her silver feet the golden Crown.
Thus, by innumerable witcheries,

She went about soliciting his eyes,
Through which she knew the robber unaware
Steals in, and takes the bosom by surprise.

Burning with her love ZULAIKHÁ
Built a chamber, wall and ceiling
Blank as an untarnisht mirror,
Spotless as the heart of YUSUF.
Then she made a cunning painter
Multiply her image round it;
Not an inch of wall or ceiling
But re-echoing her beauty.
Then amid them all in all her
Glory sat she down, and sent for
        YÚSUF—*she began a tale*
        Of Love—and lifted up her veil.
Bashfully beneath her burning
Eyes he turn'd away; but turning
Wheresoever, still about him
Saw ZULAIKHÁ, *still* ZULAIKHÁ,
Still, without a veil, ZULAIKHÁ.
But a voice as if from Canaan
Call'd him; and a Hand from Darkness
        Touch'd; and ere a living Lip
Through the mirage of bewilder'd
Eyes seduced him, he recoil'd,
        And let the skirt of danger slip.

PART II

ALAS for those who having tasted once
Of that forbidden vintage of the lips
That, press'd and pressing, from each other draw
The draught that so intoxicates them both,
That, while upon the wings of Day and Night
Time rustles on, and Moons do wax and wane,

As from the very Well of Life they drink,
And, drinking, fancy they shall never drain.
But rolling Heaven from his ambush whispers,
"So in my license is it not set down:
Ah for the sweet societies I make
At Morning, and before the Nightfall break,
Ah for the bliss that coming Night fills up,
And Morn looks in to find an empty Cup!"

———————

Once in Baghdád a poor Arab,
After weary days of fasting,
Into the Khalífah's banquet-
Chamber, where, aloft in State
HARÚN the Great at supper sate,
    Push'd and pushing, with the throng,
Got before a perfume-breathing
Pasty, like the lip of SHÍRÍN
    Luscious, or the Poet's song.
Soon as seen, the famisht clown
Seizes up and swallows down.
Then his mouth undaunted wiping—
"Oh Khalífah, hear me swear,
While I breathe the dust of Baghdád,
Ne'er at any other Table
Than at Thine to sup or dine."
Grimly laugh'd HARÚN, and answer'd;
    "Fool! who think'st to arbitrate
    What is in the hands of Fate—
    Take, and thrust him from the Gate!"

———————

WHILE a full Year was counted by the Moon,
SALÁMÁN and ABSÁL rejoiced together,
And neither SHÁH nor SAGE his face beheld.
They question'd those about him, and from them
Heard something: then himself to presence summon'd,
And all the truth was told. Then SAGE and SHÁH

Struck out with hand and foot in his redress.
And first with REASON, which is also best;
REASON that rights the wanderer; that completes
The imperfect; REASON that resolves the knot
Of either world, and sees beyond the Veil.
For REASON is the fountain from of old
From which the Prophets drew, and none beside:
Who boasts of other inspiration, lies—
There are no other Prophets than THE WISE.

AND first THE SHÁH:—"SALÁMÁN, Oh my Soul,
Light of the eyes of my Prosperity,
And making bloom the court of Hope with rose;
Year after year, SALÁMÁN, like a bud
That cannot blow, my own blood I devour'd,
Till, by the seasonable breath of God,
At last I blossom'd into thee, my Son;
Oh, do not wound me with a dagger thorn;
Let not the full-blown rose of Royalty
Be left to wither in a hand unclean.
For what thy proper pastime? Bat in hand
To mount and manage RAKHSH* along the Field;
Not, with no weapon but a wanton curl
Idly reposing on a silver breast.
Go, fly thine arrow at the antelope
And lion—let me not My lion see
Slain by the arrow eyes of a ghazál.
Go, challenge ZÁL or RUSTAM to the Field,
And smite the warriors' neck; not, flying them,
Beneath a woman's foot submit thine own.
O wipe the woman's henna from thy hand,
Withdraw thee from the minion who from thee
Dominion draws, and draws me with thee down;
Years have I held my head aloft, and all
For Thee—Oh shame if thou prepare my Fall!"

* "Lightning." The name of RUSTAM's famous Horse in the SHÁH-
NÁMEH.

When before SHIRÚYEH'S *dagger*
  KAI KHUSRAU,* *his Father, fell,*
    He declared this Parable—
"*Wretch!—There was a branch that waxing*
Wanton o'er the root he drank from,
At a draught the living water
    Drain'd wherewith himself to crown;
Died the root—and with him died
    The branch—and barren was brought down!"

THE SHÁH ceased counsel, and THE SAGE began.
"O last new vintage of the Vine of Life
Planted in Paradise; Oh Master-stroke,
And all-concluding flourish of the Pen
KUN FA YAKÚN;† Thyself prime Archetype,
And ultimate Accomplishment of MAN!
The Almighty hand, that out of common earth
Thy mortal outward to the perfect form
Of Beauty moulded, in the fleeting dust
Inscribed HIMSELF, and in thy bosom set
A mirror to reflect HIMSELF in Thee.
Let not that dust by rebel passion blown
Obliterate that character: nor let
That Mirror, sullied by the breath impure,
Or form of carnal beauty fore-possest,
Be made incapable of the Divine.
Supreme is thine Original degree,
Thy Star upon the top of Heaven; but Lust
Will bring it down, down even to the Dust!"

---

* KHUSRAU PARVÍZ (Chosroe The Victorious), Son of NOSHÍRVÁN
The Great; slain, after Thirty Years of prosperous Reign, by his Son
SHÍRÚYEH, who, according to some, was in love with his Father's mistress
SHÍRÍN. See further on one of the most dramatic Tragedies in Persian
history.

† "BE! AND IT IS"—The famous Word of Creation stolen from Genesis
by the Kurán.

Quoth a Muezzín to the crested
Cock—"Oh Prophet of the Morning,
Never Prophet like to you
Prophesied of Dawn, nor Muezzín
With so shrill a voice of warning
Woke the sleeper to confession
Crying, 'Lá ALLAH ILLÁ 'LLAH,
MUHAMMAD RASÚLUHU.'*
One, methinks, so rarely gifted
Should have prophesied and sung
In Heav'n, the Birds of Heav'n among,
Not with these poor hens about him,
Raking in a heap of dung."
"And," replied the Cock, "in Heaven
Once I was; but by my foolish
Lust to this uncleanly living
With my sorry mates about me
Thus am fallen. Otherwise,
I were prophesying Dawn
Before the gates of Paradise."

OF all the Lover's sorrows, next to that
Of Love by Love forbidden, is the voice
Of Friendship turning harsh in Love's reproof,
And overmuch of Counsel—whereby Love
Grows stubborn, and recoiling unsupprest
Within, devours the heart within the breast.

SALÁMÁN heard; his Soul came to his lips;
Reproaches struck not ABSÁL out of him,
But drove Confusion in; bitter became
The drinking of the sweet draught of Delight
And waned the splendour of his Moon of Beauty.
His breath was Indignation, and his heart
Bled from the arrow, and his anguish grew.
How bear it?—By the hand of Hatred dealt,

* "There is no God but God; Muhammad is his Prophet."

Easy to meet—and deal with, blow for blow;
But from Love's hand which one must not requite,
And cannot yield to—what resource but Flight?
Resolved on which, he victuall'd and equipp'd
A Camel, and one night he led it forth,
And mounted—he with ABSÁL at his side,
Like sweet twin almonds in a single shell.
And Love least murmurs at the narrow space
That draws him close and closer in embrace.

———————

When the Moon of Canaan YÚSUF
In the prison of Egypt darken'd,
Nightly from her spacious Palace-
  Chamber, and its rich array,
Stole ZULAIKHÁ *like a fantom*
To the dark and narrow dungeon
  Where her buried Treasure lay.
Then to those about her wond'ring—
"Were my Palace," she replied,
"Wider than Horizon-wide,
It were narrower than an Ant's eye,
Were my Treasure not inside :
And an Ant's eye, if but there
My Lover, Heaven's horizon were."

———————

SIX days SALÁMÁN on the Camel rode,
And then the hissing arrows of reproof
Were fallen far behind; and on the Seventh
He halted on the Seashore; on the shore
Of a great Sea that reaching like a floor
Of rolling Firmament below the Sky's
From KÁF to KÁF, to GAU and MÁHÍ* down

*Bull and Fish—the lowest Substantial Base of Earth. "He first made
the Mountains; then cleared the Face of the Earth from Sea; then fixed
it fast on Gau; Gau on Máhí; and Máhí on Air; and Air on what? on
NOTHING; Nothing on Nothing, all is Nothing—Enough." Attár; quoted
in De Sacy's Pendnamah, XXXV.

Descended, and its Stars were living eyes.
The Face of it was as it were a range
Of moving Mountains; or a countless host
Of Camels trooping tumultuously up,
Host over host, and foaming at the lip.
Within, innumerable glittering things
Sharp as cut Jewels, to the sharpest eye
Scarce visible, hither and hither slipping,
As silver scissors slice a blue brocade;
But should the Dragon coil'd in the abyss*
Emerge to light, his starry counter-sign
Would shrink into the depth of Heav'n aghast.

SALÁMÁN eyed the moving wilderness
On which he thought, once launcht, no foot, nor eye
Should ever follow; forthwith he devised
Of sundry scented woods along the shore
A little shallop like a Quarter-moon,
Wherein Absál and He like Sun and Moon
Enter'd as into some Celestial Sign;
That, figured like a bow, but arrow–like
In flight, was feather'd with a little sail,
And, pitcht upon the water like a duck,
So with her bosom sped to her Desire.

When they had sail'd their vessel for a Moon,
And marr'd their beauty with the wind o' the Sea,
Suddenly in mid sea reveal'd itself
An Isle, beyond imagination fair;
An Isle that all was Garden; not a Flower,
Nor Bird of plumage like the flower, but there;
Some like the Flower, and others like the Leaf;
Some, as the Pheasant and the Dove adorn'd
With crown and collar, over whom, alone,
The jewell'd Peacock like a Sultan shone;
While the Musicians, and among them Chief
The Nightingale, sang hidden in the trees

* The Sidereal Dragon, whose Head, according to the Pauránic (or poetic)
astronomers of the East, devoured the Sun and Moon in Eclipse.

Which, arm in arm, from fingers quivering
With any breath of air, fruit of all kind
Down scatter'd in profusion to their feet,
Where fountains of sweet water ran between,
And Sun and shadow chequer-chased the green.
Here Iram-garden seem'd in secresy
Blowing the rosebud of its Revelation;
Or Paradise, forgetful of the dawn
Of Audit, lifted from her face the veil.

SALÁMÁN saw the Isle, and thought no more
Of Further—there with ABSÁL he sate down,
ABSÁL and He together side by side
Together like the Lily and the Rose,
Together like the Soul and Body, one.
Under its trees in one another's arms
They slept—they drank its fountains hand in hand—
Paraded with the Peacock—raced the Partridge—
Chased the green Parrot for his stolen fruit,
Or sang divisions with the Nightingale.
There was the Rose without a thorn, and there
The Treasure and no Serpent* to beware—
Oh think of such a Mistress at your side
In such a Solitude, and none to chide!

Said to WÁMIK *one who never
Knew the Lover's passion—"Why
Solitary thus and silent
Solitary places haunting,
Like a Dreamer, like a Spectre,
    Like a thing about to die?"*
WÁMIK *answer'd—"Meditating
Flight with Azrá to the Desert :
There by so remote a Fountain
    That, whichever way one travell'd,*

* The supposed guardian of buried treasure.

211

League on league, one yet should never
See the face of Man; for ever
There to gaze on my Belovéd;
Gaze, till Gazing out of Gazing
Grew to Being Her I gaze on,
SHE and I no more, but in One
Undivided Being blended.
All that is by Nature twain
Fears, or suffers by, the pain
Of Separation: Love is only
        Perfect when itself transcends
Itself, and, one with that it loves,
        In undivided Being blends."

WHEN by and by the SHÁH was made aware
Of that heart-breaking Flight, his royal robe
He changed for ashes, and his Throne for dust,
And wept awhile in darkness and alone.
Then rose; and, taking counsel from the SAGE,
Pursuit set everywhere afoot: but none
Could trace the footstep of the flying Deer.
Then from his secret Art the Sage-Vizyr
A Magic Mirror made; a Mirror like
The bosom of All-wise Intelligence
Reflecting in its mystic compass all
Within the sev'n-fold volume of the World
Involved; and, looking in that Mirror's face,
The SHÁH beheld the face of his Desire.
Beheld those Lovers, like that earliest pair
Of Lovers, in this other Paradise
So far from human eyes in the mid sea,
And yet within the magic glass so near
As with a finger one might touch them, isled.
THE SHÁH beheld them; and compassion touch'd
His eyes and anger died upon his lips;
And arm'd with Righteous Judgment as he was,
Yet, seeing those two Lovers with one lip

Drinking that cup of Happiness and Tears*
In which Farewell had never yet been flung,†
He paused for their Repentance to recall
The lifted arm that was to shatter all.

The Lords of Wrath have perish'd by the blow
Themselves had aim'd at others long ago.
Draw not in haste the sword, which Fate, may be,
Will sheathe, hereafter to be drawn on Thee.

FARHÁD, *who the shapeless mountain*
Into human likeness moulded,
Under SHÍRÍN'S *eyes as slavish*
Potters' earth himself became.

Then the secret fire of jealous
Frenzy, catching and devouring
KAI KHUSRAU, *broke into flame.*

With that ancient Hag of Darkness
Plotting, at the midnight Banquet
FARHÁD'S *golden cup he poison'd,*
And in SHÍRÍN'S *eyes alone*
Reign'd—But Fate that Fate revenges,
Arms SHÍRÚYEH *with the dagger*
That at once from SHÍRÍN *tore,*
And hurl'd him lifeless from his throne.

BUT as the days went on, and still THE SHÁH
Beheld his Son how in the Woman lost,
And still the Crown that should adorn his head,

* Κρατῆρα μακρὸν ἡδονῆς καὶ δακρύων
  Κιρνῶντες ἐξέπινον ἄχρις ἐς μέθην.
From Theodorus Prodromus, as quoted by Sir W. Jones.
† A pebble flung into a Cup being a signal for a company to break up.

And still the Throne that waited for his foot,
Both trampled under by a base desire,
Of which the Soul was still unsatisfied—
Then from the sorrow of THE SHÁH fell Fire;
To Gracelessness ungracious he became,
And, quite to shatter that rebellious lust,
Upon SALÁMÁN all his WILL, with all*
His SAGE-VIZYR'S Might-magic arm'd, discharged.
And Lo! SALÁMÁN to his Mistress turn'd,
But could not reach her—look'd and look'd again,
And palpitated tow'rd her—but in vain!
Oh Misery! As to the Bankrupt's eyes
The Gold he may not finger! or the Well
To him who sees a-thirst, and cannot reach,
Or Heav'n above reveal'd to those in Hell!
Yet when SALÁMÁN'S anguish was extreme,
The door of Mercy open'd, and he saw
That Arm he knew to be his Father's reacht
To lift him from the pit in which he lay:
Timidly tow'rd his Father's eyes his own
      He lifted, pardon-pleading, crime-confest,
And drew once more to that forsaken Throne,
      As the stray bird one day will find her nest.

----

*One was asking of a Teacher,
"How a Father his reputed
      Son for his should recognize?"
Said the Master, "By the stripling,
As he grows to manhood, growing
Like to his reputed Father,
      Good or Evil, Fool or Wise.*

*Lo the disregarded Darnel
With itself adorns the Wheat-field,
And for all the vernal season
      Satisfies the farmer's eye;*

* He Mesmerizes him!

214

> *But the hour of harvest coming,*
> *And the thrasher by and by,*
> *Then a barren ear shall answer,*
> *'Darnel, and no Wheat, am I.'* "

YET Ah for that poor Lover! "Next the curse
Of Love by Love forbidden, nothing worse
Than Friendship turn'd in Love's reproof unkind,
     And Love from Love divorcing"—Thus I said:
Alas, a worse, and worse, is yet behind—
     Love's back-blow of Revenge for having fled!

SALÁMÁN bow'd his forehead to the dust
Before his Father; to his Father's hand
Fast—but yet fast, and faster, to his own
Clung one, who by no tempest of reproof
Or wrath might be dissever'd from the stem
She grew to: till, between Remorse and Love,
He came to loathe his Life and long for Death.
And, as from him *She* would not be divorced,
With Her he fled again: he fled—but now
To no such Island centred in the sea
As lull'd them into Paradise before;
But to the Solitude of Desolation,
The Wilderness of Death. And as before
Of sundry scented woods along the shore
A shallop he devised to carry them
Over the waters whither foot nor eye
Should ever follow them, he thought—so now
Of sere wood strewn about the plain of Death,
A raft to bear them through the wave of Fire
Into Annihilation, he devised,
Gather'd, and built; and, firing with a Torch,
Into the central flame ABSÁL and He
Sprung hand in hand exulting. But the SAGE
In secret all had order'd; and the Flame,
Directed by his self-fulfilling WILL,
Devouring Her to ashes, left untouch'd

SALÁMÁN—all the baser metal burn'd,
And to itself the authentic Gold return'd.

PART III

FROM the Beginning such has been the Fate
Of Man, whose very clay was soak'd in tears.
For when at first of common Earth they took,
And moulded to the stature of the Soul,
For Forty days, full Forty days, the cloud
Of Heav'n wept over him from head to foot:
And when the Forty days had passed to Night,
The Sunshine of one solitary day
Look'd out of Heav'n to dry the weeping clay.
And though that sunshine in the long arrear
    Of darkness on the breathless image rose,
    Yet, with the Living, every wise man knows
Such consummation scarcely shall be here!

SALÁMÁN fired the pile; and in the flame
That, passing him, consumed ABSÁL like straw,
Died his Divided Self, his Individual
Survived, and, like a living Soul from which
The Body falls, strange, naked, and alone.
Then rose his cry to Heaven—his eyelashes
Wept blood—his sighs stood like a smoke in Heaven,
And Morning rent her garment at his anguish.
And when Night came, that drew the pen across
The written woes of Day for all but him,
Crouch'd in a lonely corner of the house,
He seem'd to feel about him in the dark
For one who was not, and whom no fond word
Could summon from the Void in which she lay.

And so the Wise One found him where he sate
Bow'd down alone in darkness; and once more
Made the long-silent voice of Reason sound
In the deserted Palace of his Soul;

Until SALÁMÁN lifted up his head
To bow beneath the Master; sweet it seem'd,
Sweeping the chaff and litter from his own,
To be the very dust of Wisdom's door,
Slave of the Firmán of the Lord of Life,
Who pour'd the wine of Wisdom in his cup,
Who laid the dew of Peace upon his lips;
Yea, wrought by Miracle in his behalf.
For when old Love return'd to Memory,
And broke in passion from his lips, THE SAGE,
Under whose waxing WILL Existence rose
From Nothing, and, relaxing, waned again,
Raising a Fantom Image of ABSÁL,
Set it awhile before SALÁMÁN'S eyes,
Till, having sow'd the seed of comfort there,
It went again down to Annihilation.
But ever, as the Fantom past away,
THE SAGE would tell of a Celestial Love;
"ZUHRAH,"* he said, "ZUHRAH, compared with
    whom
That brightest star that bears her name in Heav'n
Was but a winking taper; and Absál,
Queen-star of Beauties in this world below,
But her distorted image in the stream
Of fleeting Matter; and all Eloquence,
And Soul-enchaining harmonies of Song,
A far-off echo of that Harp in Heav'n
Which Dervish-dances to her harmony."

SALÁMÁN listen'd, and inclined—again
Entreated, inclination ever grew;
Until THE SAGE beholding in his Soul
The SPIRIT† quicken, so effectually
With ZUHRAH wrought, that she reveal'd herself
In her pure lustre to SALÁMÁN'S Soul,
And blotting ABSÁL'S Image from his breast,

* "ZUHRAH." The Planetary and Celestial Venus.
† "Maaní." The Mystical pass-word of the Súfís, to express the transcendental New Birth of the Soul.

217

There reign'd instead. Celestial Beauty seen,
He left the Earthly; and, once come to know
Eternal Love, the Mortal he let go.

———

THE Crown of Empire how supreme a lot!
The Sultan's Throne how lofty! Yea, but not
For All—None but the Heaven-ward foot may dare
To mount—The head that touches Heaven to wear!—

When the Beloved of Royal augury
Was rescued from the bondage of ABSÁL,
Then he arose, and shaking off the dust
Of that lost travel, girded up his heart,
And look'd with undefiléd robe to Heaven.
Then was his Head worthy to wear the Crown,
His Foot to mount the Throne. And then THE SHÁH
From all the quarters of his World-wide realm
Summon'd all those who under Him the ring
Of Empire wore, King, Counsellor, Amír;
Of whom not one but to SALÁMÁN did
Obeisance, and lifted up his neck
To yoke it under His supremacy.
Then THE SHÁH crown'd him with the Golden
    Crown,
And set the Golden Throne beneath his feet,
And over all the heads of the Assembly,
And in the ears of all, his Jewel-word
With the Diamond of Wisdom cut, and said:—

———

"MY Son,* the Kingdom of The World is not
Eternal, nor the sum of right desire;
Make thou the Law reveal'd of God thy Law,
The voice of Intellect Divine within

* One sees Jámí taking advantage of his Allegorical Sháh to read a lesson
to the Living,—whose ears Advice, unlike Praise, scarce ever reached, unless
obliquely and by Fable. The Warning (and doubtless with good reason) is
principally aimed at the Minister.

218

Interpreter; and considering TO-DAY
TO-MORROW'S Seed-field, ere That come to bear,
Sow with the harvest of Eternity.
And, as all Work, and, most of all, the Work
That Kings are born to, wisely should be wrought,
Where doubtful of thine own sufficiency,
Ever, as I have done, consult the Wise.
Turn not thy face away from the Old ways,
That were the canon of the Kings of Old;
Nor cloud with Tyranny the glass of Justice:
By Mercy rather to right Order turn
Confusion, and Disloyalty to Love.
In thy provision for the Realm's estate,
And for the Honour that becomes a King,
Drain not thy People's purse—the Tyranny
Which Thee enriches at thy Subject's cost,
Awhile shall make thee strong; but in the end
Shall bow thy neck beneath thy People's hate,
And lead thee with the Robber down to Hell.
Thou art a Shepherd, and thy Flock the People,
To help and save, not ravage and destroy;
For which is for the other, Flock or Shepherd?
And join with thee True men to keep the Flock—
Dogs, if you will—but trusty—head in leash,
Whose teeth are for the Wolf, not for the Lamb,
And least of all the Wolf's accomplices.
For Sháhs must have Vizyrs—but be they Wise
And Trusty—knowing well the Realm's estate—
Knowing how far to Sháh and Subject bound
On either hand—not by extortion, nor
By usury wrung from the People's purse,
Feeding their Master, and themselves (with whom
Enough is apt enough to make rebel)
To such a surfeit feeding as feeds Hell.
Proper in soul and body be they—pitiful
To Poverty—hospitable to the Saint—
Their sweet Access a salve to wounded Hearts;
Their Wrath a sword against Iniquity,
But at thy bidding only to be drawn;

Whose Ministers they are, to bring thee in
Report of Good or Evil through the Realm:
    Which to confirm with thine immediate Eye,
And least of all, remember—least of all,
Suffering Accuser also to be Judge,
    By surest steps up-builds Prosperity."

MEANING OF THE STORY

UNDER the leaf of many a Fable lies
The Truth for those who look for it; of this
If thou wouldst look behind and find the Fruit,
(To which the Wiser hand hath found his way)
Have thy desire—No Tale of ME and THEE,
Though I and THOU be its Interpreters.
What signifies THE SHAH? and what THE SAGE?
And what SALÁMÁN not of Woman born?
Who was ABSÁL who drew him to Desire?
And what the KINGDOM that awaited him
When he had drawn his Garment from her hand?
What means THAT SEA? And what that FIERY PILE?
And what that Heavenly ZUHRAH who at last
Clear'd ABSÁL from the Mirror of his Soul?
Listen to me, and you shall understand
The Word that Lover wrote along the sand.

THE Incomparable Creator, when this World
He did create, created first of all
The FIRST INTELLIGENCE—First of a Chain
Of Ten Intelligences, of which the Last
Sole Agent is in this our Universe,
ACTIVE INTELLIGENCE so call'd; The One
Distributor of Evil and of Good,
Of Joy and Sorrow. Himself apart from MATTER,
In Essence and in Energy—He yet
Hath fashion'd all that is—Material Form,

And Spiritual, all from HIM—by HIM
Directed all, and in his Bounty drown'd.
Therefore is He that Firmán-issuing SHAH
To whom the World was subject. But because
What He distributes to the Universe
    Another and a Higher Power supplies,
Therefore all those who comprehend aright,
    That Higher in THE SAGE will recognise.

HIS the PRIME SPIRIT that, spontaneously
Projected by the TENTH INTELLIGENCE,
Was from no womb of MATTER reproduced
A special Essence called THE SOUL OF MAN;
A Child of Heaven, in raiment unbeshamed
Of Sensual taint, and so SALÁMÁN named.

And who ABSÁL?—The Sense-adoring Body,
Slave to the Blood and Sense—through whom THE SOUL,
Although the Body's very Life it be,
Doth yet imbibe the knowledge and delight
Of things of SENSE; and these in such a bond
United as GOD only can divide,
As Lovers in this Tale are signified.

And what the Flood on which they sail'd, with those
Fantastic creatures peopled; and that Isle
In which their Paradise awhile they made,
And thought, for ever?—That false Paradise
Amid the fluctuating Waters found
Of Sensual passion, in whose bosom lies
A world of Being from the light of God
Deep as in unsubsiding Deluge drown'd.

And why was it that ABSÁL in that Isle
So soon deceived in her Delight, and He
Fell short of his Desire?—that was to show
How soon the Senses of their Passion tire,
And in a surfeit of themselves expire.

And what the turning of SALÁMÁN'S Heart
Back to THE SHAH, and to the throne of Might
And Glory yearning?—What but the return
Of the lost SOUL to his true Parentage,
And back from Carnal error looking up
Repentant to his Intellectual Right.

And when the Man between his living Shame
Distracted, and the Love that would not die,
Fled once again—what meant that second Flight
Into the Desert, and that Pile of Fire
On which he fain his Passion with Himself
Would immolate?—That was the Discipline
To which the living Man himself devotes,
Till all the Sensual dross be scorcht away,
And, to its pure integrity return'd,
His Soul alone survives. But forasmuch
As from a darling Passion so divorced
The wound will open and will bleed anew,
Therefore THE SAGE would ever and anon
Raise up and set before Salámán's eyes
That Fantom of the past; but evermore
Revealing one Diviner, till his Soul
She fill'd, and blotted out the Mortal Love.
For what is ZUHRAH?—What but that Divine
Original, of which the Soul of Man
Darkly possesst, by that fierce Discipline
At last he disengages from the Dust,
And flinging off the baser rags of Sense,
And all in Intellectual Light arrayed,
As Conqueror and King he mounts the Throne,
And wears the Crown of Human Glory—Whence,
Throne over Throne surmounting, he shall reign
One with the LAST and FIRST INTELLIGENCE.

This is the meaning of this Mystery,
Which to know wholly ponder in thy Heart,
Till all its ancient Secret be enlarged.
Enough—The written Summary I close,
And set my Seal—

THE
TRUTH
GOD ONLY
KNOWS

RUBÁIYÁT OF
OMAR KHAYYÁM
FIRST AND
FOURTH EDITIONS

H

[Translation is hardly the word to apply to FitzGerald's *Rubáiyát*, "very unliteral as it is. Many Quatrains," he confessed, "are mashed together: and something lost, I doubt, of Omar's Simplicity which is so much a Virtue in him." "But at all Cost," he added, "a Thing must live: with a transfusion of one's own worse Life if one can't retain the Original's better. Better a live Sparrow than a stuffed Eagle."

It is in this spirit that the *Rubáiyát* of FitzGerald must be judged. We shall not find a precise English version of the original, following the Persian line by line. We shall find instead a fusion of the Oxford manuscript (which Cowell had discovered in the Bodleian Library in 1856) and the Calcutta manuscript (which Cowell copied for him in 1857). This text is sometimes shortened, sometimes lengthened, often changed in sequence, and inspired by the strangely sympathetic genius of an English writer who was born some seven centuries after Omar died.

The *Rubáiyát* was first published in 1859, but "as poor Omar is one I have great fellow feeling with, I would rather vamp him up again with a few Alterations & Additions than anything else." So FitzGerald wrote to his publisher in 1867. He did indeed alter and add to "poor Omar." The first edition had 75 stanzas, the second (for which he referred to a French text of Omar as well) 110, the third and fourth 101. Nine stanzas appeared in the second edition only; and the sequence was so radically changed from edition to edition that stanza 44 in the first edition became stanza 73 in the second version and stanza 68 in the third and fourth. Moreover, the stanzas themselves were constantly re-formed; these alterations do not always intensify the poetry, and, as FitzGerald pointed out, they do not always make the poem more accurate. "I daresay Ed[n] 1 is better in some respects than 2," he wrote blandly to Quaritch, "but I think not altogether . . . I dare say Ed[n] 1 best pleased those who read it first: as first Impressions are apt to be strongest . . . As to the relative fidelity of the two Versions, there isn't a Pin to choose—not in the opening Stanzas you send."

There were four editions of the *Rubáiyát* in FitzGerald's lifetime: in 1859, 1868, 1872 and 1879. The first and fourth are given here, taken from the Aldis Wright texts (1902–3).

J.R.]

OMAR KHAYYÁM

THE ASTRONOMER-POET
OF PERSIA

OMAR KHAYYÁM was born at Naishápúr in Khorassán in the latter half of our Eleventh, and died within the First Quarter of our Twelfth Century. The slender Story of his Life is curiously twined about that of two other very considerable Figures in their Time and Country: one of whom tells the Story of all Three. This was Nizám ul Mulk, Vizyr to Alp Arslan the Son, and Malik Shah the Grandson, of Toghrul Beg the Tartar, who had wrested Persia from the feeble Successor of Mahmúd the Great, and founded that Seljukian Dynasty which finally roused Europe into the Crusades. This Nizám ul Mulk, in his *Wasiyat*—or *Testament*—which he wrote and left as a Memorial for future Statesmen—relates the following, as quoted in the *Calcutta Review*, No. 59, from Mirkhond's History of the Assassins.

"One of the greatest of the wise men of Khorassan was the Imám Mowaffak of Naishápúr, a man highly honoured and reverenced,—may God rejoice his soul; his illustrious years exceeded eighty-five, and it was the universal belief that every boy who read the Koran or studied the traditions in his presence, would assuredly attain to honour and happiness. For this cause did my father send me from Tús to Naishápúr with Abd-us-samad, the doctor of law, that I might employ myself in study and learning under the guidance of that illustrious teacher. Towards me he ever turned an eye of favour and kindness, and as his pupil I felt for him extreme affection and devotion, so that I passed four years in his service. When I first came there, I found two other pupils of mine own age newly arrived, Hakim Omar Khayyám, and the ill-fated Ben Sabbáh. Both were endowed with sharpness of wit and the highest natural powers; and we three formed a close friendship together. When the Imám rose from his lectures, they used to join me, and we repeated to each other the lessons we had heard. Now Omar was a native of Naishápúr, while Hasan Ben Sabbáh's father was one Ali, a man of austere life and practice, but heretical in his creed and doctrine. One day Hasan said to me and to Khayyám, 'It is a universal belief that the pupils of the Imám Mowaffak will attain to fortune. Now, even if we *all* do not attain thereto, without doubt one of us will; what then shall be our mutual pledge and bond?' We answered, 'Be it what you please.' 'Well,' he said, 'let us make a vow, that to whomsoever this fortune falls, he shall share it equally with the rest, and reserve no pre-eminence for himself.' 'Be it so,' we both replied, and on those terms we mutually pledged our words. Years rolled on, and I went from Khorassan to Transoxiana, and wandered to Ghazni and Cabul; and when I returned, I was invested with office, and rose to be administrator of affairs during the Sultanate of Sultan Alp Arslán."

He goes on to state, that years passed by, and both his old school-friends found him out, and came and claimed a share in his good fortune, according to the school-day vow. The Vizier was generous and kept his word. Hasan demanded a place in the government, which the Sultan granted at the Vizier's request; but discontented with a gradual rise, he plunged into the maze of intrigue of an oriental court, and, failing in a base attempt to supplant his benefactor, he was disgraced and fell. After many mishaps and wanderings, Hasan became the head of the Persian sect of the *Ismailians*,—a party of fanatics who had long murmured in obscurity, but rose to an evil eminence under the guidance of his strong and evil will. In A.D. 1090, he seized the castle of Alamút, in the province of Rúdbar, which lies in the mountainous tract south of the Caspian Sea; and it was from this mountain home he obtained that evil celebrity among the Crusaders as the OLD MAN OF THE MOUNTAINS, and spread terror through the Mohammedan world; and it is yet disputed whether the word *Assassin*, which they have left in the language of modern Europe as their dark memorial, is derived from the *hashish*, or opiate of hemp-leaves (the Indian *bhang*), with which they maddened themselves to the sullen pitch of oriental desperation, or from the name of the founder of the dynasty, whom we have seen in his quiet collegiate days, at Naishápúr. One of the countless victims of the Assassin's dagger was Nizám-ul-Mulk himself, the old school-boy friend.

"Omar Khayyám also came to the Vizier to claim his share; but not to ask for title or office. 'The greatest boon you can confer on me,' he said, 'is to let me live in a corner under the shadow of your fortune, to spread wide the advantages of Science, and pray for your long life and prosperity.' The Vizier tells us, that, when he found Omar was really sincere in his refusal, he pressed him no further, but granted him a yearly pension of 1200 *mithkáls* of gold, from the treasury of Naishápúr.

"At Naishápúr thus lived and died Omar Khayyám, 'busied,' adds the Vizier, 'in winning knowledge of every kind, and especially in Astronomy, wherein he attained to a very high pre-eminence. Under the Sultanate of Malik Shah, he came to Merv, and obtained great praise for his proficiency in science, and the Sultan showered favours upon him.'

"When Malik Shah determined to reform the calendar, Omar was one of the eight learned men employed to do it; the result was the *Jaláli* era (so called from *Jalál-ud-din*, one of the king's names)—'a computation of time,' says Gibbon, 'which surpasses the Julian, and approaches the accuracy of the Gregorian style.' He is also the author of some astronomical tables, entitled Zíji-Maliksh5hí, and the French have lately republished and trans-lated an Arabic Treatise of his on Algebra.

"His Takhallus or poetical name (Khayyám) signifies a Tent-maker, and he is said to have at one time exercised that trade, perhaps before Nizám-ul-Mulk's generosity raised him to inde-pendence. Many Persian poets similarly derive their names from their occupations; thus we have Attár, 'a druggist,' Assár, 'an oil presser,' &c. Omar himself alludes to his name in the fol-lowing whimsical lines:—

> 'Khayyám, who stitched the tents of science,
> Has fallen in grief's furnace and been suddenly burned;
> The shears of Fate have cut the tent ropes of his life,
> And the broker of Hope has sold him for nothing!'

"We have only one more anecdote to give of his Life, and that relates to the close; it is told in the anonymous preface which is sometimes prefixed to his poems; it has been printed in the Persian in the Appendix to Hyde's *Veterum Persarum Religio*, p. 499; and D'Herbelot alludes to it in his Bibliothèque, under *Khiam*:—*

" It is written in the chronicles of the ancients that this King of the Wise, Omar Khayyám, died at Naishápúr in the year of the Hegira, 517 (A.D. 1123); in science he was unrivalled,—the very paragon of his age. Khwájah Nizámi of Samarcand, who was one of his pupils, relates the following story: 'I often used to hold conversations with my teacher, Omar Khayyám, in a garden; and one day he said to me, "My tomb shall be in a spot where the north wind may scatter roses over it." I wondered at the words he spake, but I knew that his were no idle words. Years after, when I chanced to revisit Naishápúr, I went to his final resting-place, and lo! it was just outside a garden, and trees laden with fruit stretched their boughs over the garden wall, and dropped their flowers upon his tomb, so that the stone was hidden under them.' "

Thus far—without fear of Trespass—from the *Calcutta Review*. The writer of it, on reading in India this story of Omar's Grave, was reminded, he says, of Cicero's Account of finding Archimedes' Tomb at Syracuse, buried in grass and weeds. I think Thorwaldsen desired to have roses grow over him; a wish religiously fulfilled for him to the present day, I believe. However, to return to Omar.

Though the Sultan "shower'd Favours upon him," Omar's Epicurean Audacity of Thought and Speech caused him to be regarded askance in his own Time and Country. He is said to have been especially hated and dreaded by the Súfis, whose Practice he ridiculed, and whose Faith amounts to little more than his own, when stript of the Mysticism and formal recognition of Islamism under which Omar would not hide. Their Poets, including Háfiz, who are (with the exception of Firdausi) the most considerable in Persia, borrowed largely, indeed, of

* "Philosophe Musulman qui a vécu en Odeur de Sainteté dans sa Religion, vers la Fin du premier et le Commencement du second Siècle," no part of which, except the "Philosophe," can apply to our Khayyám.

Omar's material, but turning it to a mystical Use more convenient to Themselves and the People they addressed; a People quite
as quick of Doubt as of Belief; as keen of Bodily Sense as of
Intellectual; and delighting in a cloudy composition of both, in
which they could float luxuriously between Heaven and Earth,
and this World and the Next, on the wings of a poetical expression, that might serve indifferently for either. Omar was too
honest of Heart as well as of Head for this. Having failed (however mistakenly) of finding any Providence but Destiny, and any
World but This, he set about making the most of it; preferring
rather to soothe the Soul through the Senses into Acquiescence
with Things as he saw them, than to perplex it with vain disquietude after what they *might* be. It has been seen, however,
that his Worldly Ambition was not exorbitant; and he very likely
takes a humorous or perverse pleasure in exalting the gratification
of Sense above that of the Intellect, in which he must have taken
great delight, although it failed to answer the Questions in which
he, in common with all men, was most vitally interested.

For whatever Reason, however, Omar, as before said, has
never been popular in his own Country, and therefore has been
but scantily transmitted abroad. The MSS. of his Poems, mutilated beyond the average Casualties of Oriental Transcription,
are so rare in the East as scarce to have reacht Westward at all,
in spite of all the acquisitions of Arms and Science. There is no
copy at the India House, none at the Bibliothèque Nationale of
Paris. We know but of one in England: No. 140 of the Ouseley
MSS. at the Bodleian, written at Shiráz, A.D. 1460. This contains
but 158 Rubáiyát. One in the Asiatic Society's Library at Calcutta (of which we have a Copy), contains (and yet incomplete)
516, though swelled to that by all kinds of Repetition and Corruption. So Von Hammer speaks of *his* Copy as containing about
200, while Dr Sprenger catalogues the Lucknow MS. at double
that number. The Scribes, too, of the Oxford and Calcutta
MSS. seem to do their Work under a sort of Protest; each beginning with a Tetrastich (whether genuine or not), taken out of its
alphabetical order; the Oxford with one of Apology; the Calcutta
with one of Expostulation, supposed (says a Notice prefixed to
the MS.) to have arisen from a Dream, in which Omar's mother
asked about his future fate. It may be rendered thus:—

"Oh Thou who burn'st in Heart for those who burn
In Hell, whose fires thyself shall feed in turn;
  How long be crying, 'Mercy on them, God!'
Why, who are Thou to teach, and He to learn?"

The Bodleian Quatrain pleads Pantheism by way of Justification.

"If I myself upon a looser Creed
Have loosely strung the Jewel of Good deed,
  Let this one thing for my Atonement plead:
That One for Two I never did mis-read."

The Reviewer,* to whom I owe the Particulars of Omar's Life, concludes his Review by comparing him with Lucretius, both as to natural Temper and Genius, and as acted upon by the Circumstances in which he lived. Both indeed were men of subtle, strong, and cultivated Intellect, fine Imagination, and Hearts passionate for Truth and Justice; who justly revolted from their Country's false Religion, and false, or foolish, Devotion to it; but who fell short of replacing what they subverted by such better *Hope* as others, with no better Revelation to guide them, had yet made a Law to themselves. Lucretius, indeed, with such material as Epicurus furnished, satisfied himself with the theory of a vast machine fortuitously constructed, and acting by a Law that implied no Legislator; and so composing himself into a Stoical rather than Epicurean severity of Attitude, sat down to contemplate the mechanical Drama of the Universe which he was part Actor in; himself and all about him (as in his own sublime description of the Roman Theatre) discoloured with the lurid reflex of the Curtain suspended between the Spectator and the Sun. Omar, more desperate, or more careless of any so complicated System as resulted in nothing but hopeless Necessity, flung his own Genius and Learning with a bitter or humorous jest into the general Ruin which their insufficient glimpses only served to reveal; and, pretending sensual pleasure as the serious purpose of Life, only *diverted* himself with speculative problems of Deity, Destiny, Matter and Spirit, Good and Evil, and other such questions, easier to start than to run down, and the pursuit of which becomes a very weary sport at last!

* Professor Cowell.

With regard to the present Translation. The original Rubáiyát (as, missing an Arabic Guttural, these *Tetrastichs* are more musically called) are independent Stanzas, consisting each of four Lines of equal, though varied, Prosody; sometimes *all* rhyming, but oftener (as here imitated) the third line a blank. Somewhat as in the Greek Alcaic, where the penultimate line seems to lift and suspend the Wave that falls over in the last. As usual with such kind of Oriental Verse, the Rubáiyát follow one another according to Alphabetic Rhyme—a strange succession of Grave and Gay. Those here selected are strung into something of an Eclogue, with perhaps a less than equal proportion of the "Drink and make-merry," which (genuine or not) recurs over-frequently in the Original. Either way, the Result is sad enough: saddest perhaps when most ostentatiously merry: more apt to move Sorrow than Anger toward the old Tentmaker, who, after vainly endeavouring to unshackle his Steps from Destiny, and to catch some authentic Glimpse of TO-MORROW, fell back upon TO-DAY (which has outlasted so many To-morrows!) as the only Ground he had got to stand upon, however momentarily slipping from under his Feet.

While the second Edition of this version of Omar was preparing, Monsieur Nicolas, French Consul at Resht, published a very careful and very good Edition of the Text, from a lithograph copy at Teheran, comprising 464 Rubáiyát, with translation and notes of his own.

Mons. Nicolas, whose Edition has reminded me of several things, and instructed me in others, does not consider Omar to be the material Epicurean that I have literally taken him for, but a Mystic, shadowing the Deity under the figure of Wine, Winebearer, &c., as Háfiz is supposed to do; in short, a Súfi Poet like Háfiz and the rest.

I cannot see reason to alter my opinion, formed as it was more than a dozen years ago[1] when Omar was first shown me by one to whom I am indebted for all I know of Oriental, and very much of other, literature. He admired Omar's Genius so much, that

[1] [This was written in 1868. W.A.W.

he would gladly have adopted any such Interpretation of his meaning as Mons. Nicolas' if he could. That he could not, appears by his Paper in the Calcutta Review already so largely quoted; in which he argues from the Poems themselves, as well as from what records remain of the Poet's Life.

And if more were needed to disprove Mons. Nicolas' Theory, there is the Biographical Notice which he himself has drawn up in direct contradiction to the Interpretation of the Poems given in his Notes. (See pp. xiii–xiv of his Preface.) Indeed I hardly knew poor Omar was so far gone till his Apologist informed me. For here we see that, whatever were the Wine that Háfiz drank and sang, the veritable Juice of the Grape it was which Omar used, not only when carousing with his friends, but (says Mons. Nicolas) in order to excite himself to that pitch of Devotion which others reached by cries and "hurlemens." And yet, whenever Wine, Wine-bearer, &c. occur in the text—which is often enough—Mons. Nicolas carefully annotates "Dieu," "La Divinité," &c.: so carefully indeed that one is tempted to think that he was indoctrinated by the Súfi with whom he read the Poems. (Note to Rub. ii. p. 8.) A Persian would naturally wish to vindicate a distinguished Countryman; and a Súfi to enrol him in his own sect, which already comprises all the chief Poets of Persia.

What historical Authority has Mons. Nicolas to show that Omar gave himself up "avec passion à l'étude de la philosophie des Soufis"? (Preface, p. xiii.) The Doctrines of Pantheism, Materialism, Necessity, &c., were not peculiar to the Súfi; nor to Lucretius before them; nor to Epicurus before him; probably the very original Irreligion of Thinking men from the first; and very likely to be the spontaneous growth of a Philosopher living in an Age of social and political barbarism, under shadow of one of the Two and Seventy Religions supposed to divide the world. Von Hammer (according to Sprenger's Oriental Catalogue) speaks of Omar as "a Free-thinker, and *a great opponent of Sufism;*" perhaps because, while holding much of their Doctrine, he would not pretend to any inconsistent severity of morals. Sir W. Ouseley has written a note to something of the same effect on the fly-leaf of the Bodleian MS. And in two Rubáiyát of Mons. Nicolas' own Edition Súf and Súfi are both disparagingly named.

234

No doubt many of these Quatrains seem unaccountable unless mystically interpreted; but many more as unaccountable unless literally. Were the Wine spiritual, for instance, how wash the Body with it when dead? Why make cups of the dead clay to be filled with—"La Divinité"—by some succeeding Mystic? Mons. Nicolas himself is puzzled by some "bizarres" and "trop Orientales" allusions and images—"d'une sensualité quelquefois révoltante" indeed—which "les convenances" do not permit him to translate; but still which the reader cannot but refer to "La Divinité." No doubt also many of the Quatrains in the Teheran, as in the Calcutta, Copies, are spurious; such *Rubáiyát* being the common form of Epigram in Persia. But this, at best, tells as much one way as another; nay, the Súfi, who may be considered the Scholar and Man of Letters in Persia, would be far more likely than the careless Epicure to interpolate what favours his own view of the Poet. I observe that very few of the more mystical Quatrains are in the Bodleian MS. which must be one of the oldest, as dated at Shiraz, A.H. 865, A.D. 1460. And this, I think, especially distinguishes Omar (I cannot help calling him by his—no, not Christian—familiar name) from all other Persian Poets: That, whereas with them the Poet is lost in his Song, the Man in Allegory and Abstraction; we seem to have the Man— the *Bonhomme*—Omar himself, with all his Humours and Passions, as frankly before us as if we were really at Table with him, after the Wine had gone round.

I must say that I, for one, never wholly believed in the Mysticism of Háfiz. It does not appear there was any danger in holding and singing Súfi Pantheism, so long as the Poet made his Salaam to Mohammed at the beginning and end of his Song. Under such conditions Jeláluddín, Jámí, Attár, and others sang; using Wine and Beauty indeed as Images to illustrate, not as a Mask to hide, the Divinity they were celebrating. Perhaps some Allegory less liable to mistake or abuse had been better among so inflammable a People: much more so when, as some think with Háfiz and Omar, the abstract is not only likened to, but identified with, the sensual Image; hazardous, if not to the Devotee himself, yet to his weaker Brethren; and worse for the Profane in proportion as the Devotion of the Initiated grew warmer. And all for what? To be tantalized with Images of sensual enjoyment which must be renounced if one would approximate a God, who according to the Doctrine, *is* Sensual Matter as well as Spirit, and into whose Universe one expects unconsciously to merge after Death, without hope of any posthumous Beatitude in another world to compensate for all one's self-denial in this. Lucretius' blind Divinity certainly merited, and probably got, as much self-sacrifice as this of the Súfi; and the burden of Omar's Song—if not "Let us eat"—is assuredly—"Let us drink, for Tomorrow we die!" And if Háfiz meant quite otherwise by a similar language, he surely miscalculated when he devoted his Life and Genius to so equivocal a Psalmody as, from his Day to this, has been said and sung by any rather than Spiritual Worshippers.

However, as there is some traditional presumption, and certainly the opinion of some learned men, in favour of Omar's being a Súfi—and even something of a Saint—those who please may so interpret his Wine and Cup-bearer. On the other hand, as there is far more historical certainty of his being a Philosopher, of scientific Insight and Ability far beyond that of the Age and Country he lived in; of such moderate worldly Ambition as becomes a Philosopher, and such moderate wants as rarely satisfy a Debauchee; other readers may be content to believe with me that, while the Wine Omar celebrates is simply the Juice of the Grape, he bragged more than he drank of it, in very defiance perhaps of that Spiritual Wine which left its Votaries sunk in Hypocrisy or Disgust.

RUBÁIYÁT OF OMAR KHAYYÁM OF NAISHÁPÚR

[FIRST EDITION]

I

AWAKE! for Morning in the Bowl of Night
Has flung the Stone that puts the Stars to Flight:
   And Lo! the Hunter of the East has caught
The Sultán's Turret in a Noose of Light.

II

Dreaming when Dawn's Left Hand was in the Sky
I heard a Voice within the Tavern cry,
   "Awake, my Little ones, and fill the Cup
"Before Life's Liquor in its Cup be dry."

III

And, as the Cock crew, those who stood before
The Tavern shouted—"Open then the Door!
   "You know how little while we have to stay,
"And, once departed, may return no more."

IV

Now the New Year reviving old Desires,
The thoughtful Soul to Solitude retires,
   Where the WHITE HAND OF MOSES on the Bough
Puts out, and Jesus from the Ground suspires.

V

Irám indeed is gone with all its Rose,
And Jamshýd's Sev'n-ring'd Cup where no one knows;
   But still the Vine her ancient Ruby yields,
And still a Garden by the Water blows.

[FOURTH EDITION]

I

WAKE! For the Sun, who scatter'd into flight
The Stars before him from the Field of Night,
 Drives Night along with them from Heav'n, and strikes
The Sultán's Turret with a Shaft of Light.

II

Before the phantom of False morning died,
Methought a Voice within the Tavern cried,
 "When all the Temple is prepared within,
"Why nods the drowsy Worshipper outside?"

III

And, as the Cock crew, those who stood before
The Tavern shouted—"Open then the Door!
 "You know how little while we have to stay,
"And, once departed, may return no more."

IV

Now the New Year reviving old Desires,
The thoughtful Soul to Solitude retires,
 Where the WHITE HAND OF MOSES on the Bough
Puts out, and Jesus from the Ground suspires.

V

Irám indeed is gone with all his Rose,
And Jamshýd's Sev'n-ring'd Cup where no one knows;
 But still a Ruby kindles in the Vine,
And many a Garden by the Water blows.

VI

And David's Lips are lock't; but in divine
High piping Péhlevi, with "Wine! Wine! Wine!
  "*Red* Wine!"—the Nightingale cries to the Rose
That yellow Cheek of her's to'incarnadine.

VII

Come, fill the Cup, and in the Fire of Spring
The Winter Garment of Repentance fling:
  The Bird of Time has but a little way
To fly—and Lo! the Bird is on the Wing.

VIII

And look—a thousand Blossoms with the Day
Woke—and a thousand scatter'd into Clay;
  And this first Summer Month that brings the Rose
Shall take Jamshýd and Kaikobád away.

IX

But come with old Khayyám, and leave the Lot
Of Kaikobád and Kaikhosrú forgot:
  Let Rustum lay about him as he will,
Or Hátim Tai cry Supper—heed them not.

X

With me along some Strip of Herbage strown
That just divides the desert from the sown,
  Where name of Slave and Sultán scarce is known,
And pity Sultán Máhmúd on his Throne.

VI

And David's lips are lockt; but in divine
High-piping Pehleví, with "Wine! Wine! Wine!
  "Red Wine!"—the Nightingale cries to the Rose
That sallow cheek of hers to' incarnadine.

VII

Come, fill the Cup, and in the fire of Spring
Your Winter-garment of Repentance fling:
  The Bird of Time has but a little way
To flutter—and the Bird is on the Wing.

VIII

Whether at Naishápúr or Babylon,
Whether the Cup with sweet or bitter run,
  The Wine of Life keeps oozing drop by drop,
The Leaves of Life keep falling one by one.

IX

Each Morn a thousand Roses brings, you say;
Yes, but where leaves the Rose of Yesterday?
  And this first Summer month that brings the Rose
Shall take Jamshýd and Kaikobád away.

X

Well, let it take them! What have we to do
With Kaikobád the Great, or Kaikhosrú?
  Let Zál and Rustum bluster as they will,
Or Hátim call to Supper—heed not you.

XI

With me along the strip of Herbage strown
That just divides the desert from the sown,
  Where name of Slave and Sultán is forgot—
And Peace to Mahmúd on his golden Throne!

XI

Here with a Loaf of Bread beneath the Bough,
A Flask of Wine, a Book of Verse—and Thou
    Beside me singing in the Wilderness—
And Wilderness is Paradise enow.

XII

"How sweet is mortal Sovranty!"—think some:
Others—"How blest the Paradise to come!"
    Ah, take the Cash in hand and waive the Rest;
Oh, the brave Music of a *distant* Drum!

XIII

Look to the Rose that blows about us—"Lo,
"Laughing," she says, "into the World I blow:
    "At once the silken Tassel of my Purse
    "Tear, and its Treasure on the Garden throw."

XIV

The Worldly Hope men set their Hearts upon
Turns Ashes—or it prospers; and anon,
    Like Snow upon the Desert's dusty Face
Lighting a little Hour or two—is gone.

XV

And those who husbanded the Golden Grain,
And those who flung it to the Winds like Rain,
    Alike to no such aureate Earth are turn'd
As, buried once, Men want dug up again.

XVI

Think, in this batter'd Caravanserai
Whose Doorways are alternate Night and Day,
    How Sultán after Sultán with his Pomp
Abode his Hour or two, and went his way.

XII

A Book of Verses underneath the Bough,
A Jug of Wine, a Loaf of Bread—and Thou
   Beside me singing in the Wilderness—
Oh, Wilderness were Paradise enow!

XIII

Some for the Glories of This World; and some
Sigh for the Prophet's Paradise to come;
   Ah, take the Cash, and let the Credit go,
Nor heed the rumble of a distant Drum!

XIV

Look to the blowing Rose about us—"Lo,
"Laughing," she says, "into the world I blow,
   "At once the silken tassel of my Purse
"Tear, and its Treasure on the Garden throw."

XV

And those who husbanded the Golden grain,
And those who flung it to the winds like Rain,
   Alike to no such aureate Earth are turn'd
As, buried once, Men want dug up again.

XVI

The Worldly Hope men set their Hearts upon
Turns Ashes—or it prospers; and anon,
   Like Snow upon the Desert's dusty Face,
Lighting a little hour or two—is gone.

XVII

Think, in this batter'd Caravanserai
Whose Portals are alternate Night and Day,
   How Sultán after Sultán with his Pomp
Abode his destined Hour, and went his way.

XVII

They say the Lion and the Lizard keep
The Courts where Jamshýd gloried and drank deep;
   And Bahrám, that great Hunter—the Wild Ass
Stamps o'er his Head, and he lies fast asleep.

XVIII

I sometimes think that never blows so red
The Rose as where some buried Cæsar bled;
   That every Hyacinth the Garden wears
Dropt in its Lap from some once lovely Head.

XIX

And this delightful Herb whose tender Green
Fledges the River's Lip on which we lean—
   Ah, lean upon it lightly! for who knows
From what once lovely Lip it springs unseen!

XX

Ah, my Belovéd, fill the Cup that clears
TO-DAY of past Regrets and future Fears—
   To-morrow?—Why, To-morrow I may be
Myself with Yesterday's Sev'n Thousand Years.

XXI

Lo! some we loved, the loveliest and best
That Time and Fate of all their Vintage prest,
   Have drunk their Cup a Round or two before,
And one by one crept silently to Rest.

XXII

And we, that now make merry in the Room
They left, and Summer dresses in new Bloom,
   Ourselves must we beneath the Couch of Earth
Descend, ourselves to make a Couch—for whom?

XVIII

They say the Lion and the Lizard keep
The Courts where Jamshýd gloried and drank deep:
    And Bahrám, that great Hunter—the Wild Ass
Stamps o'er his Head, but cannot break his Sleep.

XIX

I sometimes think that never blows so red
The Rose as where some buried Cæsar bled;
    That every Hyacinth the Garden wears
Dropt in her Lap from some once lovely Head.

XX

And this reviving Herb whose tender Green
Fledges the River-Lip on which we lean—
    Ah, lean upon it lightly! for who knows
From what once lovely Lip it springs unseen!

XXI

Ah, my Belovéd, fill the Cup that clears
TO-DAY of past Regrets and future Fears:
    To-morrow!—Why, To-morrow I may be
Myself with Yesterday's Sev'n thousand Years.

XXII

For some we loved, the loveliest and the best
That from his Vintage rolling Time hath prest,
    Have drunk their Cup a Round or two before,
And one by one crept silently to rest.

XXIII

And we, that now make merry in the Room
They left, and Summer dresses in new bloom,
    Ourselves must we beneath the Couch of Earth
Descend—ourselves to make a Couch—for whom?

XXIII

Ah, make the most of what we yet may spend,
Before we too into the Dust descend;
    Dust into Dust, and under Dust, to lie,
Sans Wine, sans Song, sans Singer, and—sans End!

XXIV

Alike for those who for TO-DAY prepare,
And those that after a TO-MORROW stare,
    A Muezzín from the Tower of Darkness cries
"Fools! your Reward is neither Here nor There!"

XXV

Why, all the Saints and Sages who discuss'd
Of the Two Worlds so learnedly, are thrust
    Like foolish Prophets forth; their Words to Scorn
Are scatter'd, and their Mouths are stopt with Dust.

XXVI

Oh, come with old Khayyám, and leave the Wise
To talk; one thing is certain, that Life flies;
    One thing is certain, and the Rest is Lies;
The Flower that once has blown for ever dies.

XXVII

Myself when young did eagerly frequent
Doctor and Saint, and heard great Argument
    About it and about: but evermore
Came out by the same Door as in I went.

XXVIII

With them the Seed of Wisdom did I sow,
And with my own hand labour'd it to grow:
    And this was all the Harvest that I reap'd—
"I came like Water, and like Wind I go."

XXIV

Ah, make the most of what we yet may spend,
Before we too into the Dust descend;
   Dust into Dust, and under Dust to lie,
Sans Wine, sans Song, sans Singer, and—sans End!

XXV

Alike for those who for TO-DAY prepare,
And those that after some TO-MORROW stare,
   A Muezzín from the Tower of Darkness cries,
"Fools! your Reward is neither Here nor There."

XXVI

Why, all the Saints and Sages who discuss'd
Of the Two Worlds so wisely—they are thrust
   Like foolish Prophets forth; their Words to Scorn
Are scatter'd, and their Mouths are stopt with Dust.

XXVII

Myself when young did eagerly frequent
Doctor and Saint, and heard great argument
   About it and about: but evermore
Came out by the same door where in I went.

XXVIII

With them the seed of Wisdom did I sow,
And with mine own hand wrought to make it grow;
   And this was all the Harvest that I reap'd—
"I came like Water, and like Wind I go."

XXIX

Into this Universe, and *why* not knowing,
Nor *whence*, like Water willy-nilly flowing:
　　And out of it, as Wind along the Waste,
I know not *whither*, willy-nilly blowing.

XXX

What, without asking, hither hurried *whence*?
And, without asking, *whither* hurried hence!
　　Another and another Cup to drown
The Memory of this Impertinence!

XXXI

Up from Earth's Centre through the Seventh Gate
I rose, and on the Throne of Saturn sate,
　　And many Knots unravel'd by the Road;
But not the Knot of Human Death and Fate.

XXXII

There was a Door to which I found no Key:
There was a Veil past which I could not see:
　　Some little Talk awhile of ME and THEE
There seem'd—and then no more of THEE and ME.

XXXIII

Then to the rolling Heav'n itself I cried,
Asking, "What Lamp had Destiny to guide
　　"Her little Children stumbling in the Dark?"
And—"A blind Understanding!" Heav'n replied.

XXIX

Into this Universe, and *Why* not knowing
Nor *Whence*, like Water willy-nilly flowing;
  And out of it, as Wind along the Waste,
I know not *Whither*, willy-nilly blowing.

XXX

What, without asking, hither hurried *Whence*?
And, without asking, *Whither* hurried hence!
  Oh, many a Cup of this forbidden Wine
Must drown the memory of that insolence!

XXXI

Up from Earth's Centre through the Seventh Gate
I rose, and on the Throne of Saturn sate,
  And many a Knot unravel'd by the Road;
But not the Master-knot of Human Fate.

XXXII

There was the Door to which I found no Key;
There was the Veil through which I might not see:
  Some little talk awhile of ME and THEE
There was—and then no more of THEE and ME.

XXXIII

Earth could not answer; nor the Seas that mourn
In flowing Purple, of their Lord forlorn;
  Nor rolling Heaven, with all his Signs reveal'd
And hidden by the sleeve of Night and Morn.

XXXIV

Then of the THEE IN ME who works behind
The Veil, I lifted up my hands to find
  A lamp amid the Darkness; and I heard,
As from Without—"THE ME WITHIN THEE blind!"

XXXIV

Then to this earthen Bowl did I adjourn
My Lip the secret Well of Life to learn:
    And Lip to Lip it murmur'd—"While you live
"Drink!—for once dead you never shall return."

XXXV

I think the Vessel, that with fugitive
Articulation answer'd, once did live,
    And merry-make; and the cold Lip I kiss'd
How many Kisses might it take—and give!

XXXVI

For in the Market-place, one Dusk of Day,
I watch'd the Potter thumping his wet Clay:
    And with its all obliterated Tongue
It murmur'd—"Gently, Brother, gently, pray!"

XXXV

Then to the Lip of this poor earthen Urn
I lean'd, the Secret of my Life to learn:
    And Lip to Lip it murmur'd—"While you live,
"Drink!—for, once dead, you never shall return."

XXXVI

I think the Vessel, that with fugitive
Articulation answer'd, once did live,
    And drink; and Ah! the passive Lip I kiss'd,
How many Kisses might it take—and give!

XXXVII

For I remember stopping by the way
To watch a Potter thumping his wet Clay:
    And with its all-obliterated Tongue
It murmur'd—"Gently, Brother, gently, pray!"

XXXVIII

And has not such a Story from of Old
Down Man's successive generations roll'd
    Of such a clod of saturated Earth
Cast by the Maker into Human mould?

XXXIX

And not a drop that from our Cups we throw
For Earth to drink of, but may steal below
    To quench the fire of Anguish in some Eye
There hidden—far beneath, and long ago.

XL

As then the Tulip for her morning sup
Of Heav'nly Vintage from the soil looks up,
    Do you devoutly do the like, till Heav'n
To Earth invert you—like an empty Cup.

XXXVII

Ah, fill the Cup:—what boots it to repeat
How Time is slipping underneath our Feet:
    Unborn TO-MORROW, and dead YESTERDAY,
Why fret about them if TO-DAY be sweet!

XLI

Perplext no more with Human or Divine,
To-morrow's tangle to the winds resign,
  And lose your fingers in the tresses of
The Cypress-slender Minister of Wine.

XLII

And if the Wine you drink, the Lip you press,
End in what All begins and ends in—Yes;
  Think then you are TO-DAY what YESTERDAY
You were—TO-MORROW you shall not be less.

XLIII

So when that Angel of the darker Drink
At last shall find you by the river-brink,
  And, offering his Cup, invite your Soul
Forth to your Lips to quaff—you shall not shrink.

XLIV

Why, if the Soul can fling the Dust aside,
And naked on the Air of Heaven ride,
  Were't not a Shame—were't not a Shame for him
In this clay carcase crippled to abide?

XLV

'Tis but a Tent where takes his one day's rest
A Sultán to the realm of Death addrest;
  The Sultán rises, and the dark Ferrásh
Strikes, and prepares it for another Guest.

XLVI

And fear not lest Existence closing your
Account, and mine, should know the like no more;
  The Eternal Sákí from that Bowl has pour'd
Millions of Bubbles like us, and will pour.

XXXVIII

One Moment in Annihilation's Waste,
One Moment, of the Well of Life to taste—
The Stars are setting and the Caravan
Starts for the Dawn of Nothing—Oh, make haste!

XLVII

When You and I behind the Veil are past,
Oh, but the long, long while the World shall last,
  Which of our Coming and Departure heeds
As the Sea's self should heed a pebble-cast.

XLVIII

A Moment's Halt—a momentary taste
Of BEING from the Well amid the Waste—
  And Lo!—the phantom Caravan has reach'd
The NOTHING it set out from—Oh, make haste!

XLIX

Would you that spangle of Existence spend
About THE SECRET—quick about it, Friend!
  A Hair perhaps divides the False and True—
And upon what, prithee, may life depend?

L

A Hair perhaps divides the False and True;
Yes; and a single Alif were the clue—
  Could you but find it—to the Treasure-house,
And peradventure to THE MASTER too;

LI

Whose secret Presence, through Creation's veins
Running Quicksilver-like eludes your pains;
  Taking all shapes from Máh to Máhi; and
They change and perish all—but He remains;

LII

A moment guess'd—then back behind the Fold
Immerst of Darkness round the Drama roll'd
  Which, for the Pastime of Eternity,
He doth Himself contrive, enact, behold.

XXXIX

How long, how long, in infinite Pursuit
Of This and That endeavour and dispute?
　Better be merry with the fruitful Grape
Than sadden after none, or bitter, Fruit.

XL

You know, my Friends, how long since in my House
For a new Marriage I did make Carouse:
　Divorced old barren Reason from my Bed,
And took the Daughter of the Vine to Spouse.

XLI

For "Is" and "Is-not" though *with* Rule and Line,
And "Up-and-down" *without*, I could define,
　I yet in all I only cared to know,
Was never deep in anything but—Wine.

XLII

And lately, by the Tavern Door agape,
Came stealing through the Dusk an Angel Shape
　Bearing a Vessel on his Shoulder; and
He bid me taste of it; and 'twas—the Grape!

LIII

But if in vain, down on the stubborn floor
Of Earth, and up to Heav'n's unopening Door,
   You gaze TO-DAY, while You are You—how then
TO-MORROW, You when shall be You no more?

LIV

Waste not your Hour, nor in the vain pursuit
Of This and That endeavour and dispute;
   Better be jocund with the fruitful Grape
Than sadden after none, or bitter, Fruit.

LV

You know, my Friends, with what a brave Carouse
I made a Second Marriage in my house;
   Divorced old barren Reason from my Bed,
And took the Daughter of the Vine to Spouse.

LVI

For "Is" and "Is-NOT" though with Rule and Line
And "UP-AND-DOWN" by Logic I define,
   Of all that one should care to fathom, I
Was never deep in anything but—Wine.

LVII

Ah, but my Computations, People say,
Reduced the Year to better reckoning?—Nay,
   'Twas only striking from the Calendar
Unborn To-morrow, and dead Yesterday.

LVIII

And lately, by the Tavern Door agape,
Came shining through the Dusk an Angel Shape
   Bearing a Vessel on his Shoulder; and
He bid me taste of it; and 'twas—the Grape!

I

XLIII

The Grape that can with Logic absolute
The Two-and-Seventy jarring Sects confute:
    The subtle Alchemist that in a Trice
Life's leaden Metal into Gold transmute.

XLIV

The mighty Mahmúd, the victorious Lord,
That all the misbelieving and black Horde
    Of Fears and Sorrows that infest the Soul
Scatters and slays with his enchanted Sword.

XLV

But leave the Wise to wrangle, and with me
The Quarrel of the Universe let be:
    And, in some corner of the Hubbub coucht,
Make Game of that which makes as much of Thee.

LIX

The Grape that can with Logic absolute
The Two-and-Seventy jarring Sects confute:
  The sovereign Alchemist that in a trice
Life's leaden metal into Gold transmute:

LX

The mighty Mahmúd, Allah-breathing Lord,
That all the misbelieving and black Horde
  Of Fears and Sorrows that infest the Soul
Scatters before him with his whirlwind Sword.

LXI

Why, be this Juice the growth of God, who dare
Blaspheme the twisted tendril as a Snare?
  A Blessing, we should use it, should we not?
And if a Curse—why, then, Who set it there?

LXII

I must abjure the Balm of Life, I must,
Scared by some After-reckoning ta'en on trust,
  Or lured with Hope of some Diviner Drink,
To fill the Cup—when crumbled into Dust!

LXIII

Oh threats of Hell and Hopes of Paradise!
One thing at least is certain—*This* Life flies;
  One thing is certain and the rest is Lies;
The Flower that once has blown for ever dies.

LXIV

Strange, is it not? that of the myriads who
Before us pass'd the door of Darkness through,
  Not one returns to tell us of the Road,
Which to discover we must travel too.

XLVI

For in and out, above, about, below,
'Tis nothing but a Magic Shadow-show,
   Play'd in a Box whose Candle is the Sun,
Round which we Phantom Figures come and go.

XLVII

And if the Wine you drink, the Lip you press,
End in the Nothing all Things end in—Yes—
   Then fancy while Thou art, Thou art but what
Thou shalt be—Nothing—Thou shalt not be less.

XLVIII

While the Rose blows along the River Brink,
With old Khayyám the Ruby Vintage drink:
   And when the Angel with his darker Draught
Draws up to Thee—take that, and do not shrink.

XLIX

'Tis all a Chequer-board of Nights and Days
Where Destiny with Men for Pieces plays:
   Hither and thither moves, and mates, and slays,
And one by one back in the Closet lays.

L

The Ball no Question makes of Ayes and Noes,
But Right or Left, as strikes the Player goes;
   And He that toss'd Thee down into the Field,
He knows about it all—HE knows—HE knows!

LXV

The Revelations of Devout and Learn'd
Who rose before us, and as Prophets burn'd,
    Are all but Stories, which, awoke from Sleep
They told their comrades, and to Sleep return'd.

LXVI

I sent my Soul through the Invisible,
Some letter of that After-life to spell:
    And by and by my Soul return'd to me,
And answer'd "I Myself am Heav'n and Hell:"

LXVII

Heav'n but the Vision of fulfill'd Desire,
And Hell the Shadow from a Soul on fire,
    Cast on the Darkness into which Ourselves,
So late emerged from, shall so soon expire.

LXVIII

We are no other than a moving row
Of Magic Shadow-shapes that come and go
    Round with the Sun-illumined Lantern held
In Midnight by the Master of the Show;

LXIX

But helpless Pieces of the Game He plays
Upon this Chequer-board of Nights and Days;
    Hither and thither moves, and checks, and slays,
And one by one back in the Closet lays.

LXX

The Ball no question makes of Ayes and Noes,
But Here or There as strikes the Player goes;
    And He that toss'd you down into the Field,
He knows about it all—HE knows—HE knows!

LI

The Moving Finger writes; and, having writ,
Moves on: nor all thy Piety nor Wit
    Shall lure it back to cancel half a Line,
Nor all thy Tears wash out a Word of it.

LII

And that inverted Bowl we call The Sky,
Whereunder crawling coop't we live and die,
    Lift not thy hands to *It* for help—for It
Rolls impotently on as Thou or I.

LIII

With Earth's first Clay They did the Last Man's knead,
And then of the Last Harvest sow'd the Seed:
    Yea, the first Morning of Creation wrote
What the Last Dawn of Reckoning shall read.

LIV

I tell Thee this—When, starting from the Goal,
Over the shoulders of the flaming Foal
    Of Heav'n Parwín and Mushtara they flung,
In my predestin'd Plot of Dust and Soul

LV

The Vine had struck a Fibre; which about
If clings my Being—let the Súfi flout;
    Of my Base Metal may be filed a Key,
That shall unlock the Door he howls without.

LXXI

The Moving Finger writes; and, having writ,
Moves on: nor all your Piety nor Wit
  Shall lure it back to cancel half a Line,
Nor all your Tears wash out a Word of it.

LXXII

And that inverted Bowl they call the Sky,
Whereunder crawling coop'd we live and die,
  Lift not your hands to *It* for help—for It
As impotently moves as you or I.

LXXIII

With Earth's first Clay They did the Last Man knead,
And there of the Last Harvest sow'd the Seed:
  And the first Morning of Creation wrote
What the Last Dawn of Reckoning shall read.

LXXIV

YESTERDAY *This* Day's Madness did prepare;
TO-MORROW'S Silence, Triumph, or Despair:
  Drink! for you know not whence you came, nor why:
Drink! for you know not why you go, nor where.

LXXV

I tell you this—When, started from the Goal,
Over the flaming shoulders of the Foal
  Of Heav'n, Parwín and Mushtarí they flung,
In my predestined Plot of Dust and Soul.

LXXVI

The Vine had struck a fibre: which about
If clings my Being—let the Dervish flout;
  Of my Base metal may be filed a Key,
That shall unlock the Door he howls without.

LVI

And this I know: whether the one True Light,
Kindle to Love, or Wrath consume me quite,
   One Glimpse of It within the Tavern caught
Better than in the Temple lost outright.

LVII

Oh Thou, who didst with Pitfall and with Gin
Beset the Road I was to wander in,
   Thou wilt not with Predestination round
Enmesh me, and impute my Fall to Sin?

LVIII

Oh, Thou, who Man of baser Earth didst make,
And who with Eden didst devise the Snake;
   For all the Sin wherewith the Face of Man
Is blacken'd, Man's Forgiveness give—and take!

*   *   *

LXXVII

And this I know: whether the one True Light
Kindle to Love, or Wrath consume me quite,
  One Flash of It within the Tavern caught
Better than in the Temple lost outright.

LXXVIII

What! out of senseless Nothing to provoke
A conscious Something to resent the yoke
  Of unpermitted Pleasure, under pain
Of Everlasting Penalties, if broke!

LXXIX

What! from his helpless Creature be repaid
Pure Gold for what he lent him dross-allay'd—
  Sue for a Debt he never did contract,
And cannot answer—Oh the sorry trade!

LXXX

Oh Thou, who didst with pitfall and with gin
Beset the Road I was to wander in,
  Thou wilt not with Predestined Evil round
Enmesh, and then impute my Fall to Sin!

LXXXI

Oh Thou, who Man of baser Earth didst make,
And ev'n with Paradise devise the Snake:
  For all the Sin wherewith the Face of Man
Is blacken'd—Man's forgiveness give—and take!

*   *   *

KÚZA-NÁMA

LIX

Listen again. One Evening at the Close
Of Ramazán, ere the better Moon arose,
  In that old Potter's Shop I stood alone
With the clay Population round in Rows.

LX

And, strange to tell, among that Earthen Lot
Some could articulate, while others not:
  And suddenly one more impatient cried—
"Who *is* the Potter, pray, and who the Pot?"

LXI

Then said another—"Surely not in vain
"My Substance from the common Earth was ta'en,
  "That He who subtly wrought me into Shape
"Should stamp me back to common Earth again."

LXII

Another said—"Why, ne'er a peevish Boy,
"Would break the Bowl from which he drank in Joy;
  "Shall He that *made* the Vessel in pure Love
"And Fansy, in an after Rage destroy!"

LXIII

None answer'd this; but after Silence spake
A Vessel of a more ungainly Make:
  "They sneer at me for leaning all awry;
"What! did the Hand then of the Potter shake?"

LXXXII

As under cover of departing Day
Slunk hunger-stricken Ramazán away,
  Once more within the Potter's house alone
I stood, surrounded by the Shapes of Clay.

LXXXIII

Shapes of all Sorts and Sizes, great and small,
That stood along the floor and by the wall;
  And some loquacious Vessels were; and some
Listen'd perhaps, but never talk'd at all.

LXXXIV

Said one among them—"Surely not in vain
"My substance of the common Earth was ta'en
  "And to this Figure moulded, to be broke,
"Or trampled back to shapeless Earth again."

LXXXV

Then said a Second—"Ne'er a peevish Boy
"Would break the Bowl from which he drank in joy;
  "And He that with his hand the Vessel made
"Will surely not in after Wrath destroy."

LXXXVI

After a momentary silence spake
Some Vessel of a more ungainly Make;
  "They sneer at me for leaning all awry:
"What! did the Hand then of the Potter shake?"

LXIV

Said one—"Folks of a surly Tapster tell,
"And daub his Visage with the Smoke of Hell;
   "They talk of some strict Testing of us—Pish!
"He's a Good Fellow, and 'twill all be well."

LXV

Then said another with a long-drawn Sigh,
"My Clay with long oblivion is gone dry:
   "But, fill me with the old familiar Juice,
"Methinks I might recover by-and-bye!"

LXVI

So while the Vessels one by one were speaking,
One spied the little Crescent all were seeking:
   And then they jogg'd each other, "Brother! Brother!
"Hark to the Porter's Shoulder-knot a-creaking!"

*   *   *

LXVII

Ah, with the Grape my fading Life provide,
And wash my Body whence the Life has died,
   And in a Windingsheet of Vine-leaf wrapt,
So bury me by some sweet Garden-side.

LXVIII

That ev'n my buried Ashes such a Snare
Of Perfume shall fling up into the Air,
   As not a True Believer passing by
But shall be overtaken unaware.

LXXXVII

Whereat some one of the loquacious Lot—
I think a Súfi pipkin—waxing hot—
 "All this of Pot and Potter—Tell me then,
"Who is the Potter, pray, and who the Pot?"

LXXXVIII

"Why," said another, "Some there are who tell
"Of one who threatens he will toss to Hell
 "The luckless Pots he marr'd in making—Pish!
"He's a Good Fellow, and 't will all be well."

LXXXIX

"Well," murmur'd one, "Let whoso make or buy,
"My Clay with long Oblivion is gone dry:
 "But fill me with the old familiar Juice,
"Methinks I might recover by and by."

XC

So while the Vessels one by one were speaking,
The little Moon look'd in that all were seeking:
 And then they jogg'd each other, "Brother! Brother!
"Now for the Porter's shoulder-knot a-creaking!"

   *   *   *

XCI

Ah, with the Grape my fading Life provide,
And wash the Body whence the Life has died,
 And lay me, shrouded in the living Leaf,
By some not unfrequented Garden-side.

XCII

That ev'n my buried Ashes such a snare
Of Vintage shall fling up into the Air
 As not a True-believer passing by
But shall be overtaken unaware.

LXIX

Indeed the Idols I have loved so long
Have done my Credit in Men's Eye much wrong:
    Have drown'd my Honour in a shallow Cup,
And sold my Reputation for a Song.

LXX

Indeed, indeed, Repentance oft before
I swore—but was I sober when I swore?
    And then and then came Spring, and Rose-in-hand
My thread-bare Penitence apieces tore.

LXXI

And much as Wine has play'd the Infidel,
And robb'd me of my Robe of Honour—well,
    I often wonder what the Vintners buy
One half so precious as the Goods they sell.

LXXII

Alas, that Spring should vanish with the Rose!
That Youth's sweet-scented Manuscript should close!
    The Nightingale that in the Branches sang,
Ah, whence, and whither flown again, who knows!

XCIII

Indeed the Idols I have loved so long
Have done my credit in this World much wrong:
  Have drown'd my Glory in a shallow Cup,
And sold my Reputation for a Song.

XCIV

Indeed, indeed, Repentance oft before
I swore—but was I sober when I swore?
  And then and then came Spring, and Rose-in-hand
My thread-bare Penitence apieces tore.

XCV

And much as Wine has play'd the Infidel,
And robb'd me of my Robe of Honour—Well,
  I wonder often what the Vintners buy
One half so precious as the stuff they sell.

XCVI

Yet Ah, that Spring should vanish with the Rose!
That Youth's sweet-scented manuscript should close!
  The Nightingale that in the branches sang,
Ah whence, and whither flown again, who knows!

XCVII

Would but the Desert of the Fountain yield
One glimpse—if dimly, yet indeed, reveal'd,
  To which the fainting Traveller might spring,
As springs the trampled herbage of the field!

XCVIII

Would but some wingéd Angel ere too late
Arrest the yet unfolded Roll of Fate,
  And make the stern Recorder otherwise
Enregister, or quite obliterate!

LXXIII

Ah Love! could thou and I with Fate conspire
To grasp this sorry Scheme of Things entire,
  Would not we shatter it to bits—and then
Re-mould it nearer to the Heart's Desire!

LXXIV

Ah, Moon of my Delight who know'st no wane,
The Moon of Heav'n is rising once again:
  How oft hereafter rising shall she look
Through this same Garden after me—in vain!

LXXV

And when Thyself with shining Foot shall pass
Among the Guests Star-scatter'd on the Grass,
  And in thy joyous Errand reach the Spot
Where I made one—turn down an empty Glass!

TAMÁM SHUD

XCIX

Ah Love! could you and I with Him conspire
To grasp this sorry Scheme of Things entire,
    Would not we shatter it to bits—and then
Re-mould it nearer to the Heart's Desire!

*   *   *

C

Yon rising Moon that looks for us again—
How oft hereafter will she wax and wane;
    How oft hereafter rising look for us
Through this same Garden—and for *one* in vain!

CI

And when like her, oh Sákí, you shall pass
Among the Guests Star-scatter'd on the Grass,
    And in your joyous errand reach the spot
Where I made One—turn down an empty Glass!

TAMÁM

BIRD-PARLIAMENT

[FitzGerald began this translation of Attar's *Mantik ut-tair* in 1856 and had completed most of it in 1857, but it was not published until Aldis Wright included it in the first edition of *Letters and Literary Remains* in 1889.]

BIRD-PARLIAMENT

ONCE on a time from all the Circles seven
Between the stedfast Earth and rolling Heaven
THE BIRDS, of all Note, Plumage, and Degree,
That float in Air, and roost upon the Tree;
And they that from the Waters snatch their Meat,
And they that scour the Desert with long Feet;
Birds of all Natures, known or not to Man,
Flock'd from all Quarters into full Divan,
On no less solemn business than to find
Or choose, a Sultan Khalif of their kind,
For whom, if never their's, or lost, they pined.
The Snake had his, 'twas said; and so the Beast
His Lion-lord: and Man had his, at least:
And that the Birds, who nearest were the Skies,
And went apparell'd in its Angel Dyes,
Should be without—under no better Law
Than that which lost all other in the Maw—
Disperst without a Bond of Union—nay,
Or meeting to make each the other's Prey—
This was the Grievance—this the solemn Thing
On which the scatter'd Commonwealth of Wing,
From all the four Winds, flying like to Cloud
That met and blacken'd Heav'n, and Thunder-loud
With Sound of whirring Wings and Beaks that clash'd
Down like a Torrent on the Desert dash'd:
Till by Degrees, the Hubbub and Pell-mell
Into some Order and Precedence fell,
And, Proclamation made of Silence, each
In special Accent, but in general Speech

That all should understand, as seem'd him best,
The Congregation of all Wings addrest.

And first, with Heart so full as from his Eyes
Ran weeping, up rose Tájidár* the Wise;
The mystic Mark upon whose Bosom show'd
That He alone of all the Birds THE ROAD
Had travell'd: and the Crown upon his Head
Had reach'd the Goal; and He stood forth and said:

"Oh Birds, by what Authority divine
I speak you know by *His* authentic Sign,
And Name, emblazon'd on my Breast and Bill:
Whose Counsel I assist at, and fulfil:
At His Behest I measured as he plann'd
The Spaces of the Air and Sea and Land;
I gauged the secret sources of the Springs
From Cloud to Fish:† the Shadow of my Wings
Dream'd over sleeping Deluge: piloted
The Blast that bore Sulayman's Throne: and led
The Cloud of Birds that canopied his Head;
Whose Word I brought to Balkis: and I shared
The Counsel that with Ásaf he prepared.
And now *you* want a Khalif: and I know
Him, and his whereabout, and How to go:
And go alone I could, and plead your cause
Alone for all: but, by the eternal laws,
Yourselves by Toil and Travel of your own
Must for your old Delinquency atone.
Were you indeed not blinded by the Curse
Of Self-exile, that still grows worse and worse,
Yourselves would know that, though *you* see him not,
He *is* with you this Moment, on this Spot,
Your Lord through all Forgetfulness and Crime,

---

* *Tájidár*—"*Crown-wearer*"—one Epithet of the "*Hudhud*," a beautiful kind of Lapwing, Niebuhr says, frequenting the Shores of the Persian Gulf, and supposed to have the Gift of Speech &c.

† From Máh, the Moon, to Máhi, the Fish, on which the World was fabled to repose.

Here, There, and Everywhere, and through all Time.
But as a Father, whom some wayward Child
By sinful Self-will has unreconciled,
Waits till the sullen Reprobate at cost
Of long Repentance should regain the Lost;
Therefore, yourselves to see as you are seen,
Yourselves must bridge the Gulf you made between
By such a Search and Travel to be gone
Up to the mighty mountain Káf, whereon
Hinges the World, and round about whose Knees
Into one Ocean mingle the Sev'n Seas;
In whose impenetrable Forest-folds
Of Light and Dark 'Sýmurgh'* his Presence holds;
Not to be reach'd, if to be reach'd at all
But by a Road the stoutest might apal;
Of Travel not of Days or Months, but Years—
Life-long perhaps: of Dangers, Doubts, and Fears
As yet unheard of: Sweat of Blood and Brain
Interminable—often all in vain—
And, if successful, no Return again:
'A Road whose very Preparation scared
The Traveller who yet must be prepared.
Who then this Travel to Result would bring
Needs both a Lion's Heart beneath the Wing,
And even more, a Spirit purified
Of Worldly Passion, Malice, Lust, and Pride:
Yea, ev'n of Worldly *Wisdom*, which grows dim
And dark, the nearer it approaches *Him*,
Who to the Spirit's Eye alone reveal'd,
By sacrifice of Wisdom's self unseal'd;
Without which none who reach the Place could bear
To look upon the Glory dwelling there."

———

One Night from out the swarming City Gate
Stept holy Bajazyd, to meditate

* Sýmurgh—i.e. "Thirty-Birds"—a fabulous Creature like the Griffin of our Middle Ages: the Arabian *Anka*.

Alone amid the breathing Fields that lay
In solitary Silence leagues away,
Beneath a Moon and Stars as bright as Day.
And the Saint wondering such a Temple were,
And so lit up, and scarce one worshipper,
A voice from Heav'n amid the stillness said;
"The Royal Road is not for all to tread,
Nor is the Royal Palace for the Rout,
Who, even if they reach it, are shut out.
The Blaze that from my Harím window breaks
With fright the Rabble of the Roadside takes;
And ev'n of those that at my Portal din,
Thousands may knock for one that enters in."

Thus spoke the Tájidár: and the wing'd Crowd,
That underneath his Word in Silence bow'd,
Clapp'd Acclamation: and their Hearts and Eyes
Were kindled by the Firebrand of the Wise.
They felt their Degradation: they believed
The word that told them how to be retrieved,
And in that glorious Consummation won
Forgot the Cost at which it must be done.
"They only *long'd* to follow: they would go
Whither he led, through Flood, or Fire, or Snow"—
So cried the Multitude. But some there were
Who listen'd with a cold disdainful air,
Content with what they were, or grudging Cost
Of Time or Travel that might all be lost;
These, one by one, came forward, and preferr'd
Unwise Objection: which the wiser Word
Shot with direct Reproof, or subtly round
With Argument and Allegory wound.

The Pheasant first would know by what pretence
The Tájidár to that pre-eminence
Was raised—a Bird, but for his lofty Crest
(And such the Pheasant had) like all the Rest—

Who answer'd—"By no Virtue of my own
Sulayman chose me, but by *His* alone:
Not by the Gold and Silver of my Sighs
Made mine, but the free Largess of his Eyes.
Behold the Grace of Allah comes and goes
As to Itself is good: and no one knows
Which way it turns: in that mysterious Court
Not he most finds who furthest travels for't.
For one may crawl upon his knees Life-long,
And yet may never reach, or all go wrong:
Another just arriving at the Place
He toil'd for, and—the Door shut in his Face:
Whereas Another, scarcely gone a Stride,
And suddenly—Behold he is Inside!—
But though the Runner win not, he that *stands*,
No Thorn will turn to Roses in *his* Hands:
Each one must do his best and all endure,
And all endeavour, hoping but not sure.
Heav'n its own Umpire is; its Bidding do,
And Thou perchance shalt be Sulayman's too."

————————

One day Shah Mahmúd, riding with the Wind
A-hunting, left his Retinue behind,
And coming to a River, whose swift Course
Doubled back Game and Dog, and Man and Horse,
Beheld upon the Shore a little Lad
A-fishing, very poor, and Tatter-clad
He was, and weeping as his Heart would break.
So the Great Sultan, for good humour's sake
Pull'd in his Horse a moment, and drew nigh,
And after making his Salám, ask'd why
He wept—weeping, the Sultan said, so sore
As he had never seen one weep before.
The Boy look'd up, and "Oh Amír," he said,
"Sev'n of us are at home, and Father dead,
And Mother left with scarce a Bit of Bread:
And now since Sunrise have I fish'd—and see!

281

Caught nothing for our Supper—Woe is Me!"
The Sultan lighted from his Horse. "Behold,"
Said he, "Good Fortune will not be controll'd:
And, since To-day yours seems to turn from you,
Suppose we try for once what mine will do,
And we will share alike in all I win."
So the Shah took, and flung his Fortune in,
The Net; which, cast by the Great Mahmúd's Hand,
A hundred glittering Fishes brought to Land.
The Lad look'd up in Wonder—Mahmúd smiled
And vaulted into Saddle. But the Child
Ran after—"Nay, Amír, but half the Haul
Is yours by Bargain"—"Nay, To-day take all,"
The Sultan cried, and shook his Bridle free—
"But mind—To-morrow All belongs to Me—"
And so rode off. Next morning at Divan
The Sultan's Mind upon his Bargain ran,
And being somewhat in a mind for sport
Sent for the Lad: who, carried up to Court,
And marching into Royalty's full Blaze
With such a Catch of Fish as yesterday's,
The Sultan call'd and set him by his side,
And asking him, "What Luck?" The Boy replied,
This is the Luck that follows every Cast,
Since o'er my Net the Sultan's Shadow pass'd."

———

Then came *The Nightingale*, from such a Draught
Of Ecstasy that from the Rose he quaff'd
Reeling as drunk, and ever did distil
In exquisite Divisions from his Bill
To inflame the Hearts of Men—and thus sang He—
"To me alone, alone, is giv'n the Key
Of Love; of whose whole Mystery possesst,
When I reveal a little to the Rest,
Forthwith Creation listening forsakes
The Reins of Reason, and my Frenzy takes:
Yea, whosoever once has quaff'd this wine

He leaves unlisten'd David's Song for mine.
In vain do Men for my Divisions strive,
And die themselves making dead Lutes alive:
I hang the Stars with Meshes for Men's Souls:
The Garden underneath my Music rolls.
The long, long Morns that mourn the Rose away
I sit in silence, and on Anguish prey:
But the first Air which the New Year shall breathe
Up to my Boughs of Message from beneath
That in her green Harím my Bride unveils,
My Throat bursts silence and *her* Advent hails,
Who in her crimson Volume registers
The Notes of Him whose Life is lost in hers.*
The Rose I love and worship now is here;
If dying, yet reviving, Year by Year;
But that you tell of, all my Life why waste
In vainly searching; or, if found, not taste?"

So with Division infinite and Trill
On would the Nightingale have warbled still,
And all the World have listen'd; but a Note
Of sterner Import check'd the love-sick Throat.

"Oh watering with thy melodious Tears
Love's Garden, and who dost indeed the Ears
Of men with thy melodious Fingers mould
As David's Finger Iron did of old:†
Why not, like David, dedicate thy Dower
Of Song to something better than a Flower?
Empress indeed of Beauty, so they say,
But one whose Empire hardly lasts a Day,
By Insurrection of the Morning's Breath
That made her hurried to Decay and Death:
And while she lasts contented to be seen,
And worshipt, for the Garden's only Queen,

---

* It was sometimes fancied that the Rose had as many Petals as her Lover
had Notes in his Voice.
† The Prophet David was supposed, in Oriental Legend, to have had the
power to mould Iron into a Cuirass with the miraculous Power of his Finger.

Leaving thee singing on thy Bough forlorn,
Or if she smile on Thee, perhaps in Scorn."

———————

Like that fond Dervish waiting in the throng
When some World-famous Beauty went along,
Who smiling on the Antic as she pass'd—
Forthwith Staff, Bead and Scrip away he cast,
And grovelling in the Kennel, took to whine
Before her Door among the Dogs and Swine.
Which when she often went unheeding by,
But one day quite as heedless ask'd him—"Why?"—
He told of that one Smile, which, all the Rest
Passing, had kindled Hope within his Breast—
Again she smiled and said, "Oh self-beguiled
Poor Wretch, *at* whom and not *on* whom I smiled."

———————

Then came the subtle *Parrot* in a coat
Greener than Greensward, and about his Throat
A Collar ran of sub-sulphureous Gold;
And in his Beak a Sugar-plum he troll'd,
That all his Words with luscious Lisping ran,
And to this Tune—"Oh cruel Cage, and Man
More iron still who did confine me there,
Who else with him* whose Livery I wear
Ere this to his Eternal Fount had been,
And drunk what should have kept me ever-green.
But now I know the Place, and I am free
To go, and all the Wise will follow Me.
Some"—and upon the Nightingale one Eye
He leer'd—"for nothing but the Blossom sigh:
But I am for the luscious Pulp that grows
Where, and for which the Blossom only blows:
And which so long as the Green Tree provides

* Khizar, Prophet and Keeper of the Well of Life; habited always in the
Green which the Angels were supposed to wear; and, whether from that
reason, or some peculiar Phenomenon in the Air, constantly called Sky-
colour by the Persian Poets.

What better grows along Káf's dreary Sides?
And what more needful Prophet *there* than He
Who gives me Life to nip it from the Tree?"

To whom the Tájidár—"Oh thou whose Best
In the green leaf of Paradise is drest,
But whose Neck kindles with a lower Fire—
Oh slip the collar off of base Desire,
And stand apparell'd in Heav'n's Woof entire!*
This Life that hangs so sweet about your Lips
But, spite of all your Khizar, slips and slips,
What is it but itself the coarser Rind
Of the True Life withinside and behind,
Which he shall never never reach unto
Till the gross Shell of Carcase he break through?"

For what said He, that dying Hermit, whom
Your Prophet came to, trailing through the Gloom
His Emerald Vest, and tempted—"Come with Me,
And Live." The Hermit answered—"Not with Thee.
Two Worlds there are, and *This* was thy Design,
And thou hast got it; but *The Next* is mine;
Whose Fount is *this* life's Death, and to whose Side
Ev'n now I find my Way without a Guide."

Then like a Sultan glittering in all Rays
Of Jewelry, and deckt with his own Blaze,
The glorious *Peacock* swept into the Ring:

* The Sky is constantly called *Green* in Persian Poetry: whether because of the Tree of Heaven *Sidra*: or of some fabled Emerald in Káf on which the World hinges: or because Green has been chosen (for whatever Reason) for the Colour of *Life* and Honour. The green tinge of some Oriental Skies is indeed noticed by Travellers: as we see a little also in our Northern Sunrise and Sunset: but still it must be an exceptional Phenomenon. *Blue*, or *Purple*, is rather devoted to Death and Mourning in the East. As, in this very Poem, one of the Stories is of the Sea being askt "why he dresses his Waves in Blue?"—And he answers he does so for the Loss of *One* who never will return.

And, turning slowly that the glorious Thing
Might fill all Eyes with wonder, thus said He.
"Behold, the Secret Artist, making me,
With no one Colour of the skies bedeckt,
But from its Angel's Feathers did select
To make up mine withal, the Gabriel
Of all the Birds: though from my Place I fell
In Eden, when Acquaintance I did make
In those blest Days with that Sev'n-headed Snake,*
And thence with him, my perfect Beauty marr'd
With these ill Feet, was thrust out and debarr'd.
Little I care for Worldly Fruit or Flower,
Would you restore me to lost Eden's Bower,
But first my Beauty making all complete
With reparation of these ugly Feet."

"Were it," 'twas answer'd, "only to return
To that lost Eden, better far to burn
In Self-abasement up thy pluméd Pride,
And ev'n with lamer feet to creep inside—
But all mistaken you and all like you
That long for that lost Eden as the true;
Fair as it was, still nothing but the Shade
And Out-court of the Majesty that made.
That which I point you tow'rd, and which the King
I tell you of broods over with his Wing,
With no deciduous leaf, but with the Rose
Of Spiritual Beauty, smells and glows:
No plot of Earthly Pleasance, but the whole
True Garden of the Universal Soul."

———————

For so Creation's Master-Jewel fell
From that same Eden: loving which too well,
The Work before the Artist did prefer,
And in the Garden lost the Gardener.
Wherefore one Day about the Garden went

* And, as the Tradition went, let the Snake into Eden.

A voice that found him in his false Content,
And like a bitter Sarsar of the North*
Shrivell'd the Garden up, and drove him forth
Into the Wilderness: and so the Eye
Of Eden closed on him till by and by.

Then from a Ruin where conceal'd he lay
Watching his buried Gold, and hating Day,
Hooted *The Owl.*—"I tell you, my Delight
Is in the Ruin and the Dead of Night
Where I was born, and where I love to wone
All my Life long, sitting on some cold stone
Away from all your roystering Companies,
In some dark Corner where a Treasure lies;
That, buried by some Miser in the Dark,
Speaks up to me at Midnight like a Spark;
And o'er it like a Talisman I brood,
Companion of the Serpent and the Toad.
What need of other Sovereign, having found,
And keeping as in Prison underground,
One before whom all other Kings bow down,
And with his glittering Heel their Foreheads crown?"

"He that a Miser lives and Miser dies,
At the Last Day what Figure shall he rise?"

A Fellow all his life lived hoarding Gold,
And, dying, hoarded left it. And behold,
One Night his Son saw peering through the House
A Man, with yet the semblance of a Mouse,
Watching a crevice in the Wall—and cried—
"My Father?"—"Yes," the Musulman replied,
"Thy Father!"—"But why watching thus?"—"For fear
Lest any smell my Treasure buried here."

* Sarsar—a cold Blast.

"But wherefore, Sir, so metamousified?"
"Because, my Son, such is the true outside
Of the inner Soul by which I lived and died."

"Aye," said *The Partridge*, with his Foot and Bill
Crimson with raking Rubies from the Hill,
And clattering his Spurs—"Wherewith the Ground
I stab," said he, "for Rubies, that, when found
I swallow; which, as soon as swallow'd, turn
To Sparks which through my beak and eyes do burn.
Gold, as you say, is but dull Metal dead,
And hanging on the Hoarder's Soul like Lead:
But Rubies that have Blood within, and grown
And nourisht in the Mountain Heart of Stone,
Burn with an inward Light, which they inspire,
And make their Owners Lords of their Desire."

To whom the Tájidár—"As idly sold
To the quick Pebble as the drowsy Gold,
As dead when sleeping in their mountain mine
As dangerous to Him who makes them shine:
Slavish indeed to do their Lord's Commands,
And slave-like aptest to escape his Hands,
And serve a second Master like the first,
And working all their wonders for the worst."

Never was Jewel after or before
Like that Sulayman for a Signet wore:
Whereby one Ruby, weighing scarce a grain
Did Sea and Land and all therein constrain,
Yea, ev'n the Winds of Heav'n—made the fierce East
Bear his League-wide Pavilion like a Beast,
Whither he would: yea, the Good Angel held
His subject, and the lower Fiend compell'd.
Till, looking round about him in his pride,
He overtax'd the Fountain that supplied,

Praying that after him no Son of Clay
Should ever touch his Glory. And one Day
Almighty God his Jewel stole away,
And gave it to the Div, who with the Ring
Wore also the Resemblance of the King,
And so for forty days play'd such a Game
As blots Sulayman's forty years with Shame.

Then *The Shah-Falcon*, tossing up his Head
Blink-hooded as it was—"Behold," he said,
"I am the chosen Comrade of the King,
And perch upon the Fist that wears the Ring;
Born, bred, and nourisht, in the Royal Court,
I take the Royal Name and make the Sport.
And if strict Discipline I undergo
And half my Life am blinded—be it so;
Because the Shah's Companion ill may brook
On aught save Royal Company to look.
And why am I to leave my King, and fare
With all these Rabble Wings I know not where?"—

"Oh blind indeed"—the Answer was, "and dark
To any but a vulgar Mortal Mark,
And drunk with Pride of Vassalage to those
Whose Humour like their Kingdom comes and goes;
All Mutability: who one Day please
To give: and next Day what they gave not seize:
Like to the Fire: a dangerous Friend at best,
Which who keeps farthest from does wiseliest."

A certain Shah there was in Days foregone
Who had a lovely Slave he doated on,
And cherish'd as the Apple of his Eye,
Clad gloriously, fed sumptuously, set high,
And never was at Ease were *He* not by,
Who yet, for all this Sunshine, Day by Day

Was seen to wither like a Flower away.
Which, when observing, one without the Veil
Of Favour ask'd the Favourite—"Why so pale
And sad?" thus sadly answer'd the poor Thing—
"No Sun that rises sets until the King,
Whose Archery is famous among Men,
Aims at an Apple on my Head;* and when
The stricken Apple splits, and those who stand
Around cry 'Lo! the Shah's unerring Hand!'
Then He too laughing asks me 'Why so pale
And sorrow-some? as could the Sultan fail,
Who such a master of the Bow confest,
And aiming by the Head that he loves best.' "

Then on a sudden swoop'd *The Phœnix* down
As though he wore as well as gave The Crown:†
And cried—"I care not, I, to wait on Kings,
Whose crowns are but the Shadow of my Wings!"

"Aye," was the Answer—"And, pray, how has sped,
On which it lighted, many a mortal Head?"

A certain Sultan dying, his Vizier
In Dream beheld him, and in mortal Fear
Began—"Oh mighty Shah of Shahs! Thrice-blest"—
But loud the Vision shriek'd and struck its Breast,

---

* Tell's Apple, long before his Time: and, by whomsoever invented, a
Fancy which (as was likely) would take lasting hold of the Oriental Mind.
In Chodzko's *Popular Persian Songs* (Oriental Translation Fund, 1842) is a
sort of Funeral Chaunt on Zulfakhar Khan by one of his Slaves; and the
following Passage in it: "Your Gun from the Manufactory of Loristan shines
like a Cloud gilded by the Rays of the Sun. Oh Serdar! your Place is now
empty: you were my Master: Your Gun from the Manufactory of Cabúl
shined in your Hands like a Bunch of Roses. Your Ball never missed a
Flower put in the middle of my Front Hair."

† He was supposed to be destined to Sovereignty over whom the Shadow
of the wings of the Phoenix passed.

And "Stab me not with empty Title!" cried—
"One only Shah there is, and none beside,
Who from his Throne above for certain Ends
Awhile some Spangle of his Glory lends
To Men on Earth; but calling in again
Exacts a strict account of every Grain.
Sultan I lived, and held the World in scorn:
Oh better had I glean'd the Field of Corn!
Oh better had I been a Beggar born,
And for my Throne and Crown, down in the Dust
My living Head had laid where Dead I must!
Oh wither'd, wither'd, wither'd, be the Wing
Whose overcasting Shadow made me King!"

Then from a Pond, where all day long he kept,
Waddled the dapper *Duck* demure, adept
At infinite Ablution, and precise
In keeping of his Raiment clean and nice.
And "Sure of all the Race of Birds," said He,
"None for Religious Purity like Me,
Beyond what strictest Rituals prescribe—
Methinks I am the Saint of all our Tribe,
To whom, by Miracle, the Water, that
I wash in, also makes my Praying-Mat."

To whom, more angrily than all, replied
The Leader, lashing that religious Pride,
That under ritual Obedience
To outer Law with inner might dispense:
For, fair as all the Feather to be seen,
Could one see *through*, the Maw was not so clean:
But He that made both Maw and Feather too
Would take account of, seeing through and through.

A Shah returning to his Capital,
His subjects drest it forth in Festival,

Thronging with Acclamation Square and Street,
And kneeling flung before his Horse's feet
Jewel and Gold. All which with scarce an Eye
The Sultan superciliously rode by:
Till coming to the public Prison, They
Who dwelt within those grisly Walls, by way
Of Welcome, having neither Pearl nor Gold,
Over the wall chopt Head and Carcase roll'd,
Some almost parcht to Mummy with the Sun,
Some wet with Execution that day done.
At which grim Compliment at last the Shah
Drew Bridle: and amid a wild Hurrah
Of savage Recognition, smiling threw
Silver and Gold among the wretched Crew,
And so rode forward. Whereat of his Train
One wondering that, while others sued in vain
With costly gifts, which carelessly he pass'd,
But smiled at ghastly Welcome like the last;
The Shah made answer—"All that Pearl and Gold
Of ostentatious Welcome only told:
A little with great Clamour from the Store
Of Hypocrites who kept at home much more.
But when those sever'd Heads and Trunks I saw—
Save by strict Execution of my Law
They had not parted company; not one
But told my Will not talk'd about, but *done*."

Then from a Wood was heard unseen to coo
The Ring-dove—"Yúsuf! Yúsuf! Yúsuf! Yú-"
(For thus her sorrow broke her Note in twain,
And, just where broken, took it up again)
"-suf! Yúsuf! Yúsuf! Yúsuf!"—But one Note,
Which still repeating, she made hoarse her throat:

Till checkt—"Oh You, who with your idle Sighs
Block up the Road of better Enterprize;
Sham Sorrow all, or bad as sham if true,

When once the better thing is come to *do*;
Beware lest wailing thus you meet *his* Doom
Who all too long his Darling wept, from whom
You draw the very Name you hold so dear,
And which the World is somewhat tired to hear."

When Yúsuf from his Father's Home was torn,
The Patriarch's Heart was utterly forlorn,
And, like a Pipe with but one stop, his Tongue
With nothing but the name of "Yúsuf" rung.
Then down from Heaven's Branches flew the *Bird**
Of Heav'n and said "God wearies of that word:
Hast thou not else to do and else to say?"
So Jacob's lips were sealéd from that Day.
But one Night in a Vision, far away
His darling in some alien Field he saw
Binding the Sheaf; and what between the Awe
Of God's Displeasure and the bitter Pass
Of passionate Affection, sigh'd "Alas—"
And stopp'd—But with the morning Sword of Flame
That oped his Eyes the sterner Angel's came—
"For the forbidden Word not utter'd by
Thy Lips was yet sequester'd in that Sigh."
And the right Passion whose Excess was wrong
Blinded the aged Eyes that wept too long.

And after these came others—arguing,
Enquiring and excusing—some one Thing,
And some another—endless to repeat,
But, in the Main, Sloth, Folly, or Deceit.
Their Souls were to the vulgar Figure cast
Of earthly Victual not of Heavenly Fast.
At last one smaller Bird, of a rare kind,
Of modest Plume and unpresumptuous Mind,
Whisper'd "Oh Tájidár, we know indeed

* Gabriel.

How Thou both knowest, and would'st help our Need;
For thou art wise and holy, and hast been
Behind the Veil, and there *The Presence* seen.
But we are weak and vain, with little care
Beyond our yearly Nests and daily Fare—
How should we reach the Mountain? and if there
How get so great a Prince to hear our Prayer?
For there, you say, dwells *The Symurgh* alone
In Glory, like Sulayman on his Throne,
And we but Pismires at his feet: can He
Such puny Creatures stoop to hear, or see;
Or hearing, seeing, *own* us—unakin
As He to Folly, Woe, and Death, and Sin?"—

To whom the Tájidár, whose Voice for those
Bewilder'd ones to full Compassion rose—
"Oh lost so long in Exile, you disclaim
The very Fount of Being whence you came,
Cannot be parted from, and, will or no,
Whether for Good or Evil must re-flow!
For look—the Shadows into which the Light
Of his pure Essence down by infinite
Gradation dwindles, which at random play
Through Space in Shape indefinite—one Ray
Of his Creative *Will* into *defined*
Creation quickens: We that swim the Wind,
And they the Flood below, and Man and Beast
That walk between, from Lion to the least
Pismire that creeps along Sulayman's Wall—
Yea, that in which they swim, fly, walk, and crawl—
However near the Fountain Light, or far
Removed, yet *His* authentic Shadows are;
Dead Matter's Self but the dark Residue
Exterminating Glory dwindles to.
A Mystery too fearful in the Crowd
To utter—scarcely to Thyself aloud—
But when in solitary Watch and Prayer
Consider'd: and religiously beware
Lest Thou the Copy with the Type confound;

And *Deity*, with Deity indrown'd,—
For as pure Water into purer Wine
Incorporating shall itself refine
While the dull Drug lies half-resolved below,
With Him and with his Shadows is it so:
The baser Forms, to whatsoever Change
Subject, still vary through their lower Range:
To which the *higher* even shall decay,
That, letting ooze their better Part away
For Things of Sense and Matter, in the End
Shall merge into the Clay to which they tend.
Unlike to him, who straining through the Bond
Of outward Being for a Life beyond,
While the gross Worldling to *his* Centre clings, ⎫
That draws him deeper in, exulting springs ⎬
To merge him in the central *Soul* of Things. ⎭
And shall not he pass home with other Zest
Who, with full Knowledge, yearns for such a Rest,
Than he, who with his better self at strife,
Drags on the weary Exile call'd *This Life*?—
One, like a child with outstretcht Arms and Face
Up-turn'd, anticipates his Sire's Embrace;
The other crouching like a guilty Slave
Till flogg'd to Punishment across the Grave.
And, knowing that *His* glory ill can bear ⎫
The unpurged Eye; do thou Thy Breast prepare; ⎬
And the mysterious Mirror He set there, ⎭
To temper his reflected Image in,
Clear of Distortion, Doubleness, and Sin:
And in thy Conscience understanding *this*,
The *Double* only *seems*, but The *One is*,
Thy-self to Self-annihilation give
That this false *Two* in that true *One* may live.
For this I say: if, looking in thy Heart,
Thou for *Self-whole* mistake thy *Shadow-part*,
That Shadow-part indeed into *The Sun*
Shall melt, but senseless of its Union:
But in that Mirror if with purgéd eyes
Thy Shadow Thou *for* Shadow recognize,

Then shalt Thou back into thy Centre fall
A conscious Ray of that eternal *All*."

He ceased, and for awhile Amazement quell'd
The Host, and in the Chain of Silence held:
A Mystery so awful who would dare—
So glorious who would not wish—to share?
So Silence brooded on the feather'd Folk,
Till here and there a timid Murmur broke
From some too poor in honest Confidence,
And then from others of too much Pretence;
Whom both, as each unduly hoped or fear'd,
The Tájidár in answer check'd or cheer'd.

Some said their Hearts were good indeed to go
The Way he pointed out: but they were slow
Of Comprehension, and scarce understood ⎫
Their present Evil or the promised Good: ⎬
And so, tho' willing to do all they could, ⎭
Must not they fall short, or go wholly wrong,
On such mysterious Errand, and so long?
Whom the wise Leader bid but Do their Best
In Hope and Faith, and leave to *Him* the rest,
For He who fix'd the Race, and knew its Length
And Danger, also knew the Runner's Strength.

Shah Mahmúd, absent on an Enterprize,
Ayas, the very Darling of his eyes,
At home under an Evil Eye fell sick,
Then cried the Sultan to a soldier "Quick!
To Horse! to Horse! without a Moment's Stay,—
The shortest Road with all the Speed you may,—
Or, by the Lord, your Head shall pay for it!"—
Off went the Soldier, plying Spur and Bit—
Over the sandy Desert, over green
Valley, and Mountain, and the Stream between,
Without a Moment's Stop for rest or bait,—
Up to the City—to the Palace Gate—

Up to the Presence-Chamber at a Stride—
And Lo! The Sultan at his Darling's side!—
Then thought the Soldier—"I have done my Best,
And yet shall die for it." The Sultan guess'd
His Thought and smiled. "Indeed your Best you did,
The nearest Road you knew, and well you rid:
And if *I* knew a shorter, my Excess
Of Knowledge does but justify thy Less."

And then, with drooping Crest and Feather, came
Others, bow'd down with Penitence and Shame.
They long'd indeed to go; "but how begin,
Mesh'd and entangled as they were in Sin
Which often-times Repentance of past Wrong
As often broken had but knit more strong?"

Whom the wise Leader bid be of good cheer,
And, conscious of the Fault, dismiss the Fear,
Nor at the very Entrance of the Fray
Their Weapon, ev'n if broken, fling away:
Since Mercy on the broken Branch anew
Would blossom were but each Repentance true.

For did not God his Prophet take to Task?
"*Sev'n-times* of Thee did Kárún Pardon ask;
Which, hadst thou been like Me his Maker—yea,
But present at the Kneading of his Clay
With those twain Elements of Hell and Heav'n,—
One prayer had won what Thou deny'st to Sev'n."

For like a Child sent with a fluttering Light
To feel his way along a gusty Night
Man walks the World: again and yet again
The Lamp shall be by Fits of Passion slain:
But shall not He who sent him from the Door
Relight the Lamp once more, and yet once more?

When the rebellious Host from Death shall wake
Black with Despair of Judgment, God shall take
Ages of holy Merit from the Count
Of Angels to make up Man's short Amount,
And bid the murmuring Angel gladly spare
Of that which, undiminishing his Share
Of Bliss, shall rescue Thousands from the Cost
Of Bankruptcy within the Prison lost.

Another Story told how in the Scale
Good Will beyond mere Knowledge would prevail.

In Paradise the Angel Gabriel heard
The Lips of Allah trembling with the Word
Of perfect Acceptation: and he thought
"Some perfect Faith such perfect Answer wrought,
But whose?"—And therewith slipping from the Crypt
Of Sidra,* through the Angel-ranks he slipt
Watching what Lip yet trembled with the Shot
That so had hit the Mark—but found it not.
Then, in a Glance to Earth, he threaded through
Mosque, Palace, Cell and Cottage of the True
Belief—in vain; so back to Heaven went
And—Allah's Lips still trembling with assent!
Then the tenacious Angel once again
Threaded the Ranks of Heav'n and Earth—in vain—
Till, once again return'd to Paradise,
There, looking into God's, the Angel's Eyes
Beheld the Prayer that brought that Benison
Rising like Incense from the Lips of one
Who to an Idol bowed—as best he knew
Under that False God worshipping the True.

* Sidra, the Tree of Paradise, or Heaven.

And then came others whom the summons found
Not wholly sick indeed, but far from sound:
Whose light inconstant Soul alternate flew
From Saint to Sinner, and to both untrue;
Who like a niggard Tailor, tried to match
Truth's single Garment with a worldly Patch.
A dangerous Game; for, striving to adjust
The hesitating Scale of either Lust,
That which had least within it upward flew,
And still the weightier to the Earth down drew,
And, while suspended between Rise and Fall,
Apt with a shaking Hand to forfeit all.

There was a Queen of Egypt like the Bride
Of Night, Full-moon-faced and Canopus-eyed,
Whom one among the meanest of her Crowd
Loved—and she knew it, (for he loved aloud)
And sent for him, and said "Thou lov'st thy Queen:
Now therefore Thou hast this to choose between:
Fly for thy Life: or for this one night Wed
Thy Queen, and with the Sunrise lose thy Head."
He paused—he turn'd to fly—she struck him dead.
"For had he truly loved his Queen," said She,
"He would at once have giv'n his Life for me,
And Life and Wife had carried: but he lied;
And loving only Life, has justly died."

And then came one who having clear'd his Throat
With sanctimonious Sweetness in his Note
Thus lisp'd—"Behold I languish from the first
With passionate and unrequited Thirst
Of Love for more than any mortal Bird.
Therefore have I withdrawn me from the Herd
To pine in Solitude. But Thou at last
Hast drawn a line across the dreary Past,
And sure I am by Fore-taste that the Wine
I long'd for, and Thou tell'st of, shall be mine."

But he was sternly checkt. "I tell thee this:
Such Boast is no Assurance of such Bliss:
Thou canst not even fill the sail of Prayer
Unless from *Him* breathe that authentic Air
That shall lift up the Curtain that divides
His Lover from the Harím where *He* hides—
And the Fulfilment of thy Vows must be,
Not from thy Love for Him, but His for Thee."

The third night after Bajazyd had died,
One saw him, in a dream, at his Bed-side,
And said, "Thou Bajazyd? Tell me Oh Pýr,
How fared it there with Munkar and Nakýr?"*
And Bajazyd replied, "When from the Grave
They met me rising, and 'If Allah's slave'
Ask'd me, 'or collar'd with the Chain of Hell?'
I said 'Not I but God alone can tell:
My Passion for his service were but fond
Ambition had not He approved the Bond:
Had He not round my neck the Collar thrown
And told me in the Number of his own;
And that *He* only knew. What signifies
A hundred Years of Prayer if none replies?'"

"But" said Another, "then shall none the Seal
Of Acceptation on his Forehead feel
Ere the Grave yield them on the other Side
Where all is settled?"

                    But the Chief replied—
"Enough for us to know that who is meet
Shall enter, and with unreprovéd Feet,
(Ev'n as he might upon the Waters walk)
The Presence-room, and in the Presence talk

* The two Angels who examine the Soul on its leaving the Body.

With such unbridled License as shall seem
To the Uninitiated to blaspheme."

———————

Just as another Holy Spirit fled,
The Skies above him burst into a Bed
Of Angels looking down and singing clear
"Nightingale! Nightingale! thy Rose is here!"
And yet, the Door wide open to that Bliss,⎫
As some hot Lover slights a scanty Kiss,⎬
The Saint cried "All I sigh'd for come to *this*?⎭
I who life-long have struggled, Lord, to be
Not of thy Angels one, but one with Thee!"

———————

Others were sure that all he said was true:
They were extremely wicked, that they knew:
And much they long'd to go at once—but some,
They said, so unexpectedly had come
Leaving their Nests half-built—in bad Repair—
With Children in—Themselves about to pair—
"Might he not choose a better Season—nay,
Better perhaps a Year or Two's Delay,
Till all was settled, and themselves more stout
And strong to carry their Repentance out—
And then"—

           "And then, the same or like Excuse,
With harden'd Heart and Resolution loose
With dallying: and old Age itself engaged
Still to shirk that which shirking we have aged;
And so with Self-delusion, till, too late,
Death upon all Repentance shuts the Gate;
Or some fierce blow compels the Way to choose,
And forced Repentance half its Virtue lose."

———————

As of an aged Indian King they tell
Who, when his Empire with his Army fell

Under young Mahmúd's Sword of Wrath, was sent
At sunset to the Conqueror in his Tent;
But, ere the old King's silver head could reach
The Ground, was lifted up—with kindly Speech,
And with so holy Mercy re-assured,
That, after due Persuasion, he abjured
His Idols, sate upon Mahmúd's Divan,
And took the Name and Faith of Musulman.
But when the Night fell, in his Tent alone
The poor old King was heard to weep and groan
And smite his Bosom; which, when Mahmúd knew,
He went to him and said "Lo, if Thou rue
Thy lost Dominion, Thou shalt wear the Ring
Of thrice as large a Realm." But the dark King
Still wept, and Ashes on his Forehead threw
And cried "Not for my Kingdom lost I rue;
But thinking how at the Last Day, will stand
The Prophet with *The Volume* in his Hand,
And ask of me 'How was't that, in thy Day
Of Glory, Thou didst turn from Me and slay
My People; but soon as thy Infidel
Before my True Believers' Army fell
Like Corn before the Reaper—thou didst own ⎫
His Sword who scoutedst *Me*.' Of seed so sown ⎬
What profitable Harvest should be grown?" ⎭

Then after cheering others who delay'd,
Not of the Road but of Themselves afraid,
The Tájidár the Troop of those address'd,
Whose uncomplying Attitude confess'd
Their Souls entangled in the old Deceit,
And hankering still after forbidden Meat—

"Oh ye who so long feeding on the Husk
Forgo the Fruit, and doating on the Dusk
Of the false Dawn, are blinded to the True:
That in the Maidán of this World pursue

The Golden Ball which, driven to the Goal,
Wins the World's Game but loses your own Soul:
Or like to Children after Bubbles run
That still elude your Fingers; or, if won,
Burst in Derision at your Touch; all thin
Glitter without, and empty Wind within.
So as a prosperous Worldling on the Bed
Of Death—'Behold, I am as one,' he said,
Who all my Life long have been measuring Wind,
And, dying, now leave even that behind'—
This World's a Nest in which the Cockatrice
Is warm'd and hatcht of Vanity and Vice:
A false Bazár whose Wares are all a lie,
Or never worth the Price at which you buy:
A many-headed Monster that, supplied
The faster, faster is unsatisfied;
So as one, hearing a rich Fool one day
To God for yet one other Blessing pray,
Bid him no longer bounteous Heaven tire
For Life to feed, but Death to quench, the Fire.
And what are all the Vanities and Wiles
In which the false World decks herself and smiles
To draw Men down into her harlot Lap?
Lusts of the Flesh that Soul and Body sap,
And, melting Soul down into carnal Lust,
Ev'n that for which 'tis sacrificed disgust:
Or Lust of worldly Glory—hollow more
Than the Drum beaten at the Sultan's Door,
And fluctuating with the Breath of Man
As the Vain Banner flapping in the Van.
And Lust of Gold—perhaps of Lusts the worst;
The mis-created Idol most accurst
That between Man and Him who made him stands:
The Felon that with suicidal hands
He sweats to dig and rescue from his Grave,
And sets at large to make Himself its Slave.

"For lo, to what worse than oblivion gone
Are some the cozening World most doated on

Pharaoh tried *Glory*: and his Chariots drown'd:
Kárún with all his Gold went underground:
Down toppled Nembroth* with his airy Stair:
Schedád among his Roses lived—but *where*?

"And as the World upon her victims feeds
So She herself goes down the Way she leads.
For all her false allurements are the Threads
The Spider from her Entrail spins, and spreads
For Home and hunting-ground: And by and bye
Darts at due Signal on the tangled Fly,
Seizes, dis-wings, and drains the Life, and leaves
The swinging Carcase, and forthwith re-weaves
Her Web: each Victim adding to the store
Of poison'd Entrail to entangle more.
And so She bloats in Glory: till one Day
The Master of the House, passing that way,
Perceives, and with one flourish of his Broom
Of Web and Fly and Spider clears the Room.

"Behold, dropt through the Gate of Mortal Birth,
The Knightly Soul alights from Heav'n on Earth;
Begins his Race, but scarce the Saddle feels, ⎫
When a foul Imp up from the distance steals, ⎬
And, double as he will, about his Heels ⎭
Closer and ever closer circling creeps,
Then, half-invited, on the Saddle leaps,
Clings round the Rider, and, once there, in vain
The strongest strives to thrust him off again.
In Childhood just peeps up the Blade of Ill,
That Youth to Lust rears, Fury, and Self-will:
And, as Man cools to sensual Desire,
Ambition catches with as fierce a Fire;
Until Old Age sends him with one last Lust
Of Gold, to keep it where he found—in Dust.
Life at both Ends so feeble and constrain'd
How should that Imp of Sin be slain or chain'd?

* Nimrod.

"And woe to him who feeds the hateful Beast
That of his Feeder makes an after-feast!
We know the Wolf: by Stratagem and Force
Can hunt the Tiger down: but what Resource
Against the Plague we heedless hatch within,
Then, growing, pamper into full-blown Sin
With the Soul's self: ev'n, as the wise man said,
Feeding the very Devil with God's own Bread;
Until the Lord his Largess misapplied
Resent, and drive us wholly from his Side?

"For should the Grey-hound whom a Sultan fed,
And by a jewell'd String a-hunting led,
Turn by the Way to gnaw some nasty Thing
And snarl at Him who twitch'd the silken String,
Would not his Lord soon weary of Dispute,
And turn adrift the incorrigible Brute?

"Nay, would one follow, and without a Chain,
The only Master truly worth the Pain,
One must beware lest, growing over-fond
Of even Life's more consecrated Bond,
We clog our Footsteps to the World beyond.
Like that old Arab Chieftain, who confess'd
His soul by two too Darling Things possess'd—
That only Son of his: and that one Colt
Descended from the Prophet's Thunderbolt.
'And I might well bestow the last,' he said,
'On him who brought me Word the Boy was dead.'

"And if so vain the glittering Fish we get,
How doubly vain to doat upon the Net,
Call'd Life, that draws them, patching up this thin
Tissue of Breathing out and Breathing in,
And so by husbanding each wretched Thread
Spin out Death's very Terror that we dread—
For as the Rain-drop from the sphere of God
Dropt for a while into the Mortal Clod
So little makes of its allotted Time

Back to its Heav'n itself to re-sublime,
That it but serves to saturate its Clay
With Bitterness that will not pass away."

One day the Prophet on a River Bank,
Dipping his Lips into the Channel, drank
A Draught as sweet as Honey. Then there came
One who an earthen Pitcher from the same
Drew up, and drank: and after some short stay
Under the Shadow, rose and went his Way,
Leaving his earthen Bowl. In which, anew
Thirsting, the Prophet from the River drew,
And drank from: but the Water that came up
Sweet from the Stream, drank bitter from the Cup.
At which the Prophet in a still Surprise
For Answer turning up to Heav'n his Eyes,
The Vessel's Earthen Lips with Answer ran—
"The Clay that I am made of once was *Man*,
Who dying, and resolved into the same
Obliterated Earth from which he came
Was for the Potter dug, and chased in turn
Through long Vicissitude of Bowl and Urn:
But howsoever moulded, still the Pain
Of that first mortal Anguish would retain,
And cast, and re-cast, for a Thousand years
Would turn the sweetest Water into Tears."

And after Death?—that, shirk it as we may,
Will come, and with it bring its After-Day—

For ev'n as Yúsuf, (when his Brotherhood
Came up from Egypt to buy Corn, and stood
Before their Brother in his lofty Place,
Nor knew him, for a Veil before his Face,)
Struck on his Mystic Cup, which straightway then
Rung out their Story to those guilty Ten:—

Not to *them* only, but to every one;
Whatever he have said and thought and done,
Unburied with the Body shall fly up,
And gather into Heav'n's inverted Cup,
Which, stricken by God's Finger, shall tell all
The Story whereby we must stand or fall.
And though we walk this World as if behind
There were no Judgment, or the Judge half-blind,
Beware, for He with whom we have to do
Outsees the Lynx, outlives the Phœnix too—

So Sultan Mahmúd, coming Face to Face
With mightier numbers of the swarthy Race,
Vow'd that if God to him the battle gave,
God's Dervish People all the Spoil should have.
And God the Battle gave him; and the Fruit
Of a great Conquest coming to compute,
A Murmur through the Sultan's Army stirr'd
Lest, ill committed to one hasty Word,
The Shah should squander on an idle Brood
What should be theirs who earn'd it with their Blood,
Or go to fill the Coffers of the State.
So Mahmúd's Soul began to hesitate:
Till looking round in Doubt from side to side
A raving Zealot in the Press he spied,
And call'd and had him brought before his Face,
And, telling, bid him arbitrate the case.
Who, having listen'd, said—"The Thing is plain:
If Thou and God should never have again
To deal together, rob him of his share:
But if perchance you should—why then Beware!"

So spake the Tájidár: but Fear and Doubt
Among the Birds in Whispers went about:
Great was their Need: and Succour to be sought
At any Risk: at any Ransom bought:

But such a Monarch—greater than Mahmúd
The Great Himself! Why how should he be woo'd
To listen to them? they too having come
So suddenly, and unprepared from home
With any Gold, or Jewel, or rich Thing
To carry with them to so great a King—
Poor Creatures! with the old and carnal Blind,
Spite of all said, so thick upon the Mind,
Devising how they might ingratiate
Access, as to some earthly Potentate.

"Let him that with this Monarch would engage
Bring the Gold Dust of a long Pilgrimage:
The Ruby of a bleeding Heart, whose Sighs
Breathe more than Amber-incense as it dies;
And while in naked Beggary he stands
Hope for the Robe of Honour from his Hands."
And, as no gift this Sovereign receives
Save the mere Soul and Self of him who gives,
So let that Soul for other none Reward
Look than the Presence of its Sovereign Lord."
And as his Hearers seem'd to estimate
Their Scale of Glory from Mahmúd the Great,
A simple Story of the Sultan told
How best a subject with his Shah made bold—

———————

One night Shah Mahmúd who had been of late
Somewhat distemper'd with Affairs of State
Stroll'd through the Streets disguised, as wont to do—
And, coming to the Baths, there on the Flue
Saw the poor Fellow who the Furnace fed
Sitting beside his Water-jug and Bread.
Mahmúd stept in—sat down—unask'd took up
And tasted of the untasted Loaf and Cup,
Saying within himself, "Grudge but a bit,
And, by the Lord, your Head shall pay for it!"
So having rested, warm'd and satisfied
Himself without a Word on either side,

At last the wayward Sultan rose to go.
And then at last his Host broke silence—"So?—
Art satisfied? Well, Brother, any Day
Or Night, remember, when you come this Way
And want a bit of Provender—why, you
Are welcome, and if not—why, welcome too."—
The Sultan was so tickled with the whim
Of this quaint Entertainment and of him
Who offer'd it, that many a Night again
Stoker and Shah forgather'd in that Vein—
Till, the poor Fellow having stood the Test
Of true Good-fellowship, Mahmúd confess'd
One Night the Sultan that had been his Guest:
And in requital of the scanty Dole
The Poor Man offer'd with so large a soul,
Bid him ask any Largess that he would—
A Throne—if he *would* have it, so he *should*.
The Poor Man kiss'd the Dust, and "All," said he,
"I ask is what and where I am to be;
If but the Shah from time to time will come
As now and see me in the lowly Home
His presence makes a palace, and my own
Poor Flue more royal than another's Throne."

So said the cheery Tale: and, as they heard,
Again the Heart beneath the Feather stirr'd:
Again forgot the Danger and the Woes
Of the long Travel in its glorious Close:—
"Here truly all was Poverty, Despair
And miserable Banishment—but *there*
That more than Mahmúd, for no more than Prayer
Who would restore them to their ancient Place,
And round their Shoulders fling his Robe of Grace."
They clapp'd their Wings, on Fire to be assay'd
And prove of what true Metal they were made,
Although defaced, and wanting the true Ring
And Superscription of their rightful King.

309

"The Road! The Road!" in countless voices cried
The Host—"The Road! and who shall be our Guide?"
And they themselves "The Tájidár!" replied:
Yet to make doubly certain that the Voice
Of Heav'n accorded with the People's Choice,
Lots should be drawn; and He on whom should light
Heav'n's Hand—they swore to follow him out-right.
This settled, and once more the Hubbub quell'd,
Once more Suspense the Host in Silence held,
While, Tribe by Tribe, the Birds their Fortune drew;
And Lo! upon the Tájidár it flew.
Then rising up again in wide and high
Circumference of wings that mesh'd the sky
"The Tájidár! The Tájidár!" they cry—
"The Tájidár! The Tájidár!" with Him
Was Heav'n, and They would follow Life and Limb!
Then, once more fluttering to their Places down,
Upon his Head they set the Royal Crown
As Khalif of their Khalif so long lost,
And Captain of his now repentant Host;
And setting him on high, and Silence call'd,
The Tájidár, in Pulpit-throne install'd,
His Voice into a Trumpet-tongue so clear
As all the wingéd Multitude should hear
Raised, to proclaim the Order and Array
Of March; which, many as it frighten'd—yea,
The Heart of Multitudes at outset broke,
Yet for due Preparation must be spoke.

—A Road indeed that never Wing before
Flew, nor Foot trod, nor Heart imagined—o'er
Waterless Deserts—Waters where no Shore—
Valleys comprising cloudhigh Mountains: these
Again their Valleys deeper than the Seas:
Whose Dust all Adders, and whose vapour Fire:
Where all once hostile Elements conspire
To set the Soul against herself, and tear
Courage to Terror—Hope into Despair,
And Madness; Terrors, Trials, to make stray

Or stop where Death to wander or delay:
Where when half dead with Famine, Toil, and Heat,
'Twas Death indeed to rest, or drink, or eat.
A Road still waxing in Self-sacrifice
As it went on: still ringing with the Cries
And Groans of Those who had not yet prevail'd,
And bleaching with the Bones of those who fail'd:
Where, almost all withstood, perhaps to earn
Nothing: and, earning, never to return.—

And first the *VALE OF SEARCH*: an endless Maze,
Branching into innumerable Ways
All courting Entrance: but one right: and this
Beset with Pitfall, Gulf, and Precipice,
Where Dust is Embers, Air a fiery Sleet,
Through which with blinded Eyes and bleeding Feet
The Pilgrim stumbles, with Hyæna's Howl
Around, and hissing Snake, and deadly Ghoul,
Whose Prey he falls if tempted but to droop,
Or if to wander famish'd from the Troop
For fruit that falls to ashes in the Hand,
Water that reacht recedes into the Sand.
The only word is "Forward!" Guide in sight,
After him, swerving neither left nor right,
Thyself for thine own Victual by Day,
At night thine own Self's Caravanserai.
Till suddenly, perhaps when most subdued
And desperate, the Heart shall be renew'd
When deep in utter Darkness, by one Gleam
Of Glory from the far remote *Harím*,
That, with a scarcely conscious Shock of Change,
Shall light the Pilgrim toward the Mountain Range
Of KNOWLEDGE: where, if stronger and more pure ⎫
The Light and Air, yet harder to endure;   ⎬
And if, perhaps, the Footing more secure,   ⎭
Harder to keep up with a nimble Guide,
Less from lost Road than insufficient Stride—
Yet tempted still by false Shows from the Track,
And by false Voices call'd aside or back,

Which echo from the Bosom, as if won
The Journey's End when only just begun,
And not a Mountain Peak with Toil attain'd
But shows a Top yet higher to be gain'd.
Wherefore still Forward, Forward! Love that fired
Thee first to search, by Search so re-inspired
As that the Spirit shall the carnal Load
Burn up, and double wing Thee on the Road;
That wert thou knocking at the very Door
Of Heav'n, thou still would'st cry for More, More, More!

Till loom in sight Káf's Mountain Peak ashroud
In Mist—uncertain yet Mountain or Cloud,
But where the Pilgrim 'gins to hear the Tide
Of that one Sea in which the Sev'n subside;
And not the Sev'n Seas only: but the sev'n
And self-enfolded Spheres of Earth and Heav'n—
Yea, the Two Worlds, that now as Pictures sleep
Upon its Surface—but when once the Deep
From its long Slumber 'gins to heave and sway—
Under that Tempest shall be swept away
With all their Phases and Phenomena:
Not senseless Matter only, but combined
With Life in all Varieties of Kind;
Yea, ev'n the abstract Forms that Space and Time
Men call, and Weal and Woe, Virtue and Crime,
And all the several Creeds, like those who fell
Before them, Musulman and Infidel
Shall from the Face of Being melt away,
Cancell'd and swept as Dreams before the Day.
So hast thou seen the Astrologer prepare
His mystic Table smooth of Sand, and there
Inscribe his mystic Figures, Square, and Trine,
Circle and Pentagram, and heavenly Sign
Of Star and Planet: from whose Set and Rise,
Meeting and Difference, he prophesies;
And, having done it, with his Finger clean
Obliterates as never they had been.

Such is when reacht the Table Land of *One*
And *Wonder*: blazing with so fierce a Sun
Of Unity that blinds while it reveals
The Universe that to a Point congeals,
So, stunn'd with utter Revelation, reels
The Pilgrim, when that *Double*-seeming House,
Against whose Beams he long had chafed his Brows,
Crumbles and cracks before that Sea, whose near
And nearer Voice now overwhelms his Ear.
Till blinded, deafen'd, madden'd, drunk with doubt
Of all within Himself as all without,
Nay, whether a *Without* there be, or not,
Or a *Within* that doubts: and if, then *what*?—
Ev'n so shall the bewilder'd Pilgrim seem
When nearest waking deepliest in Dream,
And darkest next to Dawn; and lost what had
When *All* is found: and just when sane quite Mad—
As one that having found the Key once more
Returns, and Lo! he cannot find the Door
He stumbles over—So the Pilgrim stands
A moment on the Threshold—with raised Hands
Calls to the eternal Sáki for one Draught
Of Light from the One Essence: which when quaff'd,
He plunges headlong in: and all is well
With him who never more returns to tell.
Such being then the Race and such the Goal,
Judge if you must not Body both and Soul
With Meditation, Watch, and Fast prepare.
For he that wastes his Body to a Hair
Shall seize the Locks of Truth: and He that prays
Good Angels in their Ministry way-lays:
And the Midnightly Watcher in the Folds
Of his own Darkness God Almighty holds.
He that would prosper here must from him strip
The World, and take the Dervish Gown and Scrip:
And as he goes must gather from all Sides
Irrelevant Ambitions, Lusts, and Prides,
Glory and Gold, and sensual Desire,
Whereof to build the fundamental Pyre

Of Self-annihilation: and cast in
All old Relations and Regards of Kin
And Country: and, the Pile with this perplext
World platform'd, from the Fables of the Next
Raise it tow'rd Culmination, with the torn
Rags and Integuments of Creeds out-worn;
And top the giddy Summit with the Scroll ⎤
Of *Reason* that in dingy Smoke shall roll ⎬
Over the true Self-sacrifice of Soul: ⎦
(For such a Prayer was his—"Oh God, do Thou
With all my Wealth in the other World endow
My Friends: and with my Wealth in *this* my Foes,
Till bankrupt in *thy* Riches I repose!")
Then, all the Pile completed of the Pelf
Of either World—at last throw on *Thyself*,
And with the Torch of Self-negation fire;
And ever as the Flames rise high and higher,
With Cries of agonizing Glory still
All of that *Self* burn up that burn up will,
Leaving the Phœnix that no Fire can slay
To spring from its own Ashes kindled—nay,
Itself an inextinguishable Spark
Of Being, *now* beneath Earth-ashes dark,
Transcending these, at last *Itself* transcends
And with the One Eternal Essence blends.

———————

The Moths had long been exiled from the Flame
They worship: so to solemn Council came,
And voted *One* of them by Lot be sent
To find their Idol. One was chosen: went.
And after a long Circuit in sheer Gloom,
Seeing, he thought, the TAPER in a Room
Flew back at once to say so. But the chief
Of *Mothistán* slighted so slight Belief,
And sent another Messenger, who flew
Up to the House, in at the window, through
The Flame itself; and back the Message brings,

With yet no sign of Conflict on his wings.
Then went a Third, who spurr'd with true Desire,
Plunging at once into the sacred Fire,
Folded his Wings within, till he became
One Colour and one Substance with the Flame.
He only knew the Flame who in it burn'd;
And only He could tell who ne'er to tell return'd.

<hr>

After declaring what of this declared
Must be, that all who went should be prepared,
From his high Station ceased the Tájidár—
And lo! the Terrors that, when told afar,
Seem'd but as Shadows of a Noon-day Sun,
Now that the talkt of Thing was to be *done*,
Lengthening into those of closing Day ⎫
Strode into utter Darkness: and Dismay ⎬
Like Night on the husht Sea of Feathers lay, ⎭
Late so elate—"So terrible a Track!
Endless—or, ending, never to come back!—
Never to Country, Family, or Friend!"—
In sooth no easy Bow for Birds to bend!—
Even while he spoke, how many Wings and Crests
Had slunk away to distant Woods and Nests;
Others again in Preparation spent
What little Strength they had, and never went:
And others, after preparation due— ⎫
When up the Veil of that first Valley drew ⎬
From whose waste Wilderness of Darkness blew ⎭
A Sarsar, whether edged of Flames or Snows,
That through from Root to Tip their Feathers froze—
Up went a Multitude that overhead
A moment darken'd, then on all sides fled,
Dwindling the World-assembled Caravan
To less than half the Number that began.
Of those who fled not, some in Dread and Doubt
Sat without stirring: others who set out
With frothy Force, or stupidly resign'd,

Before a League, flew off or fell behind.
And howsoever the more Brave and Strong
In Courage, Wing, or Wisdom push'd along,
Yet League by League the Road was thicklier spread
By the fast falling Foliage of the Dead:
Some spent with Travel over Wave and Ground;
Scorcht, frozen, dead for Drought, or drinking drown'd.
Famisht, or poison'd with the Food when found:
By Weariness, or Hunger, or Affright
Seduced to stop or stray, become the Bite
Of Tiger howling round or hissing Snake,
Or Crocodile that eyed them from the Lake:
Or raving Mad, or in despair Self-slain:
Or slaying one another for a Grain:—

Till of the mighty Host that fledged the Dome
Of Heav'n and Floor of Earth on leaving Home,
A Handfull reach'd and scrambled up the Knees
Of Káf whose Feet dip in the Seven Seas;
And of the few that up his Forest-sides
Of Light and Darkness where *The Presence* hides,
But *Thirty*—thirty desperate draggled Things,
Half-dead, with scarce a Feather on their Wings,
Stunn'd, blinded, deafen'd with the Crash and Craze
Of Rock and Sea collapsing in a Blaze
That struck the Sun to Cinder—fell upon
The Threshold of the Everlasting *One*,
With but enough of Life in each to cry,
On THAT which all absorb'd—

                                    And suddenly
Forth flash'd a wingéd Harbinger of Flame
And Tongue of Fire, and "Who?" and "Whence they
        came?"
And "Why?" demanded. And the Tájidár
For all the Thirty answer'd him—"We are
Those Fractions of the Sum of Being, far
Dis-spent and foul disfigured, that once more
Strike for Admission at the Treasury Door."

To whom the Angel answer'd—"Know ye not
That He you seek recks little who or what
Of Quantity and Kind—himself the Fount
Of Being Universal needs no Count
Of all the Drops o'erflowing from his Urn,
In what Degree they issue or return?"

Then cried the Spokesman, "Be it even so:
Let us but see the Fount from which we flow,
And, seeing, lose Ourselves therein!" And, Lo!
Before the Word was utter'd, or the Tongue
Of Fire replied, or Portal open flung,
They were *within*—they were before the *Throne*,
Before the Majesty that sat thereon,
But wrapt in so insufferable a Blaze
Of Glory as beat down their baffled Gaze,
Which, downward dropping, fell upon a Scroll
That, Lightning-like, flash'd back on each the whole
Past half-forgotten Story of his Soul:
Like that which Yúsuf in his Glory gave
His Brethren as some Writing he would have
Interpreted; and at a Glance, behold
Their own Indenture for their Brother sold!
And so with these poor Thirty: who, abasht
In Memory all laid bare and Conscience lasht,
By full Confession and Self-loathing flung
The Rags of carnal Self that round them clung;
And, their old selves self-knowledged and self-loathed,
And in the Soul's Integrity re-clothed,
Once more they ventured from the Dust to raise
Their Eyes—up to the Throne—into the Blaze,
And in the Centre of the Glory there
Beheld the Figure of—*Themselves*—as 'twere
Transfigured—looking to Themselves, beheld
The Figure on the Throne en-miracled,
Until their Eyes themselves and *That* between
Did hesitate which *Sëer* was, which *Seen*;
They That, That They: Another, yet the Same;
Dividual, yet One: from whom there came

317

A Voice of awful Answer, scarce discern'd
From *which* to Aspiration *whose* return'd
They scarcely knew; as when some Man apart
Answers aloud the Question in his Heart—
"The Sun of my Perfection is a Glass
Wherein from *Seeing* into *Being* pass
All who, reflecting as reflected see
Themselves in Me, and Me in Them: not *Me*,
But all of Me that a contracted Eye
Is comprehensive of Infinity:
Nor yet *Themselves*: no Selves, but of The All
Fractions, from which they split and whither fall.
As Water lifted from the Deep, again ⎫
Falls back in individual Drops of Rain ⎬
Then melts into the Universal Main. ⎭
All you have been, and seen, and done, and thought,
Not *You* but *I*, have seen and been and wrought:
I was the Sin that from Myself rebell'd:
I the Remorse that tow'rd Myself compell'd:
I was the Tájidár who led the Track:
I was the little Briar that pull'd you back:
Sin and Contrition—Retribution owed,
And cancell'd—Pilgrim, Pilgrimage, and Road,
Was but Myself toward Myself: and Your
Arrival but *Myself* at my own Door:
Who in your Fraction of Myself behold
Myself within the Mirror Myself hold
To see Myself in, and each part of Me
That sees himself, though drown'd, shall ever see.
Come you lost Atoms to your Centre draw,
And *be* the Eternal Mirror that you saw:
Rays that have wander'd into Darkness wide
Return, and back into your Sun subside."—

This was the Parliament of Birds: and this
The Story of the Host who went amiss,

And of the Few that better Upshot found;
Which being now recounted, Lo, the Ground
Of Speech fails underfoot: But this to tell—
Their Road is thine—Follow—and Fare thee well.

THE MIGHTY
MAGICIAN

TAKEN FROM CALDERON'S

EL MÁGICO
PRODIGIOSO

L

[Two dramas from Calderon, *The Mighty Magician*, and *Such Stuff as Dreams are Made of*, were privately printed in 1865.]

DRAMATIS PERSONÆ

AURELIO, *Viceroy of Antioch.*
LELIO, *his Son.*

FABIO, *a chief Officer in Antioch.*
FLORO, *his Son.*

LISANDRO, *an aged Christian.*
JUSTINA, *his Daughter.*
LIVIA, *their Servant.*

CIPRIANO, *a Professor of Learning.*
EUSEBIO, ⎱
JULIAN, ⎰ *his Scholars.*

LUCIFER, *the Evil Spirit.*

CITIZENS, SOLDIERS, &C.

ACT I

SCENE I.—*A retired Grove near Antioch.—Enter* CIPRIANO, EUSEBIO, *and* JULIAN, *with books.*

CIPRIANO: This is the place, this the sequester'd spot
Where, in the flower about and leaf above,
I find the shade and quiet that I love,
And oft resort to rest a wearied wing;
And here, good lads, leave me alone, but not
Lonely, companion'd with the books you bring:
That while the city from all open doors
Abroad her gaping population pours,
To swell the triumph of the pomp divine
That with procession, sacrifice, and song
Convoys her tutelary Zeus along
For installation in his splendid shrine;
I, flying from the hubbub of the throng
That overflows her thoroughfares and streets,
And here but faintly touches and retreats,
In solitary meditation may
Discount at ease my summer holiday.
You to the city back, and take your fill
Of festival, and all that with the time's,
And your own youth's, triumphant temper chimes;
Leaving me here alone to mine; until
Yon golden idol reaching overhead,
Dragg'd from his height, and bleeding out his fires
Along the threshold of the west, expires,
And drops into the sea's sepulchral lead.
EUSEBIO: Nay, sir, think once again, and go with us,
Or, if you will, without us; only, go;
Lest Antioch herself as well as we
Cry out upon a maim'd solemnity.
JULIAN: Oh, how I wish I had not brought the books,

Which you have ever at command—indeed,
Without them, all within them carry—here—
Garner'd—aloft—

EUSEBIO: In truth, if stay you will,
I scarcely care to go myself.

CIPRIANO: Nay, nay,
Good lads, good boys, all thanks, and all the more,
If you but leave it simply as I say.
You have been somewhat over-tax'd of late,
And want some holiday.

JULIAN: Well, sir, and you?

CIPRIANO: Oh, I am of that tougher age and stuff
Whose relaxation is its work. Besides,
Think you the poor Professor needs no time
For solitary tillage of his brains,
Before such shrewd ingatherers as you
Come on him for their harvest unawares?
Away, away! and like good citizens
Help swell the general joy with two such faces
As such as mine would only help to cloud.

EUSEBIO: Nay, sir—

CIPRIANO: But I say, Yea, sir! and my scholars
By yea and nay as I would have them do.

EUSEBIO: Well, then, farewell, sir.

CIPRIANO: Farewell, both of you.
                    [*Exeunt* EUSEBIO *and* JULIAN.

Away with them, light heart and wingèd heel,
Soon leaving drowsy Pallas and her dull
Professor out of sight, and out of mind.
And yet not so perhaps; and, were it so,
Why, better with the frolic herd forgetting
All in the youth and sunshine of the day
Than ruminating in the shade apart.
Well, each his way and humour; some to lie
Like Nature's sickly children in her lap,
While all the stronger brethren are at play;
When ev'n the mighty Mother's self would seem
Drest out in all her festival attire
In honour of the universal Sire

Whom Antioch as for her own to-day
Propitiates. Hark, the music!—Speed, good lads,
Or you will be too late. Ah, needless caution!
Ev'n now already half way down the hill,
Spurr'd by the very blood within their veins,
They catch up others, who catching from them
The fire they re-inflame, the flying troop
Consuming fast to distance in a cloud
Of dust themselves have kindled, whirls away
Where the shrill music blown above the walls
Tells of the solemn work begun within.
Why, ev'n the shrieking pipe that pierces here,
Shows me enough of all the long procession
Of white-robed priest and chanting chorister,
The milkwhite victim crown'd, and high aloft
The chariot of the nodding deity,
Whose brazen eyes that as their sockets see,
Stare at his loyal votaries. Ah me!—
Well, here too happier, if not wiser, those
Who, with the heart of unsuspicious youth,
Take up tradition from their father's hands
To pass it on to others in their turn;
But leaving me behind them in the race
With less indeed than little appetite
For ceremonies, and to gods, like these,
That, let the rabble shout for as they please,
Another sort begin to shake their heads at,
And heav'n to rumble with uneasily
As flinging out some antiquated gear.
So wide, since subtle Greece the pebble flung
Into the sleeping pool of superstition,
Its undulation spreads to other shores,
And saps at the foundation of our schools.
—Why, this last Roman, Caius Plinius—
Who drawing nature's growth and history
Down to her root and first cause—What says he?—
Ev'n at the very threshold of his book
A definition laying, over which
The clumsy mimic idols of our shrines

Stumble and break to pieces—oh, here it is—
"*Quapropter effigiem Dei formamque quærere,*
Imbecillitatis humanæ reor"—
"All visible effigies of God
But types of human imbecility."—
But what has Antioch to say to that,
Who at such cost of marble and of gold
Has built the very temple into which
She drags her tutelary Zeus to-day?—
Zeus veritable God, this effigy
Is none of him at all! But then, alas!
This same *Quapropter* follows a premiss
That elbows out Zeus with his effigy.
For—as I gather from his foreign word—
Wherever, or Whatever, Deity—
Si modo est alius—if distinct at all
From universal Nature—it must be
One all-informing, individual Whole,
All eye, all ear, all self, all sense, all soul—
Whereas this Zeus of ours, though Chief indeed—
Nay, *because* chief of other gods than he,
Comes from this Roman's hand no God at all!—
This is a knotty question.

LUCIFER (*without*):   Nor while I
Tangle, for you, good doctor, to untie.

CIPRIANO: What! The poor bird scarce settled on the bough,
Before the fowler after him! How now?
Who's there?

LUCIFER (*entering habited as a Merchant*): A stranger; therefore
pardon him,
Who somehow parted from his company,
And lost in his own thoughts (a company
You know one cannot lose so easily)
Has lost his way to Antioch.

CIPRIANO: Antioch!
Whose high white towers and temples ev'n from here
Challenge the sight, and scarce a random line
Traced by a wandering foot along the grass
But thither leads for centre.

LUCIFER: The old story,
    Of losing what one should have found on earth
    By staring after something in the clouds—
    Is it not so?
CIPRIANO: To-day too, when so many
    Are flocking thither to the festival,
    Whose current might have told—and taken—you
    The way you wish'd to go.
LUCIFER: To say the truth,
    My lagging here behind as much I think
    From a distaste for that same festival
    (Of which they told us as we came along)
    As inadvertency—my way of life
    Busied enough, if not too much, with men
    To care for them in crowd on holidays,
    When business stands, and neither they nor I
    Gaping about can profit one another;
    And therefore, by your leave—but only so—
    I fain would linger in this quiet place
    Till evening, under whose dusky cloak
    I may creep unobserved to Antioch.
CIPRIANO (*aside*): Humane address, at least. And why should I
    Grudge him the quiet I myself desire?—
    (*Aloud*) Nay, this is public ground—for you, as me,
    To use it at your pleasure.
LUCIFER: Still with yours—
    Whom by your sober suit and composed looks,
    And by this still society of books,
    I take to be a scholar—
CIPRIANO: And if so?
LUCIFER: Ill brooking idle company.
CIPRIANO: Perhaps;
    But that no wiser traveller need be—
    And, if I judge of you as you of me,
    Though with no book hung out for sign before,
    Perchance a scholar too.
LUCIFER: If so, more read
    In men than books, as travellers are wont.
    But, if myself but little of a bookman,

Addicted much to scholars' company,
Of whom I meet with many on my travels,
And who, you know, themselves are living books.
CIPRIANO: And you have travell'd much?
LUCIFER: Ay, little else,
One may say, since I came into the world
Than going up and down it: visiting
As many men and cities as Ulysses,
From first his leaving Troy without her crown,
Along the charmèd coasts he pass'd, with all
The Polyphemes and Circes in the way,
Right to the Pillars where his ship went down.
Nay, and yet further, where the dark Phœnician
Digs the pale metal which the sun scarce deigns
With a slant glance to ripen in earth's veins:
Or back again so close beneath his own
Proper dominion, that the very mould
Beneath he kindles into proper gold,
And strikes a living Iris into stone.
CIPRIANO: One place, however, where Ulysses was,
I think you have not been to—where he saw
Those he left dead upon the field of Troy
Come one by one to lap the bowl of blood
Set for them in the fields of Asphodel.
LUCIFER: Humph!—as to that, a voyage which if all
Must take, less need to brag of; or perchance
Ulysses, or his poet, apt to err
About the people and their doings there—
But let the wonders in the world below
Be what they may; enough in that above
For any sober curiosity,
Without one's diving down before one's time:
Not only countries now as long ago
Known, till'd, inhabited, and civilized;
As Egypt, Greece, and Rome, with all their arts,
Trades, customs, polities, and history:
But deep in yet scarce navigated seas,
Countries uncouth, with their peculiar growths
Of vegetation or of life; where men

Are savage as the soil they never till;
Or never were, or were so long ago,
Their very story blotted from the page
Of earth they wrote it on; unless perchance
From riot-running nature's overgrowth
Of swarming vegetation, peeps some scarce
Decypherable monument, which yet,
To those who find the key, perchance has told
Stories of men, more mighty men, of old,
Or of the gods themselves who walk'd the world
When with the dews of first creation wet.

CIPRIANO: Oh knowledge from the fountain freshly drawn
Without the tedious go-between of books!
But with fresh soul and senses unimpair'd
What from the pale reflexion of report
We catch at second hand, and much beside
That in our solitary cells we miss.

LUCIFER: Ay, truly we that travel see strange things,
Though said to tell of stranger; some of us,
Deceived ourselves, or seeking to deceive,
With prodigies and monsters which the world,
As wide and full of wonders as it is,
Never yet saw, I think, nor ever will:
Which yet your scholars use for clay and straw
Of which to build your mighty folios—
For instance, this same bulky Roman here,
Whose leaf you turn'd, I doubt impatiently,
When my intrusion rustled in the leaves—

CIPRIANO: Hah! But how knew you—

LUCIFER: Nay, if some stray words
Of old familiar Latin met my ear
As I stood hesitating.

CIPRIANO (*holding up the book*): This at least
You read then?

LUCIFER: One might say before 'twas written.

CIPRIANO: But how so?

LUCIFER: Oh, this same sufficient Roman
What is he but another of the many
Who having seen a little and heard more

L*   329

That others pick'd as loosely up before,
Constructs his little bird's-nest universe
Of shreds and particles of false and true
Cemented with some thin philosophy,
All filch'd from others, as from him to be
By the next pilfering philosopher,
Till blown away before the rising wind
Of true discovery, or dropt to nothing
After succeeding seasons of neglect.

CIPRIANO (*aside*): A strange man this—sharp wit and biting word.
(*Aloud*) Yet surely Man, after so many ages
Of patient observation of the world
He lives in, is entitled by the wit
Vouchsafed him by the Maker of the world
To draw into some comprehensive whole
The stray particulars.

LUCIFER: Ay, and forsooth,
Not only the material world he lives in;
But, having of this undigested heap
Composed a World, must make its Maker too,
Of abstract attributes, of each of which
Still more unsure than of the palpable,
Forthwith he draws to some consistent One
The accumulated ignorance of each
In so compact a plausibility
As light to carry as it was to build.

CIPRIANO: But, since (I know not how) you hit upon
The question I was trying when you came;
And, spite of your disclaiming scholarship,
Seem versed in that which occupies the best—
If Pliny blunder with his single God,
As in our twilight reason well he may,
Confess however that a Deity
Plural and self-discordant, as he says,
Is yet more like frail man's imagination,
Who, for his own necessities and lusts,
Splits up and mangles the Divine idea
To pieces, as he wants a piece of each;
Not only gods for all the elements

330

Divided into land, and sea, and sky;
But gods of health, wealth, love, and fortune; nay,
Of war and murder, rape and robbery;
Men of their own worse nature making gods
To serve the very vices that suggest them,
Which yet upon their fellow-men they visit
(Else were an end of human polity)
With chain and fine and banishment and death.
So that unless man made such gods as these,
Then are these gods worse than the man they made.
And for the attributes, which though indeed
You gibe at us for canvassing, yourself
Must grant—as whether one or manifold,
Deity in its simplest definition
Must be at least eternal—

LUCIFER: Well?—

CIPRIANO: Yet those
Who stuff Olympus are so little that,
That Zeus himself, the sovereign of all,
Barely escaped devouring at his birth
By his own father, who anticipated
And found some such hard measure for himself;
And as for Zeus' own progeny—some born
Of so much baser matter than his brain,
As from his eggs, which the all-mighty swan
Impregnated, and mortal Leda laid;
And whose two chicken-deities once hatch'd
Now live and die on each alternate day.

LUCIFER: Ay, but if much of this be allegory
In which the wisdom of antiquity
Veils the pure Deity from eyes profane—

CIPRIANO: —Deity taking arms against itself
Under Troy walls, wounding and wounded—ay,
And, trailing heavenly ichor from their wounds,
So help'd by others from the field to one
Who knew the leech's art themselves did not.

LUCIFER: Softly—if not to swear to allegory,
Still less to all the poets sing of heaven,
High up Parnassus as they think to sit.

CIPRIANO: But these same poets, therefore sacred call'd,
They are who these same allegories spin
Which time and fond tradition consecrate;
What might have been of the divine within
So overgrown with folly and with sin
As but a spark of God would such impure
Assimilation with himself abjure,
Which yet with all the nostril that he may
Zeus snuffs from Antioch's sacrifice to-day.
Besides, beyond the reach of allegory
The gods themselves in their own oracles
Doubly themselves convict—
As when they urge two nations on to war,
By promising the victory to each;
Whereby on one side their omniscience
Suffers, as their all-goodness on the other.

LUCIFER: What if such seeming contradictions aim
Where human understanding cannot reach?
But granting for the sake of argument,
And for that only, what you now premise;
What follows?

CIPRIANO:　　　　Why, that if, as Pliny writes,
Deity by its very definition
Be one, eternal, absolute, all wise,
All good, omnipotent, all ear, all eyes,
Incapable of disintegration—
If this be Deity indeed—

LUCIFER:　　　　　　Then what?

CIPRIANO: Simply—that we in Antioch know him not.

LUCIFER: Rash leap to necessary non-conclusion
From a premiss that quarrels with itself
More than the deity it would impugn;
For if one God eternal and all wise,
Omnipotent to do as to devise,
Whence this disorder and discordance in—
Not only this material universe,
That seems created only to be rack'd
By the rebellion of its elements,
In earthquake and tempestuous anarchy—

But also in the human microcosm
You say created to reflect it all?
For Deity, all goodness as all wise,
Why create man the thing of lust and lies
You say reflects himself in his false god?—
By modern oracle no more convicted
Of falsehood, than by that first oracle
Which first creation settled in man's heart.
No, if you must define, premise, conclude,
Away with all the coward squeamishness
That dares not face the universe it questions;
Blinking the evil and antagonism
Into its very constitution breathed
By him who, but himself to quarrel with,
Quarrels as might the many with each other.
Or would you be yourself one with yourself,
Catch hold of such as Epicurus' skirt,
Who, desperately confounded this confusion
Of matter, spirit, good and evil, yea,
Godhead itself, into a universe
That is created, roll'd along, and ruled,
By no more wise direction than blind Chance.
Trouble yourself no more with disquisition
That by sad, slow, and unprogressive steps
Of wasted soul and body lead to nothing:
And only sure of life's short breathing-while,
And knowing that the gods who threaten us
With after-vengeance of the very crimes
They revel in themselves, are nothing more
Than the mere coinage of our proper brain
To cheat us of our scanty pleasure here
With terror of a harsh account hereafter;—
Eat, drink, be merry; crown yourselves with flowers
About as lasting as the heads they garland;
And snatching what you can of life's poor feast,
When summon'd to depart, with no ill grace,
Like a too greedy guest, cling to the table
Whither the generations that succeed
Press forward famish'd for their turn to feed.

Nay, or before your time self-surfeited,
Wait not for nature's signal to be gone,
But with the potion of the spotted weed,
That peradventure wild beside your door
For some such friendly purpose cheaply grows,
Anticipate too tardy nature's call:
Ev'n as one last great Roman of them all
Dismiss'd himself betimes into the sum
Of universe; not nothing to become;
For that can never cease that was before;
But not that sad Lucretius any more.

CIPRIANO: Oh, were it not that sometimes through the dark,
That walls us all about, a random ray
Breaks in to tell one of a better day
Beyond—

Enter LELIO *and* FLORO, *as about to fight.*

LELIO: Enough—these branches that exclude the sun
Defy all other inquisition.
No need of further way.

FLORO: Nor further word;
Draw, sir, at once—

LELIO: Nay, parry that yourself
Which waited not your summons to be drawn.

CIPRIANO: Lelio, and Floro?

FLORO: What, will the leaves blab?

LELIO: And with their arms arrest a just revenge?

CIPRIANO: And well indeed may trees begin to talk,
When men as you go babbling.

FLORO: Whoso speaks
And loves his life, hold back.

LELIO: I know the voice,
But dazzled with the darkness—Cipriano?

CIPRIANO: Ay; Cipriano, sure enough; as you
Lelio and Floro.

FLORO: Well, let that suffice,
And leave us as you find us.

CIPRIANO: No, not yet—

FLORO: Not yet!

334

LELIO: Good Cipriano—
CIPRIANO: Till I know
    How it has come to pass that two such friends,
    Each of the noblest blood in Antioch,
    Are here to shed it by each other's hands.
LELIO: Sudden surprise, and old respect for you,
    Suspend my sword a moment, Cipriano,
    That else—
FLORO: Stand back, stand back! You are a scholar,
    And better versed in logic than the laws
    Of honour; and perhaps have yet to learn
    That when two noblemen have drawn the sword,
    One only must return it to the sheath.
LELIO: 'Tis so indeed—once more, stand off.
CIPRIANO: And once more
    Back, both of you, say I; if of your lives
    Regardless, not of mine, which thus, unarm'd,
    I fling between your swords—
    Lelio, I look to you—Floro, as ever
    Somewhat hot-headed and thrasonical—
    Or do you hold with him the scholar's gown
    Has smother'd all the native soldiery
    That saucy so-call'd honour to itself
    Alone mis-arrogates? You are deceived:
    I am like you by birth a gentleman,
    Under like obligation to the laws
    Of that true honour, which my books indeed
    May help distinguish from its counterfeit,
    But, older as I am, have yet not chill'd
    From catching fire at any just affront—
    And let me tell you this too—those same books,
    Ancient and modern, tell of many a hand
    That, turning most assiduously the leaf,
    When the time came, could wield as well the sword.
    I am unarm'd: but you, with all your swords,
    I say you shall not turn them on each other
    Till you have told me what the quarrel is;
    Which after hearing if I own for one
    That honour may not settle with good word,

335

I pledge my own to leave it to the sword.
Now, Lelio!—

LELIO: One answer does for both:
He loves where I love.

FLORO: No—I thus much more—
He dares to love where I had loved before;
Betrayèd friendship adding to the score
Of upstart love.

LELIO: You hear him, Cipriano?
And after such a challenge—

CIPRIANO: Yet a moment.
As there are kinds of honour, so of love—
And ladies—

LELIO: Cipriano, Cipriano!
One friend my foe for daring love where I,
Let not another, daring doubt that he
Honours himself in so dishonouring me—

FLORO: Slanting your sharp divisions on a jewel
That if the sun turn'd all his beams upon
He could not find, or make, a flaw—

CIPRIANO: Nor I then,
With far less searching scrutiny than Phœbus—
I am to understand then, such a fair
Jewel as either would in wedlock wear.

FLORO: And rather die than let another dare.

CIPRIANO: Enough, enough! of Lelio's strange logic,
And Floro's more intelligible rant,
And back to sober metaphor. Which of you
Has this fair jewel turn'd her light upon?

FLORO (after a pause): Why, who would boast—

LELIO: Indeed, how could she be
The very pearl of chastity she is,
Turn'd she her glances either left or right?

CIPRIANO: Which therefore each, as he obliquely steals,
Counts on as given him only—

FLORO: To have done
With metaphor and logic, what you will,
So as we fall to work;
Or if you must have reason, this, I say,

Resolves itself to a short syllogism—
Whether she give or we presume upon—
If one of us devote himself to win her,
How dares another cross him?

CIPRIANO: But if she
Not only turn to neither, but still worse,
Or better, turn from both?

LELIO: But love by long devotion may be won,
That only one should offer—

FLORO: And that one
Who first—

LELIO: Who first!—

CIPRIANO: And all this while, forsooth,
The lady, of whose purity one test
Is her unblemish'd unpublicity,
Is made a target for the common tongue
Of Antioch to shoot reproaches at
For stirring up two noblemen to blood.
From which she only can escape, forsooth,
By choosing one of two she cares not for
At once; or else, to mend the matter, when
He comes to claim her by the other's blood.

LELIO: At least she will not hate him, live or dead,
Who staked his life upon her love.

CIPRIANO: Small good
To him who lost the stake; and he that won—
Will she begin to love whom not before
For laying unloved blood upon her door;
Or, if she ever loved at all, love more?
Is this fair logic, or of one who knows
No more of woman's honour than of man's?
Come, come, no more of beating round the bush.
You know how I have known and loved you both,
As brothers—say as sons—upon the score
Of some few years and some few books read more—
Though two such fiery fine young gentlemen,
Put up your swords and be good boys again,
Deferring to your ancient pedagogue;
If cold by time and studies, as you say,

337

Then fitter for a go-between in love,
And warm at least in loyalty to you.
These jewels—to take up the metaphor
Until you choose to drop it of yourselves,—
These jewels have their caskets, I suppose—
Kindred and circumstance, I mean—

LELIO: Oh such

As by their honourable poverty
Do more than doubly set their jewel off!

CIPRIANO: Ev'n so? And may not one, who, you agree,
Proof-cold against suspicion of the kind,
Be so far trusted, as, if not to see,
To hear, at least, of where, and how, enshrined?

FLORO: I know not what to answer. How say you?

LELIO: Relying on your honour and tried love—
Justina, daughter of the old Lisandro.

CIPRIANO: I know them; her if scarcely, yet how far
Your praises short of her perfections are;
Him better, by some little service done
That rid him of a greater difficulty,
And would again unlock his door to me—
—And who knows also, if you both agree,
Her now closed lips; if but a sigh between
May tell which way the maiden heart may lean?

FLORO: Again, what say you, Lelio?

LELIO: I, for one,

Content with that decision.

FLORO: Be it so.

CIPRIANO: Why, after all, behold how luckily
You stumbled on this rock in honour's road,
That serves instead for Cupid's stepping-stone.
And when the knightly courage of you both
Was all at fault to hammer out the way,
Who knows but some duenna-doctor may?
And will—if but like reasonable men,
Not angry boys, you promise to keep sheathed
Your swords, while from her father or herself
I gather, from a single sigh perhaps,
To which, if either, unaware she turns;

    Provided, if to one, the other yield;
    But if to neither, both shall quit the field.
    What say you both to this?
LELIO: Ay—I for one.
FLORO: And I; provided on the instant done.
CIPRIANO: No better time than now, when, as I think,
    The city, with her solemn uproar busy,
    Shuts her we have to do with close within.
    But you must come along with me, for fear
    Your hands go feeling for your swords again
    If left together: and besides to know
    The verdict soon as spoken.
LELIO: Let us go.   [*Exeunt.*
LUCIFER (*re-appearing*): Ay, Cipriano, faster than you think;
    For I will lend you wings to burn yourself
    In the same taper they are singed withal.—
    By the quick feelers of iniquity
    That from hell's mouth reach through this lower
        world,
    And tremble to the lightest touch of mischief,
    Warn'd of an active spirit hereabout
    Of the true God inquisitive, and restless
    Under the false by which I rule the world,
    Here am I come to test it for myself.
    And lo! two fools have put into my hand
    The snare that, wanting most, I might have miss'd;
    That shall not him alone en-mesh, but *her*
    Whom I have long and vainly from the ranks
    Striv'n to seduce of Him, the woman-born,
    Who is one day to bruise the serpent's head—
    So is it written; but meanwhile my hour
    On earth is not accomplish'd, and I fain
    Of this detested race would hinder all
    From joining in the triumph of my fall
    Whom I may hinder; and of these, these twain;
    Each other by each other snaring; yea,
    Either at once the other's snare and prey.
    Oh, my good doctor, you must doubt, you must,
    And take no more the good old gods on trust;

To Antioch then away; but not so fast
But I shall be before you, starting last.   [*Exit.*

SCENE II.—*A Room in* LISANDRO'S *house.*—*Enter* LISANDRO,
JUSTINA, *and* LIVIA.

JUSTINA: At length the day draws in.
LISANDRO: And in with it
     The impious acclamation that all day,
     Block up our doors and windows as we may,
     Insults our faith, and doubly threatens it.
     Is all made fast, Justina?
JUSTINA: All shall be, sir,
     When I have seen you safely to your rest.
LISANDRO: You know how edict after edict aim'd
     By Rome against the little band of Christ—
     And at a time like this, the people drunk
     With idol-ecstasy—
JUSTINA: Alas, alas!
LISANDRO: Oh, gladly would I scatter these last drops
     That now so scarcely creep along my veins,
     And these thin locks that tremble o'er the grave,
     In such a martyrdom as swept to heav'n
     The holy Paul who planted, and all those
     Who water'd here the true and only faith,
     Were 't not for thee, for fear of thee, Justina,
     Drawing you down at once into my doom,
     Or leaving you behind, alone, to hide
     From insult and suspicion worse than death—
     I dare not think of it. Make fast; keep close;
     And then, God's will be done! You know we lie
     Under a double danger.
JUSTINA: How so, sir?
LISANDRO: Aurelio and Fabio, both, you know,
     So potent in the city, and but now
     Arm'd with a freshly whetted sword of vengeance
     Against the faith, but double-edged on us,
     Should they but know, as know they must, their sons
     Haunting the doors of this suspected house.

340

JUSTINA: Alas, alas!
    That I should draw this danger on your head!
    Which yet you know—
LISANDRO: I know, I know—God knows,
    My darling daughter; but that chaste reserve
    Serves but to quicken beauty with a charm
    They find not in the wanton Venus here:
    Drawn as they are by those withdrawing eyes
    Irradiate from a mother's, into whose
    The very eyes of the Redeemer look'd,
    And whom I dare not haste to join in heav'n
    At cost of leaving thee defenceless here.
JUSTINA: Sufficient for the day! And now the day
    Is done. Come to your chamber—lean on me—
    Livia and I will see that all is fast;
    And, that all seen to, ere we sleep ourselves,
    Come to your bedside for your blessing. Hark!
    Knocking ev'n now! See to it, Livia.
           (*She leads out* LISANDRO, *and returns.*)
    Oh, well I got my father to his chamber!
    What is it?—
LIVIA: One would see your father, madam.
JUSTINA: At such an hour! He cannot, Livia;
    You know, the poor old man is gone to rest—
    Tell him—
LIVIA: If not your father, then yourself,
    On matter that he says concerns you both.
JUSTINA: Me too!—Oh surely neither of the twain
    We both so dread?
LIVIA: No, madam; rather, one
    I think that neither need have cause to fear,—
    Cipriano.
JUSTINA: Cipriano! The great scholar,
    Who did my father service, as I think,
    And now may mean another; and God knows
    How much, or quickly, needed!
LIVIA: So he says.
JUSTINA: What shall I do! Will not to-morrow—
CIPRIANO (*entering*):   Oh, lady,

You scarce can wonder more than I myself
At such a visit, and at such an hour,
Only let what I come to say excuse
The coming, and so much unmannerly.

JUSTINA: My father is withdrawn, sir, for the night,
 Never more wanting rest; I dare not rouse him,
 And least of all with any troubled news.
 Will not to-morrow—

CIPRIANO: What I have to say
 Best told to night, at once; and not the less
 Since you alone, whom chiefly it concerns,
 Are here to listen.

JUSTINA: I!—Well, sir, relying
 On your grave reputation as a scholar,
 And on your foregone favour to my father,
 If I should dare to listen—

CIPRIANO: And alone?

JUSTINA: Livia, leave us.   [*Exit* LIVIA.

CIPRIANO: Oh, lady—oh, Justina—
 (Thus stammers the ambassador of love
 In presence of its sovereign)—
 You must—cannot but—know how many eyes
 Those eyes have wounded—

JUSTINA: Nay, sir,—

CIPRIANO: Nay, but hear.
 I do not come for idle compliment,
 Nor on my own behalf; but in a cause
 On which hang life and death as well as love.
 Two of the noblest youths in Antioch,
 Lelio and Floro—Nay, but hear me out:
 Mine, and till now almost from birth each other's
 Inseparable friends, now deadly foes
 For love of you—

JUSTINA: Oh, sir!

CIPRIANO: I have but now
 Parted their swords in mortal quarrel cross'd.

JUSTINA: Oh, that was well.

CIPRIANO: I think, for several sakes—
 Their own, their fathers', even Antioch's,

That would not lose one of so choice a pair;
And, I am sure you think so, lady, yours,
So less than covetous of public talk,
And least of all at such a fearful cost.

JUSTINA: Oh, for all sakes all thanks!

CIPRIANO: Yet little due
For what so lightly done, and it may be
So insufficiently; this feud not stopt—
Suspended only, on a single word—
Which now at this unseasonable hour
I stand awaiting from the only lips
That can allay the quarrel they have raised.

JUSTINA: Alas, why force an answer from my lips
So long implied in silent disregard?

CIPRIANO: Yet, without which, like two fierce dogs, but more
Exasperated by the holding back,
They will look for it in each other's blood.

JUSTINA: And think, poor men, to find their answer there!
Oh, sir, you are the friend, the friend of both,
A famous scholar; with authority
And eloquence to press your friendship home.
Surely in words such as you have at will
You can persuade them, for all sakes—and yet
No matter mine perhaps—but, as you say,
Their fathers', Antioch's, their own—

CIPRIANO: Alas!
I doubt you know not in your maiden calm
How fast all love and logic such as that
Burns stubble up before a flame like this.

JUSTINA (aside): And none in heav'n to help them!

CIPRIANO: All I can
But one condition hardly wringing out
Of peace, till my impartial embassy
Have ask'd on their behalf, which of the twain—
How shall I least offend?—you least disdain.

JUSTINA: Disdain is not the word, sir; oh, no, no!
I know and honour both as noblemen
Of blood and station far above my own;
And of so suitable accomplishments.

Oh, there are many twice as fair as I,
And of their own conditions, who, with half
My wooing, long ere this had worn the wreath
Tied with a father's blessing, and all Antioch
To follow them with Hymenæal home.

CIPRIANO: But if these fiery men, do what one will,
Will look no way but this?—

JUSTINA: Oh, but they will;
Divert their eyes awhile, a little while,
Their hearts will follow; such a sudden passion
Can but have struck a shallow root—perhaps
Ere this had perish'd, had not rival pride
Between them blown it to this foolish height.

CIPRIANO: Disdain is not the word then. Well, to seek,
What still as wide as ever from assent—
Could you but find it in your heart to feel
If but a hair's-breadth less—say disesteem
For one than for another—

JUSTINA: No, no, no!
Even to save their lives I could not say
What is not—cannot—nay, and if it could
And I could say that was that is not—*can* not—
How should that hair's-breadth less of hope to one
Weigh with the other to desist his suit,
Both furious as you tell me?

CIPRIANO: And both are:
But ev'n that single hair thrown in by you
Will turn the scale that else the sword must do.

JUSTINA: But surely must it not suffice for both
That they who drew the sword in groundless hope
Sheathe it in sure despair? Despair! Good God!
For a poor creature like myself, despair!
That men with souls to which a word like that
Lengthens to infinite significance,
Should pin it on a wretched woman's sleeve!
But as men talk—I mean, so far as I
Can make them, as they say, despair of that
Of which, even for this world's happiness,
Despair is better hope of better things—

Will not my saying—and as solemnly
As what one best may vouch for; that so far
As any hope of my poor liking goes,
Despair indeed they must—why should not this
Allay their wrath, and let relapsing love
In his old channel all the clearer run
For this slight interjection in the current?
Why should it not be so?

CIPRIANO: Alas, I know not:
For though as much they promised, yet I doubt
When each, however you reject him now,
Believes you might be won hereafter still,
Were not another to divide the field;
Each upon each charging the exigence
He will not see lies in himself alone,
Might draw the scarcely sheathèd sword at once;
Or stifled hate under a hollow truce
Blaze out anew at some straw's provocation,
And I perhaps not by to put it out.

JUSTINA: What can, what can be done then?

CIPRIANO: Oh Justina,
Pardon this iteration. Think once more,
Before your answer with its consequence
Travels upon my lip to destiny.
I know you more than maiden-wise reserved
To other importunities of love
Than those which ev'n the pure for pure confess;
Yet no cold statue, which, however fair,
Could not inflame so fierce a passion; but
A breathing woman with a beating heart,
Already touch'd with pity, you confess,
For these devoted men you cannot love.
Well, then—I will not hint at such a bower
As honourable wedlock would entwine
About your father's age and your own youth,
Which ev'n for him—and much less for yourself—
You would not purchase with an empty hand.
But yet, with no more of your heart within
Than what you now confess to—pity—pity,

345

For generous youth wearing itself away
In thankless adoration at your door,
Neglecting noble opportunities;
Turning all love but yours to deadly hate—
Sedate, and wise, and modestly resolved,
Can you be, lady, of yourself so sure—
(And surely they will argue your disdain
As apt to yield as their devotion)—
That, all beside so honourably faced,
You, who now look with pity, and perhaps
With gratitude, upon their blundering zeal,
May not be won to turn an eye less loath
On one of them, and blessing one, save both?

JUSTINA: Alas! I know it is impossible—
Not if they wasted all their youth in sighs,
And even slavish importunities,
I could but pity—pity all the more
That all the less what only they implore
To yield; so great a gulf between us lies.

CIPRIANO: What—is the throne pre-occupied?

JUSTINA: If so,
By one that Antioch dreams little of.
But it grows late: and if we spoke till dawn,
I have no more to say.

CIPRIANO: Nor more will hear?

JUSTINA: Alas, sir, to what purpose? When, all said,
Said too as you have said it—
And I have but the same hard answer still;
Unless to thank you once and once again,
And charge you with my thankless errand back,
But in such better terms,
As, if it cannot stop ill blood, at least
Shall stop blood-shedding 'tween these hapless
       men.

CIPRIANO: And shall the poor ambassador who fail'd
In the behalf of those who sent him here,
Hereafter dare to tell you how he sped
In making peace between them?

JUSTINA: Oh, do but that,

346

And what poor human prayer can win from Heav'n,
You shall not be the poorer. So, good-night! *[Exit.*
CIPRIANO: Good-night, good-night! Oh Lelio and Floro!
If ever friends well turn'd to deadly foes,
Wiser to fight than I to interpose. *[Exit.*
LUCIFER (*passing from behind*): The shaft has hit the mark; and
by the care
Of hellish surgery shall fester there. *[Exit.*

ACT II

SCENE I.—*The sea-shore; a storm raging.*

CIPRIANO (*cavalierly drest*): Oh, mad, mad, mad, ambition! to
    the skies
    Lifting to drop me deep as Hades down!—
    What! Cipriano—what the once so wise
    Cipriano—quit his wonted exercise
    Among the sober walks of old renown,
    To fly at love—to swell the wind with sighs
    Vainer than learning—doff the scholar's gown
    For cap and feather, and such airy guise
    In which triumphant love is wont to go,
    But wins less acceptation in her eyes—
    The only eyes in which I cared to show—
    My heart beneath the borrow'd feather bleeding—
    Than in the sable suit of long ago,
    When heart-whole for another's passion pleading.
    She loves not Floro—loves not Lelio,
    Whose quarrel sets the city's throat agape,
    And turns her reputation to reproof
    With altercation of some dusky shape
    Haunting the twilight underneath her roof—
    Which each believes the other:—and, for me,
    The guilty one of the distracted three,
    She closest veils herself, or waves aloof
    In scorn; or in such self-abasement sweet
    As sinks me deep and deeper at her feet,
    Bids me return—return for very shame
    Back to my proper studies and good name,
    Nor waste a life on one who, let me pine
    To death, will never but in death be mine.
    Oh, she says well—Oh, heart of stone and ice

Unworthy of the single sacrifice
Of one true heart's devotion! Oh divine
Creature, whom all the glory and the worth
That ever ravaged or redeem'd the earth
Were scanty worship offer'd at your shrine!
Oh Cipriano, master-fool of all
The fools that unto thee for wisdom call;
Of supercilious Pallas first the mock,
And now blind Cupid's scorn, and laughing-stock;
Who in fantastic arrogance at odds
With the Pantheon of your people's gods
Ransack'd the heavens for one more pure and whole
To fill the empty temple of the soul,
Now caught by retribution in the mesh
Of one poor piece of perishable flesh—
What baser demon of the pit would buy
With all your ruin'd aspirations?

LUCIFER (*within*):   I!—

CIPRIANO: What! The very winds and waters
                    Hear, and answer to the cry
                    She is deaf to!—Better thrown
                    On distracted nature's bosom
                    With some passion like my own
                    Torn and tortured: where the sun
                    In the elemental riot
                    Ere his daily reign half done,
                    Leaves half-quencht the tempest-drencht
                    Welkin scowling on the howling
                    Wilderness of waves that under
                    Slash of whirlwind, spur of lightning,
                    Roar of thunder, black'ning, whit'ning,
                    Fling them foaming on the shore—
                    Let confusion reign and roar!—
                    Lightnings, for your target take me!
                    Waves, upon the sharp rock break me,
                    Or into your monstrous hollow
                    Back regurgitating hurl;
                    Let the mad tornado whirl me
                    To the furthest airy circle

Dissipated of the sky,
Or the gaping earth down-swallow
To the centre!—

LUCIFER (*entering*):   By-and-bye.

CIPRIANO: Hark again! and in her monstrous
        Labour, with a human cry
        Nature yearning—what portentous
        Glomeration of the storm
        Darkly cast in human form,
        Has she bolted!—

LUCIFER: As among
        Flashes of the lightning flung
        Beside you, in its thunder now
        Aptly listen'd—

CIPRIANO: What art thou?

LUCIFER: One of a realm, though dimly in your charts
    Discern'd, so vast that as from out of it
    As from a fountain all the nations flow,
    Back they shall ebb again; and sway'd by One
    Who, without Oriental over-boast,
    Because from him all kings their crowns derive,
    Is rightfully saluted King of kings,
    Whose reign is as his kingdom infinite,
    Whose throne is heaven, and earth his footstool, and
    Sun, moon, and stars his diadem and crown.
    Who at the first disposal of his kingdom
    And distribution into sea and land—
    Me, who for splendour of my birth and grand
    Capacities above my fellows shone,
    Star of the Morning, Lucifer, alone—
    Me he made captain of the host who stand
    Clad as the morning star about his throne.
    Enough for all ambition but my own;
    Who discontented with the all but all
    Of chiefest subject of Omnipotence
    Rebell'd against my Maker; insolence
    Avenged as soon as done on me and all
    Who bolster'd up rebellion, by a fall
    Far as from heav'n to Hades. Madness, I know;

350

But worse than madness whining to repent
Under a rod that never will relent.
Therefore about the land and sea I go
Arm'd with the very instrument of hate
That blasted me: lightnings anticipate
My coming, and the thunder rolls behind;
Thus charter'd to enlarge among mankind,
And to recruit from human discontent
My ranks in spirit, not in number, spent.
Of whom, in spite of this brave gaberdine,
I recognize thee one: thee, by the line
Scarr'd on thy brow, though not so deep as mine;
Thee by the hollow circles of those eyes
Where the volcano smoulders but not dies:
Whose fiery torrent running down has scarr'd
The cheek that time had not so deeply marr'd.
Do not I read thee rightly?

CIPRIANO: But too well;
However come to read me—

LUCIFER: By the light
Of my own darkness reading yours—how deep!
But not, as mine is, irretrievable:
Who from the fulness of my own perdition
Would, as I may, revenge myself on him
By turning to fruition your despair—
What if I make you master at a blow,
Not only of the easy woman's heart
You now despair of as impregnable,
And waiting but my word to let you in,
But lord of nature's secret, and the lore
That shall not only with the knowledge, but
Possess you with the very power of him
You sought so far and vainly for before:
So far All-eyes, All-wise, Omnipotent—
If not to fashion, able yet to shake
That which the other took such pains to make—
As in the hubbub round us; I who blurr'd
The spotless page of nature at a word
With darkness and confusion, will anon

Clear it, to write another marvel on.—
    By the word of power that binds
    And loosens; by the word that finds
    Nature's heart through all her rinds,
    Hearken, waters, fires, and winds;
    Having had your roar, once more
    Down with you, or get you gone.

CIPRIANO: With the clatter and confusion
    Of the universe about me
    Reeling—all within, without me,—
    Dizzy, dazzled—if delusion,
    Waking, dreaming, seeing, seeming—
    Which I know not—only, lo!
    Like some mighty madden'd beast
    Bellowing in full career
    Of fury, by a sudden blow
    Stunn'd, and in a moment stopp'd
    All the roar, or into slow
    Death-ward-drawing murmur, leaving
    Scarce the fallen carcase heaving,
    With the fallen carcase dropp'd.—

Behold! the word scarce fallen from his lips,
Swift almost as a human smile may chase
A frown from some conciliated face,
The world to concord from confusion slips:
The winds that blew the battle up dead slain,
Or with their tatter'd standards swept amain
From heav'n; the billows of the erected deep
Roll'd with their crests into the foaming plain;
While the scared earth begins abroad to peep
And smooth her ruffled locks, as from a rent
In the black centre of the firmament,
Revenging his unnatural eclipse,
The Lord of heav'n from its ulterior blue
That widens round him as he pierces through
The folded darkness, from his sovereign height
Slays with a smile the dragon-gloom of night.

LUCIFER: All you have heard and witness'd hitherto
    But a foretaste to quicken appetite

For that substantial after-feast of power
That I shall set you down to take your fill of:
When not the fleeting elements alone
Of wind, and fire, and water, floating wrack,
But this same solid frame of earth and stone,
Yea, with the mountain loaded on her back,
Reluctantly, shall answer to your spell
From a more adamantine heart stone-cold
Than her's you curse for inaccessible.
What, you would prove it? Let the mountain there
Step out for witness. Listen, and behold.

      Monster upshot of upheaving*
      Earth, by fire and flood conceiving;
      Shapeless ark of refuge, whither,
      When came deluge creeping round,
      Man retreated—to be drown'd—
      Now your granite anchor, fast
      In creation's centre, cast,
      Come with all your tackle cleaving
      Down before the magic blast—

CIPRIANO: And the unwieldy vessel, lo!
      Rib and deck of rock, and shroud
      Of pine, top-gallanted with cloud,
      All her forest-canvas squaring,
      Down the undulating woodland
      As she flounders to and fro
      All before her tearing, bearing
      Down upon us—

LUCIFER: Anchor, ho!—
Behold the ship in port! And what if freighted
With but one jewel, worthy welcome more
Than ever full-fraught Argosy awaited,
At last descried by desperate eyes ashore;
From the first moment of her topsail showing
Like a thin cobweb spun 'twixt sea and sky;
Then momently before a full wind blowing

---

* The Phenomena that follow, and are here supposed to be the magic illusions created in Cipriano's eyes, are in the original represented by theatrical Machinery.

Into her full proportions, till athwart
The seas that bound beneath her, by and bye
She sweeps full sail into the cheering port—
 Strangest bark that ever plied
 In despite of wind and tide,
 At the captain's magic summons
 Down your granite ribs divide,
 And show the jewel hid inside.

CIPRIANO: Justina!—
LUCIFER: Soft! The leap that looks so easy
 Yet needs a longer stride than you can master.
CIPRIANO: Oh divine apparition, that I fain
 Would all my life as in Elysium lose
 Only by gazing after; and thus soon
 As rolling cloud across the long'd-for moon,
 The impitiable rocks enclose again!—
 But was it she indeed?
LUCIFER: She that shall be,
 And yours, by means that, bringing her to you,
 Possess you of all nature, which in vain
 You sigh'd for ere for nature's masterpiece.
 And thus much, as I told you, only sent
 As foretaste of that great accomplishment,
 Which if you will but try for, you can reach
 By means which, if I practise, I can teach.
CIPRIANO: And at what cost?
LUCIFER: You that have flung so many years away
 In learning and in love that came to nothing,
 Think not to win the harvest in a day!
 The God you search for works, you know, by means
 (That your philosophers call second cause),
 And we by means must underwork him—
CIPRIANO: Well!—
LUCIFER: To comprehend, and, after, to constrain
 Whose mysteries you will not count as vain
 A year in this same mountain lock'd with me?—
CIPRIANO: Where she is?—
LUCIFER: As I told you, where shall be
 At least this mountain after a short labour

Has brought forth something better than a mouse;
And what then after a whole year's gestation
Accomplish under our joint midwifery,
Under a bond by which you bind you mine
In fewer and no redder drops than needs
The leech of land or water when he bleeds?
Let us about—but first upon his base
The mountain we must study in replace,
That else might puzzle your geography.
Come, take your stand upon the deck with me,
Till with her precious cargo safe inside,
And all her forest-colours flying wide,
The mighty vessel put again to sea—
What, are you ready?—Wondrous smack,
    As without a turn or tack
    Hither come, so thither back,
    And let subside the ruffled deep
    Of earth to her primæval sleep.—
How steadily her course the good ship trims,
While Antioch far into the distance swims,
With all her follies bubbling in the wake;
Her scholars that more hum than honey make:
Muses so chaste as never of their kind
Would breed, and Cupid deaf as well as blind:
For Cipriano, wearied with the toil
Of so long working on a thankless soil,
At last embarking upon magic seas
In a more wondrous Argo than of old,
Sets sails with me for such Hesperides
As glow with more than dragon-guarded gold. [*Exeunt.*

ACT III

SCENE I.—*Before the mountain.* CIPRIANO.

CIPRIANO: Now that at last in his eternal round
    Hyperion, after skirting either pole,
    Of his own race has set the flaming goal
    In heav'n of my probation under-ground:
    Up from the mighty Titan with his feet
    Touching the centre, and his forest-hair
    Entangling with the stars; whose middle womb
    Of two self-buried lives has been the tomb;
    At last, my year's apprenticeship complete,
    I rise to try my cunning, and as one
    Arm'd in the dark who challenges the sun.
    You heav'ns, for me your azure brows with cloud
    Contract, or to your inmost depth unshroud:
    Thou sapphire-floating counterpart below,
    Obsequious of my moon-like magic flow:
    For me you mountains fall, you valleys rise,
    With all your brooks and fountains far withdrawn;
    You forests shudder underneath my sighs;
    And whatsoever breathes in earth and skies;
    You birds that on the bough salute the dawn;
    And you wild creatures that through wood and glen
    Do fly the hunter, or the hunter flies;
    Yea, man himself, most terrible to men;
    Troop to my word, about my footstep fawn;
    Yea, ev'n you spirits that by viewless springs
    Move and perplex the tangled web of things,
    Wherever in the darkest crypt you lurk
    Of nature, nature to my purpose work;
    That not the dead material element,
    But complicated with the life beyond
    Up to pure spirit, shall my charm resent,

 And take the motion of my magic wand;
 And, once more shaken on her ancient throne,
 In me old nature a new master own.
LUCIFER: But how is this, Cipriano, that misled
 By hasty passion you affront the day
 Ere master of the art of darkness?
CIPRIANO: Nay,
 By that same blazing witness overhead
 Standing in heav'n to mark the time foretold,
 Since first imprison'd in this mountain-hold
 My magic so preluded with the dread
 Preliminary kingdom of the dead,
 That not alone the womb of general earth
 Which Death has crowded thick with second birth,
 But monuments with marble lips composed
 To dream till doomsday, suddenly disclosed,
 And woke their sleepers centuries too soon
 To stare upon the old remember'd moon.
 Wearied of darkness, I will see the day:
 Sick of the dead, the living will assay:
 And if the ghastly year I have gone through
 Bear half its promised harvest, will requite
 With a too warm good-morrow the long night
 That one cold living heart consign'd me to.
LUCIFER: Justina!
CIPRIANO: Ay, Justina: now no more
 Obsequiously sighing at the door
 That never open'd, nor the heart of stone
 On which so long I vainly broke my own;
 But of her soul and body, when and how
 I will, I claim the forfeit here and now.
LUCIFER: Enough: the hour is come; do thou design
 The earth with circle, pentagram, and trine;
 The wandering airs with incantation twine;
 While through her sleep-enchanted sense I shake
 The virgin constancy I cannot break.
 (*Clouds roll before the mountain, hiding* CIPRIANO.)
 Thou nether realm of darkness and despair,
 Whose fire-enthronèd emperor am I;

Where many-knotted till the word they lie,
Your subtlest spirits at the word untie,
And breathe them softly to this upper air;
With subtle soft insinuation fair
Of foul result encompass and attaint
The chastity of the rebellious saint
Who dares the Spirit of this world defy.
Spirits that do shapeless float
In darkness as in light the mote,
At my summons straightway take
Likeness of the fairest make,
And, her sleeping sense about
Seal'd from all the world without,
Through the bolted eyelids creep;
Entheatre the walls of sleep
With an Eden where the sheen
Of the leaf and flower between
All is freshest, yet with Eve's
Apple peeping through the leaves;
Through whose magic mazes may
Melancholy fancy stray
Till she lose herself, or into
Softer passion melt away:
While the scent-seducing rose
Gazing at her as she goes
With her turning as she turns,
Into her his passion burns;
While the wind among the boughs
Whispers half-remember'd vows;
Nightingale interpreters
Into their passion translate hers;
And the murmurs of a stream
Down one current draw the dream.
While for hidden chorus, I
At her dreaming ear supply
Such a comment as her own
Heart to nature's shall atone:
Till the secret influence
Of the genial season even

Holy blood that sets to heaven
Draws into the lower sense;
Till array'd in angel guise
Earthly memories surprise
Ev'n the virgin soul, and win
Holy pity's self to sin.

(*The clouds roll away, and discover* JUSTINA *asleep in her chamber*.)

LUCIFER (*at her ear*): Come forth, come forth, Justina, come;
     for scared
    Winter is vanish'd, and victorious Spring
    Has hung her garland on the boughs he bared:
    Come forth; there is a time for everything.
JUSTINA (*in her sleep*): That was my father's voice—come, Livia—
    My mantle—oh, not want it?—well then, come.
LUCIFER: Ay, come abroad, Justina; it is Spring;
    The world is not with sunshine and with leaf
    Renew'd to be the tomb of ceaseless grief;
    Come forth: there is a time for everything.
JUSTINA: How strange it is—
    I think the garden never look'd so gay
    As since my father died.
LUCIFER: Ev'n so: for now,
    Returning with the summer wind, the hours
    Dipp'd in the sun re-dress the grave with flowers,
    And make new wreaths for the survivor's brow;
    Whose spirit not to share were to refuse
    The power that all creating, all renews
    With self-diffusive warmth, that, with the sun's,
    At this due season through creation runs,
    Nor in the first creation more express'd
    Than by the singing builder of the nest
    That waves on this year's leaf, or by the rose
    That underneath them in his glory glows;
    Life's fountain, flower, and crown; without whose giving
    Life itself were not, nor, without, worth living.
CHORUS OF VOICES: Life's fountain, flower, and crown; with-
    out whose giving
    Life itself were not, nor, without, worth living.

Song

Who that in his hour of glory
  Walks the kingdom of the rose,
And misapprehends the story
  Which through all the garden blows;
Which the southern air who brings
It touches, and the leafy strings
  Lightly to the touch respond;
And nightingale to nightingale
  Answering a bough beyond—
Chorus. Nightingale to nightingale
  Answering a bough beyond.

JUSTINA: These serenaders—singing their old songs
  Under one's window—
LUCIFER: Ay, and if nature must decay or cease
  Without it; what of nature's masterpiece?
  Not in her outward lustre only, but
  Ev'n in the soul within the jewel shut;
  What but a fruitless blossom; or a lute
  Without the hand to touch it music-mute:
  Incense that will not rise to heav'n unfired;
  By that same vernal spirit uninspired
  That sends the blood up from the heart, and speaks
  In the rekindled lustre of the cheeks?
CHORUS: Life's fountain, flower, and crown; without whose
  giving
  Life itself were not, nor, without, worth living.

Song.

Lo the golden Girasolé,
  That to him by whom she burns,
Over heaven slowly, slowly,
  As he travels ever turns;
And beneath the wat'ry main
When he sinks, would follow fain,
  Follow fain from west to east,
And then from east to west again.
Chorus. Follow would from west to east,
  And then from east to west again.

JUSTINA: He beckon'd us, and then again was gone;
 Oh look! under the tree there, Livia—
 Where he sits—reading—scholar-like indeed!—
 With the dark hair that was so white upon
 His shoulder—but how deadly pale his face!—
 And, statue-still-like, the quaint evergreen
 Up and about him creeps, as one has seen
 Round some old marble in a lonely place.
LUCIFER: Ay, look on that—for, as the story runs,
 Ages ago, when all the world was young,
 That ivy was a nymph of Latium,
 Whose name was Hedera: so passing fair
 That all who saw fell doting on her; but
 Herself so icy-cruel, that her heart
 Froze dead all those her eyes had set on fire.
 Whom the just God who walk'd that early world,
 By right-revenging metamorphosis
 Changed to a thing so abject-amorous,
 She grovels on the ground to catch at any
 Wither'd old trunk or sapling, in her way:
 So little loved as loathed, for strangling those
 Round whom her deadly-deathless arms enclose.

Song

So for her who having lighted
 In another heart the fire,
Then shall leave it unrequited
 In its ashes to expire:
After her that sacrifice
Through the garden burns and cries;
In the sultry breathing air:
In the flowers that turn and stare—
"What has she to do among us,
 Falsely wise and frozen fair?"

LUCIFER: Listen, Justina, listen and beware.
JUSTINA: Again! That voice too?—But you know my father
 Is ill—is in his chamber—
 How sultry 'tis—the street is full and close—
 Let us get home—why do they stare at us?

M*   361

And murmur something—"Cipriano?—Where
"Is Cipriano?—lost to us—some say,
"And to himself,—self-slain—mad— Where is he?"
Alas, alas, I know not—

LUCIFER: Come and see—

JUSTINA (*waking*): Mercy upon me! Who is this?

LUCIFER: Justina, your good angel,
Who, moved by your relenting to the sighs
Of one who lost himself for your disdain,
Will lead you to the cavern where he lies
Subsisting on the memory of your eyes—

JUSTINA: 'Twas all a dream!—

LUCIFER: That dreaming you fulfil.

JUSTINA: Oh, no, with all my waking soul renounce.

LUCIFER: But, dreaming or awake, the soul is one,
And the deed purposed in Heaven's eyes is done.

JUSTINA: Oh Christ! I cannot argue—I can pray,
Christ Jesus, oh, my Saviour, Jesu Christ!
Let not hell snatch away from Thee the soul
Thou gav'st Thy life to save!—Livia!—Livia!

Enter LIVIA.

Where is my father? where am I? Oh, I know—
In my own chamber—and my father—oh!—
But, Livia, who was it that but now
Was here—here in my very chamber—

LIVIA: Madam?

JUSTINA: You let none in? oh, no! I know it—but
Some one there was—here—now—as I cried out—
A dark, strange figure—

LIVIA: My child, compose yourself;
No one has come, or gone, since you were laid
In your noon-slumber. This was but a dream.
The air is heavy; and the melancholy
You live alone with since your father's death—

JUSTINA: A dream, a dream indeed—oh Livia,
That leaves his pressure yet upon my arm—
And that without the immediate help of God
I had not overcome—Oh, but the soul,

The soul must be unsteady in the faith,
So to be shaken even by a dream.
Oh, were my father here! But he's at rest—
I know he is—upon his Saviour's breast;
And—who knows!—may have carried up my cries
Ev'n to His ear upon whose breast he lies!
Give me my mantle, Livia; I'll to the church;
Where if but two or three are met in prayer
Together, He has promised to be there—
And I shall find him.

LIVIA: Oh, take care, take care!
You know the danger—in broad daylight too—
Or take me with you.

JUSTINA: And endanger two?
Best serve us both by keeping close at home,
Praying for me as I will pray for you.   [*Exeunt.*

SCENE II.—*Entrance to the mountain cavern.* CIPRIANO, *in a magician's dress, with wand, &c.*

What! do the powers of earth, and air, and hell,
Against their upstart emperor rebel?
Lo, in obedience to the rubric dark
The dusky cheek of earth with mystic mark
Of pentagram and circle I have lined,
And hung my fetters on the viewless wind,
And yet the star of stars, for whose ascent
I ransack all the lower firmament,
In unapparent darkness lags behind:
Whom once again with adjuration new
Of all the spirits whom these signs subdue,
Whether by land or water, night or day,
Whether awake or sleeping, yea or nay,
I summon now before me.—

        Enter slowly a veiled Figure of JUSTINA.

THE FIGURE: What dark spell
From the sequester'd sadness of my cell,
Through the still garden, through the giddy street,

363

And up the solitary mountain-side,
Leads me with sleep-involuntary feet?—
CIPRIANO: 'Tis she, as yet though clouded!—oh divine
Justina!—
THE FIGURE: Cipriano!—
CIPRIANO: At last here,
In such a chamber where ev'n Phœbus fails
To pierce, and baffled breezes tell no tales,
At last, to crown the labour of a year
Of solitary toil and darkness—here!—
And at a price beside—but none too dear—
Oh year-long night well borne for such a day!
Oh soul, for one such sense well sold away!
Oh Now that makes for all the past amends,
Oh moment that eternal life transcends
To such a point of ecstasy, that just
About to reap the wishes that requite
All woes—
THE FIGURE (*unveiling a skull and vanishing as it speaks*):
                    Behold, the World and its delight
Is dust and ashes, dust and ashes, dust—
CIPRIANO (*flinging down his Wand*): Lucifer! Lucifer! Lucifer!
LUCIFER: My son!
CIPRIANO: Quick! With a word—
LUCIFER: How now?—
CIPRIANO: With a word—at once—
With all your might—
LUCIFER: Well, what with it?—
CIPRIANO: The charm—
Shatter it! shatter it, I say!—Is't done?
Is't vanish'd—
LUCIFER: What has thus unsensed you?
CIPRIANO: Oh!—
You know it—saw it—did it—
LUCIFER: Come—be a man:
What, scared with a mere death's-head?
CIPRIANO: Death's, indeed!—
LUCIFER: What was it more?—
CIPRIANO: Justina's seeming self—
364

After what solitary labour wrought,
And after what re-iterated charms,
Step by step here in all her beauty brought
Within the very circle of these arms,
Then to death's grisly lineaments resign'd
Slipp'd through them, and went wailing down the wind
"Ashes and dust and ashes"—
Nay, nay, pretend not that the fault was mine—
The written incantation line by line
I mutter'd, and the mystic figure drew;
You only are to blame—you only, you,
Cajoling me, or by your own cajoled,
Bringing me fleshless death for the warm life
For which my own eternal life is sold.

LUCIFER: You were too rash,—I warn'd you, and if not,
Who thinks at a first trial to succeed?
Another time—

CIPRIANO: No, no! No more of it!
What, have I so long dabbled with the dead,
That all I touch turns to corruption?
Was it indeed herself—her living self—
Till underneath my deadly contact slain;
Or having died during the terrible year
I have been living worse than dead with you,
What I beheld not she, but what she was,
Out of the tomb that only owns my spell
Drawn into momentary lifeliness
To mock me with the phantom of a beauty
Whose lineaments the mere impalpable air
Let in upon disfeatures—Was it she?

LUCIFER: She lives, and shall be yours.

CIPRIANO: Not if herself,
In more than all her living beauty breathing,
Came to efface that deadly counterfeit.—
Oh, what have I been doing all this while,
From which I wake as from a guilty dream,
But with my guilt's accomplice at my side
To prove its terrible reality?
Where were my ears, my eyes, my senses? where

The mother-wit which serves the common boor,
Not to resent that black academy,
Mess-mating with dead men and living fiends,
And not to know no good could come of it?—
My better self—the good that in me grew
By nature, and by good instruction till'd,
Under your shadow turn'd to poisonous weed;
And ev'n the darker art you bribed me with,
To master, if by questionable ways,
The power I sigh'd for in my better days,
So little reaching to the promised height,
As sinking me beneath the lowest fiend,
Who, for the inestimable self I sold,
Pays the false self you made me with false gold!

LUCIFER: When will blind fury, falling foul of all,
Light where it should? Suppose a fault so far,
As knowledge working through unpractised hands
Might fail at first encounter; all men know
How a mere sand will check a vast machine;
And in these complicated processes
An agency so insignificant
As to be wholly overlook'd it was
At the last moment foil'd us.

CIPRIANO: But she lives!
Lives—from your clutches saved, and saved from mine—
Ev'n from that only shadow of my guilt
That could have touch'd her, saved—unguilty shame,
That now is left with all the guilt to me.
Oh that I knew a God in all the heav'ns
To thank, or ev'n of Tartarus—ev'n thee,
Thee would I bless, whatever power it be
That with that shadow saved her, and mock'd me
Back to my better senses. If not she,
What was it?

LUCIFER: What you saw.

CIPRIANO: A phantom?

LUCIFER: Well,
A phantom.

CIPRIANO: But how raised?

LUCIFER: What if by her?
　　She is a sorcerer as her father was.
CIPRIANO: A sorcerer! She a sorcerer! oh, black lie
　　To whiten your defeat! and, were it true,
　　Oh mighty doctor to be foil'd at last
　　By a mere woman!—If a sorcerer,
　　Then of a sort you deal not with, nor hell—
　　And ev'n Olympus likes the sport too well—
　　Raising a phantom not to draw me down
　　To deeper sin, but with its ghastly face
　　And hollow voice both telling of the tomb
　　They came from, warning me of what complexion
　　Were all the guilty wishes of this world.
　　But let the phantom go where gone it is—
　　Not of what mock'd me, but what saved herself,
　　By whatsoever means—ay, what was it,
　　That pitiful agency you told me of
　　So insignificant, as overlook'd
　　At the last moment thwarted us?
LUCIFER: What matter?
　　When now provided for, and which when told
　　You know not—
CIPRIANO: Which I will be told to know—
　　For as one ris'n from darkness tow'rd the light,
　　A veil seems clearing from before my sight—
　　She is a sorcerer, and of the kind
　　That old Lisandro died suspected of?—
　　Oh cunning doctor, to outwit yourself,
　　Outwitted as you have been, and shall be
　　By him who if your devilish magic fail'd
　　To teach its purposed mischief,
　　Thus on his teacher turns it back in full
　　To force him to confess the counter-power
　　That foil'd us both.
　　　　　　　　　　　　　　(*He catches up his wand.*)
LUCIFER: Poor creature that you are!
　　Did not the master from his scholars hold
　　One sleight of hand that masters all the rest,
　　What magic needed to compel the devil

To convict those who find him out too late?
Yet to increase your wrath by leaving it
Blind in the pit your guilt consigns you to,
I shall not answer—

CIPRIANO: Then if your own hell
Cannot enforce you; by that Unknown Power
That saved Justina from your fangs, although
Yourself you cannot master, if you know,
I charge you name him to me!—

LUCIFER (*after a great flash of lightning, and thunder*):
                              Jesus Christ!

CIPRIANO (*after a pause*): Ev'n so!—Christ Jesus—Jesus Christ
    —the same
That poor Lisandro died suspected of,
And I had heard and read of with the rest
But to despise, in spite of all the blood
By which the chosen few their faith confess'd—
The prophet-carpenter of Nazareth,
Poor, persecuted, buffeted, reviled,
Spit upon, crown'd with thorns, and crucified
With thieves—the Son of God—the Son of man,
Whose shape He took to teach them how to live,
And doff'd upon the cross to do away
The sin and death you and your devil-deities
Had heap'd on him from the beginning?

LUCIFER: Yea!—

CIPRIANO: Of the one sun of Deity one ray
That was before the world was, and that made
The world and all that is within it?

LUCIFER: Yea!

CIPRIANO: Eternal and Almighty then: and yet
Infinite Centre as he is of all
The all but infinite universe he made,
With eyes to see me plotting, and with ear
To hear one solitary creature pray,
From one dark corner of his kingdom?

LUCIFER: Yea!

CIPRIANO: All one, all when, all where, all good, all mighty,
All eye, all ear, all self-integrity—

Methinks this must be He of whom I read
In Greek and Roman sages dimly guess'd,
But never until now fully confess'd
In this poor carpenter of Nazareth,
With poor Justina for his confessor—
And now by thee—by thee—once and again
Spite of thyself—for answer me you must,
Convicted at the bar of your own thunder—
Is this the God for whom I sought so long
In mine own soul and those of other men,
Who from the world's beginning till to-day
Groped or were lost in utter darkness?

LUCIFER: Yea!

CIPRIANO: Enough; and your confession shall be mine—

LUCIFER: And to like purpose; to believe, confess,
     And tremble, in the everlasting fire
     Prepared for all who Him against their will
     Confess, and in their deeds deny him—

CIPRIANO: Oh,
     Like a flogg'd felon after full confession
     Released at last!

LUCIFER: To bind you mine for ever.

CIPRIANO: Thine! What art thou?

LUCIFER: The god whom you must worship.

CIPRIANO: There is no God but one, whom you and I
     Alike acknowledge, as in Jesus Christ
     Reveal'd to man. What other god art thou?

LUCIFER: Antichrist! He that all confessing Christ
     Confess; Satan, the Serpent, the first Tempter,
     Who tempted the first Father of mankind
     With the same offer to a like result
     That I have tempted thee with; yea, had power
     Even Him in his humanity to tempt,
     Though Him in vain; the god of this world; if
     False god, true devil; true angel as I was,
     Son of the morning, Lucifer, who fell
     (As first I told thee, had'st thou ears to hear)
     For my rebellion down from heaven to hell
     More terrible than any Tartarus,

Where over those who fell with me I reign.
Whom, though with them bound in the self-same chain
Of everlasting torment, God allows
To reach my hands out of my prison-house
On all who like me from their God rebel,
As thou hast done.
CIPRIANO:　　　　　Not when for God I knew him.
LUCIFER: Ay, but who but for pride and lust like mine
　　Had known Him sooner—
CIPRIANO:　　　　　And had sooner known
　　But for thy lying gods that shut Him out.
LUCIFER: Which others much less wise saw through before.
CIPRIANO: All happy they then! But all guilty I,
　　Yet thus far guiltless of denying Him
　　Whom even thou confessest.
LUCIFER:　　　　　But too late—
　　Already mine, if not so sworn before,
　　Yet by this bond—
CIPRIANO:　　　　　For service unperform'd!
　　But unperform'd, or done, and payment due,
　　　　fling myself and all my debt on Him
　　Who died to undertake them—
LUCIFER: He is the Saviour of the innocent,
　　Not of the guilty.
CIPRIANO:　　　　　Who alone need saving!
LUCIFER: Damnation is the sinner's just award,
　　And He is just.
CIPRIANO:　　　　　And being just, will not
　　For wilful blindness tax the want of light:
　　And All-good as Almighty, and therefore
　　As merciful as just, will not renounce
　　Ev'n the worst sinner who confesses Him,
　　And testifies confession with his blood.
　　Which, not to waste a moment's argument,
　　Too like the old logic that I lost my life in,
　　And hangs for ever dead upon the cross;
　　I will forthwith shout my confession,
　　Into the general ear of Antioch,
　　And from the evidence of thine own mouth,

370

Not thee alone, but all thy lying gods,
Convict; and you convicting before God,
Myself by man's tribunal judged and damn'd,
Trust by my own blood mixing with the tide
That flow'd for me from the Redeemer's side,
From those few damning drops to wash me free
That bound me thine for ever—

LUCIFER (*seizing him*):   Take my answer—

CIPRIANO (*escaping*): Oh, Saviour of Justina, save Thou me!
[*Exeunt.*

SCENE III.—*The Hall of Justice in Antioch;* AURELIO, FABIO,
SENATORS, *&c., just risen from Council.*

AURELIO: You have done well indeed; the very Church
These Christians flock'd to for safe blasphemy
Become the very net to catch them in.
How many, think you?

FABIO: Not so many, sir,
As some that are of the most dangerous.

AURELIO: Among the rest this girl, Lisandro's daughter,
As you and I know, Fabio, to our cost:
But now convicted and condemn'd is safe
From troubling us or Antioch any more.
Come, such good service asks substantial thanks;
What shall it be?

FABIO: No other, if you please,
Than my son Floro's liberation,
Whom not without good reason for so long
You keep under the city's lock and key.

AURELIO: As my own Lelio, and for a like cause;
Who both distracted by her witchery
Turn'd from fast friends to deadly enemies,
And, in each other's lives, so aimed at ours.
But no more chance of further quarrel now
For one whom Death anticipates for bride
Ere they again gird weapon at their side,
Set them both free forthwith.—   [*Exit* FABIO.
This cursèd woman whose fair face and foul

371

Behaviour was the city's talk and trouble,
Now proved a sorceress, is well condemn'd;
Not only for my sake and Fabio's,
But for all Antioch, whose better youth
She might, like ours, have carried after her
Through lust and duel into blasphemy.

Re-enter FABIO *with* LELIO *and* FLORO.

LELIO: Once more, sir, at your feet—
AURELIO: Up, both of you.
   Floro and Lelio, you understand
   What I have done was of no testy humour,
   But for three several sakes—
   Your own, your fathers', and the city's peace.
   Henceforward, by this seasonable use
   Of public law for private purpose check'd,
   Your fiery blood to better service turn.
   Take hands, be friends; the cause of quarrel gone—
LELIO: The cause of quarrel gone!—
AURELIO: Be satisfied;
   You will know better by and bye; meanwhile
   Taking upon my word that so it is;
   Which were it not indeed, you were not here
   To doubt.
FLORO (*aside*): Oh flimsy respite of revenge!—
AURELIO: And now the business of the day well crown'd
   With this so happy reconciliation,
   You and I, Fabio, to our homes again,
   Our homes once more, replenish'd with the peace
   We both have miss'd so long.—What noise is that?
(*Cries without*): Stop him! A madman! Stop him!—
AURELIO: What is it, Fabio?
FABIO: One like mad indeed,
   In a strange garb, with flaring eyes, and hair
   That streams behind him as he flies along,
   Dragging a cloud of rabble after him.
AURELIO: This is no place for either—shut the doors,
   And post the soldiers to keep peace without—
(*Cries without*): Stop him!

FLORO *and* LELIO: 'Tis Cipriano!—
AURELIO: Cipriano!—

Enter CIPRIANO.

CIPRIANO: Ay, Cipriano, Cipriano's self,
    Heretofore mad as you that call him so,
    Now first himself.—Noble Aurelio,
    Who sway'st the sword of Rome in Antioch
    And you, companions of my youthful love
    And letters; you grave senate ranged above;
    And you whose murmuring multitude below
    Do make the marble hall of justice rock
    From base to capital—hearken unto me:
    Yes, I am Cipriano: I am he
    So long and strangely lost, now strangely found—
    The famous doctor of your schools, renown'd
    Not Antioch only but the world about
    For learning's prophet-paragon forsooth;
    Who long pretending to provide the truth
    For other men in fields where never true
    Wheat, but a crop of mimic darnel grew,
    Reap'd nothing for himself but doubt, doubt, doubt.
    Then 'twas that looking with despair and ruth
    Over the blasted harvest of my youth,
    I saw Justina: saw, and put aside
    The barren Pallas for a mortal bride
    Divinelier fair than she is feign'd to be:
    But in whose deep-entempled chastity,
    That look'd down holy cold upon my fire,
    Lived eyes that but re-doubled vain desire.
    Till this new passion, that more fiercely prey'd
    Upon the wither'd spirit of dismay'd
    Ambition, swiftly by denial blew
    To fury that, transcending all control,
    I made away the ruin of my soul
    To one whom no chance tempest at my feet
    In the mid tempest of temptation threw.
    Who blinding me with the double deceit
    Of loftier aspiration and more low

Than mortal or immortal man should owe
Fulfill'd for me, myself for his I bound;
With him and death and darkness closeted
In yonder mountain, while about its head
The sun his garland of the seasons wound,
In the dark school of magic I so read,
And wrought to such a questionable power
The black forbidden art I travail'd in,
That though the solid mountain from his base
With all his forest I might counterplace,
I could not one sweet solitary flower
Of beauty to my magic passion win,
Because her God was with her in that hour
To guard her virtue more than mountain-fast:
That only God, whom all my learning past
Fail'd to divine, but from the very foe
That would have kept Him from me come to know
I come to you, to witness and make known:
One God, eternal, absolute, alone;
Of whom Christ Jesus—Jesus Christ, I say—
And, Antioch, open all your ears to-day—
Of that one Godhead one authentic ray,
Vizor'd awhile his Godhead in man's make,
Man's sin and death upon Himself to take;
For man made man; by man unmade and slain
Upon the cross that for mankind He bore—
Dead—buried—and in three days ris'n again
To His hereditary glory, bearing
All who with Him on earth His sorrow sharing
With Him shall dwell in glory evermore.
And all the gods I worship'd heretofore,
And all that you now worship and adore,
From thundering Zeus to cloven-footed Pan,
But lies and idols, by the hand of man
Of brass and stone—fit emblems as they be,
With ears that hear not; eyes that cannot see;
And multitude where only One can be—
From man's own lewd imagination built;
By that same devil held to that old guilt

Who tempted me to new. To whom indeed
If with my sin and blood myself I fee'd
For ever his—that bond of sin and blood
I trust to cancel in the double flood
Of baptism past, and the quick martyrdom
To which with this confession I am come.
Oh delegate of Cæsar to devour
The little flock of Jesus Christ! Behold
One lost sheep just admitted to the fold
Through the pure stream that rolling down the same
Mountain in which I sinn'd, and as I came
By holy hands administer'd, to-day
Shall wash the mountain of my sin away.
Lo, here I stand for judgment; by the blow
Of sudden execution, or such slow
Death as the devil shall, to maintain his lies,
By keeping life alive in death, devise.
Hack, rack, dismember, burn—or crucify,
Like Him who died to find me; Him that I
Will die to find; for whom, with whom, to die
Is life; and life without, and all his lust,
But dust and ashes, dust and ashes, dust—
                    (*He falls senseless to the ground.*)
AURELIO (*after a long pause*): So public and audacious blas-
          phemy
          Demands as instant vengeance. Wretched man,
          Arise and hear your sentence—
LELIO: Oh, sir, sir!
          You speak to ice and marble—Cipriano!
          Oh look'd for long, and best for ever lost!
          But he is mad—he knows not what he says—
          You would not, surely, on a madman visit
          What only sane confession makes a crime?
AURELIO: I never know how far such blasphemy,
          Which seems to spread like wild-fire in the world,
          Be fault or folly: only this I know,
          I dare not disobey the stern decree
          That Cæsar makes my office answer for.
          Especially when one is led away

375

Of such persuasion and authority,
Still drawing after him the better blood
Of Antioch, to better or to worse.

LELIO: Cipriano! Cipriano! Yet, pray the gods
He be past hearing me!

FABIO (*to* AURELIO): Sir, in your ear—
Justina's hour is come; and through the room
Where she was doom'd, she passes to her doom.

AURELIO: Let us be gone; they must not look on her,
Nor know she is to die until "to die"
Be past predicament. Here let her wait,
Till he she drew along with her to sin
Revive to share with her its punishment.
Come, Lelio—come, Floro—be assured
I loved and honour'd this man as yourselves
Have honour'd him—but now—

LELIO: Nay, sir, but—

AURELIO: Nay,
Not I, but Cæsar, Lelio. Come away.

[*Exeunt. Then* JUSTINA *is brought in by soldiers,
and left alone.*]

JUSTINA: All gone—all silence—and the sudden stroke,
Whose only mercy I besought, delay'd
To make my pang the fiercer.—What is here?—
Dead?—By the doom perhaps I am to die,
And laid across the threshold of the road
To trip me up with terror—Yet not so,
If but the life, once lighted here, has flown
Up to the living Centre that my own
Now trembles to!—God help him, breathing still?—
—Cipriano!—

CIPRIANO: Ay, I am ready—I can rise—
Is my time come?—Oh, God!
Have I repented and confess'd too late,
And this terrible witness of my crime
Stands at the door of death from which it came
To draw me deeper—

JUSTINA: Cipriano!

CIPRIANO: Yet
     Not yet disfeatured—nor the voice—
     Oh, if not *That*—this time unsummon'd—come
     To take me with you where I raised you from—
     Once more—once more—assure me!—
JUSTINA (*taking his hand*):   Cipriano!—
CIPRIANO: And this, too, surely, is a living hand:
     Though cold, oh, cold indeed—but yet, but yet,
     Not dust and ashes, dust and ashes—
JUSTINA: No—
     But soon to be—
CIPRIANO: But soon—but soon to be—
     But not as then?—
JUSTINA: I understand you not—
CIPRIANO: I scarce myself—I must have been asleep—
     But now not dreaming?
JUSTINA: No, not dreaming.
CIPRIANO: No—
     This is the judgment-hall of Antioch,
     In which—I scarcely mind how long ago—
     Is sentence pass'd on me?—
JUSTINA: This is indeed
     The judgment-hall of Antioch; but why
     You here, and what the judgment you await,
     I know not—
CIPRIANO: No.—But stranger yet to me
     Why you yourself, Justina,—Oh my God!
     What, all your life long giving God his due,
     Is treason unto Cæsar?—
JUSTINA: Ay, Cipriano—
     Against his edict having crept inside
     God's fold with that good Shepherd for my guide,
     My Saviour Jesus Christ!
CIPRIANO: My Saviour too,
     And Shepherd—oh, the only good and true
     Shepherd and Saviour—
JUSTINA: You confess Him! *You*
     Confess Him, Cipriano!

377

CIPRIANO: With my blood:
        Which being all to that confession pledged,
        Now waits but to be paid.
JUSTINA: Oh, we shall die,
        And go to heav'n together!
CIPRIANO: Amen! Amen!—
        And yet—
JUSTINA: You do not fear—and yet no shame—
        What I have faced so long, that present dread
        Is almost lost in long anticipation—
CIPRIANO: I fear not for this mortal. Would to God
        This guilty blood by which in part I trust
        To pay the forfeit of my soul with Heav'n
        Would from man's hand redeem the innocence
        That such atonement needs not.
JUSTINA: Oh, to all
        One faith and one atonement—
CIPRIANO: But if both,
        If both indeed must perish by the doom
        That one deserves and cries for—Oh, Justina,
        Who upward ever with the certain step
        Of faith hast follow'd unrepress'd by sin;
        Now that thy foot is almost on the floor
        Of heav'n, pray Him who opens thee the door,
        Let with thee one repenting sinner in!
JUSTINA: What more am I? And were I close to Him
        As he upon whose breast he lean'd on here,
        No intercessor but Himself between
        Himself and the worst sinner of us all—
        If but repenting we believe in Him.
CIPRIANO: I do believe—I do repent—my faith
        Have sign'd in water, and will seal in blood—
JUSTINA: I have no other hope, but, in that, all.
CIPRIANO: Oh hope that almost is accomplishment,
        Believing all with nothing to repent!
JUSTINA: Oh, none so good as not to need—so bad
        As not to find, His mercy. If you doubt
        Because of your long dwelling in the darkness
        To which the light was folly—oh 'twas shown

To the poor shepherd long before the wise;
And if to me, as simple—oh, not mine,
Not mine, oh God! the glory—nor ev'n theirs
From whom I drew it, and—Oh, Cipriano,
Methinks I see them bending from the skies
To take me up to them!

CIPRIANO: Whither could I
But into heaven's remotest corner creep,
Where I might only but discern thee, lost
With those you love in glory—

JUSTINA: Hush! hush! hush!
These are wild words—if I so speak to one
So wise, while I am nothing—
But as you know—Oh, do not think of me,
But Him, into whose kingdom all who come
Are as His angels—

CIPRIANO: Ay, but to come there!—
Where if all intercession, even thine,
Be vain—you say so—yet before we pass
The gate of death together, as we shall,—
If then to part—for ever, and for ever—
Unless with your forgiveness—

JUSTINA: I forgive!
Still I, and I, again! Oh, Cipriano,
Pardon and intercession both alike
With Him alone; and had I to forgive—
Did not He pray upon the cross for those
Who slew Him—as I hope to do on mine
For mine—He bids us bless our enemies
And persecutors; which I think, I think,
You were not, Cipriano—why do you shudder?—
Save in pursuit of that—if vain to me,
Now you know all—

CIPRIANO: I now know all—but you
Not that, which asking your forgiveness for,
I dare not name to you, for fear the hand
I hold as anchor-fast to, break away,
And I drive back to hell upon a blast
That roar'd behind me to these very doors,

379

But stopt—ev'n in the very presence stopt,
That most condemns me his.

JUSTINA: Alas, alas,
Again all wild to me. The time draws short—
Look not to me, but Him tow'rd whom alone
Sin is, and pardon comes from—

CIPRIANO: Oh, Justina,
You know not how enormous is my sin—

JUSTINA: I know, not as His mercy infinite.

CIPRIANO: To Him—to thee—to Him through thee—

JUSTINA: 'Tis written,
Not all the sand of ocean, nor the star
Of heav'n so many as His mercies are.

CIPRIANO: What! ev'n for one who, mad with pouring vows
Into an unrelenting human ear,
Gave himself up to Antichrist—the Fiend—
Though then for such I knew him not—to gain
By darkness all that love had sought in vain!
—Speak to me—if but that hereafter I
Shall never, never, hear your voice again—
Speak to me—

JUSTINA (after a long pause): By the Saviour on His cross
A sinner hung who but at that last hour
Cried out to be with Him; and was with Him
In Paradise ere night.

CIPRIANO: But was his sin
As mine enormous?—

JUSTINA: Shall your hope be less,
Offering yourself for Christ's sake on that cross
Which the other only suffer'd for his sin?
Oh, when we come to perish, side by side,
Look but for Him between us crucified,
And call to Him for mercy; and, although
Scarlet, your sin shall be as white as snow!

CIPRIANO: Ev'n as you speak, yourself, though yet yourself,
In that full glory that you saw reveal'd
With those you love transfigured, and your voice
As from immeasurable altitude
Descending, tell me that, my shame and sin

Quench'd in the death that opens wide to you
The gate, ev'n this great sinner shall pass through,
With Him, with them, with thee!—

JUSTINA: Glory to God!—
Oh blest assurance on the very verge
That death is swallow'd up in victory!
And hark! the step of death is at the door—
Courage!—Almighty God through Jesus Christ
Pardon your sins and mine, and as a staff
Guide and support us through the terrible pass
That leads us to His rest!—

CIPRIANO: My own beloved!
Whose hand—Oh let it be no sin to say it!—
Is as the staff that God has put in mine—
To lead me through the shadow—yet ev'n now—
Ev'n now—at this last terrible moment—
Which, to secure my being with thee, thee
Forbids to stand between my Judge and me,
And in a few more moments, soul and soul
May read each other as an open scroll—
Yet, wilt thou yet believe me not so vile
To thee, to Him who made thee what thou art,
Till desperation of the only heart
I ever sigh'd for, by I knew not then
How just alienation, drove me down
To that accursèd thing?

JUSTINA: My Cipriano!
Dost thou remember, in the lighter hour—
Then when my heart, although you saw it not,
All the while yearn'd to thee across the gulf
That yet it dared not pass—my telling thee
That only Death, which others disunites,
Should ever make us one? Behold! and now
The hour is come, and I redeem my vow.

(*Here the play may finish : but for any one who would follow Calderon to the end,—Enter* FABIO *with Guard, who lead away* CIPRIANO *and* JUSTINA. *Manent* EUSEBIO, JULIAN, *and* CITIZENS.)

CITIZEN 1: Alas! alas! alas! So young a pair!
  And one so very wise!
CITIZEN 2:   And one so fair!
CITIZEN 3: And both as calmly walking to their death
  As others to a marriage festival.
JULIAN: Looking as calm, at least, Eusebio,
  As when, do you remember, at the last
  Great festival of Zeus, we left him sitting
  Upon the hill-side with his books?
EUSEBIO: I think
  Almost the last we saw of him: so soon,
  Flinging his studies and his scholars by,
  He went away into that solitude
  Which ended in this madness, and now death
  With her he lost his wits for.
CITIZEN 1:   And has found
  In death whom living he pursued in vain.
CITIZEN 2: And after death, as they believe; and so
  Thus cheerfully to meet it, if the scaffold
  Divorce them to eternal union.
CITIZEN 3: Strange that so wise a man
  Should fall into so fond a superstition
  Which none but ignorance has taken up.
CITIZEN 1: Oh, love, you know, like time works wonders.
EUSEBIO: Well—
  Antioch will never see so great a scholar.
JULIAN: Nor we so courteous a Professor—
  I would not see my dear old master die
  Were all the wits he lost my legacy.

CITIZENS *talking*

One says that, as they went out hand in hand,
He saw a halo like about the moon
About their head, and moving as they went.
   — *I* saw it—
   —   Fancy! fancy!—
   —   Any how,
They leave it very dark behind them—Thunder!
   — They talk of madness and of blasphemy;
Neither of these, I think, looking much guilty.
   — And he, at any rate, I still maintain,
Least like to be deluded by the folly
For which the new religion is condemn'd.
   — Before his madness, certainly: but love
First crazed him, as I told you.
   —   Well, if mad,
How guilty?
   —   Hush! hush! These are dangerous words.
   — Be not you bitten by this madness, neighbour.
Rome's arm is long.
                 Ay, and some say her ears.
   — Then, ev'n if bitten, bark not—Thunder again!
   — And what unnatural darkness!
                    Well—a storm—
   — They say, you know, he was a sorcerer—
Indeed we saw the mystic dress he wore
All wrought with figures of astrology;
Nay, he confess'd himself as much; and now
May raise a storm to save—
                There was a crash!
   — A bolt has fallen somewhere—the walls shake—
   — And the ground under—
              Save us, Zeus—
VOICES: Away!—
The roof is falling in upon us—

(*The wall at the back falls in, and discovers a scaffold with*
CIPRIANO *and* JUSTINA *dead, and* LUCIFER *above them.*)

LUCIFER: Stay!—
    And hearken to what I am doom'd to tell.
    I am the mighty minister of hell
    You mis-call heav'n, and of the hellish crew
    Of those false gods you worship for the True;
    Who, to revenge *her* treason to the blind
    Idolatry that has hoodwinkt mankind,
    And *his*, whose halting wisdom after-knew
    What her diviner virtue fore-divined,
    By devilish plot and artifices thought
    Each of them by the other to have caught;
    But, thwarted by superior will, those eyes
    That, by my fuel fed, had been a flame
    To light them both to darkness down, became
    As stars to lead together to the skies,
    By such a doom as expiates his sin,
    And her pure innocence lets sooner in
    To that eternal bliss where, side by side,
    They reign at His right hand for whom they died.
    While I, convicted in my own despite
    Thus to bear witness to the eternal light
    Of which I lost, and they have won the crown
    Plunge to my own eternal darkness down.

HÚNDESE

AGAMEMNON
A TRAGEDY
TAKEN FROM
ÆSCHYLUS

[*Agamemnon. A Tragedy, Taken from Æschylus*, was first printed privately in 1865. Quaritch published an edition in 1876.]

This Version—or Per-version—of Æschylus was originally printed to be given away among Friends, who either knew nothing of the Original, or would be disposed to excuse the liberties taken with it by an unworthy hand.

PREFACE

ALL the Choruses in this Tragedy call for a more lyrical Interpreter than myself. But even I might have done better with the first, by mingling fragments of the so oft-told Story with such dark and ill-ominous presage as would accumulate as Time went on.

So much for the matter. As for the manner; I think that some such form as Tennyson has originated in his version of the Battle of Brunanburh might well be adopted in this case, as in many other of Æschylus' Choruses—such as in the Persæ, the Seven against Thebes, and the Eumenides—the question being whether such a trochaic gallop may not over-ride the Iambic Blank Verse Dialogue that follows it.

I suppose that a literal version of this play, if possible, would scarce be intelligible. Even were the dialogue always clear, the lyric Choruses, which make up so large a part, are so dark and abrupt in themselves, and therefore so much the more mangled and tormented by copyist and commentator, that the most conscientious translator must not only jump at a meaning, but must bridge over a chasm; especially if he determine to complete the antiphony of Strophe and Antistrophe in English verse.

Thus, encumbered with forms which sometimes, I think, hang heavy on Æschylus himself; struggling with indistinct meanings, obscure allusions, and even with *puns* which some have tried to reproduce in English; this grand play, which to the scholar and the poet, lives, breathes, and moves in the dead language, has hitherto seemed to me to drag and stifle under conscientious translation into the living; that is to say, to have lost that which I think the drama can least afford to lose all the world over. And so it was that, hopeless of succeeding where as good versifiers, and better scholars, seemed to me to have failed, I came first to break the bounds of Greek Tragedy; then to swerve from the Master's footsteps; and so, one license drawing on another to make all of a piece, arrived at the present anomalous conclusion.

If it has succeeded in shaping itself into a distinct, consistent, and animated Whole, through which the reader can follow without halting, and not without accelerating interest from beginning to end, he will perhaps excuse my acknowledged transgressions, and will not disdain the Jade that has carried him so far so well till he find himself mounted on a Thorough-bred whose thunder-clothed neck and long-resounding pace shall better keep up with the Original.

For to re-create the Tragedy, body and soul, into English, and make the Poet free of the language which reigns over that half of the world never dreamt of in his philosophy, must be reserved —especially the Lyric part—for some Poet, worthy of that name, and of congenial Genius with the Greek. Would that every one such would devote himself to one such work! whether by Translation, Paraphrase, or Metaphrase, to use Dryden's definition, whose Alexander's Feast, and some fragments of whose Plays, indicate that he, perhaps, might have rendered such a service to Æschylus and to us. Or, to go further back in our own Drama, one thinks what Marlowe might have done; himself a translator from the Greek; something akin to Æschylus in his genius; still more in his grandiose, and sometimes *authadostomous* verse; of which some lines relating to this very play fall so little short of Greek, that I shall but shame my own by quoting them before hand;

> "Is this the face that launch'd a thousand ships,
> And burnt the topless towers of Ilium?
> Sweet Helen, make me immortal with a kiss!"

AGAMEMNON

DRAMATIS PERSONÆ

AGAMEMNON,	*King of Argos.*
CLYTEMNESTRA,	*his Queen.*
ÆGISTHUS,	*his Cousin.*
CASSANDRA,	*Daughter of King* PRIAM.
HERALD.	

CHORUS *of ancient Councillors.*

The scene is at ARGOS.

AGAMEMNON'S *Palace : a Warder on the Battlements.*

WARDER: Once more, once more, and once again once more
I crave the Gods' compassion, and release
From this inexorable watch, that now
For one whole year, close as a couching dog,
On Agamemnon's housetop I have kept,
Contemplating the muster of the stars,
And those transplendent Dynasties of Heav'n
That, as alternately they rise and fall,
Draw Warmth and Winter over mortal man.
Thus, and thus long, I say, at the behest
Of the man-minded Woman who here rules,
Here have I watch'd till yonder mountain-top
Shall kindle with a signal-light from Troy.
And watch'd in vain, couch'd on the barren stone,
Night after night, night after night, alone,
Ev'n by a wandering dream unvisited,
To which the terror of my post denies
The customary passage of closed eyes.
From which, when haply nodding, I would scare
Forbidden sleep, or charm long night away
With some old ballad of the good old times,
The foolish song falls presently to tears,
Remembering the glories of this House,
Where all is not as all was wont to be,—
No, nor as should—Alas, these royal walls,
Had they but tongue (as ears and eyes, men say)
Would tell strange stories!—But, for fear they should,
Mine shall be mute as they are. Only this—
And this no treason surely—might I but,
But once more might I, see my lord again
Safe home! But once more look upon his face!
But once more take his hand in mine!—
                            Hilloa!

The words scarce from my lips.—Have the Gods heard?
Or am I dreaming wide awake? as wide
Awake I am—The Light! The Light! The Light
Long look'd for, long despair'd of, on the Height!
Oh more to me than all the stars of night!
More than the Morning-star!—more than the Sun
Who breaks my nightly watch, this rising one
Which tells me that my year-long night is done!
When, shaking off the collar of my watch,
I first to Clytemnestra shall report
Such news as, if indeed a lucky cast
For her and Argos, sure a Main to me!
But grant the Gods, to all! A master-cast,
More than compensating all losses past;
And lighting up our altars with a fire
Of Victory that never shall expire!

[*Exit* WARDER. *Daylight gradually dawns, and enter slowly*
CHORUS.]

CHORUS: Another rising of the sun
      That rolls another year away,
   Sees us through the portal dun
      Dividing night and day
  Like to phantoms from the crypt
  Of Morpheus or of Hades slipt,
   Through the sleeping city creeping,
  Murmuring an ancient song
  Of unvindicated wrong,
  Ten year told as ten year long.
  Since to revenge the great abuse
    To Themis done by Priam's son,
  The Brother-Princes that, co-heir
  Of Atreus, share his royal chair,
   And from the authentic hand of Zeus
  His delegated sceptre bear,
   Startled Greece with such a cry
  For Vengeance as a plunder'd pair
  Of Eagles over their aerial lair
  Screaming, to whirlpool lash the waves of air.

II

The Robber, blinded in his own conceit,
  Must needs think Retribution deaf and blind.
  Fool! not to know what tongue was in the wind,
When Tellus shudder'd under flying feet,
  When stricken Ocean under alien wings;
Was there no Phœbus to denounce the flight
From Heav'n? Nor those ten thousand Eyes of Night?
And, were no other eye nor ear of man
Or God awake, yet universal Pan,
  For ever watching at the heart of things,
And Zeus, the Warden of domestic Right,
  And the perennial sanctity of Kings,
Let loose the Fury who, though late
Retarded in the leash of Fate,
  Once loosed, after the Sinner springs;
Over Ocean's heights and hollows,
Into cave and forest follows,
  Into fastest guarded town,
Close on the Sinner's heel insists,
And, turn or baffle as he lists,
  Dogs him inexorably down.

III

Therefore to revenge the debt
  To violated Justice due,
Armèd Hellas hand in hand
  The iron toils of Ares drew
Over water, over land,
Over such a tract of years;
Draught of blood abroad, of tears
  At home, and unexhausted yet:
All the manhood Greece could muster,
  And her hollow ships enclose;
All that Troy from her capacious
  Bosom pouring forth oppose;
By the ships, beneath the wall,
  And about the sandy plain,

Armour-glancing files advancing,
   Fighting, flying, slaying, slain:
And among them, and above them,
Crested Heroes, twain by twain,
   Lance to lance, and thrust to thrust,
Front erect, and, in a moment,
   One or other roll'd in dust.
Till the better blood of Argos
   Soaking in the Trojan sand,
In her silent half dispeopled
   Cities, more than half unmann'd,
Little more of man to meet
Than the helpless child, or hoary
Spectre of his second childhood,
   Tottering on triple feet,
Like the idle waifs and strays
Blown together from the ways
   Up and down the windy street.

IV

But thus it is; All bides the destined Hour;
  And Man, albeit with Justice at his side,
Fights in the dark against a secret Power
  Not to be conquer'd—and how pacified?

V

For, before the Navy flush'd
   Wing from shore, or lifted oar
To foam the purple brush'd;
While about the altar hush'd
   Throng'd the ranks of Greece thick-fold,
Ancient Chalcas in the bleeding
Volume of the Future reading
   Evil things foresaw, foretold:
That, to revenge some old disgrace
   Befall'n her sylvan train,
Some dumb familiar of the Chace

By Menelaus slain,
The Goddess Artemis would vex
The fleet of Greece with storms and checks:
　That Troy should not be reach'd at all;
Or—as the Gods themselves divide
In Heav'n to either mortal side—
　If ever reach'd, should never fall—
Unless at such a loss and cost
As counterpoises Won and Lost.

VI

The Elder of the Royal Twain
Listen'd in silence, daring not arraign
　Ill omen, or rebuke the raven lips:
Then taking up the tangled skein
　Of Fate, he pointed to the ships;
He sprang aboard: he gave the sign;
　And blazing in his golden arms ahead,
Drew the long Navy in a glittering line
　After him like a meteor o'er the main.

VII

So from Argos forth: and so
　O'er the rolling waters they,
Till in the roaring To-and-fro
　Of rock-lockt Aulis brought to stay:
There the Goddess had them fast:
With a bitter northern blast
　Blew ahead and block'd the way:
Day by day delay; to ship
And tackle damage and decay;
Day by day to Prince and People
　Indignation and dismay.
"All the while that in the ribb'd
Bosom of their vessels cribb'd,
Tower-crown'd Troy above the waters
Yonder, quaffing from the horn

Of Plenty, laughing them to scorn"—
  So would one to other say;
And man and chief in rage and grief
  Fretted and consumed away.

VIII

Then to Sacrifice anew:
  And again within the bleeding
  Volume of the Future reading,
Once again the summon'd Seer
  Evil, Evil, still fore-drew.
Day by day, delay, decay
  To ship and tackle, chief and crew:
And but one way—one only way to appease
The Goddess, and the wind of wrath subdue;
One way of cure so worse than the disease,
  As, but to hear propound,
The Atreidæ struck their sceptres to the ground.

IX

After a death-deep pause,
The Lord of man and armament his voice
Lifted into the silence—"Terrible choice!
To base imprisonment of wind and flood
  Whether consign and sacrifice the band
Of heroes gathered in my name and cause;
Or thence redeem them by a daughter's blood—
  A daughter's blood shed by a father's hand;
Shed by a father's hand, and to atone
  The guilt of One—who, could the God endure
  Propitiation by the Life impure,
Should wash out her transgression with her own."

X

But, breaking on that iron multitude,
  The Father's cry no kindred echo woke:
And in the sullen silence that ensued
  An unrelenting iron answer spoke.

XI

At last his neck to that unnatural yoke
He bow'd: his hand to that unnatural stroke:
With growing purpose, obstinate as the wind
That block'd his fleet, so block'd his better mind,
To all the Father's heart within him blind—
    For thus it fares with men; the seed
    Of Evil, sown by seeming Need,
      Grows, self-infatuation-nurst,
    From evil Thought to evil Deed,
      Incomprehensible at first,
      And to the end of Life accurst.

XII

And thus, the blood of that one innocent
Weigh'd light against one great accomplishment,
At last—at last—in the meridian blaze
Of Day, with all the Gods in Heaven agaze,
And armed Greece below—he came to dare—
After due preparation, pomp, and prayer,
He came—the wretched father—came to dare—
    Himself—with sacrificial knife in hand,—
    Before the sacrificial altar stand,
To which—her sweet lips, sweetly wont to sing
    Before him in the banquet-chamber, gagg'd,
Lest one ill word should mar the impious thing;
  Her saffron scarf about her fluttering,
    Dumb as an all-but-speaking picture, dragg'd
Through the remorseless soldiery—
                But soft!—
    While I tell the more than oft-
Told Story, best in silence found,
    Incense-breathing fires aloft
Up into the rising fire,
Into which the stars expire,
    Of Morning mingle; and a sound
As of Rumour at the heel
    Of some great tiding gathers ground;

And from portals that disclose
Before a fragrant air that blows
Them open, what great matter, Sirs,
Thus early Clytemnestra stirs,
Hither through the palace gate
Torch in hand, and step-elate,
Advancing, with the kindled Eyes
As of triumphant Sacrifice?

Enter CLYTEMNESTRA.

Oh, Clytemnestra, my obeisance
Salutes your coming footstep, as her right
Who rightly occupies the fellow-chair
Of that now ten years widow'd of its Lord.
But—be it at your pleasure ask'd, as answer'd—
What great occasion, almost ere Night's self
Rekindles into Morning from the Sun,
Has woke your Altar-fire to Sacrifice?

CLYTEMNESTRA: Oh, never yet did Night—
Night of all Good the Mother, as men say,
Conceive a fairer issue than To-day!
Prepare your ear, Old man, for tidings such
As youthful hope would scarce anticipate.
CHORUS: I have prepared them for such news as such
Preamble argues.
CLYTEMNESTRA: What if you be told—
Oh mighty sum in one small figure cast!—
That ten-year-toil'd-for Troy is ours at last?
CHORUS: "If told!"—Once more!—the word escaped our ears,
With many a baffled rumour heretofore
Slipp'd down the wind of wasted Expectation.
CLYTEMNESTRA: Once more then; and with unconditional
Assurance having hit the mark indeed
That Rumour aimed at—Troy, with all the towers
Our burning vengeance leaves aloft, is ours.
Now speak I plainly?
CHORUS: Oh! to make the tears,
That waited to bear witness in the eye,
Start, to convict our incredulity!

CLYTEMNESTRA: Oh, blest conviction that enriches you
    That lose the cause with all the victory!
CHORUS: Ev'n so. But how yourself convinced before?
CLYTEMNESTRA: By no less sure a witness than the God.
CHORUS: What, in a dream?
CLYTEMNESTRA: I am not one to trust
    The vacillating witnesses of Sleep.
CHORUS: Ay—but as surely undeluded by
    The waking Will, that what we strongly *would*
    Imaginates?
CLYTEMNESTRA: Ay, like a doating girl.
CHORUS: Oh, Clytemnestra, pardon mere Old Age
    That, after so long starving upon Hope,
    But slowly brooks his own Accomplishment.
    The Ten-year war is done then! Troy is taken!
    The Gods have told you, and the Gods tell true—
    But—how? and when?
CLYTEMNESTRA: Ev'n with the very birth
    Of the good Night which mothers this best Day.
CHORUS: To-day! To-night! but of Night's work in Troy
    Who should inform the scarce awaken'd ear
    Of Morn in Argos?
CLYTEMNESTRA: Hephaistos, the lame God,
    And spriteliest of mortal messengers;
    Who, springing from the bed of burning Troy,
    Hither, by fore-devised Intelligence
    Agreed upon between my Lord and me,
    Posted from dedicated Height to Height
    The reach of land and sea that lies between.
    And, first to catch him and begin the game,
    Did Ida fire her forest-pine, and, waving,
    Handed him on to that Hermæan steep
    Of Lemnos; Lemnos to the summit of
    Zeus-consecrated Athos lifted; whence,
    As by the giant taken, so despatch'd,
    The Torch of Conquest, traversing the wide
    Ægæan with a sunbeam-stretching stride,
    Struck up the drowsy watchers on Makistos;
    Who, flashing back the challenge, flash'd it on

To those who watch'd on the Messapian height.
With whose quick-kindling heather heap'd and fired
The meteor-bearded messenger refresh'd,
Clearing Asopus at a bound, struck fire
From old Kithæron; and, so little tired
As waxing even wanton with the sport,
Over the sleeping water of Gorgopis
Sprung to the Rock of Corinth; thence to the cliffs
Which stare down the Saronic Gulf, that now
Began to shiver in the creeping Dawn;
Whence, for a moment on the neighbouring top
Of Arachnæum lighting, one last bound
Brought him to Agamemnon's battlements.
By such gigantic strides in such a Race
Where First and Last alike are Conquerors,
Posted the travelling Fire, whose Father-light
Ida conceived of burning Troy To-night.

CHORUS: Woman, your words man-metal ring, and strike
Ev'n from the tuneless fibre of Old Age
Such martial unison as from the lips
Shall break into full Pæan by and by.

CLYTEMNESTRA: Ay, think—think—think, old man, and in
your soul
As if 'twere mirror'd in your outward eye.
Imagine what wild work a-doing there—
In Troy—to-night—to-day—this moment—how
Harmoniously, as in one vessel meet
Esil and Oil, meet Triumph and Despair,
Sluiced by the sword along the reeking street,
On which the Gods look down from burning air.
Slain, slaying—dying, dead—about the dead
Fighting to die themselves—maidens and wives
Lock'd by the locks, with their barbarian young,
And torn away to slavery and shame
By hands all reeking with their Champion's blood.
Until, with execution weary, we
Fling down our slaughter-satiated swords,
To gorge ourselves on the unfinish'd feasts
Of poor old Priam and his sons; and then,

Roll'd on rich couches never spread for us,
Ev'n now our sleep-besotted foreheads turn
Up to the very Sun that rises here.
Such is the lawful game of those who win
Upon so just a quarrel—so long fought:
Provided always that, with jealous care,
Retaliation wreaking upon those
Who our insulted Gods upon them drew,
We push not Riot to *their* Altar-foot;
Remembering, on whichever mortal side
Engaged, the Gods are Gods in heav'n and earth,
And not to be insulted unavenged.
This let us take to heart, and keep in sight;
Lest, having run victoriously thus far,
And turn'd the very pillar of our race,
Before we reach the long'd-for goal of Home
Nemesis overtake, or trip us up;
Some ere safe shipp'd: or, launch'd upon the foam,
Ere touch'd the threshold of their native shore;
Yea, or that reach'd, the threshold of the door
Of their own home; from whatsoever corner
The jealous Power is ever on the watch
To compass arrogant Prosperity.
These are a woman's words; for men to take,
Or disregarded drop them, as they will;
Enough for me, if having won the stake,
I pray the Gods with us to keep it still.

                     [*Exit* CLYTEMNESTRA.

CHORUS: Oh, sacred Night,
      From whose unfathomable breast
      Creative Order formed and saw
      Chaos emerging into Law:
    And now, committed with Eternal Right,
    Who didst with star-entangled net invest
      So close the guilty City as she slept,
    That when the deadly fisher came to draw,
      Not one of all the guilty fry through crept.

II

Oh, Nemesis,
Night's daughter! in whose bosoming abyss
   Secretly sitting by the Sinner's sleeve,
   Thou didst with self-confusion counterweave
His plot; and when the fool his arrow sped,
   Thine after-shot didst only not dismiss
Till certain not to miss the guilty head.

III

Some think the Godhead, couching at his ease
Deep in the purple Heav'ns, serenely sees
   Insult the altar of Eternal Right.
   Fools! For though Fortune seem to misrequite,
   And Retribution for awhile forget;
   Sooner or later she reclaims the debt
With usury that triples the amount
Of Nemesis with running Time's account.

IV

   For soon or late sardonic Fate
      With Man against himself conspires;
      Puts on the mask of his desires:
   Up the steps of Time elate
   Leads him blinded with his pride,
   And gathering as he goes along
   The fuel of his suicide:
   Until having topp'd the pyre
   Which Destiny permits no higher,
   Ambition sets himself on fire;
   In conflagration like the crime
   Conspicuous through the world and time
   Down amidst his brazen walls
   The accumulated Idol falls
   To shapeless ashes; Demigod
   Under the vulgar hoof down-trod
   Whose neck he trod on; not an eye
   To weep his fall, nor lip to sigh

For him a prayer; or, if there were,
No God to listen, or reply.

V

And as the son his father's guilt may rue;
  And, by retort of justice, what the son
  Has sinn'd, to ruin on the father run;
So may the many help to pay the due
  Of guilt, remotely implicate with one.
And as the tree 'neath which a felon cowers,
  With all its branch is blasted by the bolt
  Of Justice launch'd from Heav'n at *his* revolt;
Thus with old Priam, with his royal line,
  Kindred and people; yea, the very towers
They crouch'd in, built by masonry divine.

VI

Like a dream through sleep she glided
  Through the silent city gate,
By a guilty Hermes guided
On the feather'd feet of Theft;
Leaving between those she left
And those she fled to lighted Discord,
  Unextinguishable Hate;
Leaving him whom least she should,
Menelaus brave and good,
Scarce believing in the mutter'd
Rumour, in the worse than utter'd
  Omen of the wailing maidens,
Of the shaken hoary head;
Of deserted board and bed.
  For the phantom of the lost one
Haunts him in the wonted places;
Hall and Chamber, which he paces
Hither, Thither, listening, looking,
  Phantom-like himself alone;
Till he comes to loathe the faces
Of the marble mute Colossi,

Godlike Forms, and half-divine,
Founders of the Royal line,
Who with all unalter'd Quiet
Witness all and make no sign.
But the silence of the chambers,
And the shaken hoary head,
And the voices of the mourning
Women, and of ocean wailing,
Over which with unavailing
Arms he reaches, as to hail
The phantom of a flying sail—
All but answer, Fled! fled! fled!
False! dishonour'd! worse than dead!

VII

At last the sun goes down along the bay,
And with him drags detested Day.
He sleeps; and, dream-like as she fled, beside
His pillow, Dream indeed, behold! his Bride
Once more in more than bridal beauty stands;
But, ever as he reaches forth his hands,
Slips from them back into the viewless deep,
On those soft silent wings that walk the ways of sleep.

VIII

Not beside thee in the chamber,
Menelaus, any more;
But with him she fled with, pillow'd
On the summer softly-billow'd
Ocean, into dimple wreathing
Underneath a breeze of amber
Air that, as from Eros breathing,
Fill'd the sail and flew before;
Floating on the summer seas
Like some sweet Effigies
Of Eirene's self, or sweeter
Aphrodite, sweeter still:
With the Shepherd, from whose luckless

Hand upon the Phrygian hill,
Of the three Immortals, She
The fatal prize of Beauty bore,
Floating with him o'er the foam
She rose from, to the Shepherd's home
On the Ionian shore.

IX

Down from the City to the water-side
　Old Priam, with his princely retinue.
　By many a wondering Phrygian follow'd, drew
To welcome and bear in the Goddess-bride,
　Whom some propitious wind of Fortune blew
From whence they knew not o'er the waters wide
Among the Trojan people to abide,
A pledge of Love and Joy for ever—Yes;
As one who drawing from the leopardess
Her suckling cub, and, fascinated by
The little Savage of the lustrous eye,
Bears home, for all to fondle and caress,
And be the very darling of the house
It makes a den of blood of by and by.

X

For the wind, that amber blew,
Tempest in its bosom drew,
　Soon began to hiss and roar;
And the sweet Effigies
That amber breeze and summer seas
　Had wafted to the Ionian shore,
By swift metamorphosis
Turn'd into some hideous, hated,
Fury of Revenge, and fated
　Hierophant of Nemesis;
Who, growing with the day and hour,
Grasp'd the wall, and topp'd the tower,
And, when the time came, by its throat
The victim City seized, and smote.

But now to be resolved, whether indeed
  Those fires of Night spoke truly, or mistold
  To cheat a doating woman; for, behold,
Advancing from the shore with solemn speed,
  A Herald from the Fleet, his footsteps roll'd
In dust, Haste's thirsty consort, but his brow
  Check-shadow'd with the nodding Olive-bough;
  Who shall interpret us the speechless sign
Of the fork'd tongue that preys upon the pine.

HERALD: Oh, Fatherland of Argos, back to whom
  After ten years do I indeed return
  Under the dawn of this auspicious day!
  Of all the parted anchors of lost Hope
  That this, depended least on, yet should hold;
  Amid so many men to me so dear
  About me dying, yet myself exempt
  Return to live what yet of life remains
  Among my own; among my own at last
  To share the blest communion of the Dead!
  Oh, welcome, welcome, welcome once again
  My own dear Country and the light she draws
  From the benignant Heav'ns; and all the Gods
  Who guard her; Zeus Protector first of all;
  And Phœbus, by this all-restoring dawn
  Who heals the wounds his arrows dealt so fast
  Beside Scamander; and not last nor least
  Among the Powers engaged upon our side,
  Hermes, the Herald's Patron, and his Pride;
  Who, having brought me safely through the war,
  Now brings me back to tell the victory
  Into my own belovèd country's ear;
  Who, all the more by us, the more away,
  Beloved, will greet with Welcome no less dear
  This remnant of the unremorseful spear.
  And, oh, you Temples, Palaces, and throned
  Colossi, that affront the rising sun,
  If ever yet, your marble foreheads now

Bathe in the splendour of returning Day
To welcome back your so long absent Lord;
Who by Zeus' self directed to the spot
Of Vengeance, and the special instrument
Of Retribution put into his hands,
Has undermined, uprooted, and destroy'd,
Till scarce one stone upon another stands,
The famous Citadel, that, deeply cast
For crime, has all the forfeit paid at last.

CHORUS: Oh hail and welcome, Herald of good news!
Welcome and hail! and doubt not thy return
As dear to us as thee.

HERALD: To me so dear,
After so long despair'd of, that, for fear
Life's after-draught the present should belie,
One might implore the Gods ev'n now to die!

CHORUS: Oh, your soul hunger'd after home!

HERALD: So sore,
That sudden satisfaction of once more
Return weeps out its surfeit at my eyes.

CHORUS: And ours, you see, contagiously, no less
The same long grief, and sudden joy, confess.

HERALD: What! Argos for her missing children yearn'd
As they for her, then?

CHORUS: Ay; perhaps and more,
Already pining with an inward sore.

HERALD: How so?

CHORUS: Nay, Silence, that has best endured
The pain, may best dismiss the memory.

HERALD: Ev'n so. For who, unless the God himself,
Expects to live his life without a flaw?
Why, once begin to open that account,
Might not *we* tell for ten good years to come
Of all we suffer'd in the ten gone by?
Not the mere course and casualty of war,
Alarum, March, Battle, and such hard knocks
As foe with foe expects to give and take;
But all the complement of miseries
That go to swell a long campaign's account.

Cramm'd close aboard the ships, hard bed, hard board:
Or worse perhaps while foraging ashore
In winter time; when, if not from the walls,
Pelted from Heav'n by Day, to couch by Night
Between the falling dews and rising damps
That elf'd the locks, and set the body fast
With cramp and ague; or, to mend the matter,
Good mother Ida from her winter top
Flinging us down a coverlet of snow.
Or worst perhaps in Summer, toiling in
The bloody harvest-field of torrid sand,
When not an air stirr'd the fierce Asian noon,
And ev'n the sea sleep-sicken'd in his bed.
But why lament the Past, as past it is?
If idle for the Dead who feel no more,
Idler for us to whom this blissful Dawn
Shines doubly bright against the stormy Past;
Who, after such predicament and toil,
Boast, once more standing on our mother soil,
    That Zeus, who sent us to revenge the crime
Upon the guilty people, now recalls
To hang their trophies on our temple walls
    For monumental heir-looms to all time.
CHORUS: Oh, but Old age, however slow to learn,
    Not slow to learn, nor after you repeat,
    Lesson so welcome, Herald of the Fleet!
    But here is Clytemnestra; be you first
    To bless her ears, as mine, with news so sweet.
CLYTEMNESTRA: I sang my Song of Triumph ere he came,
    Alone I sang it while the City slept,
    And these wise Senators, with winking eyes,
    Looked grave and weigh'd mistrustfully my word,
    As the light coinage of a woman's brain.
    And so they went their way. But not the less
    From those false fires I lit my altar up,
    And, woman-wise, held on my song, until
    The City taking up the note from me,
    Scarce knowing why, about that altar flock'd,
    Where, like the Priest of Victory, I stood,

Torch-handed, drenching in triumphant wine
The flame that from the smouldering incense rose.
Now what more needs? This Herald of the Day
Adds but another witness to the Night;
And I will hear no more from other lips,
Till from my husband Agamemnon all,
Whom with all honour I prepare to meet.
Oh, to a loyal woman what so sweet
 As once more wide the gate of welcome fling
To the loved Husband whom the Gods once more
 After long travail home triumphant bring;
Where he shall find her, as he left before,
Fix'd like a trusty watchdog at the door,
Tractable him-ward, but inveterate
Against the doubtful stranger at the gate;
 And not a seal within the house but still
Inviolate, under a woman's trust
Incapable of taint as gold of rust.

           [Exit CLYTEMNESTRA.

HERALD: A boast not misbeseeming a true woman.
CHORUS: For then no boast at all. But she says well;
 And Time interprets all. Enough for us
 To praise the Gods for Agamemnon's safe,
 And more than safe return. And Menelaus,
 The other half of Argos—What of him?
HERALD: Those that I most would gladden with good news,
 And on a day like this—with fair but false
 I dare not.
CHORUS: What, must fair then needs be false?
HERALD: Old man, the Gods grant somewhat, and withhold
 As seems them good: a time there is for Praise,
 A time for Supplication: nor is it well
 To twit the celebration of their largess,
 Reminding them of somewhat they withhold.
CHORUS: Yet till we know how much withheld or granted,
 We know not how the balance to adjust
 Of Supplication or of Praise.
HERALD: Alas,
 The Herald who returns with downcast eyes,

And leafless brow prophetic of Reverse,
Let him at once—at once let him, I say,
Lay the whole burden of Ill-tidings down
In the mid-market place. But why should one
Returning with the garland on his brow
Be stopp'd to name the single missing leaf
Of which the Gods have stinted us!

CHORUS: Alas,
The putting of a fearful question by
Is but to ill conjecture worse reply!
You bring not back then—do not leave behind—
What Menelaus was?

HERALD: The Gods forbid!
Safe shipp'd with all the host.

CHORUS: Well but—how then?
Surely no tempest—

HERALD: Ay! by that one word
Hitting the centre of a boundless sorrow!

CHORUS: Well, but if peradventure from the fleet
Parted—not lost?

HERALD: None but the eye of Day,
Now woke, knows all the havoc of the Night.
For Night it was; all safe aboard—sail set,
And oars all beating home; when suddenly,
As if those old antagonists had sworn
New strife between themselves for our destruction,
The sea, that tamely let us mount his back,
Began to roar and plunge under a lash
Of tempest from the thundering heavens so fierce
As, falling on our fluttering navy, some
Scatter'd, or whirl'd away like flakes of foam:
Or, huddling wave on wave, so ship on ship
Like fighting eagles on each other fell,
And beak, and wing, and claws, entangled, tore
To pieces one another, or dragg'd down.
So when at last the tardy-rising Sun
Survey'd, and show'd, the havoc Night had done,
We, whom some God—or Fortune's self, I think—
Seizing the helm, had steer'd as man could not,

Beheld the waste Ægæan wilderness
Strown with the shatter'd forest of the fleet,
Trunk, branch, and foliage; and yet worse, I ween,
The flower of Argos floating dead between.
Then we, scarce trusting in our own escape,
And saving such as yet had life to save,
Along the heaving wilderness of wave
Went ruminating, who of those we miss'd
Might yet survive, who lost: the saved, no doubt,
As sadly speculating after us.
Of whom, if Menelaus—and the Sun,
(A prayer which all the Gods in Heav'n fulfil!)
Behold him on the water breathing still;
Doubt not that Zeus, under whose special showers
And suns the royal growth of Atreus towers,
Will not let perish stem, and branch, and fruit,
By loss of one corroborating root.

CHORUS: Oh, Helen, Helen, Helen! oh, fair name
    And fatal, of the fatal-fairest dame
      That ever blest or blinded human eyes!
    Of mortal women Queen beyond compare,
      As she whom the foam lifted to the skies
    Is Queen of all who breathe immortal air!
      Whoever, and from whatsoever wells
      Of Divination, drew the syllables
    By which we name thee; who shall ever dare
    In after time the fatal name to wear,
    Or would, to be so fatal, be so fair?
    Whose dowry was a Husband's shame;
    Whose nuptial torch was Troy in flame;
    Whose bridal Chorus, groans and cries;
    Whose banquet, brave men's obsequies;
    Whose Hymenæal retinue,
    The winged dogs of War that flew
    Over lands and over seas,
    Following the tainted breeze,
    Till, Scamander reed among,
    Their fiery breath and bloody tongue
    The fatal quarry found and slew;

And, having done the work to which
The God himself halloo'd them, back
Return a maim'd and scatter'd pack.

II

And he for whose especial cause
   Zeus his wingéd instrument
With the lightning in his claws
   From the throne of thunder sent:
He for whom the sword was drawn:
Mountain ashes fell'd and sawn;
   And the armed host of Hellas
Cramm'd within them, to discharge
On the shore to bleed at large;
He, in mid accomplishment
Of Justice, from his glory rent!
What ten years had hardly won,
In a single night undone;
And on earth what saved and gain'd,
By the ravin sea distrain'd.

III

Such is the sorrow of this royal house;
   And none in all the City but forlorn
Under its own peculiar sorrow bows.
For the stern God who, deaf to human love,
   Grudges the least abridgment of the tale
Of human blood once pledged to him, above
The centre of the murder-dealing crowd
   Suspends in air his sanguinary scale;
And for the blooming Hero gone a-field
   Homeward remits a beggarly return
Of empty helmet, fallen sword and shield,
   And some light ashes in a little urn.

IV

Then wild and high goes up the cry
To heav'n, "So true! so brave! so fair!

The young colt of the flowing hair
And flaming eye, and now—look there!
Ashes and arms!" or, "Left behind
Unburied, in the sun and wind
To wither, or become the feast
Of bird obscene, or unclean beast;
The good, the brave, without a grave—
All to redeem *her* from the shame
To which she sold her self and name!"—
For such insinuation in the dark
About the City travels like a spark;
    Till the pent tempest into lightning breaks,
And takes the topmost pinnacle for mark.

V

But avaunt all evil omen!
    Perish many, so the State
    They die for live inviolate;
Which, were all her mortal leafage
    In the blast of Ares scatter'd,
    So herself at heart unshatter'd,
In due season she retrieves
All her wasted wealth of leaves,
And age on age shall spread and rise
To cover earth and breathe the skies.
While the rival at her side
Who the wrath of Heav'n defied,
By the lashing blast, or flashing
Bolt of Heav'n comes thunder-crashing,
Top and lop, and trunk and bough,
Down, for ever down. And now,
He to whom the Zeus of Vengeance
    Did commit the bolt of Fate—
Agamemnon—how shall I
With a Pæan not too high
For mortal glory, to provoke
From the Gods a counter-stroke,
Nor below desert so lofty,
    Suitably felicitate?

413

Such as chasten'd Age for due
May give, and Manhood take for true.
For, as many men comply
From founts no deeper than the eye
  With others' sorrows; many more,
With a Welcome from the lips,
That far the halting heart outstrips,
  Fortune's Idol fall before.
Son of Atreus, I premise,
  When at first the means and manhood
Of the cities thou didst stake
For a wanton woman's sake,
  I might grudge the sacrifice;
  But, the warfare once begun,
Hardly fought and hardly won,
Now from Glory's overflowing
Horn of Welcome all her glowing
  Honours, and with uninvidious
Hand, before your advent throwing,
I salute, and bid thee welcome,
Son of Atreus, Agamemnon,
Zeus' revenging Right-hand, Lord
  Of taken Troy and righted Greece:
Bid thee from the roving throne
  Of War the reeking steed release;
Leave the laurell'd ship to ride
Anchor'd in her country's side,
And resume the royal helm
Of thy long-abandon'd realm:
What about the State or Throne
Of good or evil since has grown,
  Alter, cancel, or complete;
And to well or evil-doer,
  Even-handed Justice mete.

Enter AGAMEMNON *in his chariot,* CASSANDRA *following
in another.*

AGAMEMNON: First, as first due, my Country I salute,
And all her tutelary Gods; all those

414

Who, having sent me forth, now bring me back,
After full retribution wrought on those
Who retribution owed us, and the Gods
In full consistory determined; each,
With scarce a swerving eye to Mercy's side,
Dropping his vote into the urn of blood.
Caught and consuming in whose fiery wrath,
The stately City, from her panting ashes
Into the nostril of revolted Heav'n
Gusts of expiring opulence puffs up.
For which, I say, the Gods alone be thank'd;
By whose connivance round about the wall
We drew the belt of Ares, and laid bare
The flank of Ilium to the Lion-horse,
Who sprung by night over the city wall,
And foal'd his iron progeny within,
About the setting of the Pleiades,
Thus much by way of prelude to the Gods.
For you, oh white-hair'd senators of Argos,
Your measured Welcome I receive for just;
Aware on what a tickle base of fortune
The monument of human Glory stands;
And, for humane congratulation, knowing
How, smile as may the mask, the man behind
Frets at the fortune that degrades his own.
This, having heard of from the wise, myself,
From long experience in the ways of men,
Can vouch for—what a shadow of a shade
Is human loyalty; and, as a proof,
Of all the Host that fill'd the Grecian ship,
And pour'd at large along the field of Troy,
One only Chief—and he, too, like yourself,
At first with little stomach for the cause—
The wise Odysseus—once in harness, he
With all his might pull'd in the yoke with me,
Through envy, obloquy, and opposition:
And in Odysseus' honour, live or dead—
For yet we know not which—shall this be said.
Of which enough. For other things of moment

To which you point, or human or divine,
We shall forthwith consider and adjudge
In seasonable council; what is well,
Or in our absence well deserving, well
Establish and requite; what not, redress
With salutary caution; or, if need,
With the sharp edge of Justice; and to health
Restore, and right, our ailing Commonwealth.
Now, first of all, by my own altar-hearth
To thank the Gods for my return, and pray
That Victory, which thus far by my side
Has flown with us, with us may still abide.

Enter CLYTEMNESTRA *from the Palace.*

CLYTEMNESTRA: Oh Men of Argos, count it not a shame
If a fond wife, and one whom riper years
From Youth's becoming bashfulness excuse,
Dares own her love before the face of men;
Nor leaving it for others to enhance,
Simply declares the wretched widowhood
Which these ten years she has endured, since first
Her husband Agamemnon went to Troy.
'Tis no light matter, let me tell you, Sirs,
A woman left in charge of house and home—
And when that house and home a Kingdom—and
She left alone to rule it—and ten years!
Beside dissent and discontent at home,
Storm'd from abroad with contrary reports,
Now fair, now foul; but still as time wore on
Growing more desperate; as dangerous
Unto the widow'd kingdom as herself.
Why, had my husband there but half the wounds
Fame stabb'd him with, he were before me now,
Not the whole man we see him, but a body
Gash'd into network; ay, or had he died
But half as often as Report gave out,
He would have needed thrice the cloak of earth
To cover him, that triple Geryon
Lies buried under in the world below.

Thus, back and forward baffled, and at last
So desperate—that, if I be here alive
To tell the tale, no thanks to me for that,
Whose hands had twisted round my neck the noose
Which others loosen'd—my Orestes too
In whose expanding manhood day by day
My Husband I perused—and, by the way,
Whom wonder not, my Lord, not seeing here;
My simple mother-love, and jealousy
Of civic treason—ever as you know,
Most apt to kindle when the lord away—
Having bestow'd him, out of danger's reach,
With Strophius of Phocis, wholly yours
Bound by the generous usages of war,
That make the once-won foe so fast a friend.
Thus, widow'd of my son as of his sire,
No wonder if I wept—not drops, but showers,
The ten years' night through which I watch'd in vain
The star that was to bring him back to me;
Or, if I slept, a sleep so thin as scared
Even at the slight incursion of the gnat;
And yet more thick with visionary terrors
Than thrice the waking while had occupied.
Well, I have borne all this: all this have borne,
Without a grudge against the wanderer,
Whose now return makes more than rich amends
For all ungrateful absence—Agamemnon,
My Lord and Husband; Lord of Argos; Troy's
Confounder; Mainstay of the realm of Greece;
And Master-column of the house of Atreus—
Oh wonder not if I accumulate
All honour and endearment on his head!
If to his country, how much more to me,
Welcome, as land to sailors long at sea,
Or water in the desert; whose return
Is fire to the forsaken winter-hearth;
Whose presence, like the rooted Household Tree
That, winter-dead so long, anew puts forth
To shield us from the Dogstar, what time Zeus

o   417

Wrings the tart vintage into blissful juice.
Down from the chariot thou standest in,
Crown'd with the flaming towers of Troy, descend,
And to this palace, rich indeed with thee,
But beggar-poor without, return! And ye,
My women, carpet all the way before,
From the triumphal carriage to the door,
With all the gold and purple in the chest
   Stored these ten years; and to what purpose stored,
   Unless to strew the footsteps of their Lord
Returning to his unexpected rest!
AGAMEMNON: Daughter of Leda, Mistress of my house,
   Beware lest loving Welcome of your Lord,
   Measuring itself by his protracted absence,
   Exceed the bound of rightful compliment,
   And better left to other lips than yours.
   Address me not, address me not, I say
   With dust-adoring adulation, meeter
   For some barbarian Despot from his slave;
   Nor with invidious Purple strew my way,
   Fit only for the footstep of a God
   Lighting from Heav'n to earth. Let whoso will
   Trample their glories underfoot, not I.
   Woman, I charge you, honour me no more
   Than as the man I am; if honour-worth,
   Needing no other trapping but the fame
   Of the good deed I clothe myself withal;
   And knowing that, of all their gifts to man,
   No greater gift than Self-sobriety
   The Gods vouchsafe him in the race of life:
   Which, after thus far running, if I reach
   The goal in peace, it shall be well for me.
CLYTEMNESTRA: Why, how think you old Priam would have
   walk'd
   Had he return'd to Troy your conqueror,
   As you to Hellas his?
AGAMEMNON: What then? Perhaps
   Voluptuary Asiatic-like,
   On gold and purple.

CLYTEMNESTRA: Well, and grudging this,
    When all that out before your footsteps flows
    Ebbs back into the treasury again;
    Think how much more, had Fate the tables turn'd,
    Irrevocably from those coffers gone,
    For those barbarian feet to walk upon,
    To buy your ransom back!

AGAMEMNON: Enough, enough!
    I know my reason.

CLYTEMNESTRA: What! the jealous God?
    Or, peradventure, yet more envious man?

AGAMEMNON: And *that* of no small moment.

CLYTEMNESTRA: No; the one
    Sure proof of having won what others would.

AGAMEMNON: No matter—Strife but ill becomes a woman.

CLYTEMNESTRA: And frank submission to her simple wish
    How well becomes the Soldier in his strength!

AGAMEMNON: And I must then submit?

CLYTEMNESTRA: Ay, Agamemnon,
    Deny me not this first Desire on this
    First Morning of your long-desired Return.

AGAMEMNON: But not till I have put these sandals off,
    That, slave-like, too officiously would pander
    Between the purple and my dainty feet.
    For fear, for fear indeed, some Jealous eye
    From heav'n above, or earth below, should strike
    The Man who walks the earth Immortal-like.
    So much for that. For this same royal maid,
    Cassandra, daughter of King Priamus,
    Whom, as the flower of all the spoil of Troy,
    The host of Hellas dedicates to me;
    Entreat her gently; knowing well that none
    But submit hardly to a foreign yoke;
    And those of Royal blood most hardly brook.
    That if I sin thus trampling underfoot
    A woof in which the Heav'ns themselves are dyed,
    The jealous God may less resent his crime,
    Who mingles human mercy with his pride.

CLYTEMNESTRA: The Sea there is, and shall the sea be dried?

Fount inexhaustibler of purple grain
Than all the wardrobes of the world could drain;
And Earth there is, whose dusky closets hide
The precious metal wherewith not in vain
The Gods themselves this Royal house provide;
For what occasion worthier, or more meet,
Than now to carpet the victorious feet
Of Him who, thus far having done their will,
Shall now their last About-to-be fulfil?

[AGAMEMNON *descends from his chariot, and goes with* CLYTEMNESTRA *into the house,* CASSANDRA *remaining.*]

CHORUS: About the nations runs a saw,
      That Over-good ill-fortune breeds;
    And true that, by the mortal law,
      Fortune her spoilt children feeds
      To surfeit, such as sows the seeds
    Of Insolence, that, as it grows,
    The flower of Self-repentance blows.
    And true that Virtue often leaves
      The marble walls and roofs of kings,
    And underneath the poor man's eaves
      On smoky rafter folds her wings.

II

Thus the famous city, flown
With insolence, and overgrown,
Is humbled: all her splendour blown
To smoke: her glory laid in dust;
Who shall say by doom unjust?
But should He to whom the wrong
Was done, and Zeus himself made strong
To do the vengeance He decreed—
At last returning with the meed
    He wrought for—should the jealous Eye
    That blights full-blown prosperity
Pursue him—then indeed, indeed,
Man should hoot and scare aloof

Good-fortune lighting on the roof;
Yea, even Virtue's self forsake
If Glory follow'd in the wake;
Seeing bravest, best, and wisest
    But the playthings of a day,
Which a shadow can trip over,
    And a breath can puff away.

CLYTEMNESTRA (*re-entering*): Yet for a moment let me look on
    her—
This, then, is Priam's daughter—
Cassandra, and a Prophetess, whom Zeus
Has giv'n into my hands to minister
Among my slaves. Didst thou prophesy that?
Well—some more famous have so fall'n before—
Ev'n Herakles, the son of Zeus, they say
Was sold, and bow'd his shoulder to the yoke.

CHORUS: And, if needs must a captive, better far
Of some old house that affluent Time himself
Has taught the measure of prosperity,
Than drunk with sudden superfluity.

CLYTEMNESTRA: Ev'n so. You hear? Therefore at once descend
From that triumphal chariot—And yet
She keeps her station still, her laurel on,
Disdaining to make answer.

CHORUS: Nay, perhaps,
Like some stray swallow blown across the seas,
Interpreting no twitter but her own.

CLYTEMNESTRA: But, if barbarian, still interpreting
The universal language of the hand.

CHORUS: Which yet again she does not seem to see,
Staring before her with wide-open eyes
As in a trance.

CLYTEMNESTRA: Ay, ay, a prophetess—
Phœbus Apollo's minion once—Whose now?
A time will come for her. See you to it:
    A greater business now is on my hands:
For lo! the fire of Sacrifice is lit,
And the grand victim by the altar stands.
                    [*Exit* CLYTEMNESTRA.

CHORUS (*continuing*): Still a mutter'd and half-blind
    Superstition haunts mankind,
     That, by some divine decree
    Yet by mortal undivined,
    Mortal Fortune must not over–
     Leap the bound he cannot see;
    For that even wisest labour
     Lofty-building, builds to fall,
    Evermore a jealous neighbour
     Undermining floor and wall.
    So that on the smoothest water
     Sailing, in a cloudless sky,
    The wary merchant overboard
    Flings something of his precious hoard
     To pacify the jealous eye,
    That will not suffer man to swell
    Over human measure. Well,
    As the Gods have order'd we
    Must take—I know not—let it be.
    But, by rule of retribution,
     Hidden, too, from human eyes,
    Fortune in her revolution,
     If she fall, shall fall to rise:
    And the hand of Zeus dispenses
     Even measure in the main:
    One short harvest recompenses
     With a glut of golden grain;
    So but men in patience wait
     Fortune's counter-revolution
    Axled on eternal Fate;
    And the Sisters three that twine,
    Cut not short the vital line;
    For indeed the purple seed
    Of life once shed—
CASSANDRA: Phœbus Apollo!
CHORUS: Hark!
  The lips at last unlocking.
CASSANDRA: Phœbus! Phœbus!
CHORUS: Well, what of Phœbus, maiden? though a name

'Tis but disparagement to call upon
In misery.

CASSANDRA: Apollo! Apollo! Again!
Oh, the burning arrow through the brain!
Phœbus Apollo! Apollo!

CHORUS: Seemingly
Possess'd indeed—whether by—

CASSANDRA: Phœbus! Phœbus!
Thorough trampled ashes, blood, and fiery rain,
Over water seething, and behind the breathing
Warhorse in the darkness—till you rose again—
Took the helm—took the rein—

CHORUS: As one that half asleep at dawn recalls
A night of Horror!

CASSANDRA: Hither, whither, Phœbus? And with whom,
Leading me, lighting me—

CHORUS: I can answer that—

CASSANDRA: Down to what slaughter-house?
Foh! the smell of carnage through the door
Scares me from it—drags me tow'rd it—
Phœbus! Apollo! Apollo!

CHORUS: One of the dismal prophet-pack, it seems,
That hunt the trail of blood. But here at fault—
This is no den of slaughter, but the house
Of Agamemnon.

CASSANDRA: Down upon the towers
Phantoms of two mangled Children hover—and
a famish'd man,
At an empty table glaring, seizes and devours!

CHORUS: Thyestes and his children! Strange enough
For any maiden from abroad to know,
Or, knowing—

CASSANDRA: And look! in the chamber below
The terrible Woman, listening, watching,
Under a mask, preparing the blow
In the fold of her robe—

CHORUS: Nay, but again at fault:
For in the tragic story of this House—

423

Unless, indeed, the fatal Helen—
No woman—

CASSANDRA: No Woman—Tisiphone! Daughter
Of Tartarus—love-grinning Woman above,
Dragon-tail'd under—honey-tongued, Harpy-claw'd,
Into the glittering meshes of slaughter
She wheedles, entices, him into the poisonous
Fold of the serpent—

CHORUS: Peace, mad woman, peace!
Whose stony lips once open vomit out
Such uncouth horrors.

CASSANDRA: I tell you the lioness
Slaughters the Lion asleep; and lifting
Her blood-dripping fangs buried deep in his mane,
Glaring about her insatiable, bellowing,
Bounds hither—Phœbus, Apollo, Apollo, Apollo!
Whither have you led me, under night alive with fire,
Through the trampled ashes of the city of my sire,
From my slaughtered kinsmen, fallen throne, insulted
      shrine,
Slave-like to be butcher'd, the daughter of a Royal
      line?

CHORUS: And so returning, like a nightingale
Returning to the passionate note of woe
By which the silence first was broken!

CASSANDRA: Oh,
A nightingale, a nightingale, indeed,
That, as she "Itys! Itys! Itys!" so
I "Helen! Helen! Helen!" having sung
Amid my people, now to those who flung
And trampled on the nest, and slew the young,
Keep crying "Blood! blood! blood!" and none will heed!
Now what for me is this prophetic weed,
And what for me is this immortal crown,
Who like a wild swan from Scamander's reed
Chaunting her death-song float Cocytus-down?
There let the fatal Leaves to perish lie!
To perish, or enrich some other brow
With that all-fatal gift of Prophecy

They palpitated under Him who now,
Checking his flaming chariot in mid sky,
With divine irony sees disadorn
The wretch his love has made the people's scorn,
The raving quean, the mountebank, the scold,
Who, wrapt up in the ruin she foretold
With those who would not listen, now descends
To that dark kingdom where his empire ends.
CHORUS: Strange that Apollo should the laurel wreath
    Of Prophecy he crown'd your head withal
    Himself disgrace. But something have we heard
    Of some divine revenge for slighted love.
CASSANDRA: Ay—and as if in malice to attest
      With one expiring beam of Second-sight
    Wherewith his victim he has cursed and blest,
      Ere quench'd for ever in descending night;
As from behind a veil no longer peeps
The Bride of Truth, nor from their hidden deeps
Darkle the waves of Prophecy, but run
Clear from the very fountain of the Sun.
Ye call'd—and rightly call'd—me bloodhound; ye
That like old lagging dogs in self-despite
Must follow up the scent with me; with me,
Who having smelt the blood about this house
Already spilt, now bark of more to be.
For, though you hear them not, the infernal Choir
Whose dread antiphony forswears the lyre,
Who now are chaunting of that grim carouse
Of blood with which the children fed their Sire,
Shall never from their dreadful chorus stop
Till all be counter-pledged to the last drop.
CHORUS: Hinting at what indeed has long been done,
    And widely spoken, no Apollo needs;
    And for what else you aim at—still in dark
    And mystic language—
CASSANDRA: Nay, then, in the speech,
    She that reproved me was so glib to teach—
    Before yon Sun a hand's-breadth in the skies
      He moves in shall have moved, those age-sick eyes
O*

Shall open wide on Agamemnon slain
Before your very feet. Now, speak I plain?
CHORUS: Blasphemer, hush!
CASSANDRA: Ay, hush the mouth you may,
But not the murder.
CHORUS: Murder! But the Gods—
CASSANDRA: The Gods!
Who even now are their accomplices.
CHORUS: Woman!—Accomplices—With whom?—
CASSANDRA: With Her,
Who brandishing aloft the axe of doom,
   That just has laid one victim at her feet,
Looks round her for that other, without whom
   The banquet of revenge were incomplete.
Yet ere I fall will I prelude the strain
Of Triumph, that in full I shall repeat
When, looking from the twilight Underland,
I welcome Her as she descends amain,
Gash'd like myself, but by a dearer hand.
For that old murder'd Lion with me slain,
Rolling an awful eyeball through the gloom
He stalks about of Hades up to Day,
Shall rouse the whelp of exile far away,
His only authentic offspring, ere the grim
Wolf crept between his Lioness and him;
Who with one stroke of Retribution, her
Who did the deed, and her adulterer,
Shall drive to hell; and then, himself pursued
By the wing'd Furies of his Mother's blood,
Shall drag about the yoke of Madness, till
Released, when Nemesis has gorged her fill,
By that same God, in whose prophetic ray
Viewing To-morrow mirror'd as To-day,
And that this House of Atreus the same wine
Themselves must drink they brew'd for me and mine;
I close my lips for ever with one prayer,
That the dark Warder of the World below
Would ope the portal at a single blow.
CHORUS: And the raving voice, that rose

Out of silence into speech
Over-shooting human reach,
Back to silence foams and blows,
 Leaving all my bosom heaving—
Wrath and raving all, one knows;
Prophet-seeming, but if ever
 Of the Prophet-God possest,
 By the Prophet's self confest
God-abandon'd—woman's shrill
Anguish into tempest rising,
Louder as less listen'd.
      Still—
Spite of Reason, spite of Will,
What unwelcome, what unholy,
Vapour of Foreboding, slowly
Rising from the central soul's
Recesses, all in darkness rolls?
What! shall Age's torpid ashes
Kindle at the ransom spark
Of a raving maiden?—Hark!
What was that behind the wall?
A heavy blow—a groan—a fall—
Some one crying—Listen further—
Hark again then, crying "Murder!"
Some one—who then? Agamemnon?
Agamemnon?—Hark again!
Murder! murder! murder! murder!
Help within there! Help without there!
Break the doors in!—

CLYTEMNESTRA (*appearing from within, where lies* AGAMEM-
 NON *dead*):   Spare your pain.
Look! I who but just now before you all
Boasted of loyal wedlock unashamed,
Now unashamed dare boast the contrary.
Why, how else should one compass the defeat
Of him who underhand contrives one's own,
Unless by such a snare of circumstance
As, once enmesh'd, he never should break through?
The blow now struck was not the random blow

Of sudden passion, but with slow device
Prepared, and levell'd with the hand of time.
I say it who devised it; I who did;
And now stand here to face the consequence.
Ay, in a deadlier web than of that loom
In whose blood-purple he divined a doom,
And fear'd to walk upon, but walk'd at last,
Entangling him inextricably fast,
I smote him, and he bellow'd; and again
I smote, and with a groan his knees gave way;
And, as he fell before me, with a third
And last libation from the deadly mace
I pledged the crowning draught to Hades due,
That subterranean Saviour—of the Dead!
At which he spouted up the Ghost in such
A burst of purple as, bespatter'd with,
No less did I rejoice than the green ear
Rejoices in the largess of the skies
That fleeting Iris follows as it flies.

CHORUS: Oh woman, woman, woman!
By what accursèd root or weed
Of Earth, or Sea, or Hell, inflamed,
Darest stand before us unashamed
And, daring do, dare glory in the deed!

CLYTEMNESTRA: Oh, I that dream'd the fall of Troy, as you
Belike of Troy's destroyer. Dream or not,
Here lies your King—my Husband—Agamemnon,
Slain by this right hand's righteous handicraft.
Like you, or like it not, alike to me;
To me alike whether or not you share
In making due libation over this
Great Sacrifice—if ever due, from him
Who, having charged so deep a bowl of blood,
Himself is forced to drink it to the dregs.

CHORUS: Woman, what blood but that of Troy, which Zeus
Foredoom'd for expiation by his hand
For whom the penalty was pledged? And now,
Over his murder'd body, Thou
Talk of libation!—Thou! Thou! Thou!

428

But mark! Not thine of sacred wine
Over his head, but ours on thine
Of curse, and groan, and torn-up stone,
To slay or storm thee from the gate,
The City's curse, the People's hate,
Execrate, exterminate—

CLYTEMNESTRA: Ay, ay, to me how lightly you adjudge
Exile or death, and never had a word
Of counter-condemnation for Him there;
Who, when the field throve with the proper flock
For Sacrifice, forsooth let be the beast,
And with his own hand his own innocent
Blood, and the darling passion of my womb—
Her slew—to lull a peevish wind of Thrace.
And him who cursed the city with that crime
You hail with acclamation; but on me,
Who only do the work you should have done,
You turn the axe of condemnation. Well;
Threaten you me, I take the challenge up;
Here stand we face to face; win Thou the game,
And take the stake you aim at; but if I—
Then, by the Godhead that for me decides,
Another lesson you shall learn, though late.

CHORUS: Man-mettled evermore, and now
            Manslaughter-madden'd! Shameless brow!
            But do you think us deaf and blind
                Not to know, and long ago,
            What Passion under all the prate
            Of holy justice made thee hate
            Where Love was due, and love where—

CLYTEMNESTRA: Nay, then, hear!
By this dead Husband, and the reconciled
Avenging Fury of my slaughter'd child,
I swear I will not reign the slave of fear
While he that holds me, as I hold him, dear,
Kindles his fire upon this hearth: my fast
Shield for the time to come, as of the past.
Yonder lies he that in the honey'd arms
Of his Chryseides under Troy walls

429

Dishonour'd mine: and this last laurell'd wench,
Prophetic messmate of the rower's bench,
Thus far in triumph his, with him along
Shall go, together chaunting one death-song
To Hades—fitting garnish for the feast
Which Fate's avenging hand through mine hath drest.

CHORUS: Woe, woe, woe, woe!
That death as sudden as the blow
That laid Thee low would me lay low
Where low thou liest, my sovereign Lord!
Who ten years long to Trojan sword
Devoted, and to storm aboard,
In one ill woman's cause accurst,
Liest slain before thy palace door
By one accursedest and worst!

CLYTEMNESTRA: Call not on Death, old man, that, call'd or no,
Comes quick; nor spend your ebbing breath on me,
Nor Helena: who but as arrows be
Shot by the hidden hand behind the bow.

CHORUS: Alas, alas! The Curse I know
That round the House of Atreus clings,
About the roof, about the walls,
Shrouds it with his sable wings;
And still as each new victim falls,
And gorged with kingly gore,
Down on the bleeding carcase flings,
And croaks for "More, more, more!"

CLYTEMNESTRA: Ay, now, indeed, you harp on likelier strings.
Not I, nor Helen, but that terrible
Alastor of old Tantalus in Hell;
Who, one sole actor in the scene begun
By him, and carried down from sire to son,
The mask of Victim and Avenger shifts:
And, for a last catastrophe, that grim
Guest of the abominable banquet lifts
His head from Hell, and in my person cries
For one full-grown sufficient sacrifice,
Requital of the feast prepared for him
Of his own flesh and blood—And there it lies.

CHORUS: Oh, Agamemnon! Oh, my Lord!
        Who, after ten years toil'd;
    After barbarian lance and sword
        Encounter'd, fought, and foil'd;
    Returning with the just award
        Of Glory, thus inglorious by
        Thine own domestic Altar die,
    Fast in the spider meshes coil'd
        Of Treason most abhorr'd!

CLYTEMNESTRA: And by what retribution more complete,
    Than, having in the meshes of deceit
    Enticed my child, and slain her like a fawn
    Upon the altar; to that altar drawn
    Himself, like an unconscious beast, full-fed
    With Conquest, and the garland on his head,
    Is slain? and now, gone down among the Ghost,
    Of taken Troy indeed may make the most,
    But not *one* unrequited murder boast.

CHORUS: Oh Agamemnon, dead, dead, dead, dead, dead!
    What hand, what pious hand shall wash the wound
    Through which the sacred spirit ebb'd and fled!
    With reverend care compose, and to the ground
    Commit the mangled form of Majesty,
    And pour the due libation o'er the mound!

CLYTEMNESTRA: This hand, that struck the guilty life away,
    The guiltless carcase in the dust shall lay
    With due solemnities: and if with no
    Mock tears, or howling counterfeit of woe,
    On this side earth; perhaps the innocent thing,
    Whom with paternal love he sent before,
    Meeting him by the melancholy shore,
    Her arms about him with a kiss shall fling,
    And lead him to his shadowy throne below.

CHORUS: Alas! alas! the fatal rent
        Which through the house of Atreus went,
        Gapes again; a purple rain
        Sweats the marble floor, and falls
        From the tottering roof and walls,
        The Dæmon heaving under; gone

The master-prop they rested on:
And the storm once more awake
Of Nemesis; of Nemesis
Whose fury who shall slake!

CLYTEMNESTRA: Ev'n I; who by this last grand victim hope
The Pyramid of Vengeance so to cope,
That—and methinks I hear him in the deep
Beneath us growling tow'rd his rest—the stern
Alastor to some other roof may turn,
Leaving us here at last in peace to keep
What of life's harvest yet remains to reap.

CHORUS: Thou to talk of reaping Peace
Who sowest Murder! Woman, cease!
And, despite that iron face—
Iron as the bloody mace
Thou bearest—boasting as if Vengeance
Centred in that hand alone;
Know that, Fury pledged to Fury,
Vengeance owes himself the debts
He makes, and while he serves thee, whets
His knife upon another stone,
Against thyself, and him with thee
Colleaguing, as you boast to be,
The tools of Fate. But Fate is Zeus;
Zeus—who for awhile permitting
Sin to prosper in his name,
Shall vindicate his own abuse;
And having brought his secret thought
To light, shall break and fling to shame
The baser tools with which he wrought.

ÆGISTHUS: CLYTEMNESTRA: CHORUS:
All hail, thou daybreak of my just revenge!
In which, as waking from injurious sleep,
Methinks I recognize the Gods enthroned
In the bright conclave of eternal Justice,
Revindicate the wrongs of man to man!
For see *this* man—so dear to me now dead—
Caught in the very meshes of the snare
By which his father Atreus netted mine.

For that same Atreus surely, was it not?
Who, wrought by false Suspicion to fix'd Hate,
From Argos out his younger brother drove,
My sire—Thyestes—drove him like a wolf,
Keeping his cubs—save one—to better purpose.
For when at last the home-heartbroken man
Crept humbly back again, craving no more
Of his own country than to breathe its air
In liberty, and of her fruits as much
As not to starve withal—the savage King,
With damnable alacrity of hate,
And reconciliation of revenge,
Bade him, all smiles, to supper—such a supper,
Where the prime dainty was—my brother's flesh,
So maim'd and clipt of human likelihood,
That the unsuspecting Father, light of heart,
And quick of appetite, at once fell to,
And ate—ate—what, with savage irony
As soon as eaten, told—the wretched man
Disgorging with a shriek, down to the ground
The table with its curst utensil dashed,
And, grinding into pieces with his heel,
Cried, lough enough for Heav'n and Hell to hear,
"Thus perish all the race of Pleisthenes!"
And now behold! the son of that same Atreus
By me the son of that Thyestes slain
Whom the kind brother, sparing from the cook,
Had with his victim pack'd to banishment;
Where Nemesis—(so sinners from some nook,
Whence least they think assailable, assailed)—
Rear'd me from infancy till fully grown,
To claim in full my father's bloody due.
Ay, I it was—none other—far away
Who spun the thread, which gathering day by day
Mesh after mesh, inch upon inch, at last
Reach'd him, and wound about him, as he lay,
And in the supper of his smoking Troy
Devour'd his own destruction—scarce condign
Return for that his Father forced on mine.

433

CHORUS: Ægisthus, only things of baser breed
   Insult the fallen; fall'n too, as you boast,
   By one who plann'd but dared not do the deed.
   This is your hour of triumph. But take heed;
   The blood of Atreus is not all outrun
   With this slain King, but flowing in a son,
   Who saved by such an exile as your own
   For such a counter-retribution—

ÆGISTHUS: Oh,
   You then, the nether benchers of the realm,
   Dare open tongue on those who rule the helm?
   Take heed yourselves; for, old and dull of wit,
   And harden'd as your mouth against the bit,
   Be wise in time; kick not against the spurs;
   Remembering Princes are shrewd taskmasters.

CHORUS: Beware thyself, bewaring me;
   Remembering that, too sharply stirr'd,
   The spurrer need beware the spurr'd;
   As thou of me; whose single word
   Shall rouse the City—yea, the very
    Stones you walk upon, in thunder
   Gathering o'er your head, to bury
    Thee and thine Adultress under!

ÆGISTHUS: Raven, that with croaking jaws
    Unorphean, undivine,
   After you no City draws;
    And if any vengeance, mine
   Upon your wither'd shoulders—

CHORUS: Thine!
   Who daring not to strike the blow
   Thy worse than woman-craft design'd,
   To worse than woman—

ÆGISTHUS: Soldiers, ho!

CLYTEMNESTRA: Softly, good Ægisthus, softly; let the sword
   that has so deep
  Drunk of righteous Retribution now within the scabbard
   sleep!
  And if Nemesis be sated with the blood already spilt,
  Even so let us, nor carry lawful Justice into Guilt.

Sheathe your sword; dismiss your spears; and you, Old
    men, your howling cease,
And, ere ill blood come to running, each unto his home
    in peace,
Recognizing what is done for done indeed, as done it is,
And husbanding your scanty breath to pray that nothing
    more amiss.
Farewell. Meanwhile, you and I, Ægisthus, shall deliber-
    ate,
When the storm is blowing under, how to settle House
    and State.

INTRODUCTION TO
READINGS IN
CRABBE

[*Readings in Crabbe's "Tales of the Hall"* was privately printed in 1879, without introduction or title-page. In 1882 Quaritch issued some of the remaining sheets bound up with the newly-printed Introduction and a title-page: *Readings in Crabbe. Tales of the Hall.* A further edition of these sheets, with a revised Introduction, was ordered by FitzGerald shortly before he died, and appeared after his death in 1883. This is the text used by Aldis Wright and in the present reprint.]

INTRODUCTION

"TALES OF THE HALL," says the Poet's son and biographer, occupied his father during the years 1817, 1818, and were published by John Murray in the following year under the present title, which he suggested, instead of that of "Remembrances," which had been originally proposed.

The plan and nature of the work is thus described by the author himself in a letter written to his old friend, Mary Leadbetter, and dated October 30, 1817:

"I know not how to describe the new, and probably (most probably) the last work I shall publish. Though a village is the scene of meeting between my two principal characters, and gives occasion to other characters and relations in general, yet I no more describe the manners of village inhabitants. My people are of superior classes, though not the most elevated; and, with a few exceptions, are of educated and cultivated minds and habits. I do not know, on a general view, whether my tragic or lighter Tales, etc., are most in number. Of those equally well executed, the tragic will, I suppose, make the greater impression; but I know not that it requires more attention."

"The plan of the work," says Jeffrey, in a succinct, if not quite exact, epitome—"for it has more of plan and unity than any of Mr Crabbe's former productions—is abundantly simple. Two brothers, both past middle age, meet together, for the first time since their infancy, in the Hall of their native Parish, which the elder and richer had purchased as a place of retirement for his declining age; and there tell each other their own history, and then that of their guests, neighbours, and acquaintances. The senior is much the richer, and a bachelor—having been a little distasted with the sex by the unlucky result of a very extravagant passion. He is, moreover, rather too reserved, and somewhat Toryish, though with an excellent heart and a powerful understanding. The younger is very sensible also, but more open, social, and talkative; a happy husband and father, with a

439

tendency to Whiggism, and some notion of reform, and a disposition to think well both of men and women. The visit lasts two or three weeks in autumn; and the Tales are told in the after-dinner *têtes-à-têtes* that take place in that time between the worthy brothers over their bottle.

"The married man, however, wearies at length for his wife and children; and his brother lets him go with more coldness than he had expected. He goes with him a stage on the way; and, inviting him to turn aside a little to look at a new purchase he had made of a sweet farm with a neat mansion, he finds his wife and children comfortably settled there, and all ready to receive them; and speedily discovers that he is, by his brother's bounty, the proprietor of a fair domain within a morning's ride of the Hall, where they may discuss politics, and tell tales any afternoon they may think proper."—*Edinburgh Review*, 1819.

The Scene has also changed with Drama and Dramatis Personæ: no longer now the squalid purlieus of old, inhabited by paupers and ruffians, with the sea on one side, and as barren a heath on the other; in place of that, a village with its tidy homesteads and well-to-do tenants, scattered about an ancient Hall, in a well-wooded, well-watered, well-cultivated country, within easy reach of a thriving country town, and

> "West of the waves, and just beyond the sound,"

of that old familiar sea, which (with all its sad associations) the Poet never liked to leave far behind him.

When he wrote the letter above quoted (two years before the publication of his book) he knew not whether his tragic exceeded the lighter stories in quantity, though he supposed they would leave the deeper impression on the reader. In the completed work I find the tragic stories fewer in number, and, to my thinking, assuredly not more impressive than such as are composed of that mingled yarn of grave and gay of which the kind of life he treats of is, I suppose, generally made up. "Nature's sternest Painter" may have mellowed with a prosperous old age, and from a comfortable grand-climacteric, liked to contemplate and represent a brighter aspect of humanity than his earlier life afforded him. Anyhow, he has here selected a subject whose character and circumstance require a lighter touch and shadow less dark than such as he formerly delineated.

Those who now tell their own as well as their neighbours' stories are much of the Poet's own age as well as condition of life, and look back (as he may have looked) with what Sir Walter Scott calls a kind of humorous retrospect over their own lives, cheerfully extending to others the same kindly indulgence which they solicit for themselves. The book, if I mistake not, deals rather with the follies than with the vices of men, with the comedy rather than the tragedy of life. Assuredly there is scarce anything of that brutal or sordid villainy, of which one has more than enough in the Poet's earlier work. And even the more sombre subjects of the books are relieved by the colloquial intercourse of the narrators, which twines about every story, and, letting in occasional glimpses of the country round, encircles them all with something of dramatic unity and interest, insomuch that of all the Poet's works this one alone does not leave a more or less melancholy impression upon me; and, as I am myself more than old enough to love the sunny side of the wall, is on that account, I do not say the best, but certainly that which best I like, of all his numerous offspring.

Such, however, is not the case, I think, with Crabbe's few readers, who, like Lord Byron, chiefly remember him by the sterner realities of his earlier work. Nay, quite recently Mr Leslie Stephen in that one of his admirable essays which analyses the Poet's peculiar genius says:

"The more humorous of these performances may be briefly dismissed. Crabbe possesses the faculty, but not in any eminent degree; his hand is a little heavy, and one must remember that Mr Tovell and his like were of the race who require to have a joke driven into their heads with a sledge-hammer. Once or twice we come upon a sketch which may help to explain Miss Austen's admiration. There is an old maid devoted to china, and rejoicing in stuffed parrots and puppies, who might have been ridiculed by Emma Woodhouse; and a Parson who would have suited the Eltons admirably."

The spinster of the stuffed parrot indicates, I suppose, the heroine of "Procrastination" in another series of tales. But Miss Austen, I think, might also have admired another, although more sensible, spinster in these, who tells of her girlish and only love while living with the grandmother who maintained her gentility in the little town she lived in at the cost of such little economies as "would scarce a parrot keep;" and the story of the romantic friend who, having proved the vanity of human bliss by the supposed death of a young lover, has devoted herself to his memory, insomuch that as she is one fine autumnal day protesting in her garden that, were he to be restored to her in all his youthful beauty, she would renounce the real rather than surrender the ideal Hero awaiting her elsewhere—behold him advancing toward her in the person of a prosperous, portly merchant, who reclaims, and, after some little hesitation on her part, retains her hand.

There is also an old Bachelor whom Miss Austen might have liked to hear recounting the matrimonial attempts which have resulted in the full enjoyment of single blessedness; his father's sarcastic indifference to the first, and the haughty defiance of the mother of the girl he first loved. And when the young lady's untimely death has settled that question, his own indifference to the bride his own mother has provided for him. And when that scheme has failed, and yet another after that, and the Bachelor feels himself secure in the consciousness of more than middle life having come upon him, his being captivated—and jilted—by a country Miss, toward whom he is so imperceptibly drawn at her father's house that

> "Time after time the maid went out and in,
> Ere love was yet beginning to begin;
> The first awakening proof, the early doubt,
> Rose from observing she went in and out."

Then there is a fair Widow, who, after wearing out one husband with her ruinous tantrums, finds herself all the happier for being denied them by a second. And when he too is dead, and the probationary year of mourning scarce expired, her scarce ambiguous refusal (followed by acceptance) of a third suitor, for whom she is now so gracefully wearing her weeds as to invite a fourth.

If "Love's Delay" be of a graver complexion, is there not some even graceful comedy in "Love's Natural Death"; some broad comedy—too true to be farce—in "William Bailey's" old house-keeper; and up and down the book surely many passages of gayer or graver humour; such as the Squire's satire on his own house and farm; his brother's account of the Vicar, whose daughter he married; the gallery of portraits in the "Cathedral Walk," besides many a shrewd remark so tersely put that I should call them epigram did not Mr Stephen think the Poet incapable of such; others so covertly implied as to remind one of old John Murray's remark on Mr Crabbe's conversation—that he said uncommon things in so common a way as to escape notice, though assuredly not the notice of so shrewd an observer as Mr Stephen if he cared to listen, or to read?

Nevertheless, with all my own partiality for this book, I must acknowledge that, while it shares with the Poet's other works in his characteristic disregard of form and diction—of all indeed that is now called "Art"—it is yet more chargeable with diffuseness, and even with some inconsistency of character and circumstance, for which the large canvas he had taken to work on, and perhaps some weariness in filling it up, may be in some measure accountable. So that, for one reason or another, but very few of Crabbe's few readers care to encounter the book. And hence this attempt of mine to entice them to it by an abstract, omitting some of the stories, retrenching others, either by excision of some parts, or the reduction of others into as concise prose as would comprehend the substance of much prosaic verse.

Not a very satisfactory sort of medley in any such case; I know not if more or less so where verse and prose are often so near akin. I see, too, that in some cases they are too patchily intermingled. But I have tried, though not always successfully, to keep them distinct, and to let the Poet run on by himself whenever in his better vein; in two cases—that of the "Widow" and "Love's Natural Death"—without any interruption of my own, though not without large deductions from the author in the former story.

On the other hand, more than as many other stories have shrunk under my hands into seeming disproportion with the Prologue by which the Poet introduces them, insomuch as they might almost as well have been cancelled were it not for carrying their introduction away with them.

And such alterations have occasionally necessitated a change in some initial article or particle connecting two originally separated paragraphs; of which I subjoin a list, as also of a few that have inadvertently crept into the text from the margin of my copy; all, I thought, crossed out before going to press. For any poetaster can amend many a careless expression which blemishes a passage that none but a poet could indite.

I have occasionally transposed the original text, especially when I thought to make the narrative run clearer by so doing. For in that respect, whether from lack or laxity of constructive skill, Crabbe is apt to wander and lose himself and his reader. This was shown especially in some prose novels, which at one time he tried his hand on, and (his son tells us), under good advice, committed to the fire.

I have replaced in the text some readings from the Poet's original MS. quoted in his son's standard edition, several of which appeared to me fresher, terser, and (as so often the case) more apt than the second thought afterward adopted.

Mr Stephen has said—and surely said well—that, with all its short and long-comings, Crabbe's better work leaves its mark on the reader's mind and memory as only the work of genius can, while so many a more splendid vision of the fancy slips away, leaving scarce a wrack behind. If this abiding impression result (as perhaps in the case of Richardson or Wordsworth) from being, as it were, soaked in through the longer process by which the man's peculiar genius works, any abridgement, whether of omission or epitome, will diminish from the effect of the whole. But, on the other hand, it may serve, as I have said, to attract a reader to an original, which, as appears in this case, scarce anybody now cares to venture upon in its integrity.

I feel bound to make all apology for thus dealing with a Poet whose works are ignored, even if his name be known, by the readers and writers of the present generation. "Pope in worsted stockings," he has been called. But, in truth, the comparison, such as it is, scarcely reaches beyond Crabbe's earliest essays. For in "The Village," which first made him popular, he set out with Goldsmith rather than with Pope, though toward a very different object than "Sweet Auburn." And then, after nearly twenty years' silence (a rare interval for a successful author),

appeared a volume of "Tales"; and after them the "Parish Register," accompanied with "Sir Eustace Grey", and by-and-by followed by "The Borough": in all of which the style differed as
much from that of Pope as the character and scene they treated
of from the Wits and Courtiers of Twickenham and Hampton
Court. But all so sharply delineated as to make Lord Byron,
according to the comprehensive and comfortable form of decision that is never out of date, pronounce him to be Nature's best,
if sternest, painter.

In the present "Tales of the Hall," the poet, as I have said,
has in some measure shifted his ground, and Comedy, whose
shrewder—not to say more sardonic—element ran through his
earlier work, here discovers something of her lighter humour.
Not that the Poet's old Tragic power, whether of Terror or
Pity, is either absent or abated; as witness the story of "Ruth";
and that of "The Sisters," of whom one, with the simple piety
that has held her up against the storm which has overtaken them
both, devotes herself to the care of her whom it has bewildered,
as she wanders alone in the deepening gloom of evening,

> "Or cries at mid-day, 'Then Good-night to all!' "

And to prove how the Poet's landscape hand has not slackened
in its cunning, we may accompany the Brothers in their morning
ramble to the farm; or Richard on his horse to the neighbouring
town; or at a respectful distance observe those two spinsters conversing in their garden on that so still autumnal day,

> "When the wing'd insect settled in our sight,
> And waited wind to recommence her flight,"

till interrupted by the very substantial apparition of him who
ought long ago to have been a Spirit in heaven.

But "Tragedy, Comedy, Pastoral," all that, applauded as it
was by contemporary critics and representatives of literature,
contributed to make this writer generally read in the first quarter
of this century, has left of him to the present generation but the
empty echo of a name, unless such as may recall the

> "John Richard William Alexander Dwyer"

of the "Rejected Addresses." Miss Austen, indeed, who is still so much renowned for her representation of genteel humanity, was so unaccountably smitten with Crabbe in his worsted hose, that she playfully declared she would not refuse him for her husband. That Sir Walter Scott, with his wider experience of mankind, could listen to the reading of him when no longer able to hold the book for himself, may pass for little in these days when the Lammermoors and Midlothians are almost as much eclipsed by modern fiction as "The Lady of the Lake" and "Marmion" by the poetic revelations which have extinguished Crabbe. Nevertheless, among the many obsolete authorities of yesterday, there is yet one—William Wordsworth—who now rules, where once he was least, among the sacred Brotherhood to which he was exclusive enough in admitting others, and far too honest to make any exception out of compliment to anyone on any occasion; he did, nevertheless, thus write to the Poet's son and biographer in 1834: "Any testimony from me to the merit of your revered father's works would, I feel, be superfluous, if not impertinent. They will last, from their combined merits as poetry and truth, full as long as anything that has been expressed in verse since they first made their appearance"—a period which, be it noted, includes all Wordsworth's own volumes except "Yarrow Revisited," "The Prelude," and "The Borderers." And Wordsworth's living successor to the laurel no less participates with him in his appreciation of their forgotten brother. Almost the last time I met him he was quoting from memory that fine passage in "Delay has Danger," where the late autumn landscape seems to borrow from the conscience-stricken lover who gazes on it the gloom which it reflects upon him; and in the course of further conversation on the subject, Mr Tennyson added, "Crabbe has a world of his own;" by virtue of that original genius, I suppose, which is said to entitle, and carry, the possessor to what we call Immortality.

Mr Mozley, in his "Recollections of Oriel College," has told us that Cardinal Newman was a great reader of Crabbe in those earlier days; and the Cardinal himself, in one of his "Addresses to the Catholics of Dublin," published in 1873, tells us that so he continued to be, and, for one reason, *why*. For in treating of what may be called his Ideal of a University, he speaks of the insufficiency of mere Book-learning toward the making of a Man,

446

as compared with that which the Richard of these "Tales" unconsciously gathered in the sea-faring village where his boyhood passed; and where—not from books (of which he had scarce more than a fisherman's cottage supplied), but from the seamen on the shore, and the solitary shepherd on the heath, and a pious mother at home—"he contrived to fashion a philosophy and poetry of his own;" which, followed as it was by an active life on land and sea, made of him the man whom his more educated and prosperous brother contemplated with mingled self-regret and pride. And the poem in which this is told is considered by Cardinal Newman as, "whether for conception or execution, one of the most touching in our language," which having read "on its first publication with extreme delight," and again, thirty years after, with even more emotion, and yet again, twenty years after *that*, with undiminished interest: he concludes by saying that "a work which can please in youth and age seems to fulfil (in logical language) the *accidental* definition of a classic."

For a notice of this passage (which may be read at large in Cardinal Newman's sixth Discourse delivered to the Catholics of Dublin, p. 150, Edit. 1873) I am indebted to Mr Leslie Stephen, against whom I ventured to break a lance, and who has thus supplied me with one that recoils upon myself for having mutilated a poem which so great an authority looks on as so perfect.

VIRGIL'S GARDEN
AND
TRANSLATION
FROM PETRARCH

P

["Virgil's Garden" first appeared in *Temple Bar* of April 1882, and "Translation from Petrarch" in the *Letters and Literary Remains* of 1889.]

VIRGIL'S GARDEN

Laid out à la Delille

―――――

"There is more pleasantness in the little platform of a Garden which he gives us about the middle of this Book" ("Georgick" IV. 115–148) "than in all the spacious Walks and Waterfalls of Monsieur Rapin."—Dryden; two of whose lines are here marked by inverted commas.

But that, my destined voyage almost done,
I think to slacken sail and shoreward run,
I would enlarge on that peculiar care
Which makes the Garden bloom, the Orchard bear,
Pampers the Melon into girth, and blows
Twice to one summer the Calabrian Rose:
Nor many a shrub with flower and berries hung,
Nor Myrtle of the seashore leave unsung.

"For where the Tower of old Tarentum stands,
And dark Galesus soaks the yellow sands,"
I mind me of an old Corycian swain,
Who from a plot of disregarded plain,
That neither Corn, nor Vine, nor Olive grew,
Yet such a store of garden-produce drew
That made him rich in heart as Kings with all
Their wealth, when he returned at even-fall,
And from the conquest of the barren ground
His table with unpurchased plenty crown'd.
For him the Rose first open'd; his, somehow,
The first ripe Apple redden'd on the bough;
Nay, even when melancholy Winter still
Congeal'd the glebe, and check'd the wandering rill,

The sturdy veteran might abroad be seen,
With some first slip of unexpected green,
Upbraiding Nature with her tardy Spring,
And those south winds so late upon the wing.
He sow'd the seed; and, under Sun and Shower,
Up came the Leaf, and after it the Flower,
From which no busier bees than his derived
More, or more honey for their Master hived:
Under his skilful hand no savage root
But sure to thrive with its adopted shoot;
No sapling but, transplanted, sure to grow,
Sizable standards set in even row;
Some for their annual crop of fruit, and some
For longer service in the years to come;
While his young Plane already welcome made
The guest who came to drink beneath the shade.

But, by the stern conditions of my song
Compell'd to leave where I would linger long,
To other bards the Garden I resign
Who with more leisure step shall follow mine.

FROM PETRARCH

(Se la mia vita dall' aspro tormento)

———

If it be destined that my Life, from thine
  Divided, yet with thine shall linger on
Till, in the later twilight of Decline,
  I may behold those Eyes, their lustre gone;
When the gold tresses that enrich thy brow
  Shall all be faded into silver-gray,
From which the wreaths that well bedeck them now
  For many a Summer shall have fall'n away:
Then should I dare to whisper in your ears
  The pent-up Passion of so long ago,
That Love which hath survived the wreck of years
  Hath little else to pray for, or bestow,
Thou wilt not to the broken heart deny
The boon of one too-late relenting Sigh.

LETTERS

The letters to Horace Basham have been taken from the originals, kindly lent to me by Mr Kenneth Basham; the letter to W. B. Scott is taken from the typescript lent to me by Mr Norman Colbeck. For the rest, I have followed the Aldis Wright edition (1902–3); *Some New Letters of Edward FitzGerald*, edited by F. R. Barton (1923); *Letters . . . to Bernard Quaritch, 1853–83*, edited by C. Q. Wrentmore (1926); *A FitzGerald Friendship*, edited by C. B. Johnson (1932); *Two Suffolk Friends*, by F. H. Groome (1895); *Edward FitzGerald and 'Posh'*, by J. Blyth (1908); and *Alfred, Lord Tennyson: a Memoir*, by Hallam, Lord Tennyson (1897). To avoid confusion, editorial dates have all been put in square brackets.

J.R.

To John Allen

London, Nov. [27, 1832]

My dear Allen,

The first thing I do in answering your letter is to tell you that I am angry at your saying that your conscience pricks you for not having written to me before. I am of that superior race of men, that are quite content to hear themselves talk, and read their own writing. But, in seriousness, I have such love of you, and of myself, that once every week, at least, I feel spurred on by a sort of gathering up of feelings, to vent myself in a letter upon you: but if once I hear you say that it makes your conscience thus uneasy till you answer, I shall give it up. Upon my word I tell you, that I do not in the least require it. You, who do not love writing, cannot think that any one else does: but I am sorry to say that I have a very young-lady-like partiality to writing to those that I love. . . . I have been reading Shakespeare's Sonnets: and I believe I am unprejudiced when I say, I had but half an idea of him, Demigod as he seemed before, till I read them carefully. How can Hazlitt call Warton's the finest sonnets? There is the air of pedantry and labour in his. But Shakespeare's are perfectly simple, and have the very essence of tenderness that is only to be found in the best parts of his Romeo and Juliet besides. I have truly been lapped in these Sonnets for some time: they seem all stuck about my heart, like the ballads that used to be on the walls of London. I have put a great many into my Paradise, giving each a fair white sheet for himself: there being nothing worthy to be in the same page. I could talk for an hour about them: but it is not fit in a letter. . . .

I shall tell you of myself, that I have been better since I wrote to you. Mazzinghi tells me that November weather breeds Blue Devils—so that there is a French proverb, 'In October, de Englishman shoot de pheasant: in November he shoot himself.' This I suppose is the case with me: so away with November, as soon as may be. 'Canst thou my Clora' is being put in proper

P*   457

musical trim: and I will write it out for you when all is right. I am sorry you are getting so musical: and if I take your advice about so big a thing as Christianity, take you mine about music. I am sure that this pleasure of music grows so on people, that many of the hours that you would have devoted to Jeremy Taylor, &c. will be melted down into tunes, and the idle train of thought that music puts us into. I fancy I have discovered the true philosophy of this: but I think you must have heard me enlarge. Therefore 'satis.'

I have gabbled on so long that there is scarce room for my quotation. But it shall come though in a shapeless manner, for the sake of room. Have you got in your Christian Poet, a poem by Sir H. Wotton—'How happy is he born or taught, that serveth not another's will'? It is very beautiful, and fit for a Paradise of any kind. Here are some lines from old Lily, which your ear will put in the proper metre. It gives a fine description of a fellow walking in Spring, and looking here and there, and pricking up his ears, as different birds sing. 'What bird so sings, but doth so wail? Oh! 'tis the ravish'd nightingale: "Jug, jug, jug, jug, terue," she cries, and still her woes at midnight rise. Brave prick-song! who is 't now we hear? It is the lark so shrill and clear: against heaven's gate he claps his wings, the morn not waking till he sings. Hark, too, with what a pretty note poor Robin Redbreast tunes his throat: Hark how the jolly Cuckoos sing "Cuckoo" to welcome in the Spring: "Cuckoo" to welcome in the Spring.' This is very English, and pleasant, I think: and so I hope you will. I could have sent you many a more sentimental thing, but nothing better. I admit nothing into my Paradise, but such as breathe content, and virtue: I count 'Back and syde' to breathe both of these, with a little good drink over.

Wednesday [28 Nov. 1832]

P.S. I sealed up my letter yesterday, forgetting to finish. I write thus soon 'becase I gets a frank.' You shall benefit by another bit of poetry. I do not admit it into my Paradise, being too gloomy: but it will please both of us. It is the prototype of the Penseroso.

> Hence all you vain delights!
> As short as are the nights

Wherein ye spend your folly!
There's nought in this life sweet,
If man were wise to see 't,
But only melancholy;
Oh sweetest melancholy!
Welcome folded arms, and fixed eyes,
A sigh, that piercing mortifies,
A look that's fasten'd to the ground,
A tongue chain'd up without a sound!

Fountain heads, and pathless groves,
Places which pale passion loves!
Moonlight walks, when all the fowls
Are warmly hous'd, save bats and owls!
A midnight dell, a passing groan!
These are the sounds we feed upon;
Then stretch our bones in a still gloomy valley;
Nothing's so dainty sweet as melancholy.
(From the *Nice Valour, or the Passionate Madman* by Fletcher).

I think these lines are quite of the finest order, and have a more headlong melancholy than Milton's, which are distinctly copied from these, as you must confess. And now this is a very long letter, and the best thing you can do when you get to the end, is to Da Capo, and read what I ordered you about answering. My dear fellow, it is a great pleasure to me to write to you; and to write out these dear poems. . . . Believe me that I am your very loving friend, E.F.G.

To John Allen

[Castle Irwell] Manchester, February 24, 1833

Dear Allen,

. . . I am fearful to boast, lest I should lose what I boast of: but I think I have achieved a victory over my evil spirits here: for they have full opportunity to come, and I often observe their approaches, but hitherto I have managed to keep them off. Lord Bacon's Essay on Friendship is wonderful for its truth: and I

459

often feel its truth. He says that with a Friend, 'a man *tosseth* his thoughts,' an admirable saying, which one can understand, but not express otherwise. But I feel that, being alone, one's thoughts and feelings, from want of conversation, become heaped up and clotted together, as it were: and so lie like undigested food heavy upon the mind: but with a friend one *tosseth* them about, so that the air gets between them, and keeps them fresh and sweet. I know not from what metaphor Bacon took his 'tosseth,' but it seems to me as if it was from the way haymakers toss hay, so that it does not press into a heavy lump, but is tossed about in the air, and separated, and thus kept sweet.

Your most affectionate friend,

E. FITZGERALD

To W. B. Donne

Geldestone, Sept. 27, [1833]

Dear Donne,

. . . As to my history since I have seen you, there is little to tell. Divinity is not outraged by your not addressing me as a Reverend—I not being one. I am a very lazy fellow, who do nothing: and this I have been doing in different places ever since I saw you last. I have not been well for the last week: for I am at present rather liable to be overset by any weariness (and where can any be found that can match the effect of two Oratorios?), since for the last three months I have lived on vegetables—that is, I have given up meat. When I was talking of this to Vipan,[1] he told me that you had once tried it, and given it up. I shall hear your account of its effect on you. The truth is, that mine is the wrong time of life to begin a change of that kind: it is either too early, or too late. But I have no doubt at all of the advantage of giving up meat: I find already much good from it, in lightness and airiness of head, whereas I was always before clouded and more or less morbid after meat. The loss of strength is to be expected: I shall keep on and see if that also will turn, and

[1] [D. J. Vipan, one of a family of well-known brewers at Thetford, Norfolk. He was a scholar and friend of John Kemble's, and travelled much in Germany and Hungary. He is often mentioned in Donne's correspondence.]

change into strength. I have almost Utopian notions about *vegetable diet*, begging pardon for making use of such a vile, Cheltenhamic, phrase. Why do you not bring up your children to it? To be sure, the chances are, that, after guarding their vegetable morals for years, they would be seduced by some roast partridge with bread sauce, and become ungodly. This actually happened to the son of a Dr Newton who wrote a book about it and bred up his children to it—but all such things I will tell you when I meet you. Gods! it is a pleasant notion that one is about to meet an old acquaintance in a day or two.

Believe me then your most sincere friend,

E. FitzGerald

Pipes—are their names ever heard with you? I have given them up, except at Cambridge. But the word has something sweet in it—Do you ever smoke?

To W. B. Donne

7, Southampton Row, Bloomsbury, [Oct. 25, 1833]
Dear Donne,

. . . As to myself, and my diet, about which you give such excellent advice: I am still determined to give the diet I have proposed a good trial: a year's trial. I agree with you about vegetables, and soups: but my diet is chiefly *bread*: which is only a little less nourishing than flesh: and, being compact, and baked, and dry, has none of the washy, diluent effects of green vegetables. I scarcely ever touch the latter: but only pears, apples, &c. I have found no benefit yet; except, as I think, in more lightness of spirits: which is a great good. But I shall see in time.

I am living in London in the quarter of the town which I have noticed above: in a very happy bachelor-like way. Would you would come up here for a few days. I can give you bed, board, &c. Do have some business in town, please. Spedding[1] is here:

[1] [James Spedding (1808–81) was a school friend of EFG. On leaving Cambridge, he served in the Colonial Office until 1841. He then devoted himself to the study of Bacon, and published a monumental edition of Bacon's work, as well as his life and letters. He was secretary to Lord Ashburton's mission to America in 1842, and to the Civil Service Commission when it was instituted in 1855.]

taking lessons of drawing, before he goes for good into Cumberland: whither, for my sake and that of all his friends, I wish he never would go: for there are few such men, as far [as] I know. He and I have been theatricalizing lately. We saw an awful Hamlet the other night—a Mr Serle—and a very good Wolsey, in Macready: and a very bad Queen Catherine, in Mrs Sloman, whom you must remember. I am going to-night to see Macready in Macbeth: I have seen him before in it: and I go for the sake of his two last acts, which are amazingly fine, I think. . . . I am close to the British Museum, in which I take great pleasure in reading in my rambling way. I hear of Kemble[1] lately that he has been making some discoveries in Anglo-Saxon MSS. at Cambridge that, they say, are important to the interests of the church: and there is talk of publishing them, I believe. He is a strange fellow for that fiery industry of his: and, I am sure, deserves some steady recompence.

Tennyson has been in town for some time: he has been making fresh poems, which are finer, they say, than any he has done. But I believe he is chiefly meditating on the purging and subliming of what he has already done: and repents that he has published at all yet. It is fine to see how in each succeeding poem the smaller ornaments and fancies drop away, and leave the grand ideas single. . . .

I have lately bought a little pamphlet which is very difficult to be got, called The Songs of Innocence, written and adorned with drawings by W. Blake (if you know his name) who was quite mad: but of a madness that was really the elements of great genius ill-sorted: in fact, a genius with a screw loose, as we used to say. I shall shew you this book when I see you: to me there is particular interest in this man's writing and drawing, from the strangeness of the constitution of his mind. He was a man that used to see visions: and make drawings and paintings of Alexander the Great, Cæsar, &c. who, he declared, stood before him while he drew . . .

Your very affectionate friend,
E. FitzGerald

[1] [John Mitchell Kemble (1807–57), brother of Fanny Kemble, and school-friend of EFG. He was an Anglo-Saxon scholar and historian.]

To W. B. Donne

7 Southampton Row, Nov. 19, 1833

Dear Donne,

Your book I got: and read through all that seemed to concern me the first day. I have doubted whether it would be most considerate to return you thanks for it, making you pay for a letter: or to leave you thankless, with a shilling more in your pocket. You see I have taken the latter [? former], and God forgive me for it. The book is a good one, I think, as any book is, that notes down *facts alone*, especially about health. I wish we had diaries of the lives of half the unknown men that have lived. Like all other men who have got a theory into their heads, I can only see things in the light of that theory; and whatever is brought to me to convince me to the contrary is only wrought and tortured to my view of the question. This lasts till a reaction is brought about by some of the usual means: as time, and love of novelty, &c. I am still very obstinate and persist in my practices. I do not think Stark[1] is an instance of vegetable diet: consider how many things he tried grossly animal: lard, and butter, and fat: besides thwarting Nature in every way by eating when he wanted not to eat, and the contrary. Besides the editor says in the preface that he thinks his death was brought about as much by vexation as by the course of his diet: but I suppose the truth is that vexation could not have had so strong hold except upon a weakened body. However, altogether I do not at all admit Stark to be any instance: to be set up like a scarecrow to frighten us from the corn &c. Last night I went to hear a man lecture at Owen of Lanark's establishment (where I had never been before) and the subject happened to be about Vegetable Diet: but it was only the termination of a former lecture, so that I suppose all the good arguments (if there were any) were gone before. Do you know anything of a book by a Doctor Lamb[2] upon this subject? I do not feel it to be disgusting to talk of myself upon this subject, because

[1] [Dr William Stark (1740–70) was a victim of his own experiments on diet.]

[2] [Dr William Lambe, an advocate of vegetarianism, had attended Keats. Mrs Gisborne recorded in her journal on 12 July 1820 that 'poor Keats' was 'under sentence of death from Dr Lamb.']

I think there is great interest in the subject itself. So I shall say that I am just now very well: in fine spirits. I have only eaten meat once for many weeks: and that was at a party where I did not like to be singled out. Neither have I tasted wine, except two or three times. If I fail at last I shall think it a very great bore: but assuredly the first cut of a leg of mutton will be some consolation for my wounded judgement: that first cut is a fine thing. So much for this . . . Have you heard that Arthur Malkin is to be married? to a Miss Carr, with what Addison might call a pleasing fortune: or perhaps Nicholas Rowe. 'Sweet, pleasing friendship, &c. &c.' Mrs Malkin is in high spirits about it, I hear: and I am very glad indeed. God send that you have not heard this before: for a man likes to be the first teller of a pretty piece of news. Spedding and I went to see Macready in Hamlet the other night: with which he was pretty well content, but not wholly. For my part, I have given up deciding on how Hamlet should be played: or rather have decided it shouldn't be played at all. I take pleasure in reading things I don't wholly understand; just as the old women like sermons: I think it is of a piece with an admiration of all Nature around us. I think there is a greater charm in the half meanings and glimpses of meaning that come in through Blake's wilder visions: though his difficulties arose from a very different source from Shakespeare's. But somewhat too much of this. I suspect I have found out this as an useful solution, when I am asked the meaning of any thing that I am admiring, and don't know it.

Believe me, dear Donne, to be ever your affect. friend,

E. FitzGerald

To John Allen

Geldestone Hall, Sept. 9 [1834]

Dear Allen,

I have really nothing to say, and I am ashamed to be sending this third letter all the way from here to Pembrokeshire for no earthly purpose: but I have just received yours: and you will know how very welcome all your letters are to me when you see how the perusal of this one has excited me to such an instant reply. It has indeed been a long time coming: but it is all the more delicious. Perhaps you can't imagine how wistfully I have looked for it: how, after a walk, my eyes have turned to the table, on coming into the room, to see it. Sometimes I have been tempted to be angry with you: but then I thought that I was sure you would come a hundred miles to serve me, though you were too lazy to sit down to a letter. I suppose that people who are engaged in serious ways of life, and are of well filled minds, don't think much about the interchange of letters with any anxiety: but I am an idle fellow, of a very ladylike turn of sentiment: and my friendships are more like loves, I think. Your letter found me reading the Merry Wives of Windsor too: I had been laughing aloud to myself: think of what another coat of happiness came over my former good mood. You are a dear good fellow, and I love you with all my heart and soul. The truth is I was anxious about this letter, as I really didn't know whether you were married or not—or ill—I fancied you might be anything, or anywhere . . .

As to reading, I have not done much. I am going through the Spectator: which people nowadays think a poor book: but I honour it much. What a noble kind of Journal it was! There is certainly a good deal of what may be called '*pill*,' but there is a great deal of wisdom, I believe, only it is couched so simply that people can't believe it to be absolute wisdom. The little book you speak of I will order and buy. I heard from Thackeray,[1] who is just upon the point of going to France; indeed he may be there by this time. I shall miss him much . . .

Farewell, my dearest fellow: you have made me very happy to hear from you: and to know that all is so well with you. Believe me to be your ever affectionate friend,

E. FitzGerald

To John Allen

Manchester, May 23, 1835

Dear Allen,

I think that the fatal two months have elapsed, by which a letter shall become due to me from you. Ask Mrs Allen if this is

[1] [William Makepeace Thackeray (1811–63). Cambridge friend of EFG and author of *Vanity Fair*.]

not so. Mind, I don't speak this upbraidingly, because I know that you didn't know where I was. I will tell you all about this by degrees. In the first place, I staid at Mirehouse till the beginning of May, and then, going homeward, spent a week at Ambleside, which, perhaps you don't know, is on the shore of Winandermere. It was very pleasant there: though it was to be wished that the weather had been a little better. I have scarce done anything since I saw you but abuse the weather: but these four last days have made amends for all: and are, I hope, the beginning of summer at last. Alfred Tennyson staid with me at Ambleside: Spedding was forced to go home, till the last two days of my stay there. I will say no more of Tennyson than that the more I have seen of him, the more cause I have to think him great. His little humours and grumpinesses were so droll, that I was always laughing: and was often put in mind (strange to say) of my little unknown friend, Undine—I must however say, further, that I felt what Charles Lamb describes, a sense of depression at times from the overshadowing of a so much more lofty intellect than my own: this (though it may seem vain to say so) I never experienced before, though I have often been with much greater intellects: but I could not be mistaken in the universality of his mind; and perhaps I have received some benefit in the now more distinct consciousness of my dwarfishness. I think that you should keep all this to yourself, my dear Allen: I mean, that it is only to you that I would write so freely about myself. You know most of my secrets, and I am not afraid of entrusting even my vanities to so true a man . . .

Pray, do not forget to say how the Freestone party are. My heart jumped to them, when I read in a guide book at Ambleside, that from Scawfell (a mountain in Westmoreland) you could see Snowdon. Perhaps you will not see the chain of ideas: but I suppose there was one, else I don't know how it was that I tumbled, as it were, from the very summit of Scawfell, upon the threshold of Freestone. The mind soon traverses Wales. I have not been reading very much—(as if you ever expected that I did!)—but I mean, not very much for me—some Dante, by the aid of a Dictionary: and some Milton—and some Wordsworth—and some Selections from Jeremy Taylor, Barrow &c., compiled by Basil Montagu—of course you know the book: it is published by

Pickering. I do not think that it is very well done: but it has served to delight, and, I think, to instruct me much. Do you know South? He must be very great, I think. It seems to me that our old Divines will hereafter be considered our Classics—(in Prose, I mean)—I am not aware that any other nations have such books. A single selection from Jeremy Taylor is fine: but it requires a skilful hand to put many detached bits from him together: for a common editor only picks out the flowery, metaphorical, morsels: and so rather cloys: and gives quite a wrong estimate of the Authour, to those who had no previous acquaintance with him: for, rich as Taylor's illustrations, and grotesque as his images, are, no one keeps a grander proportion: he never huddles illustration upon the matter so as to overlay it, nor crowds images too thick together: which these Selections might make one unacquainted with him to suppose. This is always the fault of Selections: but Taylor is particularly liable to injury on this score. What a man he is! He has such a knowledge of the nature of man, and such powers of expressing its properties, that I sometimes feel as if he had had some exact counterpart of my own individual character under his eye, when he lays open the depths of the heart, or traces some sin to its root. The eye of his portrait expresses this keen intuition: and I think I should less like to have stood with a lie on my tongue before him, than before any other I know of. . . .

I beg you to give my best remembrances to your lady, who may be always sure that in all I wish of well for you, she is included: so that I take less care to make mention of her separately. . . .

To John Allen

Wherstead, July 4, 1835

Dear Allen,

. . . My brother John's[1] wife, always delicate, has had an attack this year, which she can never get over: and while we are all living in this house cheerfully, she lives in separate rooms, can

[1] [John FitzGerald (1803–79), eldest brother of EFG, was educated at Trinity College, Cambridge. He married twice; he was a philanthropist, but inclined to eccentricity.]

scarcely speak to us, or see us: and bears upon her cheek the marks of death. She has shewn great Christian dignity all through her sickness: was the only cheerful person when they supposed she could not live: and is now very composed and happy. You say sometimes how like things are to dreams: or, as I think, to the shifting scenes of a play. So does this place seem to me. All our family, except my mother, are collected here: all my brothers and sisters, with their wives, husbands, and children: sitting at different occupations, or wandering about the grounds and gardens, discoursing each their separate concerns, but all united into one whole. The weather is delightful: and when I see them passing to and fro, and hear their voices, it is like scenes of a play. I came here only yesterday. I have much to tell you of: I mean, much in my small way: I will keep all till I see you, for I don't know with what to begin in a letter. . . .

Edgeworth[1] introduced me to his wife and sister in law, who are very handsome Spanish ladies, seemingly of excellent sense. The wife is the gentler, and more feminine: and the sister more regularly handsome, and vivacious. I think that he is a very remarkable man: and I like him more the more I see of him.

What you say of Tennyson and Wordsworth is not, I think, wholly just. I don't think that a man can turn himself so directly to the service of morality, unless naturally inclined: I think Wordsworth's is a natural bias that way. Besides, one must have labourers of different kinds in the vineyard of morality, which I certainly look up to as the chief object of our cultivation: Wordsworth is first in the craft: but Tennyson does no little by raising and filling the brain with noble images and thoughts, which, if they do not direct us to our duty, purify and cleanse us from mean and vicious objects, and so prepare and fit us for the reception of the higher philosophy. A man might forsake a drunken party to read Byron's Corsair: and Byron's Corsair for Shelley's Alastor: and the Alastor for the Dream of Fair Women or the Palace of Art: and then I won't say that he would forsake these two last for anything of Wordsworth's, but his mind would be sufficiently refined and spiritualised to admit Wordsworth, and profit by him, and he might keep all the former imaginations

[1] [Francis Beaufort Edgeworth, half-brother of the novelist, Maria. He had been EFG's contemporary at Cambridge.]

as so many pictures, or pieces of music, in his mind. But I think that you will see Tennyson acquire all that at present you miss: when he has *felt* life, he will not die fruitless of instruction to man as he is. But I dislike this kind of criticism, especially in a letter. I don't know any one who has thought out any thing so little as I have. I don't see to any end, and should keep silent till I have got a little more, and that little better arranged.

I am sorry that all this page is filled with this botheration, when I have a thousand truer and better things that I want to talk to you about. I will write to you again soon. If you please to write (but consider it no call upon you, for the letter I have just got from you is a stock that will last me in comfort this long while) I shall be at Wherstead all July—after that I know not where, but probably in Suffolk. Farewell, my best of fellows: there is no use saying how much I wish that all your sorrow will be turned to hope, and all your hope to joy. As far as we men can judge, you are worthy of all earthly happiness.

To W. B. Donne

London. Oct: 23: 1836

Dear Donne,

What have you been doing, and where have you been? To the sea side yet? And did Blakesley[1] find you?—Pray when you have a spare half hour, and are not disinclined, let me know of your doings—I conclude that you are safe at Mattishall by this time— I have been to Ireland: and after that in Northamptonshire, till last Wednesday when I came to London. To-morrow I go into Suffolk: where I shall be for a fortnight: in which space of time if you can manage to write to me I shall be glad. My abode, Boulge Hall, Woodbridge—

Spedding is coming back to London this dientical [*sic*] night, so that I shall just miss him—which is a bore. Allen is in town, & as merry as good—Otter, the former Principal of King's College,

---

[1] [J. W. Blakesley (1808–85), had been an "Apostle" at Cambridge, and became a Fellow of Trinity in 1831. In 1872 he was made Dean of Lincoln on Mr Gladstone's recommendation. His chief work was an edition of Herodotus.]

is made Bishop of Chichester: and he will, I think, give my Divine Doctor a living in the course of time: for he is very fond of him— I always thought Providence would do something for Johnny: and lay an easy pillow in the corner where Johnny was only thinking to hide his head in humility— I am afraid for his wife's health: but I don't know that her friends or Doctors think her in a bad state—

I have been to the play nearly every night since I have been here: and they have really mustered all the strength of England at Covent Garden, even at the present low prices— I have seen King John, and Othello, there—Charles Kemble has lost all his lightness in Falconbridge & Cassio: and is become very burdensome on the stage, I think. Vandenhoff really plays Iago very well: not so well as Young, to my taste: I don't think he has made up his mind so clearly as to Iago's real character— But he plays with great ease, and point—Macready's Othello is fine: in parts, very fine: but not so good as some of his other parts— Miss Helen Faucit is a very considerable bore: and Mrs W. West persists in softening whore into *whoore*: an old item of stage delicacy— Liston is delicious at the Olympic: he should always be seen at the beginning of a season: for he becomes fagged and careless towards the end of it— He and Mrs Orger played last night as well as I could wish to see. So now you have heard all that I have seen. When will you come up and see some of these things according to your promise? My movements are not quite certain just now: but I shall be in town again in the middle of November, for I have to go to the Isle of Wight at that time— I should like hugely to sit with you before the green curtain again— I have also got Blake's book of Job for you to see: terrible, awful, and wonderful—and Retsch's Romeo & Juliet, and no end of Epicureanisms in store— I am ashamed of living in such Epicurean ease: and really think I ought to marry, or open a book at a Banker's, that I may not be more happy than my fellows— Seriously, I do not mean to speak disrespectfully of marriage &c but I only mean that it must bring some cares, and anxieties— However, don't divulge what I say: for it sounds pert and awkward— Edgeworth is still at Eltham with one pupil, I hear: I am sorry that I have not had time to go and see him— Thackeray is married and happy as the day is long— John

Kemble is in town, I believe: but I have not seen him. Now you have heard about men you do know, and about men you know no more of than Alexander the Coppersmith— So now I will bid you good bye: and go to pack up a trunk— But remember me very kindly to Mrs Donne: why will not she come to London some day?— Then we will all go to the Boxes, ye Gods—"which that we may all do &c" How's Padden?—

Yrs ever
E.F.G.

To John Allen

[Boulge Hall, Woodbridge, 21 April, 1837]

Dear Allen,

Have you done with my Doctor? If you have, will you send him to me here: Boulge Hall, Woodbridge, per Shannon Coach? You may book it at the Boar and Castle, Oxford Street, close by Hanway Passage. This is not far out of your beat. Perhaps I should not have sent for this book (it is Bernard Barton the Quaker who asks to read it) but that it gives me an excuse also to talk a little to you. Ah! I wish you were here to walk with me now that the warm weather is come at last. Things have been delayed but to be more welcome, and to burst forth twice as thick and beautiful. This is boasting however, and counting of the chickens before they are hatched: the East winds may again plunge us back into winter: but the sunshine of this morning fills one's pores with jollity, as if one had taken laughing gas. Then my house is getting on: the books are up in the bookshelves and do my heart good: then Stothard's Canterbury Pilgrims are over the fireplace: Shakespeare in a recess: how I wish you were here for a day or two! My sister is very well and cheerful and we have kept house very pleasantly together. My brother John's wife is, I fear, declining very fast: it is very probable that I shall have to go and see her before long: though this is a visit I should gladly be spared. They say that her mind is in a very beautiful state of peacefulness. She *may* rally in the summer: but the odds are much against her. We shall lose a perfect Lady, in the complete sense of the word, when she dies.

I have been doing very little since I have been here: having accomplished only a few Idylls of Theocritus, which harmonize with this opening of the fine weather. Is all this poor occupation for a man who has a soul to account for? You think so certainly. My dear Allen, you, with your accustomed humility, asked me if I did not think you changed when I was last in London: never did I see man less so: indeed you stand on too sure a footing to change, I am persuaded. But you will not thank me for telling you these things: but I wish you to believe that I rejoice as much as ever in the thought of you, and feel confident that you will ever be to me the same best of friends that you ever have been. I owe more to you than to all others put together. I am sure, for myself, that the main difference in our opinions (considered so destructive to friendship by so many pious men) is a difference in the Understanding, not in the Heart: and though you may not agree entirely in this, I am confident that it will never separate you from me.

Mrs Schutz is much delighted with the books you got for her: and still enquires if you hurt your health in searching. This she does in all simplicity and kindness. She has been very ill all the winter: but I see by a letter I have just had from her that her mind is still cheerful and the same. The *mens sana in corpore sano* of old age is most to be wondered at.

To Bernard Barton

London, April, 1838

Dear Sir,

John, who is going down into Suffolk, will I hope take this letter and despatch it to you properly. I write more on account of this opportunity than of anything I have to say: for I am very heavy indeed with a kind of Influenza, which has blocked up most of my senses, and put a wet blanket over my brains. This state of head has not been improved by trying to get through a new book much in fashion—Carlyle's French Revolution—written in a German style. An Englishman writes of French Revolutions in a German style. People say the book is very deep: but it appears to me that the meaning *seems* deep from lying under mystical language. There is no repose, nor equable movement in it: all cut up into short sentences half reflective, half narrative; so that one labours through it as vessels do through what is called a short sea—small, contrary going waves caused by shallows, and straits, and meeting tides &c. I like to sail before the wind over the surface of an even-rolling eloquence, like that of Bacon or the Opium Eater. There is also pleasant fresh water sailing with such writers as Addison; is there any *pond*-sailing in literature? that is, drowsy, slow, and of small compass? Perhaps we may say, some Sermons. But this is only conjecture. Certainly Jeremy Taylor rolls along as majestically as any of them. We have had Alfred Tennyson here; very droll, and very wayward: and much sitting up of nights till two and three in the morning with pipes in our mouths: at which good hour we would get Alfred to give us some of his magic music, which he does between growling and smoking; and so to bed. All this has not cured my Influenza as you may imagine: but these hours shall be remembered long after the Influenza is forgotten.

I have bought scarce any new books or prints: and am not sorry to see that I want so little more. One large purchase I have made however, the Biographie Universelle, 53 Octavo Volumes. It contains everything, and is the very best thing of its kind, and so referred to by all historians &c. Surely nothing is more pleasant than, when some name crosses one, to go and get acquainted with the owner of the name: and this Biographie really has found places for people whom one would have thought almost too small for so comprehensive a work—which sounds like a solecism, or Bull, does it not?

Now I must finish my letter: and a very stupid one it is. Here is a sentence of Warburton's that, I think, is very wittily expressed: though why I put it in here is not very discoverable. "The Church, like the Ark of Noah, is worth saving: not for the sake of the unclean beasts that almost filled it, and probably made most noise and clamour in it, but for the little corner of rationality, that was as much distressed by the stink within, as by the tempest without." Is it not good? It is out of his letters: and the best thing in them. It is also the best thing in mine.

473

With kind remembrances to Miss Barton,[1] believe me
Yours very affectionately
E. FitzGerald

To Bernard Barton

[London, 8 June, 1838]

Dear Sir,

I have just come home after accompanying my Father and
Lusia to their starting place in the City: they are off for Suffolk
for some days. I should have written to you by them: but I only
just now found your letter on the mantelpiece: there it has lain
some days during which I have been ruralising in Bedfordshire.
Delicious has it been there: such weather, such meadows, to
enjoy: and the Ouse still wandering along at his ease through
pretty villages and vales of his own beautifying. I am much in
love with Bedfordshire: it beats our part of the world: and I am
sure you would like it. But here I am come back to London for
another three weeks I suppose. . . .

I should much like to see your Platonic Brother. By your
account he must have a very perfect mental organization: or,
phrenologically speaking, he must be fully and equally furnished
with the bumps of ideality and causality: which, as Bacon would
say, are the two extreme poles on which the perfect 'sound and
roundabout' intellect is balanced. A great deficiency of the
causality bump causes me to break short in a long discussion
which I meant to have favoured you with on this subject. I hope
to meet your Brother one of these days: and to learn much from
him. 'Guesses at Truth' I know very well: the two Brothers are
the Hares: one a fellow of Trinity College Cambridge; the other
Author of some Sermons which I think you had from me this
winter. 'The Guesses' are well worth reading; nay, buying: very
ingenious, with a good deal of pedantry and *onesidedness* (do you

---

[1] [Lucy Barton was to become EFG's wife in November 1856, and to
separate from him the following August; and 'if,' he wrote, 'people want to
go further for the cause of all this Blunder than the fact of two People of
very determined habits and Temper, first trying to change them at close on
fifty—they may lay nine-tenths of the Blame on me.' Mrs FitzGerald died
in 1898, at the age of ninety.]

474

know this German word?), which, I believe, chiefly comes from the Trinity Fellow, who was a great pedant. I have just read Mrs Austin's Characteristics of Goethe: which I will bring for you when I come. It is well worth knowing something of the mind of certainly a great man, and who has had more effect on his age than any one else. There is something almost fearful in the energy of his intellect. I wish indeed you were in London to see all these pictures: I am sure their greatness would not diminish your pleasure in your own small collection. Why should it? There is as genuine a feeling of Nature in one of Nursey's[1] sketches as in the Rubenses and Claudes here: and if that is evident, and serves to cherish and rekindle one's own sympathy with the world about one, the great end is accomplished. I do not know very much of Salvator: is he not rather a melodramatic painter? No doubt, very fine in his way. But Claude and the two Poussins are the great ideal painters of Landscape. Nature looks more stedfast in them than in other painters: all is wrought up into a quietude and harmony that seem eternal. This is also one of the mysterious charms in the Holy Families of Raffaelle and of the early painters before him: the faces of the Madonnas are beyond the discomposure of passion, and their very draperies betoken an Elysian atmosphere where wind never blew. The best painter of the unideal Christ is, I think, Rembrandt: as one may see in his picture at the National Gallery, and that most wonderful one of our Saviour and the Disciples at Emmaus in the Louvre: there they sit at supper as they might have sat. Rubens and the Venetian Painters did neither one thing nor the other: their Holy figures are neither ideal nor real: and it is incongruous to see one of Rubens' brawny boors dressed up in the ideal red and blue drapery with which the early Italians clothed their figures of Christ. But enough of all this. I have seen Trench's Sabbation, and like it much: how do you like those centuries of couplets, which are a German fashion? they are very much in the style of Quarles' Emblems, and other pithy epigrams of that time: only doubtless more artistically polished: perhaps profounder. There were some of the same kind in Blackwood some months ago. My paper is out: and I must again say Good Bye.

[1] [Perry Nursey, a Suffolk artist.]

To John Allen

[28 April, 1839]

My dear Allen,

Some one from this house is going to London: and I will try and write you some lines now in half an hour before dinner: I am going out for the evening to my old lady who teaches me the names of the stars, and other chaste information. You see, Master John Allen, that if I do not come to London (and I have no thought of going yet) and you will not write, there is likely to be an end of our communication: not by the way that I am never to go to London again: but not just yet. Here I live with tolerable content: perhaps with as much as most people arrive at, and what if one were properly grateful one would perhaps call perfect happiness. Here is a glorious sunshiny day: all the morning I read about Nero in Tacitus lying at full length on a bench in the garden: a nightingale singing, and some red anemones eyeing the sun manfully not far off. A funny mixture all this: Nero, and the delicacy of Spring: all very human however. Then at half past one lunch on Cambridge cream cheese: then a ride over hill and dale: then spudding up some weeds from the grass: and then coming in, I sit down to write to you, my sister winding red worsted from the back of a chair, and the most delightful little girl in the world chattering incessantly. So runs the world away. You think I live in Epicurean ease: but this happens to be a jolly day: one isn't always well, or tolerably good, the weather is not always clear, nor nightingales singing, nor Tacitus full of pleasant atrocity. But such as life is, I believe I have got hold of a good end of it. . . .

Give my love to Thackeray from your upper window across the street. So he has lost a little child: and moreover has been sorry to do so. Well, goodbye my dear John Allen: Auld Lang Syne. My kind regards to your Lady.

> Down to the vale this water steers,
>   How merrily it goes:
>   'T will murmur on a thousand years,
>   And flow as now it flows.[1]

Geldestone Hall, Beccles.   E.F.G.

[1] [Wordsworth, *The Fountain.*]

To W. F. Pollock

[July 20, 1839]

My dear Pollock,

I have not such a pen as yours that can be inspirited to indite a jolly long letter under such circumstances as you describe. My circumstances are not much more enlivening: but then I have the advantage of your letter to begin upon: a great advantage. So here goes for an answer: for though few men have ever sat down with less to say, yet it is good to have such a starting-point as a letter just received. We have more books in our Library here than you found at your lodging in York—an Encyclopedia, a Johnson's Dictionary, Bailey's Navigation, etc., but nothing so new or striking as to make me suppose that you would be interested with any remarks I could make. Have you ever read Smith's Wealth of Nations? I never have. *Smellie's* Moral Philosophy?—Better than his Physical, I should think—Drury's Madagascar, Alison on Taste, Kett's Elements of Knowledge, etc.? All these we have, well bound, upon the shelves of the room in which I write: and we have had them for years—and shall have them, I dare say: they will never wear out. Grammont we have also, not so visible, however: he is in a private corner of a book-case in the drawing-room. I read him once twelve years ago, I believe: and have forgotten all about him. At your recommendation I shall read him again. I have also heard Thackeray speak well of him: but he is naturally prejudiced in favour of the dirty and immoral. I like Horace Walpole: he's capital fun, and the most easy reading in the world: no small praise, for easy reading does not presume easy writing by any means. Walpole I suppose wrote easily: but then it is not easy to have such a head as would write so easily. Q.E.D.

Can you shoot with a pistol, Pollock? Can you hit an oak tree (they grow large in this part of the country) at the distance of about ten yards? I tell you how it is with me: I generally miss; and when I hit, the bullet returns with great violence back upon me. So if you read of an inquest sitting upon me one of these days, don't wonder: I think they'll find it hard to bring in a verdict, whether Felo-de-se or Accidental Death. For I go on with my eyes open: though to be sure I am taking the quickest course to put them both out. A worse shot never existed.

Morton recommended me to read Alfieri's Life of Himself. So I bought it in London and have been reading it by bits ever since. It is in very easy Italian, and is entertaining, as far as I have read: just half. He was a very fine fellow, was Alfieri: they say his plays are very dull, and I think the Life becomes duller as he begins the Literary part of it. For he only began to *read* his own language at twenty-five; and his first plays were written first in French Prose and then drafted into Italian verse. What a process! Up to that time of his life he only rode horses over every country in Europe, and kept mistresses: his loves were very heroic and poetical: so perhaps he would have aided the cause of poetry more by leaving it to others to write about him. I wonder the French Playwrights haven't got hold of him: perhaps they have though. He was such a fellow for Liberty too: he calls Catherine the 2nd *codesta Clitennestra filosofessa*, which words have the whistling of the lash about them, I think. He would have been a capital Middle Age Italian: especially for Dante to put into Hell. But perhaps he'll meet him there yet.

To Bernard Barton

Bedford, July 24, 1839.

Dear Barton,

. . . I have brought down here with me Sidney Smith's Works, now first collected: you will delight in them: I shall bring them to Suffolk when I come: and it will not be long, I dare say, before I come, as there is to be rather a large meeting of us at Boulge this August. I have got the fidgets in my right arm and hand (how the inconvenience redoubles as one mentions it)— do you know what the fidgets are?—a true ailment, though perhaps not a dangerous one. Here I am again in the land of old Bunyan—better still in the land of the more perennial Ouse, making many a fantastic winding and going much out of his direct way to fertilize and adorn. Fuller supposes that he lingers thus in the pleasant fields of Bedfordshire being in no hurry to enter the more barren fens of Lincolnshire. So he says. This house is just on the edge of the town: a garden on one side skirted by the public road which again is skirted by a row of such Poplars as only the Ouse knows how to rear—and pleasantly they rustle now—and the room in which I write is quite cool and opens into a greenhouse which opens into said garden: and it's all deuced pleasant. For in half an hour I shall seek my Piscator,[1] and we shall go to a Village two miles off and fish, and have tea in a pot-house, and so walk home. For all which idle ease I think I must be damned. I begin to have dreadful suspicions that this fruitless way of life is not looked upon with satisfaction by the open eyes above. One really ought to dip for a little misery: perhaps however all this ease is only intended to turn sour by and bye, and so to poison one by the very nature of self-indulgence. Perhaps again as idleness is so very great a trial of virtue, the idle man who keeps himself tolerably chaste &c. may deserve the highest reward: the more idle, the more deserving. Really I don't jest: but I don't propound these things as certain.

There is a fair review of Shelley in the new Edinburgh: saying the truth on many points where the truth was not easily enunciated, as I believe.

Now, dear sir, I have said all I have to say: and Carlyle says, you know, it is dangerous to attempt to say more. So farewell for the present: if you like to write soon, direct to the Post Office, Bedford: if not, I shall soon be at Woodbridge to anticipate the use of your pen.

To W. F. Pollock

Boulge Hall, Aug. 14 [1839]

My dear Pollock,

I came here only yesterday, and your letter was brought up into my bedroom this morning. What are you doing at Binfield? rusticating there for fun with your family, or are there Assizes at such a place? And is the juvenile party you speak of assisting

---

[1] [William Kenworthy Browne (1817–59). EFG had met him on a steam packet in 1833, and though Browne was eight years his junior, they had become close friends. Browne was the original of Phidippus, the cultured man of action, in *Euphranor*.]

479

at, one of juvenile depredators? Well, I have been in my dear old Bedfordshire ever since I saw you: lounging in the country, lying on the banks of the Ouse, smoking, eating copious teas (prefaced with beer) in the country pot-houses, and have come mourning here: finding an empty house when I expected a full one, and no river Ouse, and no jolly boy to whistle the time away with. Such are the little disasters and miseries under which I labour: quite enough, however, to make one wish to kill oneself at times. This all comes of having no occupation or sticking-point: so one's thoughts go floating about in a gossamer way. At least, this is what I hear on all sides. So you are going with Monteith's party to Ireland. Well, I think you will have a plea-sant trip. I think I shall probably be in Ireland all September, but far away from your doings. Not to mention that I shall be on shore and you at sea. You will go and see the North Coast: which I am anxious to see, and shall not unlikely go too about the time of the Equinoctial gales, when such places should be seen. I love Ireland very much, I don't know why: the country and the people and all are very homogeneous: mournful and humor-ous somehow: just like their national music. Some of Tommy Moore's Irish Ballads (the airs, I mean) are the spirits of the Waterford women made music of. You should see them, Pollock, on a Sunday, as they come from Chapel in their long blue cloaks. Don't you think that blue eyes with black hair, and especially with long black eyelashes, have a mystery about them? This day week a dozen poor fellows who had walked all the way from the county Mayo into Bedfordshire came up to the door of the Inn where we were fishing, and called for small beer. We made their hearts merry with good Ale: and they went off flourishing their sticks, hoping all things, enduring all things, and singing some loose things. You must contrive to see some-thing of the people when you go to Ireland: I think that is the great part of the fun. You should certainly go some miles in or on an Irish Stage Coach, and also on a jaunting Car. I never saw Wimpole near Cambridge till the other day when I passed it in my way from Bedfordshire. Did you ever go and see it? People always told me it was not worth seeing: which is another reason for believing nothing that people tell one: it is a very noble old Queen Anne's building of red brick, in the way of

Hampton Court (not half so fine, but something in that way), looking down two miles of green sward as broad as itself, skirted on each side with fine elms. I did not go inside, but I believe the pictures are well worth seeing. Houses of that style have far more mark and character than Woburn and the modern bastard Grecian. I see they have built a new chapel at Barnwell —of red brick and very well done. I should think Peacock must have done it. Fancy his being Dean of Barnwell. Cambridge looked very ghastly, and the hard-reading, pale, dwindled students walking along the Observatory road looked as if they were only fit to have their necks wrung. I scorn my nerveless carcase more and more every day—but there's no good in talking. Farewell, my dear Pollock: I know this is a very worthless letter: but it is very good of you to write, and I have nothing better to do to-day than to write ever such vapid stuff. I would ask you if Spedding were still in London if your Yes or No (never very clamorously uttered by you) could reach me from Binfield. But even then I should not be much the better for the Information.

To Bernard Barton

Halverstown,[1] Sunday Oct. 20, [1839]

My dear Sir,

I am very glad you lifted yourself at last from your mahogany desk, and took such a trip as you describe in your last letter. I don't think you could have made a better in the same given space of time. It is some years since I have seen the Castle at Windsor, except from Eton. The view from the Terrace is the noblest I know of, taking it with all its associations together. Gray's Ode rises up into the mind as one looks around—does it not?—a sure proof that, however people may condemn certain conceits and expressions in the poem, the spirit of it is genuine. 'Ye distant spires, ye antique towers'—very large and noble, like the air that breathes upon one as one looks down along the view. My brother John told me he thought the Waterloo gallery very fine: the portraits by Sir Thomas almost as fine as Vandyke. You saw them of course. You say nothing of having seen the

[1] [Where FitzGerald's uncle Peter Purcell lived.]

National Gallery in London: indeed I rather fear it is closed these two months. This is a great loss to you: the Rubens landscape you would never have forgot. Thank you for the picture of my dear old Bredfield which you have secured for me: it is most welcome. Poor Nursey once made me a very pretty oil sketch of it: but I gave it to Mr Jenney. By all means have it engraved for the pocket book: it is well worthy. Some of the tall ash trees about it used to be visible at sea: but I think their topmost branches are decayed now. This circumstance I put in, because it will tell in your verse illustration of the view. From the road before the lawn, people used plainly to see the topmasts of the men-of-war lying in Hollesley bay during the war. I like the idea of this; the old English house holding up its enquiring chimneys and weathercocks (there is great physiognomy in weathercocks) toward the far off sea, and the ships upon it. How well I remember when we used all to be in the Nursery, and from the window see the hounds come across the lawn, my Father and Mr Jenney in their hunting caps &c. with their long whips: all Daguerreotyped into the mind's eye now—and that is all. Perhaps you are not civilized enough to know what Daguerreotype is: no more do I well. We were all going on here as merrily as possible till this day week, when my Piscator got an order from his Father to go home directly. So go he would the day after. I wanted to go also: but they would have me stay here ten days more. So I stay: I suppose I shall be in London toward the end of this week however: and then it will not be long before I pay you a visit. . . .

I have gone through Homer's Iliad—sorry to have finished it. The accounts of the Zoolu people, with Dingarn their king &c. give one a very good idea of the Homeric heroes, who were great brutes: but superior to the Gods who governed them: which also has been the case with most nations. It is a lucky thing that God made Man, and that Man has not to make God: we should fare badly, judging by the specimens already produced—Frankenstein Monster Gods, formed out of the worst and rottenest scraps of humanity—gigantic—and to turn destructively upon their Creators—

'But be ye of good cheer! I have overcome the world—'

So speaks a gentle voice.

I found here a Number of Tait's Magazine for August last, containing a paper on Southey, Wordsworth &c. by De Quincey. Incomplete and disproportioned like his other papers: but containing two noble passages: one, on certain years of his own Life when Opium shut him out from the world; the other, on Southey's style: in which he tells a truth which is obvious, directly it is told. Tait seems to be very well worth a shilling a month: that is the price of him, I see. You have bought Carlyle's Miscellanies, have you not? I long to get them: but one must wait till they are out of print before the Dublin booksellers shall have heard of them. Now here is really a very long letter, and what is more, written with a pen of my own mending—more consolatory to me than to you. Mr Macnish's inscription for Milton is—

> His lofty spirit was the home
> Of inspirations high,
> A mighty temple whose great dome
> Was hidden in the sky.

Who Mr Macnish is, I don't know. Didn't he write some Essays on Drunkenness once? or on Dreams?

Farewell for the present, my dear Sir. We shall soon shake hands again. Ever yours,

E. FitzGerald

To W. F. Pollock

Hastings, Febr. 3/40

My dear Pollock,

When I got here I found the letter you had sent after me into Suffolk. I keep it as a perfect specimen of a Penny Post letter: this is meant for a compliment. Not being able to write such a one myself, I send the enclosed advertisement from an Atlas of two weeks ago.* A Roman Dictator could not pronounce more emphatically: nor Tacitus relate more concisely. Have you heard if there has been a general Suicide among all the Brown Bread

* "No. 118 Jermyn Street. *Jan.* 5, 1840. BEAUFOY'S DIGESTIVE BREAD. —The sale of this article is DISCONTINUED from this day: any Bread offered under this designation is, therefore, deceptious. Brown Bread, as usually made, and Beaufoy's Digestive Bread, are very different articles."

Makers, not to say of London, but of England generally? When I read the last line of the Advertisement, I felt glad I was not a Brown Bread Maker.

There is an excellent Review on Carlyle's Chartism in the same Atlas. Tell Spedding of this. But what will he care? Carlyle is universally believed here to be *the* Carlile—the more decided one, I mean. All the invalids are warned by the Clergymen to be on their guard against him. He is all the more dangerous now that his meaning cannot be discovered. What do you think of Sterling's review of him? Some very good remarks: but I never was so suffocated by words in my life. I declare it gives me a shortness of breath to think of it.

I shall return to London either to-morrow week or fortnight. As I depend on others, I am not certain. Here I have got a good lodging looking on the sea—books, tobacco, etc. But I know nobody. So much for all things. Goodbye, my dear Pollock. I hope we shall smoke a cigar together ere long.

To Bernard Barton

[London, 17 February 1840]

My dear Sir,

You will by this time, I dare say, have seen Isabella,[1] who will have told you of my abode &c. for the last month. I expect to be at Boulge very shortly, as I have some things to do there: and I shall be very glad to see you again— Why it is a long time since we met—I left Lusia[2] certainly better at Hastings: and a note I had from her this morning tells me she has been walking about at the rate of 2 and 3 hours a day—I really liked Hastings very much: more than any watering-place I ever was at. The seas were very high. I am now come to London to see my friends, to go to a play or two (from which wicked and foolish amusement I am not yet weaned), and to abstain entirely from buying either books or pictures (money failing)—If I can pay my lodgings, and for a place in the Pit once or twice I shall do—I went last

---

[1] [Isabella FitzGerald (1810–64) was EFG's youngest sister. She married Gaetano Vignati.]

[2] [Andalusia FitzGerald (?–1879), married Rev. Francis De Soyres.]

Saturday night to see a new play by poor Leigh Hunt,[1] who has at last done something to put a few pounds into his pocket. His Play is very pretty, though not so dramatic as to ensure any long success on the stage:—it is very well acted—Poor L. H. is delighted with his new friends the Actors—When I got to my lodgings, I found A. Tennyson installed in them: he has been here ever since in a very uneasy state: being really ill, in a nervous way: what with an hereditary tenderness of nerve, and having spoiled what strength he had by incessant smoking &c.— I have also made him very out of sorts by desiring a truce from complaints and complainings—Poor fellow: he is quite magnanimous, and noble natured, with no meanness or vanity or affectation of any kind whatever—but very perverse, according to the nature of his illness—So much for Poets, who, one must allow, are many of them a somewhat tetchy race—There's that great metaphysical, Doric, moral, religious, psychological, poet of the Age, W. Wordsworth, who doesn't like to be contradicted at all: nor to be neglected in any way.

Well, my dear Sir, you are made of a happier compound, and take the world easily—Your nerves will not irritate you with a sense of neglected genius, if I do not quite fill up this sheet to the end—Prepare yourself: take a little bottled Porter if you have it: now I am going to end: no offence intended: now are you ready?—quite ready?—Well then, I am ever yours

E. F<small>ITZ</small>G<small>ERALD</small>

To W. F. Pollock

[Postmark May 3, 1840]

My dear Pollock,

I received a second letter of yours from York—how many months ago? certainly when no leaves were out as they are now in a wonderful way for this season of the year. You in London do not know that the country is in great want of rain. What does it signify to you? What effect would it have on your dry wigs, which, like Achilles' sceptre, will never, never bud again? To-day we have been drinking the Duke of Wellington's health, as my

[1] [*A Legend of Florence* at Covent Garden.]

brother-in-law is a staunch Tory, and I am not disinclined—so far. Then, after a walk which was illuminated by a cigar—*lanterna pedibus meis*—we are come back to the library: where, after tea, we are in some danger of falling asleep. So I take this sheet of paper and this pen that lie opposite me on the table, and write to you. So far so good.

You told me to read Clarendon—which I have begun to do: and like him much. It is really delightful to read his manly, noble English after Lord Brougham's spick-and-span Birmingham ware in the Edinburgh. Is the article on Sir W. Raleigh by Macaulay? It is not so good as most of his, I think. I never was one of those who cared much for the vindication of Raleigh's character: he was a blackguard, it seems: and the chief defence is that he lived among blackguards—Bacon, for instance. Does Spedding think him immaculate? I think the portraits of Raleigh are not favourable: there is great finesse in his eyes and in the shape of his face. Old James the First was a better man than any of his courtiers, I do believe.

It must be very nearly half-past 9 I am sure: ring the bell for the tea-things to be removed—pray turn the lamp—at 10 the married people go to bed: I sit up till 12, sometimes diverging into the kitchen, where I smoke amid the fumes of cold mutton that has formed (I suppose) the maids' supper. But the pleasant thing is to wake early, throw open the window, and lie reading in bed. Morning, noon, and night we look at the barometer, and make predictions about the weather. The wheat begins to look yellow; the clover layers are beginning to blossom, before they have grown to any height; and the grass won't grow: stock, therefore, will be very cheap, because of the great want of keep. That is poetry. Have you been down to Kitlands with that mad wag Spedding?

My brother-in-law is fallen fast asleep over Buckland's Bridge-water Treatise—his breathing approaches a snore. Now could I drink hot blood. I will write no more. Clarendon shall wind up the night with me. What do people say of Dickens's new work?[1] I saw the 1st No.—a very seedy framework, I thought: but the little conversation between the Lord Mayor and Mr. Toddyhigh

[1] [*Master Humphrey's Clock.*]

wonderful. Thackeray writes to me that he is going to show up D. Lardner in a quiz.[1] Ever yours.

Geldestone Hall, Friday Night [May 1]

To Frederick Tennyson[2]

The Corporate Town of Bedford, June 7, 1840

Dear Frederic,

Your letter dated from the Eternal City on the 15th of May reached me here two days ago. Perhaps you have by this time left Naples to which you bid me direct: or will have left it by the time my letter gets there. . . . Our letters are dated from two very different kinds of places: but perhaps equally well suited to the genius of the two men. For I am becoming more hebete every hour: and have not even the ambition to go up to London all this spring to see the Exhibitions &c. I live in general quietly at my brother in law's in Norfolk and I look with tolerable composure on vegetating there for some time to come, and in due time handing out my eldest nieces to waltz &c. at the County Balls. People affect to talk of this kind of life as very beautiful and philosophical: but I don't: men ought to have an ambition to stir, and travel, and fill their heads and senses: but so it is. Enough of what is now generally called the subjective style of writing. This word has made considerable progress in England during the year you have been away, so that people begin to fancy they understand what it means. I have been striving at it, because it is a very *sine qua non* condition in a book which I have just been reading, Eastlake's translation of Goethe's Theory of Colours. I recommend it to you, when you can get hold of it. Come back to England quick and read my copy. Goethe is all in opposition to Newton: and reduces the primitive colours to two. Whewell, I believe, does not patronise it: but it is certainly very Baconically put together. While you are wandering among ruins,

[1] [Probably in *The History of Dionysius Diddler*, which was written about this time, though it was not published till 1864.

[2] [EFG persistently spelt Frederick Tennyson's christian name without the 'k.' In proper-nouns, as in everything else, he followed his own fancy, and we shall find him addressing Horace Basham as 'Arthur' and apparently referring to Lucy Barton as 'Nellie'.]

waterfalls, and temples, and contemplating them as you sit in your lodgings, I poke about with a book and a colour box by the side of the river Ouse—quiet scenery enough—and make horrible sketches. The best thing to me in Italy would be that you are there. But I hope you will soon come home and install yourself again in Mornington Crescent. I have just come from Leamington: while there, I met Alfred by chance: we made two or three pleasant excursions together: to Stratford upon Avon and Kenilworth &c. Don't these names sound very thin amid your warm southern nomenclature? But I'll be bound you would be pleased to exchange all your fine burnt up places for a look at a Warwickshire pasture every now and then during these hot days. . . .

The sun shines very bright, and there is a kind of bustle in these clean streets, because there is to be a grand True Blue dinner in the town Hall. Not that I am going: in an hour or two I shall be out in the fields rambling alone. I read Burnet's History—Ex pede Herculem. Well, say as you will, there is not, and never was, such a country as Old England—never were there such a Gentry as the English. They will be the distinguishing mark and glory of England in History, as the Arts were of Greece, and War of Rome. I am sure no travel would carry me to any land so beautiful, as the good sense, justice, and liberality of my good countrymen make this. And I cling the closer to it, because I feel that we are going down the hill, and shall perhaps live ourselves to talk of all this independence as a thing that has been. To none of which you assent perhaps. At all events, my paper is done, and it is time to have done with this solemn letter. I can see you sitting at a window that looks out on the bay of Naples, and Vesuvius with a faint smoke in the distance: a half naked man under you cutting up watermelons &c. Haven't I seen it all in Annuals, and in the Ballet of Massaniello long ago?

To Bernard Barton

Bedford, Aug. 31/40

Dear Sir,

I duly received your letter. I am just returned from staying three days at a delightful Inn by the river Ouse, where we always go to fish. I dare say I have told you about it before. The Inn is the cleanest, the sweetest, the civillest, the quietest, the liveliest, and the cheapest that ever was built or conducted. Its name, the Falcon of Bletsoe. On one side it has a garden, then the meadows through which winds the Ouse: on the other, the public road, with its coaches hurrying on to London, its market people halting to drink, its farmers, horsemen, and foot travellers. So, as one's humour is, one can have whichever phase of life one pleases: quietude or bustle; solitude or the busy hum of men: one can sit in the principal room with a tankard and a pipe and see both these phases at once through the windows that open upon either. But through all these delightful places they talk of leading railroads: a sad thing, I am sure: quite impolitic. But Mammon is blind.

I went a week ago to see Luton, Lord Bute's place; filled with very fine pictures, of which I have dreamt since. It is the gallery in England that I most wish to see again: but I by no means say it is the most valuable. A great many pictures seemed to me misnamed—especially Correggio has to answer for some he never painted.

I am thinking of going to Naseby for a little while: after which I shall return here: and very likely find my way back to Norfolk before long. At all events, the middle of October will find me at Boulge, unless the Fates are very contrary.

To Bernard Barton

Holbrook [October 1840]

Dear Sir,

The faith of man—it is proverbially bad—I cannot get home till Monday: and the sun of toasted Cheese must set for this week—But next week it shall rise anew, and warm us with redoubled ray—"Foul impious man" &c. Crabbe—toasted Cheese—Gin and Water—what else is wanted but a Pipe—to complete the perfect Square of comfort. One night, devote your little room to *that*: let it be said for once—

Farewell. Ever yrs

E.F.G.

Q*

489

To Frederick Tennyson

London, Jan. 16, 1841

Dear Frederic,

I have just concluded, with all the throes of imprudent plea-sure, the purchase of a large picture by Constable: of which, if I can continue in the mood, I will enclose you a sketch. It is very good: but how you and Morton[1] would abuse it! Yet this, being a sketch, escapes some of Constable's faults, and might escape some of your censures. The trees are not splashed with that white sky-mud, which (according to Constable's theory) the Earth scatters up with her wheels in travelling so briskly round the Sun: and there is a dash and felicity in the execution that gives one a thrill of good digestion in one's room, and the thought of which makes one inclined to jump over the children's heads in the streets. But if you could see my great enormous Venetian Picture you would be extonished. Does the thought ever strike you, when looking at pictures in a house, that you are to run and jump at one, and go right through it into some behind-scene world on the other side, as Harlequins do? A steady por-trait especially invites one to do so: the quietude of it ironically tempts one to outrage it: one feels it would close again over the panel, like water, as if nothing had happened. That portrait of Spedding, for instance, which Laurence has given me: not swords, nor cannon, nor all the Bulls of Bashan butting at it, could, I feel sure, discompose that venerable forehead. No won-der that no hair can grow at such an altitude: no wonder his view of Bacon's virtue is so rarefied that the common consciences of men cannot endure it. Thackeray and I occasionally amuse our-selves with the idea of Spedding's forehead: we find it somehow or other in all things, just peering out of all things: you see it in a milestone, Thackeray says. He also draws the forehead rising with a sober light over Mont Blanc, and reflected in the lake of Geneva. We have great laughing over this. The forehead is at

[1] [Savile Morton was 'a wild Irishman' and, according to EFG, 'an ill-starred man of genius.' An 'Apostle' at Cambridge, he went to Italy to study art, but found travelling more to his taste. He was a fine correspondent and conversationalist.]

present in Pembrokeshire, I believe: or Glamorganshire: or Monmouthshire: it is hard to say which. It has gone to spend its Christmas there.

[A water-colour sketch of Constable's picture.]

This you see is a sketch of my illustrious new purchase. The two animals in the water are cows: that on the bank a dog: and that in the glade of the wood a man or woman as you may choose. I can't say my drawing gives you much idea of my picture, except as to the composition of it: and even that depends on the colour and disposition of light and shade. The effect of the light breaking under the trees is very beautiful in the original: but this can only be given in water-colours on thick paper, where one can scratch out the lights. One would fancy that Constable had been looking at that fine picture of Gainsborough's in the National: the Watering Place: which is superior, in my mind, to all the Claudes there. But this is perhaps because I am an Englishman and not an Italian.

To Bernard Barton

19 Charlotte St., Rathbone Place. [April 1841]
Dear Barton,

Have I not sent to Flook's Stationery warehouse over the way, and bought one Quire of Bath Post—and paid a shilling for it— (for they don't like trusting lodgers)—and have I not turned away from the fire to the table, and devoted the end of a pipe, which was consecrated to the Spirit of inactivity, to the inferior calling of letter-writing—all for the sake of writing a letter to you?—I have. My Father tells me that you were not well enough to dine with him last week. Now this is not as it should be— Your sound heart should have a sound body to dwell in, Mr Barton; and in short it is not proper that you should be ill. Seriously, you should take exercise: walk even half an hour in your garden up and down, with a book, or (better still) with a pipe as a companion: you should eat and drink little—except when t-s-t-d cheese is on the table—and be careful of what you do eat and drink—and then you would be well, I am sure; your sound head and heart would do the rest. One can't afford to lose the full use of good men in this world—Now "be by your friends advised, too rash, too hasty Dad"—

I am afraid you will be much disappointed with the Constable sketch when you see it: but I have found nothing else that seemed in your way: and I don't like to ransack the pawnbrokers' shops without giving you a specimen of my doings. Three doors off me is a Constable which is worth a journey from Woodbridge to London to see: it is a large one—of Salisbury Cathedral. It was bought at his sale for £200: and the owner adds £100 to its value every year, he tells me: he now wants £600—It is worth it: being as fine as Rubens. It ought to be in the National Gallery.[1] Why don't you come up here and see it: I can give you bed and board.

It is not yet certain when my sisters will go down to Boulge. I am trying to make my Father keep them in London till Xmas: which, I am sure, would be better for them both: but I know not if I shall succeed. When they go, I shall not be long in following. If we do not go down yet, I will send you your picture: which will do very well to hang in your bedroom: it is not spick and span enough for your state sitting room.

I saw a portrait by Sir Joshua Reynolds so tender and delicious that it almost brought the tears into my eyes—A Lady, with a little child clinging round her neck, passing through a wood: to the left, the branches opening, and the golden Autumn light peeping in. It seemed like the type of all that is fair and transitory—A. Tennyson and I pass some hours together every day and night: with pipes and Brandy and water—I hope he will publish ere long. He is a great fellow. But he is ruining himself by mismanagement and neglect of all kinds. He must smoke 12 hours out of the 24—

We are enjoying very fine London fogs, of the colour of sage cheese. Red herrings are very good just now: don't you like them?—Isabella has become a great Oxford Divine: she attends matins, vigils &c. but she does not fast, which would do her more good than anything. This is the chief news of the day.

---

[1] [This picture of Salisbury Cathedral is probably the one now in the National Gallery. Constable had died in 1836.]

Now write to me and tell me you are well, and moreover taking measures to keep so. It is possible I may run down to Bedford for 2 days: but all depends on what my Papa decides and also on the state of the weather. Please to make my respects and remembrances to Miss Barton: and believe me ever yours

E.F.G.

To W. F. Pollock

Dear Pollock,

Thank you for your advertisement, which was and is very charming. I have waited to see if I could send you back anything so short and so good: but I have scarce read an advertisement since I have been down here, and since the weather has become so delightful. I live in a house full of jolly children; and the day passes in eating, drinking, swinging, riding, driving, talking and doing nonsense; the intervals being filled with idleness. I hear a nephew of eight years old say his Latin Grammar: to-day we say the verb moneo—in this way—moneo, mones, monui, monuorum, monuarum, monuorum—then I thought it was time to stop. But it was a good shot.

When one talks in this sort of way, I am sure it must seem as if one considered oneself very sublimely philosophical, etc.— but I don't—my digestion is very good: and everybody here is very kind and well-behaved, and there never was such fine weather since the world began. Also, I have had Fielding to read, while smoking in the garden.

You see that all this is a mighty pleasant kind of life to lead, but not easy to write about. You must *therefore* (a pretty consequence) write to me: and tell Spedding to do so: and if old Alfred is in London, or at his country house, stir him up. Not that he will be stirred up. But I really do very much like to hear of my friends, and about pyroglyphs, etc.[1] I wish very much also

[1] [Tennyson was concerned in a project to manufacture machine-made sculpture, originally called by this name. But in 1842 he wrote to Rawnsley, "We have dropt the name 'Pyroglyph' as too full of *meaning* (a singular reason for rejecting a word!) and now call ourselves 'The Patent Decorative Carving and Sculpture Company!' "]

to step into the pit of Drury Lane and to hear Fidelio once a week.

So take pity, and ask others to take pity, on a poor devil who is rather too well off: and let a London letter slide once in a while out of the Beccles postbag.

Does the word Beccles put you in mind of hooks and eyes?

Geldestone Hall, Beccles, May 29/41

To Bernard Barton

Edgeworthstown, September 2/41

My dear Barton,

You must allow I am a good correspondent—this half year at least. This is Septr. 2, a most horrible day for a Bazaar, judging at least by the weather here. But you may be better off. I came to this house a week ago to visit a male friend, who duly started to England the day before I got here. I therefore found myself domiciled in a house filled with ladies of divers ages—Edgeworth's wife, aged—say 28—his mother aged 74—his sister (the great Maria)[1] aged 72—and another cousin or something—All these people very pleasant and kind: the house pleasant: the grounds ditto: a good library: . . . so here I am quite at home. But surely I must go to England soon: it seems to me as if that must take place soon: and so send me a letter directed to me at Mr Watcham's, Naseby, Thornby. Those places are in England. You may put Northampton after Thornby if you like. I am going to look at the winding up of the harvest there.

I am now writing in the Library here: and the great Authoress is as busy as a bee making a catalogue of her books beside me, chattering away. We are great friends. She is as lively, active, and cheerful as if she were but twenty; really a very entertaining person. We talk about Walter Scott whom she adores, and are merry all the day long. I have read about thirty-two sets of novels since I have been here: it has rained nearly all the time.

I long to hear how the Bazaar went off: and so I beg you to tell me all about it. When I began this letter I thought I had something to say: but I believe the truth was I had nothing to

[1] [Maria Edgeworth, the novelist (1767–1849).]

494

do. When you see my dear Major[1] give him my love, and tell him I wish he were here to go to Connemara with me: I have no heart to go alone. The discomfort of Irish inns requires a companion in misery. This part of the country is poorer than any I have yet seen: the people becoming more Spanish also in face and dress. Have you read The Collegians?

I have now begun to sketch heads on the blotting paper on which my paper rests—a sure sign, as Miss Edgeworth tells me, that I have said quite enough. She is right. Good-bye. In so far as this country is Ireland I am glad to be here: but inasmuch as it is not England I wish I were there.

To Bernard Barton

Jan. 24/42

Dear Barton,

You mistake. The Poacher was bought in his shell—for £3— did I not name that price? As you desire a packing case, I will order one to day: and I hope you will have him down on Wednesday, just when your Bank work is over, and you will be glad of such good company. One of my friends thought the picture must have been an anticipation of Bill Sykes: put a cap and feathers on his head and you make him Iago, Richard the Third, or any other aristocratic villain. I really think the picture is a very good one of its kind: and one that you will like.

I am going to get my large Constable very lightly framed, and shall bring it down into Suffolk with me to shew you and others. I like it more and more.

. . . There is something poetical, and almost heroic, in this Expedition to the Niger—the motives lofty and Christian—the issue so disastrous. Do you remember in A. Cunningham's Scottish Songs one called 'The Darien Song'? It begins

> We will go, maidens, go,
> To the primrose woods and mourn, &c.

Look for it. It applies to this business. Some Scotch young folks went out to colonize Darien, and never came back.

[1] [Presumably Major Edward Moor, a retired officer of the Indian Army, who lived at Great Bealings. He was a student of Oriental literature, though EFG did not credit him with stimulating his interest in Persian.]

Oh there were white hands wav'd,
  And many a parting hail,
As their vessel stemm'd the tide,
  And stretch'd her snowy sail.

I remember reading this at Aldbro', and the sound of the sea hangs about it always, as upon the lips of a shell.

Farewell for the present. We shall soon be down amongst you.

P.S. I think Northcote drew this picture from life: and I have no doubt there is some story attached to it. The subject may have been some great malefactor. You know that painters like to draw such at times. Northcote could not have painted so well but from life.

To Frederick Tennyson

London, February 6, 1842

Dear Frederic,

These fast-following letters of mine seem intended to refute a charge made against me by Morton: that I had only so much impulse of correspondence as resulted from the receipt of a friend's letter. Is it very frivolous to write all these letters, on no business whatsoever? What I think is, that one will soon be going into the country, where one hears no music, and sees no pictures, and so one will have nothing to write about. I mean to take down a Thucydides, to feed on: like a whole Parmesan. But at present here I am in London: last night I went to see Acis and Galatea brought out, with Handel's music, and Stanfield's scenery: really the best done thing I have seen for many a year. As I sat alone (alone in spirit) in the pit, I wished for you: and now Sunday is over: I have been to church: I have dined at Portland Place:[1] and now I come home to my lodgings: light my pipe: and will whisper something over to Italy. You talk of your Naples: and that one cannot understand Theocritus without having been on those shores. I tell you, you can't understand Macready without coming to London and seeing his revival of Acis and Galatea. You enter Drury Lane at a quarter to seven: the pit is already nearly full: but you find a seat, and a very

------

[1] [No. 39, where his parents lived.]

pleasant one. Box doors open and shut: ladies take off their shawls and seat themselves: gentlemen twist their side curls: the musicians come up from under the stage one by one: 'tis just upon seven. Macready is very punctual: Mr T. Cooke is in his place with his marshal's baton in his hand: he lifts it up: and off they set with old Handel's noble overture. As it is playing, the red velvet curtain (which Macready has substituted, not wisely, for the old green one) draws apart: and you see a rich drop scene, all festooned and arabesqued with River Gods, Nymphs, and their emblems; and in the centre a delightful, large, good copy of Poussin's great landscape (of which I used to have a print in my rooms) where the Cyclops is seen seated on a mountain, looking over the sea-shore. The overture ends, the drop scene rises, and there is the sea-shore, a long curling bay: the sea heaving under the moon, and breaking upon the beach, and rolling the surf down—the stage! This is really capitally done. But enough of description. The choruses were well sung, well acted, well dressed, and well grouped; and the whole thing creditable and pleasant. Do you know the music? It is of Handel's best: and as classical as any man who wore a full-bottomed wig could write. I think Handel never gets out of his wig: that is, out of his age: his Hallelujah chorus is a chorus not of angels, but of well-fed earthly choristers, ranged tier above tier in a Gothic cathedral, with princes for audience, and their military trumpets flourishing over the full volume of the organ. Handel's gods are like Homer's, and his sublime never reaches beyond the region of the clouds. Therefore I think that his great marches, triumphal pieces, and coronation anthems, are his finest works. There is a little bit of Auber's, at the end of the Bayadère when the God resumes his divinity and retires into the sky, which has more of pure light and mystical solemnity than anything I know of Handel's: but then this is only a scrap: and Auber could not breathe in that atmosphere long: whereas old Handel's coursers, with necks with thunder clothed and long resounding pace, never tire. Beethoven thought more deeply also: but I don't know if he could sustain himself so well. I suppose you will resent this praise of Beethoven: but you must be tired of the whole matter, written as it is in this vile hand: and so here is an end of it. . . . And now I am going to put on my night-cap: for my paper is nearly ended, and the iron tongue of St Paul's, as reported by an East wind, has told twelve. This is the last news from the City. So Good night. I suppose the violets will be going off in the Papal dominions by the time this letter reaches you: my country cousins are making much of a few aconites. Love to Morton.

P.S. I hope these foolish letters don't cost you and Morton much: I always pay 1s. 7d. for them here: which ought to carry such levities to Hindostan without further charge.

To Bernard Barton

Sat: Febr 19/42

Dear Barton,

That this wonderful correspondence may not languish till it dies a natural sudden death, I send you such a Report on the Fine Arts as has been laid on your table every Sunday morning, I think, for several weeks. Your temptations have ended in a fall: you have bought the box:[1] well—I have had smaller temptations which I have resisted. In particular, a little bit of evening landscape by some body: very like what I remember of a village near Cambridge: a small bit of canvas, but well suggestive of the Spirit of the time: that is, of Twilight. £4. 10 they want: but the picture has been rubbed in parts, especially in the sky: so that it is not in keeping. I don't know however if I can yet pronounce myself safe: I walk insensibly *that* way: flutter round the shop-window—there it is: meeting my gaze with a kind of ironical quiet—I have also seen a picture of Highland shooting by Ward: and fortunately recollecting that my Uncle goes every year to shoot in Perthshire, I think I cant do better than lay out £7 for him—What I gain by buying pictures for my friends is the keeping those pictures for a time in my room, and then seeing them from time to time afterward. Besides, the price of making a good purchase and shewing one's taste: all that contributes to health and long life. I hope you like the Gainsborough still: I shall be really glad to see that little picture again. I knew it would want varnishing soon: indeed it was varnished (by the dealer's mistake) too soon after I had cleaned it with oil—There

[1] [Barton collected snuff-boxes.]

are three genuine pictures of Gainsborough now to be seen in Conduit St. I understand: the property of some Suffolk man. Laurence saw them: says they are copies of Wynant's manner: do you know whose they are? I dare say Mr. C.[1] does—Poor old Nursey—I think I remember his sketch of Bealings Bridge in the good old picturesque days: when little rivers were suffered to run wild.

I have cut down my great Opie, and think I have done well: I am going to paint it on Monday, as it has suffered during the late operation: it will then be cleaned, and left at a dealer's shop to earn what it can. Never was a stupider purchase. I am glad you have got rid of your sham Constable. Only wait till I come down and shew you a real one. You have some picture of a Holy Family, or some sacred subject—people in red and yellow—by Rubens or P. Veronese—which you must get rid of one day. It has no merit if I recollect rightly—

My dear Barton, I hope you keep all this nonsense of mine to yourself. You have a bad habit of reading letters out, have you not?—Pray, pray dont these. I have lost some of my confidence in you since I hear that you read those lines of mine to my Mother! My dear fellow! You have no idea of what FitzGeralds are. If you betray me further, you shall learn what they are by my abusing you like a pick pocket. So look out. Does not your little Nellie laugh at two elderly gentlemen (for am not I 33— which is certainly elderly in a damsel's eyes) corresponding in this way?—She hasn't those eyes for nothing—rather mischievous eyes if I remember. Now goodbye again.

To Bernard Barton

London, February 21/42

I have just got home a new coat for my Constable: which coat cost 33 shillings: just the same price as I gave for a Chesterfield wrapper (as it is called) for myself some weeks ago. People told me I was not improved by my Chesterfield wrapper: and I am vext to see how little my Constable is improved by his coat of

---

[1] [Presumably Thomas Churchyard, the Woodbridge solicitor. He was a talented artist.]

Cloth of Gold. But I have been told what is the use of a frame lately: only as it requires nice explanation I shall leave it till I see you. Don't you wish me to buy that little Evening piece I told you of? worth a dozen of your Paul Veroneses put together.

When I rate you (as you call it) about shewing my verses, letters &c. you know in what spirit I rate you: thanking you all the time for your generous intention of praising me. It would be very hard, and not desirable, to make you understand why my Mama need not have heard the verses: but it is a very little matter: so no more of it. As to my doing anything else in that way, I know that I could write volume after volume as well as others of the mob of gentlemen who write with ease: but I think unless a man can do better, he had best not do at all: I have not the strong inward call, nor cruel-sweet pangs of parturition, that prove the birth of anything bigger than a mouse. With you the case is different, who have so long been a follower of the Muse, and who have had a kindly, sober, English, wholesome, religious spirit within you that has communicated kindred warmth to many honest souls. Such a creature as Augusta—John's wife— a true Lady, was very fond of your poems: and I think that is no mean praise: a very good assurance that you have not written in vain. I am a man of taste, of whom there are hundreds born every year: only that less easy circumstances than mine at present are compel them to one calling: that calling perhaps a mechanical one, which overlies all their other, and naturally perhaps more energetic impulses. As to an occasional copy of verses, there are few men who have leisure to read, and are possessed of any music in their souls, who are not capable of versifying on some ten or twelve occasions during their natural lives: at a proper conjunction of the stars. There is no harm in taking advantage of such occasions.

This letter-writing fit (one must suppose) can but happen once in one's life: though I hope you and I shall live to have many a little bargain for pictures. But I hold communion with Suffolk through you. In this big London all full of intellect and pleasure and business I feel pleasure in dipping down into the country, and rubbing my hand over the cool dew upon the pastures, as it were. I know very few people here: and care for fewer: I believe I should like to live in a small house just outside a pleasant English town all the days of my life, making myself useful in a humble way, reading my books, and playing a rubber of whist at night. But England cannot expect long such a reign of inward quiet as to suffer men to dwell so easily to themselves. But Time will tell us:

> Come what come may,
> Time and the Hour runs through the roughest day.

It is hard to give you so long a letter, so dull an one, and written in so cramped a hand, to read in this hardworking part of your week. But you can read a bit at odd times, you know: or none at all. Anyhow 'tis time to have done. I am going to walk with Lusia. So farewell.

P.S. I always direct to you as 'Mr Barton' because I know not if Quakers ought to endure Squiredom. How I long to shew you my Constable!

Pray let me know how Mr Jenney is. I think that we shall get down to Suffolk the end of next week.

To Bernard Barton

[London, March 2, 1842]

And now, Barton, know that I really have made my last purchase in the picture line for the season—today at Phillips' I fell —my virtue fell under the Auctioneer's hammer—an early Venetian picture the seducer—a Holy Family—to think such families should be painted to allure unwary youths into Sin!— There they sit collected in a quiet group just outside the walls of Nazareth, or Bethlehem—sweet St Catherine with the palm in her hand, her yellow hair encircled with a row of pearls. The child is an ugly swollen child:—but I skip him—This picture pleases me hugely—But my encouragement to buy afresh has been this: that Mr. Browne the elder (long life to him!) came to town yesterday: eat a meat tea at my rooms: and was pleased to express himself laudatorily of my Opie Fruit Girl:—I said nothing then: but I hope to make him buy her for what I gave —£4. She has cost me some shillings more in getting her curtailed: and then have I not painted her myself?—Besides

501

this I understand a man at Bedford has offered to buy a picture I have there: good fellow: so he shall: and then I shant have to borrow monies this quarter, shall I?—And as for the future, I utterly scorn it—I bought the best picture in to-day's auction: and this over the dealers' heads: who had agreed the picture had been painted on:—"Look there—there's a patch" &c.—whereas the picture has been *rubbed*, not re-painted, and probably was but a sketch at first. I exult over the whole tribe.

Alfred Tennyson suddenly appeared in town to-day: I carried him off to the auction: and then with violence to Moxon: who is to call on him to-morrow, and settle the publishing of a new volume. And only think: 2 new volumes are just coming out: one by Daddy Wordsworth:[1] another by Campbell[2]—the Daddy's Tragedy!—what a lamentable one it will be—and Campbell's book is to get money—Then Trench is coming out!—such wonders is this Spring to call forth. Milnes[3] talks of a popular edition of his poems!—poor devil, as if he could make one by any act of typography.

Goodbye. Given under our hand in the exultation of a new purchase this 2nd or 1st day of March in the year 1842.

E. FitzGerald

To W. F. Pollock

[1842]

Dear Pollock,

I think the man[4] who shot at the dear little Queen must have been mad. Surely no sane man would choose such a place as he did for his purpose: I mean, where he was sure to be taken whether he succeeded or not. What is your Uncle doing in India? I see manifestoes by General Pollock: but I always hope to be told the result of politics by some good friend.

I have been on a visit to my friend Donne. He is very busy with history:[5] which must inevitably be a great bore. This I

[1] [*The Borderers.*]

[2] [*The Pilgrim of Glencoe*, by Thomas Campbell.]

[3] [Richard Monckton Milnes, 1st Baron Houghton (1809–85), politician and patron of letters.]

[4] [John Francis shot at the Queen May 30, 1842. He was condemned to death, but afterwards transported for life.]

[5] [*The History of Rome.*]

regret: for Donne had such fun in him, only when he gets a pen in his hand he forgets it all. So his style is of the Quaker-coat cut.

I read at his house Venables'[1] Article on Carlyle. I thought it most admirable. He seems to me in the first rank of Reviewers: and I hope we shall see much more. I also read his Hegel, which I did not so much admire: but then the subject is a more perplexed one: and I suspect Venables is more at home in matters of the understanding than of the Arts. And how did you and Thackeray like Penshurst? I should like well to have seen it. We are calling out for rain loudly here: no hay: corn looking yellow. This does not touch you in London: except that I suppose the Opera is rather too hot at times. You see what a lofty sense of rustic superiority I can assume. As to your sea trip, I wish it all success: it is a pity you are not about it now with these long cheery days, and a fine steady breeze always blowing. Perhaps, however, autumn weather has more variety and excitement about it. I should like one good toss on the sea again, not in a steamer: but somehow or other I seldom get far from my kennel. Pray ask Thackeray if he has done anything for poor Pandurang Hari[2]—I wish he could. Is Alfred in town still? I have got his books. It is a pity he did not publish the new volume separately. The other will drag it down. And why reprint the Merman, the Mermaid, and those everlasting Eleanores, Isabels,—which always were, and are, and must be, a nuisance, though Mrs Butler (who recognised herself in the portrait, of course) said that Eleanore (what a bore) was the finest thing he ever wrote. She has sat for it ever since, I believe. Every woman thinks herself the original of one of that stupid Gallery of Beauties. The sonnet to J.M.K. also remains: there's a beauty too.

[1] [George Stovin Venables (1810–88). He was to become a Q.C. in 1863, and do much to maintain the highest type of political thought in journalism.]
[2] [*A Tale of the Mahrattas* by W. B. Hockley.]

To Frederick Tennyson

Bedford, August 16, 1842

Dear Tennyson,

I have been long hoping for a letter from you: it has come this morning, and repays me for all waiting. While you and Morton write to me about Italy I shall never go to see it. And yet your account of Cicero's villa, I confess, gives me a twinge. But of this I am sure: if I saw all these fine things with the bodily eye, I should but see them as a scene in a play, with the additional annoyance of being bitten with fleas perhaps, and being in a state of transition which is not suitable to me: whereas while you see them, and will represent them to me, I see them through your imagination, and that is better than any light of my own. This is very true, I assure you: and you and Morton have given me quite a different view of Italy to what I had before: a much more enchanting one, but not the more likely to seduce me into making the false step of trying to realize it for myself. . . . In the mean time how tired and bored would you be to take one of my travels—a voyage of eight miles from Bedford perhaps—travelled twenty times before—every winding of the river, every church spire, every country pot house and the quality of its beer, well known. No surprise at all. Nil admirari—I find that old Horace is a good fellow traveller in England: so is Virgil. It is odd that those fellows living in the land they did live in should have talked so coldly about it. As to Alfred's book, I believe it has sold well: but I have not seen him for a long while, and have had no means of hearing about the matter except from Thompson, who told me that very many copies had been sold at Cambridge, which indeed will be the chief market for them. Neither have I seen any notice of them in print except that in the Examiner; and that seemed so quiet that I scarce supposed it was by Forster. Alfred himself is, I believe, in Kent at present. And now, my dear Frederic, why do you think of returning to England? Depend upon it you are better off as you are. You will never turn magistrate nor bean-dibbler, nor make yourself of use in the country, and therefore why should you not live where you like to live best? When I read of your laughing and singing and riding into Naples with huge self-supplying beakers full of the warm South[1] I am sure you had best stay where you are. I should indeed be very glad to see you again: but then I should miss hearing from you: and you would only come here to abuse us all and then go back again. You Tennysons are born for warm climates. As to poor England, I never see a paper, but I think with you that she is on the go. I used to dread this: but somehow I now contemplate it as a necessary thing, and, till the shoe begins to pinch me sorely, walk on with some indifference. It seems impossible the manufacturers can go on as they are: and impossible that the demand for our goods can continue as of old in Europe: and impossible but that we must get a rub and licking in some of our colonies: and if all these things come at once, why then the devil's in it. I used to think as you do about France and the French: and we all agreed in London that France should be divided among the other powers as Poland was: but Donne has given me pause: he says that France is the great counter-acting democratic principle to Russia. This may be: though I think Russia is too unwieldy and rotten-ripe ever to make a huge progress in conquest. What is to be thought of a nation where the upper classes speak the language of another country, and have varnished over their honest barbarism with the poorest French profligacy and intrigue? Russia does not seem a whole to me. In the mean time, all goes on toward better and better, as is my firm belief: and humanity grows clear by flowing, (very little profited by any single sage or hero) and man shall have wings to fly and something much better than that in the end . . .

I draw a very little, and think of music as I walk in the fields: but have no piano in this part of the world. . . . I hear there is a fine new Symphony by Mendelssohn, who is by far our best writer now, and in some measure combines Beethoven and Handel. I grow every day more and more to love only the old God save the King style: the common chords, those truisms of music, like other truisms so little understood in the full. Just look at the mechanism of Robin Adair.

----

[1] [This unacknowledged quotation from Keats is remarkable, for Monckton Milnes was not to popularise him for another six years. His *Life, Letters and Literary Remains of John Keats* was published in 1848. EFG repeats the quotation on page 516.]

Now pray write to me again when you can. You don't know how much I rejoice in your letters.

To Bernard Barton

London. Friday, Septr. [16] 1842

Dear Barton,

Have you supposed me dead or what? Well, so far from it, I have grown more fat than ever, which is quite as much reason for not writing. I have been staying at Naseby, and, having come up here for two days, return to that place by railroad to-morrow. I went to see Carlyle last night. He had just returned from the neighbourhood of Bury. He is full of Cromwell, and, funnily enough, went over from Rugby to Naseby this spring with poor Dr Arnold. They saw nothing, and walked over what was not the field of battle. I want him to go down with me: but he thinks it would be too expensive. So I have engaged to collect what matter I can for him on the spot. At the beginning of October I expect to be back in East Anglia for the winter. Frail is human virtue. I thought I had quite got over picture-dealing, when lo! walking in Holborn this day I looked into a shop just to shew the strength of my virtue, and fell. That accursed Battle Piece— I have bought it—and another picture of dead chaffinches, which Mr C[hurchyard] will like, it is so well done: I expect you to give high prices for these pictures—mind that: and begin to economize in household matters. Leave off sugar in tea and make all your household do so. Also write to me at Naseby, Welford, Northampton. That's my direction—such a glorious country, Barton. I wrote you a letter a week ago, but never posted it. So now goodbye. I shall bring down the Chaffinches with me to Suffolk. Trade has been very bad, the dealers tell me. My fruit Girl still hangs up at a window—an unpleasant sight. Nobody is so hard set as to bid for her.

To Bernard Barton

[Naseby,] Septr. 22/42

My dear Barton,

The pictures are left all ready packed up in Portland Place, and shall come down with me, whenever that desirable event takes place. In the mean while here I am as before: but having received a long and interesting letter from Carlyle asking information about this Battle field, I have trotted about rather more to ascertain names of places, positions &c. After all he will make a mad book. I have just seen some of the bones of a dragoon and his horse who were found foundered in a morass in the field— poor dragoon, much dismembered by time: his less worthy members having been left in the owner's summer-house for the last twenty years have disappeared one by one: but his skull is kept safe in the hall: not a bad skull neither: and in it some teeth yet holding, and *a bit of the iron heel of his boot*, put into the skull by way of convenience. This is what Sir Thomas Browne calls 'making a man act his Antipodes.'[1] I have got a fellow to dig at one of the great general graves in the field: and he tells me to-night that he has come to bones: to-morrow I will select a neat specimen or two. In the mean time let the full harvest moon wonder at them as they lie turned up after lying hid 2400 revolutions of hers. Think of that warm 14th of June when the Battle was fought, and they fell pell-mell: and then the country people came and buried them so shallow that the stench was terrible, and the putrid matter oozed over the ground for several yards: so that the cattle were observed to eat those places very close for some years after. Every one to his taste, as one might well say to any woman who kissed the cow that pastured there.

Friday, 23rd. We have dug at a place, as I said, and made such a trench as would hold a dozen fellows: whose remains positively make up the mould. The bones nearly all rotted away, except the teeth which are quite good. At the bottom lay the *form* of a perfect skeleton: most of the bones gone, but the pressure

---

[1] [Perhaps referring to a passage in the *Christian Morals*, part III, sect. xiv: "Let the Divine part be upward, and the Region of Beast below. Otherwise, 'tis but to live invertedly, and with thy Head unto the Heels of thy Antipodes."]

distinct in the clay: the thigh and leg bones yet extant: the skull a little pushed forward, as if there were scanty room. We also tried some other reputed graves, but found nothing: indeed it is not easy to distinguish what are graves from old marl-pits &c. I don't care for all this bone-rummaging myself: but the identification of the graves identifies also where the greatest heat of the battle was. Do you wish for a tooth?

As I began this antiquarian account in a letter to you, so I have finished it, that you may mention it to my Papa, who perhaps will be amused at it. Two farmers insisted on going out exploring with me all day: one a very solid fellow who talks like the justices in Shakespeare: but who certainly was inspired in finding out this grave: the other a Scotchman full of intelligence, who proposed the flesh-soil for manure for turnips. The old Vicar, whose age reaches half-way back to the day of the Battle, stood tottering over the verge of the trench. Carlyle has shewn great sagacity in guessing at the localities from the vague descriptions of contemporaries: and his short *pasticcio* of the battle is the best I have seen. But he will spoil all by making a demi-god of Cromwell, who certainly was so far from wise that he brought about the very thing he fought to prevent—the restoration of an unrestricted monarchy.

To Bernard Barton

Ballysax,[1] Kilcullen. August, 17/43

My dear Barton,

. . . That old Suffolk comes over here sometimes, as I say; and greets one's eyes with old familiar names: Sales at Yoxford, Aldeburgh &c., regattas at Lowestoft, and at Woodbridge. I see Major Moor turning the road by the old Duke of York; the Deben winding away in full tide to the sea; and numberless little pictures of this kind.

I am going the day after tomorrow to Edgeworth's, for a week, it may be a fortnight before I set sail for England. Where shall I pitch my tent? that is the question. Whither shall those treasures of ancient art descend, and be reposited there for ever?

[1] [Where his brother Peter FitzGerald lived.]

I have been looking over the old London Magazine. Lamb's papers come in delightfully: read over the Old China the night you get this, and sympathize with me. The account of the dish of green pease &c. is the true history of lawful luxury. Not Johnson nor Adam Smith told so much. It is founded not on statistics but on good humanity.

We have at last delightful weather, and we enjoy it. Yesterday we went to Pool-a-Phooka, the Leap of the Goblin Horse. What is that, do you suppose? Why, a cleft in the mountains down and through which the river Liffey (not very long born from the earth) comes leaping and roaring. Cold veal pies, champagne &c. make up the enchantment. We dabbled in the water, splashed each other, forded the river, climbed the rocks, laughed, sang, eat, drank, and were roasted, and returned home the sun sinking red.

[A pen-and-ink sketch.]

This is not like Pool-a-Phooka.

To Bernard Barton

Naseby. Welford. Septr. [12. 1843]

Dear Barton,

I have been suffering for these last 4 days with an attack, which I partly attribute to my having walked to Thornby under a burning sun, then eaten unripe peaches, and then gone to sleep upon long wet grass! A pretty mixture—I have paid for it: and am even now in a state of water gruel, shiverings, headache like a thundercloud over the eyes &c. The Doctor told me my tongue was very white: I told him the tongues of all Suffolk men were said to be white. He looked rather as if he was affronted. Haven't you heard this before, as a saying?—We have had a famous harvest at Naseby. Today a little rain begins to fall: but we are nearly all safely housed. I talk of going the end of this week to Bedford, at the Post Office of which place a letter will find me. I do not mean to wait for Carlyle—He did not return from Scotland by Liverpool, but by Edinburgh packet &c. and I doubt if he will be much inclined to set off here again soon.

Still he writes that he is very earnest so to do: since he has been to see the field of Dunbar, and verified all its position. He stood on the spot where Cromwell stood when the sun broke out, and Oliver broke out too with "Arise O Lord" &c and led such a charge as won the battle. "Worthy man!" Carlyle calls him.

When I got home I found my brother married and come down here. These little surprises are common in our family. She seems a decent woman. We have other rumours of marriage afloat too: but what the issue will be nobody knows. The wind bloweth where it listeth.

You should have stated the reason why Mr. Churchyard left off smoking, for the benefit of survivors. Why did he? Let him leave off cigars: that is good: but pipes!—Not that I can boast, for I believe some of my headache originates from them—

I am glad our dear Major has taken up the Privy Council —as a wit once called it. Do you also read the book and see if it is not more interesting than Gaities and Gravities.[1] "The health of the whole world!" Is not this a poetical subject? —Poetry has done its duty by daisies, heart-breakings &c.—it must now turn to the real views of mankind at large—or be lost. The ideal and the actual are about to meet!—Therefore be wise in time and send me a sonnet to a Privy in return for mine. The diver may be a night man,[2] and he may bring up a fragrant treasure which may tell him how it became so fragrant. Farewell.

E.F.G.

> A diver springing darkly to the brim
> Of the full sapphire river as it rolled
> Under palm shadows over sands of gold
> Along the balmy vales of Almahim:
> Brought up what seem'd a piece of common mould,
> But of so rare a fragrance that he cried—
> "My eyes are dim with diving—thou'rt no piece
> Of common earth, but musk or ambergrease"—
> "I am but common earth" the clod replied—
> "But once within my dusky bosom grew
> The Rose, and so insinuated through

[1] [By Horace Smith.]
[2] [The sanitary collector who came at night to empty the privies.]

Her aromatic fibres day by day,
That time her virtue never will subdue,
Nor all the rambling water wash away—"

This I found in my desk tonight—I remember versifying it out of a passage in one of old D'Israeli's books[1]—when, I forget—But it turned up opportunely as a counter stench to the subject of the last part of my letter. The last line is a good one—But my poetical farthing candle is almost burnt out. Is your *Liar* silent?

To Frederick Tennyson

Boulge Hall, Woodbridge. Sunday, Dec. 10/1843
Dear Frederic,

Either you wrote me word yourself, or some one told me, that you meant to winter at Florence. So I shall direct to the Poste Restante there. You see I am not settled at the Florence of Suffolk, called Ipswich, yet: but I am perhaps as badly off; being in this most dull country house quite alone; a grey mist, that seems teeming with half formed snow, all over the landscape before my windows. It is also Sunday morning: ten of the clock by the chime now sounding from the stables. I have fed on bread and milk (a dreadfully opaque diet) and I await the morning Church in humble hope. It will begin in half an hour. We keep early hours in the country. So you will be able to measure my aptitude and fullness for letter writing by the quantity written now, before I bolt off for hat, gloves, and prayerbook. I always put on my thickest great coat to go to our Church in: as fungi grow in great numbers about the communion table. And now, to turn away from Boulge, I must tell you that I

---

[1] [Isaac D'Israeli's *Mejnoun and Leila*. The passage reads: "I was once in the bath, and they gave me a piece of scented clay. It was more than fragrant. And I asked of it, —Art thou pure musk, or ambergris? for thy scent delights my soul. It answered, —I was but Common Earth till I lived in the company of my Rose; then every day I became sweeter, till all her aromatic spirit was infused into mine. Oh! had I not lived with my Rose, I should still have been but a lump of Earth!" Sádi's version of this allegory was transcribed in the original Persian in Lucy Barton's autograph album by Major Moor who added his own translation of it. This is perhaps the first evidence of Fitz-Gerald's interest in the Persian poets.]

went up to London a month ago to see old Thackeray, who had come there to have his eyes doctored. I stayed with him ten days and we were as usual together. Alfred came up 'in transitu' from Boxley to Cheltenham; he looked, and said he was, ill: I have never seen him so hopeless: and I am really anxious to know how he is. . . . I remember the days of the summer when you and I were together, quarrelling and laughing—these I remember with pleasure. Our trip to Gravesend has left a perfume with me. I can get up with you on that everlastingly stopping coach on which we tried to travel from Gravesend to Maidstone that Sunday morning: worn out with it, we got down at an inn, and then got up on another coach—and an old smiling fellow passed us holding out his hat—and you said, 'That old fellow must go about as Homer did'—and numberless other turns of road and humour, which sometimes pass before me as I lie in bed. . . . Now before I turn over, I will go and see about Church, as I hear no bell, pack myself up as warmly as I can, and be off. So goodbye till twelve o'clock.—'Tis five minutes past twelve by the stable clock: so I saw as I returned from Church through the garden. Parson and Clerk got through the service see-saw like two men in a sawpit. In the garden I see the heads of the snow-drops and crocuses just out of the earth. Another year with its same flowers and topics to open upon us. Shenstone somewhere sings

> Tedious again to mark the drizzling day,
>   Again to trace the same sad tracts of snow:
> Or, lull'd by vernal airs, again survey
>   The selfsame hawthorn bud, and cowslips blow.

I rely on you and all your family sympathizing in this. So do I sometimes—anyhow, people complimenting each other on the approach of Spring and such like felicitations are very tiresome. Our very year is of a paltry diameter. But this is not proper language for Mark Tapley—whose greatest bore just now is having a bad pen—but the letter is ended. So he is jolly and yours as ever.

To Frederick Tennyson

Boulge, Woodbridge, February 24/44

My dear Frederic,

I got your letter all right. But you did not tell me where to direct to you again; so I must send to the Poste Restante at Florence. I have also heard from Morton, to whom I despatched a letter yesterday: and now set about one to you. As you live in two different cities, one may write about the same things to both. You told me of the Arno being frozen, and even Italian noses being cold: he tells me the Spring is coming. I tell you that we have had the mildest winter known; but as good weather, when it does come in England, is always unseasonable, and as an old proverb says that a green Yule makes a fat kirk yard, so it has been with us: the extraordinary fine season has killed heaps of people with influenza, debilitated others for their lives long, worried everybody with colds, &c. I have had three influenzas: but this is no wonder: for I live in a hut with walls as thin as a sixpence: windows that don't shut: a clay soil safe beneath my feet: a thatch perforated by lascivious sparrows over my head. Here I sit, read, smoke, and become very wise, and am already quite beyond earthly things. I must say to you, as Basil Montagu once said, in perfect charity, to his friends: 'You see, my dear fellows, I like you very much, but I continue to advance, and you remain where you are (you see), and so I shall be obliged to leave you behind me. It is no fault of mine.' You must begin to read Seneca, whose letters I have been reading; else, when you come back to England, you will be no companion to a man who despises wealth, death &c. What are pictures but paintings— what are auctions but sales! All is vanity. Erige animum tuum, mî Lucili &c. I wonder whether old Seneca was indeed such a humbug as people now say he was: he is really a fine writer. About three hundred years ago, or less, our divines and writers called him the divine Seneca; and old Bacon is full of him. One sees in him the upshot of all the Greek philosophy, how it stood in Nero's time, when the Gods had worn out a good deal. I don't think old Seneca believed he should live again. Death is his great resource. Think of the *rococicity* of a gentleman studying

R   513

Seneca in the middle of February 1844 in a remarkably damp cottage.

I have heard from Alfred also, who hates his water life—βίος ἄβιος he calls it—but hopes to be cured in March. Poor fellow, I trust he may. He is not in a happy plight, I doubt. I wish I lived in a pleasant country where he might like to come and stay with me—but this is one of the ugliest places in England —one of the dullest—it has not the merit of being bleak on a grand scale—pollard trees over a flat clay, with regular hedges. I saw a stanza in an old book which seemed to describe my condition rather—

> Far from thy kyn cast thee:
> Wrath not thy neighbour next thee,
> In a good corn country rest thee,
> And sit down, Robin, and rest thee.

Funny advice, isn't it? I am glad to hear Septimus[1] is so much improved. I beg you will felicitate him from me: I have a tacit regard of the true sort for him, as I think I must have for all of the Tennyson build. I see so many little natures about that I must draw to the large, even if their faults be on the same scale as their virtues. You and I shall I suppose quarrel as often as we meet: but I can quarrel and never be the worse with you. How we pulled against each other at Gravesend! You would stay—I wouldn't—then I would—then we did.—Do you remember the face of that girl at the Bazaar, who kept talking to us and looking all round the room for fresh customers—a way women have —that is, a way of doing rather gracefully? Then the gentleman who sang Ivy green; a very extraordinary accentuation, it seemed to me: but I believe you admired it very much. Really if these little excursions in the company of one's friends leave such a pleasant taste behind in the memory one should court them oftener. And yet then perhaps the relish would grow less: it is the infrequency that gives them room to expand. I shall never get to Italy, that seems clear. My great travel this year will be to Carlisle. Quid prosit ista tua longa peregrinatio &c. Travelling, you know, is a vanity. The *soul* remains the

[1] [Septimus Tennyson (1815–66), younger brother of Alfred and Frederick. He had long suffered from melancholia, and was now living in Italy.]

same. An amorem possis fugare, an libidinis exsiccari, an timorem mortis depellere? What then will you say to Pollock's being married! I hear he is to be. Ad matrimonium fugis? Miser! Scævola noster dicere solebat &c. Excuse my overflowing with philosophy. I am going this evening to eat toasted cheese with that celebrated poet Bernard Barton. And I must soon stir, and look about for my great coat, brush myself &c. It blows a harrico, as Theodore Hook used to say, and will rain before I get to Woodbridge. Those poor mistaken lilac buds there out of the window! and an old Robin, ruffled up to his thickest, sitting mournfully under them, quite disheartened. For you must know the mild winter is just giving way to a remarkably severe spring. . . . I wish you were here to smoke a pipe with me. I play of evenings some of Handel's great choruses which are the bravest music after all. I am getting to the true John Bull style of music. I delight in Handel's Allegro and Penseroso. Do you know the fine pompous joyous chorus of 'These pleasures, Mirth, if thou canst give &c.'? Handel certainly does in music what old Bacon desires in his Essay on Masques, 'Let the songs be loud and cheerful—not puling &c.' One might think the Water music was written from this text.

To Bernard Barton

London [April 1844]

My dear Barton,

While waiting for some books in the British Museum, I have the honour of informing you that, having enquired of the Saracen himself at Aldgate, he swears my pictures *did* go down last Tuesday, and would arrive at Woodbridge on *Wednesday*. It is possible therefore that Smith having a waggon at market may have taken back my pictures by way of ballast when the corn was disposed of. I hope so. But if the box exploded by the way—if the Holy Families were laid in the dirt—if the Magi, forbearing to stop at Woodbridge as they ought, chose to go on foolishly to Halesworth—why—I say again, I snap my fingers at them. I will buy no more things that cause me to go to Aldgate on such a morning as this.

I have not seen Churchyard: had I known his put-up I would have called on him. I saw his Linnell's sketch for sale at Christie's, as also a true Constable—Salisbury Cathedral: which he would have liked. Indeed I think he had seen it somewhere, and spoken to me of it.

We hear Major Moor is come back no better to London. I shall go down to Westminster to hear of him this evening. Are John's lectures over at Woodbridge?—

Ah—your trees are coming out, hedges and willows I know. But I shall soon be down to welcome them and introduce them with all good will to my garden at Boulge. My heart sucks at the fresh air from afar. I have seen nobody here, and all I want is to go away from the detestable dunghill. This is true, in spite of what the Squire says—I was obliged to come up to see Thackeray. I have scarce seen him.

My books come, and so I must make the best of the time and bid you farewell. You can write long letters: but are not you inspired with beakers full of the warm South wind that breathes of sweet briar and violets—The fishmongers' shops here are nearly as bad as the churchyards. Farewell.

ever yrs

E.F.G.

To Bernard Barton

19 Charlotte St., April 11/44

Dear Barton,

I am still indignant at this nasty place London. Thackeray, whom I came up to see, went off to Brighton the night after I arrived, and has not re-appeared: but I must wait some time longer for him. Thank Miss Barton much for the *kit*; if it is but a kit: my old woman is a great lover of cats, and hers has just *kitted*, and a wretched little blind puling tabby lizard of a thing was to be saved from the pail for me: but if Miss Barton's is a *kit*, I will gladly have it: and my old lady's shall be disposed of —not to the pail. Oh rus, quando te aspiciam? Construe that, Mr Barton.—I am going to send down my pictures to Boulge, if I can secure them: they are not quite secure at present. If they vanish, I snap my fingers at them Magi and all—there is a world (alas!) elsewhere beyond pictures—Oh, oh, oh, oh—

I smoked a pipe with Carlyle yesterday. We ascended from his dining room carrying pipes and tobacco up through two stories of his house, and got into a little dressing room near the roof: there we sat down: the window was open and looked out on nursery gardens, their almond trees in blossom, and beyond, bare walls of houses, and over these, roofs and chimneys, and roofs and chimneys, and here and there a steeple, and whole London crowned with darkness gathering behind like the illimitable resources of a dream. I tried to persuade him to leave the accursed den, and he wished—but—but—perhaps he *didn't* wish on the whole.

When I get back to Boulge I shall recover my quietude which is now all in a ripple. But it is a shame to talk of such things. So Churchyard has caught another Constable. Did he get off our Debach boy that set the shed on fire? Ask him that. Can'st thou not minister to a mind diseased, etc.

A cloud comes over Charlotte Street and seems as if it were sailing softly on the April wind to fall in a blessed shower upon the lilac buds and thirsty anemones somewhere in Essex; or, who knows? perhaps at Boulge. Out will run Mrs Faiers,[1] and with red arms and face of woe haul in the struggling windows of the cottage, and make all tight. Beauty Bob[2] will cast a bird's eye out at the shower, and bless the useful wet. Mr Loder[3] will observe to the farmer for whom he is doing up a dozen of Queen's Heads, that it will be of great use: and the farmer will agree that his young barleys wanted it much. The German Ocean will dimple with innumerable pin points, and porpoises rolling near the surface sneeze with unusual pellets of fresh water—

> Can such things be,
> And overcome us like a summer cloud,
> Without our special wonder?

Oh this wonderful wonderful world, and we who stand in the middle of it are all in a maze, except poor Matthews of Bedford,

[1] [Mrs Faiers was EFG's old-fashioned Suffolk housekeeper at Boulge Cottage.]
[2] [His parrot.]
[3] [John Loder, stationer and bookseller at Woodbridge.]

who fixes his eyes upon a wooden Cross and has no misgivings whatsoever. When I was at his chapel on Good Friday, he called at the end of his grand sermon on some of the people to say merely this, that they believed Christ had redeemed them: and first one got up and in sobs declared she believed it: and then another, and then another—I was quite overset:—all poor people: how much richer than all who fill the London Churches. Theirs is the kingdom of Heaven!

This is a sad farrago. Farewell.

To Frederick Tennyson

Boulge, Woodbridge, May 24/44

My dear Frederic,

I think you mean never to write to me again. But you should, for I enjoy your letters much for years after I have got them. They tell me all I shall know of Italy, beside many other good things. I received one letter from you from Florence, and as you gave me no particular direction, I wrote to you at the Poste Restante there. I am now inditing this letter on the same venture. As my location is much more permanent, I command you to respond to me the very day you get this, warmed into such faint inspiration as my turnip radiance can kindle. You have seen a turnip lantern perhaps. Well, here I continue to exist: having broken my rural vegetation by one month in London, where I saw all the old faces—some only in passing, however—saw as few sights as possible, leaving London two days before the Exhibition opened. This is not out of moroseness or love of singularity: but I really supposed there could be nothing new: and therefore the best way would [be] to come new to it oneself after three or four years absence. I see in Punch a humorous catalogue of supposed pictures; Prince Albert's favourite spaniel and bootjack, the Queen's Macaw with a Muffin &c., by Land-seer &c., in which I recognize Thackeray's fancy. He is in full vigour play and pay in London, writing in a dozen reviews, and a score of newspapers: and while health lasts he sails before the wind. I have not heard of Alfred since March. . . . Spedding devotes his days to Lord Bacon in the British Museum: his

nights to the usual profligacy. . . . My dear Frederic, you must
select some of your poems and publish them: we want some bits
of strong genuine imagination to help put to flight these——&c.
Publish a book of fragments, if nothing else but single lines, or
else the whole poems. When will you come to England and do it?
I dare say I should have stayed longer in London had you been
there: but the wits were too much for me. Not Spedding, mind:
who is a dear fellow. But one finds few in London *serious* men:
I mean *serious* even in fun: with a true purpose and character
whatsoever it may be. London melts away all individuality into
a common lump of cleverness. I am amazed at the humour and
worth and noble feeling in the country, however much railroads
have mixed us up with metropolitan civilization. I can still find
the heart of England beating healthily down here though no one
will believe it.

You know my way of life so well that I need not describe it
to you, as it has undergone no change since I saw you. I read of
mornings; the same old books over and over again, having no
command of new ones: walk with my great black dog of an
afternoon, and at evening sit with open windows, up to which
China roses climb, with my pipe, while the blackbirds and
thrushes begin to rustle bedwards in the garden, and the nightingale to have the neighbourhood to herself. We have had such a
spring (bating the last ten days) as would have satisfied even
you with warmth. And such verdure! white clouds moving over
the new fledged tops of oak trees, and acres of grass striving with
buttercups. How old to tell of, how new to see! I believe that
Leslie's Life of Constable (a very charming book) has given me a
fresh love of Spring. Constable loved it above all seasons: he
hated Autumn. When Sir G. Beaumont who was of the old
classical taste asked him if he did not find it difficult to place *his
brown tree* in his pictures, 'Not at all,' said C., 'I never put one
in at all.' And when Sir George was crying up the tone of the old
masters' landscapes, and quoting an *old violin* as the proper tone
of colour for a picture, Constable got up, took an old Cremona,
and laid it down on the sunshiny grass. You would like the book.
In defiance of all this, I have hung my room with pictures, like
very old fiddles indeed: but I agree with Sir George and Constable both. I like pictures that are not like nature. I can have

nature better than any picture by looking out of my window. Yet I respect the man who tries to paint up to the freshness of earth and sky. Constable did not wholly achieve what he tried at: and perhaps the old masters chose a soberer scale of things as more within the compass of lead paint. To paint dew with lead!

I also plunge away at my old Handel of nights, and delight in the Allegro and Penseroso, full of pomp and fancy. What a pity Handel could not have written music to some great Masque, such as Ben Jonson or Milton would have written, if they had known of such a musician to write for.

To Samuel Laurence

May, 1844

Dear Laurence,

I hope your business is settled by this time. I have seen praise of your picture in the Athenæum, which quoted also the Chronicle's good opinion. I am very glad of all this and I hope you will now set to work, and paint away with ease and confidence, forgetting that there is such a hue as bottle-green* in the universe (it was tastefully omitted from the rainbow, you see); and, in spite of what Moore says, paint English people in English atmospheres. Your Coningham was rather orange, wasn't he? But he was very good, I thought. Dress your ladies in cheerful dresses, not quite so vulgar as Chalon's. . . . I heard from my sister that you had finished Wilkinson[1] to the perfect content of all: I had charged her particularly not to allow Mrs W. to intercede for any smirk or alteration whatever.

My Venetian pictures look very grand on my walls, which previously had been papered with a still green (not bottled) on purpose to receive them. On my table is a long necked bottle with three flowers just now in it . . . a tuft of rhododendron, a tuft of scarlet geranium, and a tuft of white gilliflower. Do you see these in your mind's eye? I wish you could come down here and refresh your sodden eyes with pure daylight, budding oak trees, and all

* Also, bottle-brown: in general all bottled things are not so fresh coloured as before they were put in. A gherkin loses considerably in freshness. The great triumph of a housekeeper is when her guests say, 'Why, are these *really* bottled gooseberries! They look like fresh &c.' [FitzGerald's note.]

[1] [Rev. J. B. Wilkinson, husband of EFG's sister Jane.]

the changes of sky and cloud. To live to make sonnets about these things, and doat upon them, is worse Cockneyism than rejoicing in the sound of Bow Bells for ever so long: but here one has them whether one will or no: and they are better than Lady Morgan and —— at a rout in Harley Street. Maclise is a handsome and fine fellow, I think: and Landseer is very good natured. I long for my old Alfred portrait here sometimes: but you had better keep it for the present. W. Browne and Spedding are with me, good representatives one of the Vita Contemplativa, the other of the Vita Attiva. Spedding, if you tell him this, will not allow that he has not the elements of Action in him: nor has he not: nor has not the other those of contemplation: but each inclines a different way notwithstanding. I wish you and Spedding could come down here: though there is little to see, and to eat. When you write you must put *Woodbridge* after Boulge. This letter of yours went to Bury St Edmunds, for want of that. I hear Alfred Tennyson is in very good looks: mind and paint him *quickly* when he comes to town; looking full at you.

To Bernard Barton

Leamington, Sept. 28/44

My dear Barton,

. . . I expect to be here about a week, and I mean to give a day to looking over the field of Edgehill, on the top of which, I have ascertained, there is a very delightful pothouse, commanding a very extensive view. Don't you wish to sit at ease in such a high tower, with a pint of porter at your side, and to see beneath you the ground that was galloped over by Rupert and Cromwell two hundred years ago, in one of the richest districts of England, and on one of the finest days in October, for such my day is to be?

In the meanwhile I cast regretful glances of memory back to my garden at Boulge, which I want to see dug up and replanted. I have bought anemone roots which in the Spring shall blow Tyrian dyes, and Irises of a newer and more brilliant prism than Noah saw in the clouds. I have bought a picture of my poor quarrelsome friend Moore, just to help him; for I don't know what to do with his picture.

R*

To Frederick Tennyson

Boulge, Woodbridge. Oct. 10/44

My dear Frederic,

You will think I have wholly cut you. But I wrote half a letter to you three months ago; and mislaid it; spent some time in looking for it, always hoping; and then some more time despairing; and we all know how time goes when [we] have got a thing to do which we are rather lazy about doing. As for instance, getting up in a morning. Not that writing a letter to you is so bad as getting up; but it is not easy for mortal man who has heard, seen, done, and thought, nothing since he last wrote, to fill one of these big foreign sheets full as a foreign letter ought to be. I am now returned to my dull home here after my usual pottering about in the midland counties of England. A little Bedfordshire —a little Northamptonshire—a little more folding of the hands —the same faces—the same fields—the same thoughts occurring at the same turns of road—this is all I have to tell of; nothing at all added—but the summer gone. My garden is covered with yellow and brown leaves; and a man is digging up the garden beds before my window, and will plant some roots and bulbs for next year. My parsons come and smoke with me &c. 'The round of life from hour to hour'—alluding doubtless to a mill-horse. Alfred is reported to be still at Park House, where he has been sojourning for two months, I think; but he never writes me a word. Hydropathy has done its worst; he writes the names of his friends in water. . . . I spent two days in London with old Morton about five weeks ago; and pleasant days they were. The rogue bewitches me with his wit and honest speech. He also staid some while at Park House, while Alfred was there, and managed of course to frighten the party occasionally with some of his sallies. He often writes to me; and very good his letters are all of them.

When do you mean to write me another? Morton told me in his last that he had heard from Brotherton you were gone, or going, to Naples. I dare say this sheet of mine will never get to your hands. But if it does, let me hear from you. Is Italy becoming stale to you? Are you going to Cairo for fresh sensations?

Thackeray went off in a steamboat about the time the French were before Mogadore; he was to see those coasts and to visit Jerusalem! Titmarsh at Jerusalem will certainly be an era in Christianity. But I suppose he will soon be back now. Spedding is yet in his highlands, I believe, considering Grouse and Bacon.

I expect to run up to London some time during the winter just to tell over old friends' faces and get a sup of music and painting. I have bought very few more pictures lately; and [heard] no music but Mendelssohn's M. Night's Dream. The overture, which was published long ago, is the best part; but there is a very noble triumphal march also.

Now I feel just in the same fix as I did in that sheet of paper whose fate is uncertain. But if I don't put in a word more, yet this shall go, I am determined. Only consider how it is a matter of necessity that I should have nothing to say. If you could see this place of Boulge! You who sit and survey marble palaces rising out of cypress and olive. There is a dreadful vulgar ballad, composed by Mr Balfe, and sung with the most unbounded applause by Miss Rainforth,

> 'I dreamt that I dwelt in marble Halls,'

which is sung and organed at every corner in London. I think you may imagine what kind of flowing $\frac{6}{8}$ time of the last degree of imbecillity it is. The words are written by Mr Bunn! Arcades ambo.

I say we shall see you over in England before long: for I rather think you want an Englishman to quarrel with sometimes. I mean quarrel in the sense of a good strenuous difference of opinion, supported on either side by occasional outbursts of spleen. Come and let us try. You used to irritate my vegetable blood sometimes.

To Frederick Tennyson

Boulge, Woodbridge, Dec. 8/44

My dear Frederic,

What is a poor devil to do? You tell me quite truly that my letters have not two ideas in them, and yet you tell me to write my two ideas as soon as I can. So indeed it is so far easy to write down one's two ideas, if they are not very abstruse ones; but then what the devil encouragement is it to a poor fellow to expose his nakedness so? All I can say is, to say again that if you lived in this place, you would not write so long a letter as you have done, full of capital description and all good things; though without any compliment I am sure you would write a better than I shall. But you see the original fault in me is that I choose to be in such a place as this at all; that argues certainly a talent for dullness which no situation nor intercourse of men could much improve. It is true; I really do like to sit in this doleful place with a good fire, a cat and dog on the rug, and an old woman in the kitchen. This is all my live stock. The house is yet damp as last year; and the great event of this winter is my putting up a trough round the eaves to carry off the wet. There was discussion whether the trough should be of iron or of zinc: iron dear and lasting; zinc the reverse. It was decided for iron; and accordingly iron is put up.

Why should I not live in London and see the world? you say. Why then *I* say as before, I don't like it. I think the dullness of country people is better than the impudence of Londoners; and the fresh cold and wet of our clay fields better than a fog that stinks *per se*; and this room of mine, clean at all events, better than a dirty room in Charlotte St. If you, Morton, and Alfred, were more in London, I should be there more; but now there is but Spedding and Allen whom I care a straw about. I have written two notes to Alfred to ask him just to notify his existence to me; but you know he is obstinate on that point. I heard from Carlyle that he (Alfred) had passed an evening at Chelsea much to C's delight; who has opened the gates of his Valhalla to let Alfred in. Thackeray is at Malta, where I am told he means to winter. . . .

As I have no people to tell you of, so have I very few books, and know nothing of what is stirring in the literary world. I have read the Life of Arnold of Rugby, who was a noble fellow; and the letters of Burke, which do not add to, or detract from, what I knew and liked in him before. I am meditating to begin Thucydides one day; perhaps this winter. . . .

Old Seneca, I have no doubt, was a great humbug in deed,

and his books have plenty of it in word; but he had got together a vast deal of what was not humbug from others; and, as far as I see, the old philosophers are available now as much as two thousand years back. Perhaps you will think that is not saying much. Don't suppose I think it good philosophy in myself to keep here out of the world, and sport a gentle Epicurism; I do not; I only follow something of a natural inclination, and know not if I could do better under a more complex system. It is very smooth sailing hitherto down here. No velvet waistcoat and ever-lustrous pumps to be considered; no bon mots got up: no information necessary. There is a pipe for the parsons to smoke, and quite as much bon mots, literature, and philosophy as they care for without any trouble at all. If we could but feed our poor! It is now the 8th of December; it has blown a most desperate East wind, all razors; a wind like one of those knives one sees at shops in London, with 365 blades all drawn and pointed; the wheat is all sown; the fallows cannot be ploughed. What are all the poor folks to do during the winter? And they persist in having the same enormous families they used to do; a woman came to me two days ago who had seventeen children! What farmers are to employ all these? What landlord can find room for them? The law of generation must be repealed. The London press does nothing but rail at us poor country folks for our cruelty. I am glad they do so; for there is much to be set right. But I want to know if the Editor of the Times is more attentive to his devils, their wives and families, than our squires and squiresses and parsons are to their fellow parishioners. Punch also assumes a tone of virtuous satire, from the mouth of Mr Douglas Jerrold! It is easy to sit in arm chairs at a club in Pall Mall and rail on the stupidity and brutality of those in High Suffolk.

Come, I have got more than two ideas into this sheet; but I don't know if you won't dislike them worse than mere nothing. But I was determined to fill my letter. Yes, you are to know that I slept at Woodbridge last night, went to church there this morning, where every one sat with a purple nose, and heard a dismal well-meant sermon; and the organ blew us out with one grand idea at all events, one of old Handel's Coronation Anthems; that I dined early, also in Woodbridge; and walked up here with a tremendous East wind blowing sleet in my face from over the German Sea, that I found your letter when I entered my room; and reading it through, determined to spin you off a sheet incontinently, and lo! here it is! Now or never! I shall now have my tea in, and read over your letter again while at it. You are quite right in saying that Gravesend excursions with you do me good. When did I doubt it? I remember them with great pleasure; few of my travels so much so. I like a short journey in good company; and I like you all the better for your English-man's humours. One doesn't find such things in London; some-thing more like it here in the country, where every one, with whatever natural stock of intellect endowed, at least grows up his own way, and flings his branches about him, not stretched on the espalier of London dinner-table company.

P.S. Next morning. Snow over the ground. We have our wonders of inundation in Suffolk also, I can tell you. For three weeks ago such floods came, that an old woman was carried off as she was retiring from a beer house about 9 p.m., and drowned. She was probably half seas over before she left the beer house.

And three nights ago I looked out at about ten o'clock at night, before going to bed. It seemed perfectly still; frosty, and the stars shining bright. I heard a continuous moaning sound, which I knew to be, not that of an infant exposed, or female ravished, but of the sea, more than ten miles off! What little wind there was carried to us the murmurs of the waves circulating round these coasts so far over a flat country. But people here think that this sound so heard is not from the waves that break, but a kind of prophetic voice from the body of the sea itself announcing great gales. Sure enough we have got them, however heralded. Now I say that all this shows that we in this Suffolk are not so completely given over to prose and turnips as some would have us. I always said that being near the sea, and being able to catch a glimpse of it from the tops of hills, and of houses, redeemed Suffolk from dullness; and at all events that our turnip fields, dull in themselves, were at least set all round with an undeniably poetic element. And so I see Arnold says; he enumerates five inland counties as the only parts of England for which nothing could be said in praise. Not that I agree with him there neither;

I cannot allow the valley of the Ouse about which some of my pleasantest recollections hang to be without its great charm. W. Browne, whom you despised, is married, and I shall see but little of him for the future. I have laid by my rod and line by the willows of the Ouse for ever. 'He is married and cannot come.' This change is the true meaning of those verses,[1]

> Friend after friend departs;
> Who has not lost a friend?

and so on. If I were conscious of being stedfast and good humoured enough I would marry to-morrow. But a humourist is best by himself.

To Bernard Barton

London, Saturday [Jany. 11th 1845]

Dear Barton,

My illness has been no more than a cold—which made me snivel for 3 days—and is now gone—Thank you for your enquiries however. Land is in sight! Yo ho!—in the middle of next week I shall form a trio with dog and cat in the cottage parlour! I have visited here chiefly for my Father; whom I have just left till dinner time—He dines with the Woods tomorrow— I am going to call on them today—now—in half an hour—

I spent one evening with Carlyle, but was very dull somehow, and delighted to get out into the street. An organ was playing a polka even so late in the street: and Carlyle was rather amazed to see me polka down the pavement—He shut his street door— to which he always accompanies you—with a kind of groan— He was looking well—but he says he gets no sleep of nights. This comes of having a great idea, which germinating once in the mind, grows like a tape worm, and consumes the vitals. What a nasty idea—

Last night I went to hear Handel's Messiah—nobly done. But here again I was glad to get into the street before it was half over. So I doubt I cant hold out the heroic long. "Let me plant cabbages!" was the well considered prayer of Panurge; and it is rather mine. But honour to the Carlyles, who, giving up their

[1] [By James Montgomery.]

own prospect of cabbages, toil and sweat in the spirit that we may plant ours in peace.

Dont you like to get a letter upon a Sunday more than on any other day in the week?—Have you read a foolish looking letter by Mr. Edge in the Ipswich Journal? It is about Dissent. I say foolish-looking, because I only looked at it in Portland Place just now. So I am the fool, by that logic. But Edge combats an ultra Churchman who asserted that a Dissenting Chapel was the cradle of all vice; and Edge says it is not *quite* so bad as that. This is a wretched position to take—And he says "Let us be just before we are logical"!!! My powers! What would Plato say to this! As if justice were not the very outcome of logic—The old saying "Be just before you are generous" distinguishes this well.

I dont think this letter is heroic enough to make *you* dance the Polka when you've got through it—And now it is high time for you to be off to your meeting: so mind you dont *polk* there. That would be worse than a Quaker murdering. You ought not to be ashamed of one murderer: your community should keep his body in a glass case for ever.

Farewell. Ever yrs
E F G.

To Bernard Barton

[Boulge Cottage 1845]

Dear B. B.

Come by all means tomorrow, an thou wilt. Do not come if it rains like this. I will ask Crabbe, who I have no doubt will come; for though Woodbridge is far for him to go out to in the evening, we may reckon Boulge as a midway place where happy spirits may alight between Bredfield and Woodbridge.

I have a letter from Cowell. Perhaps he also will ride over tomorrow—

Bring up with thee a pound of Derby Cheese, for a toast: and some oysters, with knives; that thou mayst eat. And I will pay thee the cost—I have a fowl hanging up: and if my Father's cook arrive, as I think she will, tonight, she shall handsell her skill on my fowl. For I doubt Mrs. Faiers' powers of Bread-sauce—I doubt she would produce a sort of dumpling. But Sarah knows about these things.

Only think. Robert Peel has given A. Tennyson £200 pension —I suppose so much a year—

I dont think him the less a humbug for this.

Yrs

E. F.

To W. B. Donne

Boulge, Jan. 29/45

My dear Donne,

. . . A. T. has near a volume of poems—elegiac—in memory of Arthur Hallam. Don't you think the world wants other notes than elegiac now? Lycidas is the utmost length an elegiac should reach. But Spedding praises: and I suppose the elegiacs will see daylight, public daylight, one day. Carlyle goes on growling with his Cromwell: whom he finds more and more faultless every day. So that *his* paragon also will one day see the light also, an elegiac of a different kind from Tennyson's; as far apart indeed as Cromwell and Hallam.

Barton comes and sups with me to-morrow, and George Crabbe, son of the poet, a capital fellow.

To W. B. Donne

[Postmark: Feb. 28, 1845]

My dear Donne

I was very glad to hear of you; & glad to hear you say you will come & see me this Spring. I dare say it will be in London then: for I doubt I shall have to go there for some time. This will be no evil to you, however: and indeed it will be better you should make your little holiday there, as you are a Londoner at heart; & we shall see all our friends together—

I had not heard of Geldart's paper: & as for him, he never writes. He must be a very odd man. I suppose it is a religious paper, is it?—

If one could have good Lyrics, I think the World wants them as much as ever. Tennyson's are good: but not of the *kind* wanted. We have surely had enough of men reporting their sorrows: especially when one is aware all the time that the poet wilfully protracts what he complains of, magnifies it in the Imagination, puts it into all the shapes of Fancy: and yet we are to condole with him, and be taught to ruminate our losses & sorrows in the same way. I felt that if Tennyson had got on a horse & ridden 20 miles, instead of moaning over his pipe, he would have been cured of his sorrows in half the time. As it is, it is about 3 years before the Poetic Soul walks itself out of darkness & Despair into Common Sense—Plato w^d. not have allowed such querulousness to be published in his Republic, to be sure: and when we think of the Miss Barretts, Brownes, Jewsburys &c who will set to work to feel friends' losses in melodious tears, in imitation of A.T's—one must allow Plato was no such prig as some say he was.

I saw Antigone:[1] but, as Vipan says, the music &c which was what I went to hear, was execrable. The Audience seemed pleased with the plot & dialogue; I can only say it would have been fine if properly done. It should be done in the Senate House at Cambridge.

You are very good not to hate me for hinting to you what I did about your boys. If one had seen sickly mopes, one would not have troubled oneself about what they wore & what they did— but your boys are handsome, lusty, and spirited. If they are let out free, they run all sorts of hazards to be sure; but then if they don't run these hazards they wil[l] be worth nothing. Have you ever read *Andrew* [torn out] Book on Physiology & Education? —It is not very good: but better than other books: and so all ought to read it.

Where is Vipan?—Well, come & see me in London. I will give you due notice of my going thither & place of abode. I shall be very sorry to leave the Country just when the fine weather is coming.

Ever yrs. EDWARD FitzGerald

---

[1] [The *Antigone* of Sophocles, with music by Mendelssohn, was performed at Covent Garden for forty-five nights in January and February of 1845.]

To W. B. Donne

Boulge. Woodbridge. [1845 ?]

Dear Donne

Procter[1] is the only literatus I have seen in London that I care to see again, (saving Tom Carlyle) as he has the heart of a good fellow about him: & as I think his songs poor Cockney things that had better never have been printed, I would not for the world have to say so. Besides, his wife made me a present of the new little volume. I never could understand how Barry, being what he is & always must have been, could have written such things: but no one of his day escaped the Cockney twang then rising—Keats *only* just managed to carry off his share of it—I wish the B. & F.[2] would leave Barry alone: but I suppose many men will be found who will admire the poems & praise them in excellent English—

> Go fetch to me a pint of wine,
>   And fill it in a silver tassie:
> For I maun drink before I go
>   A bumper to my bonnie lassie!

Could one find a stanza like that in the whole book one might cry "Well Done": but yet not be able to write an article on it: for God only who made the rose smell so knows why such verses are from the heart, & go to it—

I am glad you are yet in Norfolk: for little advantage as I take of y^{r.} being so near yet I am always glad to think you are there: which shews there is something in it. I really mean to go to Norwich before long: not to Geldestone yet—

Are you dried up in Norfolk?—We are beginning to cry out here: but in other parts of England people are worse off. Is Vipan still in England?—Ever yrs

E. FitzGerald

[1] [Bryan Waller Procter, the poet, better known as Barry Cornwall (1787–1874).]
[2] [*British and Foreign Review*, edited by John Mitchell Kemble.]

To Bernard Barton

Geldestone, April 3/45

My dear Barton,

. . . I have been loitering out in the garden here this golden
day of Spring. The wood-pigeons coo in the covert; the frogs
croak in the pond; the bees hum about some thyme: and some
of my smaller nieces have been busy gathering primroses, 'all to
make posies suitable to this present month.' I cannot but think
with a sort of horror of being in London now: but I doubt I must
be ere long . . . I have abjured all Authorship, contented at
present with the divine Poem which Great Nature is now composing about us. These primroses seem more wonderful and
delicious Annuals than Ackermann ever put forth. I suppose no
man ever grew so old as not to feel younger in Spring. Yet,
poor old Mrs. Bodham[1] lifted up her eyes to the windows, and
asked if it were a clear or a dull day!

To Bernard Barton

39 Norton St., FitzRoy Sqr. [? May 1845]

Dear Barton,

You see my address. I only got into it yesterday, though I
reached London on Friday, and hung loose upon it for all that
interval. I spent four days at Cambridge pleasantly enough; and
one at Bedford where I heard my friend Matthews preach.

Last night I appeared at the Opera, and shall do so twice a
week till further notice. Friends I have seen but few; for I have
not yet found time to do anything. Alfred Tennyson was here;
but went off yesterday to consider the sea from the top of Beachy
Head. Carlyle gets on with his book which will be in two big
volumes. He has entirely misstated all about Naseby, after all my
trouble. . . .

Did Churchyard see in London a picture at the address I
enclose? The man's card, you see, proclaims 'Silversmith,' but
he is 'Pawnbroker.' A picture hangs up at the door which he

_____
[1] [Great-aunt of William Bodham Donne.]

calls by 'Williams,' but I think is a rather inferior Crome; though the figure in it is not like Crome's figures. The picture is about three feet high by two broad; good in the distance; very natural in the branching of the trees; heavy in the foliage; all common to Crome. And it seems painted in that fat substance he painted in. If C. come to London let him look at this picture, as well as come and see me.

I have cold, head-ache, and London disgust. Oh that I could look on my Anemones! and hear the sighing of my Scotch firs. The Exhibition is full of bad things: there is a grand Turner, however; quite unlike anything that was ever seen in Heaven above, or in Earth beneath, or in the waters under the Earth.

The reign of primroses and cowslips is over, and the oak now begins to take up the empire of the year and wear a budding garland about his brows. Over all this settles down the white cloud in the West, and the Morning and Evening draw toward Summer.

To Frederick Tennyson

Boulge, Woodbridge. June 12/45

Dear Frederic,

Though I write from Boulge you are not to suppose I have been here ever since I last wrote to you. On the contrary, I am but just returned from London, where I spent a month, and saw all the sights and all the people I cared to see. But what am I to tell you of them? Spedding, you know, does not change: he is now the same that he was [at] fourteen years old when I first knew him at school more than twenty years ago; wise, calm, bald, combining the best qualities of Youth and Age. And then as to things seen; you know that one Exhibition tells another, and one Panorama certifieth another &c. If you want to know something of the Exhibition however, read Fraser's Magazine for this month; there Thackeray has a paper on the matter, full of fun. I met Stone[1] in the street the other day; he took me by the button, and told me in perfect sincerity, and with increasing warmth, how, though he loved old Thackeray, yet these yearly

[1] [Frank Stone, the artist; EFG had probably met him through Samuel Laurence.]

out-speakings of his sorely tired him; not on account of himself (Stone), but on account of some of his friends, Charles Landseer, Maclise &c. Stone worked himself up to such a pitch under the pressure of forced calmness that he at last said Thackeray would get himself horse-whipped one day by one of these infuriated Apelleses. At this I, who had partly agreed with Stone that ridicule, though true, needs not always to be spoken, began to laugh: and told him two could play at that game. These painters cling together, and bolster each other up, to such a degree, that they really have persuaded themselves that any one who ventures to laugh at one of their drawings, exhibited publickly for the express purpose of criticism, insults the whole corps. In the mean while old Thackeray laughs at all this; and goes on in his own way; writing hard for half a dozen Reviews and Newspapers all the morning; dining, drinking, and talking of a night; managing to preserve a fresh colour and perpetual flow of spirits under a wear-and-tear of thinking and feeding that would have knocked up any other man I know two years ago, at least. . . .

Alfred was in London the first week of my stay there. He was looking well, and in good spirits; and had got two hundred lines of a new poem in a butcher's book. He went down to Eastbourne in Sussex; where I believe he now is. He and I made a plan to go to the coast of Cornwall or Wales this summer; but I suppose we shall manage never to do it. I find I must go to Ireland; which I had not intended to do this year.

I have nothing new to tell you of Music. The Operas were the same old affair; Linda di Chamouni, the Pirata &c. Grisi coarse, . . . only Lablache great. There is one singer also, Brambelli, who, with a few husky notes, carries one back to the days of Pasta. I did not hear 'Le Désert'; but I fancy the English came to a fair judgment about it. That is, they did not want to hear it more than once. It was played many times, for new batches of people; but I doubt if any one went twice. So it is with nearly all French things; there is a clever showy surface; but no Holy of Holies far withdrawn; conceived in the depth of a mind, and only to be received into the depth of ours after much attention. Poussin must spend his life in Italy before he could paint as he did; and what other Great Man, out of the exact Sciences, have they to show? This you will call impudence. Now Beethoven, you see by your own experience, has a depth not to be reached all at once. I admit with you that he is too bizarre, and, I think, morbid. But he is original, majestic, and profound. Such music *thinks*; so it is with Gluck; and with Mendelssohn. As to Mozart, he was, as a musical Genius, more wonderful than all. I was astonished at the Don Giovanni lately. It is certainly the Greatest Opera in the world. I went to no concert, and am now sorry I did not.

Now I have told you all my London news. You will not hear of my Cottage and Garden; so now I will shut up shop and have done. We have had a dismal wet May; but now June is recompensing us for all, and Dr Blow may be said to be leading the great Garden Band in full chorus. This is a pun, which, profound in itself, you must not expect to enjoy at first reading. I am not sure that I am myself conscious of the full meaning of it. I know it is very hot weather; the distant woods steaming blue under the noonday sun. I suppose you are living without clothes in wells, where you are. Remember me to your brothers; write soon; and believe me ever yours,

E. FitzGerald

As to going to Italy, alas! I have less call to do that than ever: I never shall go. You must come over here about your Railroad land.

To Bernard Barton

Geldestone. Monday [Dec. 29. 1845]

Dear Barton,

Thanks for your letter. I am glad Turkey and Sausage did so well. We had our Feast here also, which did as well as most things of the kind. The children mostly eat as much as they could, and more than was good for them, and looked paler all next day in consequence.

I expect to be home by the end of this week, or early in next week. I want to see how my draining at the Cottage goes on. One may rejoice, I think, in the Snow forbearing us so long. What a day, however, was this day week, when I came hither!—

This note is but to acknowledge yours: for I have positively

535

nothing to say. Such total bankruptcies will happen in men's wits every now and then. I have sat over this little sheet of paper a quarter of an hour, looking up and asking intelligence of the ceiling, the furniture of the room, and the lawn before the window—But no thought reducible to paper comes. Take will for deed, and believe me yrs as ever

EDWARD FITZGERALD

Do give the enclosed paper to Daddy Loder, and bid him get me the book.

To Bernard Barton

60 Charlotte St. Rathbone Place. [April 1846]

My dear Barton,

I have been very bilious and very resentful of this London atmosphere. And all epistolary power has left me. I have been able to manage no book but Mrs. Trollope's novels: of which one, "the Robertses on their Travels," is very entertaining and, I think, instructive. I wish our good folks who go abroad yearly to stare, make fools of themselves, and learn much less good than evil, would read and take to heart the true picture of so many of them drawn in that novel—

I sent Churchyard a note some days ago, apprizing him of my locality, and hoping I should see him ere long. I keep all my picture expeditions till he comes up. Indeed, I have lost all appetite for sights: and I think would go further to see a bit of clear blue sky over a furze-blossomed heath than any Titian in the world.

On Thursday I dined with a large party at Portland Place, among the company your friend *Ainsworth* figures: and your other friend *Wilson* comes to sing to us in the evening. Ainsworth is, in my opinion, a *Snob*; but I don't reveal my opinion at P. P.—Tennyson and I sometimes get a walk and a talk together. He is no Snob. He has lately been standing as Godfather to one of Dickens's children—Count d'Orsay being the other Godfather—insomuch that the poor child will be named "Alfred d'Orsay Tennyson Dickens"! proving clearly enough, I think, that Dickens is a *Snob*—For what is Snobbishness and Cockney-

536

ism but all such pretension and parade? It is one thing to worship Heroes; and another to lick up their spittle—

I expect Edward Cowell to-day. He comes to London to see his Lady, and to buy Persian books. I shall be glad to see him; he will bring up a waft of Suffolk air with him—O! the bit of salmon I eat yesterday! I feel it within me like churchyard fat— I scratch out a capital C because I mean a burial place and not any person. Farewell for the present.

Ever yrs, E. F. G.

To Bernard Barton

60 Charlotte St., Rathbone Place. [May 4th 1846]
My dear Barton,

You will think me very negligent. Crabbe, I suppose, will think I am offended with him. For I owe him and you a letter this long while, I think. But I have no wits to write with in this London, where, positively, I have not enjoyed one hour's clear health since I have been in it.

Tomorrow Tennyson and I are going to get a pint or two of fresh air at Richmond: and we are to wind up our day at Carlyle's by way of a refreshing evening's entertainment. I met C. last night at Tennyson's; and they two discussed the merits of this world and the next, till I wished myself out of *this*, at any rate. Carlyle gets more wild, savage, and unreasonable every day; and, I do believe, will turn mad. "What is the use of ever so many rows of stupid, fetid, animals in cauliflower wigs—and clean lawn sleeves—calling themselves Bishops—Bishops, I say, of the Devil—not of God—obscene creatures, parading between men's eyes, and the eternal light of Heaven," &c. &c. This, with much abstruser nonconformity for 2 whole hours!—and even as it was yesterday, so shall it be to-morrow, and the day after that —in sæcula sæculorum!—

I met Ainsworth at P. P. but had not much talk with him, and did not give him your love. He works very hard at gentility now. Churchyard has doubtless told you of his jaunt with me: and I suppose you have fallen greatly in love with his two little fruit pieces. I have done nothing since. Indeed, I don't go into the streets now, but get out by the Regent's Park to Primrose Hill, where the air is a little purer.

Thank Miss Barton for the book extracts she sent me. And drive over round by Boulge Cottage one afternoon, and tell me if my anemones and irises are in full glow. My heart would leap up to see them.

Farewell. Ever yrs   E. F. G.

To W. B. Donne

Boulge Hall, Woodbridge [1846]

My dear Donne,

I don't know which of us is most to blame for this long gulph of silence. Probably I; who have least to do. I have been for two months to London; where (had I thought it of any use) I should have written to try and get you up for a few days; as I had a convenient lodging, and many beside myself would have been glad to see you.

I came back a week ago; and on looking in at Barton's last evening he showed me your letter with such pleasure as he is wont to receive your letters with. And there I read all the surprising story of your moving to old Bury. When I passed through Cambridge two months ago, Thompson said (I think) that he had seen you; and that you had given up thoughts of Bury. But now you are going. As you say, you will then be nearer to us than you now are at Mattishall; especially when our Railroad shall be completed. In my journeys to and from Bedfordshire, I shall hope to stay a night at the good old Angel, and so have a chat with you.

I saw very little of Spedding in London; for he was out all day at State paper offices and Museums; and I out by night at Operas &c. with my Mother. He is however well and immutable. A. Tennyson was in London; for two months striving to spread his wings to Italy or Switzerland. It has ended in his flying to the Isle of Wight till Autumn, when Moxon promises to convoy him over; and then God knows what will become of him and whether we shall ever see his august old body over here again. He was in a ricketty state of body; brought on wholly by neglect &c., but in fair spirits; and one had the comfort of seeing the Great Man. Carlyle goes on fretting and maddening as usual. Have you read his Cromwell? Are you converted, or did you ever need conversion? I believe I remain pretty much where I was. I think Milton, who is the best evidence Cromwell has in his favour, warns him somewhat prophetically at the end of his Second Defence against taking on him Kingship &c. and in the tract on the State of England in 1660 (just before it was determined to bring back Charles 2) he says *nothing at all* of Cromwell, no panegyric; but glances at the evil ambitions men in the Army have done; and, now that all is open to choose, prays for a pure Republic! So I herd with the flunkies and lackies, I doubt; but am yours notwithstanding, E. F. G.

To E. B. Cowell

[1846]

Dear Cowell,

I am glad you have bought Spinoza. I am in no sort of hurry for him: you may keep him a year if you like. I shall perhaps never read him now I have him. Thank you for the trouble you took. . . .

Your Hafiz is fine: and his tavern world is a sad and just idea. I did not send that vine leaf to A. T. but I have not forgotten it. It sticks in my mind—

> "In Time's fleeting river
> The image of that little vine-leaf lay,
> Immovably unquiet—and for ever
> It trembles—but it cannot pass away."

I have read nothing you would care for since I saw you. It would be a good work to give us some of the good things of Hafiz and the Persians; of bulbuls and ghuls we have had enough.

Come and bring over Spinoza; or I must go and bring him.

To E. B. Cowell

[1847]

Dear Cowell.

. . . I am only got half way in the third book of Thucydides: but I go on with pleasure; with as much pleasure as I used to read a novel. I have also again taken up my Homer. That is a noble and affecting passage where Diomed and Glaucus, being about to fight, recognize each other as old family friends, exchange arms, and vow to avoid each other henceforth in the fray. (N.B. and this in the tenth year of the war!) After this comes, you know, the meeting of Hector and Andromache, which we read together; altogether a truly Epic canto indeed.

Yet, as I often think, it is not the poetical imagination, but bare Science that every day more and more unrolls a greater Epic than the Iliad; the history of the World, the infinitudes of Space and Time! I never take up a book of Geology or Astronomy but this strikes me. And when we think that Man must go on to discover in the same plodding way, one fancies that the Poet of to-day may as well fold his hands, or turn them to dig and delve, considering how soon the march of discovery will distance all his imaginations, [and] dissolve the language in which they are uttered. Martial, as you say, lives now, after two thousand years; a space that seems long to us whose lives are so brief; but a moment, the twinkling of an eye, if compared (not to Eternity alone) but to the ages which it is now known the world must have existed, and (unless for some external violence) must continue to exist. Lyell in his book about America, says that the falls of Niagara, if (as seems certain) they have worked their way back southwards for seven miles, must have taken over 35,000 years to do so, at the rate of something over a foot a year! Sometimes they fall back on a stratum that crumbles away from behind them more easily: but then again they have to roll over rock that yields to them scarcely more perceptibly than the anvil to the serpent. And those very soft strata which the Cataract now erodes contain evidences of a race of animals, and of the action of seas washing over them, long before Niagara came to have a distinct current; and the rocks were compounded ages and ages before those strata! So that, as Lyell says, the Geologist looking at

Niagara forgets even the roar of its waters in the contemplation of the awful processes of time that it suggests. It is not only that this vision of Time must wither the Poet's hope of immortality; but it is in itself more wonderful than all the conceptions of Dante and Milton.

As to your friend Pliny, I don't think that Time can use his usual irony on that saying about Martial. Pliny evidently only suggests that "at non erunt æterna quæ scripsit" as a question of his correspondent; to which he himself replies "Non erunt *fortasse.*" Your Greek quotations are very graceful. I should like to read Busbequius. Do *you* think Tacitus *affected* in style, as people now say he is?

To Samuel Laurence

Geldestone Hall, Beccles. [June 20, 1847]

My dear Laurence,

I have had another letter from the Bartons asking about your advent. In fact Barton's daughter is anxious for her Father's to be done, and done this year. He is now sixty-three; and it won't do, you know, for grand-climacterical people to procrastinate— nay, to *proannuate*—which is a new, and, for all I see, a very bad word. But, be this as it may, do you come down to Woodbridge this summer if you can; and that you can, I doubt not; since it is no great things out of your way to or from Norwich.

The means to get to Ipswich are—A steamboat will bring you for five shillings (a very pretty sail) from the Custom House to Ipswich, the Orwell steamer; going twice a week, and heard of directly in the fishy latitudes of London Bridge. Or, a railroad brings you for the same sum; if you will travel third class, which I sometimes do in fine weather. I should recommend *that*; the time being so short, so certain: and no eating and drinking by the way, as must be in a steamer. At Ipswich, I pick you up with the washerwoman's pony and take you to Woodbridge. There Barton sits with the tea already laid out; and Miss about to manage the urn; plain, agreeable people. At Woodbridge too is my little friend Churchyard, with whom we shall sup off toasted cheese and porter. Then, last and not least, the sweet retirement of Boulge: where the Graces and Muses &c.

I write thus much because my friends seem anxious; my friend, I mean, Miss Barton: for Barton pretends he dreads having his portrait done; which is 'my eye.' So come and do it. He is a generous, worthy, simple-hearted, fellow: worth ten thousand better wits. Then you shall see all the faded tapestry of country town life: London jokes worn threadbare; third rate accomplishments infinitely prized; scandal removed from Dukes and Duchesses to the Parson, the Banker, the Commissioner of Excise, and the Attorney.

Let me hear from you soon that you are coming. I shall return to Boulge the end of this week.

P.S. Come if you can the latter part of the week; when the Quaker is most at leisure. There is a daily coach from Woodbridge to Norwich.

To Frederick Tennyson

[Leamington, 4 Sept. 1847]

My dear Frederic,

I believe I must attribute your letter to your having skipped to Leghorn, and so got animated by the sight of a new place. *I* also am an Arcadian: have been to Exeter—the coast of Devonshire—the Bristol Channel—and to visit a Parson in Dorsetshire.[1] He wore cap and gown when I did at Cambridge—together did we roam the fields about Granchester, discuss all things, thought ourselves fine fellows, and that one day we should make a noise in the world. He is now a poor Rector in one of the most out-of-the-way villages in England—has five children—fats and kills his pig—smokes his pipe—loves his home and cares not ever to be seen or heard of out of it. I was amused with his company; he much pleased to see me: we had not met face to face for fifteen years—and now both of us such very sedate unambitious people! Now I am verging homeward; taking Leamington and Bedford in my way.

[1] [Francis Duncan, rector of West Chelborough.]

You persist in not giving me your clear direction at Florence. It is only by chance that you give the name 'Villa Gondi' of the house you describe so temptingly to me. I should much like to visit you there; but I doubt shall never get up the steam for such an expedition. And now know that, since the last sentence was written, I have been to Cheltenham, and called at your Mother's; and seen her, and Matilda, and Horatio, all well: Alfred is with the Lushingtons and is reported to be all the better for the water-cure. Cheltenham seemed to me a woeful place: I had never seen it before. I now write from Leamington; where I am come to visit my Mother for a few days. . . .

All the world has been, as I suppose you have read, crazy about Jenny Lind: and they are now giving her £400 to sing at a Concert. What a frightful waste of money! I did not go to hear her: partly out of contradiction perhaps; and partly because I could not make out that she was a great singer, like my old Pasta. Now I will go and listen to any pretty singer whom I can get to hear easily and unexpensively: but I will not pay and squeeze much for any canary in the world. Perhaps Lind is a nightingale: but I want something more than that. Spedding's cool blood was moved to hire stalls several times at an advanced rate: the Lushingtons (your sister told me) were enraptured: and certainly people rushed up madly from Suffolk to hear her but once and then die. I rather doubted the value of this general appreciation. But one cause of my not hearing her was that I was not in London for more than a fortnight in the Spring: and she came out but at the close of my fortnight. . . .

. . . You are wrong, as usual, about Moore and Eastlake: all the world say that Moore had much the best of the controversy, and Eastlake only remains cock of the walk because he is held up by authority. I do not pretend to judge which of the two is right in art: but I am sure that Moore argues most logically, and sets out upon finer principles; and if two shoemakers quarrelled about the making of a shoe, I should be disposed to side with him who argued best on the matter, though my eyes and other senses could not help me to a verdict. Moore takes his stand on high ground, and appeals to Titian, Michel Angelo, and Reynolds. Eastlake is always shifting about, and appealing to Sir

Robert Peel, Etty, and the Picture-dealers.[1] Now farewell. Write when you can to Boulge.

To W. B. Donne

[Postmark: Woodbridge, Nov. 5, 1847]

My dear Donne

I am not so exorbitant as Barton in demanding letters: I supposed you were busy to some better purpose—Indeed, *my* letter the less called for an answer, being of itself a sort of apology for not calling upon you in propriâ personâ. How do you stand engaged next week?— I think I might contrive to run over to Bury for 2 days in it;—but am not quite sure, as we expect my Father & the Kerrich party here very soon. Kerrich[2] *is* somewhat better. Will you give me one line as to your liabilities & conveniences next week?—

I do not think my brother knows Lord —— any longer. Did not my Lord go crazy, & get into confinement? I think so—

Tell *Miss Johnson* I think she has a spite against me, (probably arising from my accidentally calling her *Miss Donne* last year) and that she makes the worst of my sayings— Seriously, I would not have you suppose that I made any heavy charge on you behind your back, or said what I would not say before you. Surely, we have had many fights about *"the Blimbers"*[3] face to face— Besides words lightly spoken seem grave when reported; —perhaps, only when *written*, as I see them in your letter—

As to Jenny Lind, I don't care what I say about her. I cannot endure that she should clutch more money on the strength of her good character than the Italian whores ever stand out for— At

---

[1] [Morris Moore's letters on the Abuses of the National Gallery were addressed to *The Times* at the end of 1846 and the beginning of 1847 with the signature "Verax." They were collected and published in a pamphlet by Pickering in 1847.]

[2] [John Kerrich, of Geldestone Hall, had married EFG's sister Mary Eleanor (1805–63).]

[3] [FitzGerald's name—from the tyrannical schoolmaster in *Dombey and Son*—for Dr Donaldson, of Bury Grammar School, who, he thought, overworked the young Doesnn unduly.]

Norwich I hear she got £12,000[1] & gave back £200—something like Mrs Blaize's[2] Charity— Of all Avarices the worst is that which apes Liberality, surely.

Barton is overworked in his Bank; they ought to be more considerate to the old man— Pray write him a letter out of kindness. I never see Geldart's paper; but I know his prejudices might easily turn savage—

Farewell, ever yrs

E. F.G.

To E. B. Cowell

Boulge, Wednesday. [Jan. 25, 1848]

My dear Cowell,

I liked your paper on the Mesnavi very much; both your criticism and your Mosaic legend. That I may not seem to give you careless and undistinguishing praise, I will tell you that I could not quite hook on the latter part of Moses to the former; did you leave out any necessary link of the chain in the hiatus you made? or is the inconsequence only in my brains? So much for the legend: and I must reprehend you for one tiny bit of Cockney about Memory's rosary at the end of your article, which, but for that, I liked so much.

So judges Fitz-Dennis; who, you must know by this time, has the judgment of Molière's old woman, and the captiousness of Dennis.[3] Ten years ago I might have been vext to see you striding along in Sanscrit and Persian so fast; reading so much; remembering all; writing about it so well. But now I am glad to see any man do any thing well; and I know that it is my vocation to stand and wait, and know within myself whether it *is* done well.

I have just finished, all but the last three chapters, the fourth Book of Thucydides, and it is now no task to me to go on. This fourth book is the most interesting I have read; containing all

[1] [Jenny Lind is more likely to have received £1,200 or less, for her "quite unprecedented" fee at Norwich the following year was 1,000 guineas. She was far from avaricious and gave many large bequests to charity besides the £200 mentioned in the letter.]

[2] [The pawnbroker about whom Goldsmith wrote a punning elegy.]

[3] [John Dennis (1657–1735), a savage critic who quarrelled with Pope.]

that blockade of Pylos; that first great thumping of the Athenians at Oropus, after which they for ever dreaded the Theban troops. And it came upon me 'come stella in ciel,' when, in the account of the taking of Amphipolis, Thucydides, ὃς ταῦτα ξυνέγραψεν, comes with seven ships to the rescue! Fancy old Hallam sticking to his gun at a Martello tower! This was the way to write well; and this was the way to make literature respectable. Oh, Alfred Tennyson, could you but have the luck to be put to such employment! No man would do it better; a more heroic figure to head the defenders of his country could not be.

To Frederick Tennyson

Boulge, May 4, 1848

My dear Frederic, When you talk of two idle men not taking the trouble to keep up a little intercourse by letters, you do not, in conscience, reflect upon me; who, you know, am very active in answering almost by return of post. It is some six months since you must have got my last letter, full of most instructive advice concerning my namesake; of whom, and of which, you say nothing. How much has he borrowed of you? Is he now living on the top of your hospitable roof? Do you think him the most ill-used of men? I see great advertisements in the papers about your great Grimsby Railway . . . Does it pay? does it pay all but you? who live only on the fine promises of the lawyers and directors engaged in it? You know England has had a famous winter of it for commercial troubles: my family has not escaped the agitation: I even now doubt if I must not give up my daily twopennyworth of cream and take to milk: and give up my Spectator and Athenæum. I don't trouble myself much about all this: for, unless the kingdom goes to pieces by national bankruptcy, I shall probably have enough to live on: and, luckily, every year I want less. What do you think of my not going up to London this year; to see exhibitions, to hear operas, and so on! Indeed I do not think I shall go: and I have no great desire to go. I hear of nothing new in any way worth going up for. I have never yet heard the famous Jenny Lind, whom all the world raves about. Spedding is especially mad about her, I understand: and, after that, is it not best for weaker vessels to keep out of her way? Night after night is that bald head seen in one particular position in the Opera house, in a stall; the miserable man has forgot Bacon and philosophy, and goes after strange women. There is no doubt this lady is a wonderful singer; but I will not go into hot crowds till another Pasta comes; I have heard no one since her worth being crushed for. And to perform in one's head one of Handel's choruses is better than most of the Exeter Hall performances. I went to hear Mendelssohn's Elijah last spring: and found it wasn't at all worth the trouble. Though very good music it is not original: Haydn much better. I think the day of Oratorios is gone, like the day for painting Holy Families &c. But we cannot get tired of what has been done in Oratorios more than we can get tired of Raffaelle. Mendelssohn is really original and beautiful in *romantic* music: witness his Midsummer Night's Dream, and Fingal's Cave.

I had a note from Alfred three months ago. He was then in London: but is now in Ireland, I think, adding to his new poem, the Princess. Have you seen it? I am considered a great heretic for abusing it; it seems to me a wretched waste of power at a time of life when a man ought to be doing his best; and I almost feel hopeless about Alfred now. I mean, about his doing what he was born to do. . . . On the other hand, Thackeray is progressing greatly in his line: he publishes a Novel in numbers—Vanity Fair—which began dull, I thought: but gets better every number, and has some very fine things indeed in it. He is become a great man I am told: goes to Holland House, and Devonshire House: and for some reason or other, will not write a word to me. But I am sure this is not because he is asked to Holland House. Dickens has fallen off in his last novel,[1] just completed; but there are wonderful things in it too. Do you ever get a glimpse of any of these things?

As to public affairs, they are so wonderful that one does not know where to begin. If England maintains her own this year, she must have the elements of long lasting in her. I think People begin to wish we had no more to do with Ireland: but the Whigs will never listen to a doctrine which was never heard of in Holland House. I am glad Italy is free: and surely there is

[1] [*Dombey and Son.*]

nothing for her now but a Republic. It is well to stand by old kings who have done well by us: but it is too late in the day to *begin* Royalty.

If anything could tempt me so far as Italy, it would certainly be your presence in Florence. But I boggle about going twenty miles, and *cui bono*? deadens me more and more.

July 2. All that precedes was written six weeks ago, when I was obliged to go up to London on business. . . . I saw Alfred, and the rest of the sçavans. Thackeray is a great man: goes to Devonshire House &c : and *his* book (which is capital) is read by the Great: and will, I hope, do them good. I heard but little music: the glorious Acis and Galatea; and the redoubtable Jenny Lind, for the first time. I was disappointed in her: but am told this is all my fault. As to naming her in the same Olympiad with great old Pasta, I am sure that is ridiculous. The Exhibition is like most others you have seen; worse perhaps. There is an 'Aaron' and a 'John the Baptist' by Etty far worse than the Saracen's Head on Ludgate Hill. Moore is turned Picture dealer: and that high Roman virtue in which he indulged is likely to suffer a Picture-dealer's change, I think. Carlyle writes in the Examiner about Ireland: raves and foams, but has nothing to propose. Spedding prospers with Bacon. Alfred seemed to me in fair plight: much dining out: and his last Poem is well liked I believe. Morton is still at Lisbon, I believe also: but I have not written to him, nor heard from him. And now, my dear Frederic, I must shut up. Do not neglect to write to me sometimes. Alfred said you ought to be in England about your Grimsby Land.

To E. B. Cowell

19, Charlotte Street, Rathbone Place, [November 1848] My dear Cowell,

It is a long time since we have corresponded. The truth is, I have read so little of late—indeed, next to nothing—that I have no heart to address you who are always reading—who have probably read more since you last wrote to me than I shall read in the next ten years, should I live so long. Here is a letter, however; and let me have one from you to tell me how you and [your] gude-wife are; and also what realms of gold you have discovered since I last heard of you.

I have been some time in London, chiefly on business; indeed it is a business that still promises to end and still will not end, that has detained me thus long. I shall have to go to Brighton before I return home.

I have seen Carlyle but once; he was very grim, very eloquent; and altogether I have not been tempted there again. A. Tennyson is now residing in London, at 25 Mornington Place, Hampstead Road; a short walk from me. I particularise all this because, should you come to London, you can call upon him without any further introduction. I have often spoken about you to him, and he will be very glad to make your acquaintance. Can you not run up here for a day or two before I leave? I can give you a crib, and all board but dinner; but do not come without giving me notice; as I may have to be at Brighton at any time. Altogether, I hope to reach Boulge by the beginning of December.

If you come, we will go and see Carlyle, whom I must visit once before my return. Tennyson is emerged half-cured, or half-destroyed, from a water establishment: has gone to a new Doctor who gives him iron pills; and altogether this really great man thinks more about his bowels and nerves than about the Laureate wreath he was born to inherit. Not but he meditates new poems; and now the Princess is done, he turns to King Arthur—a worthy subject indeed—and has consulted some histories of him, and spent some time in visiting his traditionary haunts in Cornwall. But I believe the trumpet can wake Tennyson no longer to do great deeds; I may mistake and prove myself an owl; which I hope may be the case. But how are we to expect heroic poems from a valetudinary? I have told him he should fly from England and go among savages.

Well, you see I have not forgot to talk confidently, in proportion as I grow more ignorant perhaps.

To W. B. Donne

[Early 1849]

My dear Donne

Thanks for y^r. letter. As far as I can see nothing of B. B's would have a general interest except a Small Selection of his Poems: & *a short Memoir*, with a few letters, by way of specimen of the Man.[1] From what I have seen of his letters, I cannot imagine there is any more in them than ease and good humour: of which a little is enough for the world at large.

I have now looked over *all* his Volumes with some care; and have selected what will fill about 200 pages of print—as I suppose —really all the best part out of 9 *volumes*! Some of the poems I take entire—some half—some only a few stanzas, & these dovetailed together—with a change of a word, or even of a line here & there, to give them logic and fluency. It is wonderful when you come to look close into most of these poems to see the elements of repetition, indistinctness &c which go to make them diffuse and weary. I am sure I have distilled many pretty little poems out of long dull ones which the world has discarded—I do not pretend to be a poet: but I have faculty enough to mend some of B. Bs'. dropped stitches, though I really could not make any whole poem so good as many of his. As a matter of *Art*, I have no doubt whatsoever I am right: whether I am right in *morals* to use a dead man so I am not certain. Tell me candidly what you think of this. I only desire to go a good little job for his memory, & make a presentable book for Miss B's profit—

You say Selections are *Extracts*: and as such are permissible even from Copyrights. But are Selections of *whole pieces extracts*? —Was it ruled in Southey v. Grimshawe[2] that *whole* letters might be taken without penalty?

We have had "May you like It" Tayler[3] here lately—a man versed in books & booksellers. He approves of all that has been

---

[1] [Bernard Barton had died on 19 February 1849.]

[2] [A bitter dispute between Robert Southey and the Rev. T. S. Grimshawe, rival editors of Cowper, about publication of a portion of his private correspondence.]

[3] [For twenty years or more B.B. had corresponded with the Rev. Charles Benjamin Tayler, curate of Hadleigh, Suffolk: a prolific writer of devotional and didactic books.]

done—advises Subscription—and a *London Publisher*—Whom do you recommend for one?—

I must go over one day & show you something of our doings—I do nothing without Miss B's approbation.

Yrs E. F.G.

I find that Tayler & Miss B. rather desire *more* letters—

P.S. We think 300 pages including letters &c (perhaps 50 letters of B. B's—)—There are also some of Southeys—C Llofts[1]—What ought these 300 pages to *cost* per volume for subscribers?

To Frederick Tennyson

Boulge, Woodbridge, June 19, 1849

My dear old Frederic,

I often think of you: often wish to write to you—often intend to do so—determine to do so—but perhaps should not do so for a long time, but that this sheet of thin paper happens to come under my fingers this 19th of June 1849. You must not believe however that it is only chance that puts me up to this exertion; I really should have written but that the reports we read of Italian and Florentine troubles put me in doubt first whether you are still at Florence to receive my letter: and secondly whether, if you be there, it would ever reach your hands. But I will brace myself up even to that great act of Friendship, to write a long letter with all probability of its miscarrying. Only look here; if it ever does reach you, you must really write to me directly: to let me know how you and yours are, for I am sincerely anxious to know this. I saw great reports in the paper too some months back of Prince Albert going to open Great Grimsby Docks. Were not such Docks to be made on your land? and were you not to be a rich man if they were made? And have you easily consented to forego being paid in money, and to accept in lieu thereof a certain quantity of wholly valueless shares in said Docks, which will lead you into expense, instead of enriching you? This is what I suppose will be the case. For though you

[1] [Capell Lofft (1751–1824), name misspelt by EFG; a barrister with a taste for letters, especially poetry.]

have a microscopic eye for human character, you are to be diddled by any knave, or set of knaves, as you well know.

Of my own affairs I have nothing agreeable to tell. . . . When I met you in London, I was raising money for myself on my reversionary property: and so I am still: and of course the lawyers continue to do so in the most expensive way; a slow torture of the purse. But do not suppose I want money: I get it, at a good price: nor do I fret myself about the price: there will be quite enough (if public securities hold) for my life under any dispensation the lawyers can inflict. As I grow older I want less. I have not bought a book or a picture this year: have not been to a concert, opera, or play: and, what is more, I don't care to go. Not but if I meet you in London again I shall break out into shilling concerts &c. and shall be glad of the opportunity.

After you left London, I remained there nearly to the end of December; saw a good deal of Alfred &c. Since then I have been down here except a fortnight's stay in London, from which I have just returned. I heard Alfred had been seen flying through town to the Lushingtons: but I did not see him. He is said to be still busy about that accursed Princess. By the by, beg, borrow, steal, or buy Keats' Letters and Poems; most wonderful bits of Poems, written off hand at a sitting, most of them: I only wonder that they do not make a noise in the world. By the by again, it is quite necessary *your* poems should be printed; which Moxon, I am sure, would do gladly. Except this book of Keats, we have had *no* poetry lately, I believe; luckily, the ——, ——, —— &c. are getting older and past the age of conceiving—*wind*. Send your poems over to Alfred to sort and arrange for you: he will do it: and you and he are the only men alive whose poems I want to see in print. By the by, thirdly and lastly, and in total contradiction to the last sentence, I am now helping to edit some letters and poems of—Bernard Barton! Yes: the poor fellow died suddenly of heart disease; leaving his daughter, a noble woman, almost unprovided for: and we are getting up this volume by subscription. If you were in England *you* must subscribe: but as you are not, you need only give us a share in the Great Grimsby Dock instead.

Now there are some more things I could tell you, but you see where my pen has honestly got to in the paper. I remember you did not desire to hear about my garden, which is now gorgeous with large red poppies, and lilac irises—satisfactory colouring: and the trees murmur a continuous soft *chorus to the solo which my soul discourses within.* If that be not Poetry, I should like to know what is? and with it I may as well conclude. I think I shall send this letter to your family at Cheltenham to be forwarded to you:—they may possibly have later intelligence of you than I have. Pray write to me if you get this; indeed you *must*; and never come to England without letting me know of it.

To E. B. Cowell

Boulge, Saturday, [1849]

My dear Cowell,

How is it I have not heard from you these two months? Surely, I was the last who wrote. I was told you had influenza, or cold: but I suppose that is all over by this time. How goes on Sanscrit, Athenæus, etc. I am reading the sixth Book of Thucydides—the Sicilian expedition—very interesting—indeed I like the old historian more and more and shall be sorry when I have done with him. Do you remember the fine account of the great armament setting off from the Piraeus for Sicily—B. 6, ch. 30, etc.? If not, read it now.

One day, I mean to go and pay you another visit, perhaps soon. I heard from Miss Barton you were reading, and even liking, the Princess—is this so? I believe it is greatly admired in London coteries. I remain in the same mind about [it]. I am told the Author means to republish it, with a character of each speaker between each canto; which will make the matter worse, I think; unless the speakers are all of the Tennyson family. For there is no indication of any change of speaker in the cantos themselves. What do you say to all this?

Can you tell me any passages in the Romans of the Augustan age, or rather before, telling of decline in the people's morals, hardihood, especially as regards the youth of the country?

Kind remembrances to Miladi, and I am yours ever,

E. FitzGerald

To Frederick Tennyson

Bedford, Dec. 7/49

My dear old Frederic,

Your note came to me to day. I ought to have written to you long ago: and indeed did half do a letter before the summer was half over: which letter I mislaid. I shall be delighted indeed to have your photograph: insufficient as a photograph is. You are one of the few men whose portrait I would give a penny to have: and one day when you are in England we must get it done by Laurence; half at your expense and half at mine, I think. I wish you had sent over to me some of your poems which you told me you were printing at Florence: and often I wish I was at Florence to give you some of my self-satisfied advice on what you should select. For though I do not pretend to write Poetry you know I have a high notion of my judgment in it.

Well, I was at Boulge all the summer: came up thence five weeks ago: stayed three weeks with my mother at Richmond; a week in London: and now am come here to try and finish a money bargain with some lawyers which you heard me beginning a year ago. They utterly failed in any part of the transaction except bringing me in a large bill for service unperformed. However, we are now upon another tack. . . .

In a week I go to London, where I hope to see Alfred. Oddly enough, I had a note from him this very day on which I receive yours: he has, he tells me, taken chambers in Lincoln's Inn Fields. Moxon told me he was about to publish another edition of his Princess, with interludes added between the parts: and also that he was about to print, but (I think) not to publish, those Elegiacs on Hallam. I saw poor old Thackeray in London: getting very slowly better of a bilious fever that had almost killed him. Some one told me that he was gone or going to the Water Doctor at Malvern. People in general thought Pendennis got dull as it got on; and I confess I thought so too: he would do well to take the opportunity of his illness to discontinue it altogether. He told me last June he himself was tired of it: must not his readers naturally tire too? Do you see Dickens' David Copperfield? It is very good, I think: more carefully written than his

554

later works. But the melodramatic parts, as usual, bad. Carlyle says he is a showman whom one gives a shilling to once a month to see his raree-show, and then sends him about his business.

I have been obliged to turn Author on the very smallest scale. My old friend Bernard Barton chose to die in the early part of this year . . . We have made a Book out of his Letters and Poems, and published it by subscription . . . and I have been obliged to contribute a little dapper Memoir, as well as to select bits of Letters, bits of Poems, &c. All that was wanted is accomplished: many people subscribed. Some of B. B's letters are pleasant, I think, and when you come to England I will give you this little book of incredibly small value. I have heard no music but two concerts at Jullien's a fortnight ago; very dull, I thought: no beautiful new Waltzes and Polkas which I love. It is a strange thing to go to the Casinos and see the coarse whores and apprentices in bespattered morning dresses, pea-jackets and bonnets, twirl round clumsily and indecently to the divine airs played in the Gallery; 'the music yearning like a God in pain' indeed. I should like to hear some of your Florentine Concerts; and I do wish you to believe that I do constantly wish myself with you: that, if I ever went anywhere, I would assuredly go to visit the Villa Gondi. I wish you to believe this, which I know to be true, though I am probably further than ever from accomplishing my desire. Farewell: I shall hope to find out your Consul and your portrait in London: though you do not give me very good directions where I am to find them. And I will let you know soon whether I have found the portrait, and how I like it.

To W. B. Donne

19 Charlotte St., FitzRoy Square, London. [18 Jan. 1850]
Dear Donne,

. . . After I left Richmond, whence I last wrote to you, I went to Bedford, where I was for five weeks: then returned to spend Christmas at Richmond: and now dawdle here hoping to get some accursed lawyers to raise me some money on what remains of my reversion. This they *can* do, and *will* do, in time: but, as usual, find it their interest to delay as much as possible.

I found A. Tennyson in chambers at Lincoln's Inn: and recreated myself with a sight of his fine old mug, and got out of him all his dear old stories, and many new ones. He is republishing his Poems, the Princess with songs interposed. I cannot say I thought them like the old vintage of his earlier days, though perhaps better than other people's. But, even to you, such opinions appear blasphemies. A. T. is now gone on a visit into Leicestershire: and I miss him greatly. Carlyle I have not seen; but I read an excellent bit of his in the Examiner, about Ireland. Thackeray is well again, except not quite strong yet. Spedding is not yet returned: and I doubt will not return before I have left London.

I have been but to one play; to see the Hypocrite, and Tom Taylor's burlesque[1] at the Strand Theatre. It was dreadfully cold in the pit: and I thought dull. Farren almost unintelligible: Mrs Glover good in a disagreeable part.[2] Diogenes has very good Aristophanic hits in it, as perhaps you know: but its action was rather slow, I thought: and I was so cold I could not sit it half through.

To Frederick Tennyson

Direct to Boulge, Woodbridge. March 7/50.
My dear old Frederic,

. . . I saw Alfred in London—pretty well I thought. He has written songs to be stuck between the cantos of the Princess, none of them of the old champagne flavour, as I think. But I am in a minority about the Princess, I believe. If you print any poems, I especially desire you will transmit them to me. I wish I was with you to consider about these: for though I cannot write poems, you know I consider that I have the old woman's faculty of judging of them: yes, much better than much cleverer and wiser men; I pretend to no Genius, but to Taste: which, according to my aphorism, is the feminine of Genius. . . .

. . . Please to answer me directly. I constantly think of you: and, as I have often sincerely told you, with a kind of love which I feel towards but two or three friends. Are you coming to England? How goes on Grimsby? Doesn't the state of Europe

1 [*Diogenes and his Lantern.*]   2 [Old Lady Lambert.]

sicken you? Above all, let me have any poems you print: you are now the only man I expect verse from; such gloomy grand stuff as you write. Thackeray, to be sure, can write good ballads, half serious. His Pendennis is very stupid, I think: Dickens' Copperfield on the whole, very good. He always lights one up somehow. There is a new volume of posthumous poems by Ebenezer Elliott: with fine things in it. I don't find myself growing old about Poetry; on the contrary. I wish I could take twenty years off Alfred's shoulders, and set him up in his youthful glory: . . . He is the same magnanimous, kindly, delightful fellow as ever; uttering by far the finest prose sayings of any one.

To John Allen

Boulge: March 9/50

My dear Allen,

. . . I have now been home about three weeks, and, as you say, one sees indications of lovely spring about. I have read but very little of late; indeed my eyes have not been in superfine order. I caught a glimpse of the second volume of Southey's Life and Letters; interesting enough. I have also bought Emerson's 'Representative Men,' a shilling book of Bohn's: with very good scattered thoughts in it: but scarcely leaving any large impression with one, or establishing a theory. So at least it has seemed to me: but I have not read very carefully. I have also bought a little posthumous volume of Ebenezer Elliott: which is sure to have fine things in it.

I believe I love poetry almost as much as ever: but then I have been suffered to doze all these years in the enjoyment of old childish habits and sympathies, without being called on to more active and serious duties of life. I have not put away childish things, though a man. But, at the same time, this visionary inactivity is better than the mischievous activity of so many I see about me; not better than the useful and virtuous activity of a few others: John Allen among the number.

To Frederick Tennyson

Portland Coffee House, London. April 17/50

My dear Frederic,

You tell me to write soon: and this letter is begun, at least, on the day yours reaches me. This is partly owing to my having to wait an hour here in the Coffee room of the Portland Hotel: whither your letter has been forwarded to me from Boulge. I am come up for one week: once more to haggle with Lawyers; once more to try and settle my own affairs as well as those of others for a time. . . .

I don't think of drowning myself yet: and what I wrote to you was a sort of safety escape for my poor flame . . . it is only idle and well-to-do people who kill themselves; it is ennui that is hopeless: great pain of mind and body 'still, still, on hope relies': the very old, the very wretched, the most incurably diseased never put themselves to rest. It really gives me pain to hear you or any one else call me a philosopher, or any good thing of the sort. I am none, never was; and, if I pretended to be so, was a hypocrite. Some things, as wealth, rank, respectability, I don't care a straw about; but no one can resent the toothache more, nor fifty other little ills beside that flesh is heir to. But let us leave all this.

I am come to London; but I do not go to Operas or Plays: and have scarce time (and, it must be said, scarce inclination) to hunt up many friends. Dear old Alfred is out of town; Spedding is my sheet-anchor, the truly wise and fine fellow: I am going to his rooms this very evening: and there I believe Thackeray, Venables &c. are to be. I hope not a large assembly: for I get shyer and shyer even of those I knew. Thackeray is in such a great world that I am afraid of him; he gets tired of me: and we are content to regard each other at a distance. You, Alfred, Spedding, and Allen, are the only men I ever care to see again. If ever I leave this country I will go and see you at Florence or elsewhere; but my plans are at present unsettled. I have refused to be Godfather to all who have ever asked me; but I declare it will give me sincere pleasure to officiate for your Child. I got your photograph at last: it is a beastly thing: not a bit like: why did you not send your Poems, which are like you; and reflect your dear old face well? As you know I admire your poems, the only poems by a living writer I do admire, except Alfred's, you should not hesitate. I can have no doubt whatever they ought to be published in England: I believe Moxon would publish them: and I believe you would make some money by them. But don't send them to Alfred to revise or select: only for this reason, that you would both of you be a little annoyed by gossip about how much share each of you had in them. Your poems can want no other hand than your own to meddle with them, except in respect of the choice of them to make a volume which would please generally: a little of the vulgar faculty of popular tact is all that needs to be added to you, as I think. You will know I do not say this presumptuously: since I think the power of writing one fine line transcends all the 'Able-Editor' ability in the ably-edited Universe.

Do you see Carlyle's 'Latter Day Pamphlets'? They make the world laugh, and his friends rather sorry for him. But that is because people will still look for practical measures from him: one must be content with him as a great satirist who can make us feel when we are wrong though he cannot set us right. There is a bottom of truth in Carlyle's wildest rhapsodies. I have no news to tell you of books or music, for I scarce see or hear any. And moreover I must be up, and leave the mahogany coffee-room table on which I write so badly: and be off to Lincoln's Inn. God bless you, my dear fellow. I ask a man of business here in the room about Grimsby: he says, 'Well, all these railways are troublesome; but the Grimsby one is one of the best: railway property must look up a little: and so will Grimsby.'

To Frederick Tennyson

Boulge, Woodbridge, August 15/50

My dear Frederic,

Let me hear something of you. The last I heard was three months and more ago, when you announced I was a Godfather. I replied instantly. Since all this, Alfred has got married. Spedding has seen him and his wife at Keswick: and speaks very highly of her. May all turn out well! Alfred has also published his Elegiacs on A. Hallam: these sell greatly: and will, I fear, raise a host of Elegiac scribblers.

Since I wrote to you, I have been down here, leading a life of my usual vacuity. My garden shows Autumn asters about to flower: chrysanthemums beginning to assert their places in the beds. The corn cutting all round. I have paid no visits except where the Lady of my old Love resides. A week ago Spedding came down into Suffolk: and we all met: very delightfully. I propose being here till October, and then must, I believe, pay John Allen a visit in Shropshire. Sometimes I turn my thoughts to paying you a visit in Florence this winter: but I doubt that would end in nothing. Yet I have several reasons for going: yourself not the least, pray believe. I have begun to nibble at Spanish: at their old Ballads: which are fine things—like *our*, or rather the North Country, old Ballads. I have also bounced through a play of Calderon with the help of a friend—a very fine play of its kind. This Spanish literature is alone of its kind in Europe, I fancy: with some *Arabian* blood in it. It was at one time overrated perhaps: I think lately it has undergone the natural reaction of undervaluing. But I am not a fit judge perhaps: and after all shall never make much study of it.

I was in London only for ten days this Spring: and those ten days not in the thick of the season. So I am more than usually deficient in any news. The most pleasurable remembrance I had of my stay in town was the last day I spent there; having a long ramble in the streets with Spedding, looking at Books and Pictures: then a walk with him and Carlyle across the Park to Chelsea, where we dropped that Latter Day Prophet at his house; then getting upon a steamer, smoked down to Westminster: dined at a chop-house by the Bridge: and then went to Astley's; old Spedding being quite as wise about the Horsemanship as about Bacon and Shakespeare. We parted at midnight in Covent Garden: and this whole pleasant day has left a taste on my palate like one of Plato's lighter, easier, and more picturesque dialogues.

When I speak of the Latter Day Prophet, I conclude you have read, or heard of, Carlyle's Pamphlets so designed. People are tired of them and of him: he only foams, snaps, and howls, and no progress, people say: this is almost true: and yet there is vital good in all he has written. Spedding, beside his Bacon labours, which go on with the quietude and certainty of the Solar System, contributes short and delightful bits to the Gentleman's Magazine: which has now turned over a new leaf, and is really the best Magazine we have. No pert Criticism; but laborious and unaffected information.

Merivale is married! to a daughter of George Frere's, a lawyer in London. I have not heard of M. since this fatal event: but I stayed two days with him in his Essex parsonage just before it He is grown very fat—an Archdeacon, if ever there were one—and tries to screw himself down to village teaching, etc. He does all he can, I dare say: but what use is an historical Fellow of a College in a Country parish? It is all against the grain with him, and with his people.

You see Daddy Wordsworth is dead, and there is a huge subscription going on for his monument in Westminster Abbey. I believe he deserves one; but I am against stuffing Westminster Abbey with any one's statue till a hundred years or so have proved whether Posterity is as warm about a Man's Merits as we are. What a vast monument is erected to Cider Phillips—to Gay?—the last of whom I love, but yet would not interfere with the perfect Gothic of the Abbey to stick up his ugly bust in it.

I went to one Opera in London—*Zora*—Rossini's own *re*-version of his Moïse. I stayed about an hour and came away. It was good music, well sung, well acted, but the house was hot! To this complexion do we come at last.

Thackeray goes on with Pendennis: which people think very clever, of course, but rather dull. It is nothing but about selfish London people. Dickens's novel[1] is much like his others. I should be sorry not to read it, and not to like it.

Pray let me hear from you soon. How do Grimsby railways get on? Give my love to my Godchild. Why don't you send me your Poems? You really ought to do that. Damn the Daguerrotype.

[1] [*David Copperfield.*]

To Frederick Tennyson

[Boulge.] Decr. 31/50

My dear old Frederic,

If you knew how glad I am to hear from you, you would write to me oftener. You see I make a quick return whenever I get an epistle from you. I should indeed have begun to indite before, but I had not a scrap of serviceable paper in the house: and I am only this minute returned from a wet walk to Woodbridge bringing home the sheet on which I am now writing, along with the rest of a half quire, which may be filled to you, if we both live. I now count the number of sheets: there are nine. I do not think we average more than three letters a year each. Shall both of us, or either, live three years more, beginning with the year that opens to morrow? I somehow believe *not*: which I say not as a doleful thing (indeed you may look at it as a very ludicrous one). Well, we shall see. I am all for the short and merry life. Last night I began the sixth Book of Lucretius in bed. You laugh grimly again? I have not looked into it for more than a year, and I took it up by mistake for one of Swift's dirty volumes; and, having got into bed with it, did not care to get out to change it.

The delightful lady . . . is going to leave this neighbourhood and carry her young Husband to Oxford, there to get him some Oriental Professorship one day. He is a delightful fellow, and, *I* say, will, if he live, be the best Scholar in England. Not that I think Oxford will be so helpful to his studies as his counting house at Ipswich was. However, being married he cannot at all events become Fellow, and, as so many do, dissolve all the promise of Scholarship in Sloth, Gluttony, and sham Dignity. I shall miss them both more than I can say, and must take to Lucretius! to comfort me. I have entirely given up the *Genteel* Society here about; and scarce ever go anywhere but to the neighbouring Parson, with whom I discuss Paley's Theology, and the Gorham Question. I am going to him to night, by the help of a Lantern, in order to light out the Old Year with a Cigar. For he is a great Smoker, and a very fine fellow in all ways.

I have not seen any one you know since I last wrote; nor heard from any one: except dear old Spedding, who really came down and spent two days with us, me and that Scholar and his Wife in their Village, in their delightful little house, in their pleasant fields by the River side. Old Spedding was delicious there; always leaving a mark, as I say, in all places one has been at with him, a sort of Platonic perfume. For has he not all the beauty of the Platonic Socrates, with some personal Beauty to boot? He explained to us one day about the laws of reflection in water: and I said then one never could look at the willow whose branches furnished the text without thinking of him. How beastly this reads! As if he gave us a lecture! But you know the man, how quietly it all came out; only because I petulantly denied his plain assertion. For I really often cross him only to draw him out; and vain as I may be, he is one of those that I am well content to make shine at my own expense.

Don't suppose that this or any other ideal day with him effaces my days with you. Indeed, my dear Frederic, you also mark many times and many places in which I have been with you. Gravesend and its ἀνήριθμοι shrimps cannot be forgotten. You say I shall never go to see you at Florence. I have said to you before and I now repeat it, that if ever I go abroad it shall be to see you and my Godchild. I really cannot say if I should not have gone this winter (as I hinted in my last) in case you had answered my letter. But I really did not know if you had not left Florence; and a fortnight ago I thought to myself I would write to Horatio at Cheltenham and ask him for news of you. As to Alfred, I have heard of his marriage &c. from Spedding, who also saw and was much pleased with her indeed. But you know Alfred himself never writes, nor indeed cares a halfpenny about one, though he is very well satisfied to see one when one falls in his way. You will think I have a spite against him for some neglect, when I say this, and say besides that I cannot care for his In Memoriam. Not so, if I know myself: I always thought the same of him, and was just as well satisfied with it as now. His poem I never did greatly affect: nor can I learn to do so: it is full of finest things, but it is monotonous, and has that air of being evolved by a Poetical Machine of the highest order. So it seems to be with him now, at least to me, the Impetus, the Lyrical œstrus, is gone . . . It is the cursed inactivity (very pleasant to me who am no Hero) of this 19th century which has spoiled Alfred, I mean spoiled him for the great work he ought now to be entering upon; the lovely and noble things he has done must remain. It is dangerous work this prophesying about great Men. . . . I beg you very much to send me your poems, the very first opportunity; as I went them very much. Nobody doubts that you ought to make a volume for Moxon. Send your poems to Spedding to advise on. No doubt Alfred would be best adviser of all: but then people would be stupid and say that he had done all that was good in the Book—(wait till I take my tea, which has been lying on the table these ten minutes—) Now, animated by some very inferior Souchong from the village shop, I continue my letter, having reflected during my repast that I have seen two College men you remember since I last wrote, Thompson and Merivale. The former is just recovering of the water cure, looking blue: the latter, Merivale, is just recovering from—Marriage! —which he undertook this Midsummer, with a light-haired daughter of George Frere's. Merivale lives just on the borders of Suffolk: and a week before his marriage he invited me to meet F. Pollock and his wife at the Rectory. There we spent two easy days, and I heard no more of Merivale till three weeks ago when he asked me to meet Thompson just before Christmas. . . . Have you seen Merivale's History of Rome, beginning with the Empire? Two portly volumes are out, and are approved of by Scholars, I believe. I have not read them, not having money to buy, nor any friend to lend.

I hear little music but what I make myself, or help to make with my Parson's son and daughter. We, with not a voice among us, go through Handel's Coronation Anthems! Laughable it may seem; yet it is not quite so; the things are so well-defined, simple, and grand, that the faintest outline of them tells; my admiration of the old Giant grows and grows: his is the Music for a Great, Active, People. Sometimes too, I go over to a place elegantly called *Bungay*, where a Printer[1] lives who drills the young folks of a manufactory there to sing in Chorus once a week. . . . They sing some of the English Madrigals, some of Purcell, and some of Handel, in a way to satisfy me, who don't want perfection, and

[1] [Charles Childs. He was recommended by Carlyle to print the *Selections from the Poems and Letters of Bernard Barton*, and printed most of EFG's works.]

who believe that the *grandest* things do not depend on delicate finish. If you were here now, we would go over and hear the Harmonious Blacksmith sung in Chorus, with words, of course. It almost made me cry, when I heard the divine Air rolled into vocal harmony from the four corners of a large Hall. One can scarce comprehend the Beauty of the English Madrigals till one hears them done (though coarsely) in this way and on a large scale: the play of the parts as they alternate from the different quarters of the room.

I have taken another half sheet to finish my letter upon: so as my calculation of how far this half-quire is to spread over Time is defeated. Let us write oftener, and longer, and we shall not tempt the Fates by inchoating too long a hope of letter-paper. I have written enough for to-night: I am now going to sit down and play one of Handel's Overtures as well as I can—Semele, perhaps, a very grand one—then, lighting my lantern, trudge through the mud to Parson Crabbe's. Before I take my pen again to finish this letter the New Year will have dawned—on some of us. 'Thou fool! this night thy soul may be required of thee!' Very well: while it is in this Body I will wish my dear old F. T. a happy New Year. And now to drum out the Old with Handel. Good Night.

New Year's Day, 1851. A happy new Year to you! I sat up with my Parson till the Old Year was past, drinking punch and smoking cigars, for which I endure some headache this morning. Not that we took much; but a very little punch disagrees with me. Only I would not disappoint my old friend's convivial expectations. He is one of those happy men who has the boy's heart throbbing and trembling under the snows of sixty-five.

To George Crabbe

60 Lincoln's Inn Fields, [Feb. 27, 1851]

My dear George,

. . . My heart saddens to think of Bramford all desolate;[1] and I shall now almost turn my head away as any road, or railroad brings me within sight of the little spire! I write once a

[1] [The Cowells had gone to live in Oxford.]

week to abuse both of them for going. But they are quite happy at Oxford.

I felt a sort of horror when I read in your letter you had ordered the Book[1] into your Club, for fear some one might guess. But if *your* folks don't guess, no one else will. I have heard no more of it since I wrote to you last, except that its sale does not stand still. Pickering's foreman blundered in the Advertisements; quoting an extract about the use of the Book, when he should have quoted about its amusement, which is what the world is attracted by. But I left it to him. As it would be a real horror to me to be known as the writer, I do not think I can have much personal ambition in its success; but I should sincerely wish it to be read for what little benefit it may do. . . .

I have seen scarce anybody here: Thackeray only once; neither Tennyson nor Carlyle. Donne came up for a day to see as to the morality of the 'Prodigal Son'[2] at Drury Lane, which the Bishop of London complained of. Donne is deputy Licenser for Jack Kemble. I went to see it with him; it was only stupid and gaudy.

To W. B. Donne

[Late 1851]

My dear Donne,

I was not surprised at your kind and partial letter—for I have long known your feeling toward me—I have so often said that you over-estimate my talents, and under-rate your own, that it only looks like scratching for a return to say so again—And yet this is very clear to myself, and others—I have what Goethe calls the "Barber's talent" of easy narrative of easy things—can tell of Barton, & Chesterton Inn,[3] but not of Atreus, and the Alps—Nor do I pretend to do so—You have a far stronger head —a better Understanding—more *active* Humour—and a Memory that supplies your Understanding with unfailing stuff to grind. I have come to a time of life, or perhaps (as I hope) a

---

[1] [*Euphranor.*]

[2] [*Azaël the Prodigal*, adapted from Scribe and Auber's *L'Enfant Prodigue.*]

[3] [The Three Tuns Inn, Chesterton, near Cambridge, described in *Euphranor.*]

time of philosophy, which enables me to see these things pretty
clearly, undimmed by much Ambition or (I fondly hope again)
Vanity—And what I say of us both I say with at least as much
Sincerity as I am capable of saying anything.

This little Book[1] is no sudden push at Authordom: it was
written some years ago: but with-held because Puseyism &
Catholicism were ascendant, and I w^d. not help even by a f—t
to fill their sails. When they got into disgrace, I brushed up my
Dialogue—& printed it—Except a letter to the Ipswich Journal,
or a few words of Preface to some Book of Extracts, I do not
really meddle with Print—and, *I believe*, never shall. For it
really is more *labour* to me to put anything together than you
who write so much can imagine—And I know that others will
do and can do much better with pleasure, ease, and profit, to
themselves.

Enough of this. As I believe you honestly like much of my
Book, & think it may be useful, I shall be undoubtedly glad to
have you say so in print—so as I may stick "a plum of praise"
in an advertisement. For certainly if I do not want, or expect,
to *gain* much, I also do not want to lose; & at least I hope I shall
do no harm—If you cannot give me a whole Review, you can
give me *a glance* in a Review on some one else, may be. All this
I leave to y^r. discretion & opportunities—Only do not *bore*
yourself in my small service.

Pickering publishes—and I suppose the Book will be to be
had at his Shop in a Week. I leave it to Childs & him to fix a
price—2^s ought to be the utmost—It is to be done up in plain
green cloth: which is all ready, I believe, waiting only the title-
page to be made up at once.

Tell Charles I had his pleasant letter this morning. If he comes
over to Jackson's while I am here, he must also come over here
and smoke a pipe with old Crabbe. But this place is not lovely
in this weather: and I live the life of a Polar Bear in it.

Ah those Cowells! Going away for ever, it seems to me!—I
delight in what you say of them—yet with a remorse-ful delight—

Did I tell you about my visit to Merivale's?—He wanted
much to know about you, & why you did not go to see him.
Thompson was ill of a cold. *Madame* was, I presume, *enceinte*.

She seemed an unaffected, sensible, woman—but I had just left Bramford!

Burn this. ever yr E. F.G.

To Frederick Tennyson

[19 Charlotte St., Fitzroy Square, Dec. 1851]

My dear old Frederic,

I have long been thinking I would answer a long and kind letter I had from you some weeks ago, in which you condoled with me about my finances, and offered me your house as a Refuge for the Destitute. I can never wonder at generosity in you: but I am sorry I should have seemed to complain so much as to provoke so much pity from you. I am not worse off than I have been these last three years; and so much better off than thousands who deserve more that I should deserve to be kicked if I whined over my decayed fortunes. If I go to Italy, it will be to see Florence and Fred. Tennyson: I do not despair of going one day: I believe my desire is gathering, and my indolence warming up with the exhilarating increase of Railroads.

But for the present here I am, at 19 Charlotte Street Fitzroy Square, come up to have a fresh squabble with Lawyers, and to see an old College friend who is gone mad, and threatens to drive his wife mad too, I think. Here are troubles, if you like: I mean, these poor people's. Well, I have not had much time except to post about in Omnibi between Lincoln's Inn and Bayswater: but I have seen Alfred once; Carlyle once; Thackeray twice; and Spedding many times. I did not see Mrs A.: but am to go and dine there one day before I leave. Carlyle has been undergoing the Water System at Malvern, and says it has done him a very little good. He would be quite well, he says, if he threw his Books away, and walked about the mountains: but that would be 'propter vitam &c.' Nature made him a Writer: so he must wear himself out writing Lives of Sterling etc. for the Benefit of the World. Thackeray says he is getting tired of being witty, and of the great world: he is now gone to deliver his Lectures[1] at Edinburgh: having already given them at Ox-

[1] [On the English humourists of the eighteenth century.]

ford and Cambridge. Alfred, I thought looking pretty well. Spedding is immutably wise, good, and delightful: not so immutably well in Body, I think: though he does not complain. But I will deal in no more vaticinations of Evil. I can't think what was the oracle in my Letters you allude to, I mean about the three years' duration of our lives. I have long felt about England as you do, and even made up my mind to it, so as to sit comparatively, if ignobly, easy on that score. Sometimes I envy those who are so old that the curtain will probably fall on them before it does on their Country. If one could save the Race, what a Cause it would be! not for one's own glory as a member of it, nor even for its glory as a Nation: but because it is the only spot in Europe where Freedom keeps her place. Had I Alfred's voice, I would not have mumbled for years over In Memoriam and the Princess, but sung such strains as would have revived the Μαραθωνομάχους ἄνδρας to guard the territory they had won. What can 'In Memoriam' do but make us all sentimental? . . .

My dear Frederic, I hope to see you one day: I really do look forward one day to go and see you in Italy, as well as to see you here in England. I know no one whom it would give me more pleasure to think of as one who might perhaps be near me as we both go down the hill together, whether in Italy or England. You, Spedding, Thackeray, and only one or two more. The rest have come like shadows and so departed.

To George Crabbe

Ham, June 2/52

My dear George,

. . . Order into your Book Club 'Trench on the Study of Words'; a delightful, good, book, not at all dry (unless to fools); one I am sure you will like. Price but three and sixpence and well worth a guinea at least.

In spite of my anti-London prejudices, I find this Limb of London (for such it is) very beautiful: the Thames with its Swans upon it, and its wooded sides garnished with the Villas of Poets, Wits, and Courtiers, of a Time which (I am sorry to say) has more charms to me than the Middle Ages, or the Heroic.

I have seen scarce any of the living London Wits; Spedding

and Donne most: Thackeray but twice for a few minutes. He finished his Novel[1] last Saturday and is gone, I believe, to the Continent.

To Frederick Tennyson

Goldington, Bedford, June 8/52

My dear Frederic,

It gave me, as always, the greatest pleasure to hear from you. Your letter found me at my Mother's house, at Ham, close to Richmond; a really lovely place, and neighbourhood, though I say it who am all prejudiced against London and 'all the purtenances thereof.' But the copious woods, green meadows, the Thames and its swans gliding between, and so many villas and cheerful houses and terraced gardens with all their associations of Wits and Courtiers on either side, all this is very delightful. I am not heroic enough for Castles, Battlefields &c. Strawberry Hill for me! I looked all over it: you know all the pictures, jewels, curiosities, were sold some ten years ago; only bare walls remain: the walls indeed here and there stuck with Gothic woodwork, and the ceilings with Gothic gilding, sometimes painted Gothic to imitate woodwork; much of it therefore in less good taste: all a Toy, but yet the Toy of a very clever man. The rain is coming through the Roofs, and gradually disengaging the confectionary Battlements and Cornices. Do you like Walpole? did you ever read him? Then close by is Hampton Court: with its stately gardens, and fine portraits inside; all very much to my liking. I am quite sure gardens should be formal, and unlike general Nature. I much prefer the old French and Dutch gardens to what are called the English.

I saw scarce any of our friends during the three weeks I passed at Ham. Though I had to run to London several times, I generally ran back as fast as I could; much preferring the fresh air and the fields to the smoke and the 'wilderness of monkeys' in London. Thackeray I saw for ten minutes: he was just in the agony of finishing a Novel: which has arisen out of the Reading necessary for his Lectures, and relates to those Times—of Queen Anne, I mean. He will get £1000 for his Novel. He was wanting

[1] [*Henry Esmond.*]

570

to finish it, and rush off to the Continent, I think, to shake off the fumes of it. Old Spedding, that aged and most subtle Serpent, was in his old haunt in Lincoln's Inn Fields, up to any mischief. It was supposed that Alfred was somewhere near Malvern: Carlyle I did not go to see, for I really have nothing to tell him, and I have got tired of hearing him growl: though I do not cease to admire him as much as ever. I also went once to the pit of the Covent Garden Italian Opera, to hear Meyerbeer's Hugue-nots, of which I had only heard bits on the Pianoforte. But the first Act was so noisy, and ugly, that I came away, unable to wait for the better part, that, I am told, follows. Meyerbeer is a man of Genius: and works up *dramatic* Music: but he has scarce any melody, and is rather grotesque and noisy than really powerful. I think this is the fault of modern music; people can-not believe that Mozart is *powerful* because he is so Beautiful: in the same way as it requires a very practised eye (more than I possess) to recognize the consummate power predominating in the tranquil Beauty of Greek Sculpture. I think Beethoven is rather spasmodically, than sustainedly, grand.

Well, I must take to my third side after all, which I meant to have spared you, partly because of this transparent paper, and my more than usually bad writing. I came down here four days ago: and have this morning sketched for you the enclosed, the common that lies before my Bedroom window, as I pulled up my blind, and opened my shutter upon it, early this morning. I never draw now, never drew well; but this may serve to give a hint of poor old dewy England to you who are, I suppose, begin-ning to be dried up in the South. W. Browne, my host, tells me that your Grimsby Rail is looking up greatly, and certainly will pay well, sooner or later: which I devoutly hope it may.

I do not think I told you my Father was dead; like poor old Sedley in Thackeray's Vanity Fair, all his Coal schemes at an end. He died in March, after an illness of three weeks, saying 'that engine works well' (meaning one of his Colliery steam engines) as he lay in the stupor of Death. I was in Shropshire at the time, with my old friend Allen; but I went home to Suffolk just to help to lay him in the Grave.

Pray do send me your Poems, one and all: I should like very much to talk them over with you, however much you might resent me, who am no Poet, presuming to advise you who as certainly are one. That you ought to publish some of these Poems (as I think, somewhat condensed, or, at least, curtailed) I am more and more sure, having seen the very great pleasure, and deep interest, some of them have caused when read to persons of very different talents and tastes.

And now, my dear Frederic, farewell for the present. Remember, you cannot write to me too often, as far as I am concerned. ☞Don't write Politics—I agree with you beforehand.

To W. B. Donne

Boulge, August 10/52

My dear Donne,

It is very good of you to write to me, so much as you have to do. I am much obliged to you also for taking the trouble to go and see my Mother. You may rely on it she feels as pleased with your company as she says she is: I do not know any one who has the power of being so agreeable to her as yourself.

And dear old Thackeray is really going to America! I must fire him a letter of farewell.

The Cowells are at Ipswich, and I get over to see them &c. They talk of coming here too. I have begun again to read Calderon with Cowell: the Magico we have just read, a very grand thing. I suppose Calderon was over-praised some twenty years ago: for the last twenty it has been the fashion to underpraise him, I am sure. His Drama may not be the finest in the world: one sees how often too he wrote in the fashion of his time and country: but he is a wonderful fellow; one of the Great Men of the world.

To Elizabeth Cowell

Boulge, Woodbridge, April 4/53

My dear Lady,

Let me hear from you. As to Cowell, he is too steeped in Pracrit. Did you leave Oxford this Easter? I concluded I should hear of you if you went to Ipswich. I have been to Geldestone:

and returned from it a fortnight ago. Do you know I am really going to leave this poor little Cottage this Autumn:—a sort of sorrowful thing to do too: and I am not yet decided where I am to go and live for a while—Cambridge—Bury—*Oxford*?

I think I told you I kept on translating Calderon at odd times: and shall put up some five or six plays into a small Volume I think. But I want Cowell for some passages: and my Translation would be so free as to be rather a dangerous Experiment. But I think you can hardly make Calderon interesting to English Readers unless with a large latitude of interpretation.

I saw Mrs. Smith to-day—took tea there indeed: and she talked of you. Shall we all live and be in cue to meet somewhere here about this summer? Don't let Cowell forget us all in Pracrit. Is the Grammar out? I had a letter from Thackeray, from America: he flourishes greatly; but I thought his letter a disagreeable one, though kind as usual to me.

To W. F. Pollock

Boulge, Woodbridge, July 25/53
My dear Pollock,

Thank you for your letter. Though I believed the Calderon to be on the whole well done and entertaining, I began to wish to be told it was so by others, for fear I had made a total mistake: which would have been a bore. And the very free and easy translation lies open to such easy condemnation, unless it be successful.

Your account of Sherborne rouses all the Dowager within me. I shall have to leave this cottage, I believe, and have not yet found a place sufficiently dull to migrate to. Meanwhile to-morrow I am going to one of my great treats: viz. the Assizes at Ipswich: where I shall see little Voltaire Jervis,[1] and old Parke,[2] who I trust will have the gout, he bears it so Christianly.

[1] [Sir John Jervis (1802–56), Lord Chief Justice of Common Pleas.]
[2] [Baron Parke, afterwards Lord Wensleydale.]

To George Crabbe

Boulge, Woodbridge, Sept. 12/53

My dear George,

I enclose you a scrap from 'The Leader' as you like to see criticisms on my Calderon. I suppose your sisters will send you the Athenæum in which you will see a more determined spit at me. I foresaw (as I think I told you) how likely this was to be the case: and so am not surprized. One must take these chances if one will play at so doubtful a game. I believe those who read the Book, without troubling themselves about whether it is a free Translation or not, like it: but Critics must be supposed to know all, and it is safe to condemn. On the other hand, the Translation may not be good on any ground: and then the Critics are all right.

To E. B. Cowell

3 Park Villas West, Richmond, Surrey, October 25/53

My dear Cowell,

. . . I think I forgot to tell you that Mr Maccarthy (my literal Rival in Calderon) mentions in his Preface a masterly Critique on Calderon in the Westminster 1851, which I take to be yours.[1] He says it, and the included translations, are the best Commentary he has seen on the subject.

I have ordered Eastwick's Gulistan: for I believe I shall potter out so much Persian. The weak Apologue[2] goes on (for I have not had time for much here) and I find it difficult enough even with Jones's Translation.

I am now going to see the last of the Tennysons[3] at Twickenham.

[1] [It was.]
[2] ['The Gardener and the Nightingale' in Sir William Jones's *Persian Grammar*.]
[3] [Hallam Tennyson, born 11 August 1852.]

To Frederick Tennyson

Bredfield Rectory, Woodbridge. December 27/53
My dear Frederic,

I am too late to wish you a Happy Christmas; so must wish you a happy New Year. Write to me here, and tell me (in however few words) how you prospered in your journey to Italy: how you all are there: and how your Book progresses. I saw Harvest Home advertised in Fraser: and I have heard from Mrs Alfred it is so admired that Parker is to print two thousand copies of the Volume. I am glad of this, and I think, little ambitious or vain as you really are, you will insensibly be pleased at gaining your proper station in public Celebrity. Had I not known what an invidious office it is to meddle with such Poems, and how assuredly people would have said that one had helped to clip away the Best Poems, and the best part of them, I should have liked to advise you in the selection: a matter in which I feel confidence. But you would not have agreed with me any more than others: though on different grounds: and so in all ways it was, and is, and will be, best to say nothing more on the subject. I am very sure of that, of whatever your Volume is composed, you will make public almost the only Volume of Verse, except Alfred's, worthy of the name.

I hear from Mrs Alfred they are got to their new abode in the Isle of Wight. I have been into Norfolk: and am now come to spend Christmas in this place, where, as you have been here, you can fancy me. Old Crabbe is as brave and hearty as ever: drawing designs of churches: and we are all now reading Moore's Memoirs with considerable entertainment: I cannot say the result of it in one's mind is to prove Moore a Great Man: though it certainly does not leave him altogether 'The Poor Creature' that Mr Allingham reduced him to. I also amuse myself with poking out some Persian which E. Cowell would inaugurate me with: I go on with it because it is a point in common with him, and enables us to study a little together. He and his wife are at Oxford: and his Pracrit Grammar is to be out in a few days.

I have settled upon no new Abode: but have packed up my few

goods in a neighbouring Farm-House[1] (that one near Woodbridge I took you to), and will now float about for a year and visit some friends. Perhaps I shall get down to the Isle of Wight one day: also to Shropshire, to see Allen: to Bath to a Sister.[2] But you can always direct hither, since old Crabbe is only too glad to have some letters to pay for, and forward to me . . . We have one of the old fashioned winters, snow and frost: not fulfilling the word of those who were quite sure the seasons were altered. Farewell, my dear Frederic. E.F.G.

To W. F. Pollock

1 Long Wall Street, Oxford, March 15/54

My dear Pollock,

The whole history of my mighty Books is simply this. Wishing to do something as far as I could against a training System of which I had seen many bad effects, I published the little Dialogue;[3] but not having (for several other reasons) any desire to appear Author, I only told it to three men whom I wanted to puff the little Book in case they honestly thought it worth puffing in a good cause. Spedding did 'give me a wind' and Cowell (with whom I am here) another. Donne (who was my third man) for some reason or other did not puff the Book in print, but told my name in private; so as at last I was saluted with it in many quarters (above all in my own country neighbourhood where I least wanted it). So as at last, when Pickering broke up, and I put my small affairs into Parker's hand, I let him do as he liked, and lump all under one name. The Calderon I was obliged to print with some name because of a rival in the field; and so thought it as well at once to put my own.

N.B. I don't tell this long story for the Book's sake; but, as you have been so good as to write on the subject, to account for what might seem a whim, and moreover, a change of Whim, which I don't wish my friends to think me too lightly guilty of. I should almost write to Spedding on the subject, but it would only trouble him: and he has charity enough to guess a kind

[1] [Farlingay Hall.]   [2] [Mrs De Soyres.]   [3] [*Euphranor.*]

reason for his friend's actions. Pray thank Mrs Pollock for her message; this is not the proper occasion for me to say how much I value her opinion (except on Jenny Lind), which really is the case, though.

I was detained in London by accidentally meeting some country Ladies whose *Beau* had been called away from them. So I offered my services in Street and Theatre. You may tell Spedding I saw Kean's Richard III twice; and liked his Dress very much as King. Such very good colours.

At last I have got down to this delightful Oxford. With many so pleasant personal associations with Cambridge, I have never got to like the *place*; which has always a sordid look to me. Here, as you know, are wide clean streets, and the Colleges themselves more presentable on the whole than the unsatisfactory new Gothic at Cambridge. The façade of Christ Church to the Street (by Wren, I believe) is what most delights me: and the Voice of Tom in his Tower.

No—no—my dear Donne is not meant to be Lexilogised by me any way, nor any one else. You don't know Donne's fun yet.

To Frederick Tennyson

Bath, May 7/54

My dear Frederic. You see to what fashionable places I am reduced in my old Age. The truth is however I am come here by way of Visit to a sister I have scarce seen these six years; my visit consisting in this that I live alone in a lodging of my own by day, and spend two or three hours with her in the Evening. This has been my way of Life for three weeks, and will be so for some ten days more: after which I talk of flying back to more native countries. I was to have gone on to see Alfred in his 'Island Home' from here: but it appears he goes to London about the same time I quit this place; so I must and shall defer my Visit to him. Perhaps I shall catch a sight of him in London; as also of old Thackeray who, Donne writes me word, came suddenly on him in Pall Mall the other day: while all the while

T   577

people supposed the Newcomes were being indited at Rome or Naples.

If ever you live in England you must live here at Bath. It really is a splendid City in a lovely, even a noble, Country. Did you ever see it? One beautiful feature in the place is the quantity of Garden and Orchard it is all through embroidered with. Then the Streets, when you go into them, are as handsome and gay as London, gayer and handsomer because cleaner and in a cleaner Atmosphere; and if you want the Country you get into it (and a very fine Country) on all sides and directly. Then there is such Choice of Houses, Cheap as well as Dear, of all sizes, with good Markets, Railways &c. I am not sure I shall not come here for part of the Winter. It is a place you would like, I am sure: though I do not say but you are better in Florence. Then on the top of the hill is old Vathek's Tower, which he used to sit and read in daily, and from which he could see his own Fonthill, while it stood. Old Landor quoted to me 'Nullus in orbe locus &c.' apropos of Bath: he, you may know, has lived here for years, and I should think would die here, though not yet. He seems so strong that he may rival old Rogers; of whom indeed one Newspaper gave what is called an 'Alarming Report of Mr Rogers' Health' the other day, but another contradicted it directly and indignantly, and declared the Venerable Poet never was better. Landor has some hundred and fifty Pictures; each of which he thinks the finest specimen of the finest Master, and has a long story about, how he got it, when &c. I dare say some are very good: but also some very bad. He appeared to me to judge of them as he does of Books and Men; with a most uncompromising perversity which the Phrenologists must explain to us after his Death.

By the bye, about your Book, which of course you wish me to say something about. Parker sent me down a copy 'from the Author' for which I hereby thank you. If you believe my word, you already know my Estimation of so much that is in it: you have already guessed that I should have made a different selection from the great Volume which is now in Tatters. As I differ in Taste from the world, however, quite as much as from you, I do not know but you have done very much better in choosing as you have; the few people I have seen are very much pleased with it, the Cowells at Oxford delighted. A Bookseller there sold all his Copies the first day they came down: and even in Bath a Bookseller (and not one of the Principal) told me a fortnight ago he had sold some twenty Copies. I have not been in Town since it came out: and have now so little correspondence with literati I can't tell you about them. There was a very unfair Review in the Athenæum; which is the only Literary Paper I see: but I am told there are laudatory ones in Examiner and Spectator.

I was five weeks at Oxford, visiting the Cowells in just the same way that I am visiting my Sister here. I also liked Oxford greatly: but not so well I think as Bath: which is so large and busy that one is drowned in it as much as in London. There are often concerts &c. for those who like them; I only go to a shilling affair that comes off every Saturday at what they call the Pump Room. On these occasions there is sometimes some Good Music if not excellently played. Last Saturday I heard a fine Trio of Beethoven. Mendelssohn's things are mostly tiresome to me. I have brought my old Handel Book here and recreate myself now and then with pounding one of the old Giant's Overtures on my sister's Piano, as I used to do on that Spinnet at my Cottage. As to Operas, and Exeter Halls, I have almost done with them: they give me no pleasure, I scarce know why.

I suppose there is no chance of your being over in England this year, and perhaps as little Chance of my being in Italy. All I can say is, the latter is not impossible, which I suppose I may equally say of the former. But pray write to me. You can always direct to me at Donne's, 12 St James' Square, or at Rev. G. Crabbe's, Bredfield, Woodbridge. Either way the letter will soon reach me. Write soon, Frederic, and let me hear how you and yours are: and don't wait, as you usually do, for some inundation of the Arno to set your pen agoing. Write ever so shortly and whatever-about-ly. I have no news to tell you of Friends. I saw old Spedding in London; only doubly calm after the death of a Niece he dearly loved and whose death-bed at Hastings he had just been waiting upon. Harry Lushington wrote a martial Ode on seeing the Guards march over Waterloo Bridge towards the East: I did not see it, but it was much admired and handed about, I believe. And now my paper is out: and I am going through the rain (it is said to rain very much here) to my

Sister's. So Good Bye, and write to me, as I beg you, in reply to this long if not very interesting letter.

To E. B. Cowell

31 Great Portland Street, P. Place [1855]

My dear Cowell,

. . . You never say a word about your Hafiz. Has that fallen for the present, Austin not daring to embark in it in these days of war, when nothing that is not warlike sells except Macaulay? Don't suppose I bandy compliments; but, with moderate care, any such Translation of such a writer as Hafiz by you into pure, sweet, and partially measured Prose must be better than what I am doing for Jámí;[1] whose ingenuous prattle I am stilting into too Miltonic verse. This I am very sure of. But it is done.

To Thomas Carlyle

Bredfield Rectory, Woodbridge, August 1, [1855]

Dear Carlyle,

I came down here yesterday: and saw my Farming Friends to-day, who are quite ready to do all service for us at any time. They live about two miles nearer Woodbridge than this place I write from and I am certain they and their place will suit you very well. I am going to them any day: indeed am always fluctuating between this place and theirs; and you can come down to me there, or here, any day—(for Crabbe and his Daughter will, they bid me say, be very glad if you will come; and I engage you shan't be frightened, and that the place shall suit you as well as the Farmer's)—I say you can come to either place any day, and without warning if you like; only in that case I can't go to meet you at Ipswich: Beds etc. are all ready whether here or at the Farmer's. If you like to give me notice, you can say which place you will come to first: and I will meet you at any time at Ipswich.

[1] [Salámán and Absál.]

I think if you come you had best come as soon as possible, before harvest, and while the Days are long and fine. Why not come directly? while all the Coast is so clear?

Now as to your mode of going. There are Rail Trains to Ipswich from Shoreditch, at 7 a.m. 11 a.m. and 3 p.m. all of which come to Ipswich in time for Coaches which carry you to Woodbridge; where, if you arrive unawares, any one will show you the way to Mr Smith's, or Farlingay Hall, about half a mile from Woodbridge; or direct you to Parson Crabbe's, at Bredfield, about three miles from Woodbridge. You may take my word (will you?) that you will be very welcome at either or both of these places; I mean, to the owners as well as myself.

Well, then there is a Steamer every Wednesday and Sunday; which starts from Blackwall at 9 a.m.; to go by which you must be at the Blackwall Railroad Station in Fenchurch Street by half past eight. This Steamer gets to Ipswich at $\frac{1}{2}$ past 5 or 6; probably in time for a Woodbridge Coach, but not certainly. It is a very pleasant sail. The Rail to Ipswich takes three or two and a half hours.

Have I more to say? I can't think of it if I have. Only, dear Mrs Carlyle, please to let me know what C. is "*To Eat—Drink—and Avoid.*" As I know that his wants are in a small compass, it will be as easy to get what he likes as not, if you will only say. If you like Sunday Steam, it will be quite convenient whether here or at Farlingay. Crabbe only is too glad if one doesn't go to his church.

Bredfield, Sunday

Scrap for Scrap! I go tomorrow to stay at Farlingay, where you will find me, or I will find you, as proposed in my last. Do not let it be a burden on you to come now, then, or at all; but, if you come, I think this week will be good in weather as in other respects. You will be at most entire Liberty; with room, garden, and hours, to yourself, whether at Farlingay or here, where you must come for a day or so. Pipes are the order of the house at both places; the Radiator always lighting up after his 5 o'clock dinner, and rather despising me for not always doing so. At both places a capital sunshiny airy Bedroom without any noise. I wish Mrs C. could come, indeed; but I will not propose this; for though my Farm has good room, my Hostess would fret herself to entertain a Lady suitably, and that I would avoid, especially toward Harvest time. Will Mrs Carlyle believe this?

E. F. G.

P. S. Bring some Books. If you don't find yourself well, or at ease, with us, you have really but to go off without any sort of Ceremony as soon as you like: so don't tie yourself to any time at all. If the weather be fair, I predict you will like a week; and I shall like as much more as you please; leaving you mainly to your own devices all the while.

To Elizabeth Cowell

London. Friday [April 25, 1856]

My dear Lady,

The Picture after all did not go down yesterday as I meant, but shall and will go to-morrow (Saturday). Also I shall send you dear Major Moor's "Oriental Fragments"; an almost worthless Book, I doubt, to those who did not know him—which means, *love* him! And somehow all of us in our corner of Suffolk knew something of him: and so again loved something of him. For there was nothing at all about him not to be beloved. Ah! I think how interested he would have been with all this Persian: and how we should have disputed over parts and expressions over a glass of his Shiraz wine (for he had some) in his snug Parlour, or in his Cornfields when the Sun fell upon the latest Gleaners! He is dead, and you will go where he lived, to be dead to me!

Remember to take poor Barton's little Book with you to India; better than many a better Book to you there!

I got a glimpse of Professor Müller's Essay[1]—full of fine things; but I hardly gather it up into a good whole, which is very likely my fault; from hasty perusal, ignorance, or other Incapacity. Perhaps, on the other hand, he found the Subject too great for his Space; and so has left it disproportioned, which the German is not inapt to do. But one may well be thankful for such admirable fragments, perhaps left so in the very honesty

---

[1] ["Comparative Mythology," in the *Oxford Essays* for 1856.]

582

that is above rounding them into a specious Theory which will not hold.

To George Crabbe

31, Great Portland Street, Jan. 1, 1857

My dear George,

A good New Year to you! Here I am, and have been for the last Fortnight, *alone*: my Wife[1] having gone to Mr. Gurney's, and afterwards to Geldestone: and I remaining here partly to see through that mortgage with W. Browne which you remember my telling you about. There has been plenty of Bother, but I suppose it will be done, like some other things, for Better or Worse.

I am still in a total Quandary about a Place of Abode. My Wife has been asking about Norwich, where she heard of nothing except a Furnisht House in The Close, and an Unfurnisht on the Thorpe Road. So if we be in East Anglia now, I think we shall have to go to Lowestoft for a time. I want my wife to learn all she can of Housekeeping, and employ herself in it: I think she is given to Profusion, and her Hand is out of practice, of course.

I shall be down at Geldestone myself in a few days, and then settle where to go for a time. It is not Inclination that keeps me unsettled: but the not seeing my way at all clear; a matter in which I may perhaps know some more reason than you or others who would otherwise be far more competent to judge of any such matter than I am.

I have scarce seen any one here: but put my Eyes quite out over a silly Persian Manuscript by Day, and look into the Pit of a Theatre for an Hour at night when I can see no longer. What a waste of Life—if *my* Life ever could be worth living. I am rather weary of it.

Give my kind Remembrances to Barlow and his Lady. Tell him I will gladly accept the arm-chair he promises me: but let it not be a luxurious or ornamental one, but a plain Oak Chair: for I like, and will have, all of the plainest in my House . . .

[1] [EFG married Lucy Barton 4 November 1856.]

To E. B. Cowell

My dearest Cowell,

As usual I blunder. I have been taking for granted all this while that of course we could not write to you till you had written to us! Else how several times I could have written! Hafiz or Jámí or Nizámí that I thought wanted Comment of some kind: so as the Atlantic should have been no greater Bar between us than the two hours rail to Oxford. And now I have forgot many things, or have left the Books scattered in divers places; or, if I had all here 'twould be too much to send. So I must e'en take up with what the present Hour turns up.

It was only yesterday I heard from your Brother of a Letter from you, telling of your safe Arrival; of the Dark Faces about you at your Calcutta Caravanserai! Methinks how I should like to be there! Perhaps should not, though, were the Journey only half its length! Write to me one day . . .

I have now been five weeks alone at my old Lodgings in London where you came this time last year! My wife in Norfolk. She came up yesterday; and we have taken Lodgings for two months in the Regent's Park. And I positively stay behind here in the old Place on purpose to write to you in the same condition you knew me in and I you! I believe there are new Channels fretted in my Cheeks with many unmanly Tears since then, "remembering the Days that are no more," in which you two are so mixt up. Well, well; I have no news to tell you. Public Matters you know I don't meddle with; and I have seen scarce any Friends even while in London here. Carlyle but once; Thackeray not once; Spedding and Donne pretty often. Spedding's first volume of Bacon is out; some seven hundred pages; and the Reviews already begin to think it over-commentaried. How interested would you be in it! and from you I should get a good Judgment, which perhaps I can't make for myself. I hear Tennyson goes on with King Arthur; but I have not seen or heard from him for a long long while.

Oddly enough, as I finished the last sentence, Thackeray was announced; he came in looking gray, grand, and good-humoured;

and I held up this Letter and told him whom it was written to and he sends his Love! He goes Lecturing all over England; has fifty pounds for each Lecture: and says he is ashamed of the Fortune he is making. But he deserves it.

And now for my poor Studies. I have read really very little except Persian since you went: and yet, from want of Eyes, not very much of that. I have gone carefully over two thirds of Hafiz again with Dictionary and Von Hammer:[1] and gone on with Jámí and Nizámí. But my great Performance all lies in the last five weeks since I have been alone here; when I wrote to Napoleon Newton to ask him to lend me his MS. of Attár's Mantic uttair; and, with the help of Garcin de Tassy[2] have nearly made out about two-thirds of it. For it has greatly interested me, though I confess it is always an old Story. The Germans make a Fuss about the Súfi Doctrine; but, as far as I understand, it is not very abstruse Pantheism, and always the same. One becomes as wearied of the *man-i* and *du-i* in their Philosophy as of the *bulbul* &c. in their Songs. Attár's Doctrine seems to me only Jámí and Jeláleddín (of whom I have poked out a little from the MS. you bought for me), but his Mantic has, like Salámán, the advantage of having a Story to hang all upon; and some of his illustrative Stories are very agreeable: better than any of the others I have seen. He has not so much Fancy or Imagination as Jámí, nor I dare say, so much depth as Jeláleddín; but his touch is lighter. I mean to make a Poetic Abstract of the Mantic, I think: neither De Tassy nor Von Hammer gives these Stories which are by far the best part, though there are so many childish and silly ones. Shah Máhmúd figures in the best. I am very pleased at having got on so well with this MS. though I doubt at more cost of Eyesight than it is worth. I have exchanged several Letters with Mr Newton, though by various mischances we have not yet met; he has however introduced me to Mr Dowson of the Asiatic, with whom, or with a certain Seyd Abdúllah recommended by Allen, I mean (I think) to read a little. No need of this had you remained

[1] [J. von Hammer-Purgstall: *Geschichte der schönen Redekünste Persiens.*]
[2] [*Mémoire sur la poésie philosophique et religieuse chez les Persans.* His edition of the text of Attár's poem came out in 1857, but the French translation only in 1863.]

T*

behind! Oh! how I should like to read the Mantic with you! It is very easy in the main. But I believe I shall never see you again; I really do believe that. And my Paper is gradually overcome as I write this: and I must say Good Bye. Good Bye, my dear dear Friends! I dare not meddle with Mr and Mrs Charlesworth.[1] Thackeray coming in overset me, with one thing and another. Farewell. Write to me; direct—whither? For till I see better how we get on I dare fix on no place to live or die in. Direct to me at Crabbe's, Bredfield, till you hear further.

To E. B. Cowell

24 Portland Terrace, Regent's Park
Saturday January 23 [?24] 1857

My dear E. B. C.,

I must write you a second Letter (which will reach you, I suppose, by the same Post as that which I posted on Thursday Jan. 22) to tell you that not half an hour after I had posted that first Letter, arrived yours! And now, to make the Coincidence stranger, your brother Charles, who is now with us for two days, tells me that very Thursday Jan. 24 [? 22] is your Birthday! I am extremely obliged to you for your long, kind, and interesting Letter: yes, yes: I should have liked to be on the Voyage with you, and to be among the Dark People with you even now. Your Brother Charles, who came up yesterday, brought us up your Home Letter, and read it to us last night after Tea to our great Satisfaction. I believe that in my already posted Letter I have told you much that you enquire about in yours received half an hour after: of my poor Studies at all events. This morning I have been taking the Physiognomy of the 19th Birds. . . . There are, as I wrote you, very pleasant stories. One, of a Shah returning to his Capital, and his People dressing out a Welcome for him, and bringing out Presents of Gold, Jewels, &c. all which he rides past without any Notice, till, coming to the Prison, the Prisoners, by way of their Welcome, toss before him the Bloody Heads and Limbs of old and recent Execution. At which the Shah for the first time stops his Horse—smiles—casts Largess

[1] [Mrs Cowell's parents.]

586

among the Prisoners &c. And when asked why he neglected all
the Jewels &c. and stopped with satisfaction at such a grim welcome as the Prisoners threw him, he says, 'The Jewels &c. were
but empty Ostentation—but those bloody Limbs prove that my
Law has been executed, without which none of those Heads and
Carcases would have parted Company &c.' De Tassy notices a
very agreeable Story of Mahmúd and the Lad fishing: and I
find another as pleasant about Mahmúd consorting 'incog:' with
a Bath-Stove-Keeper, who is so good a Fellow that, at last,
Mahmúd, making himself known, tells the Poor Man to ask
what he will—a Crown, if he likes. But the poor Fellow says,
'All I ask is that the Shah will come now and then to me as I am,
and here where I am; here, in this poor Place, which he has
made illustrious with his Presence, and a better Throne to me
with Him, than the Throne of Both Worlds without Him &c.'
You observed perhaps in De Tassy's Summary that he notices
an Eastern Form of William Tell's Apple? A Sultan doats on a
beautiful Slave, who yet is seen daily to pine away under all the
Shah's Favour, and being askt why, replies, 'Because every day
the Shah, who is a famous Marksman with the Bow, shoots at an
Apple laid on my Head, and always hits it; and when all the
Court cries "Lo! the Fortune of the King!" he also asks me
why I turn pale under the Trial, he being such a Marksman, and
his Mark an Apple set on the Head he most doats upon?' I am
going to transcribe on the next Page a rough Draft of a Version
of another Story, because all this will amuse you, I think. I
couldn't help running some of these Apologues into Verse as I
read them: but they are in a very rough state as yet, and so perhaps may continue, for to correct is the Bore.

When Yúsúf from his Father's House was torn,
His Father's Heart was utterly forlorn;
And, like a Pipe with but one note, his Tongue
Still nothing but the name of Yúsúf rung.
Then down from Heaven's Branches came the Bird
Of Heaven, and said 'God wearies of that Word.
Hast thou not else to do, and else to say?'
So Yacúb's lips were sealed from that Day.
But one Night in a Vision, far away

His Darling in some alien Home he saw,
And stretch'd his Arms forth; and between the Awe
Of God's Displeasure, and the bitter Pass
Of Love and Anguish, sigh'd forth an *Alas!*
And stopp'd—But when he woke The Angel came,
And said, 'Oh, faint of purpose! Though the Name
Of that Belovèd were not utter'd by
Thy Lips, it hung sequester'd in that Sigh.'

You see this is very imperfect, and I am not always quite certain of always getting the right Sow by the Ear; but it is pretty anyhow. In this, as in several other Stories, one sees the fierce vindictive Character of the Eastern Divinity and Religion: a 'jealous God' indeed! So there is another Story of a poor Hermit, who retires into the Wilderness to be alone with God, and lives in a Tree, and there in the Branches a little Bird has a Nest, and sings so sweetly that the poor old Man's Heart is drawn to it in spite of Himself; till a Voice from Heaven calls to Him—'What are you about? You have bought *Me* with your Prayers &c. and I *You* by some Largess of Grace: and is this Bargain to be cancelled by the Piping of a little Bird?'[1] So I construe at least right or wrong. . . .

---

[1] [This Apologue FitzGerald afterwards turned into verse; but it remained an unfinished fragment. The words in square brackets were supplied by Cowell.

A Saint there was who threescore Years and ten
In holy Meditation among Men
Had spent, but, wishing, ere he came to close
With God, to meet him in complete Repose,
Withdrew into the Wilderness, where he
Set up his Dwelling in an agèd Tree
Whose hollow Trunk his Winter Shelter made,
And whose green branching Arms his Summer Shade.
And like himself a Nightingale one Spring
Making her Nest above his Head would sing
So sweetly that her pleasant Music stole
Between the Saint and his severer Soul,
And made him sometimes [heedless of his] Vows
Listening his little Neighbour in the Boughs.
Until one Day a sterner Music woke
The sleeping Leaves, and through the Branches spoke—
"What! is the Love between us two begun

Monday Jan. 25 [? 26]. Like your Journal, you see, I spread my Letter over more than a Day. On Saturday Night your Brother and I went to hear Thackeray lecture on George III.— very agreeable to me, though I did not think highly of the Lecture. . . . I should like to see Nizámí's Shírín, though I have not yet seen enough to care for in Nizámí. Get me a MS. if you can get a fair one; as also one of Attár's Birds; of which however Garcin de Tassy gives hint of publishing a Text. There might be a good Book made of about half the Text of the Original; for the Repetitions are many, and the stories so many of them not wanted. What a nice Book too would be the Text of some of the best Apologues in Jámí, Jeláleddín, Attár, &c. with literal Translations! . . .

I was with Borrow a week ago at Donne's, and also at Yarmouth three months ago: he is well, but not yet agreed with Murray. He read me a long Translation he had made from the Turkish: which I could not admire, and his Taste becomes stranger than ever.

24 Portland Terrace, Regent's Park

My dear Cowell,

. . . March 12. You see I leave this Letter like an unfinished Picture; giving it a touch every now and then. Meanwhile it lies in a volume of Sir W. Ouseley's Travels. Meanwhile also I keep putting into shape some of that Mantic which however would never do to publish. For this reason; that anything like a literal Translation would be, I think, unreadable; and what I have done for amusement is not only so unliteral, but I doubt unoriental, in its form and Expression, as would destroy the value of the Original without replacing it with anything worth reading of my own. It has amused me however to reduce the Mass into something of an Artistic Shape. There are lots of Passages which— how should I like to talk them over with you! Shall we ever meet again? I think not; or not in such plight, both of us, as will make Meeting what it used to be. Only to day I have been

> And waxing till we Two were nearly One,
> For three score Years of Intercourse unstirr'd
> Of Men, now shaken by a little Bird;
> And such a precious Bargain, and so long
> A making, [put in peril] for a Song?"]

opening dear old Salámán: the original Copy we bought and began this time three years ago at Oxford; with all my scratches of Query and Explanation in it, and the Notes from you among the Leaves. How often I think with Sorrow of my many Harshnesses and Impatiences! which are yet more of manner than intention. My wife is sick of hearing me sing in a doleful voice the old Glee of 'When shall we Three Meet again?' Especially the Stanza, 'Though in foreign Lands we sigh, Parcht beneath a hostile Sky &c.' How often too I think of the grand Song written by some Scotch Lady, which I sing to myself for you on Ganges Banks!

> Slow spreads the Gloom my Soul desires,
> The Sun from India's Shore retires:
> To *Orwell's* Bank, with temperate ray—
> Home of my Youth!—he leads the Day:
> Oh Banks to me for ever dear,
> Oh Stream whose Murmur meets my Ear;
> Oh all my Hopes of Bliss abide
> Where Orwell mingles with the Tide.

The Music has come to me for these Words, little good otherwise than expressive: but there is no use sending it to India. To India! It seems to me it would be easy to get into the first great Ship and never see Land again till I saw the Mouth of the Ganges! and there live what remains of my shabby Life.

But there is no good in all such Talk. I never write to you about Politics in which you know I little meddle. . . . March 20. Why, see how the Time goes! And here has my Letter been lying in Sir W. Ouseley for the last ten days, I suppose: To-day I have been writing twenty pages of a metrical Sketch of the Mantic, for such uses as I told you of. It is an amusement to me to take what Liberties I like with these Persians, who (as I think) are not Poets enough to frighten one from such excursions, and who really do want a little Art to shape them. I don't speak of Jeláleddín whom I know so little of (enough to show me that he is no great Artist, however), nor of Hafiz, whose *best* is untranslatable because he is the best Musician of Words. Old Johnson said the Poets were the best Preservers of a Language: for People must go to the Original to relish them. I am sure that what

Tennyson said to you is true: that Hafiz is the most Eastern—
or, he should have said, most *Persian*—of the Persians. He is
the best representative of their character, whether his Sáki and
Wine be real or mystical. Their Religion and Philosophy is soon
seen through, and always seems to me *cuckooed* over like a
borrowed thing, which people, once having got, don't know how
to parade enough. To be sure, their Roses and Nightingales are
repeated enough; but Hafiz and old Omar Khayyám ring like
true Metal. The Philosophy of the Latter is, alas, one that never
fails in the World! 'To-day is ours, &c.'

While I think of it, why is the Sea[1] (in that Apologue of Attár
once quoted by Falconer) supposed to have lost God? Did the
Persians agree with something I remember in Plato about the
Sea and all in it being of an inferior Nature, in spite of Homer's
'divine Ocean &c.' And here I come to the end of my sheet,
which you will hardly get through, I think. I scarce dare to think
of reading it over. But I will try.

To E. B. Cowell and Elizabeth Cowell

24 Portland Terrace, Regent's Park. March 29, [1857]

My dear Cowell,

I only posted my last long letter four days ago: and how far
shall I get with this? Like the other, I keep it in Sir W. Ouseley,
and note down a bit now and then. When the time for the Mail
comes, the sheet shall go whether full or not. I had a letter from
your Mother telling me she had heard from you—all well—but
the Heats encreasing. I suppose the Crocuses we see even in
these poor little Gardens hereabout would wither in a Glance of
your Sun. Now the black Trees in the Regent's Park opposite
are beginning to show green Buds; and Men come by with great
Baskets of Flowers; Primroses, Hepaticas, Crocuses, great
Daisies &c. calling as they go, 'Growing, Growing, Growing!
All the Glory going!' So my wife says she has heard them call:

[1] [This struck EFG so much that he introduced it into Omar Khayyám,
stanza xxxvi.]

some old Street cry, no doubt, of which we have so few now remaining. It will almost make you smell them all the way from Calcutta. 'All the Glory going!' What has put me upon beginning with this Sheet so soon is, that, (having done my Will for the present with the Mantic—one reason being that I am afraid to meddle more with N. Newton's tender MS., and another reason that I now lay by what I have sketched out so as to happen on it again one day with fresh eyes)—I say, this being shelved, I took up old Hafiz again, and began with him where I left off in November at Brighton. And this morning came to an ode we did together this time two years ago when you were at Spiers' in Oxford . . . How it brought all back to me! Oriel opposite, and the Militia in Broad Street, and the old Canary-coloured Sofa and the Cocoa or Tea on the Table! . . .

I should think Bramford begins to look pretty about this time, hey, Mr Cowell? And Mrs Cowell? There is a house there constantly advertised to let in the Papers. I think that one by the Mill; not the pleasant place where *Trygæus* looked forth on the Rail! 'The Days are gone when Beauty bright &c.' . . .

Spedding has been once here in near three months. His Bacon keeps coming out: his part, the Letters &c. of Bacon, is not come yet; so it remains to be seen what he will do then: but I can't help thinking he has let the Pot boil too long. Well, here is a great deal written to-day: and I shall shut up the Sheet in Ouseley again. March 30. Another reason for thinking the *máhi* which supports the world to be only a *myth* of the simple Fish genus is that the stage next above him is *Gau*, the Bull, as the Symbol of *Earth*. It seems to me one sees this as it were pictured in those Assyrian Sculptures; just some waving lines and a fish to represent Water &c. And it hooks on, I think, to Max Müller's Theory in that Essay of his. Saturday, April 4. Why, we are creeping toward another Post day! another 25th when the 'Viâ Marseilles' Letters go off! And I now renew this great Sheet, because in returning to old Hafiz two or three days ago, I happened on a line which you will confer with a Tetrastich of Omar's . . . Donne has got the Licenser's Post; given him in the handsomest way by Lord Bre[a]dalbane to whom the Queen as handsomely committed it. The said Donne has written an Article on Calderon in Fraser, in which he says very handsome things of me, but is not accurate in what he says. I suppose it was he wrote an Article in the Saturday Review some months ago to the same effect; but I have not asked him. I find people like that Calderon book. By the bye again, what is the passage I am to write out for you from the Volume you gave me, the old Bramford Volume, 'E. B. Cowell, Bramford, Aug. 20, 1849'? Tell me, and I will write it in my best style: I have the Volume here in my room, and was looking into it only last night; at that end of the Magico which we read together at Elmsett! I don't know if I could translate it now that the '*æstus*' caught from your sympathy is gone! . . . April 5. In looking into the 'Secreto Agravio' I saw an Oriental superstition, which was likely enough however to be a poetical fancy of any nation: I mean, the Sun turning Stone to Ruby &c. Enter Don Luis: 'Soy mercador, y trato en los Diamantes, que hoy son Piedras, y rayos fueron antes de Sol, que perficiona é ilumina rústico Grano en la abrasada Mina.' The Partridge in the Mantic tells something of the same; he digs up and swallows Rubies which turn his Blood to Fire inside him and sparkle out of his Eyes and Bill. This volume of Calderon is marked by the Days on which you finished several Plays, all at Bramford! Wednesday, April 8. I have been reading the 'Mágico' over and remembering other days; I saw *us* sitting at other tables reading it. Also I am looking over old Æschylus—Agamemnon—with Blackie's Translation. . . . Is it in Hafiz we have met the Proverb (about *pregnant* Night) which Clytemnestra also makes her Entry with [264, 5]? εὐάγγελος μὲν, ὥσπερ ἡ παροιμία, ἕως γένοιτο μητρὸς εὐφρόνης πάρα. I think one sees that the Oriental borrowed this Fancy, which smacks of the Grecian Deification of Mother Night. What an Epitaph for a Warrior are those two Greek words by which the Chorus express all that returns to Mycenæ of the living Hero who went forth [435] τεύχη καὶ σποδός!

Well; and I have had a note from Garcin de Tassy whom I had asked if he knew of any copy of Omar Khayyám in all the Paris Libraries: he writes 'I have made, by means of a Friend &c.' But I shall enclose his Note to amuse you. Now what I mean to do is, in return for his politeness to me, to copy out as well as I can the Tetrastichs as you copied them for me, and send them as a Present to De Tassy. Perhaps he will edit them.

I should not wish him to do so if there were any chance of your ever doing it; but I don't think you will help on the old Pantheist, and De Tassy really, after what he is doing for the Mantic, deserves to make the acquaintance of this remarkable little Fellow. Indeed I think you will be pleased that I should do this. Now for some more Æschylus. Friday, April 17. I have been for the last five days with my brother at Twickenham; during which time I really copied out Omar Khayyám, in a way! and shall to-day post it as a '*cadeau*' to Garcin de Tassy in return for his Courtesy to me. I am afraid, a bad return: for my MS. is but badly written and it would perhaps more plague than profit an English 'savant' to have such a present made him. But a Frenchman gets over all this very lightly. Garcin de Tassy tells me he has printed four thousand lines of the Mantic. And here is April running away and it will soon be time to post you another Letter! When I once get into the Country I shall have less to write you about than now; and that, you see, is not much.

Tuesday, April 21. Yours and your wife's dear good Letters put into my hand as I sit in the sunshine in a little Balcony outside the Windows looking upon the quite green hedge side of the Regent's Park. For Green it is thus early, and such weather as I never remember before at this Season. Well, your Letters, I say, were put into my hand as I was there looking into Æschylus under an Umbrella, and waiting for Breakfast. My wife cried a good deal over your wife's Letter, I think, I think so. Ah me! I would not as yet read it, for I was already sad; but I shall answer hers to me which I did read indeed with many thoughts: perhaps I can write this post; at least I will clear off this letter to you, my dear Cowell. E. F. G.

April 21.

My dear Lady, I have told E. B. C. at the close of my long letter to him how his and yours were put into my hand this morning. Well, as in telling him that I finished that sheet of Paper, I will e'en take one scrap more to thank you; and (since you have, I believe, some confidences together) some things I have yet got to say to him shall be addressed to you; and you can exercise your own discretion as to telling him. One thing tell

594

him however, which my overflowing Sheet had not room for, and was the very thing that most needed telling: viz. that he, a busy man, must not feel bound to write me as long Letters in return. Who knows how long I shall keep up any thing like to my own mark; for I daily grow worse with the Letter-pen: and beside his other employments, the Sun of India will '*belaze*' him (I doubt if the word be in Johnson). But 'vogue la Galère' while the wind blows! Again you may give him the enclosed instead of a former Letter from the same G. de T. For is it not odd he should not have time to read a dozen of those 150 Tetrastichs? I pointed out such a dozen to him of the best, and told him if he liked them I would try and get the rest better written for him than I could write. I had also told him that the whole thing came from E. B. C. and I now write to tell him I have no sort of intention of writing a paper in the Journal Asiatique, nor I suppose E. B. C. neither. G. de Tassy is very civil to me however. How much I might say about your Letter to me! you will hardly comprehend how it is I almost turn my Eyes from it in this Answer, and dally with other matter. You make me sad with old Memories; yet, I don't mean quite disagreeably sad, but enough to make me shrink recurring to them. I don't know whether to be comforted or not when *you* talk of India as a Land of Exile— . . .

Wednesday, April 22. Now this morning comes a second Letter from Garcin de Tassy saying that his first note about Omar Khayyám was 'in haste': that he has read some of the Tetrastichs which he finds not very difficult; some difficulties which are probably errors of the 'copist'; and he proposes his writing an Article in the Journal Asiatique on it in which he will 'honourably mention' E. B. C. and E. F. G. I now write to deprecate all this: putting it on the ground (and a fair one) that we do not yet know enough of the matter: that I do not wish E. B. C. to be made answerable for errors which E. F. G. (the '*copist*') may have made: and that E. F. G. neither merits nor desires any honourable mention as a Persian Scholar: being none. Tell E. B. C. that I have used his name with all caution, referring De Tassy to Vararuchi &c. But these Frenchmen are so self-content and superficial, one never knows how they will take up anything. To turn to other matters—we are talking of leaving this place almost directly . . . I often wonder if I shall ever see you both again! Well, for the present Adieu, Adieu, Adieu!

To E. B. Cowell

London, May 7/57

My dear Cowell,

Owing partly to my own Stupidity, and partly to a change in the India Post days, my last two letters (to you and wife) which were quite ready by the Marseilles Post of April 25th will not get off till the Southampton Mail of this May 10. Your Letter of March 21 reached me three days ago. Write only when you have Leisure and Inclination, and only as much as those two good things are good for: I will do the same. I will at once say (in reply to a kind offer you make to have Hatifi's 'Haft Paikar' copied for me) that it will [be] best to wait till you have read it; you know me well enough to know whether it will hit my taste. However, if it be but a very short poem, no harm would be done by a Copy: but do let me be at the Charges of such things. I will ask for Hatifi's Laili: but I didn't (as you know) take much to what little I saw. As to any copies Allen might have had, I believe there is no good asking for them: for, only yesterday going to put into Madden's hands Mr Newton's MS. of the Mantic, I saw Allen's house *kharáb*. There had been a Fire there, Madden told me, which had destroyed stock &c., but I could not make much out of the matter, Madden putting on a Face of foolish mystery. You can imagine it? We talked of you, as you may imagine also: and I believe in that he is not foolish. Well, and to-day I have a note from the great De Tassy which announces, 'My dear Sir, Definitively I have written a little Paper upon Omar with some Quotations taken here and there at random, avoiding only the too badly sounding *rubayát*. I have read that paper before the Persian Ambassador and suite, at a meeting of the Oriental Society of which I am Vice President, the Duc de Dondeauville being president. The Ambassador has been much pleased of my quotations.' So you see I have done the part of an ill Subject in helping France to ingratiate herself with Persia when England might have had the start! I suppose it probable

Ferukh Khan himself had never read or perhaps heard of Omar. I think I told you in my last that I had desired De Tassy to say nothing about you in any Paper he should write; since I cannot have you answerable for any blunders I may have made in my Copy, nor may you care to be named with Omar at all. I hope the Frenchman will attend to my desire; and I dare say he will, as he will then have all credit to himself. He says he can't make out the metre of the *rubayát* at all—never could—though 'I am enough skilful in scanning the Persian verses as you have seen' (Qy?) 'in my Prosody of the languages of Musulman Countries &c.' So much for De Tassy. No; but something more yet: and better, for he tells me his Print of the Mantic is finisht, 'in proofs,' and will be out in about a Month: and he will send me one. Now, my dear Cowell, can't I send one to you? Yes, we must manage that somehow.

Well, I have not turned over Johnson's Dictionary for the last month, having got hold of Æschylus. I think I want to turn his Trilogy into what shall be readable English Verse; a thing I have always thought of, but was frightened at the Chorus. So I am now; I can't think them so fine as People talk of: they are terribly maimed; and all such Lyrics require a better Poet than I am to set forth in English. But the better Poets won't do it; and I cannot find one readable translation. I shall (if I make one) make a very free one; not for Scholars, but for those who are ignorant of Greek, and who (so far as I have seen) have never been induced to learn it by any Translations yet made of these Plays. I think I shall become a bore, of the Bowring order, by all this Translation: but it amuses me without any labour, and I really think I have the faculty of making some things readable which others have hitherto left unreadable. But don't be alarmed with the anticipation of another sudden volume of Translations; for I only sketch out the matter, then put it away; and coming on it one day with fresh eyes trim it up with some natural impulse that I think gives a natural air to all. So I have put away the Mantic. When I die, what a farrago of such things will be found! Enough of such matter . . .

Friday, June 5! What an interval since the last sentence! And why? Because I have been moving about nearly ever since till yesterday, and my Letter, thus far written, was packt up in a

Box sent down hither, namely, Gorlestone Cliffs, Great Yarmouth. Instead of the Regent's Park and Regent Street, here before my windows are the Vessels going in and out of this River: and Sailors walking about with fur caps and their brown hands in their Breeches Pockets. Within hail almost lives George Borrow who has lately published, and given me, two new Volumes of Lavengro called 'Romany Rye,' with some excellent things, and some very bad (as I have made bold to write to him —how shall I face him!). You would not like the Book at all, I think. But I must now tell you an odd thing, which will also be a sad thing to you. I left London last Tuesday fortnight for Bedfordshire, meaning to touch at Hertford in passing; but, as usual, bungled between two Railroads and got to Bedford, and not to Hertford, on the Tuesday Evening. To that latter place I had wanted to go, as well to see it, as to see N. Newton, who had made one or two bungled efforts to see me in London. So, when I got to Bedford, I wrote him a line to say how it was I had missed him. On the very Saturday immediately after, I received a Hertford Paper announcing the sudden Death of N. Newton on the very Tuesday on which I had set out to see him! He had been quite well till the Saturday preceding: had then caught some illness (I suppose some infectious fever) which had been visiting some in his house; died on the Tuesday, and was buried on the Thursday after! What will Austin do without him? He had written to me about your Hafiz saying he had got several subjects for Illustration, and I meant to have a talk with him on the matter. What should be done? I dare not undertake any great responsibility in meddling in such a matter even if asked to do so, which is not likely to be unless on your part; for I find my taste so very different from the Public that what I think good would probably be very unprofitable.

When in Bedfordshire I put away almost all Books except Omar Khayyám!, which I could not help looking over in a Paddock covered with Buttercups and brushed by a delicious Breeze, while a dainty racing Filly of W. Browne's came startling up to wonder and snuff about me. 'Tempus est quo Orientis Aurâ mundus renovatur, Quo de fonte pluviali dulcis Imber reseratur; *Musi-manus* undecumque ramos insuper splendescit; Jesu-spiritusque Salutaris terram pervagatur.' Which is to be read as Monkish Latin, like 'Dies Iræ' &c., retaining the Italian value of the Vowels, not the Classical. You will think me a perfectly Aristophanic Old Man when I tell you how [much] of Omar I could not help running into such bad Latin. I should not confide such follies but to you who won't think them so, and who will be pleased at least with my still harping on our old Studies. You would be sorry, too, to think that Omar breathes a sort of Consolation to me! Poor Fellow; I think of him, and Oliver Basselin, and Anacreon; lighter Shadows among the Shades, perhaps, over which Lucretius presides so grimly.— Thursday, June 11. Your letter of April is come to hand, very welcome; and I am expecting the MS. Omar which I have written about to London. And now with respect to your proposed Fraser Paper on Omar. You see a few lines back I talk of some lazy Latin Versions of his Tetrastichs, giving one clumsy example. Now I shall rub up a few more of those I have sketched in the same manner, in order to see if you approve, if not of the thing done, yet of

[Letter breaks off abruptly at the end of the page.]

June 23. I begin another Letter because I am looking into the Omar MS. you have sent me, and shall perhaps make some notes and enquiries as I go on. I had not intended to do so till I had looked all over and tried to make out what I could of it; since it is both pleasant to oneself to find out for oneself if possible, and also saves trouble to one's friends. But yet it will keep me talking with you as I go along: and if I find I say silly things or clear up difficulties for myself before I close my Letter (which has a month to be open in!) why, I can cancel or amend, so as you will see the whole Process of Blunder. I think this MS. furnishes some opportunities for one's critical faculties, and so is a good exercise for them, if one wanted such! First however I must tell you how much ill poor Crabbe has been: a sort of Paralysis, I suppose, in two little fits, which made him think he was sure to die: but Dr Beck at present says he may live many years with care. Of this also I shall be able to tell you more before I wind up. The brave old Fellow! he was quite content to depart, and had his Daughter up to give her his Keys, and tell her where the different wines were laid! I must also tell you that Borrow is greatly delighted with your MS. of Omar which I showed him: delighted at the terseness so unusual in Oriental Verse. But his Eyes are apt to cloud: and his wife has been obliged, he tells me, to carry off even the little Omar out of reach of them for a while. . . .

June 27. Geldestone Hall. I brought back my two Nieces here yesterday: and to-day am sitting as of old in my accustomed Bedroom, looking out on a Landscape which your Eyes would drink. It is said there has not been such a Flush of Verdure for years: and they are making hay on the Lawn before the house, so as one wakes to the tune of the Mower's scythe-whetting, and with the old Perfume blowing in at open windows. . . .

July 1. June over! A thing I think of with Omar-like sorrow. And the Roses here are blowing—and going—as abundantly as even in Persia. I am still at Geldestone, and still looking at Omar by an open window which gives over a Greener Landscape than yours. To-morrow my eldest Nephew, Walter Kerrich, whom I first took to school, is to be married in the Bermudas to a young Widow. He has chosen his chosen sister Andalusia's Birthday to be married on: and so we are to keep that double Festival. . . .

[Extract from letter begun 3 July 1857.]

Monday, July 13. This day year was the last I spent with you at Rushmere! We dined in the Evening at your Uncle's in Ipswich, walking home at night together. The night before (yesterday year) you all went to Mr Maude's Church, and I was so sorry afterward I had not gone with you too; for the last time, as your wife said. One of my manifold stupidities, all avenged in a Lump now! I think I shall close this letter to-morrow: which will be the Anniversary of my departure from Rushmere. I went from you, you know, to old Crabbe's. Is he too to be wiped away by a yet more irrecoverable exile than India? By to-morrow I shall have finisht my first Physiognomy of Omar, whom I decidedly prefer to any Persian I have yet seen, unless perhaps Salámán.

Tuesday, July 14. Here is the Anniversary of our Adieu at Rushmere. And I have been (rather hastily) getting to an end of my first survey of the Calcutta Omar, by way of counterpart to

600

our joint survey of the Ouseley MS. then. I suppose we spoke of it this day year; probably had a final look at it together before I went off, in some Gig, I think, to Crabbe's. We hear rather better Report of him, if the being likely to live a while longer is better. I shall finish my Letter to-day; only leaving it open to add any very particular word. I must repeat I am sure this Calcutta Omar is, in the same proportion with the Ouseley, by as good a hand as the Ouseley: by as good a hand, if not Omar's; which I think you seemed to doubt if it was, in one of your letters. . . .

Have I previously asked you to observe 486, of which I send a poor Sir W. Jones' sort of Parody which came into my mind walking in the Garden here; where the Rose is blowing as in Persia? And with this poor little Envoy my Letter shall end. I will not stop to make the Verse better.

> I long for wine! oh Sáki of my Soul,
> Prepare thy Song and fill the morning Bowl;
> For this first Summer month that brings the Rose
> Takes many a Sultan with it as it goes.

To George Borrow

Wednesday [June 1857]

Dear Borrow,

My wife writes to yours. Let me say to you, that as I have declined two or three little Invitations from some of our near Neighbours here, I cannot go with any face to your House on such Invitation, can I? If one happens to drop in at tea, or Grog, time—all very well. I shall hope to give you a look before you go; perhaps bringing a gay little Niece who is just now brightening my Life.

Will you have poor old Omar to travel with? I find the Calcutta MS. abounding with as good things as what you saw; as good, not better, and too much to the same tune. But for all that, he is the best Persian I have seen.

'You, oh God, who gave me such a turn for drinking—may it be, you were drunk, when you created me!' says he. Yet here is a more pious one, tersely expressed.

Alas, that life is gone in vain!
My every mouthful is unlawful, every breath is tainted;
Commands not fulfilled have disgraced me;
And alas for my unlawful deeds![1]

Written in pencil because of a vile pen, and so Adieu.

E. FitzGerald

I hear from old Donne, who is got with satisfaction to his new house—rejoiced to leave London and its Libraries.[2]

To George Crabbe the Younger

Goldington, Sat., Septr. 19/57

My dear George,

I got your Letter to-day. In case I should not go to the Funeral, it will only be from my nervous fear of making any Figure in it: and I can't feel sure but I might make too much of one, for it is certain I feel your Father's loss more than any I have felt—except Major Moor's perhaps, whom, if I had known longer, I had not lived nearly so much with. If I go, it will be rather for the sake of the Living. I want your Sisters so much to go to my Wife at Gorlestone, when they can, and for as long as they can: and I have had a Letter from her to-day, hoping so they *will* but let her in that way return them some of the Sympathy they showed her when *her* Trial was. I am convinced that their going to her would be the very thing for herself, poor Soul; taking her out of herself, and giving her the very thing she is pining for; namely, some one to devote herself to. I write to your Sister to say this. And mind you tell me any use I can be to you, for I can't say what a pleasure it will be to me, and what a heap of unrepaid obligations I feel always on my Shoulders for the kindness and all the happy peaceful Times I have experienced at Bredfield for the last ten years.

In case I do go to the Funeral, I can put up at the Castle, or at Mrs Garrod's, can't I? I want to keep clear of Woodbridge and all Friends, and to talk to nobody about one who has left

[1] [The lines are written in Persian in the original letter.]
[2] [W. B. Donne resigned the Librarianship of the London Library in 1857.]

nobody I care to talk to him about; except Drew; and I almost dread becoming too sad with remembering our old Days!

My dear George, don't misunderstand me in case I don't appear on the Day; and don't mistrust all my little Professions of Sympathy. I shall know better to-morrow: but I do not like putting off writing.

I will think over the Ipswich Journal; but have become afraid of meddling with another's Memory: and of one worth many hundred wretches like myself.

To E. B. Cowell

Rushmere, October 3/57

My dear Cowell,

I hope things will not be so black with you and us by the time this Letter reaches you, but you may be amused and glad to have it from me. Not that I have come into Suffolk on any cheerful Errand: I have come to bury dear old Mr Crabbe! I suppose you have had some Letters of mine telling you of his Illness; Epileptic Fits which came successively and weakened him gradually, and at last put him to his Bed entirely, where he lay some while unable to move himself or to think! They said he might lie so a long time, since he eat and drank with fair Appetite: but suddenly the End came on and after a twelve hours Stupor he died. On Tuesday September 22 he was buried; and I came from Bedfordshire (where I had only arrived two days before) to assist at it. I and Mr Drew were the only persons invited not of the Family: but there were very many Farmers and Neighbours come to pay respect to the remains of the brave old Man, who was buried, by his own desire, among the poor in the Churchyard in a Grave that he wishes to be no otherwise distinguisht than by a common Head and Footstone. . . .

You may imagine it was melancholy enough to me to revisit the house when He who had made it so warm for me so often lay cold in his Coffin unable to entertain me any more! His little old dark Study (which I called the 'Cobblery') smelt strong of its old Smoke: and the last Cheroot he had tried lay three quarters smoked in its little China ash-pan. This I have taken as a Relic, as also a little silver Nutmeg Grater which used to give the finishing Touch to many a Glass of good hot Stuff, and also had belonged to the Poet Crabbe. . . .

Last night I had some of your Letters read to me: among them one but yesterday arrived, not very sunshiny in its prospects: but your Brother thinks the Times Newspaper of yesterday somewhat bids us look up. Only all are trembling for Lucknow crowded with Helplessness and Innocence! I am ashamed to think how little I understand of all these things: but have wiser men, and men in Place, understood much more? or, understanding, have they *done* what they should? . . .

Love to the dear Lady, and may you be now and for time to come safe and well is the Prayer of yours E. F. G.

To E. B. Cowell

[Merton Rectory.] September 3/58

My dear Cowell,

. . . Now about my Studies, which, I think, are likely to dwindle away too. I have not turned to Persian since the Spring; but shall one day look back to it: and renew my attack on the 'Seven Castles,'[1] if that be the name. I found the Jámí MS. at Rushmere: and there left it for the present: as the other Poem will be enough for me for my first onslaught. I believe I will do a little a day, so as not to lose what little knowledge I had. As to my Omar: I gave it to Parker in January, I think: he saying Fraser was agreeable to take it. Since then I have heard no more; so as, I suppose, they don't care about it: and may be quite right. Had I thought they would be so long however I would have copied it out and sent it to you: and I will still do so from a rough and imperfect Copy I have (though not now at hand) in case they show no signs of printing me. My Translation will interest you from its *Form*, and also in many respects in its *Detail*: very unliteral as it is. Many Quatrains are mashed together: and something lost, I doubt, of Omar's Simplicity, which is so much a Virtue in him. But there it is, such as it is. I purposely said in the very short notice I prefixed to the Poem that it was so short

[1] [Hatifi's Haft Paikar, a poem on the Seven Castles of Bahrám Gúr.]

because better Information might be furnished in another Paper, which I thought *you* would undertake. So it rests. Nor have I meddled with the Mantic lately: nor does what you say encourage me to do so. For what I had sketcht out was very paraphrase indeed. I do not indeed believe that any readable Account (unless a prose Analysis for the History and Curiosity of the Thing) will be possible, for *me* to do, at least. But I took no great pleasure in what I had done: and every day get more and more a sort of Terror at re-opening any such MS. My '*Go*' (such as it was) is *gone*, and it becomes *Work*: and the Upshot is not worth *working* for. It was very well when it was a Pleasure. So it is with Calderon. It is well enough to sketch such things out in warm Blood; but to finish them in cold! I wish I could finish the 'Mighty Magician' in my new way: which I know you would like, in spite of your caveat for the Gracioso. I have not wholly dropt the two Students, but kept them quite under; and brought out the religious character of the Piece into stronger Relief. But as I have thrown much, if not into Lyric, into Rhyme, which strikes a more Lyric Chord. I have found it much harder to satisfy myself than with the good old Blank Verse, which I used to manage easily enough, The 'Vida es Sueño' again, though blank Verse, has been difficult to arrange; here also Clarin is not quenched, but subdued: as is all Rosaura's Story, so as to assist, and not compete with, the main Interest. I really wish I could finish these some lucky day: but, as I said, it is so much easier to leave them alone; and when I had done my best, I don't know if they are worth the pains, or whether any one (except you) would care for them even if they were worth caring for. So much for my grand Performances, except that I amuse myself with jotting down materials (out of Vocabularies etc.) for a Vocabulary of *rural* English, or *rustic* English: that is, only the best country words selected from the very many Glossaries etc. relating chiefly to country matters, but also to things in general: words that carry their own story with them, without needing Derivation or Authority, though both are often to be found. I always say I have heard the Language of Queen Elizabeth's, or King Harry's Court, in the Suffolk Villages: better a great deal than that spoken in London Societies, whether Fashionable or Literary: and the homely [strength] of which has made Shakespeare, Dryden, South, and Swift, what they could not have been without it. But my Vocabulary if ever done will be a very little Affair—if ever done: for here again it is pleasant enough to jot down a word now and then, but not to equip all for the Press.

To E. B. Cowell

Farlingay, Woodbridge. Nov. 2/58.

My dear Cowell,

. . . No. I have not read the Jámí Díwán; partly because I find my Eyes are none the better, and partly because I have now no one to "prick the sides of my Intent"; not even "Vaulting Ambition" now. I have got the Seven Castles in my Box here and old Johnson's Dictionary; and these I shall strike a little Fire out of by and by: Jámí also in time perhaps. I have nearly finisht a metrical Paraphrase and Epitome of the Mantic: but you would scarce like it, and who else would? It has amused me to give a 'Bird's Eye' View of the Bird Poem in some sixteen hundred lines. I do not think one could do it as Salámán is done. As to Omar, I hear and see nothing of it in Fraser yet: and so I suppose they don't want it. I told Parker he might find it rather dangerous among his Divines: he took it however, and keeps it. I really think I shall take it back; add some Stanzas which I kept out for fear of being too strong; print fifty copies and give away; one to you, who won't like it neither. Yet it is most ingeniously tesselated into a sort of Epicurean Eclogue in a Persian Garden.

To E. B. Cowell

88 Gt. Portland St., London, Jan. 13/59

My dear Cowell,

I have been here some five weeks: but before my Letter reaches you shall probably have slid back into the Country somewhere. This is my old Lodging, but new numbered. I have been almost alone here: having seen even Spedding and Donne but two or three times. They are well and go on as before. Spedding has got out the seventh volume of Bacon, I believe:

with Capital Prefaces to Henry VII. &c. But I have not yet seen it. After vol. viii. (I think) there is to be a Pause: till Spedding has set the Letters to his Mind. Then we shall see what he can make of his Blackamoor. . . .

I am almost ashamed to write to you, so much have I forsaken Persian, and even all good Books of late. There is no one now to "prick the Sides of my Intent"; Vaulting Ambition having long failed to do so! I took my Omar from Fraser [? Parker], as I saw he didn't care for it; and also I want to enlarge it to near as much again, of such Matter as he would not dare to put in Fraser. If I print it, I shall do the impudence of quoting your Account of Omar, and your Apology for his Freethinking: it is not wholly my Apology, but you introduced him to me, and your excuse extends to that which you have not ventured to quote, and I do. I like your Apology extremely also, allowing its Point of View. I doubt you will repent of ever having showed me the Book. I should like well to have the Lithograph Copy of Omar which you tell of in your Note. My Translation has its merit: but it misses a main one in Omar, which I will leave you to find out. The Latin Versions, if they were corrected into decent Latin, would be very much better. . . . I have forgotten to write out for you a little Quatrain which Binning found written in Persepolis; the Persian Tourists having the same propensity as English to write their Names and Sentiments on their national Monuments.

To W. H. Thompson

10 Marine Terrace, Lowestoft. Nov. 27, 1859.
My dear Thompson,

After a Fortnight's Visit to my Sister's (where I caught Cold which flew at once to my Ears, and there hangs) I returned hither, as the nearest Place to go to, and here shall be till Christmas at all Events. I wish to avoid London this winter: and indeed seem almost to have done with it, except for a Day's Business or Sightseeing every now and then. Often should I like to roam about old Cambridge, and hear St Mary's Chimes at Midnight —but—but! This Place of course is dull enough: but here's the Old Sea (a dirty Dutch one to be sure) and Sands, and Sailors, a very fine Race of Men, far superior to those in Regent Street. Also the Dutchmen (an ugly set whom I can't help liking for old Neighbours) come over in their broad Bottoms and take in Water at a Creek along the Shore. But I believe the East winds get very fierce after Christmas, when the Sea has cooled down. You won't come here, to be sure: or I should be very glad to smoke a Cigar, and have a Chat: and I would take care to have a Fire in your Bedroom this time: a Negligence I was very sorry for in London.

I read, or was told, they wouldn't let old Alfred's Bust into your Trinity. They are right, I think, to let no one in there (as it should be in Westminster Abbey) till a hundred Years are past; when, after too much Admiration (perhaps) and then a Reaction of undue Dis-esteem, Men have settled into some steady Opinion on the subject: supposing always that the Hero survives so long, which of itself goes far to decide the Question. No doubt A. T. will do *that.* . . .

To George Crabbe the Younger

Market Hill, Woodbridge. Decr. 28/60

My dear George,

. . . I forgot to tell you I really ran to London three weeks ago: by the morning Express, and was too glad to rush back by the Evening Ditto. I went up for a Business I of course did not accomplish: did not call on, or see, a Friend: couldn't get into the National Gallery: and didn't care a straw for Holman Hunt's Picture. No doubt, there is Thought and Care in it: but what an outcome of several Years and sold for several Thousands! What Man with the Elements of a Great Painter could come out with such a costive Thing after so long waiting! Think of the Acres of Canvas Titian or Reynolds would have covered with grand Outlines and deep Colours in the Time it has taken to niggle this Miniature! The Christ seemed to me only a wayward Boy: the Jews, Jews no doubt: the Temple I dare say very correct in its Detail: but think of even Rembrandt's Woman in Adultery at the National Gallery; a much smaller Picture, but how much vaster in Space and Feeling! Hunt's Picture stifled me with its Littleness. I think Ruskin must see what his System has led to.

I have just got Lady Waterford's 'Babes in the Wood,' which are well enough, pretty in Colour: only, why has she made so bad a Portrait of one of her chief Performers, whose Likeness is so easily got at, the Robin Redbreast? This Lady Waterford was at Gillingham this Summer: and my Sister Eleanor said (as Thackeray had done) she was something almost to worship for unaffected Dignity.

To W. M. Donne

Market hill: Woodbridge. [February 1861]
My dear Mowbray,

I am very much obliged to you indeed for taking Trouble about the Cigars. I am so bad a Judge myself that I try to get others to judge for me: & I don't think Woodbridge abounds in Conoisseurs. *Three* of the most reliable I can get hold of, however, pronounce the *Cabanas* to be much better than the *Partages*: and a very good Cigar—A Banker's Clerk indeed wrote me word it was "such a Weed as the Gods might smoke when they went *a nutting.*" My Lad also from Aldboro, whose Mouth one w^d. have thought desecrated by Shag & Cavendish, pronounced at once for Cabanas over Partages:—so I will have more of *Cabanas* when I want. Indeed, it might be well to lay in a little Store now. However I enclose P. O. with many Thanks for what I have had.

I can only wonder your dear old Dad has kept his Head well so long with all the work he has given it: and Heart too. Mine would have given way long, long ago. You must not let him hack away his Brain at Reviews &c. He surely *need* not: you must get him out. I certainly hope he will come for a *Blow* here: when fine weather comes: not before: for the place is only for "Mark Tapley" as F. Tennyson calls me, at present.

I have had my young Sailor here for a Visit: it is now his turning Point of Life: whether he is to stay with Father, Mother, & Sweetheart, fishing at Aldbro:—or go out in a *Square-rigg'd* Vessel (humph!) for 5 or 6 years, & learn what will qualify him to come home & be a *Pilot*. *This* w^{d.} be best for *him*: but "Father & Mother & Sue"—& even E. F.G.—don't want to lose Sight of him so long, perhaps for ever, some of us.

February 17

Since writing the foregoing, I have been over to Aldboro, & we are to stay on shore with a Boat which was to be begun yesterday—to be finished (it is hoped) in time for Herrings & *Pleasuring*—I have made Acquaintance with the *"Sweetheart"* too: (a nice looking Girl) & have even proposed *that* for the Name of the New Boat—No doubt the Lad would have done best going out to Sea, as I said: it will be a Life of something near Penury on Shore, I think, when the Sweetheart becomes *M^{rs}* & breeds accordingly. As it is, they scarce get a Bit of Meat once a Week: whereas, on Board, they have plenty—as you have of the Subject—

I was not surprized to hear of Donaldson's Death after what your Dad had written to me about him. One begins to look for one's Contemporaries falling from the Bough—as also—but one must not be egotistical.

My love to Dad & Sisters. Always yrs
E. F.G.

I should really like to know if one could make *sure* of Don Pereira sending one a Pound more of the *Cabanas* if one wanted. The *Partages* are said to be coarse, & very inferior.

To George Crabbe the Younger

Market-hill, Woodbridge. Whitmonday [May 20, 1861]
My dear George,

. . . I take pleasure in my new little Boat: and last week went with her to Aldbro; and she *'behaved'* very well both going and returning; though, to be sure there was not much to try her Temper. I am so glad of this fine Whit-Monday, when so many Holiday-makers will enjoy *their*selves, and so many others make a little money by their Enjoyment. Our 'Rifles' are going to march to Grundisburgh, *manuring* and *skrimmaging* as they go, and also (as the Captain[1] hopes) recruiting. He is a right good little Fellow, I do believe. It is a shame the Gentry hereabout are so indifferent in the Matter: they subscribe next to nothing: and give absolutely nothing in the way of Entertainment or Attention to the Corps. But we are split up into the pettiest possible Squirarchy, who want to make the utmost of their little territory: cut down all the Trees, level all the old Violet Banks, and stop up all the Footways they can. The old pleasant way from Haske-ton to Bredfield is now a Desert. I was walking it yesterday and had the pleasure of breaking down and through some Bushes and Hurdles put to block up a fallen Stile. I thought what your Father would have said of it all. And really it is the sad ugliness of our once pleasant Fields that half drives me to the Water where the Power of the Squirarchy stops. . . .

To George Crabbe the Younger

Market-hill: Woodbridge. June 4/61.

My dear George,

Let me know when you come into these Parts, and be sure I shall be glad to entertain you as well as I can if you come while I am here. Nor am I likely to be away further than Aldbro', so far as I see. I do meditate crossing one fine Day to Holland: to see the Hague, Paul Potter: and some Rembrandts at Rotterdam. This, however, is not to be done in my little Boat: but in some Trader from Ipswich. I also talk of a cruise to Edinburgh in one of their Schooners. But both these Excursions I reserve for such hot weather as may make a retreat from the Town agreeable. I make no advances to Farlingay, because (as yet) we have not had any such Heat as to bake the Houses here: and, beside, I am glad to be by the River. It is strange how sad the Country has become to me. I went inland to see Acton's Curiosities before the Auction: and was quite glad to get back to the little Town again. I am quite clear I must live the remainder of my Life in a Town; but a little one, and with a strip of Garden to saunter in. . . .

I go sometimes to see the Rifles drill, and shoot at their Target;

[1] [Major Rolla Rouse of Melton.]

and have got John to ask them up to Boulge to practise some day: I must insinuate that he should offer them some Beer when they get there. It is a shame the Squires do nothing in the matter: take no Interest: offer no Encouragement, beyond a Pound or two in Money. And who are those who have most interest at stake in case of Rifles being really wanted? But I am quite assured that this Country is dying, as other Countries die, as Trees die, atop first. The lower Limbs are making all haste to follow. . . .

By the bye, don't let me forget to ask you to bring with you my Persian Dictionary in case you come into these Parts. I read very very little: and get very desultory: but when Winter comes again must take to some dull Study to keep from Suicide, I suppose. The River, the Sea, &c. serve to divert one now.

Adieu. These long Letters prove one's Idleness.

To W. H. Thompson

Market-hill, Woodbridge. July 15/61

My dear Thompson,

I was very glad to hear of you again. You need never take it to Conscience, not answering my Letters, further than that I really do want to hear you are well, and where you are, and what doing, from time to time. I have absolutely nothing to tell about myself, not having moved from this place since I last wrote, unless to our Sea coast at Aldbro', whither I run, or sail, from time to time to idle with the Sailors in their Boats or on their Beach. I love their childish ways: but they too degenerate. As to reading, my Studies have lain chiefly in some back Volumes of the New Monthly Magazine and some French Memoirs. Trench was good enough to send me a little unpublished Journal by his Mother: a very pretty thing indeed. I suppose he did this in return for one or two Papers on Oriental Literature which Cowell had sent me from India, and which I thought might interest Trench. I am very glad to hear old Spedding is really getting *his* Share of Bacon into Print: I doubt if it will be half as good as the "*Evenings*," where Spedding was in the *Passion* which is wanted to fill his Sail for any longer Voyage.

I have not seen his Paper on English Hexameters[1] which you tell me of: but I will now contrive to do so. I, however, believe in them: and I think the ever recurring attempts that way show there is some ground for such belief. To be sure, the Philosopher's Stone, and the Quadrature of the Circle, have had at least as many Followers. . . . Mrs Browning's Death is rather a relief to me, I must say: no more Aurora Leighs, thank God! A woman of real Genius, I know: but what is the upshot of it all? She and her Sex had better mind the Kitchen and their Children; and perhaps the Poor: except in such things as little Novels, they only devote themselves to what Men do much better, leaving that which Men do worse or not at all.

It was finding some Bits of Letters and Poems of old Alfred's that made me wish to restore those I gave you to the number, as marking a by-gone time to me. That they will not so much do to you, who did not happen to save them from the Fire when the Volumes of 1842 were printing. But I would waive that if you found it good or possible to lay them up in Trinity Library in the Closet with Milton's! Otherwise, I would still look at them now and then for the few years I suppose I have to live . . .

This is a terribly long Letter: but, if it be legible sufficiently, will perhaps do as if I were spinning it in talk under the walls of the Cathedral. I dare not now even talk of going any visits: I can truly say I wish you could drop in here some Summer Day and take a Float with me on our full River, which does lead to THE SEA some ten miles off.

You must think I have become very nautical, by all this: haul away at ropes, swear, dance Hornpipes &c. But it is not so: I simply sit in Boat or Vessel as in a moving Chair, dispensing a little Grog and Shag to those who do the work.

To George Crabbe the Younger

Woodbridge, Sept. 25/61

My dear George,

What Cheer, ho! I can't remember how long ago it was that you paid me a very pleasant Visit here, which I wish had been

[1] ["Arnold on translating Homer," *Fraser's Magazine*, June 1861.]

thrice as long. Since you went, William Airy[1] came over to Playford: and I went to see him there, and he came to see me here: and then we went together to Bury to ramble over our old School haunts. This also was really a pleasant thing to me. After this I went to Geldestone for some Days: called on your Aunt: did not see her: but heard from W. Crowfoot she was about to set off with your Cousin to Brighton, in order to hear their favourite Preachers. Donne talks of coming here for a Day on his road to Norfolk: whither I shall perhaps run with him: at least so far as a Day's Railway goes.

These are all the Dissipations I have had: except buying a great ugly dish of what was called *Majolica* (which I read means *Majorca*, where the Ware was first made), and a party-coloured Mop, so agreeable to my colour-loving eyes that I have kept it in my Sitting-room instead of giving it over to be trundled in the Kitchen. I still persist with my Boat: and have been half perished with Cold in it this very Day. But one must have some such—Amusement!

In three Ipswich Journals have been long Letters about foreign Travel by 'one of your Subscribers,' who, I am told (by Peter Parley), is no other than the great Capitaine Brooke! They are very well written indeed, whomsoever by. I keep on being very much pleased with my Causeries du Lundi, by Sainte Beuve, of which I told you, and which you may well recommend to Lady Walsingham. I almost think they are worth buying, which is saying one's utmost for a Book: especially for one in some dozen small volumes. I wish there were many Dozen, so long as one could get them from the London Library.

The Chimes have just played 'Ye Banks and Braes' for 6 P.M., and it is so dark I can scarce see how to write. So Summer is gone, and terrible old Winter coming, which I dread. What shall I do without my Boat? Sometimes I think I should like to try a winter—one—in Italy: but Indolence of Action carries it. I think I *must* go to Dresden to see the Madonna. Oh, there is a Book of Travel by a Lady Charlotte Pepys, incredible for its inanity, and I dare say much admired by the Sir Leicester

---

[1] [Rev. William Airy, school friend of EFG at Bury St Edmunds, Vicar of Keysoe, Bedfordshire, and brother of Sir George Airy, the Astronomer Royal.]

Dedlocks. It is called From Rieu to Eaux-bonnes, and is *almost* worth buying too, though only in two Volumes.

To W. F. Pollock

Market Hill, Woodbridge, Nov. 20/61

My dear Pollock,

'Vox clamantis' once again, at something of the usual Season. You have had your Summer Excursions, I suppose: and pray let me hear how you both do after them, and how well prepared to face the Winter. I rather dread it: having, I think, suffered with the Cold last year: and moreover sorry to exchange Boating on the River, in such glorious Summer as we have had, for poring one's Eyes out over Mudie's Books at a Sea-coal Fire. Oh, if you were to hear 'Where and oh where is my Soldier Laddie gone' played every three hours in a languid way by the Chimes of Woodbridge Church, wouldn't you wish to hang yourself? On Sundays we have the 'Sicilian Mariner's Hymn'— very slow indeed. I see, however, by a Handbill in the Grocer's Shop that a Man is going to lecture on the Gorilla in a few weeks. So there is something to look forward to.

Donne very kindly came and stayed some days with me: and I think went away looking better than when he arrived. Then Laurence has been painting a Sister of mine: I wouldn't go to look at it for fear of not liking it. He goes on talking of Colour, etc., just as he did twenty years ago—and was about, I believe, to finish my Sister through some '*Amber Medium*' which nobody seemed to wish at all for. (Don't tell Spedding what I say.)

I am extremely pleased with Sainte Beuve's Causeries du Lundi, which I get from the London Library: and try to make the most and longest of its 12 Vols.! Do you know the Book? I suppose it is now almost out of Date in London: but it is as new as 'Soldier Laddie' here.

Fechter's Othello?

To E. B. Cowell

Market Hill, Woodbridge. December 7/61

My dear Cowell,

. . . I shall look directly for the passages in Omar and Hafiz which you refer to and clear up, though I scarce ever see the Persian Character now. I suppose you would think it a dangerous thing to edit Omar: else, who so proper? Nay, are you not the only Man to do it? And he certainly is worth good re-editing. I thought him from the first the most remarkable of the Persian Poets: and you keep finding out in him Evidences of logical Fancy which I had not dreamed of. I dare say these logical Riddles are not his best: but they are yet evidences of a Strength of mind which our Persian Friends rarely exhibit, I think. I always said about Cowley, Donne &c. whom Johnson calls the metaphysical Poets, that their very Quibbles of Fancy showed a power of Logic which could follow Fancy through such remote Analogies. This is the case with Calderon's Conceits also. I doubt I have given but a very one-sided version of Omar: but what I do only comes up as a Bubble to the Surface, and breaks: whereas you, with exact scholarship, might make a lasting impression of such an Author. So I say of Jeláluddín, whom you need not edit in Persian, perhaps, unless in selections, which would be very good work: but you should certainly translate for us some such selections exactly in the way in which you did that apologue of Azräel. I don't know the value of the Indian Philosophy &c. which you tell me is a fitter exercise for the Reason: but I am sure that you should give us some of the Persian I now speak of, which you can do all so easily to yourself; yes, as a holiday recreation, you say, to your Indian Studies. As to India being 'your Place,' it may be: but as to your being lost in England, that could not be. You know I do not flatter. . . .

I declare I should like to go to India as well as any where: and I believe it might be the best thing for me to do. But, always slow at getting under way as I have been all my Life, what is to be done with one after fifty! I am sure there is no longer any great pleasure living in this Country, so tost with perpetual Alarms as it is. One Day we are all in Arms about France. To-day we are doubting if To-morrow we may not be at War to the Knife with America! I say still, as I used, We have too much Property, Honour &c. on our Hands: our outward Limbs go on lengthening while our central Heart beats weaklier: I say, as I used, we should give up something before it is forced from us. The World, I think, may justly resent our being and interfering all over the Globe. Once more I say, would we were a little, peaceful, unambitious, trading, Nation, like—the Dutch! . . .

Adieu, my dear Cowell; once more, Adieu. I doubt if you can read what I have written. Do not forget my Love to your Wife. I wonder if we are ever to meet again: you would be most disappointed if we were!

To W. H. Thompson

Market hill, Woodbridge. Dec. 9/61

My dear Thompson,

The MS. came safe to hand yesterday, thank you: and came out of its Envelope like a Ray of Old Times to my Eyes. I wish I had secured more leaves from that old *"Butcher's Book"* torn up in old Spedding's Rooms in 1842 when the Press went to work with, I think, the Last of old Alfred's Best. But that, I am told, is only a 'Crotchet.' However, had I taken some more of the Pages that went into the Fire, after serving in part for Pipe-lights, I might have enriched others with that which A himself would scarce have grudged, jealous as he is of such sort of Curiosity.

I have seen no more of Tannhäuser than the Athenæum showed me; and certainly do not want to see more. One wonders that Men of some Genius (as I suppose these are) should so disguise it in Imitation: but, if they be very young men, this is the natural course, is it not? By and by they may find their own Footing.

As to my own Peccadilloes in Verse, which never pretend to be original, this is the story of *Rubáiyát.* I had translated them partly for Cowell: young Parker asked me some years ago for something for Fraser, and I gave him the less wicked of these to use if he chose. He kept them for two years without using: and as I saw he didn't want them I printed some copies with Quaritch; and, keeping some for myself, gave him the rest. Cowell, to whom I sent a Copy, was naturally alarmed at it; he being a very religious Man: nor have I given any other Copy but to George Borrow, to whom I had once lent the Persian, and to old Donne when he was down here the other Day, to whom I was showing a Passage in another Book which brought my old Omar up.

[End of letter lost.]

To George Crabbe the Younger

Market Hill, Woodbridge, Jan. 31/62

Dear George,

Thank you always for your Invitations to Merton: why don't I go there? as well as to London, etc. Ah, why! You know, I hope, that you will always be welcome to my seedy home. Board here, Bed at the Bull. But I am (as for the last ten years) looking out for a House, and indeed have gone so far as to have (though without my asking for it) a Plan of Alterations drawn up for a wretched little House (where Mr Reynolds, once Parson here, used to live), at the end of Seckford Street. But, little as I want, I doubt this would be almost too little, with scarce a Scrap of Garden ground. I had even thoughts of that House where Mr Causton once lived at foot of the Bredfield Sandhill—do you remember? which has a Bit of Garden, and might be altered to my Use. But the House lies low in a Corner where one can't get out except one way—up the hill—and into the Town by those *Ship-meadows*, whereas Seckford Street is high and dry, and leads out to Far-lingay, Ipswich Road, etc. But all the better houses are occupied by Dowagers like Myself: the Miss Tolls: Mrs Pulham: the Miss Silvers: and Billy Whincupp: and none of them will die, or otherwise migrate, for Love or Money: so here I go floundering on and teasing everybody without any Progress at all. I wish you were here, or could give me any Advice from where you are: for I am so certain to blunder in all I do that I quite lose heart to decide. I do really want, however, to get into a house of my own with my own servants (where and with whom, of course, I shan't do half as well as here), and this for several reasons. Do not forget me in case you hear of any likely Housekeeper or Servant, though I can't yet engage the former because I have no house for her to keep. But a good Maidservant I would almost undertake here, paying her instead of Mrs. Berry's[1] doing so: who hires at 1s. a week such a Slut as even I cannot put up with. We are now, I hope, getting rid of the third since I have been here, and I yesterday went to see about another at Hasketon. Also, if when you are at Norwich, you should see any pretty and quaint Furniture, I should be glad to hear of it, and would even go to Norwich if you knew of a Place where such things were in plenty. When I took my Niece to London in November, I went to the Baker Street Bazaar: but spent what Time and Money I had in the new Chinese Department, where I bought a heap of Things which, however, have chiefly gone in Presents. I however like Oriental Things: their quaint shapes, fine Colours, and musky sandal-wood Scents; and, though I do not so much look at these things individually, yet their Presence in the Room creates a cheerfulness which is good as one grows old, blind, deaf, and dull. A little time in London would soon set one up in such Things: but I don't care to go there, and perhaps it is as well to have to pick up such Things now and then only.

I have not yet hung up my Pictures, which are now got back to the Room they were ou[s]ted from: but the Truth is they look so much better on the Floor. I have cleaned and put a thick coat of varnish on the Secretary; this fills up some cracks, though it makes him a little too glossy. Laurence was delighted with my hideous larger Spanish woman, which is certainly Velasquez, he says: I have turpentined her, which (as I have learned from Mr. Churchyard) will freshen up old Varnish, and so do better than overlaying a new Coat of *that*. But what do you think of my Impudence in actually rubbing down my Titian Landscape! which Mr. C. was frightened to think of my doing, but says it is certainly improved, now it's done. I will not have green skies at any Price. . . .

I should like some of the old light Cane Chairs such as one used to see in old Inns, Watering Places, etc. Do keep me and my wants of this kind in your Eye, as you have an Eye

[1] [EFG's landlady.]

for such things, and may not be unamused at thus keeping it open.

Here is a stupendous Letter: all about myself. You seem too much engaged, or too little inclined, to write much: and indeed I can't expect other People to repay me with such Coin as my own Idleness can spare so easily. I am reading a Book of almost as dull Letters as my own: the second series of Mrs Delany: five thick volumes of five hundred pages apiece of almost the poorest twaddle, and often very vulgar Twaddle, from the very greatest People to one another.

To W. H. Thompson

Market Hill, Woodbridge. March 19/62

My dear Thompson,

Thanks for your Letter in the middle of graver occupations. It will give me very great pleasure if you will come here: but not if you only do so out of kindness; I mean, if you have no other call of Business or Pleasure to yourself. For I don't deserve—

You should have sent me some Photograph[s]. I hate them nearly all: but S[tephen Spring] Rice was very good. I wonder you don't turn out well: I suppose, too black, is it? It is generally florid people, I think, who fail: yet, strange to say, my Brother Peter has come quite handsome in the Process. . . .

I am all for a little Flattery in Portraits: that is, so far as, I think, the Painter or Sculptor should try at something more agreeable than anything he sees sitting to him: when People look either bored, or smirking: he should give the best possible Aspect which the Features before him *might* wear, even if the Artist had not seen that Aspect. Especially when he works for Friends or Kinsfolk: for even the plainest face has looked handsome to them at some happy moment, and just such we like to have perpetuated.

Now, I really do feel ashamed when you ask about my Persian Translations, though they are all very well: only very little affairs. I really have not the face to send to Milnes direct: but I send you four Copies which I have found in a Drawer here to do as you will with. This will save Milnes, or any one else, the bore of writing to me to acknowledge it.

My old Boat has been altered, I hope not spoiled; and I shall soon be preparing for the Water—and Mud. I don't think one can reckon on warm weather till after the Longest Day: but if you should come before, it will surely be warm enough to walk, or drive, if not to sail; and Leaves will be green, if the Tide should be out.

You would almost think I wanted to repay you in Compliment if I told you I regarded even your hasty Letters as excellent in all respects. I do, however: but I do not wish you to write one when you are busy or disinclined.

To George Crabbe the Younger

Market Hill, Woodbridge, April 18, 1862

My dear George,

No—I won't go to Norwich on Saturday, though I should like then, or at any time, to meet you.

I ran to London for one day at the beginning of this week: saw nobody: but tore about to Shops where I bought some things I wanted, and some I didn't want. I got a look at the National Gallery, and admired the New Room: but the Devotion of one whole Room to Turner seems to me to be a national Absurdity. I didn't see one good Picture in the Shop windows, except a Wilson at Bryant's: but I saw the beautiful Venetian Portrait of a Lady which used to hang at Boulge Cottage, and which I gave to my Sister Lusia, quite spoiled by having been cleaned and restored by Seguier. Quite spoiled, I say, as a whole and perfect Work, so far as it went: it is now in uneven patches. I also managed to rush to the Crystal Palace—always, I think, the Sight of the Century: there were Chinese Trees in Blossom, and M. Angelo's Statues striving into Life, as it were, and the Grand Organ preparing itself by reverberating Preludes for some Handel Commemoration.

Now, after this flourish of the Tupper Trumpet, how can you

expect I am to descend to Questions of Trusteeships, etc. Or how could you ever ask *my* opinion on such a Subject? I, who run about asking every one else's!

To Emily Tennyson

[1862]

How is it that your note has been unanswered this month or more? Why, a fortnight of the month I didn't see it at all: being away with a sister in Norfolk; and the remaining fortnight? Why I kept thinking I might tell you something about the *fishing* questions you ask me:[1] I mean, about telling you "*anything*" about fishermen, etc. Well, somehow, what little I know on such matters won't turn up on demand: perhaps it would undemanded if you and A. T. were in my boat one summer day on this poor river, or plunging over its bar into the German Seas. Ah! Alfred should never have left his old county with its Mable-thorpe sea. As to the definite questions you ask on the subject, I can only answer for the customs in such matters *hereabout*.

1. There is no *apprenticeship* to fishing: anyone takes anyone who comes handy, etc., even in the *Deep-Sea* fishing, i.e. not along the coast, but out to the Dogger bank, Scotland, Ireland, etc. (for cod-fish); anyone *may* go who *can* get a berth. Only a little while ago, a lad was telling me at Aldbro' how *he* first went, as a boy of 13: he *hid* himself in the *stern* of the boat that was pushing off to the *smack*: and when they were well off shore, he pushed up his head from under ropes, etc., and the "Master" only said, "What! is thee that devil of a boy? You'll be glad enough to be at home again before along!" and so took him out to sea; and now the lad has his 14s. a week (grown to 19 years old) like the rest.

2. "May *fishermen* act as pilots, or must they be of a *Guild* of pilots?" *Yes*, properly: no one is *authorized* to become a pilot, unless he has served his time as *mate* in a *square-rigged vessel* (i.e. nothing under *a brig*: even a *schooner* won't do). When he has so

[1] [Mrs Tennyson had asked EFG to help her husband with details for *Enoch Arden*.]

served a certain time, he has to pass examinations before (I *think*) the *Trinity Board* and so is admitted or not to be of the Guild. But, when all the authorized pilots in a place are exhausted (as will happen when many foreign ships pass, etc.), then a *fisherman* or other *un*authorized sailor will go: being called a *"Brummagem Pilot."*

Oh, dear! this is very learned, very useless, I dare say. But you ask me and I tell my best. I have been almost tempted to write you out some morsels of Dampier's *Voyages* which I copied out for myself: so fine as they are in their way I think, but they would be no use unless A. T. fell upon them by chance: for, of all horses, Pegasus least likes to be dragged to drink. I love Captain Cook too: what fine English his, in the Johnsonian days! I remember, 10 years ago, telling Alfred at Brighton of some poor little verses found in the Prayer-Book of a seafaring son of our old coachman, who died at sea: and Alfred took the pipe out of his blessed old lips to remurmur one, which *Thackeray* pooh-poohed. Along the coast here are many peculiar and fine Scandinavian words, which are not registered even by our provincial glossarists (who have dealt chiefly with the inland husbandman people).

Well, I shan't go on more about this unless you desire some more. About the photographs of A. T., thank you for them: as *you* think one of them very good, I have no doubt it is so: but what becomes of the eyes? I had seen some bigger ones, which made a sort of Rembrandt Burgomaster of him: but in reality I don't much love photographs: though I asked you for one, because I knew they were always going on: and I sincerely thank you for sending me (I dare say) the best.

This is vile weak scribbling, after two glasses of b-r-n-d-y and water too (Sunday evening).

I saw (in Norfolk) that Yarrell does give that human note to the plover: so I dare say he is right, and my friends on the river here wrong. I see too that Yarrell writes the word "Curlew" as French *"Couvre lieu"* (*I think*), supposed to be from its *cry*. (Query. Will A. T. say anything better than an Aldbro' fisherman said of *a* boat—(Humph) "Ah!—She go like *a Wiolin*, she do!")

Some Summer—some Summer day send the old wretch here,

where nobody scarce knows his name (don't be angry, Mrs A. T.), though a duller place is not! but an ugly river
(and a dirty sea)
(and E. F. G.)
which is my poem Q. E. D.

(P.S. Leave the scrap of *Cook* on the floor, in Alfred's way: don't give it him.)

To Herman Biddell

Market Hill, Woodbridge. Thursday [1863]

My dear Sir,

Airy first proposed to come this present week: I should have let you know if he had, in hope you would come and meet him here. He now talks of August 10; of which you shall hear in time.

As to my going to meet him at your's—beside that you know I may say I go nowhere—(alas! I have not yet found my way to Boulge, where my Brother has been these two months)—I feel it rather indelicate only to break that rule in order to meet an old School-fellow because he happens to be staying at a house where I know I am always kindly invited, and yet don't go. I can tell you truly, that if I went anywhere I should have been much more than once at Playford, where I find sensible, unaffected, and (best of all) unconventional People; and (next best) no formal Dinner: the stupid Dulness of which determined to drive me out of the Society hereabout as much as anything else. However, we must see when Airy does come; he is very obstinate, you know; and makes a rather truculent mouth if one doesn't follow where he bids. You know how I mean all this; he is a real loyal Fellow, as well as a clever; and I am sure I value his old Regard, and like well a Talk of Old Times, and take it very kind that he should give up any holiday, and go to the Expense, for the sake of coming so far to me.

Now, as to Frith, etc., I didn't half read the Review: but sent it to you to see what you would make of it. I quite agree with you about Hogarth, who (I always thought) made his pictures unnatural by overcrowding what was natural in Part, as also by caricature. For this reason, I always thought his Apprentices his best Series. But there are passages of Tragedy and Comedy in his Works that go very deep into Human Nature, and into one's Soul. He was also an Artist in Composition, Colour, etc., though in all respects, I think, a little over-rated of late years.

I don't say that Frith is not more natural (in the sense you use the word, I suppose) than Hogarth; but then does he take so difficult a Face of Nature to deal with, and, even on his own lower ground, does he go to the bottom of it? Is there in his Derby Day the one typical Face and Figure of the Jockey, the Gambler, etc., such as Hogarth would have painted for ever on our Imaginations? Is Frith at all better (if so good) as Leech in Punch? If as good or better, are his Pictures worth a thousandth Part of the Prices given for them? Which, I think, is the Question with the Reviewer. I don't know about his Colour; but I have never heard of it as beyond the usual.

If we take the mere representation of common Nature as the sum total of Art, we must put the modern Everyday life Novel above Shakespeare: for certainly Macbeth and Coriolanus, etc., did not spout Blank Verse, etc. But they dealt in great, deep, and terrible Passions, and Shakespeare has made them live again out of the dead Ashes of History by the force of his Imagination, and by the 'Thoughts that breathe, and Words that burn' that he has put into their Mouths. Nor can I think that Frith's veracious Portraitures of people eating Luncheons at Epsom are to be put in the Scale with Raffaelle's impossible Idealisation of the Human made Divine.

As you are a sensible Man, I drop 'Mr' and 'Esq.' in directing to you. I wish others would do so to me.

To George Crabbe the Younger

Woodbridge, June 8/63

My dear George,

Your sister wrote me a very kind letter to tell of her safe Return home. I must repeat to you very sincerely that I never recollect to have passed a pleasanter week. As far as Company went, it was like old Times at Bredfield; and the Oak-trees were divine! I never expected to care so very much for Trees, nor for your flat Country: but I really feel as one who has bathed in Verdure. I suppose Town-living makes one alive to such a Change.

I spent a long Day with Thompson: and much liked the painted Roof. On Thursday I went to Lynn: which I took a Fancy to: the odd old Houses: the Quay: the really grand Inn (Duke's Head in the Market place) and the civil, Norfolk-talking, People. I went to Hunstanton, which is rather dreary: one could see the Country at Sandringham was good. I enquired fruitlessly about those Sandringham Pictures &c.: even the Auctioneer, whom I found in the Bar of the Inn, could tell nothing of where they had gone.

To George Crabbe the Younger

Woodbridge, August 4, [1863]

My dear George,

I have at last done my Holland—you won't be surprised to hear that I did it in two days, and was too glad to rush home on the first pretence, after (as usual) seeing nothing I cared the least about. The Country itself I had seen long before in Dutch Pictures, and between Beccles and Norwich: the Towns I had seen in Picturesque Annuals, Drop Scenes &c.

But the Pictures—the Pictures—themselves?

Well, you know how I am sure to mismanage: but you will hardly believe, even of me, that I never saw what was most worth seeing, the Hague Gallery! But so it was: had I been by myself, I should have gone off directly (after landing at Rotterdam) to that: but Mr Manby was with me: and he thought best to see about Rotterdam first: which was last Thursday, at whose earliest Dawn we arrived. So we tore about in an open Cab: saw nothing: the Gallery not worth a visit: and at night I was half dead with weariness. Then again on Friday I, by myself, should have started for the Hague: but as Amsterdam was also to be done, we thought best to go there (as furthest) first. So we went: tore about the town in a Cab as before: and I raced through the Museum seeing (I must say) little better than what I have seen

626

over and over again in England. I couldn't admire the Night-watch much: Van der Helst's very good Picture seemed to me to have been cleaned: I thought the Rembrandt Burgomasters worth all the rest put together. But I certainly looked very flimsily at all.

Well, all this done, away we went to the Hague: arriving there just as the Museum closed for that day; next Day (Saturday) it was not to be open at all (I having proposed to wait in case it should), and on Sunday only from 12 to 2. Hearing all this, in Rage and Despair I tore back to Rotterdam: and on Saturday Morning got the Boat out of the muddy Canal in which she lay and tore back down the Maas &c. so as to reach dear old Bawdsey shortly after Sunday's Sunrise. Oh my Delight when I heard them call out 'Orford Lights!' as the Boat was plunging over the Swell.

All this is very stupid, really wrong: but you are not surprised at it in me. One reason however of my Disgust was, that we (in our Boat) were shut up (as I said) in the Canal, where I couldn't breathe. I begged Mr Manby to let me take him to an Inn: he would stick to his Ship, he said: and I didn't like to leave him. Then it was Murray who misled me about the Hague Gallery: he knew nothing about its being shut on Saturdays. Then again we neither of us knew a word of Dutch: and I was surprised how little was known of English in return.

But I shall say no more. I think it is the last foreign Travel I shall ever undertake; unless I should go with you to see the Dresden Madonna; to which there is one less impediment now Holland is not to be gone through. . . . I am the Colour of a Lobster with Sea-faring: and my Eyes smart: so Good-Bye. Let me hear of you. Ever yours E. F. G.

Oh dear!—Rembrandt's Dissection—where and how did I miss that?

To W. B. Donne

Market Hill: Woodbridge Jan: 3/64

My dear Donne—

Thank you for your very kind Letter, & take back in full all Good Wishes for this same /64—

It is very good of you (but only as usual) to offer all Entertainment &c. However, I am better: whether owing to M^r. Gissing's Pills & Draughts; or to giving up Alcohol in it's many Shapes; or to tearing about out of doors till knocked up: or to the change of Weather; or all these Things together—So here I am again a Candidate for /64, & may perhaps, smoke a Cigar & drink some Dilution of Alc-h-l this very night with Manby, should he look in after Evening Church: whither he goes punctually as Church-warden as well as Christian—He is very proud of a Porch he has had re-fronted at the expense of refractory Dissenters—

I wrote to Charles about Thackeray. I have been reading his Books, as well as Letters, and can scarce believe the Great Spirit is quite quench'd—*Now* I wish he were alive that I might write & tell him how the Newcomes were illuminating my long Evenings. But, if he were alive, I don't think he'd care to be told so by me now; I think he had ceased to remember me; and I'm sure I can't wonder, nor (least of all) blame him.

Last night I wrote to Mrs Kemble (taking the Hampshire Address you gave me) & told her how sincerely well I liked her Play.[1] As to her Stage Criticism, perhaps I don't *understand* her Definitions; I should have thought that "*intuitive*" and "*intellectual*" would have served well enough to distinguish the Styles.

[Remainder of letter wanting.]

To Samuel Laurence

Market Hill: Woodbridge. Jan. 7/64

Dear Laurence,

. . . I want to know about your two Portraits of Thackeray: the first one (which I think Smith and Elder have) I know by the Print: I want to know about one you last did (some two years ago?) whether you think it as good and characteristic: and also who has it. Frederic Tennyson sent me a Photograph of W. M. T. old, white, massive, and melancholy, sitting in his Library.

I am surprized almost to find how much I am thinking of him:

[1] [Probably *An English Tragedy*.]

so little as I had seen him for the last ten years; not once for the last five. I had been told—by you, for one—that he was spoiled. I am glad therefore that I have scarce seen him since he was 'old Thackeray'. I keep reading his Newcomes of nights, and as it were hear him saying so much in it; and it seems to me as if he might be coming up my Stairs, and about to come (singing) into my Room, as in old Charlotte Street &c. thirty years ago.

To George Crabbe the Younger

Woodbridge, March 20 [1864]

Dear George,

I went to London to see Thackeray's House before the Auction cleared all off. To the Auction I did not go. I was much pleased at the Kensington Museum; Crome's Picture really seemed to me to cut over everything there. Then I went to several Dealers, and two Picture Sales; but have come away with two Pictures I don't want, having missed one which I did much want. This was a Portrait of Pope, in so neglected and battered a Condition I thought to be sure I should buy it for £10 at the end of a Sale. But when some People had bid £3 or £4, a voice called out £10; then £20—£30—£40—and so would have gone on, I suppose to any amount, for it was the great Farrer. The Portrait was, I was sure, done from the Man: and I had planned so nicely how I was to cut it down and make oval! I spoke to Farrer, who had bought my Father's Lady Castlemaine (Lely). He said it was now at Narboro'; we will go see it one day, eh? At this last Sale was a great tawdry Lely sold for £200; I said to Farrer I could not believe it to be Lely; and he said No, it was by Lely's Pupil, Mrs. Beale, who did much for him.

Well, I went to my dear Crystal Palace; was all day upon my Legs in the Streets and half the night too; saw countless Silver Teapots!—just the thing! and ended by buying a Plated Service! Oh, how base! You would have kept me from such Cowardice; as would the poor Captain, whom I kept thinking of as I went about; also, much of W. M. T. Then I bought some perfectly useless Things at the Baker Street Bazaar; in short, have frittered away in Things I don't care for what might have bought something I should have cared for. Ass!

Bence Jones gave me some Prescription to cool my head of Nights; I still wake up in a Bother. He talked to me a good deal of W. M. T., having known him of late years. He thought he had a foible for Great Folks; I wonder if this was really so.

To Samuel Laurence

Market hill: Woodbridge. April 23/64

Dear Laurence,

I only got home last Night, from Wiltshire, where I had been to see Miss Crabbe, daughter of the old Vicar whom you remember. I found your two Letters: and then your Box. When I had unscrewed the last Screw, it was as if a Coffin's Lid were raised; there was the Dead Man.[1] I took him up to my Bedroom; and when morning came, he was there—reading; alive, and yet dead. I am perfectly satisfied with it on the whole; indeed, could only have suggested a very, very, slight alteration, if any. . . .

As I passed through London, I saw that wonderful Collection of Rubbish, the late Bishop of Ely's Pictures; but I fell desperately in Love with a Sir Joshua, a young Lady in white with a blue Sash, and a sweet blue Sky over her sweet, noble, Head; far above Gainsboro' in its Air and Expression. I see in the Papers that it went for £165; which, if I thought well to give so much for any Picture, I could almost have given, by some means, for such a delightful Work.

To W. H. Thompson

Woodbridge: March 15/66

My dear Thompson,

To-day's Post brings me a Letter from Robert Groome, which tells me (on "Times" authority) that you are Master of Trinity. Judging by your last Letter, I suppose this was unexpected by yourself: I have no means of knowing whether it was expected

---

[1] [A copy by Laurence of his portrait of Thackeray.]

by others beside those who voted you to the Honour. For I had heard nothing further of the whole matter, even of Whewell's accident, than you yourself told me. Well, at our time of Life, any very vehement Congratulations are, I suppose, irrelevant on both sides. But I am very sure I do congratulate you heartily, if you are yourself gratified. Whether you are glad of the Post itself or not, you must, I think, be gratified with the Confidence in your Scholarship and Character which has made your Society elect you. And so far one may unreservedly congratulate you. . . .

To-day I was looking at the Carpenters &c. carrying away Chips &c. of a Tree I had cut down: and, coming home, read—

δρυὸς πεσούσης πᾶς ἀνὴρ ξυλεύεται—

Whose Line ?—Certainly not of

Yours ever sincerely E. F. G.

To R. H. Groome

11, Marine Terrace, Lowestoft, March 28, 1866
. . . The change has been of some use, I think, in brightening me. My long solitary habit of Life now begins to tell upon me, and I am got past the very cure which only could counteract it: Company or Society: of which I have lost the Taste too long to endure again. So, as I have made my Bed, I must lie in it—and Die in it . . .

To R. H. Groome

Lowestoft, April 2, '66
. . . I am going to be here another week: as I think it really has freshened me up a bit. Especially going out in a Boat with my good Fletcher, though I get perished with the N. E. wind. I believe I never shall do unless in a Lodging, as I have lived in these 40 years. It is too late, I doubt, to reform in a House of one's own . . . Dove,[1] unlike Noah's Dove, brings no report of a green leaf when I ask him about the Grass seed . . .

[1] [The builder of Little Grange.]
631

To R. H. Groome

Lowestoft, Dec. 4, 1866.

I am sorry you can't come, but have no doubt that you are right in *not* coming. You may imagine what I do with myself here: somehow, I do believe the Seaside is more of my Element than elsewhere, and the old Lodging Life suits me best. That, however, I have at Woodbridge; and can be better treated nowhere than there.

I have just seen Posh, who had been shooting his Lines in the Morning: had fallen asleep after his Sunday Dinner, and rose up like a Giant refreshed when I went into his house. His little Wife, however, told him he must go and tidy his Hair, which he was preparing to obey. Oh! these are the People who somehow interest me; and if I were not now too far advanced on the Road to Forgetfulness, I should be sad that my own Life had been such a wretched Concern in comparison. But it is too late, even to lament, now . . .

There is a Wedding-party next door: at No. 11; I being in 12; *Becky* having charge of both houses. There is incessant vulgar Giggling and Tittering, and 5 meals a Day, Becky says. Oh! these are not such Gentlefolks as my Friends on the Beach, who have not 5 meals a Day. I wonder how soon I shall quarrel with them, however—I don't mean the Wedding Party . . . At Eight or half-past I go to have a Pipe at Posh's, if he isn't half-drunk with his Friends.

To W. B. Donne

Woodbridge: Wednesday. [1867?]

My dear Donne,

I had your Letter this morning: and by Noon comes a huge Box—very heavy, my Landlord says—"Shall he unpack it?"— "If he likes"— He finds a heap of Sawdust: & by & bye comes up again to tell me he can't make out what is forth-coming— "something like the end of a dead Nose"— So I went down: &

632

directly I saw the Address on the Box, knew what it must be.[1]
At last we get out A. T. all safe & sound—

Did you forget to apprize me in your Letter? Anyhow, thank you very, very much for the Trouble—and Expense—you have had about it—

Oddly enough, I had said to Spedding in a Letter a few days ago, that the Reason why I had never sent for his handsome Present, now that I have a house to put it in, is simply—that I dared not have it where my poor Epileptic Niece, who takes great pleasure in coming to my House, might be frightened at it; I am obliged to take down all my dark Italian Faces from the Walls: she would dream of them: and I shall now have to send Tennyson away into a Barn, when she comes next—

I take for granted that Spedding had not spoken of my Letter to you: & that is why I call this an odd Coincidence— It is very good of you to provide for all this.

I am very glad you are going to Mrs Kemble—

Mr Woodward is a clever, diligent, good—but somehow absurd—creature. Old Childs, his great Patron & Admirer (I always wonder'd how) said he "wanted Ballast"— He is something of the Bladder Species—

I am very glad of the Scheme of Tacitus. Now, mind not to let it slip from you, as Schemes do from that Woodwardian Professor—

Ever your's, my dear Donne,

E. FG.

To Joseph Fletcher

Markethill, Woodbridge, Thursday [Early January 1867]
My dear Poshy,

My Lawyer can easily manage the Assignment of the Lugger to me, leaving the Agreement as it is between you and Fuller. But you must send the Agreement here to him to see.

As we shall provide that the Lugger when built shall belong to me; so we will provide that, in case of my dying *before* she is built, you may come on my executors for any money due.

I think you will believe that I shall propose, and agree to,

[1] [It was a cast of a bust of Tennyson by Thomas Woolner.]

nothing which is not for your good. For surely I should not have meddled with it at all, but for that one purpose.

And now, Poshy, I mean to read you a short Sermon which you can keep till Sunday to read. You know I told you of *one* danger—and I do think the only one—you are liable to—*Drink*.

I do not the least think you are *given* to it: but you have, and will have, so many friends who will press you to it: perhaps *I* myself have been one. And when you keep so long without *food*; *could* you do so, Posh, without a Drink—of some your bad Beer too—now and then? And then, does not the Drink—and of bad Stuff—take away Appetite for the time? And will, if continued, so spoil the stomach that it will not bear anything *but* Drink. And this evil comes upon us gradually, without our knowing how it grows. That is why I warn you, Posh. If I am wrong in thinking you want my warning, you must forgive me, believing that I should not warn at all if I were not much interested in your welfare. I know that you do your best to keep out at sea, and watch on shore, for anything that will bring home something for Wife and Family. But do not do so at any such risk as I talk of.

I say, I tell you all this for your sake: and something for my own also—not as regards the Lugger—but because, thinking you, as I do, so good a Fellow, and being glad of your Company; and taking *Pleasure* in seeing you prosper; I should now be sorely vext if you went away from what I believe you to be. Only, whether you do well or ill, *show me all above-board*, as I really think you have done; and do not let a poor old, solitary, and sad Man (as I really am, in spite of my Jokes), do not, I say, let me waste my Anxiety in vain.

I thought I had done with new Likings: and I had a more easy Life perhaps on that account: now I shall often think of you with uneasiness, for the very reason that I have so much Liking and Interest for you.

There—the Sermon is done, Posh. You *know* I am not against Good Beer while at Work: nor a cheerful Glass after work: only do not let it spoil the stomach, or the Head.

Your's truly,
E. FG.

To R. H. Groome

Lowestoft, Jan. 5/67

I really was to have gone home To-day, but made a little Business with Posh an excuse for waiting over Sunday. This very Day he signs an Agreement for a new Herring-lugger, of which he is to be Captain, and to which he will contribute some Nets and Gear. I daresay I had better have left all this alone: but, if moderately lucky, the Vessel will pay *something*, at any rate: and in the meanwhile it really does me some good, I believe, to set up this little Interest here: and even if I lose money, I get some Fun for it. So now I shall be very glad to drop *Esquire*, and be addressed as '*Herring-merchant*,' for the future.

Posh has been doing well this week with Cod-fishing, as only one other Boat has been out (owing to the others not having a *Set-net* to catch bait with). His fish have fetched a good price, even from the old Jew, Levi. I believe I have smoked my Pipe every evening but one with Posh at his house, which his quiet little Wife keeps tidy and pleasant. The Man is, I do think, of a Royal Nature. I have told him he is liable to one Danger (the Hare with many Friends)—so many wanting him to drink. He says, it's quite true, and that he is often obliged to run away: as I believe he does: for his House shows all Temperance and Order. This little Lecture I give him—to go the way, I suppose, of all such Advice . . .

To Frederick Tennyson

Woodbridge: Jan. 29/67

My dear Frederick,

Let me hear from you one Day. I would send you my MS. Book of Morton's Letters: but I scarce know if the Post would carry it to you; though not so very big: and I am still less sure that you would ever return it to me. And what odds if you didn't? It might as well die in your Possession as in mine.

In answer to my yearly Letter to Alfred and Co. I heard (from Mrs) that they were about to leave Freshwater, frightened away

by Hero-worshippers &c. and were going to a Solitude called
Greyshott Hall, Haslemere; which, I am told, is in Hants.
Whether they go to settle there I don't know. Lucretius' Death
is thought to be too free-spoken for Publication, I believe; not
so much in a religious, as an amatory, point of View. I should
believe Lucretius more likely to have expedited his Departure
because of Weariness of Life and Despair of the System, than
because of any Love-philtre. I wrote also my yearly Letter to
Carlyle, begging my compliments to his Wife: who, he replies,
died, in a very tragical way, last April. I have since heard that the
Papers reported all the Circumstances. So, if one lives so much
out of the World as I do, it seems better to give up that Ghost
altogether. Old Spedding has written a Pamphlet about 'Authors
and Publishers'; showing up, or striving to show up, the Publishers' system. He adduces his own Edition of Bacon as a sample
of their mismanagement, in respect of too bulky Volumes &c.
But, as he says, Macaulay and Alison are still bulkier; yet they
sell. The truth is that a solemnly-inaugurated Edition of all
Bacon was not wanted. The Philosophy is surely superseded; not
a Wilderness of Speddings can give men a new interest in the
Politics and Letters. The Essays will no doubt always be in
request, like Shakespeare. But I am perhaps not a proper Judge
of these high matters. How should I? who have just, to my great
sorrow, finished 'the Woman in White' for the third time, once
every last three winters. I wish Sir Percival Glyde's death were
a little less of the minor Theatre sort; then I would swallow all
the rest as a wonderful Caricature, better than so many a sober
Portrait. I really think of having a Herring-lugger I am building
named 'Marian Halcomb,' the brave Girl in the Story. Yes, a
Herring-lugger; which is to pay for the money she costs unless
she goes to the Bottom: and which meanwhile amuses me to
consult about with my Sea-folks. I go to Lowestoft now and
then, by way of salutary Change: and there smoke a Pipe every
night with a delightful Chap, who is to be Captain. I have been,
up to this time, better than for the last two winters: but feel a
Worm in my head now and then, for all that. You will say, only
a Maggot. Well, we shall see. When I go to Lowestoft, I take
Montaigne with me; very comfortable Company. One of his
Consolations for *The Stone* is, that it makes one less unwilling

to part with Life. Oh, you think that it didn't need much Wisdom to suggest that? Please yourself, Ma'am. January, just gone! February, only 28 Days: then March with Light till six p.m.: then April with a blush of Green on the Whitethorn hedge: then May, Cuckoos, Nightingales &c.; then June, Ship, launched, and nothing but Ship till November, which is only just gone. The Story of our lives from Year to Year. This is a poor letter: but I won't set The Worm fretting. Let me hear how you are and don't be two months before you do so.

To W. F. Pollock

Woodbridge, May 8/67

My dear Pollock,

Unless you are predestined to vote for a German to fill the chair of Sanskrit to be set up at Cambridge, do vote, and get those you can to vote, for Edward Cowell. What the other Candidates may be, I don't know; I am sure he is fit for the Place; first, because, though I am not a proper Judge of Sanskrit, or any other Scholarship, I believe I am a Judge of the Stuff a Scholar should be made of: and, of all my learned Friends, I have known none of so unmistakeable Metal as Cowell. And, secondly, among the Qualities that so clearly distinguish him, none is more to be trusted than his Reverence and Modesty, which I know would not let him set up for any Office he was not competent to fill: for which very reason he may not profess the Omniscience, or the sublime Theories, which the Germans have dazzled us with: but he will be sure of what he does profess. Beside having studied Oriental Literature these twenty years, he has been for eight years at Calcutta (Professor of English Literature there), where he studied Sanskrit with the native Pundits, etc. He told me, on his return two years ago, that he had been surprised to find how extremely inaccurate the German Scholars were in that direction: that their grand and plausible Theories would not stand Examination: this he told me long before this Cambridge Professorship was talked of. It was Thompson who first told me of the Scheme, and asked if Cowell would stand: I believe Cowell is now with him at Trinity. I repeat that, whatever the other Candidates may be, I am certain Cowell is a fit man; and if he be so, I should wish him success over a German, even were he not my Friend, but only an Englishman: whose national Good Sense I have more respect for than all the German Æsthetics, etceterorum.

I have nothing to tell you of mine self—only the old Story—Dormouse Existence here all Winter: now boating on the River: and soon about to put to Sea. I have been reading Thackeray's Novels a third time: I am sure that Fielding is common and coarse work in Comparison.

To Bernard Quaritch

Market Hill, Woodbridge [1867]

Dear Sir,

Pray dont waste your learned Catalogues on me who now buy nothing but Mudie's Secondhand Memoirs.

One Catalogue you sent me some weeks ago recalled to me what Edward Cowell had told me a year ago; viz. that you had partly sold, partly lost, the copies of Omar Khayyám; and thought a small Edition would sell.

Well—I have done with such things; and I suppose you find that such *"livraisons"* even if they do sell, are not worth the trouble of keeping &c.

But as poor Omar is one I have great fellow feeling with, I would rather vamp him up again with a few Alterations & Additions than anything else.

You must tell me, Busy and Great Man as you now are, whether you care to take charge of such a shrimp of a Book if I am silly enough to reprint it.

Yours truly, E. FG.

If you ever come down here I will give you a sail in my Great Ship (of 14 Tons) and Good Entertainment at the famous *Bull Inn*, opposite; where I find better Fare for my Friends than I can give them in this Lodging.

Can't you tell me of a good, readable, Edition of Ste Beuve's Causeries du Lundi, not in a dozen little Volumes.

Yours truly, EDWARD FITZGERALD

To Bernard Quaritch

Market Hill, Woodbridge October 14/67
Dear Sir,

Please to post me *9244 Nicolas' Omar Khayyám*: for which I enclose 19ˢ for postage &c.

This Book, and No. 9245 (with my Name too!) remind me of what Cowell has told me more than once; viz, that you thought a small Edition of my Omar would sell in time.

I had always wished to add some 20 or 30 more Stanzas to it and some additional matter: but it seemed absurd to reprint a thing for that alone; and I have no other object. I might also have added to it the translation of Jámi's Salámán & Absál—printed in the same form—of which I have several copies left after Parker's Firm broke up.

These two would make a Pamphlet more worth 2/6 than the present Omar (I blush to see it!) at 3/6.

Yours EDWARD FITZGERALD

To W. M. Donne

Woodbridge: Octʳ· 16 [1867?]
My dear Mowbray,

I have just come back from our Harbour mouth for two hours (to go back in Ship there) and, finding your Letter, dated Sunday, *will* answer it, in part, at any rate. You conclude from what I have already said that I am not yet shut up for the Winter: I thought I shᵈ· have had to give up the Ghost last week, when the Cold came on like a Giant, & made me shake in my Cabin, under all the Coats, Waistcoats & Breeches I could pile upon me. But *this* week comes a lovely warm S. Wester, & so I keep at our Harbour: cruising about a little by day, & by night walking on the Sands under the Moon. After that, Grog at the small Inn: Sailors jabbering inside. My Captain's Wife is going fast into a Decline: he does all he can for her: and I see thinks much about her. The other day she began to despair of herself: & he told her (in all sincerity & Affection) that, once she despaired, it would "clew her up in no time"— My Lugger did *nothing* in the North Sea: & the Crew began to despair a little: This last Fortnight they have begun the *Home* Voyage, as it's called, and Today only I find a Letter to say they have at last caught something. I have not sailed to Lowestoft myself lately: because one gets jammed in among the Luggers very uncomfortably.

I assure you, my dear Mowbray, that I thoroughly enjoyed your visit to Lowestoft—in a way that is now very rare with me —really to feel sorry when you departed—you and Wife. My old friend W Airy has been to see me here—only for two days—& him also I was not glad to lose— Oh yes: & Edward Cowell was staying near our Harbour a month ago: & came several times on board me: & we had some Sophocles (Philoctetes) together: & he comes like Daylight upon obscurities that the German Editors quarrel & blunder about. I have not the least doubt that E B C would have been the best Greek Professor, as well as Sanscrit; he is certainly *the* Scholar I have known—

Airy sent me a capital Photograph of *Thompson*,—not Master of Trinity—but second Master of Bury in *our* Day. I shall send one to old Spedding, I think, to try & make him remember me, & even write a Line to me—

I have been sunning myself with Boccacio's Decameron on board: but all these Immortals—D Quixote—Sophocles—Montaigne &c I somehow keep for Summer & Ship:—when *they* fail me, then Mudie comes in. I fancied I could always read A. Trollope: but his last Barset has made me skip here & there. The Account of old Harding with his Violoncello in Vol II is— *better* than Sterne—inasmuch as it is more unaffected & true—

Now do write to me now & then, Mowbray. You see, at any rate, by the present speedy reply, that your Remembrance is welcome.

> *Another Ham* has come & gone
> Since you did sail the Scandal on;
> And other Bards must come & try
> To sing your praise, friantic Guy.

P.S. The Pencil all right: will be used before this Sun sets.

To W. F. Pollock

Market hill: Woodbridge. October 28, [1867]

Now, my dear Pollock, I have put on a new Goose-quill Nib on purpose to write my best MS. to you. But the new Nib has very little to say for me: the old Story: dodging about in my Ship for these last five months: indeed during all that time not having lain, I believe, for three consecutive Nights in Christian Sheets. But now all that is over: this very day is my little Ship being dismantled, and to-morrow will she go up to her middle in mud, and here am I anchored to my old Desk for the Winter; and beginning, as usual, by writing to my Friends, to tell them what little there is to tell of myself, and asking them to tell what they can of themselves in return. I shall even fire a shot at old Spedding; who would not answer my last Letters at all: innocent as they were, I am sure: and asking definite Questions, which he once told me he required if I wanted any Answer. I suppose he is now in Cumberland. What *is* become of Bacon? Are you one of the Converted, who go the whole Hog?

Thompson—no, I mean the Master of Trinity—has replied to my half-yearly Enquiries in a very kind Letter. He tells me that my friend Edward Cowell has pleased all the Audience he had with an inaugural Lecture about Sanskrit. Also, that there is such an Article in the Quarterly about the Talmud as has not been seen (so fine an Article, I mean) for years. I have had Don Quixote, Boccaccio, and my dear Sophocles (once more) for company on board: the first of these so delightful, that I got to love the very Dictionary in which I had to look out the words: yes, and often the same words over and over again. The Book really seemed to me the most delightful of all Books: Boccaccio, delightful too, but millions of miles behind; in fact, a whole Planet away.

To W. F. Pollock

Woodbridge, Nov. 11 [1867]

My dear Pollock,

I must thank you for your Letter—good Fellow as you were to write it. I must say that you never leave one long in doubt as to whether one is any longer acceptable or not. Not like that Wretch Spedding; who, since I wrote you, did write to me at last, and confessed that he slightly repented of not writing before. However, I am contented that he thinks it worth while to think twice about the matter. He now talks of two more Volumes of Bacon in the Spring: and then he says he will take the reins into his own hands, and publish Volume by Volume as it is finished. He is now *entêté* (I forget how it's spelt) about some sort of Phonetic Alphabet.

I have not yet revived my appetite for Novels: not even for my dear 'Woman in White': which I should like to have read to me; and which even now exerts a sort of magnetism in drawing me toward the corner of a dark Cupboard, or Closet, in which (like the proprietary Skeleton) she lies.

I have heard from *Mrs* Alfred, who (as you may know) answers for Husband and Self. She does not give a good Account of one Son (I believe the Eldest): and Frederic Tennyson, who was at Farringford this Autumn, thinks them both very delicate. Is it to be with A. T., as is said to be the Fate of your great Men: to leave no Posterity?

Well—and I have heard from the Master of Trinity: who encloses me a Leaf of Proof-sheet of Plato, with good English Notes, corrected, and therefore, I doubt not, written by himself. The Page he encloses is meant to answer a Question I put to him years ago. I don't know when, nor on what occasion. However, I find the Question is left ambiguous even by Scholars.

Are you overrun in London with 'Champagne Charlie is my Name'? A brutal Thing; nearly worthless—the Tune, I mean—but yet not quite—else it would not become so great a Bore. No: I can see, to my Sorrow, that it has some Go—which Mendelssohn had not. But Mozart, Rossini, and Handel had.

I can't help thinking that Opera will have to die for a time: certainly there seems to be no new Blood to keep it alive: and the Old Works of Genius want rest. I have never heard Faust: only Bits—which I suppose were thought the best Bits. They were expressive—musically ingenious, etc.—but the part of Hamlet— the one Divine Soul of Music, Melody—was not there. I think that such a Fuss can be made about it only because there is nothing better.

To W. A. Wright

Market hill, Woodbridge. Dec. 11 [1867]

Dear Sir,

When Robert Groome was with me a month ago, I was speaking to him of having found some Bacon in Montaigne: and R. G. told me that you had observed the same, and were indeed collecting some instances; I think, quotations from Seneca, so employed as to prove that Bacon had them from the Frenchman. It has been the fashion of late to scoff at Seneca; whom such men as Bacon and Montaigne quoted: perhaps not Seneca's own, but cribbed from some Greek which would have been admired by those who scoff at the Latin.

I had not noticed this Seneca coincidence: but I had observed a few passages of Montaigne's own, which seemed to me to have got into Bacon's Essays. I dare say I couldn't light upon all these now; but, having been turning over Essai 9, Lib. III. De la Vanité, I find one sentence which comes to the point: 'Car parfois c'est bien choisir de ne choisir pas.' In the same Essay is a piece of King Lear, perhaps; 'De ce mesme papier où il vient d'escrire l'arrest de condemnation contre un Adultere, le Juge en desrobe un lopin pour en faire un poulet à la femme de son compaignon.' One doesn't talk of such things as of plagiarisms, of course; as if Bacon and Shakespeare couldn't have said much better things themselves; only for the pleasure of tracing where they read, and what they were struck by. I see that 'L'Appetit vient en mangeant' is in the same Essay.

If I light some other day on the other passages, I will take the liberty of telling you. You see I have already taken the liberty of writing to a man, not unknown to me in several ways, but with whom I have not the pleasure of being acquainted personally. Perhaps I may have that pleasure one of these days; we are both connected with the same town of Beccles, and may come together. I hope so.

But I have also another reason for writing to you. Your 'Master' wrote me word the other day, among other things, that you as well as he wished for my own noble works in your Library. I quite understand that this is on the ground of my being a Trinity man. But then one should have done something worthy of ever so little a niche in Trinity Library; and that I do know is not my case. I have several times told the Master what I think, and know, of my small Escapades in print; nice little things, some of them, which may interest a few people (mostly friends, or through friends) for a few years. But I am always a little ashamed of having made my leisure and idleness the means of putting myself forward in print, when really so many much better people keep silent, having other work to do. This is, I know, my sincere feeling on the subject. However, as I think some of the Translations I have done are all I can dare to show, and as it would be making too much fuss to wait for any further asking on the subject, I will send them if you think good one of these days all done up together; the Spanish, at least, which are, I think, all of a size. Will you tell the Master so if you happen to see him and mention the subject?

Allow me to end by writing myself yours sincerely

EDWARD FITZGERALD

To Herman Biddell

Woodbridge, Decr. 22/67

My dear Biddell,

It occurs to me that, when I last saw you, you gave me hopes of finding a *Chanticleer* to replace that aged fellow you saw in my Domains. *He* came from Grundisburgh; and surely you spoke of some such Bird flourishing in Grundisburgh still. I will not hold out for the identical plumage—worthy of an Archangel— I only stipulate for one of the sort: such as are seen in old Story books; and on Church-vanes; with a plume of Tail, a lofty Crest and Walk, and a shrill trumpet-note of Challenge: any splendid colours; black and red; black and Gold; white, and red, and Gold! Only so as he be 'gay,' according to old Suffolk speech.

Well, of course you won't trouble yourself about this: only don't *forget* it, next time you ride through Grundisburgh. Or if, in the course of any Ride, you should see any such Bird, catch him up at once upon your Saddle-bow, and bring him to the distressed Widows on my Estate.

644

Now, I gladly take this opportunity of wishing you and yours a Happy Christmas and New Year. You know you will be welcome here whenever you choose to come.

To E. B. Cowell

12 Marine Terrace, Lowestoft. Dec. 28 [1867]
My dear Cowell

. . . I don't think I told you about Garcin de Tassy. He sent me (as no doubt he sent you) his annual Oration. I wrote to thank him: and said I had been lately busy with another countryman of his, Mons. Nicolas, with his Omar Khayyám. On which De Tassy writes back by return of post to ask 'Where I got my Copy of Nicolas? He had not been able to get one in all Paris!' So I wrote to Quaritch: who told me the Book was to be had of Maisonneuve, or any Oriental Bookseller in Paris; but that probably the Shopman did not understand, when 'Les Rubáiyát d'Omar &c.' were asked for, that it meant 'Les Quatrains &c.' This (which I doubt not is the solution of the Mystery) I wrote to Garcin: at the same time offering one of my two Copies. By return of Post comes a frank acceptance of one of the Copies; and his own Translation of Attár's Birds by way of equivalent. τοιόνδ' ἀπέβη τόδε πρᾶγμα. Well, as I got these Birds just as I was starting here, I brought them with me, and looked them over. Here, at Lowestoft, in this same row of houses, two doors off, I was writing out the Translation I made in the Winter of 1859. I have scarce looked at Original or Translation since. But I was struck by this; that eight years had made little or no alteration in my idea of the matter: it seemed to me that I really had brought in nearly all worth remembering, and had really condensed the whole into a much compacter Image than the original. This is what I think I can do, with such discursive things: such as all the Oriental things I have seen are. I remember you thought that I had lost the Apologues towards the close; but I believe I was right in excluding them, as the narrative grew dramatic and neared the Catastrophe. Also, it is much better to glance at the dangers of the Valley when the Birds are in it, than to let the Leader recount them before: which is not good policy, morally or dramatically. When I say all this, you need not suppose that I am vindicating the Translation as a Piece of Verse. I remember thinking it from the first rather disagreeable than not: though with some good parts. Jam satis.

There is a pretty story, which seems as if it really happened (p. 201 of De Tassy's Translation, referring to v. 3581 of the original), of the Boy falling into a well, and on being taken out senseless, the Father asking him to say but a word; and then, but one word more: which the Boy says and dies. And at p. 256, Translation iv. 4620), I read, 'Lorsque Nizâm ul-mulk fut à l'agonie, il dit: "O mon Dieu, je m'en vais en tre les mains du vent."' Here is our Omar in his Friend's mouth, is it not?

I have come here to wind up accounts for our Herring-lugger: much against us, as the season has been a bad one. My dear Captain, who looks in his Cottage like King Alfred in the Story, was rather saddened by all this, as he had prophesied better things. I tell him that if he is but what I think him—and surely my sixty years of considering men will not so deceive me at last! —I would rather lose money with him than gain it with others. Indeed I never proposed Gain, as you may imagine: but only to have some Interest with this dear Fellow. Happy New Year to you Both!

I wish you would have Semelet's Gulistan which I have. You know I never cared for Sadi.

To W. M. Donne

Lowestoft: Decr. 31/67

My dear Mowbray,

Your letter only came to hand here this morning. But I am just in time to wish you both a Good 1868. So be it!

I came here a week ago to wind up accounts for the Lugger— all on the wrong side, at present—but we look to 1868. *Posh* has fretted at his unsuccess: though in fact he has done better than half the Boats. It has been a bad Season: spoilt by the strong Winds in the last month. Yesterday we had a grand Bill paying: I told him there was *less* to pay than I expected: &, if he were what I thought, I would rather lose money with him than win it with many others. The dear old Boy got happy: and of course made me angry by coming home *rather unsteady* after settling the Bills. So I look glum Today: & all the while know I'm not worthy to grease his Boots—

What is all this to you!—I should like to see a Westminster Play: but I never could care for Terence—Very easy, elegant, & sensible: but no Devil. I have a Virgil with me here; he has no Devil neither: but then what an Angel! Talking of Devil, I am really reprinting that old Persian: all the copies of which have gone off, at a steady sale of 2 per annum: the greater portion having, I believe, been lost by Quaritch when he changed house. It is the only one of all my Great Works that ever has been asked for:—I am persuaded, *because* of the Wickedness, which is now at the heart of so much—Goodness! Not that the Persian has anything at all new: but he has dared to *say* it, as Lucretius did: and now it is put into tolerable English Music—That is all—

Edmund Kerrich & Wife are here for a while: after which they go to Boulge, and then perhaps to *My Château* at Woodbridge. My Brother told them he expected Gerald at Boulge—I was rejoiced to see your Dad so well & in such good Spirits: more amiable & good you know he could not be. I was sorry to have heard from him that Mrs. Fred & Co were come over.

Oh, it's cold enough here now! And all the time my old Brother Peter is sitting under a Parasol, I believe, amid Oranges in Blossom, at Cannes. I had a very kind Letter from Mrs. Kemble: she seems glad to hear from England.

Now, my dear *Mow*, give my kind Regards to the *Missis*, & believe me ever your's

E. F.G.

To R. H. Groome

Lowestoft, Tuesday, June 16, 1868

. . . Thank you for the Books, which were all right: except in so far that they were anointed by the oozings of some Rhubarb Jam which Miss Berry very kindly introduced among them. I am at my Don Quixote again; and really only sorry that I can read it so much more easily this year than last that I shall be all the sooner done with it. Mackerel still come in very slow, sometimes none at all: the dead-calm nights play the deuce with the Fishing, and I see no prospect of change in the weather till the Mackerel shall be changing their Quarters. I am vexed to see the Lugger come in Day after day so poorly stored after all the Labour of Time and Anxiety given to the work by her Crew; but I can do no more, and at any rate take my own share of the Loss very lightly. I can afford it better than they can. I have told Newson[1] to set sail and run home any Day, Hour, or Minute, when he wishes to see his Wife and Family. But at present he seems contented to eat Fish here: whether some of the few '*Stulls*'[2] which Posh brings in, or what his now innumerable friends the Trawlers are always offering. In fact, I think Newson looks to Lowestoft as a Summer Pasture, and is in no hurry to leave it. He lives there well for nothing, except Bread, Cheese, and Tea and Sugar. He has now taken to Cocoa, however, which he calls 'Cuckoo' to my hearing; having become enamoured of that Beverage in the Lugger, where it is the order of the day . . .

To Joseph Fletcher

Markethill, Woodbridge, Wednesday. [1869?]
Now then, Posh, here is a letter for you, sooner than you looked for, and moreover you will have to answer it as soon as you can.

I want you to learn from your friend *Dan Fuller* what particulars you can about that Lugger we saw at Mutford Bridge. Draft of Water, Length of Keel, What sails and Stores; and what *Price*; and any other Questions you may think necessary to ask. If the man here who has a notion of buying such a Vessel to make a Yacht of on this river sees any hope of doing so at a reasonable rate, and with a reasonable hope of Success, he will go over next week to look at the Vessel. He of course knows he would have to alter all her inside: but I told him your Opinion that she would do well *cutter rigged*.

So now, Poshy, do go down as soon as is convenient, to Dan, and stand him *half a pint* and don't tell him what you are come about, but just turn the conversation (in a *Salvaging* sort of way)

[1] [Thomas Newson, EFG's captain on the *Scandal*.]
[2] [Stull—an extra large mackerel.]

to the old Lugger and get me the particulars I ask for. Perhaps Dan's heart will open—*over Half a Pint*—as yours has been known to do. And if you write to me as soon as you can what you can learn, why I take my Blessed Oath that I'll be d—d if I don't stand you Half a Pint, so help me Bob, the next time I go to Lowestoft. I hope I make myself understood.

The Elsie is being gutted, and new timbered, and Mr Silver had bought a new dandy of forty tons, and Ablett Percival is to be Captain. I think of going down the river soon to see Captain Newson. I have been on the River To-day and thought that I should have been with you on the way to Yarmouth or South-wold if I had stayed at Lowestoft. Instead of which I have been to the Lawyer here.

Good-bye, Poshy, and believe me always yours to the last Half Pint.

E. FG.

I enclose a paper with my questions marked, to which you can add short answers.

To W. F. Pollock

[1869]

My dear Pollock,

I meant to have thanked you for your first long, and capital, letter, even had it not been followed by that of yesterday. You think to mystify a poor Country man? Well, it is all capital fooling. Do, pray, when you have an idle half-hour, send me any such letters. I cannot return them in kind, *you* know as *I* know: I have not the material, nor the Wit to work upon it. That is quite true.

I have not seen Forster's Landor; not caring much for either party. Forster seems to me a genuine Cockney: be-heroing Goldsmith, Landor, etc., *à outrance*. I remember so well his being red-hot in admiration of Coventry Patmore's first Poems: 'By God, they came up to Tennyson's,' etc. Talking of Tennyson, by the way, I had the curiosity to ask Carlyle (in my yearly Letter) what he thought of Browning's Book.[1] I dare say you have heard him talk on the subject. He writes to me: 'I have

---

[1] [*The Ring and the Book.*]

read—insisted on reading—Browning's Book. It is full of talent, energy, and effort: but actually without *Backbone* or basis of Common-sense. I think it among the absurdest books ever written by a gifted Man.'

Such is the opinion of all the men I know, whose opinion is certainly worth as much as the Newspaper Critics. Then why don't some of you step out into the Newspapers and Magazines, and tell the Truth of the Case? Why does not Venables? Stephen? Pollock? I am sure I would if I could: but I have not the faculty. I can only say, 'I do not like you, Doctor Fell,' but there I stop—knowing I'm right. If Browning were half as great as they say, he would himself write to disclaim any approximation to Tennyson . . .

To E. B. Cowell

Woodbridge: March 1/69

My dear Cowell,

. . . My lugger Captain has just left me to go on his Mackerel Voyage to the Western Coast; and I don't know when I shall see him again. Just after he went, a muffled bell from the Church here began to toll for somebody's death: it sounded like a Bell under the sea. He sat listening to the Hymn played by the Church chimes last evening, and said he could hear it all as if in Lowestoft church when he was a Boy, 'Jesus our Deliverer!' You can't think what a grand, tender, Soul this is, lodged in a suitable carcase.

To Mrs W. H. Thompson

[1869]

Dear Mrs Thompson—

(I must get a new Pen for you—which doesn't promise to act as well as the old one—Try another.)

Dear Mrs Thompson—Mistress of Trinity—(this does better)—

I am both sorry, and glad, that you wrote me the Letter you have written to me: sorry because I think it was an effort to you, disabled as you are; and glad, I need not say why.

I despatched Spedding's Letter to your Master yesterday;

I dare say you have read it: for there was nothing extraordinary wicked in it. But, he to talk of *my* perversity! . . .

My Sir Joshua is a darling. A pretty young Woman ("Girl" I won't call her) sitting with a turtle-dove in her lap, while its mate is supposed to be flying down to it from the window. I say 'supposed' for Sir J. who didn't know much of the drawing of Birds, any more than of Men and Women, has made a thing like a stuffed Bird clawing down like a Parrot. But then, the Colour, the Dove-colour, subdued so as to carry off the richer tints of the dear Girl's dress; and she, too, pensive, not sentimental: a Lady, as her Painter was a Gentleman. Faded as it is in the face (the Lake, which he would use, having partially flown), it is one of the most beautiful things of his I have seen: more varied in colour; not the simple cream-white dress he was fond of, but with a light gold-threaded Scarf, a blue sash, a green chair &c. . . .

I was rather taken aback by the Master's having discovered my last—yes, and bonâ-fide my last—translation in the volume I sent to your Library. I thought it would slip in unobserved, and I should have given all my little contributions to my old College, without after-reckoning. Had I known you as the wife of any but the 'quondam' Greek Professor, I should very likely have sent it to you: since it was meant for those who might wish for some insight into a Play[1] which I must think they can scarcely have been tempted into before by any previous Translation. It remains to be much better done; but if Women of Sense and Taste, and Men of Sense and Taste (who don't know Greek) can read, and be interested in such a glimpse as I give them of the Original, they must be content, and not look the Horse too close in the mouth, till a better comes to hand.

My Lugger has had (along with her neighbours) such a Season hitherto of Winds as no one remembers. We made £450 in the North Sea; and (just for fun) I did wish to realize £5 in my Pocket. But my Captain would take it all to pay Bills. But if he makes another £400 this Home Voyage! Oh, then we shall have money in our Pockets. I do wish this. For the anxiety about all these People's lives has been so much more to me than all the amusement I have got from the Business, that I think I will draw out of it if I can see my Captain sufficiently firm on his

[1] [The *Agamemnon*.]

legs to carry it on alone. True, there will then be the same risk to him and his ten men, but they don't care; only I sit here listening to the Winds in the Chimney, and always thinking of the Eleven hanging at my own fingers' ends.

This Letter is all desperately about me and mine, Translations and Ships. And now I am going to walk in *my* Garden: and feed my Captain's Pony with white Carrots; and in the Evening have *my* Lad come and read for an hour and a half (he stumbles at every third word, and gets dreadfully tired, and so do I; but I renovate him with Cake and Sweet Wine), and I can't just now smoke the Pipe nor drink the Grog. "These are my Troubles, Mr Wesley"; but I am still the Master's and Mistress' loyal Servant,

EDWARD FITZGERALD

To W. F. Pollock

Woodbridge, May 10 [1869]

My dear Pollock,

I am like old Mr Barton, who, as he never left Woodbridge, could only talk by letter to Friends beyond. (Dear me! it is now just ten years since I made my last bow before the London Lights.) Like him, too, I take a pinch of snuff between-whiles: and, now I think of it, from the very box he held in his hand five minutes before his death. What agreeable Associations!

However, you know that I never expect you to answer me unless I put a particular question; and that is not very often; and I think you are generally good enough to reply to it. This present Letter wants no such notice at all. I am not got on board my Ship as yet; she is now making her Toilet, or 'toilette' as I see it now written, to meet me at the end of the month; and after that I dare say we shall be living together, for better or worse, till November. It seems to me but a few weeks since I parted with her.

Your notion of J. S. and the Velocipede (I know it's yours only) is capital. I remember one day talking with my poor friend W. Browne as to what forms Drunkenness would take with our friends in case they should ever get overtaken. How with old

Spedding? W. B. said at once, 'I can fancy him turning a chair bottom upwards and fancying himself an Applewoman.' A touch of Genius, I thought: I don't know how it will strike you.

I have made three vain attempts at Vol. I. of Browning—did I tell you? It seems to me an audacious piece of defiance to the Public whom he had found so long blind to his Merits—'Now you have at last come to accept me, I'll ride over you rough-shod.' But A. T. tells me he 'finds greatness' in the work, call it Poem or what you will. And I should say no more, only I remember old Alfred trying to make us worship Bailey's Festus—magnanimous Great Dog!

Laurence I have given up as hopeless these twenty years, since he himself gave up his sketches in Crayon and Oil to seek after Venetian colour. Old Spedding encouraged him; was as sure of his finding that secret out as of redressing Bacon; and in both cases leaves his Heroes worse off than he found them.

There are interesting Notes of Conversation with Rossini in some back Numbers of Once a Week, showing how perfectly sane and comprehensive was the mind of that great Genius, at any rate.

To Herman Biddell

Woodbridge, Guy Faux Day [1869]

Dear Biddell,

I have thought once or twice that Tennyson himself ought to have that illustration of one of his Poems which Thackeray made, and which I gave to you. If you do not set any particular store by it, let us arrange that, and do you take any other you please from the Book you know of. But if you *do* set store by that particular drawing, why, keep it by all means. I have never mentioned it to Tennyson, and do not suppose that *he* would care very much for it. Yet it seems the right thing to do: for he was a great friend of Thackeray's, and admired *the Man*, without (I suppose) having ever read any of his Books through. I remember his taking up a No. of Pendennis in my Lodging twenty years ago, reading awhile, and then saying—'How *mature* it is!'— perfectly ripe, seasonable, and perfect, a produce of the Man's Wit and Experience of the World.

I am *sure* that Thackeray's drawing must be better than any of *Doré's*—which I have never seen!

To W. F. Pollock

Woodbridge, Nov. 20 [1869]

My dear Pollock,

I am ashamed to lay you under any tax for more letters, since I really can send such poor repayment. And just now, I doubt, worse than usual: for I'm not quite in sorts, nor have been these last ten days. Perhaps from a change of Life from being out all day long in Sea Air, to being shut up here.

I have bought and looked over (*that*, I must say, is all) Mrs. Ward's Clarissa (Routledge's 2s. affair), and seem to have a few scraps and bones of the original Book served up to me—the best part of the meat gone. I shall one day see from Mudie how Dallas has managed; but our Mudie-man here is terribly slow. He tells me he has ordered Books over and over again; perhaps you great Londoners think anything will do for us Country chaps.

I remember when I was busy with Clarissa, being frightened at Montaigne's 'Tout abrégé d'un bon livre est sot abrégé,' which I think coincided something with the opinion of F. Pollock. I should, however, have done it; but now these people have spoilt my Market, and saved me money.

I am about to write my yearly letter to Carlyle. I suppose he still lives at Chelsea. His Niagara Pamphlet was almost tragic to me: such a helpless outcry from the Prophet who has so long told us what not to do, but never what *to* do. I don't know if he still maintains his Fame at the former height.

There was an absurd Article in my old Athenæum comparing the relative merits of Tennyson and Browning: awarding the praise of Finish, etc., to A. T., and of originality to B.! I am not perhaps sufficiently read in the latter: for I never could read him: and I have reliance on my own intuition that, such being the case, he is not a rival to A. T., whom I judge of by his earlier poems (up to 1842). In Browning I could but see little but Cockney Sublime, Cockney Energy, etc.; and as you once very wittily said to me that Miss Brontë was a 'great Mistress of the Disagreeable,' so, if B. has power, I must consider it of that sort. Tennyson has stocked the English language with lines which once knowing one can't forgo. Cowell tells me that even at Oxford and Cambridge Browning is considered the deepest! But 'this also will pass away.' But not A. T.

To W. F. Pollock

Woodbridge, Dec. 7/69

My dear Pollock,

It is very good of you to write to me. You have plenty to do, and I have nothing to do, or to tell in return. So it is, however, that only last night, or this morning, as I was lying awake in bed, I thought to myself that I would write to you—yes, and have a letter from you—once before Christmas—before New Year 1870, at any rate. And when I came down this morning with the pleasing prospect of half-an-hour's walk in the East wind before breakfast, here was your letter anticipating mine.

It is capital, your going to see old Alfred in his lordly Pleasure-house looking over the Weald: I think one misses water in those otherwise fine sweeps of Down and Weald. But then water is the only thing we East Anglians have to show: and dismal cold it shows now. I don't know if the woodland look better. This time of Year is certainly next door to Death. I half long to be at Rome, which Mrs Kemble, who winters there, tells me about. But then the packing, unpacking, rushing to packets, railways, hotels, etc., with the probable chance of wishing oneself back in one's own dull Woodbridge after all!

Leave well—even 'pretty well'—alone: that is what I learn as I get old. I have only been pretty well myself lately: diminished of Grog and Pipe, which made the happiest hour of the twenty-four, and actually trying some Homeopathic Nux Vomica instead—whether for better or worse I won't say: for, directly one has said it, you know——

Then, my dear Eyes not having quite recovered the paraffin, a lad comes to read at half-past seven till nine—stumbling at every other word, unless it be some Story that carries him along. So now we are upon the Woman in White: third time of reading in my case: and I can't help getting frightened now. I see a new Story[1] advertised from Dickens.

Did I tell you that when I ran to London some weeks ago to consult Bowman,[2] I saw at a framer's in Leicester Square, a Sir Joshua Portrait, and bought it? The face faded, but the expression and air all delightful, and the Dress and 'entourage' of Venetian Colour. It is of a young and pretty woman—pensive, not sentimental—holding a Dove in her lap, while its mate is coming down (very heavily), through a Window, I suppose. I wonder how it was that such lots of Virtuosos, Artists, Academicians, etc., should be passing, as they must, that way, and not have troubled themselves to offer, or get some one to offer £20 for it. Well, if they saw it with me they would say it was no Sir Joshua at all; I am very glad they never thought it was so. I should tell Tom Taylor of it, as I see he advertises a list of Sir Joshua's as forthcoming from Murray: but he would take for granted it was a pleasant delusion.

Mrs A. T. is all you say, indeed: a Lady of a Shakespearian type, as I think A. T. once said of her: that is, of the Imogen sort, far more agreeable to me than the sharp-witted Beatrices, Rosalinds, etc. I do not think she has been (on this very account perhaps) so good a helpmate to A. T.'s Poetry as to himself. But the time is come (if it never were before) that makes the latter [? former] a very secondary consideration.

This is very dull, all this, my dear Pollock: and now growing too much of it: in bad MS. too. Besides, I begin to think I told you all about my Picture before. And, after all, I haven't looked at it half-a-dozen times since it has been down: but then it is at my *Château*—where I don't live.

Now in ten minutes the Mate of a Three-masted Schooner is coming to say Goodbye before he starts to Genōa (they call it) with a cargo of—Red Herring. And then my reader! He is the son of a Cabinet-maker: and last night read 'her future husband' as 'her *furniture* husband.' This is true.

[1] [*The Mystery of Edwin Drood.*]
[2] [Sir William Bowman (1816–92), a distinguished ophthalmic surgeon.]

To Samuel Laurence

Market hill: Woodbridge. Jan. 13/70

My dear Laurence,

Can you tell me (in a line) how I should treat some old Pictures of mine which have somehow got rusty with the mixt damp and then fires (I suppose) of my new house, which, after being built at near double its proper cost, is just what I do not want, according to the usage of the Ballyblunder Family, of which I am a very legitimate offshoot?

If you were down here, I think I should make you take a life-size Oil Sketch of the Head and Shoulders of my Captain of the Lugger. You see by the enclosed that these are neither of them of a bad sort: and the Man's Soul is every way as well proportioned, missing in nothing that may become A Man, as I believe. He and I will, I doubt, part Company; well as he likes me, which is perhaps as well as a sailor cares for any one but Wife and Children: he likes to be, what he is born to be, his own sole Master, of himself, and of other men. So now I have got him a fair start, I think he will carry on the Lugger alone: I shall miss my Hobby, which is no doubt the last I shall ride in this world: but I shall also get eased of some Anxiety about the lives of a Crew for which I now feel responsible. And this last has been a Year of great Anxiety in this respect.

I had to run to London for one day about my Eyes (which, you see by my MS., are not in prime order at all) and saw a Sir Joshua at a Framer's window, and brought it down. The face faded, but elegant and lady-like always; the dress in colour quite Venetian. It was in Leicester Square; I can't think how all the world of Virtuosos kept passing and would not give twenty pounds for it. But you don't rate Sir Joshua in comparison with Gainsboro'.

To Samuel Laurence

Woodbridge: Jan. 20/70

My dear Laurence,

. . . My Captain lives at Lowestoft, and is there at present: he also in anxiety about his Wife who was brought to bed the very same day my Landlady died, and (as a letter from him this morning tells me) has a hard time of it. I should certainly like a large Oil-sketch, like Thackeray's, done in your most hasty, and worst, style, to hang up with Thackeray and Tennyson, with whom he shares a certain Grandeur of Soul and Body. As you guess, the colouring is (when the Man is all well) as fine as his form: the finest Saxon type: with that complexion which Montaigne calls 'vif, mâle, et flamboyant;' blue eyes; and strictly auburn hair, that any woman might sigh to possess. He says it is coming off, as it sometimes does from those who are constantly wearing the close hot Sou'westers. We must see what can be done about a Sketch.

To Samuel Laurence

Lowestoft, February 27 [1870]

My dear Laurence,

. . . I came here a few days ago, for the benefit of my old Doctor, The Sea, and my Captain's Company, which is as good. He has not yet got his new Lugger home; but will do so this week, I hope; and then the way for us will be somewhat clearer.

If you sketch in a head, you might send it down to me to look at, so as I might be able to guess if there were any likelihood in that way of proceeding. Merely the Lines of Feature indicated, even by Chalk, might do. As I told you, the Head is of the large type, or size, the proper Capital of a six foot Body, of the broad dimensions you see in the Photograph. The fine shape of the Nose, less than Roman, and more than Greek, scarce appears in the Photograph; the Eye, and its delicate Eyelash, of course will remain to be made out; and I think you excel in the Eye.

When I get home (which I shall do this week) I will send you two little Papers about the Sea words and Phrases used hereabout, for which this Man (quite unconsciously) is my main Authority. You will see in them a little of his simplicity of Soul; but not the Justice of Thought, Tenderness of Nature, and all the other good Gifts which make him a Gentleman of Nature's grandest Type.

To Bernard Quaritch

Market Hill, Woodbridge July 8 [1870]

Dear Sir,

Thank you for your note about poor old Omar's first "*fiasco*" —I suppose he does not fare much better now, in spite of all those Gentlemen's good opinions; which might not have been the case had one of them given him a good word years ago. But I never *ask* anyone to do such a Job for me, as someone I hear has now done in Fraser's Magazine.

However Omar does not take up much room on your shelves, & will go off one day—when probably I shall be out of reach of a third Edition of 150 copies.

Meanwhile I console myself with my little ship, & am

Yours truly, EDWARD FITZOMAR

To Samuel Laurence

Suffolk Hotel, Lowestoft, August 2/70

Dear Laurence,

. . . The Lugger is now preparing in the Harbour beside me; the Captain here, there, and everywhere; with a word for no one but on business; the other side of the Man you saw looking for Birds' Nests; all things in their season. I am sure the Man is fit to be King of a Kingdom as well as of a Lugger. To-day he gives the customary Dinner to his Crew before starting, and my own two men go to it; and I am asked too: but will not spoil the Fun.

I declare, you and I have seen A Man! Have we not? Made in the mould of what Humanity should be, Body and Soul, a poor Fisherman. The proud Fellow had better have kept me for a Partner in some of his responsibilities. But no; he must rule alone, as is right he should too.

I date from the Inn where my Letters are addressed; but I write in the little Ship which I live in. My Nieces are now here; in the Town, I mean; and my friend Cowell and his Wife; so I have more company than all the rest of the year. I try to shut my Eyes and Ears against all tidings of this damnable War, seeing that I can do no good to others by distressing myself.

To Bernard Quaritch

TELEGRAM[1]

Lowestoft Septr. 20/70. 10 a.m.
From on board Ship where Professor Cowell is just going for a sail with yours truly E. FG.

$10\frac{1}{2}$ a.m.
A Melton Mowbray Pork Pie & a Bottle of Sherry just hoisted on board for the Professor's Luncheon.

11 a.m.
Professor himself just hoisted on board. He begs his Compliments.

$11\frac{1}{4}$ a.m.
Topsail just hoisting in order to get the Professor & the Pork Pie out of Harbour. Wind very light. S. E.

Please to tell Count Bismarck that, if he could batter down Paris, without killing the Parisians, it would do more to keep France quiet for the next 20 years than the cession of Alsace & Lorraine.

To W. F. Pollock

Bridgewood, Nov. 1, [1870]

My dear Pollock,

I must say that my savageness against France goes no further than wishing that the new and gay part of Paris were battered down; not the poor working part, no, nor any of the People destroyed. But I wish ornamental Paris down, because then I

---

[1] [This communication was not really a telegram, but was written on the back of a receipted bill for Mirabeau's Correspondence, 3 vols., sent to "E. FitzGerald, Esqre, Suffolk Hotel, Lowestoft," by Bernard Quaritch, 2 September 1870.]

think the French would be kept quiet till they had rebuilt it. For what would France be without a splendid Palace? I should not wish any such Catastrophe, however, if Paris were now as I remember it: with a lot of old historic houses in it, old Gardens &c., which I am told are now made away with. Only Notre Dame, the Tuileries, and perhaps the beautiful gilt Dome of the Invalides do I care for. They are historical and beautiful too.

But I believe it would be a good thing if the rest of Europe would take possession of France itself, and rule it for better or worse, leaving the French themselves to amuse and enlighten the world by their Books, Plays, Songs, Bon Mots, and all the Arts and Sciences which they are so ingenious in. They can do all things but manage themselves and live at peace with others: and they should themselves be glad to have their volatile Spirits kept in order by the Good Sense and Honesty which other Nations certainly abound in more than themselves.

I see what I think very good remarks about them in old Palmerston's Papers quoted in my Athenæum. He was just the Man they wanted, I think.

To Fanny Kemble

Woodbridge, July 4, [1871]

Dear Mrs Kemble,

I asked Donne to tell you, if he found opportunity, that some two months ago I wrote you a letter, but found it so empty and dull that I would not send it to extort the Reply which you feel bound to give. I should have written to tell you so myself; but I heard from Donne of the Wedding soon about to be, and I would not intrude then. Now that is over[1]—I hope to the satisfaction of you all—and I will say my little say, and you will have to Reply, according to your own Law of Mede and Persian.

It is a shame that one should only have oneself to talk about; and yet that is all I have; so it shall be short. If you will but tell

[1] [Mrs Kemble's daughter, Frances Butler, was married to the Hon. and Rev. James Wentworth Leigh, 29 June 1871.]

me of yourself, who have read, and seen, and done, so much more, you will find much more matter for your pen, and also for my entertainment.

Well, I have sold my dear little Ship, because I could not employ my Eyes with reading in her Cabin, where I had nothing else to do. I think those Eyes began to get better directly I had written to agree to the Man's proposal. Anyhow, the thing is done; and so now I betake myself to a Boat, whether on this River here, or on the Sea at the Mouth of it.

Books you see I have nothing to say about. The Boy who came to read to me made such blundering Work that I was forced to confine him to a Newspaper, where his Blunders were often as entertaining as the Text which he mistook. We had 'hangarues' in the French Assembly, and, on one occasion, 'iron-clad Laughter from the Extreme Left.' Once again, at the conclusion of the London news, 'Consolations closed at 91, ex Div.'—And so on. You know how illiterate People will jump at a Word they don't know, and twist it in[to] some word they are familiar with. I was telling some of these Blunders to a very quiet Clergyman here some while ago, and he assured me that a poor Woman, reading the Bible to his Mother, read off glibly, 'Stand at a Gate and swallow a Candle.' I believe this was no Joke of his: whether it were or not, here you have it for what you may think it worth.

I should be glad to hear that you think Donne looking and seeming well. Archdeacon Groome, who saw him lately, thought he looked very jaded: which I could not wonder at. Donne, however, writes as if in good Spirits—brave Man as he is— and I hope you will be able to tell me that he is not so much amiss. He said that he was to be at the Wedding.

You will tell me too how long you remain in England: I fancy, till Winter: and then you will go to Rome again, with its new Dynasty installed in it. I fancy I should not like that so well as the old; but I suppose it's better for the Country.

I see my Namesake (Percy) Fitzgerald advertizes a Book about the Kembles. That I shall manage to get sight of. He made far too long work of Garrick. I should have thought the Booksellers did not find that pay, judging by the price to which Garrick soon came down. Half of it would have been enough.

Now I am going for a Sail on the famous River Deben, to pass by the same fields of green Wheat, Barley, Rye, and Beet-root, and come back to the same Dinner. Positively the only new thing we have in Woodbridge is a Waxen Bust (Lady, of course) at the little Hairdresser's opposite. She turns slowly round, to our wonder and delight; and I caught the little Barber the other day in the very Act of winding her up to run her daily Stage of Duty. Well; she has not got to answer Letters, as poor Mrs Kemble must do to hers always sincerely

E. F.G.

To W. A. Wright

Woodbridge: Septr. 4/71

I run over to Lowestoft occasionally for a few days, but do not abide there long: no longer having my dear little Ship for company. I saw her there looking very smart under her new owner ten days ago, and I felt so at home when I was once more on her Deck that—Well: I content myself with sailing on the river Deben, looking at the Crops as they grow green, yellow, russet, and are finally carried away in the red and blue Waggons with the sorrel horse.

To Fanny Kemble

[Nov. 1871]

Dear Mrs Kemble,

I ought to be much obliged to you for answering my last letter with an uneasy hand, as you did. So I do thank you: and really wish that you would not reply to this under any such pain: but how do I know but that very pain will make you more deter-mined to reply? I must only beg you not to do so: and thus wash *my* hands of any responsibilities in the matter.

And what will you say when I tell you that I can hardly pity one who suffers from Gout; though I would undoubtedly prefer that you should be free from that, or any other ailment. But I have always heard that Gout exempts one from many other

663

miseries which Flesh is heir to: at any rate, it almost always leaves the Head clear: and that is so much! My Mother, who suffered a good deal, used often to say how she was kept awake of nights by the Pain in her feet, or hands, but felt so clear aloft that she made Night pass even agreeably away with her reflections and recollections.

And you have your recollections and Reflections which you are gathering into Shape, you say, in a Memoir of your own Life. And you are good enough to say that you would read it to me if I—were good enough to invite you to my House here some Summer Day! I doubt that Donne has given you too flattering an account of my house, and me: you know he is pleased with every one and everything: I know it also, and therefore no longer dissuade him from spending his time and money in a flying Visit here in the course of his Visits to other East Anglian friends and Kinsmen. But I feel a little all the while as if I were taking all, and giving nothing in return: I mean, about Books, People, etc., with which a dozen years discontinuance of Society, and, latterly, incompetent Eyes, have left me in the lurch. If you indeed will come and read your Memoir to me, I shall be entitled to be a Listener only: and you shall have my Château all to yourself for as long as you please: only do not expect me to be quite what Donne may represent.

It is disgusting to talk so much about oneself: but I really think it is better to say so much on this occasion. If you consider my circumstances, you will perhaps see that I am not talking unreasonably: I am sure, not with sham humility: and that I am yours always and sincerely

E. F.G.

P.S. I should not myself have written so soon again, but to apprise you of a brace of Pheasants I have sent you. Pray do not write expressly to acknowledge them:—only tell me if they don't come. I know you thank me.

To W. F. Pollock

Woodbridge, Dec. 29 [1871]

My dear Pollock,

If you come here, come some very fine weather, when we look at our best inland, and you may take charge of my Boat on the River. I doubt I did my Eyes damage this Summer by steering in the Sun, and peering out for the Beacons that mark the Channel; but your Eyes are proof against this, and I shall resign the command to you, as you wrote that you liked it at Clovelly. . . .

I had thought Beauty was the main object of the Arts: but these people, not having Genius, I suppose, to create any new forms of that, have recourse to the Ugly, and find their Worshippers in plenty. In Poetry, Music, and Painting, it seems to me the same. And people think all this finer than Mozart, Raffaelle, and Tennyson—as he *was*—but he never ceases to be noble and pure. There was a fine passage quoted from his Last Idyll: about a Wave spending itself away on a long sandy Shore: that was Lincolnshire, I know.

Carlyle has written to remind me of putting up a Stone on the spot in Naseby field where I dug up the Dead for him thirty years ago. I will gladly have the Stone cut, and the Inscription he made for it engraved: but will I go again to Northamptonshire to see it set up? And perhaps the people there have forgotten all about the place, now that a whole Generation has passed away, and improved Farming has passed the Plough over the Ground. But we shall see.

To Anna Biddell

Woodbridge. Feb. 22, [1872]

. . . I have lost the Boy who read to me so long and so profitably: and now have another; a much better Scholar, but not half so agreeable or amusing a Reader as his Predecessor. We go through Tichborne without missing a Syllable, and, when Tichborne is not long enough, we take to Lothair! which has entertained me well. So far as I know of the matter, his pictures of the manners of English High Life are good: Lothair himself I

665

do not care for, nor for the more romantic parts, Theodora, &c. Altogether the Book is like a pleasant Magic Lantern: when it is over, I shall forget it: and shall want to return to what I do not forget, some of Thackeray's monumental Figures of 'pauvre et triste Humanité,' as old Napoleon called it: Humanity in its Depths, not in its superficial Appearances.

To Fanny Kemble

[27 Feb. 1872]

Dear Mrs Kemble,

Had I anything pleasant to write to you, or better Eyes to write it with, you would have heard from me before this. An old Story, by way of Apology—to one who wants no such Apology, too. Therefore, true though it be there is enough of it.

I hear from Mowbray Donne that you were at his Father's Lectures, and looking yourself. So that is all right. Are your Daughters—or one of them—still with you? I do not think you have been to see the Thanksgiving Procession,[1] for which our Bells are even now ringing—the old Peal which I have known these—sixty years almost—though at that time it reached my Eyes [sic] through a Nursery window about two miles off. From that window I remember seeing my Father with another Squire passing over the Lawn with their little pack of Harriers—an almost obliterated Slide of the old Magic Lantern. My Mother used to come up sometimes, and we Children were not much comforted. She was a remarkable woman, as you said in a former letter: and as I constantly believe in outward Beauty as an Index of a Beautiful Soul within, I used sometimes to wonder what feature in her fine face betrayed what was not so good in her Character. I think (as usual) the Lips: there was a twist of Mischief about them now and then, like that in—the Tail of a Cat!—otherwise so smooth and amiable. I think she admired your Mother as much as any one she knew, or had known.

And (I see by the Athenæum) Mr. Chorley[2] is dead, whom I

[1] [27 February 1872, for the recovery of the Prince of Wales.]

[2] [Henry Fothergill Chorley (1808–72), author and critic. He joined the staff of the *Athenaeum* in 1833, and took charge of the music criticism.]

used to see at your Father's and Sister's houses. Born in 1808 they say: so, one year older than yours truly E. F.G.—who, however, is going to live through another page of Letter-paper. I think he was a capital Musical Critic, though he condemned Piccolomini, who was the last Singer I heard of Genius, Passion, and a Voice that told both. I am told she was no Singer: but that went some way to make amends. Chorley, too, though an irritable, nervous creature, as his outside expres⁀ ᵈ, was kind and affectionate to Family and Friend, I always heard. But I think the Angels must take care to keep in tune when he gets among them.

This is a wretched piece of Letter to extort the Answer which you feel bound to give. But I somehow wished to write: and not to write about myself; and so have only left room to say—to repeat—that I am yours ever sincerely

E. F.G.

To E. B. Cowell

Woodbridge, March 17 [1872]

My dear Cowell,

Let me hear if you be coming this way this Easter, and if you do, contrive to run over here for half a day.

My Eyes have let me read a little for the last month, though I am obliged to be very tender of them. But I have managed to read a little of some of the old 'Standards'—a little Shakespeare, to wit: which seemed astonishingly fresh to me: some of De Quincey's Essays: and some of Ste. Beuve's. Tichborne, you know, is no more: that Light has departed: so now my Boy and I console ourselves of a night with a Novel: one of Wilkie Collins' being now in course of reading. This Boy is a new Boy (the former having left Woodbridge), and one of two in the uppermost class of the school here: there been reading Euripides' Medea, Cicero's Officia, and Plato's Crito with Dr Tait. I enquire, and hear, a little about all this between readings, and made the Boy read me a bit of the Oedipus Coloneus the other night. I wish he could read it all over to me; but he would not understand it, and I am not Scholar enough to teach him as he ought to learn. Last night he came when the Curfew was tolling: I quoted to him the first Line of Gray's Elegy, which he had never heard of. This shows how things have altered since my young days: and, I suppose, since yours also: then we only heard too much of Gray's Curfew. And now farewell, ὦ φίλτατ' Αἰγέως παῖ.

To Bernard Quaritch

Woodbridge March 31 [1872]
Easter Sunday my own Birthday (64). I wonder how it is with Omar but I think I know.

Dear Sir,
You must think I have followed Omar underground, not to have answered you sooner—But I have been looking over him in consequence of your letter, to see what I could make of him. I wonder that, with all your great Business, you care to be troubled again with this little one: but if you really wish to set off old Omar once more to America, I would do what I could for his outfit.

I daresay Ed^n 1 is better in some respects than 2, but I think not altogether. Surely, several good things were added—perhaps too much of them which also gave Omar's thoughts room to turn in, as also the Day which the Poem occupies. He begins with Dawn pretty sober & contemplative: then as he thinks & drinks, grows savage, blasphemous &c., and then again sobers down into melancholy at nightfall. All which wanted rather more expansion than the first Ed^n gave. I dare say Ed^n 1 best pleased those who read it first: as first Impressions are apt to be strongest.

By the same rule might not those who read the 2nd Ed^n first go the other way? The Gentleman in Fraser & some others seemed well satisfied.

As to the relative fidelity of the two Versions, there isn't a Pin to choose—not in the opening Stanzas you send.

All this seems making too much fuss about a small thing. But the truth is, that on looking over the two Versions, and ready to adopt your plan of reconciling two in one, I considered that such a scheme, with brackets &c *would be* making too much of the thing: and you and I might both be laughed at for treating my Omar as if it were some precious fragment of Antiquity.

668

Besides I doubt if the two Versions could now—as altered—
separately dove-tail into one another without some fresh alteration—which I have lost heart and even Eyes for.

I doubt therefore that, if Omar be republished, he must go
forth in one Shape or another—in his first, or second, suit. And
I certainly vote for Version 2, with some whole Stanzas which
may be "de trop" cut out, & some of the old readings replaced.

On all which I would ask advice of you & of such as you rely
on, who would take the trouble of advising.

I said that I have looked over the two Versions and therefore I
can repeat about them now. My Eyes have been so bad these last
two years that I have read scarce anything: and feel a little
reluctant to revert even to my little Omar for any purpose of
revision.

If, however, you still wish it, I will send you the Poem curtailed,
& altered back, as I have proposed.

Yours truly, E. FG.

By the by, Cowell wrote me some months ago that Edⁿ 1 had
been reprinted by someone in India. So I have not lived in vain,
if I have lived to be *Pirated!*

To Fanny Kemble

[1872]

Dear Mrs Kemble,

I set off with a Letter to you, though I do not very well know
how I am to go on with it. But my Reader has been so disturbed
by a Mouse in the room that I have dismissed him—9½ p.m.—
and he has been reading (so far as he could get on) Hawthorne's
Notes of Italian Travel: which interest me very much indeed,
as being the Notes of a Man of Genius who will think for himself
independently of Murray &c. And then his Account of Rome
has made me think of you more than once. We have indeed left
off to-night at Radicofani: but, as my Boy is frightened away by
the Mouse, I fancy I will write to you before I take my one Pipe
—which were better left alone, considering that it gives but half
an hour's rather pleasant musing at the expense of a troubled
night. Is it not more foolish then to persist in doing this than

being frightened at a Mouse? This is not a mere fancy of the Boy
—who is not a Fool, nor a 'Betty,' and is seventeen years old:
he inherits his terror from his Mother, he says: positively he has
been in a cold Sweat because of this poor little thing in the room:
and yet he is the son of a Butcher here. So I sent him home, and
write to you instead of hearing him read Hawthorne. He is to
bring some poisoned Wheat for the Mouse to-morrow.

Another Book he read me also made me think of you: Harness:
whom I remember to have seen once or twice at your Father's
years ago. The Memoir of him (which is a poor thing) still makes
one like—nay, love—him—as a kindly, intelligent, man. I think
his latter letters very pleasant indeed.

I do not know if you are in London or in your 'Villeggiatura'
in Kent. Donne must decide that for me. Even my Garden and
Fields and Shrubs are more flourishing than I have yet seen
them at this time of Year: and with you all is in fuller bloom,
whether you be in Kent or Middlesex. Are you going on with
your Memoir? Pray read Hawthorne. I dare say you do not
quite forget Shakespeare now and then: dear old Harness,
reading him to the last!

Pray do you read Annie Thackeray's new Story in Cornhill?
She wrote me that she had taken great pains with it, and so
thought it might not be so good as what she took less pains with.
I doated on her Village on the Cliff, but did not care for what I
had read of hers since: and this new Story I have not seen!
And pray do you doat on George Eliot?

Here are a few questions suggested for you to answer—as
answer I know you will. It is almost a Shame to put you to it by
such a piece of inanity as this letter. But it is written: it is
10 p.m. A Pipe—and then to Bed—with what Appetite for Sleep
one may.

And I am yours sincerely always

E. F.G.

To W. F. Pollock

[1872]

My dear Pollock,
I went to London at the end of last week, on my way to
Sydenham, where my second Brother is staying, whom I had

not seen these six years, nor his Wife . . . On Saturday I went to the Academy, for little else but to see Millais, and to disagree with you about him! I thought his three Women and his Highlanders brave pictures, which you think also; but braver than you think them. The Women looked alive: the right Eye so much smaller than the left in the Figure looking at you that I suppose it was so in the original, so that I should have chosen one of the other Sisters for the position. I could not see any analogy between the Picture and Sir Joshua's Graces, except that there were Three. Nor could I think the Highlanders in the Landscape vulgar; they seemed to me in character with the Landscape. Both Pictures want tone, which may mean Glazing: wanting which they may last the longer, and sober down of themselves without danger of cracking by any transparent Colour laid over them.

I scarce looked at anything else, not having much time. Just as I was going out, who should come up to me but Annie Thackeray, who took my hands as really glad to see her Father's old friend. I am sure she was; and I was taken aback somehow; and, out of sheer awkwardness, began to tell her that I didn't care for her new Novel! And then, after she had left her Party to come to me, I ran off! It is true, I had to be back at Sydenham: but it would have been better to forgo all that: and so I reflected when I had got halfway down Piccadilly: and so ran back, and went into the Academy again: but could not find A. T. She told me she was going to Normandy this week: and I have been so vext with myself that I have written to tell her something of what I have told you. It was very stupid indeed.

To Bernard Quaritch

Woodbridge August 24 [1872]

Dear Sir,

I found Omar on my return home yesterday. I can only say that I doubt you have put him into a finer Dress than he deserves —and that some other Critics will have their Bile raised to say so—if they take any notice now of the old Offender. I only hope you have not overestimated your Transatlantic friends who I fancy are our chief Patrons—The Americans (as I found from

Mrs. Wister[1]—a daughter of Mrs. Kemble's) taking up a little *Craze* of this sort now and then.

Well—you have chosen to run the risk: and you are such a clever man that I suppose you know that your Edition may evaporate in time: and I hope you may live to see it.

Meanwhile, when Ed[n] II is exhausted, you will owe me something for it—of so little consequence to me, or to you, that I shall desire you to give it to some Charity—public or private. If the Persian *Famine Fund* still subsists, the money might properly be added to that—as I daresay old Omar would have done—had he translated the Works of your truly

E. FG.

I should like a *bound* Copy, such as you have sent me, to be sent to Cowell: and one also to "Alfred Tennyson, Farringford, Freshwater, Isle of Wight."

A dozen other Copies will, I daresay, quite suffice for myself: and these, I think, *not* bound, as I would do them up with a Revision of Salámán which I amused myself with two years ago. So I can stitch up the Saint & the Sinner together, for better or worse.

To W. F. Pollock

Woodbridge: November 1, [1872]

My dear Pollock,

The Spectator, and also the Athenæum, somewhat over-praise Gareth, I think: but I am glad they do so. . . . The Poem seems to me scarce more worthy of what A. T. was born to do than the other Idylls; but you will almost think it is out of contradiction that I like it better: except, of course, the original Morte. The Story of this young Knight, who can submit and conquer and do all the Devoir of Chivalry, interests me much more than the Enids, Lily Maids &c. of former Volumes. But Time *is*—Time *was*—to have done with the whole Concern: pure and noble as all is, and in parts more beautiful than any one else can do. . . .

Rain—Rain—Rain! What will become of poor Italy? I think

---

[1] [It was Sarah Wister who first decided, almost intuitively, that EFG was the anonymous translator of Omar Khayyám.]

we ought to subscribe for her. Did you read of one French Caricature of the Pope leaving Rome with the Holy Ghost in a Bird Cage?

To W. B. Donne

Lowestoft: March 6/75

My dear Donne

I have not received your Letter $\frac{1}{4}$ of an hour ago, when I try to send an Answer by our morning's Post: so as you may have it this same Ev^g instead of Monday Morning. You understand, I am sure, why I have written to Mowbray & Blanche rather than to yourself: I do not wish to put you to the least "conscience" about answering: which I doubt you would feel, however much I protested that no answer was needed. So far as your MS. is to be taken as a proof of your health, I do not see, I assure you, why it is not very good: not a word causing delay to me, who read off "currente oculo."

Yes, this has been a Year indeed for Death & Sickness: Doctors & Chemists hereabout say they never had such demand. I saw in yesterdays Telegraph that *Helps* Sir A. was seriously ill —with Pleurisy—one form of Cold, I believe. I got on pretty well till last week: when Cold came which began to *wheeze*: but went about till yesterday, when the Doctor, meeting me at my niece's Door, ordered me in, & sent Pill, Draught, & Embrocation after me. I think the East Wind, *plus* Sun, is worse than *minus*: I suppose one fries & freezes on different sides at the same time.

I have not seen Greville:[1] only a few extracts in Athenæum when first the Book came out. There was something sharp about M^{rs} K's American Journal.[2] I wondered if Greville were he whom I once—one evening—met at her house in Savile Row; a man who brought some *knitting* to do while talking—à la Chorley. Dear Chorley! I write it in earnest, for his Memoir sufficiently proves to me that he was a brave, good, fellow; though as Mrs K. says "*ludicrous*." I love him for his Love of Dickens & of Dickens Regard for him.

[1] [The first series of Greville's memoirs was published in 1875.]
[2] [Fanny Kemble had published *Autobiographical Recollections* in the *Atlantic Monthly*.]

I always wish I was *thoroughly* up in Virgil: so as to read him with accuracy & ease, which I cannot. He is my Love among the Romans, spite of Niebuhrs (I forget his name) and I was thinking the other day I would begin on Conington directly I got home. I have been once more trying La Fontaine, & Gil Blas; but cannot get on with either. I believe I see the naiveté & finesse of the first, Frenchman though I am not: but Birds & Birds should talk in rougher terms. Montaigne or Rabelais or any one *before* Louis XIV wd, have done them better. I think I understand too something of the Spirit of Gil Blas; all so easy going &c. But there seems to me no *Colour*, nor *Body*, in it, nor with any of the *Beauty* of my dear Don Q. Oh, the two Books can't be named together.

I bought a dirty Copy of Blackwood from it's Beginning to 1830; and have the first 6 Vols in reading here. There is capital Fun even so early: and one knows the Fun will become faster as Wilson gets ahead. *He* is the only one of the Critics, I think, who can be read *after*: having Genius of his own as well as Discernment of others. Indeed, I suppose he had more of the First than of the last. I find "Timothy Tickler" very good too.

I am writing against Time: for our early Post closes at $10\frac{1}{2}$ and I was not down till past 9, I believe. But I want you to have my Letter, such as it is, this same Day. You will know, without my saying, that I wish Blanche & Valentia to be well. I have not touched on poor *Fred*:[1] for I think you know what my Feelings are about him also. And now I shall "shut up" to make sure, if I can— You may know how glad I am to hear from you: but never *wish* you to write unless quite easy to you. Believe all this; and believe me your's ever & always

E. FG.

To W. B. Donne

[March 1873]

My dear Donne—

After many years solicitation from Nieces, Crabbes, and two or three other old Friends, I got myself Photo'ed at the Beginning of this Year. And I don't like not to send a Copy to you, one of

[1] [Major Frederick Donne, youngest son of W. B. Donne, died 3 February 1875.]

my very oldest & dearest Friends—The Artist always does *three* of every Sitter: but my bad Eyes blinked so (I suppose) in the Full face, turned toward the Machine, that we only took Copies of the two which turn away: and here they are for you to choose from—as also for Mowbray, if he likes. They are so unexpectedly complimentary, that I should not know either was meant for me: but also I must say I should not send them to my Friends if they were not so complimentary. For I think one should only hand over a presentable Likeness of oneself to those who have a Regard for one: and they, as well as I, must *believe* in the Likeness, though they wouldn't know it, inasmuch as Phoebus Apollo struck it off; and he should be the God of Truth. I shall send Pollock one, if you and your's will tell me which is best. I call one *The Statesman*: and the other, *The Philosopher*.

I have read in the Papers of your Censorship Bothers: in which I see the Knavery of the Managers.[1] I suppose your hide is sufficiently thick by this time not to mind Newspaper pelting.

I was in London three weeks ago, & saw the old Masters, and heard part of a delicious Opera of Mozart, which was in Music what Titian & Raffelle were in Painting. I saw no one but poor Mr Rowe whom I mainly went up to see; and have no more to say than I have said so many times before as to my not looking for you. If I went to see any one, depend upon it, I should not wait for any other occasion than the simple one of going up expressly to see you, and one or two others, who I know never fail in wishing me to do so.

I do not like to trouble you to write, you having so much else to do with your Time, and Pen. But you will feel bound to thank me for these Photos: and then I shall be very glad to hear about you & your's. I have nothing more to tell of myself than you know from other years; for one thing (I hope you believe) that I am your's as ever

E. FG.

[1] [Marie Litton put on *The Happy Land*, a political satire and burlesque of W. S. Gilbert's *Wicked World*, at the Court Theatre, on 3 March 1873. It included "Three Right Honourables" made up to look like Gladstone and two other politicians, and some passages which had not been in the copy licensed by the Lord Chamberlain. It was suppressed on 6 March.]

To Fanny Kemble

[1873]

Dear Mrs Kemble,

It is scarce fair to assail you on your return to England with another Letter so close on that to which you have only just answered—you who *will* answer! I wish you would consider this Letter of mine an Answer (as it really is) to that last of yours; and before long I will write again and call on you then for a Reply.

What inspires me now is, that, about the time you were writing to me about Burns and Béranger, I was thinking of them 'which was the Greater Genius?'—I can't say; but, with all my Admiration for about a Score of the Frenchman's almost perfect Songs, I would give all of them up for a Score of Burns' Coup-lets, Stanzas, or single Lines scattered among those quite *im*perfect Lyrics of his. Béranger, no doubt, was The *Artist*; which still is not the highest Genius—witness Shakespeare, Dante, Æschylus, Calderon, to the contrary. Burns assuredly had more *Passion* than the Frenchman; which is not Genius either, but a great Part of the Lyric Poet still. What Béranger might have been, if born and bred among Banks, Braes, and Mountains, I cannot tell: Burns had that advantage over him. And then the Highland Mary to love, amid the heather, as compared to Lise the Grisette in a Parisian Suburb! Some of the old French Virelays and *Vaux-de-vire* come much nearer the Wild Notes of Burns, and go to one's heart like his; Béranger never gets so far as that, I think. One knows he will come round to his pretty *refrain* with perfect grace; if he were more Inspired he couldn't.

> 'My Love is like the red, red, Rose
> That's newly sprung in June,
> My Love is like the Melody
> That's sweetly play'd in tune.'

and he will love his Love,

> 'Till a' the Seas gang Dry'

Yes—Till a' the Seas gang dry, my Dear. And then comes some

weaker stuff about Rocks melting in the Sun. All Imperfect; but that red, red Rose has burned itself into one's silly Soul in spite of all. Do you know that one of Burns' few almost perfect stanzas was perfect till he added two Syllables to each alternate Line to fit it to the lovely Music which almost excuses such a dilution of the Verse?

> 'Ye Banks and Braes o' bonnie Doon,
>   How can ye bloom (so fresh) so fair?
> Ye little Birds how can ye sing,
>   And I so (weary) full of care!
> Thou'lt break my heart, thou little Bird,
>   That sings (singest so) upon the Thorn:
> Thou minds me of departed days
>   That never shall return
>   (Departed never to) return.'

Now I shall tell you two things which my last Quotation has recalled to me.

Some thirty years ago A. Tennyson went over Burns' Ground in Dumfries. When he was one day by Doon-side—'I can't tell how it was, Fitz, but I fell into a Passion of Tears'—And A. T. not given to the melting mood at all.

No. 2. My friend old Childs of the romantic town of Bungay (if you can believe in it!) told me that one day he started outside the Coach in company with a poor Woman who had just lost Husband or Child. She talked of her Loss and Sorrow with some Resignation; till the Coach happened to pull up by a roadside Inn. A 'little Bird' was singing somewhere; the poor Woman then broke into Tears, and said—'I could bear anything but that.' I dare say she had never even heard of Burns: but he had heard the little Bird that he knew would go to all Hearts in Sorrow.

Béranger's Morals are Virtue as compared to what have followed him in France. Yet I am afraid he partly led the way. Burns' very *Passion* half excused him; so far from its being Refinement which Burke thought deprived Vice of half its Mischief!

Here is a Sermon for you, you see, which you did not compound for: nor I neither when I began my Letter. But I think I have told you the two Stories aforesaid which will almost deprive my sermon of half its Dulness. And I am now going to transcribe you a *Vau-de-vire* of old Olivier de Basselin,[1] which will show you something of that which I miss in Béranger. But I think I had better write it on a separate Paper. Till which, what think you of these lines of Clément Marot on the Death of some French Princess who desired to be buried among the Poor?[2]

(P.S.—These also must go on the Fly-leaf: being too long, Alexandrine, for these Pages.)

What a Letter! But if you are still at your Vicarage, you can read it in the Intervals of Church. I was surprised at your coming so early from Italy: the famous Holy Week there is now, I suppose, somewhat shorn of its Glory.—If you were not so sincere I should think you were persiflaging me about the Photo, as applied to myself, and yourself. Some years ago I said—and now say—I wanted one of you; and if this letter were not so long, would tell you a little how to sit. Which you would not attend to; but I should be all the same, your long-winded Friend

E. F.G.

To W. F. Pollock

[March 1873]

My dear Pollock,

7¼ p.m. After a stroll in mine own Garden, under the moon—shoes kicked off—Slippers and Dressing Gown on—A Pinch of Snuff—and hey for a Letter—to my only London Correspondent!

And to London have I been since my last Letter: and have seen the Old Masters; and finished them off by such a Symphony

[1] [Probably the piece beginning:

"On plante des pommiers ès bords
Des cimitières, près des morts," &c.

Olivier Basselin ("Vaux-de-Vire," ed. Jacob, 1858, xv, p. 28).]

[2] [De Damoyselle Anne de Marle (Marot, "Cimetière," xiv):

"Lors sans viser au lieu dont elle vint,
Et desprisant la gloire que l'on a
En ce bas monde, icelle Anne ordonna,
Que son corps fust entre les pauures mys
En cette fosse. Or prions, chers amys,
Que l'ame soit entre les pauures mise,
Qui bien heureux sont chantez en l'Église."]

as was worthy of the best of them, two Acts of Mozart's 'Così.'
You wrote me that you had 'assisted' at that also: the Singing,
as you know, was inferior: but the Music itself! Between the
Acts a Man sang a song of Verdi's: which was a strange Contrast,
to be sure: one of Verdi's heavy Airs, however: for he has a true
Genius of his own, though not Mozart's. Well: I did not like
even Mozart's two Bravuras for the Ladies: a bad Despina for
one: but the rest was fit for—Raffaelle, whose Christ in the
Garden I had been looking at a little before. I had thought
Titian's Cornaro, and a Man in Black, by a Column, worth
nearly all the rest of the Gallery till I saw the Raffaelle: and I
couldn't let that go with the others. All Lord Radnor's Pictures
were new to me, and nearly all very fine. The Vandykes delightful: Rubens' Daniel, though all by his own hand, not half so
good as a Return from Hunting, which perhaps was not: the
Sir Joshuas not first rate, I think, except a small life Figure of a
Sir W. Molesworth in Uniform: the Gainsboros scratchy and
superficial, *I* thought: the Romneys better, *I* thought. Two fine
Cromes: Ditto Turners: and— I will make an End of my
Catalogue Raisonnée . . .

I suppose you never read Béranger's Letters: there are four
thick Volumes of these, of which I have as yet only seen the
Second and Third: and they are well worth reading. They make
one love Béranger: partly because (odd enough) he is so little
of a Frenchman in Character, French as his works are. He hated
Paris, Plays, Novels, Journals, Critics, &c., hated being monstered
himself as a Great Man, as he proved by flying from it; seems
to me to take a just measure of himself and others, and to be
moderate in his Political as well as Literary Opinions.

I am hoping for Forster's second volume of Dickens in
Mudie's forthcoming Box. Meanwhile, my Boy (whom I
momently expect) reads me Trollope's 'He knew he was right,'
the opening of which I think very fine: but which seems to be
trailing off into 'longueur' as I fancy Trollope is apt to do. But
he 'has a world of his own' as Tennyson said of Crabbe.

To W. F. Pollock

March 30/73

My dear Pollock,

. . . You have never told me how you thought him [Spedding] looking &c. though you told me that your Boy Maurice went to sit with him. It really reminds me of some happy Athenian lad who was privileged to be with Socrates. Some Plato should put down the Conversation.

I have just finished the second volume of Forster's Dickens: and still have no reason not to rejoice in the Man Dickens. And surely Forster does his part well; but I can fancy that some other Correspondent but himself should be drawn in as Dickens' Life goes on, and thickens with Acquaintances.

We in the Country are having the best of it just now, I think, in these fine Days, though we have nothing to show so gay as Covent Garden Market. I am thinking of my Boat on the River . . .

You say I did not date my last letter: I can date this: for it is my Birthday. This it was that made me resolve to send you the Photos. Hey for my 65th year! I think I shall plunge into a Yellow Scratch Wig to keep my head warm for the Remainder of my Days.

To C. E. Norton

Woodbridge, April 17/73

Dear Sir,

Two days ago Mr Carlyle sent me your Note, enclosing one from Mr Ruskin 'to the Translator of Omar Khayyám.' You will be a little surprized to hear that Mr Ruskin's Note is dated September 1863: all but ten years ago! I dare say he has forgotten all about it long before this: however, I write him a Note of Thanks for the good, too good, messages he sent me; better late than never; supposing that he will not be startled and bored by my Acknowledgments of a forgotten Favor rather than gratified. It is really a funny little Episode in the Ten years' Dream. I had asked Carlyle to thank you also for such trouble as you have taken in the matter. But, as your Note to him carries your Address, I think I may as well thank you for myself. I am very glad to gather from your Note that Carlyle is well, and able to walk, as well as talk, with a congenial Companion. Indeed, he speaks of such agreeable conversation with you in the Message he appends to your Letter. For which thanking you once more, allow me to write myself yours sincerely,

EDWARD FITZGERALD

To Fanny Kemble

Woodbridge, May 1, [1873]

Dear Mrs Kemble,

I am very glad that you will be Photographed: though not by the Ipswich Man who did me, there are no doubt many much better in London.

Of course the whole Figure is best, if it can be artistically arranged. But certainly the safe plan is to venture as little as possible when an Artist's hand cannot harmonize the Lines and the Lights, as in a Picture. And as the Face is the Chief Object, I say the safest thing is to sit for the Face, neck, and Shoulders only. By this, one not only avoids any conflict about Arms and Hands (which generally disturb the Photo), but also the Lines and Lights of Chair, Table, etc.

For the same reason, I vote for nothing but a plain Background, like a Curtain, or sober-coloured Wall.

I think also that there should be no White in the Dress, which is apt to be too positive for the Face. Nothing nearer White than such material as (I think) Brussels Lace (?) of a yellowish or even dirty hue; of which there may be a Fringe between Dress and Skin. I have advised Men Friends to sit in a—dirty Shirt!

I think a three-quarter face is better than a Full; for one reason, that I think the Sitter feels more at ease looking somewhat away, rather than direct at the luminous Machine. This will suit you, who have a finely turned Head, which is finely placed on Neck and Shoulders. But, as your Eyes are fine also, don't let them be turned too much aside, nor at all downcast:

but simply looking as to a Door or Window a little on one side.

Lastly (!) I advise sitting in a lightly clouded Day; not in a bright Sunlight at all.

You will think that I am preaching my own Photo to you. And it is true that, though I did not sit with any one of these rules in my head; but just as I got out of a Cab, etc., yet the success of the Thing made me consider afterward why it succeeded; and I have now read you my Lecture on the Subject. Pray do not forgo your Intention—nay, your Promise, as I regard it—to sit, and send me the result.

Here has been a bevy of Letters, and long ones, from me, you see. I don't know if it is reasonable that one should feel it so much easier to write to a Friend in England than to the same Friend abroad; but so it is, with me at least. I suppose that a Letter directed to Stoneleigh will find you before you leave— for America!—and even after that. But I shall not feel the same confidence and ease in transcribing for you pretty Norman Songs, or gossiping about them as I have done when my Letters were only to travel to Kenilworth: which very place—which very name of a Place—makes the English world akin. I suppose you have been at Stratford before this—an event in one's Life. It was not the Town itself—or even the Church—that touched me most: but the old Footpaths over the Fields which He must have crossed three Centuries ago.

Spedding tells me he is nearing Land with his Bacon. And one begins to think Macready a Great Man amid the Dwarfs that now occupy his Place.

Ever yours sincerely
E. F.G.

To W. F. Pollock

[16 Dec. 1873.]

. . . What do you think I am reading? Voltaire's 'Pucelle': the Epic he was fitted for. It is poor in Invention, I think: but wonderful for easy Wit, and the Verse much more agreeable to me than the regularly rhymed Alexandrines. I think Byron was indebted to it in his Vision of Judgment, and Juan: his best works. There are fine things too: as when Grisbourdon suddenly slain tells his Story to the Devils in Hell where he unexpectedly makes his Appearance,

'Et tout l'Enfer en rit d'assez bon cœur.'

This is nearer the Sublime, I fancy, than anything in the Henriade. And one Canto ends:

'J'ai dans mon temps possédé des maîtresses,
Et j'aime encore à retrouver mon cœur'—

is very pretty in the old Sinner. . . .

I am engaged in preparing to depart from these dear Rooms where I have been thirteen years, and don't know yet where I am going.

To Horace Basham

Woodbridge: Thursday [18 December 1873]
Dear Arthur Basham[1]—

Your Note which is dated the *16th* only reached me Today, which is the *18th*.

We are unlucky in our proposals to meet: and the very same cause that prevented you coming here before must prevent it now; the leaving of a Servant, who left *yesterday*; and only one Girl to do the work left me. But beside this, I am actually moving from these Lodgings where I have been 13 years; and I have waited on for the last two months till now almost kicked out; so loath am I to leave *the Place*—not the People. However, go I must: and have been sending away some of my Goods, and want to send off more before the end of the week: as Christmas is coming on so close. Beside, I should be sorry to expose a Friend to the Neglect with which I am studiously treated myself so long as I do remain. So I will not let you come now—Do you think you could come over to me *at* Christmas, which I shall keep either at *my own* house here, or at Lowestoft, where you know I have more than once invited you? I am waiting for another young Friend from London if he can get Holyday enough at Christmas; and I could house you both at my house, or Lowestoft. I cannot ask you to my house so soon as *tomorrow* as

[1] [The name was apparently a private joke.]

nothing is ready there: but by the middle of next week—I can get things ready.

You see, I hope, that it is not for want of Will that I defer your coming now. Believe me on the contrary yours sincerely

E. FG.

I shall send back Fisher's hamper with a little Xmas Dinner in it.

To Horace Basham

Woodbridge, Dec 24th [? 1873]

Dear Horace

You should have touched at my house here on your way from Aldbro to London. I dont know whether I shall not be at Lowestoft by the time you return and I really do not like you going all the way there only for a day or two. I have not been so long away from Lowestoft these dozen years. I enclose you (you see) the account of Charles' Death as given in our "Woodbridge Reporter." I think possibly that you may not have heard this much of the Particulars if you left Aldbro before it happened. My former Captain Newson lost a son off the Norfolk Coast in one of the late Gales. He (Newson) and my best of Good Fellows his Nephew Jack, went all the way in the snow to claim the poor Remains of the Lad and bring them home to be laid in the Churchyard with the rest of the family. Newson is a strange wild creature, but very tender hearted to his Family.

Christmas is not a dull time to me alone as I am, the young Fellow who was with me in the summer would have come, but I advised to go among his own kinfolk who are kind to him. I had a few cigars for you in case you called here or I found my way to Aldbro. But I get worse at moving as I get older a common case. But I am none the less

Yours Sincerely

E. FG.

To Bernard Quaritch

[March 1874]

Dear Sir,

Surely it was Edition I of Ray that I wanted, not Edⁿ IV at all? So I must send it back to you with the Carriage paid up and down.

As to Polonius, I did not, and do not advise Advertisement: only sending you that bit of Leader, in case you shᵈ ever advertise in any way again. I must now leave it to you to give me what you think it *may be* worth in time, if you choose to let it drain away or if you knock it off by some sudden *swop*.

Poor old Pol! He would do people more good than harm even at 2ˢ cost:—but having now let him go I must leave it to your conscience (which has been duly instructed by Omar and other such Worthies) to account for him. If I had had 250 Friends I would have made away all the Copies by way of Gift to them:—but having only about a Dozen, I had satisfied them 20 years ago. I suppose your Illness is cold with the hot sun & East-wind. This has been an unhealthy Winter hereabouts: but I am expecting to celebrate my 65th year on March 31—which is all but April Fool Day, you know: as is your truly, E. FG.

I enclose you a Photo of our *Great Author*: as he appeared under the Sun's Rays 3 months ago. Nobody knows it: I should not myself know it; it is *a Miracle* of 1 favourable Sitting. By such means I, a Sinner, turn out [a] much better man than my Brother, who is a Saint: only he didn't know how to sit for one. Isn't it quite *Beautiful*? Had the Original Omar a more contemplative look—even when drunk? or Polonius, the Original?

By the by I didn't send what Copies I had of Calderon as I saw my Rival Macarthy¹ in your List: and one of us is enough. I hope *he* won't sell!

---

¹ [Denis Florence MacCarthy's edition.]

To W. F. Pollock

Little Grange, Woodbridge. July 23, [1874]

But I did get to Abbotsford, and was rejoiced to find it was not at all Cockney, not a Castle, but only in the half-castellated style of heaps of other houses in Scotland; the Grounds simply and broadly laid out before the windows, down to a field, down to the Tweed, with the woods which he left so little, now well aloft and flourishing, and I was glad. I could not find my way to Maida's Grave in the Garden, with its false Quantity,

Ad jănuam Domini &c.

which the Whigs and Critics taunted Scott with, and Lockhart had done it. 'You know I don't care a curse about what I write;' nor about what was imputed to him. In this, surely like Shakespeare: as also in other respects. I will worship him, in spite of Gurlyle, who sent me an ugly Autotype of Knox whom I was to worship instead.

Then I went to see Jedburgh[1] Abbey, in a half ruined corner of which he lies entombed—Lockhart beside him—a beautiful place, with his own Tweed still running close by, and his Eildon Hills looking on. The man who drove me about showed me a hill which Sir Walter was very fond of visiting, from which he could see over the Border &c. This hill is between Abbotsford and Jedburgh: and when his Coach horses, who drew his Hearse, got there, to that hill, they could scarce be got on.

My mission to Scotland was done; but some civil pleasant people, whom I met at Abbotsford, made me go with them (under Cook's guidance) to the Trossachs, Katrine, Lomond &c. which I did not care at all about; but it only took a day. After which, I came in a day to London, rather glad to be in my old flat land again with a sight of my old Sea as we came along.

And in London I went to see my dear old Donne, because of wishing to assure myself with my own eyes of his condition: and I can safely say he looked better than before his Illness, near two years ago. He had a healthy colour; was erect, alert, and with his old humour, and interest in our old topics. . . .

[1] [Dryburgh.]

I looked in at the Academy, as poor a Show as ever I had seen, I thought; only Millais attracted me: a Boy with a red Sash, and that old Seaman with his half-dreaming Eyes while the Lassie reads to him. I had no Catalogue: and so thought the Book was —The Bible—to which she was drawing his thoughts, while the sea-breeze through the half open Window whispered of his old life to him. But I was told afterwards (at Donne's indeed) that it was some account of a N. W. Passage she was reading. The Roll Call I could not see, for a three deep file of worshippers before it: I only saw the 'hairy Cap' as Thackeray in his Ballad,[1] and I supposed one would see all in a Print as well as in the Picture. But the Photo of Miss Thompson herself gives me a very favourable impression of her. It really looks, in face and dress, like some of Sir Joshua's Women. . . .

Another Miss Austen! Of course under Spedding's Auspices, the Father of Evil.

To Horace Basham

12 Marine Terrace. Lowestoft. Jan: 7/75

Dear Horace.

When you are back from your London Visit, let me know when you like to come over here; and I will be here to meet you. I want a few days notice as, otherwise, I may have run home to Woodbridge—to pay Bills &c. I am not sure if I shall be next week, as I depend a little on the arrangements of others: but, if you like to fix a time—next week or any other—I *can* be here. Only, come in literally good weather—for your own sake.

The Fishing, as you know—is all over: and I have seen Jemmy this very morning on his way to the Shipyard to clean the Owner's Boat. But Jemmy has now one of his own, in partnership with three other men—one of the *Scotch Boats* such as his Brother has, and such as are becoming much the fashion here. So, he will have to show you all this when you come.

You can let me know when you are most likely to come: and I will let you know when I am sure to be here.

Yours truly E. FG.

[1] [See "The Chronicle of the Drum."]

To Anna Biddell

12 Marine Terrace, Lowestoft. Jan. 18/75

Dear Miss Biddell,

I am sending you a Treat. The old Athenæum told me there was a Paper by 'Mr Carlyle' in this month's Magazine; and never did I lay out half-a-crown better. And you shall have the Benefit of it, if you will. Why, Carlyle's Wine, so far from weak evaporation, is only grown better by Age: losing some of its former fierceness, and grown mellow without losing Strength. It seems to me that a Child might read and relish this Paper, while it would puzzle any other Man to write such a one. I think I must write to T. C. to felicitate him on this truly 'Green Old Age.' Oh, it was good too to read it here, with the old Sea (which also has not sunk into Decrepitude) rolling in from that North: and as I looked up from the Book, there was a Norwegian Barque beating Southward, close to the Shore, and nearly all Sail set. Read—Read! you will, you must, be pleased; and write to tell me so.

This Place suits me, I think, at this time of year: there is Life about me: and that old Sea is always talking to one, telling its ancient Story.

To Alfred Tennyson

Woodbridge, July 9th, 1875

My dear old Alfred,

I had bought your Play[1] a few days before your gift-copy reached me. I have not had sufficient time to digest either you see, though I have read through twice. I must leave it for the Papers and Magazines to judge in a few hours, what took you, I suppose, weeks and months in concocting. I could speak of parts, I think: but not yet of the whole: and you can very well afford (can't you?) to wait till "The Great Twalmley" pronounces? One thing, I don't quite understand why you have so much relinquished "*thee*" and "*thou*" with their relative verbs

[1] [*Queen Mary: A Drama* was published in 1875, and performed at the Lyceum the following year.]

688

for "*you*," etc. I know that we have had more than enough of "Thee" and "Thou" in modern Plays and Poems; but it should surely rule in the common *talk* of Mary's time. I suppose however that you have some very good reason for so often supplying the old form by the new.

Still your old Fitzcrotchet, you see, still! And so will be to the end, I suppose. I am not over-well just now, and see very little of books; all day on the river, and talking to the ducks and barn-doors.

But ever yours the same,
"OLD FITZ"

To Fanny Kemble

Woodbridge, Aug. 24 [1875]
Now, my dear Mrs. Kemble, you will have to call me 'a Good Creature,' as I have found out a Copy of your capital Paper,[1] and herewith post it to you. Had I not found this Copy (which Smith & Elder politely found for me) I should have sent you one of my own, cut out from a Volume of Essays by other friends, Spedding, etc., on condition that you should send me a Copy of such Reprint as you may make of it in America. It is extremely interesting; and I always think that your Theory of the Intuitive *versus* the Analytical and Philosophical applies to the other Arts as well as that of the Drama. Mozart couldn't tell how he made a Tune; even a whole Symphony, he said, unrolled itself out of a leading idea by no logical process. Keats said that no Poetry was worth [anything] unless it came spontaneously as Leaves to a Tree, etc. I have no faith in your Works of Art done on Theory and Principle, like Wordsworth, Wagner, Holman Hunt, etc.

But, one thing you can do on Theory, and carry it well into Practice: which is—to write your Letter on Paper which does not let the Ink through, so that (according to your mode of paging) your last Letter was crossed: I really thought it so at first, and really had very hard work to make it out—some parts indeed still defying my Eyes. What I read of your remarks on

[1] ["On the Stage," in the *Cornhill Magazine*, December 1863. Reprinted as an introduction to Mrs Kemble's *Notes upon some of Shakespeare's Plays*.]

689

Portia, etc., is so good that I wish to keep it: but still I think I shall enclose you a scrap to justify my complaint. It was almost by Intuition, not on Theory, that I deciphered what I did. Pray you amend this. My MS. is bad enough, and on that very account I would avoid diaphanous Paper. Are you not ashamed?

I shall send you Spedding's beautiful Paper on the Merchant of Venice if I can lay hands on it: but at present my own room is given up to a fourth Niece (Angel that I am!) You would see that S[pedding] agrees with you about Portia, and in a way I am sure that must please you. But (so far as I can decipher that fatal Letter) you say nothing at all to me of the other Spedding Paper I sent to you (about the Cambridge Editors, etc.), which I must have back again indeed, unless you wish to keep it, and leave me to beg another Copy. Which to be sure I can do, and will, if your heart is set upon it—which I suppose it is not at all.

I have not heard of Donne for so long a time, that I am uneasy, and have written to Mowbray to hear. M[owbray] perhaps is out on his Holyday, else I think he would have replied at once. And 'no news may be Good News.'

I have no news to tell of myself; I am much as I have been for the last four months: which is, a little ricketty. But I get out in my Boat on the River three or four hours a Day when possible, and am now as ever yours sincerely

E. F.G.

To Bernard Quaritch

Woodbridge Septr. 12/75

Dear Sir,

I should like to know the *date* of the two Editions of Sévigné you tell me of—in 8, & 6 Vols. I doubt that none are exact till the *last Edition*—edited by Regnier, I think: and that I fear is in *many* volumes—Can you tell me about this also?

I shall be glad of Berlioz's Memoirs and, when I have it, I can send [an] Order for that, & the two others sent before.

And by the by—If you have made any so fair profit of Omar &c as to repay you for trouble as well as outlay, I think you should give of it something towards the relief of the Toulouse Floods and also of my poor Icelanders.[1]

I have already given some little to both—scarce enough I think. It is a shame that the English Nobility & Gentry who travel in France, adopt its fashions, read its Books—in short almost *depend upon it* for Civilisation have done so little—next to nothing—for them in this case of need.

Yours truly, E. FG.

To Bernard Quaritch

[1875]

Dear Sir,

I am sorry to have troubled you about Sévigné: that 14 Vols. Régnier, with its blazing large type, is too much for me. You did not mention the *date* of the 6 Vol. Ed[n,] But it is not worth your while to take more trouble about it. If a good clear *Type* it might do "pro tempore."

I should not have adverted to Omar at all, but for your having given me to understand (a year ago, I think) that his last Edition was almost coming to an end:—insomuch that you even hinted at another. I am only surprised that there should have been any such likelihood; I daresay you now find he has pretty well run his course which has been much better run than ever I thought of. Why, he has had an immortality of nearly 15 years!

Yours &c. E. FG.

To Bernard Quaritch

[1875]

Dear Sir,

I enclose you a P.O. for £1. 6 for the Sévigné—which pleases me well for its' Binding, at any rate.

As to old Omar—I think he has done well, considering that he began his English Life as an "Enfant Trouvé"—or rather "perdu" in Castle Street 15 years ago.

I only wonder he has survived up to this time. We will leave at present to smoulder away what Life is in him—perhaps as

[1]["£5. Q." in red ink.]

much as in myself. I had once wished to associate him with the Jámi—which I altered, but which I suppose no one would care for with all my alterations—

Enough for the present from

Yours truly, E. FG.

I should give to the Herzegovinians if I knew what was proper to do: though I *fancy* they ought to be released from Turkish Rule. But I don't know the Rights of the case, and do not suppose Lord John Russell could tell me.

I dare say Mr. Magnússon will report himself in time. I think it was he to whom I sent my Name as a Subscriber to some Icelandic Work: but I never was called on for my Subscription, nor ever received the Book; though it came out, I believe. I did not want it, but was asked to subscribe by Aldis Wright.

To W. F. Pollock

Lowestoft, Sept. 22, [1875]

My dear Pollock,

You will scarce thank me for a letter in pencil: perhaps you would thank me less if I used the steel pen, which is my other resource. You could very well dispense with a Letter altogether: and yet I believe it is pleasant to get one when abroad.

I dare say I may have told you what Tennyson said of the Sistine Child, which he then knew only by Engraving. He first thought the Expression of his Face (as also the Attitude) almost too solemn, even for the Christ within. But some time after, when A T was married, and had a Son, he told me that Raffaelle was all right: that no Man's face was so solemn as a Child's, full of Wonder. He said one morning that he watched his Babe 'worshipping the Sunbeam on the Bedpost and Curtain.' I risk telling you this again for the sake of the Holy Ground you are now standing on.

Which reminds me also of a remark of Béranger's not out of place. He says God forgot to give Raffaelle to Greece, and made a 'joli cadeau' of him to the Church of Rome.

I brought here some Volumes of Lever's 'Cornelius O'Dowd' Essays, very much better reading than Addison, I think. Also some of Sainte Beuve's, better than either. A sentence in O'Dowd reminded me of your Distrust of Civil Service Examinations: 'You could not find a worse Pointer than the Poodle which would pick you out all the letters of the Alphabet.' And is not this pretty good of the World we live in? 'You ask me if I am going to "*The Masquerade*." I am at it: Circumspice!'

So I pick out and point to other Men's Game, this Sunday Morning, when the Sun makes the Sea shine, and a strong head wind drives the Ships with shortened Sail across it. Last night I was with some Sailors at the Inn: some one came in who said there was a Schooner with five feet water in her in the Roads: and off they went to see if anything beside water could be got out of her. But, as you say, one mustn't be epigrammatic and clever. Just before Grog and Pipe, the Band had played some German Waltzes, a bit of Verdi, Rossini's 'Cujus animam,' and a capital Sailors' Tramp-chorus from Wagner, all delightful to me, on the Pier: how much better than all the dreary oratorios going on all the week at Norwich, Elijah, St Peter, St Paul, Eli, &c. There will be an Oratorio for every Saint and Prophet; which reminds me of my last Story. Voltaire had an especial grudge against Habakkuk. Some one proved to him that he had misrepresented facts in Habakkuk's history. 'C'est égal,' says V., 'Habakkuk était capable de tout.' Cornewall Lewis, who (like most other Whigs) had no Humour, yet tells this: I wonder if it will reach Dresden.

To Mrs W. H. Thompson

Little Grange, Woodbridge. Sept. 23, [1875]

Dear Mrs Thompson,

It is very good of you to write to me, so many others as, I know, you must have to write to. I can tell you but little in return for the Story of your Summer Travel: but what little I have to say shall be said at once. As to Travel, I have got no further than Norfolk, and am rather sorry I did not go further North, to the Scottish Border, at any rate. But now it is too late. I have contented myself with my Boat on the River here: with my Garden, Pigeons, Ducks &c.; a great Philosopher indeed! But (to make an end of oneself) I have not been well all the summer; unsteady in head and feet; the Beginning of the End, I suppose; and if the End won't be too long spinning out, one cannot complain of its coming too soon. . . .

I had a kindly Letter from Carlyle some days ago: he was summering at some place near Bromley in Kent, lent him by a Lady Derby; once, he says, Lady Salisbury, which I don't understand. He had also the use of a Phaeton and Pony; which latter he calls "*Shenstone*" from a partiality to stopping at every Inn door. Carlyle had been a little touched in revisiting Eltham, and remembering Frank Edgeworth who resided there forty years ago "with a little Spanish Wife, but no pupils." Carlyle would name him with a sort of sneer in the Life of Sterling; could not see that any such notice was more than needless, just after Edgeworth's Death. This is all a little Scotch indelicacy to other people's feelings. But now Time and his own Mortality soften him. I have been looking over his Letters to me about Cromwell: the amazing perseverance and accuracy of the Man, who writes so passionately! In a letter of about 1845 or 6 he says he has burned at least six attempts at Cromwell's Life: and finally falls back on sorting and elucidating the Letters, as a sure Groundwork. . . .

I have this Summer made the Acquaintance of a great Lady, with whom I have become perfectly intimate, through her Letters, Madame de Sévigné. I had hitherto kept aloof from her, because of that eternal Daughter of hers; but "it's all Truth and Daylight," as Kitty Clive said of Mrs Siddons. Her Letters from Brittany are best of all, not those from Paris, for she loved the Country, dear Creature; and now I want to go and visit her "Rochers," but never shall.

To E. B. Cowell

My dear Cowell,

. . . I told Elizabeth, I think, all I had to write about Arthur C. I had a letter from him a few days ago, hoping to see me in London, where I thought I might be going about this time, and where I would not go without giving him notice to meet me, poor lad. As yet however I cannot screw my Courage to go up: I have no Curiosity about what is to be seen or heard there; my Day is done. I have not been very well all this Summer, and fancy that I begin to 'smell the Ground,' as Sailors say of the Ship that slackens speed as the Water shallows under her. I can't say I have much care for long Life: but still less for long Death: I mean a lingering one.

Did you ever read Madame de Sévigné? I never did till this summer, rather repelled by her perpetual harping on her Daughter. But it is all genuine, and the same intense Feeling expressed in a hundred natural yet graceful ways: and beside all this such good Sense, good Feeling, Humour, Love of Books and Country Life, as makes her certainly the Queen of all Letter writers.

To Frederick Tennyson

Woodbridge, Sept. 29/75

My dear Frederic,

It is now 9½ P.M. I have written two Letters: but since that have drunk three Glasses of *1870* Port (which only wants about twenty-five years over its head to make it a very fine Wine), and so I am inspired to 'take up my Pen' again and write to you. For it is now some time since I have heard from you: and, when I write, it is more to get an answer than for the mere pleasure of writing which some people feel—chiefly Women, I suppose. Well: I want to know how you are: that is the main thing; I suppose not *doing* much beyond reading, writing, and ruminating. I cannot say much for myself: though every one tells me in what rude health I look, etc.; and in spite of taking countless Bottles of which a sixth part is marked out by so many stages in each Bottle. But I shall not say any more on this score: let me hear *you* are well, at any rate.

I am so vexed that I cannot find a bundle of your Letters from Italy thirty years ago, which I carefully preserved: which I know I had on Market Hill: and which I am now wanting to transcribe extracts from, as I had done (you know) from Morton and from Carlyle. I have looked where I can: but my Nieces have been taking up all my home except one room, and I still hope to find the letters in some Box where I deposited them before I moved from Market Hill hither. They were becoming faint and yellow in their Ink: and that is why I wanted to transcribe parts: as was the case with Morton's.

I have been proposing to go up to London, and hear a Selection from Lohengrin at the Promenade Concerts: but Indolence, and Despair of any Satisfaction, has left me where I am. Malim Mozartii recordari quam cum Wagnero versari—if that be Latin. Tell me: tell me of yourself also, and believe me ever yours,

E. F. G.

Now—To Bed. But—To Sleep! That is the Question.

To Alfred Tennyson

[December 1875]

My dear Alfred,

The time of year has come about when I have earned a right to hear a little about you all—Mrs Tennyson especially. But I suppose I must wait till one of your boys is at home; which must soon be, for here is Christmas close by. Then a son must write me a bit of a letter. You know that I wish you all well and happy at Christmas and after. I have been told of Mrs Leslie Stephen's death, which must be a terrible thing for Annie Thackeray. Only about a fortnight ago she was telling me by letter what a sister she had.

As Spedding and Pollock (whom I asked about it) told me they had given their names to the Carlyle conspiracy, so did I, much wondering how Masson came to know of my existence. But I must say I thought the whole thing rather a cockney affair—*Address and Medal and White Satin Scroll*, which some dozen years ago, I think Carlyle would have been tempted to blow his nose upon, as the Sandwich Islanders did with their playbills at the Theatre. Only I never did see Carlyle use a handkerchief. . . . It is fine of him to be eighty: I shall write him also my best 1875 letter. He seems to have passed the summer cheerfully and well in Kent. I see [Browning] has another of his uncouth works out: I call him the great Prophet of the Gargoyle School: in France they have a man equally disagreeable to me—

696

Victor Hugo. I think it partly is because the beautiful things have been done from the time of the Greeks to A.T., and so those who can't do them better prove their originality by descanting on the Ugly; and they have their day. And I am your sincere and trusty old bedesman,

E. F. G.

To Samuel Laurence

Woodbridge. Dec. 30/75

My dear Laurence,

. . . I cannot get on with Books about the Daily Life which I find rather insufferable in practice about me. I never could read Miss Austen, nor (later) the famous George Eliot. Give me People, Places, and Things, which I don't and can't see; Antiquaries, Jeanie Deans, Dalgettys &c. . . . As to Thackeray's, they are terrible; I really look at them on the shelf, and am half afraid to touch them. He, you know, could go deeper into the Springs of Common Action than these Ladies: wonderful he is, but not Delightful, which one thirsts for as one gets old and dry.

To C. E. Norton

Little Grange, Woodbridge. Jan. 23/76

My dear Sir,

. . . I suppose you may see one of the Carlyle Medallions: and you can judge better of the Likeness than I, who have not been to Chelsea, and hardly out of Suffolk, these fifteen years and more. I dare say it is like him: but his Profile is not his best phase. In two notes dictated by him since that Business he has not adverted to it: I think he must be a little ashamed of it, though it would not do to say so in return, I suppose. And yet I think he might have declined the Honours of a Life of 'Heroism.' I have no doubt he would have played a Brave Man's Part if called on; but, meanwhile, he has only sat pretty comfortably at Chelsea, scolding all the world for not being Heroic, and not always very precise in telling them how. He has, however, been so far heroic, as to be always independent, whether of Wealth,

Rank, and Coteries of all sorts: nay, apt to fly in the face of some who courted him. I suppose he is changed, or subdued, at eighty: but up to the last ten years he seemed to me just the same as when I first knew him five and thirty years ago. What a Fortune he might have made by showing himself about as a Lecturer, as Thackeray and Dickens did; I don't mean they did it for Vanity: but to make money: and that to spend generously. Carlyle did indeed lecture near forty years ago before he was a Lion to be shown, and when he had but few Readers. I heard his 'Heroes' which now seems to me one of his best Books. He looked very handsome then, with his black hair, fine Eyes, and a sort of crucified Expression.

I know of course (in Books) several of those you name in your Letter: Longfellow, whom I may say I love, and so (I see) can't call him *Mister*: and Emerson whom I admire, for I don't feel that I know the Philosopher so well as the Poet: and Mr Lowell's 'Among my Books' is among mine. I also have always much liked, I think rather loved, O. W. Holmes. I scarce know why I could never take to that man of true Genius, Hawthorne. There is a little of my Confession of Faith about your Countrymen, and I should say mine, if I were not more Irish than English.

To Bernard Quaritch

Woodbridge Jan. 25/76

Dear Sir,

I am much obliged to Mr. Wilson[1] for his Good Word, and Good Deed, "*re*" Omar and myself.

As for my *Name*. I always told you it wᵈ do both of us more harm than good by appearing on Title page or in Advertisement. *Good* it could not; so many E. FG's; no one of them celebrated but the Lord of that name[2].

Why, there is one beside myself in this very Woodbridge, an

[1] [H. Schütz Wilson—who, in a letter to Quaritch of 21 January 1786 announced he was about to write a paper on the *Rubáiyát* "for a leading magazine," and asked if he might record FitzGerald as the translator.]

[2] [Lord Edward FitzGerald, M.P., 1763–98, Irish rebel, fought with the Americans in the War of Independence.]

Ex-policeman; there lately was another, a Parson, in a neighbouring Village; you knew another to your Cost.[1] In fact *one* of us
was generally hanged in Ireland once a Year till the Law was
altered—

Shall all these dispute my Glory?

My name was only put to those first 6 Plays of Calderon to
distinguish them from those of Mr. Macarthy which came out
the same year, and almost the same month.

So much for Title pages &c. As to Reviews; as I suppose that
one of us is known to be the Culprit by several among the small
Circles of *Omarians*, Mr. Wilson[1] will do as he finds most convenient to himself in naming *one of us* as the *understood* Translator, or simply saying "The Translator" in the Review he kindly
proposes, and which of course I shall be glad of.

You can if you choose advertize Ag^n in your Catalogue as "by
the Translator of Omar"—which will have all the more force
after Mr. Wilson's Review, I hope.

But I am afraid you will only provoke the Jealous Gods by
printing me as if I were a Browning. And the Danger more
because of so many of The Gods knowing more of Greek than
Persian. But I suppose you make your Calculation.

Thank you—as once before—for your Invitation to your
pleasant Haverstock. But I scarce ever go to London now; and
when I do, only to be back the same Day, without looking up
even 50 year-old Friends. But I remain theirs & your's always,

One of the E. FG's.

To C. E. Norton

[Woodbridge. Feb. 7/76]

My dear Sir,

I will not look on the Book you have sent me as any Return for
the Booklet I sent you, but as a free and kindly Gift. I really
don't know that you could have sent me a better. I have read it
with more continuous attention and gratification than I now
usually feel, and always (as Lamb suggested) well disposed to
say Grace after reading.

[1] [A book-thief named FitzGerald.]

Seeing what Mr Lowell has done for Dante, Rousseau, &c. one does not wish him to be limited in his Subjects: but I do wish he would do for English Writers what Ste. Beuve has done for French. Mr Lowell so far goes along with him as to give so much of each Writer's Life as may illustrate his Writings; he has more Humour (in which alone I fancy S. B. somewhat wanting), more extensive Reading, I suppose; and a power of metaphorical Illustration which (if I may say so) seems to me to want only a little reserve in its use: as was the case perhaps with Hazlitt. But Mr Lowell is not biassed by Hazlitt's—(by any-body's, so far as I see)—party or personal prejudices; and altogether seems to me the man most fitted to do this Good Work, where it has not (as with Carlyle's Johnson) been done, for good and all, before. Of course, one only wants the Great Men, in their kind: Chaucer, Pope (Dryden being done), and perhaps some of the 'minora sidera' clustered together, as Hazlitt has done them. Perhaps all this will come forth in some future Series even now gathering in Mr Lowell's Head. How-ever that may be, this present Series will make me return to some whom I have not lately looked up. Dante's face I have not seen these ten years: only his Back on my Book Shelf. What Mr Lowell says of him recalled to me what Tennyson said to me some thirty-five or forty years ago. We were stopping before a shop in Regent Street where were two Figures of Dante and Goethe. I (I suppose) said, 'What is there in old Dante's Face that is missing in Goethe's?' And Tennyson (whose Profile then had certainly a remarkable likeness to Dante's) said: 'The Divine.' Then Milton; I don't think I've read him these forty years; the whole Scheme of the Poem, and certain Parts of it, looming as grand as anything in my Memory; but I never could read ten lines together without stumbling at some Pedantry that tipped me at once out of Paradise, or even Hell, into the School-room, worse than either. Tennyson again used to say that the two grandest of all Similes were those of the Ships hanging in the Air, and 'the Gunpowder one,' which he used slowly and grimly to enact, in the Days that are no more. He certainly then thought Milton the sublimest of all the Gang; his Diction modelled on Virgil, as perhaps Dante's.

Spenser I never could get on with, and (spite of Mr Lowell's good word) shall still content myself with such delightful Quotations from him as one lights upon here and there: the last from Mr Lowell.

Then, old 'Daddy Wordsworth,' as he was sometimes called, I am afraid, from my Christening, he is now, I suppose, passing under the Eclipse consequent on the Glory which followed his obscure Rise. I remember fifty years ago at our Cambridge, when the Battle was fighting for him by the Few against the Many of us who only laughed at 'Louisa in the Shade' &c. His Brother was then Master of Trinity College; like all Wordsworths (unless the drowned Sailor) pompous and priggish. He used to drawl out the Chapel responses so that we called him the 'Mēēserable Sinner' and his brother the 'Meeserable Poet.' Poor fun enough: but I never can forgive the Lakers all who first despised, and then patronized 'Walter Scott,' as they loftily called him: and He, dear, noble, Fellow, thought they were quite justified. Well, your Emerson has done him far more Justice than his own Countryman Carlyle, who won't allow him to be a Hero in any way, but sets up such a cantankerous narrow-minded Bigot as John Knox in his stead. I did go to worship at Abbotsford, as to Stratford on Avon: and saw that it was good to have so done. If you, if Mr Lowell, have not lately read it, pray read Lockhart's account of his Journey to Douglas Dale on (I think) July 18 or 19, 1831. It is a piece of Tragedy, even to the muttering Thunder, like the Lammermuir, which does not look very small beside Peter Bell and Co.

My dear Sir, this is a desperate Letter; and that last Sentence will lead to another dirty little Story about my Daddy: to which you must listen or I should feel like the Fine Lady in one of Vanbrugh's Plays, 'Oh my God, that you won't listen to a Woman of Quality when her Heart is bursting with Malice!' And perhaps you on the other Side of the Great Water may be amused with a little of your old Granny's Gossip.

Well then: about 1826, or 7, Professor Airy (now our Astronomer Royal) and his Brother William called on The Daddy at Rydal. In the course of Conversation Daddy mentioned that sometimes when genteel Parties came to visit him, he contrived to slip out of the room, and down the garden walk to where 'The Party's' travelling Carriage stood. This Carriage he would look into to see what Books they carried with them: and he observed it was generally 'WALTER SCOTT'S.' It was Airy's Brother (a very veracious man, and an Admirer of Wordsworth, but, to be sure, more of Sir Walter) who told me this. It is this conceit that diminishes Wordsworth's stature among us, in spite of the mountain Mists he lived among. Also, a little stinginess; not like Sir Walter in that! I remember Hartley Coleridge telling us at Ambleside how Professor Wilson and some one else (H. C. himself perhaps) stole a Leg of Mutton from Wordsworth's Larder for the fun of the Thing.

Here then is a long Letter of old world Gossip from the old Home. I hope it won't tire you out: it need not, you know.

P.S. By way of something better from the old World, I post you Hazlitt's own Copy of his English Poets, with a few of his marks for another Edition in it. If you like to keep it, pray do: if you like better to give it to Hazlitt's successor, Mr Lowell, do that from yourself.

To Fanny Kemble

Woodbridge: Febr: 17/76

Dear Mrs Kemble,

I ought to have written before to apprise you of your Mother's Miniature being sent off—by Post. On consideration, we judged that to be the safest and speediest way: the Post Office here telling us that it was not too large or heavy so to travel: without the Frame. As, however, our Woodbridge Post Office is not very well-informed, I shall be very glad to hear it has reached you, in its double case: wood within, and tin without (quite unordered and unnecessary), which must make you think you receive a present of Sardines. You lose, you see, the Benefit of my exalted Taste in respect of Framing, which I had settled to perfection. Pray get a small Frame, concaving inwardly (Ogee pattern, I believe), which leads the Eyes into the Picture: whereas a Frame convexing outwardly leads the Eye away from the Picture; a very good thing in many cases, but not needed in this. I dare say the Picture (faded as it is) will look poor to you till enclosed and set off by a proper Frame. And the way is, as with a Bonnet (on which you know much depends even with the fairest face), to try one on before ordering it home. That is, if you choose to indulge in some more ornamental Frame than the quite simple one I have before named. Indeed, I am not sure if the Picture would not look best in a plain gold Flat (as it is called) without Ogee, or any ornament whatsoever. But try it on first: and then you can at least please yourself, if not the Terrible Modiste who now writes to you. My Brother is very anxious you should have the Picture, and wrote to me again to send you his hereditary kind Regards. I ought to be sending you his Note—which I have lost. Instead of that, I enclose one from poor Laurence to whom I wrote your kind message; and am as ever

Yours
E. F.G.

You will let me know if the Picture has not arrived before this Note reaches you?

To Fanny Kemble

[Lowestoft, April, 1876]

My dear Mrs Kemble,

From Lowestoft still I date: as just ten years ago when I was about building a Lugger, and reading Montaigne. The latter holds his own with me after three hundred years: and the Lugger does not seem much the worse for her ten years' wear, so well did she come bouncing between the Piers here yesterday, under a strong Sou'-Wester. My Great Captain has her no more; he has what they call a 'Scotch Keel' which is come into fashion: her too I see: and him too steering her, broader and taller than all the rest: fit to be a Leader of Men, Body and Soul; looking now Ulysses-like. Two or three years ago he had a run of constant bad luck; and, being always of a grand convivial turn, treating Everybody, he got deep in Drink, against all his Promises to me, and altogether so lawless, that I brought things to a pass between us. 'He should go on with me if he would take the Tee-total Pledge for one year'—'No—he had broken his word,' he said, 'and he would not pledge it again,' much as he wished to go on with me. That, you see, was very fine in him; he is altogether fine—A Great Man, I maintain it: like one of Carlyle's old Norway Kings, with a wider morality than we use; which is very good and fine (as this Captain said to me) 'for you who are born with a silver spoon in your mouths.' I did not forget what Carlyle too says about Great Faults in Great Men: even in David, the Lord's Anointed. But I thought best to share the Property with him and let him go his way. He had always resented being under any Control, and was very glad to be his own sole Master again: and yet clung to me in a wild and pathetic way. He has not been doing better since: and I fear is sinking into disorder.

This is a long story about one you know nothing about except what little I have told you. But the Man is a very remarkable Man indeed, and you may be interested—you must be—in him.

'Ho! parlons d'autres choses, ma Fille,' as my dear Sévigné says. She now occupies Montaigne's place in my room: well—worthily: she herself a Lover of Montaigne, and with a spice of his free thought and speech in her. I am sometimes vext I never made her acquaintance till last year: but perhaps it was as well to have such an acquaintance reserved for one's latter years. The fine Creature! much more alive to me than most Friends—I *should* like to see her 'Rochers' in Brittany.

'Parlons d'autres choses'—your Mother's Miniature. You seemed at first to think it was taken from the Engraving: but the reverse was always clear to me. The whole figure, down to the Feet, is wanted to account for the position of the Legs; and the superior delicacy of Feature would not be gained *from* the Engraving, but the contrary. The Stars were stuck in to make an 'Urania' of it perhaps. I do not assert that your Miniature is the original: but that such a Miniature is. I did not expect that Black next the Picture would do: had you 'tried on the Bonnet' first, as I advised? I now wish I had sent the Picture over in its original Frame, which I had doctored quite well with a strip of Black Paper pasted over the Gold. It might really have gone through Quaritch's Agency: but I got into my head that the Post was safer. (How badly I am writing!) I had a little common Engraving of the Cottage bonnet Portrait: so like Henry. If I did not send it to you, I know not what is become of it.

Along with your Letter came one from Donne telling me of

your Niece's Death.[1] He said he had written to tell you. In reply, I gave him your message; that he must 'hold on' till next year when peradventure you may see England again, and hope to see him too.

Sooner or later you will see an Account of 'Mary Tudor'[2] at the Lyceum. It is just what I expected: a 'succès d'estime,' and not a very enthusiastic one. Surely, no one could have expected more. And now comes out a new Italian Hamlet—Rossi—whose first appearance is recorded in the enclosed scrap of *Standard*. And (to finish Theatrical or Dramatic Business) Quaritch has begun to print Agamemnon—so leisurely that I fancy he wishes to wait till the old Persian is exhausted, and so join the two. I certainly am in no hurry; for I fully believe we shall only get abused for the Greek in proportion as we were praised for the Persian—in England, I mean: for you have made America more favourable.

'Parlons d'autres choses.' 'Eh? mais de quoi parler,' etc. Well: a Blackbird is singing in the little Garden outside my Lodging Window, which is frankly opened to what Sun there is. It has been a singular half year; only yesterday Thunder in rather cold weather; and last week the Road and Rail in Cambridge and Huntingdon was blocked up with Snow; and Thunder then also. I suppose I shall get home in ten days: before this Letter will reach you, I suppose: so your next may be addressed to Woodbridge. I really don't know if these long Letters are more of Trouble or Pleasure to you: however, there is an end to all: and that End is that I am yours as truly as ever I was

E. F.G.

To Elizabeth Cowell

12 Marine Terrace, Lowestoft. April 8/76

. . . If you go to Brittany you must go to my dear Sévigné's 'Rochers.' If I had the 'Go' in me, I should get there this Summer too: as to Abbotsford and Stratford. She has been my Companion here; quite alive in the Room with me. I sometimes

---

[1] [Mrs Charles Donne, daughter of John Mitchell Kemble, died 15 April 1876.]

[2] [*Queen Mary*, by Tennyson.]

lament I did not know her before: but perhaps such an Acquaintance comes in best to cheer one toward the End.

To C. E. Norton

Little Grange, Woodbridge. June 10,[1] [1876]

My dear Sir,

I don't know that I should trouble you so soon again—(only, don't trouble yourself to answer for form's sake only)—but that there is a good deal of Wordsworth in the late Memoir of Haydon by his Son. All this you might like to see; as also Mr Lowell. And do you, or he, know of some dozen very good Letters of Wordsworth's addressed to a Mr Gillies who published them in what he calls the Life of a Literary Veteran some thirty years ago, I think? This Book, of scarce any value except for those few Letters, and a few Notices of Sir Walter Scott, all good, is now not very common, I think. If you or Mr Lowell would like to have a Copy, I can send you one, through Quaritch, if not per Post: I have the Letters separately bound up from another Copy of long ago. There is also a favorable account of a meeting between Wordsworth and Foscolo in an otherwise rather valueless Memoir of Bewick the Painter. I tell you of all this Wordsworth, because you have, I think, a more religious regard for him than we on this side the water: he is not so much honoured in his own Country, I mean, his Poetry. I, for one, feel all his lofty aspiration, and occasional Inspiration, but I cannot say that, on the whole, he makes much of it; his little pastoral pieces seem to me his best: less than a Quarter of him. But I may be wrong.

I am very much obliged to you for wishing me to see Mr Ticknor's Life &c. I hope to make sure of that through our Briareus-handed Mudie; and have marked the Book for my next Order. For I suppose that it finds its way to English Publishers, or Librarians. I remember his Spanish Literature coming out, and being for a long time in the hands of my friend Professor Cowell, who taught me what I know of Spanish. Only a week ago I began my dear Don Quixote over again; as welcome and fresh as the Flowers of May. The Second Part is my favorite, in

[1] [10 June 1876 was a Saturday. Perhaps the letter was finished on Sunday.]

spite of what Lamb and Coleridge (I think) say; when, as old Hallam says, Cervantes has fallen in Love with the Hero whom he began by ridiculing. When this Letter is done I shall get out into my Garden with him, Sunday though it be.

We have also Memoirs of Godwin, very dry, I think; indeed with very little worth reading, except two or three Letters of dear Charles Lamb, 'Saint Charles,' as Thackeray once called him, while looking at one of his half-mad Letters, and remember[ing] his Devotion to that quite mad Sister. I must say I think his Letters infinitely better than his Essays; and Patmore says his Conversation, when just enough animated by Gin and Water, was better than either: which I believe too. Procter said he was far beyond the Coleridges, Wordsworths, Southeys &c. And I am afraid I believe that also.

I am afraid too this is a long letter nearly [all] about my own Likes and Dislikes. 'The Great Twalmley's.' But I began only thinking about Wordsworth. Pray do believe that I do not wish you to write unless you care to answer on that score. And now for the Garden and the Don: always in a common old Spanish Edition. Their coarse prints always make him look more of the Gentleman than the better Artists of other Countries have hitherto done.

Carlyle, I hear, is pretty well, though somewhat shrunk: scolding away at Darwin, The Turk, &c.

To Bernard Quaritch

Little Grange, Woodbridge July 30 [1876]

Dear Sir,

Agam^n came safe & sound. I am only ashamed at his looking so fine: but that is your doing, you know: and I only hope it won't lose you money, nor draw the "Evil Eye" on myself.

If you advertize it in your Catalogue, please do so *without any encomium* till someone else offers you a Quotation. "*By the Translator of Omar K.*" will be enough as to the Authorship.

As to Copies: I would have a Dozen Copies sent me please (one I have, you know): as also one to Mr Schütz Wilson, and one to Mr Kerney, for their respective kind services to me.

Now for Don Quixote. If your present Copy be *well* & *handsomely* bound—strong, well-opening, well-*margined*, and well-looking it will do for me. If not, I will wait till another Copy turns up.

I hope you are about to take your Holyday; & am yours truly,
E. FG.

I should like a copy of *Heinrich Heine's* shorter Poems: if in the compass of one or two Vols.

To Fanny Kemble

Woodbridge: Septr. 21/76

Dear Mrs Kemble,

Have your American Woods begun to hang out their Purple and Gold yet? on this Day of Equinox. Some of ours begin to look rusty, after the Summer Drought; but have not turned Yellow yet. I was talking of this to a Heroine of mine who lives near here, but visits the Highlands of Scotland, which she loves better than Suffolk—and she said of those Highland Trees— 'O, they give themselves no dying Airs, but turn Orange in a Day, and are swept off in a Whirlwind, and Winter is come.'

Now too one's Garden begins to be haunted by that Spirit which Tennyson says is heard talking to himself among the flower-borders. Do you remember him?

And now—Who should send in his card to me last week—but the old Poet himself—he and his elder Son Hallam passing through Woodbridge from a Tour in Norfolk. 'Dear old Fitz,' ran the Card in pencil, 'We are passing thro'.' I had not seen him for twenty years—he looked much the same, except for his fallen Locks; and what really surprised me was, that we fell at once into the old Humour, as if we had only been parted twenty Days instead of so many Years. I suppose this is a Sign of Age— not altogether desirable. But so it was. He stayed two Days, and we went over the same old grounds of Debate, told some of the old Stories, and all was well. I suppose I may never see him again: and so I suppose we both thought as the Rail carried him off: and each returned to his ways as if scarcely diverted from them. Age again!—I liked Hallam much; unaffected, unpretending—no Slang—none of Young England's nonchalance —speaking of his Father as 'Papa' and tending him with great Care, Love, and Discretion. Mrs A. T. is much out of health, and scarce leaves Home, I think.

I have lately finished Don Quixote again, and I think have inflamed A. T. to read him too—I mean in his native Language. For this *must* be, good as Jarvis' Translation is, and the matter of the Book so good that one would think it would lose less than any Book by Translation. But somehow that is not so. I was astonished lately to see how Shakespeare's Henry IV. came out in young V. Hugo's Prose Translation: Hotspur, Falstaff and all. It really seemed to show me more than I had yet seen in the original.

Ever yours,
E. F.G.

To Alfred Tennyson

Woodbridge, Sept. 26th, 1876

I am glad you were pleased with your short visit here. Perhaps you will one day, one or both of you, come again: and, if you will but give warning, and no nieces are in possession of the house, it shall be ready for you, and some *tender* meat provided. Somehow I, when you were gone, felt somewhat abroad, and a few hours after went to an old village by the sea, Dunwich, once a considerable town, now swept into the sea, with the remains of a church on the cliff and the walls of an ancient priory beside. I was wishing that I had made you come with me, over a stretch of wild heath too, but there was no room in the little Inn: and dare say *very tough meat*! *That* fatal reed sticks in my side you see. But I am still yours, and all yours, sincerely,

E. F. G.

To E. B. Cowell

Woodbridge. October 5/76

My dear Cowell,

. . . I bought Clemencin's Quixote after all: but have looked little into him as yet, as I had finished my last Reading of the Don before he came. . . . I fear his Notes are more than one wants about errors, or inaccuracies of Style &c. Cervantes had some of the noble carelessness of Shakespeare, Scott &c., as about Sancho's stolen Dicky.[1] But why should Clemencin, and his Predecessors, decide that Cervantes changed the title of his second Part from 'Hidalgo' to 'Caballero' from negligence? Why should he not have intended the change for reasons of his own? Anyhow, they should have printed the Title as he printed it, and pointed out what they thought the oversight in a Note. This makes one think they may have altered other things also: which perhaps I shall see when I begin another Reading: which (if I live) won't be very far off. I think I almost inspired Alfred Tennyson (who suddenly came here a Fortnight ago) to begin on the Spanish. Yes: A. T. called one day, after near twenty years' separation, and we were in a moment as if we had been together all that while. He had his son Hallam with him: whom I liked much: unaffected and unpretentious: so attentive to his Father, with a humorous sense of his Character as well as a loving and respectful. It was good to see them together. We went one day down the Orwell and back again by Steamer: but the weather was not very propitious. Altogether, I think we were all pleased with our meeting.

To Horace Basham

Little Grange, Woodbridge. October 5/76

Dear Horace—

I was sorry not to have seen you last Monday, though I c^d have seen but little of you:—as my short Visit was made mainly for the purpose of seeing my Sister for an hour or two. You would always be welcome *here*: but I have so little to repay time and trouble lost in coming over that I do not press it. When I am at Lowestoft, it is another matter: there *is* something going on there, as you know; and I hope you will come over there when next I go:—which I will let you know of. I have not been there for *6 months*; as I never go during *the Season*, as they call it. But I have been told that *Jemmy* Fletcher was the *top Boat* on the North Sea:—and that *my* man—Joseph—had also done well,

[1] [Suffolk for donkey.]

only lost Nets. *Fisher* told me he had heard the Lowestoft Boats had done well with *Mackerel*: I suppose Joseph F. has been among them—He keeps all right, I believe, so long as he is at Sea: but gets all wrong on shore—oh, what a Pity that such a Grand, Noble, and *Good*, Nature shd. get spoiled—by that accursed Drink, which *is* the Curse of Lowestoft.

I was glad to see Fisher again, and to see him looking well. I think he is a very honest, and sincere, man; and now something of an *old Friend*.

I get out in my Boat on the River when Tides serve—as they do this week. My House is painting, too, which drives me abroad. I meant to have brought you a little Batch of Cigars: but forgot them at last.

Yours sincerely (—Why do *you* write Yours *Respectfully*?)

E. FG.

To Horace Basham

Woodbridge Oct 12th [1876]

Dear Horace

A Hamper of very good opening came to me two days ago: were they from you or Fisher? Today comes a Parcel of very fine Grapes off which (with Bread) I have Dined and the remainder will make my Dinner tomorrow if I live. These Grapes I know come from no one else but yourself, so let me thank you for them.

I am going through Saxmundham today on my road to Lowestoft. I shall leave your hamper there directed to Aldbro: and also the Grape-box within it containing the Cigars I told you of which I hope you will find pretty good.

I shall be at Lowestoft 12 Marine Terrace I *suppose* for I dont know till I get there if there be room for a week at least while Painters and Whitewashers are doing up my house here. If you should care to come to Lowestoft I shall be glad to see you, but I suppose this fine weather will send you after the Herrings.

Yours truly

E. FG.

To Horace Basham

Little Grange, Woodbridge, October, 18 [1876]

Dear Horace

It is odd but it is true that only yesterday I was thinking I would write to you: and this Eve your Box of Grapes comes. It is very kind of you to think of me: the Grapes will (together with a lump of Bread) be my Dinner tomorrow.

Now what I had thought of writing to you about was—and is —to know if Fisher (the Father) would do me a good lot of his best salt Herrings (when the Herrings come!) His have always been much better than any I have had from Lowestoft, and as I have no doubt that this superiority results mainly from the superior care Fisher takes in his curing the fish, I am willing and indeed wish to pay him a better Price: in fact what he and you consider a *good* price for him.

I do not eat much of this Herring myself: but I like to give some away and to give only—*the Best*. I have hitherto said nothing to you about a visit to me, because (first) I supposed from your last note that you would be busy about this time after the Herrings, and secondly I thought there would be more to amuse you if you should come to me at Lowestoft: where I shall doubtless be this winter, off and on. But you will always be welcome, here or there.

Jemmy has done well on the North Sea: my old Chum Joseph did not do much here, but made some £190 and over in a few days catching *Mackrel*. I hold no communication with him, but he is a very extraordinary man, and I do not believe that *he* thought wrong what I said, and then did think so.

Yours sincerely,
E. FitzGerald

To Fanny Kemble

Lowestoft: October 24/76

Dear Mrs Kemble,

Little—Nothing—as I have to write, I am nevertheless beginning to write to you, from this old Lodging of mine, from which I think our Correspondence chiefly began—ten years ago. I am

in the same Room: the same dull Sea moaning before me: the
same Wind screaming through the Windows: so I take up the
same old Story. My Lugger was then about building: she has
passed into other hands now: I see her from time to time bouncing into Harbour, with her '244' on her Bows. Her Captain
and I have parted: I thought he did very wrongly—Drink,
among other things: but he did not think he did wrong: a different Morality from ours—that, indeed, of Carlyle's ancient Sea
Kings. I saw him a few days ago in his house, with Wife and
Children; looking, as always, too big for his house: but always
grand, polite, and unlike anybody else. I was noticing the many
Flies in the room—'Poor things,' he said, 'it is the warmth of our
Stove makes them alive.' When Tennyson was with me, whose
Portrait hangs in my house in company with those of Thackeray
and this Man (the three greatest men I have known), I thought
that both Tennyson and Thackeray were inferior to him in respect
of Thinking of Themselves. When Tennyson was telling me of
how The Quarterly abused him (humorously too), and desirous
of knowing why one did not care for his later works, etc., I
thought that if he had lived an active Life, as Scott and Shakespeare; or even ridden, shot, drunk, and played the Devil, as
Byron, he would have done much more, and talked about it
much less. 'You know,' said Scott to Lockhart, 'that I don't care
a Curse about what I write,' and one sees he did not. I don't
believe it was far otherwise with Shakespeare. Even old Wordsworth, wrapt up in his Mountain mists, and proud as he was,
was above all this vain Disquietude: proud, not vain, was he:
and that a Great Man (as Dante) has some right to be—but not
to care what the Coteries say. What a Rigmarole!

Donne scarce ever writes to me (Twalmley the Great), and if
he do not write to you, depend upon it he thinks he has nothing
worth sending over the Atlantic. I heard from Mowbray quite
lately that his Father was very well.

Yes: you told me in a previous Letter that you were coming to
England after Christmas. I shall not be up to going to London
to see you, with all your Company about you; perhaps (don't
think me very impudent!) you may come down, if we live till
Summer, to my Woodbridge Château, and there talk over some
old things.

z*

I make a kind of Summer in my Room here with Boccaccio. What a Mercy that one can return with a Relish to these Books! As Don Quixote can only be read in his Spanish, so I do fancy Boccaccio only in his Italian: and yet one is used to fancy that Poetry is the mainly untranslateable thing. How prettily innocent are the Ladies, who, after telling very loose Stories, finish with 'E cosí Iddio faccia [noi] godere del nostro Amore, etc.,' sometimes, *Domeneddio*, more affectionately.

Anyhow, these Ladies are better than the accursed Eastern Question; of which I have determined to read, and, if possible, hear, no more till the one question be settled of Peace or War. If war, I am told I may lose some £5000 in Russian Bankruptcy: but I can truly say I would give that, and more, to ensure Peace and Good Will among Men at this time. Oh, the Apes we are! I must retire to my Montaigne—whom, by the way, I remember reading here, when the Lugger was building! Oh, the Apes, etc. But there was A Man in all that Business still, who is so now, somewhat tarnished.—And I am yours as then sincerely

E. F.G.

To C. E. Norton

Woodbridge, Novr. 8/76

My dear Sir,

'Vita Nuova' reached me safe, and 'siempre verde,' untarnished by its Voyage. I am afraid I liked your account of it more than itself: I mean, I was more interested: I suppose it is too mystical for me. So I felt when I tried to read it in the original twenty years ago: and I fear I must despair of relishing it as I ought now I have your Version of it, which, it seems to me, must be so good. I don't think you needed to bring in Rossetti, still less Theodore Martin, to bear Witness, or to put your Work in any other Light than its own.

After once more going through my Don Quixote ('siempre verde' too, if ever Book was), I returned to another of the Evergreens, Boccaccio, which I found by a Pencil mark at the Volume's end I had last read on board the little Ship I then had, nine years ago. And I have shut out the accursed 'Eastern

Question' by reading the Stories, as the 'lieta Brigata' shut out the Plague by telling them. Perhaps Mr Lowell will give us Boccaccio one day, and Cervantes? And many more, whom Ste. Beuve has left to be done by him. I fancy Boccaccio must be read in his Italian, as Cervantes in his Spanish: the Language fitting either 'like a Glove' as we say. Boccaccio's Humour in his Country People, Friars, Scolds &c. is capital: as well, of course, as the easy Grace and Tenderness of other Parts. One thinks that no one who had well read him and Don Quixote would ever write with a strain again, as is the curse of nearly all modern Literature. I know that 'Easy Writing is d—d hard Reading.' Of course the Man must be a Man of Genius to take his Ease: but, if he be, let him take it. I suppose that such as Dante, and Milton, and my Daddy, took it far from easy: well, they dwell apart in the Empyrean; but for Human Delight, Shakespeare, Cervantes, Boccaccio, and Scott!

Tennyson (a Man of Genius, who, I think, has crippled his growth by over-elaboration) came suddenly upon me here six weeks ago: and, many years as it was since we had met, there seemed not a Day's Interval between. He looked very well; and very happy; having with him his eldest Son, a very nice Fellow, who took all care of 'Papa,' as I was glad to hear him say, not 'Governor' as the Phrase now is. One Evening he was in a Stew because of some nasty Paragraph in a Newspaper about his not allowing Mr Longfellow to quote from his Poems. And he wrote a Note to Mr L. at once in this room, and his Son carried it off to the Post that same Night, just in time. So my House is so far becoming a Palace, being the Place of a Despatch from one Poet to the other, all over that Atlantic!

We never had the trees in Leaf so long as this Year: they are only just rusty before my window, this Nov. 8. So I thought they would die of mere Old Age: but last night came a Frost, which will hasten their End. I suppose yours have been dying in all their Glory as usual.

You must understand that this Letter is to acknowledge the Vita Nuova (which, by the by, I think ought to be the Title on the Title page as well as outside), so do not feel obliged to reply, but believe me yours truly, E. F. G.

To Alfred Tennyson

Lowestoft, December 30th, 1876

My dear old Alfred,

"Harold"[1] came, King Harold. But I still yearn after a Fairy Prince who came from other skies than these rainy ones, with his joyful eyes, "foxfooted step," and his mantle glittering on the rocks. Impute this to my old prejudice, childish taste, whatever you will, except my ceasing to be your loyal old Fitz.

I scarce know if it be worth writing to say this: you knew it all beforehand: still, I suppose it is proper to acknowledge such a present. At any rate it gives me an opportunity to wish you and all yours all good for coming 1877, a wish that I think you would also guess without my writing. Here I have a book of old Spanish Romances familiar to Don Quixote and Sancho. I shall write you out a *rather* pretty one which I read yesterday, and remain

Yours as ever, E. F. G.

There is not much in it, if you take the trouble to construe; but I like the lady with her old husband partner, managing to address the young Count, perhaps as she passes him in the dance, bit by bit as the figure brings her round again.

To Samuel Laurence

Woodbridge. Jan. 15/77

My dear Laurence,

Then I sent you the Greek instead of the Persian whom you asked for? The two are the same size and binding: so of course I sent the wrong one. But I will send the right one directly: and you need not make a trouble of acknowledging it: I know you will thank me, and I think you will feel a sort of 'triste Plaisir' in it, as others beside myself have felt. It is a desperate sort of thing, unfortunately at the bottom of all thinking men's minds;

[1] [Tennyson's *Harold* was published in November 1876; it was not performed publicly until 1928.]

but made Music of . . . I shall soon be going to old ugly Lowestoft again to be with Nephews and Nieces. The Great Man . . . is yet there: commanding a Crew of those who prefer being his Men to having command of their own. And they are right; for the Man is Royal, tho' with the faults of ancient Vikings. . . . His Glory is somewhat marred; but he looks every inch a King in his Lugger now. At home (when he is there, and not at the Tavern) he sits among his Dogs, Cats, Birds &c., always with a great Dog following abroad, and aboard. This is altogether the Greatest Man I have known.

To Elizabeth Cowell

12 Marine Terrace, Lowestoft. March 11/77

. . . I scarce like your taking any pains about my Works, whether in Verse, Prose, or Music. I never see any Paper but my old Athenæum, which, by the way, now tells me of some Lady's Edition of Omar which is to discover all my Errors and Perversions. So this will very likely turn the little Wind that blew my little Skiff on. Or the Critic who incautiously helped that may avenge himself on Agamemnon King, as he pleases. If the Pall Mall Critic knew Greek, I am rather surprised he should have vouchsafed even so much praise as the words you quoted. But I certainly have found that those few whom I meant it for, not Greek scholars, have been more interested in it than I expected. Not you, I think, who, though you judge only too favourably of all I do, are not fond of such Subjects.

I have here two Volumes of my dear Sévigné's Letters lately discovered at Dijon; and I am writing out for my own use a Dictionary of the Dramatis Personæ figuring in her Correspondence, whom I am always forgetting and confounding.

To Fanny Kemble

Little Grange: Woodbridge. February 22, [1878]

My dear Lady,

I am calling on you earlier than usual, I think. In my 'Academy'[1] I saw mention of some Notes on Mrs. Siddons in some article of this month's 'Fortnightly'[2]—as I thought. So I bought the Number, but can find no Siddons there. You probably know about it; and will tell me?

If you have not already read—*buy* Keats' Love-Letters to Fanny Brawne. One wishes she had another name; and had left some other Likeness of herself than the Silhouette (cut out by Scissors, I fancy) which dashes one's notion of such a Poet's worship. But one knows what misrepresentations such Scissors make. I had—perhaps have—one of Alfred Tennyson, done by an Artist on a Steamboat—some thirty years ago; which, though not inaccurate of outline, gave one the idea of a respectable Apprentice. But Keats' Letters—It happened that, just before they reached me, I had been hammering out some admirable Notes on Catullus[3]—another such fiery Soul who perished about thirty years of age two thousand years ago; and I scarce felt a change from one to other. From Catullus' better parts, I mean; for there is too much of filthy and odious—both of Love and Hate. Oh, my dear Virgil never fell into that: he was fit to be Dante's companion beyond even Purgatory.

I have just had a nice letter from Mr Norton in America: an amiable, modest man surely he must be. His aged Mother has been ill: fallen indeed into some half-paralysis: affecting her Speech principally. He says nothing of Mr Lowell; to whom I would write if I did not suppose he was very busy with his Diplomacy, and his Books, in Spain. I hope he will give us a Cervantes, in addition to the Studies in his 'Among my Books,' which seem to me, on the whole, the most conclusive Criticisms we have on their several subjects.

Do you ever see Mrs Ritchie? Fred. Tennyson wrote me that

---

[1] [9 February 1878.]

[2] [It was not in the *Fortnightly* but in the *Nineteenth Century*.]

[3] [*Criticisms and Elucidations of Catullus* by H. A. J. Munro.]

Alfred's son (Lionel, the younger, I suppose) was to be married in Westminster Abbey: which Fred. thinks an ambitious flight of Mrs A. T.

I may as well stop in such Gossip. Snowdrops and Crocuses out: I have not many, for what I had have been buried under an overcoat of Clay, poor little Souls. Thrushes tuning up; and I hope my old Blackbirds have not forsaken me, or fallen a prey to Cats.

And I am ever yours

E. F.G.

To W. A. Wright

Woodbridge. March 3/78

My dear Wright,

. . . You may infer that I have been reading—yes, and with great Interest, however little Scholarship—your Fellow-Collegian's new Book of Notes &c. And just as I had done my best with his Catullus, came to hand the Love Letters of a kindred Spirit, Keats; whose peevish Jealousy might, two thousand years ago, have made him as bitter and indecent against his friend Armitage Brown, as Catullus against Cæsar. But in him too Malice was not stronger than Love, any more than in Catullus, not only of the Lesbia-Brawne, but of the Fraternal, kind. Keats sighs after 'Poor Tom' as well as he whose 'Frater ave atque vale' continues sighing down to these times. (I hope I don't misquote, more Hibernorum.)

That is a fine Figure of old Cæsar entertaining his Lampooner at the Feast. And I have often thought what a pretty picture, for Millais to do, of the child Keats keeping guard outside his sick Mother's Chamber with a drawn Sword. If Catullus, however, were only *Fescennining*, his 'Malice' was not against Cæsar but against the Nemesis that might else be revenged on him—eh? But I don't understand how Suetonius, or those he wrote for, could have forgotten, though for party purposes they may have ignored, the nature and humour of that *Fescennine* which is known to Scholars two thousand years after. How very learned, and probably all wrong, have I become, since becoming interested in this Book!

To Fanny Kemble

The Old (Curiosity) Shop. Woodbridge, April 16 [1878]
(Where, by the by, I heard the Nightingale for the first time
yesterday Morning. That is, I believe, almost its exact date of
return, wind and weather permitting. Which being premised—)

Dear Mrs Kemble,

I think it is about time for you to have a letter from me; for I
think I am nearly as punctual as the Nightingale, though at
quicker Intervals; and perhaps there may be other points of
Unlikeness. After hearing that first Nightingale in my Garden,
I found a long, kind, and pleasant, Letter from Mr Lowell in
Madrid: the first of him too that I have heard since he flew
thither. Just before he wrote, he says, he had been assigning
Damages to some American who complained of having been
fed too long on Turtle's Eggs:—and all that sort of Business,
says the Minister, does not inspire a man to Letter-writing. He
is acclimatizing himself to Cervantes, about whom he must write
one of his fine, and (as I think) final Essays: I mean such as (in
the case of others he has done) ought to leave no room for a
reversal of Judgment. Amid the multitude of Essays, Reviews,
etc., one still wants *that*: and I think Lowell does it more than
any other Englishman. He says he meets Velasquez at every
turn of the street; and Murillo's Santa Anna opens his door for
him. Things are different here: but when my Oracle last night
was reading to me of Dandie Dinmont's blessed visit to Bertram
in Portanferry Gaol, I said—'I know it's Dandie, and I shouldn't
be at all surprized to see him come into this room.' No—no more
than—Madame de Sévigné! I suppose it is scarce right to live
so among Shadows; but—after near seventy years so passed—
'Que voulez-vous?'

Still, if any Reality would—of its own Volition—draw near to
my still quite substantial Self; I say that my House (if the
Spring do not prove unkindly) will be ready to receive—and the
owner also—any time before June, and after July; that is, before
Mrs Kemble goes to the Mountains, and after she returns from

them. I dare say no more, after so much so often said, and all about oneself.

Yesterday the Nightingale; and To-day a small, still, Rain which we had hoped for, to make 'poindre' the Flower-seeds we put in Earth last Saturday. All Sunday my white Pigeons were employed in confiscating the Sweet Peas we had laid there; so that To-day we have to sow the same anew.

I think a Memoir of Alfred de Musset, by his Brother, well worth reading. I don't say the best, but only to myself the most acceptable of modern French Poets; and, as I judge, a fine fellow —of the moral French type (I suppose some of the Shadow is left out of the Sketch), but of a Soul quite abhorrent from modern French Literature—from V. Hugo (I think) to E. Sue (I am sure). He loves to read—Clarissa! which reminded me of Tennyson, some forty years ago, saying to me *à propos* of that very book, 'I love those large, *still*, Books.' During a long Illness of A. de M. a Sister of the Bon Secours attended him: and, when she left, gave him a Pen worked in coloured Silks, 'Pensez à vos pro-messes,' as also a little 'amphore' she had knitted. Seventeen years (I think) after, when his last Illness came on him, he desired these two things to be enclosed in his Coffin.

And I am ever yours

E. F.G.

To J. R. Lowell

Woodbridge. April 17/78

My dear (Sir—)—(Lowell)?

Your letter reached me just after hearing this year's first Nightingale in my Garden: both very welcome. I am very glad you did not feel bound to answer me before; I should not write otherwise to you or to some very old Friends who, like most sensible men as they grow older, dislike all unnecessary writing more and more. So that I scarce remind them of myself more than once a year now. I shall feel sure of your good Will toward me whether you write or not; as I do of theirs.

Mr Norton thinks, as a Gentleman should, that Keats' Letters should not have been published. I hope I should not have bought them, had I not gathered from the Reviews that they were not derogatory to him. You know, I suppose, that she of whom K. wrote about to others so warmly, his Charmian, was not Fanny Brawne. Some years ago Lord Houghton wrote me it was: but he is a busy man of the World, though really a very good Fellow: indeed, he did not deserve your *skit* about his 'Finsbury Circus gentility,' which I dare say you have forgotten. I have not seen him, any more than much older and dearer friends, for these twenty years: never indeed was very intimate with him; but always found him a good natured, unaffected, man. He sent me a printed Copy of the first draught of the opening of Keats' Hyperion; very different from the final one: if you wished, I would manage to send it to you, quarto size as it is. This now reminds me that I will ask his Lordship why it was not published (as I supposed it was not). For it ought to be. He said he did not know if it were not the second draught rather than the first. But he could hardly have doubted if he gave his thoughts to it, I think. . . .

I want you to do De Quincey; certainly a very remarkable Figure in Literature, and not yet decisively drawn, as you could do it. There is a Memoir of him by one Page, showing a good deal of his familiar, and Family, Life: all amiable: perhaps the frailties omitted. It is curious, his regard to Language even when writing (as quite naturally he does) to his Daughter, 'I was disturbed last night at finding no natural, or spontaneous, opening —how barbarous by the way, is this collision of *ings*—find*ing*—open*ing* &c.' And some other instances.

I cannot understand why I have not yet taken to Hawthorne, a Man of real Genius, and that of a kind which I thought I could relish. I will have another Shot. His Notes of Travel seemed to me very shrewd, original, and sincere. Charles Sumner, of so different a Genius, also appears to me very truthful, and, I still fancy, strongly attached to the few he might care for. I am sorry he got a wrong idea of Sir Walter from Lord Brougham, and the Whigs, who always hated Scott. Indeed (as I well remember) it was a point of Faith with them that Scott had not written the Novels, till the Catastrophe discovered him: on which they changed their Cry into a denunciation of his having written them only for money, 'Scott's weak point,' Sumner quotes from

Brougham. As if Scott loved Money for anything else than to spend it: not only on Lands and House (which I maintain were simply those of a Scotch Gentleman) but to help any poor Devil that applied to him. Then that old Toad Rogers must tell Sumner that Manzoni's 'Sposi' were worth any ten of Scott's; yes, after Scott's Diary spoke of 'I really like Rogers &c.' and such moderate expressions of regard as Scott felt for him and his Breakfast of London Wits.

Here am I running over to Chapter II. You will be surfeited, like your Captain, if not on Turtles' Eggs. But you can eat me at intervals, you know, or not at all. Only you will certainly read my last Great Work,[1] which I enclose, drawn up first for my own benefit, in reading Lamb's Letters, as now printed in batches to his several Correspondents; and so I thought others than myself might be glad of a few Data to refer the letters to. Pollock calls my Paper 'Côtelette d'Agneau à la minute.'

As to my little Dialogue, I can't send it: so pretty in Form, I think, and with some such pretty parts: but then some odious smart writing, which I had forgotten till I looked it over again before sending to you. But I will send you the Calderon which you already like.

And, if you would send me any samples of Spanish, send me some Playbill (of the old Drama, if now played), or some public Advertisement, or Newspaper; this is what I should really like. As to Books, I dare say Quaritch has pretty well ferreted them out of Spain. Give a look, if you can, at a Memoir of Alfred de Musset written by his Brother. Making allowance for French morals, and Absinthe, (which latter is not mentioned in the Book) Alfred appears to me a fine Fellow, very un-French in some respects. He did not at all relish the new Romantic School, beginning with V. Hugo, and now alive in [Browning] and Co.— (what I call The *Gurgoyle* School of Art, whether in Poetry, Painting, or Music)—he detested the modern 'feuilleton' Novel, and read Clarissa! . . . Many years before A. de M. died he had a bad, long, illness, and was attended by a Sister of Charity. When she left she gave him a Pen with '[Pensez] à vos promesses' worked about in coloured silks: as also a little worsted 'Amphore' she had knitted at his Bed side. When he came to die, some

[1] [A calendar of Charles Lamb's Life.]

seventeen years after, he had these two little things put with him in his Coffin.

To J. R. Lowell

Woodbridge. May 1878

Ecce iterum Crispin! I think you will soon call me '*Les* FitzGerald*s*' as Madame de Sévigné called her too officious friend '*Les* Hacquevilles.' However, I will risk that in sending you a Copy of that first Draught of an opening to Hyperion. I have got it from that Finsbury Circus Houghton, who gave me the first Copy, which I keep: so you shall have this, if you please; I know no one more worthy of it; and indeed I told Lord H. I wanted it for you; so you see he bears no malice. He is in truth a very good natured fellow. . . .

Well, to leave that, he writes me that he had the original MS.: it was stolen from him. Fortunately, a friend of his (Edmund Lushington) had taken a MS. copy, and from that was printed what I send you. The corrections are from Lushington. I do not understand why Lord H. does not publish it. He says he has just written to Bendizzy to do something from the state purse for an aged Sister of Keats, now surviving in great Poverty. Her name is 'Fanny.' Ben might do much worse: some say he is about worse, now: I do not know; I cannot help: and I distress myself as little as I can. 'Lisons tout Madame de Sévigné,' said Ste. Beuve one day to some Friends in the Country; and Doudan (whom Mr Norton admires, as I do) bids a Friend take that advice in 1871. One may be glad of it here in England ere 1879.

A short while ago we were reading the xith Chapter of Guy Mannering, where Colonel Mannering returns to Ellangowan after seventeen years. A long gap in a Story, Scott says: but scarcely so in Life, to any one who looks back so far. And, at the end of the Novel, we found a pencil note of mine, 'Finished 10½ p.m. Tuesday Decr. 17/1861.' Not on this account, but on account of its excellence, pray do read the Chapter if you can get the Book: it is altogether admirable—Cervantes—Shakespeare. I mean that Chapter of the Colonel's return to Mrs MacCandlish's Inn at Kippletringan.

We are now reading 'Among the Spanish People,' by the Mr
Rose who wrote 'Untrodden Spain;' a really honest, good-hearted,
fellow, I think: with some sentimentality amid his Manhood, and
(I suppose) rather too rose-coloured in his Estimate of the People
he has long lived among. But he can't help recalling Don
Quixote. He has a really delightful account of a Visit he pays to a
pueblo he calls Baños up the Sierra Morena: one would expect
Don and Sancho there, by one of the old Houses with Arms over
the Door. Pray get hold of this Book also if you can: else 'les
Hacquevilles' will have to buy it second hand from Mudie and
send—'Coals to Newcastle.'

With Keats I shall send you an Athenæum with a rather
humorous account of a Cockney squabble about whether Shelley
called his Lark an '*un*-bodied,' or '*em*-bodied,' Spirit. I really
forget which way was settled by MS. Shelley is now the rage in
Cockayne; but he is too unsubstantial for me.

It is now hot here: I suppose something [like] February in
Andalusia. Do you find Madrid Climate as bad as Rose and
others describe it? He has also a very pleasant [chapter] about
the Lavanderas of the Manzanares. What delightful words!

To Frederick Tennyson

Woodbridge, May 8/78

My dear Frederic,

I wish you had retained Keats if you cared for him: but perhaps once read is enough: I suppose I shall hardly look further
than the sad portrait hereafter: but I do not regret having read
the Letters. I shall post you now (pray keep it—or don't send it
back) a small Volume in which you may like to read a good
Article on old Carlyle. I suppose it was in some American Paper
or Magazine. The Author (Lowell) has published two volumes of
longer Essays on some great Authors; I think on the whole the
best yet written on their several Subjects. I would send you
either, or both, of these if I knew whether you would care to
read them: but you say you are engaged in other speculations,
and so they might become rather a burden than a pleasure to
you. Lowell (the writer) has written a good deal of Poetry which,

725

so far as I have seen of it, has not interested me; but I think he can judge of it, as well as of the Authors thereof: and is a very able and independent Man. This I thought long before I had any acquaintance with the Man, whom I now know only by Letter. He is a Professor at the American Cambridge: but is now gone as Minister to Spain: where he is imbibing Cervantes, one of his chief Idols. A merit about him is, that he is in no hurry to write on any matter, but lets it gather and form within him till as complete as he can make it.

I suppose you see the Athenæum or some such Paper as tells you of new Books, etc. The last Athenæum gave a remarkable account of Trelawny's reprint of his remarkable account of Shelley and Byron, published over thirty years ago, I think. He seems to have loved Shelley as a Man: Byron, not so well: which I think one can sympathise with. The Cockneys are now making a tremendous effort to set up Shelley as *the* Apollo of his time: for a true Poet I recognise him: but too unsubstantial for me: and poor Keats' little finger worth all his Body: not to mention Byron, with all his faults. Lord Houghton (Dicky Milnes of old) sent me some years ago Keats' first Draught of the opening of Hyperion, printed from a MS. which he (Lord H.) had, but which was stolen from him by one of his many Friends. This I would post you if you cared to see it. But I really don't know if my doing so be not a bore to you.

I fancy we must now be having Jersey weather here: very warm and wet. All our younger trees are in leaf, fresh if not full: the old Oaks and Elms, whose blood, I suppose, circulates more slowly, still reserving themselves. I have been kept in for two days; and, as my Eyes happen to be rusty just now, am rather puzzled how to get through the Day—

> And hence arises ancient Men's Report—
> The Days are tedious, but the Years are short.

So says old Crabbe: who elsewhere says:

> So with the aid that Shops and Sailing (Books and
>   Letters?) give,
> Life passes on—'tis Labour—but we live.

There is Mark Tapley for you, at his favourite recreation.

726

I saw another Copy of your Days and Hours in a Bristol Catalogue; sent for it, but it had been sold. You know I have the large Volume from which the publisht one was drawn: but I buy the latter to give away. I see your old friend Browning is in the field again, with another of his odd titles: De Saisiez—or Croisic—or some such name. I tried to read his Dramatic Lyrics again: they seemed to me Ingoldsby Legends.

To C. E. Norton

July 2/78

My dear Norton,

You wrote me a very kind Invitation—to your own home—in America! But it is all too late for that; more on account of habit than time of life: I will not repeat what I feel sure I have told you before on that subject. You will be more interested by the enclosed note: of which this is the simple Story. Some three weeks ago I wrote my half-yearly note of enquiry to Carlyle's Niece; he was, she said, quite well; walking by the river before Breakfast: driving out of an Afternoon: constantly reading: just then reading Goethe of whom he never tired: and glancing over Magazines and Reviews which he called 'Floods of Nonsense, Cataracts of Twaddle' &c. I had sent him the enclosed paper,[1] written by a Suffolk Archdeacon for his Son's East Anglian Notes and Queries: and now reprinted, with his permission, by me, for the benefit of others, yourself among the number. Can you make out the lingo, and see what I think the pretty Idyll it tells of? If I were in America, at your home, I would recite it to you; nay, were the Telephone prepared across the Atlantic! Well: it was sent, as I say, to Carlyle: who, by what his Niece replied, I suppose liked it too. And, by way of return, I suppose, he sends me a Volume of Norway Kings and Knox: which I was very glad to have, not only as a token of his Good Will, but also because Knox was, I believe, the only one of his works I had not read. And I was obliged to confess to him in my acknowledgment of his kindly Present, that I relished these two children of his old Age as much as any of his more fiery Manhood. I had

[1] [*The only Darter, A Suffolk Clergyman's Reminiscence.* Written in the Suffolk Dialect by R. H. Groome under the name of John Dutfen.]

727

previously asked if he knew anything of John Wesley's Journal,
which I was then re-perusing; as he his Goethe: yes, he knew
that Wesley too, and 'thought as I did about it' his Niece said;
and in reply to my Question if he knew anything of two 'mountains' (as English people called hills a hundred years ago) which
Wesley says were called 'The Peas' at Dunbar[1]—why, here is his
Answer: evincing the young Blood in the old Man still.

Wesley's Journal is very well worth reading, and having; not
only as an outline of his own singular character, but of the conditions of England, Ireland, and Scotland, in the last Century.
Voilà par exemple un Livre dont Monsr Lowell pourrait faire
une jolie critique, s'il en voudrait, mais il s'occupe de plus
grandes choses, du Calderon, du Cervantes. I always wish to
run on in bad French: but my friends would not care to read it.
But pray make acquaintance with this Wesley; if you cannot find
a copy in America, I will send you one from here: I believe I have
given it to half a dozen Friends. Had I any interest with Publishers, I would get them to reprint parts of it, as of my old
Crabbe, who still sticks in my Throat.

I have taken that single little Lodging at Dunwich for the
next three months, and shall soon be under those Priory Walls
again. But the poor little 'Dunwich Rose,' brought by those
monks from the North Country, will have passed, after the hot
weather we are at last having. Write when you will, and not till
then; I believe in your friendly regard, with, or without, a Letter
to assure me of it.

To C. E. Norton

Woodbridge. October 15/78

My dear Norton,

. . . I got little more than a Fortnight at that old Dunwich;
for my Landlady took seriously ill, and finally died: and the
Friend[2] whom I went to meet there became so seriously ill also

---

[1] [Wesley's Journal, 30 May 1786, and 22 May 1788.]

[2] [Edwin Edwards (1823–79) was a Suffolk man who left a clerkship at the
Admiralty to become a painter and etcher in London. EFG said he had
"a strong understanding, much intuitive perception, Humour, and Love for
Literature as well as Art." His wife was "a very clever, shrewd, and good
woman: the very woman for an Artist's wife."]

as to be obliged to return to London before August was over. So then I went to an ugly place[1] on the sea shore also, some fifteen miles off the old Priory; and there was with some Nephews and Nieces, trying to read the Novels from a Circulating Library, with indifferent Success. And now here am I at home once more; getting my Garden, if not my House, in order; and here I shall be probably all Winter, except for a few days visit to that sick Friend in London, if he desires it. . . .

We too have been having a Fortnight of delightful weather, so as one has been able to sit abroad all the Day. And now, that Spirit which Tennyson sung of in one of his early Poems is heard, as it were, walking and talking to himself among the decaying flower-beds. This Season (such as we have been enjoying)—my old Crabbe sings of it too, in a very pathetic way to me: for it always seems to me an Image of the Decline of Life also.

'It was a Day ere yet the Autumn closed,
When Earth before her Winter's War reposed;
When from the Garden as we look'd above,
No Cloud was seen, and nothing seem'd to move;
[When the wide River was a silver Sheet,
And upon Ocean slept the unanchor'd fleet;][2]
When the wing'd Insect settled in our sight,
And waited wind to recommence its flight.'

You see I cross out two lines which, fine as they are, go beyond the Garden: but I am not sure if I place them aright. The two last lines you will feel, I think: for I suppose some such Insect is in America too. (You must not mind Crabbe's self-contradiction about 'nothing moving.') . . .

I have two Letters I want to send Lowell: but I do not like writing as if to extort answers from him. You see Carlyle's Note within: I do not want it back, thank you. Good Night: for Night it is: and my Reader is coming. We look forward to The Lammermoor, and Old Mortality before long. I made another vain attempt on George Eliot at Lowestoft, Middlemarch.

[1] [Lowestoft.]
[2] [These two lines are crossed out.]

To Charles Merivale

Woodbridge, December 15 [1878]

My dear Dean,

Donne gave me your letter when I last saw him, on Friday afternoon. My scrap appended to his letter did not deserve so good acknowledgment from you: so now, you see, I try to make up for it, especially as you in some measure ask me about Mrs. Kemble.

I did not see much of her acting, nor hear much of her reading, for in truth I did not much admire either. She herself admits she had no liking for the stage, and (in a capital paper in some magazine) that she had not a *Theatrical* gift, though she had, she thinks, a *Dramatic*, a distinction which I leave for herself to explain. In such readings of hers as I heard, she seemed to me to do the men and the soldiers best, such as the warlike lords in King John. I did not hear her Hotspur, which should have been good, as was her brother Jack's at school. I never heard such capital declamation as *his* Hotspur, and Alexander's Feast, when we were at Bury together, he about eighteen, and then with the profile of Alexander himself, as I have seen it on medals, etc. When *you* knew him he had lost, I suppose, his youthful freshness. His sister, Fanny, I say, I did not much admire in public: but she was, and is, a noble-hearted and noble-souled woman, however wayward; and no one more loyal, not only to her own, but to her brother's friends and schoolfellows. And does she not write finely too? Sometimes in long sentences too, which spin out without entanglement from her pen.

When I remember your viva voce, and when I read your letters, Merivale, I always wish some one would make notes of your table and letter talk: so witty, so humorous, so just. You would not do this yourself; if you thought about what you said and wrote for such a purpose it would not, I suppose, be as good; but I wish others would do it for you—and—I must not say 'for *me*' at my time of day, but for those who come after us both.

I had not seen Donne for three years, I think: he seemed to me feebler in body and mind, but the same dear old Donne still.

And I am still yours, as his,

OLD FITZ

To Bernard Quaritch

Little Grange, Woodbridge Decr. 17 [1878]

Dear Sir,

I was away from home when your last letter came and did not return till Saturday Night.

About your proposal I will say:—

1st That an Edition of *1000* Copies would—at the rate I sell at—amount to a *final* Edition—for *my* Life assuredly.

2nd I still demur at the *4to* size you propose. I suppose, the same as previous Omars. I quite understand that only *the few* buy me, and you suppose that those few will be willing to pay such a price as will make up for *many* at a cheaper rate. But even were that so, you see *Osgood* made a very small Vol. of Omar, though doubling its size by blank pages; and if *Jámi* were added to Omar, those pages might be occupied. All *Verse* should, I feel sure, be in a *handy, pocketable*, size: as much better Verse than mine is generally printed in. And I have a dislike to see my minor things swelled out into 4to margin as if they were precious things. You said in a former letter that I could choose my own shape of Book: and, unless you care to trouble yourself with further Argument on so small a matter, I am for the usual size.

All This you can consider if you choose: there *can* be no hurry for I suppose no one will think of printing till Xmas is over and 1879 come.

Meanwhile now you have seen Salámán so as to judge of what space he would occupy, I wish you would send him safely back to me, as I would consult Cowell about some points which are better certified in MS. than in Print.

Yours E. FG.

Direct always Little Grange, Woodbridge.

To Horace Basham

Little Grange Woodbridge Feb 8/79

Dear Horace

I am not quite sure of old James Fisher's address, therefore it is that I trouble you to cash the enclosed, and to give him the money. Whether all at once or in two halves, as you see best.

Please to thank him for some herring which he sent me. He says his *Dropsy* has returned, I did not know that he ailed anything else than *Rheumatism*. Whatever it be, if it is not likely that he can work again, I shall allow him something weekly, poor Fellow, 2s, I think, but of this I will talk to you when I go over to Aldbro: I should be going over *now* (having only just returned home since August) but have a Friend coming today till over tomorrow. I hope to hear that your prospects have cleared up since I last saw you, and

am always sincerely yours

E. FITZGERALD

To Fanny Kemble

Woodbridge: April 25, [1879]

Dear Mrs Kemble,

I think I have let sufficient time elapse before asking you for another Letter. I want to know how you are: and, if you can tell me that you are as well as you and I now expect to be—anyhow, well rid of that Whooping Cough—that will be news enough for one Letter. What else, you shall add of your own free will:—not feeling bound.

When you last wrote me from Leamington, you crossed over your Address: and I (thinking perhaps of America) deciphered it 'Baltimore.' I wonder the P. O. did not return me my Letter: but there was no Treason in it, I dare say.

My Brother keeps waiting—and hoping—for—Death: which will not come: perhaps Providence would have let it come sooner, were he not rich enough to keep a Doctor in the house, to keep him in Misery. I don't know if I told you in my last that he was

732

ill; seized on by a Disease not uncommon to old Men—an
'internal Disorder' it is polite to say; but I shall say to you,
disease of the Bladder. I had always supposed he would be
found dead one good morning, as my Mother was—as I hoped
to be—quietly dead of the Heart which he had felt for several
Years. But no; it is seen good that he shall be laid on the Rack—
which he may feel the more keenly as he never suffered Pain
before, and is not of a strong Nerve. I will say no more of this.
The funeral Bell, which has been at work, as I never remember
before, all this winter, is even now, as I write, tolling from St
Mary's Steeple.

'Parlons d'autres choses,' as my dear Sévigné says.

I—We—have finished all Sir Walter's Scotch Novels; and I
thought I would try an English one: Kenilworth—a wonderful
Drama, which Theatre, Opera, and Ballet (as I once saw it represented) may well reproduce. The Scene at Greenwich, where
Elizabeth 'interviews' Sussex and Leicester, seemed to me as
fine as what is called (I am told, wrongly) Shakespeare's Henry
VIII. Of course, plenty of melodrama in most other parts:—
but the Plot wonderful.

Then—after Sir Walter—Dickens' Copperfield, which came
to an end last night because I would not let my Reader read the
last Chapter. What a touch when Peggotty—the man—at last
finds the lost Girl, and—throws a handkerchief over her face
when he takes her to his arms—never to leave her! I maintain it
—a little Shakespeare—a Cockney Shakespeare, if you will: but
as distinct, if not so great, a piece of pure Genius as was born in
Stratford. Oh, I am quite sure of that, had I to choose but one
of them, I would choose Dickens' hundred delightful Caricatures
rather than Thackeray's half-dozen terrible Photographs.

In Michael Kelly's Reminiscences (quite worth reading about
Sheridan) I found that, on January 22, 1802, was produced at
Drury Lane an Afterpiece called Urania, by the Honourable
W. Spencer, in which 'the scene of Urania's descent was entirely
new to the stage, and produced an extraordinary effect.' Hence
then the Picture which my poor Brother sent you to America.

'D'autres choses encore.' You may judge, I suppose, by the
N.E. wind in London what it has been hereabout. Scarce a tinge
of Green on the hedgerows; scarce a Bird singing (only once the

733

Nightingale, with broken Voice), and no flowers in the Garden but the brave old Daffydowndilly, and Hyacinth—which I scarce knew was so hardy. I am quite pleased to find how comfortably they do in my Garden, and look so Chinese gay. Two of my dear Blackbirds have I found dead—of Cold and Hunger, I suppose; but one is even now singing—across that Funeral Bell. This is so, as I write, and tell you—Well: we have Sunshine at last—for a day—'thankful for small Blessings,' etc.

I think I have felt a little sadder since March 31 that shut my seventieth Year behind me, while my Brother was—in some such way as I shall be if I live two or three years longer—'Parlons d'autres'—that I am still able to be sincerely yours

E. F.G.

To C. E. Norton

Woodbridge. May 18/79

My dear Norton:

It is over six months, I believe, since we exchanged a letter; mine the last shot: which I mention only because that has been my reason for not writing again till I should hear from you that all was well enough with you and yours to justify my writing an idle letter. You have spoken of an aged Mother:—if your Winter has been such as ours! And not over yet, as scarce a leaf on the trees, and a N. E. wind blowing Cold, Cough, Bronchitis &c. and the confounded Bell of a neighbouring Church announcing a Death, day after day. I certainly never remember so long, and so mortal a Winter: among young as well as old. Among the latter, I have just lost my elder, and only surviving Brother. But I shall close this Bill of Mortality before turning over the leaf.

Well: it is Mr Clarke's pamphlet which has encouraged me to 'take up the pen,' for I think it was you who sent it to me. All I am qualified to say about it is, that it is very well and earnestly written; but on a Subject, like your own Olympia, that I am no Judge of. I think of forwarding it to Cowell at our Cambridge, who is a Judge of Everything, I think, while pretending to Nothing. . . .

This reminds me of all the pains he bestowed on me five and twenty years ago; of which the result is one final Edition of

Omar and Jámí. . . . Omar remains as he was; Jámí (Salámán) is cut down to two-thirds of his former proportion, and very much improved, I think. It is still in a wrong key: Verse of Miltonic strain, unlike the simple Eastern; I remember trying that at first, but could not succeed. So there is little but the Allegory itself (not a bad one), and now condensed into a very fair Bird's Eye view; quite enough for any Allegory, I think. . . .

And—(this Letter is to be all about myself)—by this post I send you my Handbook of Crabbe's Tales of the Hall, of which I am so doubtful that I do not yet care to publish it. I wished to draw a few readers to a Book which nobody reads, by an Abstract of the most readable Parts connected with as little of my Prose as would tell the story of much prosaic Verse, but that very amount of prosy Verse may help to soak the story into the mind (as Richardson &c.) in a way that my more readable Abstract does not. So it may only serve to remind any one of a Book— which he never read! The Original must be more obsolete in America than here in England; however, I should like to know what you make of it: and you see that you may tell me very plainly, for it is not as an Author, but only as Author's Showman that I appear.

It is rather shameful to take another Sheet because of almost filling the first with myself. And I have but little to tell in it. Carlyle I have not heard of for these six months: nor Tennyson: I must write to hear how they have weathered this mortal Winter. Tennyson's elder, not eldest, Brother Charles is dead: and I was writing only yesterday to persuade Spedding to insist on Macmillan publishing a complete edition of Charles' Sonnets: graceful, tender, beautiful, and quite original, little things. Two thirds of them would be enough: but no one can select in such a case, you know. I have been reading again your Hawthorne's Journal in England when he was Consul here; this I have: I cannot get his 'Our Old Home,' nor his Foreign Notes: can you send me any small, handy, Edition of these two last? I delight in them because of their fearless Truthfulness as well as for their Genius. I have just taken down his Novels, or Romances, to read again, and try to relish more than I have yet done; but I feel sure the fault must be with me, as I feel about Goethe, who is yet as sealed a book to me as ever. . . . I have (alas!) got through all

Sir Walter's Scotch Novels this winter, even venturing further on Kenilworth: which is wonderful for Plot: and one Scene, Elizabeth reconciling her Rival Earls at Greenwich, seeming to me as good as Shakespeare's Henry VIII., which is mainly Fletcher's, I am told. I have heard nothing of Mr Lowell since I heard of you, and do think that I will pitch him a Crabbe into the midst of Madrid, if he be still there. (N.B. Some of Crabbe is not in the Text but from MS. first (and best) readings printed in the Son's edition.)

The Nightingale is now telling me that he is not dead.

To J. R. Lowell

Woodbridge. May 20/79

My dear Sir,

By this post I send you a bit of a Book, in which you see that I only play very second Fiddle. It is not published yet, as I wait for a few friends to tell me if it be worth publishing, or better kept among ourselves, who know Crabbe as well as myself. You could tell me better than any one, only that I doubt if any Transatlantic Man can care, even if he knows of a Writer whose Books are all but unread by his own Countrymen, so obsolete as has become his Subject (in this Book) as well as his way of treating it. So I think I may exonerate you from giving an opinion, and will only send it to you for such amusement as it may afford you in your Exile. I fancied I could make a pleasant Abstract of a much too long and clumsy Book, and draw a few Readers to the well-nigh forgotten Author. But, on looking over my little work, I doubt that my short and readable Handybook will not leave any such impression as the long, rather un-readable, original; mere length having, you know, the inherent Virtue of soaking it in: so as my Book will scarce do but as a reminder of the original, which nobody reads! . . .

Voilà assez sur ce sujet là. I think that you will one day give us an account of your Spanish Consulship, as Hawthorne did of his English: a noble Book which I have just been reading over again. His 'Our old Home' is out of print here; and I have asked Mr Norton to send me any handy Edition of it, as also of the Italian

Journal, my Copies having been lent out past recovery. I am going to begin again with his Scarlet Letter and Seven Gables; which (oddly to myself) I did not take to. And yet I think they are not out of my line, or reach, I ought to say.

We have had such a long, and mortal Winter as never do I remember in my seventy years, which struck 70 on March 31 last. I have just lost a Brother—75. Proximus ardet &c. But I escaped through all these seven months Winter, till a week or ten days ago, when a South Wind and Sunshine came for a Day, and one expatiated abroad, and then down comes a North Easter &c. I was like the Soldier in Crabbe's Old Bachelor (now with you), who compares himself to the Soldier stricken by a random Shot, when resting on his Arms &c. So Cold, Cough, Bronchitis &c. And To-day Sunshine again, and Ruiseñor (do you know him?) in my Shrubs only just be-greening, and I am a Butterfly again. I have heard nothing of Carlyles, Tennysons &c. save that the latter had written some Ballad about Lucknow. I shall be glad to hear a word of yourself, Calderon, and Don Quixote, the latter of whom σαίνει με from my Bookshelf. Yes, yes, I am soon coming.

To Fanny Kemble

Woodbridge: Nov. 13/79

My dear Lady,

Now that your anxieties are, as I hope, over, and that you are returned, as I suppose, to London, I send you a budget. First: the famous *Belvidere Hat*; which I think you ought to stick into your Records. Were I a dozen years younger, I should illustrate all the Book in such a way; but, as my French song says, 'Le Temps est trop court pour de si longs projets.'

Next, you behold a Photo of Carlyle's Niece, which he bid her send me two or three years ago in one of her half-yearly replies to my Enquiries. What a shrewd, tidy, little Scotch Body! Then you have her last letter, telling of her Uncle, and her married Self, and thanking me for a little Wedding gift which I told her was bought from an Ipswich Pawnbroker—a very good, clever fellow, who reads Carlyle, and comes over here now and then for a talk with me. Mind, when you return me the Photo, that you secure it around with your Letter paper, that the Postman may not stamp into it. Perhaps this trouble is scarce worth giving you.

'Clerke Sanders' has been familiar to me these fifty years almost; since Tennyson used to repeat it, and 'Helen of Kirkconnel,' at some Cambridge gathering. At that time he looked something like the Hyperion shorn of his Beams in Keats' Poem: with a Pipe in his mouth. Afterwards he got a touch, I used to say, of Haydon's Lazarus. Talking of Keats, do not forget to read Lord Houghton's Life and Letters of him: in which you will find what you may not have guessed from his Poetry (though almost unfathomably deep in that also) the strong, masculine, Sense and Humour, etc., of the man: more akin to Shakespeare, I am tempted to think, in a perfect circle of Poetic Faculties, than any Poet since.

Well: the Leaves which hung on more bravely than ever I remember are at last whirling away in a Cromwell Hurricane—(not quite that, neither)—and my old Man says he thinks Winter has set in at last. We cannot complain hitherto. Many summer flowers held out in my Garden till a week ago, when we dug up the Beds in order for next year. So now little but the orange Marigold, which I love for its colour (Irish and Spanish) and Courage, in living all Winter through. Within doors, I am again at my everlasting Crabbe! doctoring his Posthumous Tales *à la mode* of those of 'The Hall,' to finish a Volume of simple 'Selections' from his other works: all which I will leave to be used, or not, whenever old Crabbe rises up again: which will not be in the Lifetime of yours ever

E. F.G.

I dared not decypher all that Mrs Wister wrote in my behalf—because I knew it must be sincere! Would she care for my Eternal Crabbe?

To Fanny Kemble

Woodbridge, Febr: 3/80

My dear Lady,

I do not think it is a full month since I last taxed you for some account of yourself: but we have had hard weather, you know, ever since: your days have been very dark in London, I am told, and as we have all been wheezing under them down here, I want to know how you stand it all. I only hope my MS. is not very bad; for I am writing by Candle, before my Reader comes. He eat such a Quantity of Cheese and Cake between the Acts that he could scarce even see to read at all after; so I had to remind him that, though he was not quite sixteen, he had much exceeded the years of a Pig. Since which we get on better. I did not at all like to have my Dombey spoiled; especially Captain Cuttle, God bless him, and his Creator, now lying in Westminster Abbey. The intended Pathos is, as usual, missed: but just turn to little Dombey's Funeral, where the Acrobat in the Street suspends his performance till the Funeral has passed, and his Wife wonders if the little Acrobat in her Arms will so far outlive the little Boy in the Hearse as to wear a Ribbon through his hair, following his Father's Calling. It is in such Side-touches, you know, that Dickens is inspired to Create like a little God Almighty. I have read half his lately published letters, which, I think, add little to Forster's Account, unless in the way of showing what a good Fellow Dickens was. Surely it does not seem that his Family were not fond of him, as you supposed?

I have been to Lowestoft for a week to see my capital Nephew. Edmund Kerrich, before he goes to join his Regiment in Ireland, I wish you could see him make his little [child] (six years old) put him through his Drill. That is worthy of Dickens: and I am always yours sincerely—and I do hope not just now very illegibly—

LITTLEGRANGE

739

To Horace Basham

Little Grange, Woodbridge April 1/80

Dear Horace:

I ought to have sent you the enclosed yesterday: but you will duly get it, I hope, in time for old Fisher's weekly payment, which (as I think) I had made up to the end of March.

I *suppose* he is not much better—if at all better—since winter: and, if that be so, my Enclosure can be paid at 2s a week till the end of June.

If he *should* be able to work before that, I leave it to your Discretion to keep on [paying?], or to withhold for any future occasion.

As you are generally very busy, I enclose you a Card, on which you can just write a few words, with just your *Initials* at the end, only just saying how you & Fisher are, without anything further.

If I have not to go to Lowestoft next week, I may very possibly run over to Aldbro' for a few hours.

I am fairly well myself, having entered on my 72nd year yesterday: and am

Yours' sincerely
E. FitzGerald

To R. C. Trench

Woodbridge. May 18/80

My dear Lord:

I should have sent a line before now to thank you for your Calderon, had I not waited for some tidings of Donne from Mowbray, to whom I wrote some days ago. Not hearing from him, I suppose that he is out holyday-making somewhere; and therefore I will delay no longer.

You gave me your Calderon when it first came out, now some five and twenty years ago! I am always glad to know that it, or any of your writings, Prose or Verse, still flourish—which I think not many others of the kind will do after the Generation they are born in. I remember that you regretted having tried the asonante, and you now decide that Prose is best for English Translation. It may be so; in a great degree it must be so; but I think this experiment might yet be tried; namely, the short trochaic line, regardless of an assonant that will not speak in our thin vowels, but looped up at intervals with a strong monosyllabic rhyme, without which the English trochaic, assonant or not, is apt to fray out, or run away too watery-like without some such interruption; I mean when running to any considerable length, as I should think would be the case in Longfellow's Hiawatha; which I have not however seen since it appeared. Were I a dozen years younger I might try this with Calderon which I have found to succeed in some much shorter flights: but it is too late now, and you may think it well that it is so, with one who takes such great liberties with great Poets, himself pretending to be little more than a Versifier. I know not how it is with you who are really a Poet; and perhaps you may think I am as wrong about my trochee as about my iambic.

As for the modern Poetry, I have cared for none of the last thirty years, not even Tennyson, except in parts: pure, lofty and noble as he always is. Much less can I endure the *Gurgoyle* school (I call it) begun, I suppose, by V. Hugo. . . . I do think you will find something better than that in the discarded Crabbe; whose writings Wordsworth (not given to compliment any man on any occasion) wrote to Crabbe's Son and Editor would continue as long at least as any Poetry written since, on account of their mingled 'Truth and Poetry.' And this includes Wordsworth's own. So I must think my old Crabbe will come up again, though never to be popular.

This reminds me that just after I had written to you, Crabbe's Grandson, one of the best, most amiable, and most agreeable, of my friends, paid me a two days' Visit, and told me that a Nephew of yours was learning to farm with a Steward of Lord Walsingham at Merton in Norfolk, George Crabbe's own parish; I mean the living George, who spoke of your Nephew as a very gentlemanly young man indeed. I think *he* will not gainsay what I write to you of his 'Parson.'

Your kind Letter has encouraged me to write all this. I felt some hesitation in addressing you again after an interval of some fifteen years, I think; and now I think I shall venture on writing to you once again before another year be gone, if we both live to see 1881 in, and out.

To Fanny Kemble

Woodbridge: June 23, [1880]

My dear Mrs Kemble,

You smile at my 'Lunacies' as you call my writing periods; I take the Moon as a signal not to tax you too often for your inevitable answer. I have now let her pass her Full: and June is drawing short: and you were to be but for June at Leamington: so—I must have your answer, to tell me about your own health (which was not so good when last you wrote) and that of your Family; and when, and where, you go from Leamington. I shall be sorry if you cannot go to Switzerland.

I have been as far as—Norfolk—on a week's visit (the only visit of the sort I now make) to George Crabbe, my Poet's Grandson, and his two Grand-daughters. It was a very pleasant visit indeed; the people all so sensible, and friendly, talking of old days; the Country flat indeed, but green, well-wooded, and well-cultivated: the weather well enough.

I carried there two volumes of my Sévigné: and even talked of going over to Brittany, only to see her Rochers, as once I went to Edinburgh only to see Abbotsford. But (beside that I probably should not have gone further than talking in any case) a French Guide Book informed me that the present Proprietor of the place will not let it be shown to Strangers who pester him for a view of it, on the strength of those 'paperasses,' as he calls her Letters. So this is rather a comfort to me. Had I gone, I should also have visited my dear old Frederick Tennyson at Jersey. But now I think we shall never see one another again.

Spedding keeps on writing Shakespeare Notes in answer to sundry Theories broached by others: he takes off copies of his MS. by some process he has learned; and, as I always insist on some Copy of all he writes, he has sent me these, which I read by instalments, as Eyesight permits. I believe I am not a fair Judge between him and his adversaries; first, because I have but little, if any, faculty of critical Analysis; and secondly, because I

742

am prejudiced with the notion that old Jem is Shakespeare's Prophet, and must be right. But, whether right or wrong, the way in which he conducts, and pleads, his Case is always Music to me. So it was even with Bacon, with whom I could not be reconciled: I could not like Dr. Fell: much more so with 'the Divine Williams,' who is a Doctor that I do like.

It has turned so dark here in the last two days that I scarce see to write at my desk by a window which has a hood over it, meant to exclude—the Sun! I have increased my Family by two broods of Ducks, who compete for the possession of a Pond about four feet in diameter: and but an hour ago I saw my old Seneschal escorting home a stray lot of Chickens. My two elder Nieces are with me at present, but I do not think will be long here, if a Sister comes to them from Italy.

Pray let me hear how you are. I am pretty well myself:— though not quite up to the mark of my dear Sévigné, who writes from her Rochers when close on sixty—'Pour moi, je suis d'une si parfaite santé, que je ne comprends point ce que Dieu veut faire de moi.'

But yours always and a Day,
LITTLEGRANGE

To Fanny Kemble

Woodbridge: Decr. 6 [1880]

My dear Lady,

I was surprised to see a Letter in your MS. which could not be in answer to any of mine. But the Photos account for it. Thank you: I keep that which I like best, and herewith return the other.

Why will you take into your head that I could suppose you wanting in Hospitality, or any other sort of Generosity! That, at least, is not a Kemble failing. Why, I believe you would give me—and a dozen others—£1000 if you fancied one wanted it— even without being asked. The Law of Mede and Persian is that you *will* take up—a perverse notion—now and then. There! It's out.

As to the Tea—'pure and simple'—with Bread and Butter—

it is the only meal I do care to join in:—and this is why I did not see Mowbray Donne, who has not his Dinner till an hour and a half after my last meal is done.

I should very gladly have 'crushed a Cup of Tea' with you that last Evening, coming prepared so to do. But you had Friends coming; and so (as Mrs Edwards was in the same plight) I went to the Pit of my dear old Haymarket Opera: remembering the very corner of the Stage where Pasta stood when Jason's People came to tell her of his new Marriage; and (with one hand in her Girdle—a movement (Mrs. Frere said) borrowed from Grassini) she interrupted them with her "Cessati—intesi!"—also when Rubini, feathered hat in hand, began that "Ah te, oh Cara"— and Taglioni hovered over the Stage. There was the old Omnibus Box too where D'Orsay flourished in ample white Waistcoat and Wristbands: and Lady Blessington's: and Lady Jersey's on the Pit tier; and my own Mother's, among the lesser Stars, on the third. In place of all which I dimly saw a small Company of less distinction in all respects; and heard an Opera (*Carmen*) on the Wagner model: very beautiful Accompaniments to no Melody: and all very badly sung except by Trebelli, who [was] excellent. I ran out in the middle to the dear Little Haymarket opposite— where Vestris and Liston once were: and found the Theatre itself spoilt by being cut up into compartments which marred the beautiful Horse-shoe shape, once set off by the flowing pattern of Gold which used to run round the house.

Enough of these Old Man's fancies—But—Right for all that!

I would not send you Spedding's fine Article[1] till you had returned from your Visit, and also had received Mrs Leigh at Queen Anne's. You can send it back to me quite at your leisure, without thinking it necessary to write about it.

It is so mild here that the Thrush sings a little, and my Anemones seem preparing to put forth a blossom as well as a leaf. Yesterday I was sitting on a stile by our River side.

You will doubtless see Tennyson's new Volume,[2] which is to my thinking far preferable to his later things, though far inferior to those of near forty years ago: and so, I think, scarce wanted.

[1] ["The Story of the Merchant of Venice," in the *Cornhill Magazine*, March 1880.]

[2] [*Ballads and other Poems*, 1880.]

There is a bit of Translation from an old War Song which shows what a Poet can do when he condescends to such work: and I have always said that 'tis for the old Poets to do some such service for their Predecessors.

I hope this long letter is tolerably legible: and I am in very truth

Sincerely yours

THE LAIRD OF LITTLEGRANGE

To C. E. Norton

Woodbridge. February 20, 1881

My dear Norton,

. . . I have little to say about Carlyle, but that my heart did follow him to Ecclefechan, from which place I have, or had, several letters dated by him. I think it was fine that he should anticipate all Westminster Abbey honours, and determine to be laid where he was born, among his own kindred, and with all the simple and dignified obsequies of (I suppose) his own old Puritan Church. The Care of his Posthumous Memory will be left in good hands, I believe, if in those of Mr Froude. His Niece, who had not answered a Note of Enquiry I wrote her some two months ago, answered it a few days after his Death: she had told him, she said, of my letter, and he said, 'You must answer that.'

To Fanny Kemble

[March,] 1881

My dear Lady,

It was very, very good and kind of you to write to me about Spedding. Yes: Aldis Wright had apprised me of the matter just after it happened, he happening to be in London at the time; and but two days after the accident heard that Spedding was quite calm, and even cheerful; only anxious that Wright himself should not be kept waiting for some communication that S. had promised him! Whether to live, or to die, he will be Socrates still.

Directly that I heard from Wright, I wrote to Mowbray Donne to send me just a Post Card daily, if he or his Wife could, with

2A*   745

but one or two words on it, 'Better,' 'Less well,' or whatever it might be. This morning I hear that all is going on even better than could be expected, according to Miss Spedding. But I suppose the Crisis, which you tell me of, is not yet come; and I have always a terror of that French Adage, 'Monsieur se porte mal—Monsieur se porte mieux—Monsieur est—!' Ah, you know, or you guess, the rest.

My dear old Spedding, though I have not seen him these twenty years and more, and probably should never see again; but he lives, his old Self, in my heart of hearts; and all I hear of him does but embellish the recollection of him, if it could be embellished; for he is but the same that he was from a Boy, all that is best in Heart and Head, a man that would be incredible had one not known him.

I certainly should have gone up to London, even with Eyes that will scarce face the lamps of Woodbridge, not to see him, but to hear the first intelligence I could about him. But I rely on the Post-card for but a Night's delay. Laurence, Mowbray tells me, had been to see him, and found him as calm as had been reported by Wright. But the Doctors had said that he should be kept as quiet as possible.

I think, from what Mowbray also says, that you may have seen our other old friend Donne in somewhat worse plight than usual because of his being much shocked at this accident. He would feel it indeed!—as you do.

I had even thought of writing to tell you all this, but could not but suppose that you were more likely to know of it than myself; though sometimes one is greatly mistaken with these 'of course you knows &c.' But you have known it all: and have very kindly written of it to me, whom you might also have supposed already informed of it: but you took the trouble to write, not relying on 'of course you know &c.'

I have thought lately that I ought to make some enquiry about Arthur Malkin, who was always very kind to me. I had meant to send him my Crabbe, who was a great favourite of his Father's, 'an excellent Companion for Old Age' he told—Donne, I think. But I do not know if I ever did send him the Book; and now, judging by what you tell me, it is too late to do so, unless for Compliment.

The Sun, I see, has put my Fire out, for which I only thank him, and will go to look for him himself in my Garden, only with a Green Shade over my Eyes. I must get to London to see you before you move away to Leamington; when I can bear Sun or Lamp without odious blue glasses &c. I dare to think those Eyes are better, though not Sun-proof.

To C. E. Norton

Woodbridge. March 13, [1881]

My dear Norton,

I send you along with this Letter Part II. of Œdipus, with some corrections or suggestions which I have been obliged to make in Pencil, because of the Paper blotting under the lightest Penwork. And, along with it, a preliminary Letter, which I believe I told you of also, addressed to your Initial: for I did not wish to compromise you even with yourself in such a Business. I know you will like it probably more than it deserves, and excuse its inroads on the Original, though you may, and probably will, think I might better have left it alone, or followed it more faithfully. As to those Students you tell me of who are meditating, or by this time may have accomplisht, their Representation, they could only look on me as a Blasphemer. . . .

It seems almost wrong or unreasonable of me to be talking thus of myself and my little Doings, when not only Carlyle has departed from us, but one, not so illustrious in Genius, but certainly not less wise, my dear old Friend of sixty years, James Spedding:[1] whose name you will know as connected with Lord Bacon. To re-edit his Works, which did not want any such re-edition, and to vindicate his Character which could not be cleared, did this Spedding sacrifice forty years which he might well have given to accomplish much greater things; Shakespeare, for one. But Spedding had no sort of Ambition, and liked to be kept at one long work which he knew would not glorify himself. He was the wisest man I have known: not the less so for plenty of the Boy in him; a great sense of Humour, a Socrates in Life and in Death, which he faced with all Serenity so long as

[1] [Spedding had died on 9 March.]

747

Consciousness lasted. I suppose something of him will reach America, I mean, of his Death, run over by a Cab and dying in St George's Hospital to which he was taken, and from which he could not be removed home alive. I believe that had Carlyle been alive, and but as well as he was three months ago, he would have insisted on being carried to the Hospital to see his Friend, whom he respected as he did few others. I have just got the Carlyle Reminiscences, which will take me some little time to read, impatient as I may be to read them. What I have read is of a stuff we can scarce find in any other Autobiographer: whether his Editor Froude has done quite well in publishing them as they are, and so soon, is another matter. Carlyle's Niece thinks, not quite. She sent me a Pipe her Uncle had used, for Memorial. I had asked her for the Bowl, and an Inch of stem, of one of the Clay Pipes such as I had smoked with him under that little old Pear Tree in his Chelsea garden many an Evening. But she sent me a small Meerschaum which Lady Ashburton had given him, and which he used when from home.

To Samuel Laurence

March 13/81

My dear Laurence,

It was very very good of you to think of writing to me at all on this occasion:[1] much more, writing to me so fully, almost more fully than I dared at first to read: though all so delicately and as you always write. It is over! I shall not write about it. He was all you say.

So I turn to myself! And that is only to say that I am much as usual: here all alone for the last six months, except a two days visit to London in November to see Mrs Kemble, who is now removed from Westminster to Marshall Thompson's Hotel Cavendish Square: and Mrs Edwards who is naturally better and happier than a year ago, but who says she never should be happy unless always at work. And that work is taking off impressions of yet another—and I believe last—batch of her late Husband's Etchings. I saw and heard nothing else than these two Ladies: and some old Nurseys at St John's Wood: and dear

[1] [The death of Spedding.]

748

Donne, who was infirmer than when I had seen him before, and, I hear, is infirmer still than when I saw him last.

By the by, I began to think my own Eyes, which were blazed away by Paraffin some dozen years ago, were going out of me just before Christmas. So for the two dreary months which followed I could scarce read or write. And as yet I am obliged to use them tenderly: only too glad to find that they are better; and not quite going (as I hope) yet. I think they will light me out of this world with care. On March 31 I shall enter on my seventy-third year: and none of my Family reaches over seventy-five.

When I was in London I was all but tempted to jump into a Cab and just knock at Carlyle's door, and ask after him, and give my card, and—run away. . . .

The cold wind will not leave us, and my Crocuses do not like it. Still I manage to sit on one of those Benches you may remember under the lee side of the hedge, and still my seventy-third year approaches.

To Fanny Kemble

[April, 1881]

My dear Mrs Kemble,

Somewhat before my usual time, you see; but Easter comes, and I shall be glad to hear if you keep it in London, or elsewhere. Elsewhere there has been no inducement to go until To day: when the Wind though yet East has turned to the Southern side of it; one can walk without any wrapper; and I dare to fancy we have turned the corner of Winter at last. People talk of changed Seasons: only yesterday I was reading in my dear old Sévigné, how she was with the Duke and Duchess of Chaulnes at their Château of Chaulnes in Picardy all but two hundred years ago: that is in 1689: and the green has not as yet ventured to shew its 'nez' nor a Nightingale to sing. You see that I have returned to her as for some Spring Music, at any rate. As for the Birds, I have nothing but a Robin who seems rather pleased when I sit down on a Bench under an old Ivied Pollard, where I suppose he has a Nest, poor little Fellow. But we have terrible Superstitions about him here; no less than that he always kills his Parents if he can: my young Reader is quite determined on this head:

749

and there lately has been a Paper in some Magazine to the same effect.

My dear old Spedding sent me back to old Wordsworth too, who sings (his best songs I think) about the Mountains and Lakes they were both associated with: and with a quiet feeling he sings that somehow comes home to me more than ever it did before.

As to Carlyle, I thought on my first reading that he must have been *égaré* at the time of writing: a condition which I well remember saying to Spedding long ago that one of his temperament might likely fall into. And now I see that Mrs Oliphant hints at something of the sort. Her's I think an admirable Paper:[1] better than has yet been written, or (I believe) is likely to be written by any one else. . . . I must think Carlyle's judgments mostly, or mainly, true; but that he must have 'lost his head' if not when he recorded them, yet when he left them in any one's hands to decide on their publication. Especially when not about Public Men, but about their Families. It is slaying the Innocent with the Guilty. But of all this you have doubtless heard in London more than enough. 'Pauvre et triste Humanité!' One's heart opens again to him at the last: sitting alone in the middle of her Room. 'I want to die.' 'I want—a Mother.' 'Ah mamma Letizia!' Napoleon is said to have murmured as he lay. By way of pendant to this recurs to me the Story that when Ducis was wretched his Mother would lay his head on her Bosom—'Ah, mon homme! mon pauvre homme!' . . .

And now I have written more than enough for yourself and me: whose Eyes may be the worse for it to-morrow. I still go about in Blue Glasses, and flinch from Lamp and Candle. Pray let me know about your own Eyes, and your own Self; and believe me always sincerely yours

LITTLEGRANGE

[1] [In *Macmillan's Magazine* for April 1881.]

To Fanny Kemble

[Jan. 1882]

I see my poor little Aconites—'New Year's Gifts'—still surviving in the Garden-plot before my window: 'still surviving,' I say, because of their having been out for near a month agone. I believe that Messrs Daffodil, Crocus and Snowdrop are putting in appearance above ground, but (old Coward) I have not put my own old Nose out of doors to look for them. I read (Eyes permitting) the Correspondence between Goethe and Schiller (translated) from 1798 to 1806, extremely interesting to me, though I do not understand, and generally skip, the more purely Æsthetic Parts: which is the Part of Hamlet, I suppose. But in other respects, two such men so freely discussing together their own, and each other's, works interest me greatly. At night, we have the Fortunes of Nigel; a little of it, and not every night: for the reason that I do not wish to eat my Cake too soon. The last night but one I sent my Reader to see Macbeth played by a little Shakespearian company at a Lecture Hall here. He brought me one new Reading: suggested, I doubt not by himself, from a remembrance of Macbeth's tyrannical ways: 'Hang out our *Gallows* on the outward walls.' Nevertheless, the Boy took great Interest in the Play, and I like to encourage him in Shakespeare rather than in the Negro Melodists.

To Fanny Kemble

[Spring, 1882]

My dear Mrs Kemble,

I scarce think, judging by my old Recorder the Moon, that it is a month since I last wrote to you. But not far off, neither. Be that as it may, just now I feel inclined to tell you that I lately heard from Hallam Tennyson by way of acknowledgment of the Programme of a Recital of his Father's verse at Ipswich, by a quondam Tailor there. This, as you may imagine, I did for fun, such as it was. But Hallam replies, without much reference to the Reading: but to tell me how his Father had a fit of Gout in his hand while he was in London: and therefore it was that he had

751

not called on you as he had intended. Think of my dear old Fellow with the Gout! In consequence of which he was forbidden his daily allowance of Port (if I read Hallam's scrawl aright), which, therefore, the Old Boy had stuck to like a fine Fellow with a constancy which few modern Britons can boast of. This reminded me that when I was on my last visit to him, Isle of Wight, 1854, he stuck to his Port (I do not mean too much) and asked me, who might be drinking Sherry, if I did not see that his was 'the best Beast of the two.' So he has remained true to his old Will Waterproof Colours—and so he was prevented from calling on you—his hand, Hallam says, swelled up like 'a great Sponge.' Ah, if he did not live on a somewhat large scale, with perpetual Visitors, I might go once more to see him.

Now, you will, I know, answer me (unless your hand be like his!) and then you will tell me how you are, and how your Party whom you were expecting at Leamington when last you wrote. I take for granted they arrived safe, in spite of the Wind that a little alarmed you at the time of your writing. And now, in another month, you will be starting to meet your American Family in Switzerland, if the Scheme you told me of still hold—with them, I mean. So, by the Moon's law, I shall write to you once again before you leave, and you—will once more answer!

I shall say thus much of myself, that I do not shake off the Cold and Cough that I have had, off and on, these four months: I certainly feel as if some of the internal timbers were shaken; which is not to be wondered at, nor complained of. Tell me how you fare; and believe me

Your sincere as ancient
LITTLEGRANGE

I now fancy that it must be Bentley who delays your Book, till Ballantine & Co. have blown over.[1]

---

[1] [Serjeant Ballantine's *Experiences of a Barrister's Life* appeared in March 1882.]

To W. B. Scott[1]

Little Grange: Woodbridge. July: 9 (I think) [1882]

My dear Sir,

Thank you for your pretty Book, which I ought to deserve by a somewhat better title than that of Translator of other Men's Thoughts. But so it is: and I must feel all the more flattered by your thinking me worthy of your gift.

I shall trust that you will agree with me that in cases of giving an already published Book, one does not call, or even wish, for any return of Praise from the Receiver. I always distinctly *deprecate* it in the case of my own mighty works: even (as is usual with me) when *not* published, and when some honest comment, whether of praise or censure, might be available. *This* our friend C Keene[2] will avouch for, among others, and I have this very day a letter from an American friend complying with the conditions I made in sending him one of the mighty works—which he may like or not at pleasure, without the trou[ble] of measuring what he has to say about it.

So, my dear Sir, I will treat you; and so, shall you treat me in return, when I one day send you a mighty work—perhaps of some 60 pages. Which, therefore, you will not ask for; which would be doing next thing to praising when sent.

I hope all this does not bore you; I remain yours faithfully

EDWARD FITZGERALD

To Fanny Kemble

[August 1882]

My dear Mrs. Kemble,

I have let the Full Moon go by, and very well she looked, too

---

[1] [This letter was sent to Scott on receipt of his *Harvest Home*.]

[2] [Charles Samuel Keene (1823–91), the *Punch* artist. EFG met him in 1877 at the Edwards' at Dunwich; Keene described him as "an old *literato*, . . . and quite a character—an Irishman, an author, and bookworm."]

—over the Sea by which I am now staying. Not at Lowestoft: but at the old extinguished Borough of Aldeburgh, to which—as to other 'premiers Amours,' I revert—where more than sixty years ago I first saw, and first felt, the Sea—where I have lodged in half the houses since; and where I have a sort of traditional acquaintance with half the population. 'Clare Cottage' is where I write from; two little rooms—enough for me—a poor civil Woman pleased to have me in them—oh, yes,—and a little spare Bedroom in which I stow a poor Clerk, with his Legs out of the window from his bed—like a Heron's from his nest—but rather more horizontally. We dash about in Boats whether Sail or Oar—to which latter I leave him for his own good Exercise. Poor fellow, he would have liked to tug at that, or rough-ride a horse, from Boyhood: but must be made Clerk in a London Lawyer's Office: and so I am glad to get him down for a Holyday when he can get one, poor Fellow!

The Carlyle 'Reminiscences' had long indisposed me from taking up the Biography. But when I began, and as I went on with that, I found it one of the most interesting of Books: and the result is that I not only admire and respect Carlyle more than ever I did: but even love him, which I never thought of before. For he loved his Family, as well as for so long helped to maintain them out of very slender earnings of his own; and, so far as these two Volumes show me, he loved his Wife also, while he put her to the work which he had been used to see his own Mother and Sisters fulfil, and which was suitable to the way of Life which he had been used to. His indifference to her sufferings seems to me rather because of Blindness than Neglect; and I think his Biographer has been even a little too hard upon him on the score of Selfish disregard of her. Indeed Mr Norton wrote to me that he looked on Froude as something of an Iago toward his Hero in respect of all he has done for him. The publication of the Reminiscences is indeed a mystery to me: for I should [have] thought that, even in a mercantile point of view, it would indispose others, as me it did, to the Biography. But Iago must have bungled in his work so far as I, for one, am concerned, if the result is such as I find it—or unless I am very obtuse indeed. So I tell Mr Norton; who is about to edit Carlyle's Letters to

Emerson, and whom I should not like to see going to his work with such an 'Animus' toward his Fellow-Editor.

Yours always,

E. F.G.

Faites, s'il vous plaît, mes petits Compliments à Madame Wister.

To Bernard Quaritch

Little Grange, Woodbridge October [1882]

My dear Sir,

Will you put your name as Publisher to a little Volume of "Readings in Crabbe" (of whom you probably never heard) and Edited by me, and charge yourself with 50 copies to sell—of which 50 Copies you may perhaps sell about 25 if you will bestow on them the usual Publisher's care, at the usual Publisher's remuneration.

If you agree to undertake this very lucrative business, I will have the Title page with your name as Publisher, and my own under the name of my dwelling place,—and

Yours sincerely, "LITTLEGRANGE"

I shall be glad to hear of your being well, during a year that has proved very vindictive to many of my friends, and has settled Bronchitis on myself——

And pray how does Omar do?

To Bernard Quaritch

Woodbridge February 18/83

My dear Sir,

As you consented to undertake the very unprofitable charge of publishing my Crabbe—I send you up some 47 Copies which, with all due deductions for Museums &c. I honestly think you will scarce get rid of.

You will judge if there be any good in sending Copies to Athenæums, & Academies &c who will only quite overlook, or give a paragraph to bid others do so. *Advertizing* is, I think, out of the question. So if you are willing to do me—or much rather my old Poet—a good turn, you can do little more than let a copy or two lie on your Counter, perhaps also saying a word to one or two of your Customers about our Existence. For, as to our merits, you are too busy a man to look into them. As usual I do not put my illustrious name on the Title page: but I don't care who knows it—for no one is likely to publish it.

I wish you would give a copy to the Gentleman who did me so much service in revising my other "Broachers" (as we say hereabout) while in the course of printing. I was never told his name or I would send him a Copy direct, bidding him, as my rule is, simply say "Thank you" *and no more*.

And so I will bid you farewell for the present, being

Yours truly, *The Laird of Littlegrange*

P.S. About the *price*—I suppose it may be 3ˢ. 6.? *Certainly* not more: *less* if you think better.

To W. A. Wright

Woodbridge: May 1/83

My dear Wright

I do not suppose it likely that any of my works should be reprinted after my Death. Possibly the three Plays from the Greek, and Calderon's Mágico: which have a certain merit in the Form they are cast into, and also in the Versification.

However this may be, I venture to commit to you this Box containing Copies of all that I have corrected in the way that I would have them appear, if any of them ever should be resuscitated.

The C. Lamb papers are only materials for you, or any one else, to use at pleasure.

The Crabbe volume would, I think, serve for an almost sufficient Selection from him; and some such Selection will have to be made, I believe, if he is to be resuscitated. Two of the Poems —'The Happy Day' and 'The Family of Love'—seem to me to have needed some such abridgement as the 'Tales of the Hall,' for which I have done little more than hastily to sketch the Plan. For all the other Poems, simple Extracts from them will suffice: with a short notice concerning their Dates of Composition &c. at the Beginning.

My poor old Lowestoft Sea-slang may amuse yourself to look over perhaps.

And so, asking your pardon for inflicting this Box upon you, I am ever sincerely yours

E. F. G.

To Horace Basham

Woodbridge: Friday [25 May 1883]

Dear Horace:

Your Herrings came up here yesterday afternoon, & are pronounced *very good* by myself & Mr Keene who has been staying with me for the last week. He has not been very well of late; otherwise I think we should have run over to Aldbro' together: but I dare say that he will join me there some time in the Summer (D.V.). He is just now in my little Green house, playing on his Bag-pipe—that is to say, on the *Pipe* part: for he has not brought the Bag with him. He has desired me to remember him kindly to you.

The Roads are so dusty & the Sun so hot that we are scarce minded to go out in a Carriage; but we shall, I think, try for a Boat on the River this Afternoon.

Pray take my thanks for Remembering me always, & thinking of sending such a token of your doing so as these good herrings.

. . . Kind remembrances to your Wife, I remain sincerely your's   E. FG.

Mr Keene finds that your Uncle is remembered with honour by some London Physicians that he is acquainted with.

"*Horace* has sent me some very nice smoked Herring from Aldbro:—which he says is 'not very grand' as yet."

(This is what I have written to Miss Lynn)

To Fanny Kemble

Woodbridge, May 27/83.

My dear Mrs Kemble:

I feel minded to write you a word of Farewell before you start off for Switzerland: but I do not think it will be very welcome to you if, as usual, you feel bound to answer it on the Eve of your Departure. Why not let me hear from you when you are settled for a few days somewhere among your Mountains?

I was lately obliged to run to London on a disagreeable errand: which, however, got itself over soon after midday; when I got into a Cab to Chelsea, for the purpose of seeing Carlyle's Statue on the Embankment, and to take a last look at his old House in Cheyne Row. The Statue very good, I thought, though looking somewhat small for want of a good Background to set it off: but the old House! Shut up—neglected—'To Let'—was sad enough to me. I got back to Woodbridge before night.

Since then I have had Charles Keene (who has not been well) staying with me here for ten days. He is a very good Guest, inasmuch as he entertains himself with Books, and Birds'-nests, and an ancient Viol which he has brought down here: as also a Bagpipe (his favourite instrument), only leaving the 'Bag' behind: he having to supply its functions from his own lungs. But he will leave me to-morrow or next day; and with June will come my two Nieces from Lowestoft: and then the Longest Day will come, and we shall begin declining toward Winter again, after so shortly escaping from it.

This very morning I receive the Diary of John Ward, Vicar of Stratford on Avon from 1648 to 1679—with some notices of W. S. which you know all about. And I am as ever

Sincerely yours

LITTLEGRANGE

Is not this Letter legible enough?

To Samuel Laurence

Woodbridge. Tuesday, [June 12, 1883]

My dear Laurence,

It is very kind of you to remember one who does so little to remind you of himself. Your drawing of Allen always seemed to me excellent, for which reason it was that I thought his Wife should have it, as being the Record of her husband in his younger days. So of the portrait of Tennyson which I gave his Wife. Not that I did not value them myself, but because I did value them, as the most agreeable Portraits I knew of the two men; and, for that very reason, presented them to those whom they were naturally dearer to than even to myself. I have never liked any Portrait of Tennyson since he grew a Beard; Allen, I suppose, has kept out of that.

If I do not write, it is because I have absolutely nothing to tell you that you have not known for the last twenty years. Here I live still, reading, and being read to, part of my time; walking abroad three or four times a day, or night, in spite of wakening a Bronchitis, which has lodged like the household "Brownie" within; pottering about my Garden (as I have just been doing) and snipping off dead Roses like Miss Tox; and now and then a visit to the neighbouring Seaside, and a splash to Sea in one of the Boats. I never see a new Picture, nor hear a note of Music except when I drum out some old Tune in Winter on an Organ, which might almost be carried about the Streets with a handle to turn, and a Monkey on the top of it. So I go on, living a life far too comfortable as compared with that of better, and wiser men: but ever expecting a reverse in health such as my seventy-five years are subject too. What a tragedy is that of [Mrs Donne]! So brisk, bright, good, a little woman, who seemed made to live! And now the Doctors allot her but two years longer at most, and her friends think that a year will see the End! And poor [Mowbray], tender, true, and brave! His letters to me are quite fine in telling about it. Mrs Kemble wrote me word some two or three months ago that he was looking very old: no wonder. I am told that she keeps up her Spirits the better of the two. Ah, Providence might have spared 'pauvre et triste Humanité' that Trial, together

759

with a few others which (one would think) would have made no difference to its Supremacy. 'Voilà ma petite protestation respectueuse à la Providence,' as Madame de Sévigné says.

To-morrow I am going (for my one annual Visit) to G. Crabbe's, where I am to meet his Sisters, and talk over old Bredfield Vicarage days. Two of my eight Nieces are now with me here in my house, for a two months' visit, I suppose and hope. And I think this is all I have to tell you of

Yours ever sincerely

E. F. G.[1]

[1] [This was probably FitzGerald's last letter; he died two days later on 14 June 1883.]

BIOGRAPHICAL INDEX OF
CORRESPONDENTS

ALLEN, REV. JOHN: Cambridge friend of EFG. Lecturer in mathematics, King's College, London; Chaplain to the College (1833); Archdeacon of Salop (1846). 457, 459, 464, 465, 467, 471, 476, 557

BARTON, BERNARD (1784–1849): A well-known resident of Woodbridge, generally called the Quaker Poet. Barton, who was a bank clerk from 1810 until his death, published his first book of poems in 1812, and corresponded with Byron, Southey, Lamb and Hogg. EFG contributed a memoir of Barton to a posthumous selection from his letters and poems. He also married Barton's daughter, Lucy. 472, 478, 481, 484, 488, 489, 491, 494, 495, 498, 499, 501, 506, 508, 509, 515, 516, 521, 527, 528, 532, 535, 536, 537

BASHAM, HORACE, was born in Aldeburgh in 1854 and died there in 1911. The youngest son of George Basham, of Staples Inn, London, and a nephew of W. R. Basham, the senior surgeon of Westminster Hospital, he was educated at Westminster School and Cambridge. He followed no profession, but spent all his life in Aldeburgh, where he took an interest in the fishing. 683, 687, 710, 711, 712, 732, 740, 757

BIDDELL, ANNA, sister of Herman Biddell. She suggested the name of 'Little Grange' for EFG's house. 665, 688

BIDDELL, HERMAN, a cousin of William Airy. A successful farmer, he lived at Playford, near Ipswich, and often called on EFG on Woodbridge market days. 624, 644, 653

BORROW, GEORGE HENRY (1803–81): Linguist and author of *The Bible in Spain, Lavengro*, and *The Romany Rye*. EFG first met him at W. B. Donne's, and later at Yarmouth and Lowestoft. He lent him Persian MSS., and gossiped about translation (Borrow translated from thirty-five languages), but they never became intimate. 601

CARLYLE, THOMAS (1795–1881): EFG first met the essayist and historian in 1842. He was not drawn to Chelsea through admiration of the man or his writings, indeed he condemned *The French Revolution* and *Heroes and Hero-Worship*; but their common interest in the Battle of Naseby seems to have overcome this prejudice, and the two men eventually became fast friends. 580

COWELL, EDWARD BYLES (1826–1903): Born at Ipswich and educated at Ipswich Grammar School and Magdalen Hall, Oxford, Cowell went to

INDEX TO THE LETTERS

For references to recipients of letters, the reader should also consult the Biographical Index of Correspondents on pp. 761-4.

Beethoven, Ludwig van, 497, 505,
534-5, 571, 579
Bentley, George, 752
Béranger, P. J. de, 676, 677, 678,
679, 692
Berlioz, Hector, 690
Berry, Mrs, 619, 647, 658
Bewick, Thomas, 706
Bickerstaffe, Isaac; *The Hypocrite*,
556
Biographie Universelle, 473
Bismarck, Count, 661
Bizet, Georges; *Carmen*, 744
Blackie, J. S., 592
Blackwood's Magazine, 674
Blake, William, 462, 464, 470
Blakesley, J. W., 469
Blessington, Lady, 744
Blow, John, 535
Boccaccio, Giovanni; *Decameron*,
640, 641, 714-5
Bohn, H. G., 557
Bonaparte, Napoleon, 750
Borrow, George, 589, 598, 599-600,
618; *Romany Rye*, 598
Bottled fruit, 520n
Bowman, Sir William, 656
Bowring, Sir John, 597
"Brambelli," *see* Brambilla
Brambilla, Marietta, 534
Brawne, Fanny, 718, 722
Breadalbane, Lord, 592
British and Foreign Review, 531
British Museum, 462, 515, 518
Brontë, Charlotte, 654
Brooke, Captain F. C., 614
Brougham, Lord, 486, 722-3
Browne, Gerald, 647
Browne, Joseph, 501
Browne, Sir Thomas, 507; *Christian
Morals*, 507n
Browne, W. K., 479, 482, 521, 527,
571, 583, 652-3
Browne, Sir W., 598
Browning, Elizabeth Barrett, 530,
613
Browning, Robert, 654-5, 696, 723,
727; *The Ring and the Book*, 649-
650, 653; *La Saisiaz*, 727
Buckland, William; "Bridgewater
Treatise," 486
Bunn, Alfred; "I dreamt I dwelt in
marble halls," 523
Bunyan, John, 478

Burns, Robert, 676-7; "My bonie
Mary" (The Silver Tassie), 531;
"O my Luve's like a red, red Rose,'
676; "Ye banks and braes o' bonie
Doon," 677
Burke, Edmund, 524, 677
Bute, Lord, 489
Butler, Frances, 661n, 744
Byron, Lord, 713, 726; *The Corsair*,
468; *Vision of Judgment*, 682

Caesar, 719
Calderon, Pedro, 560, 572, 573, 574,
592-3, 616, 728, 737, 741; *El
Magico Prodigioso*, 572, 593, 605;
Six Dramas of Calderon, 573, 574,
576, 699, 723
Campbell, Thomas, 502; *The Pilgrim
of Glencoe*, 502n
Carlile, Richard, 484
Carlyle, Jane Welsh, 581, 582, 639,
754
Carlyle, Thomas; Sterling on, 484;
Venables on, 503; EFG sees, 506,
517, 527, 537, 549, 560, 568, 584;
and Naseby, 506-10, 665; pipe-
smoking, 517, 748; on Tennyson,
524; EFG's regard for, 531, 754;
raves, 537, 539, 548, 750; on
Dickens, 555; and Childs, 564n;
EFG fails to see, 566; EFG tired
of growling, 571; on Browning,
649-50; and Ruskin, 680-1; and
Scott, 686, 701; mellows, 688,
694; revisits Eltham, 694; extracts
from, 695; eightieth birthday,
696, 697; as lecturer, 698; on
Johnson, 700; on Great Faults,
704; shrunk, scolds Darwin, 707;
Lowell on, 725; sends books, 727;
on Wesley, 728; no news of, 735,
737; death of, 745, 747; statue of,
758; *Chartism*, 484; "Early Kings
of Norway," 713, 727, 688; "Essay
on the Portraits of John Knox,"
727; *The French Revolution*, 472-3;
Latterday Pamphlets, 559, 560-1;
"Legislation for Ireland," 548,
556; *Life of Sterling*, 568, 694;
Miscellanies, 483; *Oliver Cromwell*,
507, 508, 510, 529, 532, 539, 694;
Reminiscences, 754; "Shooting
Niagara," 554
Catullus, 718, 719

2B